Constraint Programming

NATO ASI Series

Advanced Science Institutes Series

A series presenting the results of activities sponsored by the NATO Science Committee, which aims at the dissemination of advanced scientific and technological knowledge, with a view to strengthening links between scientific communities.

The Series is published by an international board of publishers in conjunction with the NATO Scientific Affairs Division

A Life Sciences	Plenum Publishing Corporation
B Physics	London and New York
C Mathematical and Physical Sciences	Kluwer Academic Publishers Dordrecht, Boston and London
D Behavioural and Social Sciences	
E Applied Sciences	
F Computer and Systems Sciences	Springer-Verlag Berlin Heidelberg New York
G Ecological Sciences	London Paris Tokyo Hong Kong
H Cell Biology	Barcelona Budapest
I Global Environmental Change	

NATO-PCO DATABASE

The electronic index to the NATO ASI Series provides full bibliographical references (with keywords and/or abstracts) to more than 30000 contributions from international scientists published in all sections of the NATO ASI Series. Access to the NATO-PCO DATABASE compiled by the NATO Publication Coordination Office is possible in two ways:

- via online FILE 128 (NATO-PCO DATABASE) hosted by ESRIN, Via Galileo Galilei, I-00044 Frascati, Italy.

- via CD-ROM "NATO Science & Technology Disk" with user-friendly retrieval software in English, French and German (© WTV GmbH and DATAWARE Technologies Inc. 1992).

The CD-ROM can be ordered through any member of the Board of Publishers or through NATO-PCO, Overijse, Belgium.

Series F: Computer and Systems Sciences Vol. 131

Constraint Programming

Edited by

Brian Mayoh

Aarhus University
Computer Science Department
Ny Munkegade, Building 540
DK-8000 Aarhus C, Denmark

Enn Tyugu

Royal Institute of Technology
Computer Science Department
S-10044 Stockholm, Sweden

Jaan Penjam

Estonian Academy of Sciences
Institute of Cybernetics
21 Adadeemia tee
EE-0026 Tallinn, Estonia

Springer-Verlag
Berlin Heidelberg GmbH

Proceedings of the NATO Advanced Study Institute on Constraint Programming, held in Pärnu, Estonia, August 13–24, 1993

CR Subject Classification (1991): D.1.6, D.3.2, I.2.5, I.2.8

ISBN 978-3-642-85985-4   ISBN 978-3-642-85983-0 (eBook)
DOI 10.1007/978-3-642-85983-0

CIP data applied for

© Springer-Verlag Berlin Heidelberg 1994
Originally published by Springer-Verlag Berlin Heidelberg New York in 1994
Softcover reprint of the hardcover 1st edition 1994

Typesetting: Camera ready by authors
SPIN: 10130734   45/3140 - 5 4 3 2 1 0 - Printed on acid-free paper

Preface

Constraint programming is like an octopus spreading its tentacles into databases, operations research, artificial intelligence, and many other areas. The concept of constraint programming was introduced in artificial intelligence and graphics in the 1960s and 1970s. Now the related techniques are used and studied in many fields of computing. Different aspects of constraint processing are investigated in theoretical computer science, logic programming, knowledge representation, operations research, and related application domains. Constraint programming has been included in the lists of related topics of many conferences. Nevertheless, only in 1993 were the first forums held, devoted as a whole to this field of knowledge. These were the *First Workshop on Principles and Practice of Constraint Programming (PPCP'93)* which was held in Newport, Rhode Island, USA, April 28-30, the *International Workshop on Constraint Processing (at CSAM'93)* held in St. Petersburg, Russia, July 20-21, and the *NATO Advanced Study Institute (NATO ASI) on Constraint Programming* held in Pärnu, Estonia, August 13-24.

NATO ASIs are aimed to be schools bringing together leading researchers and practitioners from industry and academia in some area of knowledge to provide a concise picture of the work done and results obtained by different groups. This is intended for dissemination of advanced knowledge not yet taught regularly in university. However, ASIs must also encourage the introduction of new topics into university curricula as well as foster international scientific contacts.

All Pärnu ASI lectures are represented by chapters in this book, except: "A Constraint-Based Approach to Full First Order Logic" and "A Constraint-Based Approach to Intelligent Networked Colocation in Concurrent Engineering" by J. Bowen and "Constraint-Based Reasoning About Geometry" by W. Keirouz. At this NATO ASI on constraint programming there were 16 original papers by participants; all but one of these are listed in the Appendix, and published as a separate technical report.

Highlights of the ASI social activity were probably evening volleyball on the beach (won by the Estonian team) and the slogan competition. The winning slogan was "Perfect Relaxation for Total Satisfaction".

The NATO ASI on constraint programming and the publishing of this book were funded by NATO grant no. 920880. This financial support is gratefully acknowledged. We are also grateful for the enthusiastic support of the Estonian scientific and secretarial staff. I would like to thank Marianne Dammand Iversen and Karen K. Moeller for their strenuous efforts to get this book out in time, also Tatjana Yakhno and Adriana Paniou for their assistance in the Pärnu presentation.

April 1994   B. Mayoh

Contents

1. Introduction

1.1 Constraint Satisfaction and Constraint Programming: A Brief Lead-In

Brian Mayoh[1], Enn Tyugu[2] and Tarmo Uustalu[2]

[1]Aarhus University, Computer Science Dept,
Ny Munkegade 540, DK-8000 Aarhus, Denmark,
brian@daimi.aau.dk

[2]The Royal Institute of Technology, Dept of Teleinformatics,
Electrum 204, S-164 40 Kista, Sweden

This paper presents the authors' vision about the achievements and expected further developments in the paradigm and techniques of constraint solving, and in applying these in programming

1.1.1 Introduction

Recently, constraints have become a hot topic in several computer science communities. Constraints are fashionable these days. However, apart from this trendy side of the matter, we believe the field to have a steadier significance. After all, the rise of the constraint paradigm resulted from certain developments within AI and computing science. Constraint solving is basically about search in huge search spaces, which in bad cases possess little or almost no guidance-providing structure, and lots of practical problems that daily pop up in AI applications and in computing in general can only be solved by wise search management.

One possible way to classify various constraint problems is the following:

- *Synthesis problems*. We are given requirements in a form of a huge set of constraints, and our task is to find an object that satisfies this set (fully, or at least the important ones of them, or all, but only up to certain precision). Examples are simulation (=reconstruction), where the laws (e.g. physical) that govern the situation or process under investigation are the constraints, and various design (=construction) problems, where the requirements on the end product and the properties of the available construction elements are the constraints. For example, in program synthesis, the I/O relations of the expected program and of the available modules act as constraints; in scheduling, constraints are temporal.

- *Analysis problems.* These are about objects that have visible attributes (an outer appearance) and invisible attributes (an inner essence). The relationships between the visible and invisible attributes are known to us. Our task is, given the values of some object's visible attributes, find what the values of its invisible attributes could be. Examples are all sorts of fault diagnosis problems (medical, technical, etc.), where malfunction manifestations are the visible attributes and faults are the invisible ones; and vision, where a bitmap is what we see, and the lines, angles, shapes etc. that give rise to this, are the underlying essence we are interested in.

Problems that involve much search will always remain, and this sets forth three challenges:

- Find out commonalities between different approaches that tackle search problems, and from upon this basis, advance the general *philosophy* of constraint manipulation. Because of the infamous trade-off between generality and usefulness (efficiency), this requires delicacy, but can give valuable broad insights. Besides, this helps to develop common terminology, and to avoid duplication in the efforts that different communities undertake.

- Seek for efficient constraint satisfaction *algorithms*, both universally applicable and domain-specific. This is very practical and of immediate use.

- Make machines solve our problems elegantly and efficiently, *program machines in new ways.*

A good philosophy of constraints is a basis for constraint programming languages that users will like, and good algorithms are a basis for constraint programming languages that machines will like.

This sketch is a brief presentation of our subjective vision about these three challenges, i.e. about the achievements and expectable further developments in the paradigm and techniques of constraint solving, and in applying these in programming.

1.1.2 How It All Started

The concept of a constraint network was formed gradually. Sketchpad (Sutherland 1963), one of the first interactive graphical interfaces, solved geometrical constraints. Relations in the form of equations or tables were used as problem specifications in several CAD systems, but no generalization was made.

One of the earliest generalizations close to constraint networks of today was the concept of computational models, which was initially developed for specifications of engineering problems and used in a problem solver **Utopist** (Tyugu 1970), which was a value propagation planner.

Research in image processing led Montanari to the first systematic algebraic treatment of constraint networks (Montanari 1974), which originally appeared as a technical report already in 1970, and contained a path consistency algorithm. A very basic consistency technique—Waltz filtering—originated also from a work on image processing (Waltz 1972).

An IFIP workshop in Grenoble in 1978 on applications of AI and pattern recognition in computer aided design (Latombe 1978) gave strong impetus to the research in constraint solving. Present were a number of people who later have made significant contributions in the area: Montanari, Sussman, McDermott etc. The AI people discussed intelligent problem-solving with engineers and discovered a very promising application field for their methods. In particular, applications based on value propagation (then called constraint propagation) ideas were discussed, and a number of reports on research in this direction was published thereafter. A good example system is **CONSTRAINTS** (Sussman, Steele Jr. 1980).

Elegant, but for some reason not widely acknowledged work in finite-domain constraint satisfaction was done in France in the end of the 1970s by Lauriere, who developed a system called **ALICE** and applied it to several practical problems, including prediction/detection problems in geology (Lauriere 1978).

1.1.3 The Constraint Satisfaction Problem (CSP)

There is much confusion in constraint terminology, partly for historical reasons, partly due to the young age of the area. A *constraint network (CN)* (if cleanly described) involves three components:

- *Variables.* These are something that have names and can take values which are elements of some universal domain.

- *Constraints.* These, too, have names, and can take values. Their values are relations of finite arity on the universal domain, and these values are usually given. A relation can be given either extensionally (by plainly enumerating the tuples it contains) or intensionally (by some effective characterization of its extension).

- *A connection (binding) function.* This important component of a network is a function from constraint names to tuples of variable names.

A *valuation* is a value assignment for the variables of a given CN, i.e. a function that maps the variables into elements of the universal domain. A valuation *satisfies a constraint* if, under it, the constraint holds on the variables it connects. A valuation *satisfies a CN* if it satisfies all of its constraints. A goal of *solving* a CN is to find either one satisfying valuation (*solution*) or all such ones, and this is obviously a search problem formulation.

It is quite straightforward to represent CNs as *labelled hypergraphs*. Variable names and values correspond to nodes and their labels respectively. Similarly, constraint names and values correspond to hyperarcs and their labels respectively. Finally, the connection function of a CN corresponds to the incidence function of a hypergraph.

1.1.4 Relation to Logic

There is a clear meaning for CNs in 1st order predicate logic (FOPL). Variables correspond to (individual) variables, constraints correspond to predicates, and the connection function helps to turn the "name part" of the CN into a formula, according to the following prescription. Guided by connections, form atoms from the predicate and variable names, and conjoin these. The interpretation of the formula is partly open: the interpretations of the predicates are pre-determined, while the interpretations of the variables are yet to be found.

As classical CSP benchmark, the Zebra problem, is described in the next chapter; figure 1.4.1 gives its constraint net, and figure 1.4.2 gives the logical reformation

In logical terms, CN solving amounts to completing a partial model. In fact, we need not speak about partial models, but just restrict the class of models we consider to those where the predicates are interpreted as prescribed by a given CN. In this context, CN solving is simply model-construction.

Algorithms for model-construction are something that usually is too down-to-earth to interest pure logicians. The issue of whether a model class can be constructed for some theory, i.e. consistency of a theory, is, of course, of high importance, but the question whether a model can be found for some simple formula of FOPL in some given model class, and if yes, then how, is not interesting.

In applied logic, however, the situation is different. In applications of logic to computer science (e.g. in program reasoning), one often faces the following problems, and therefore there is research going on in finding efficient algorithms to solve them:

- *Model-checking.* Given a formula and a model, check whether the formula is satisfied by the model. E.g. given a specification and a program, does the program meet the specification?

- *Model-construction.* Given a formula, construct a model that satisfies it. E.g. given a specification, construct a program that meets it.

- *Entailment-checking.* Given two formulae, does one entail the other (wrt the model class under consideration)? E.g. given two specifications, does one refine the other?

- *Entailer-construction.* Given a formula, construct another that entails it (the other formula must be in some sense better manageable). E.g. given a specification, construct another that refines it.

On the basic level, CN solving is mostly about model-construction, as we have pointed out. But there are signs already, that in the future, the three other listed problems, especially the third, gain acuteness.

The formulae that result from CNs are of very simple structure—conjuctions of atoms. Model-checking for such formulae is usually quite trivial (it depends on how the relations are given). But this is not the case with model-checking in general: verification of a transition system against a temporal-logic-of-actions formula is far from trivial. The situtation may change also in the constraint community, when partial constraint satisfaction (see subsection 1.1.6) and higher-order constraints (see subsection 1.1.7) gain more attention.

In the cc programming paradigm (see subsection 1.1.8.2), one of the two fundamental operations that can be applied to a program's data state (which is a constraint store) is **ask**, and this checks whether the store yields a given constraint, i.e. in logical terms, whether one formula entails another.

Stepwise specification refinement is a technique in program synthesis relying on entailer-construction. Roughly speaking, a given initial specification is gradually transformed into stronger and more specific ("finer") versions, the last of which is turned into a program. In constraint solving there is a clear analogue to specification refinement—the consistency techniques (see subsection 1.1.5.1). These techniques gradually transform a CN into more and more explicit versions (atoms in the corresponding formulae become more and more restricting), and the last version is solved directly (a model for the last formula is found directly).

As a part of the work on the foundations of the cc framework (see subsection 1.1.8.2), Saraswat et al. have been developing a theory of *constraint systems* as logical theories (Panangaden et al. 1991; Saraswat 1992a). A constraint system consists of a set of *tokens*, all carrying partial information about certain states-of-affairs, and an *entailment relation* between finite sets of tokens. Constraints on states-of-affairs can be stated as finite sets of tokens (understood as conjunctions of primitive constraints). The only requirements that an entailment relation is required to fulfill are transitivity and the property that any set of tokens must entail all of its subsets. In constraint systems, the concept of constraint is very general: one abstracts away from the extensions of constraints, being interested only in the entailment relation between them.

These were some links between CN solving and logic. Probably there will be many more upcoming. From among the work done within the AI community, we can mention (Bibel 1988; Mackworth 1992). The latter paper presents a very basic comparison of various ways of treating finite-domain constraint satisfaction in terms of different fragments of FOPL (including propositional logic).

1.1.5 CN Solving Techniques

Provided that the universal domain can be effectively enumerated, the most straightforward CN solving technique is backtrack search for a satisfying valuation. Blind backtrack search is only applicable, if the domain is finite, since in this case such search is always terminating. But even for finite domains, backtrack search is grossly inefficient, and therefore researchers have tried to develop more efficient algorithms for various special cases. Infinite domains require domain-specific algorithms.

Many algorithms assume binary CNs. A CN is *binary* if all its constraints are either unary or binary. Another assumption often made in algorithms is that, for every subset of the variables of a CN, there is exactly one constraint connecting them. Any CN can easily be transformed into such a form. If, for some subset of variables, there are several connecting constraints, replace these by one, whose extension is the intersection of the old ones. If, for some subset of variables, there is no connecting constraint, then connect them with a mock one of suitable arity, which is universally true (i.e. essentially non-constraining).

1.1.5.1 Consistency Techniques A major idea in the various improvements to the brute-force backtracking is to cut down the search space by first modifying the original CN into a more "explicit" one, and then running brute-force backtracking on this new CN. The modification is done by repeatedly enforcing consistency on certain (small) sub-CNs with distinguished constraints. A sub-CN is *consistent* if every solution of its distinguished constraint can be extended to a solution of the sub-CN (what an inaccurate term from the logical point-of-view!!). A sub-CN is made consistent by tightening up the distinguished constraint (i.e. by restricting its extension). It is easy to see that each solution of the modified CN is a solution of the original CN. Moreover, if consistency is enforced carefully (and most algorithms do that), then even the converse holds, and the original and modified CNs are equivalent. As the extensions of constraints become smaller in the course of modification, backtrack search on the modified CN is more efficient than on the original CN (it becomes possible to backtrack earlier in the failing branches).

The early consistency-enforcing algorithms processed arcs and paths. An *arc* is a sub-CN consisting of two variables, two unary constraints (one per each variable), and a binary constraint, the distinguished constraint being one of the unary constraints. A *path* is a sub-CN consisting of three variables, three unary constraints (one per each variable), and three binary constraints (one per each (unordered) pair of variables), the distinguished constraint being one of the binary constraints. Making an arc or path consistent amounts to applying simple operations on relations, much like those that one encounters in relational databases. A CN is called *arc-consistent* (resp. *path-consistent*) if all its arcs (resp. paths) are consistent. The goal of an arc- (resp. path-)consistency algorithm is to make a CN arc- (resp. path-)consistent.

A problem with making one sub-CN consistent is that this may make other sub-CNs inconsistent. That is why repetitions are generally needed if we insist on achieving simultaneous consistency of several sub-CNs. By subtle bookkeeping over the changes that modifications introduce into the original CN, one can get algorithms with low worst-case time complexity, but the space complexity increases. The first arc- and path-consistency algorithms, AC-1, AC-2, AC-3, and PC-1, PC-2 were proposed in (Mackworth 1977; Mackworth, Freuder 1985). They were impoved by Mohr and Henderson's (1986) AC-4 and PC-3 . Finally, Van Hentenryck, Deville and Teng (1992) gave a generic arc-consistency algorithm AC-5, which can be instantiated to reduce to AC-3 and AC-4, and, for a number of important special classes of constraints (functional, anti-functional, and monotonic constraints, and constraints that are piecewise of any one of these kinds), can be instantiated to yield special fast algorithms.

If a CN (as a hypergraph) is dense, arc- and path-consistency algorithms may not improve the CN, and one might be tempted therefore to try to make larger sub-CNs consistent. Here a difficulty arises. Sub-CNs with more than two variables generally involve loops of constraints, and so a general algorithm for solving them is backtrack search. We face a dilemma: either to pre-process a CN extensively (which involves some backtrack search), and have the search space for the final backtrack search for the solutions of the modified CN smaller, or to pre-process less, and do all the backtrack search in the final end and in a larger search space. To choose adequately the sub-CNs to be made consistent is a critical problem. Guidance can be sought from the global structure of the network (see Section 1.1.5.2).

Some authors (especially Montanari and Rossi) used to call consistency-enforcing 'relaxation', though individual constraints become tighter in this process and the overall CN typically remains equivalent to the original one. This was motivated by the consistency-enforcing process being one always dampening in a stable state where no futher changes can occur. In a way, 'relaxation' is a more beautiful term than 'consistency-enforcing', but it must be noted that a number of researchers apply the word 'relaxation' in relation to weakening of constraints in partial constraint satisfaction (see subsection 1.1.6), which is a very different thing.

Yet another name for consistency-enforcing, 'consistency propagation', is most adequate in situations where CNs can be made consistent "in one pass", without repetitions, e.g. in case of tree-structured binary CNs.

An important special form of (hyperedge) consistency enforcing is *value propagation*, which is applicable if the constraints of a CN are functional, i.e. if the value of some one variable participating in a constraint becomes uniquely determined once the values of the other variables of that constraint are known. If it is known in advance that a CN has a solution (e.g. in analysis situations), so that no conflicts can arise despite that in propagation there possibly are several potential sources for values of some variables, the variable values can be decided in one pass.

1.1.5.2 Network Structure Based Techniques Dechter and Pearl have worked on how to exploit the structure of a CN in choosing an appropriate tactic for solving a CN. They have proposed a number of techniques, which include the following:

- *Adaptive consistency enforcing.* This is a consistency technique that avoids repeated considering of sub-CNs. The sub-CN to be made consistent next is decided at run-time.

- *Cycle-cutset decomposition.* This technique is based on two facts: one is that by fixing the values of certain variables, the connectivity of a CN can be decreased, and the other is that tree-structured CNs can be solved very efficiently (by a repetition-free arc-consistency algorithm).

- *Tree clustering.* This technique operates on the so-called dual graphs of binary CNs.

For descriptions of these techniques, see (Dechter, Pearl 1988; Dechter, Pearl 1989; Dechter 1990).

In (Montanari, Rossi 1991a) it is pointed out that, if a CN was formed incrementally by a series of substitutions of smaller CNs for single constraints (in graph terms, by hyperedge replacements), then this CN can be solved without repetitions, by making the "building blocks" consistent in the order inverse to that of substitutions. Montanari and Rossi call this *perfect relaxation*. The problem with perfect relaxation is: how to find a appropriate decomposition of a given CN into a series of substitutions, such that it is not too costly to make the substituted CNs consistent. In some cases, however, the decomposition ("the evolution history") of a CN is known, and then perfect relaxation may be useful. An natural example of an evolving CN is the constraint store in CLP (see Section 1.1.8.1) (Montanari, Rossi 1991b).

1.1.5.3 Domain-Specific Techniques We do not intend to say much on domain-specific techniques. Although most practical and much exploited, they are not too interesting from a philosophical point of view due to their limited applicability.

The best-studied domain is *rational/real arithmetic*. Typically, linear equations and inequalities are considered, and solving systems of these is the classical problem of linear programming, the most famous method in this area being the simplex algorithm. In case if we only have linear equations, the Gaussian elimination is sufficient. An algebraic technique of Gröbner bases (Buchberger 1985) can be applied to tackle non-linear real equations, whereas another algebraic technique of quantifier elimination (Collins 1975) can handle arbitrary predicates definable in arithmetic.

Another useful domain is that of *Boolean values*. The techniques are various Boolean unification algorithms (see e.g. Martin, Nipkov 1990), Gröbner bases, and saturation methods.

A consistency technique for the domain of inexact arithmetical data, i.e. intervals, is tolerance propagation (Hyvönen 1992).

1.1.6 Partial Constraint Satisfaction and Approximate Constraints

Often, it is unnecessary or too costly to find out an exact solution to a CN, or exact solutions do not even exist. Then different goals might be posed:

- To satisfy as many constraints as possible.

- Find the least degree of priority such that all the constraints with higher priority can be satisfied simultaneously, and satisfy these. This assumes a priority ordering on the constraints.

- To satisfy all constraints, but up to some precision. This assumes that we have a metric for measuring errors.

Freuder and Wallace have written a paper on maximal constraint satisfaction (Freuder, Wallace 1992), containing many references. Borning and colleagues have worked a lot on the so-called constraint hierarhies and introduced several priority orderings and error metrics (see e.g. Borning et al. 1987; Borning et al. 1992).

One uses constraint networks to describe some reality. If the reality is complex, one cannot do without simplifications in specifying the structure of the network and the extensions of its constraints. If "real relations" are approximated by more restrictive ones, the worst that can happen is losing part of solutions. Thus, in cases where there is no risk that all solutions disappear, approximations may be a convenient means to make the search easier. A typical example is approximating a non-functional relation by a function.

1.1.7 Modular and Higher-Order CNs

Conventional CNs are flat, i.e. they do not have a modular structure. By this we mean that if there is some "homogeneity" in a CN with huge number of variables and constraints, we cannot take advantage of it, when writing down a description of the CN, or when reasoning about it, simply because there are no concepts in the constraint jargon for expressing this.

A way to formalize one kind of "homogeneity" are the so-called *dynamic CNs* (Guesgen, Hertzberg 1992). The term 'dynamic CNs' is quite unfortunate, since dynamicity in this context has nothing to do with time and change, and we will use '*modular CNs*' instead. The idea is as follows.

It happens often that a subset of variables of a CN participates together in several constraints, and that only certain valuations of this subset's variables can be extended to satisfy all of them. In such a case, we have to do with an implicit constraint on these variables. If this implicit constraint has a meaning on the conceptual level, it might well be worth of having an own name. Suppose we give it a name, and we reorganize the constraints which connected our variables so that they connect the new constraint instead. Then we find ourselves in a situation, where constraints connect variables and/or constraints. The values of constraints are relations on single elements and/or tuples of elements of the universal domain. At this stage the distinction between variables and constraints becomes blurring. Now there is only one step to be taken—to abandon variables completely. Guesgen and Hertzberg do this by regarding variables as constraints connecting nothing, i.e. 0-ary constraints. (In some respect, this identification is not very neat, since the extension of a 0-ary constraint ought to be a subset of the direct product of an empty family of sets.) The networks where constraints connect constraints are called modular CNs.

In modular CNs, constraint values are relations between tuples. One could also think of giving another meaning for constraint-connecting constraints, where their values would be relations between relations. Such networks (let us call them *higher-order CNs*) ought to be a promising research direction.

In (Tyugu, Uustalu 1994), it is shown that computability statements with nested implications in structural synthesis of programs (see e.g. Mints, Tyugu 1983) can be viewed as higher-order functional constraints.

1.1.8 Programming with Constraints

1.1.8.1 The CLP Framework The most natural programming paradigm for combining with constraints is logic programming (LP).

Roughly speaking, in the conventional LP, data are ground terms of some language, and control is governed by a resolution strategy. A program's data state is the set of variable instantiations made so far (since instantiations equate variables to terms, a single instantiation is generally just a little concretization of some variable's value), and its control state is the set of atomic goals yet to be demonstrated. Instantiations happen at unification, which is part of the resolution step. The final values of variables are determined by the set of instantiations accumulated in the course of the program's run. Instantiations are equality statements and can well be viewed as constraints.

From this observation, it is not a long way to the following generalization. As computation of variable values in LP is always about solving a constraint network, although a simple one, why not liberalize the form of constraints? Let us choose an interesting domain and a set of predicates over it with fixed interpretation (e.g. real numbers and the machinery for writing down linear equations). Now, besides the usual predicates, whose meaning is defined by program clauses (we now call them *control predicates*), we have *constraint predicates* for which we allow no defining clauses, as we assume their meaning is known. We modify the concept of clause, so that a clause body now has a constraint part and a control part, which are finite sets of constraint and control atoms, respectively. We also modify the resolution rule, so that constraint atoms play no active role in resolution—they are merely accumulated, similarly to instantiations. Now, likewise as it is checked at the resolution step in conventional LP whether unification succeeds (otherwise, backtrack occurs), there must be a check at resolution steps in our generalization, but a much stronger one. Namely, it must be verified that it is consistent to add to the current constraint store the constraint atoms from the input clause and the instantiations the unification suggests. This is not cheap.

The paradigm we just outlined is called *constraint logic programming (CLP)* (Jaffar, Lassez 1987; Jaffar, Lassez 1988). A CLP interpreter must have two components: an *inference engine* which deals with resolutions, and a domain-specific *constraint engine* which maintains the constraint store in a standard form, and, upon a request from the inference engine, is able to inform it whether the new constraints it suggests can be consistently added to the store.

There are a number of CLP systems around, some of them commercially available. Examples are CHIP (Dincbas et al. 1988), CLP($\mathcal{R}$) (Jaffar, Michaylov 1987), Prolog-III (Colmerauer 1990), CAL (Aiba et al. 1988), Trilogy (Voda 1988). For references and a tutorial survey on CLP, see either (Cohen 1990) or (Frühwirth et al. 1992).

In the mainstream paradigm of concurrent logic programming, originally due to Shapiro, OR-parallelism is restricted to processing of the guards of the definition clauses of a given predicate, after which a decisive commitment is made in favour of one of them (for a survey on concurrent LP, see (Shapiro 1989)). AKL (Franzén et al. 1991) is a constraint programming language stemming from this tradition that facilitates deep guards, i.e. guards involving user-defined predicates. The rôle of guards in concurrent LP languages is similar that of **ask** actions in cc languages (on these, see the next subsection).

1.1.8.2 The cc Framework Saraswat et al. have developed a *concurrent constraint programming* paradigm, called cc (Saraswat, Rinard 1990). cc languages are similar to Milner's CCS in that a program is a set of agent definitions. But the communication mechanism of cc is radically different from that of CCS: communication in cc occurs through a constraint store, which is a program's data state. The basic actions of agents are **ask**ing and **tell**ing constraints. An **ask** action succeeds if the store entails the given constraint, fails if the given constraint is inconsistent with the store, and is suspended otherwise. A **tell** action adds a constraint to the store, and succeeds if the store remains consistent, otherwise it fails. Complex behaviours are built from simpler ones by means of prefixing, indeterministic choice, interleaving, hiding, and mutual recursion. Although cc is outwardly different from committed choice concurrent LP paradigm, it adequately captures it.

The first denotational and SOS interleaving semantics of cc appeared in (Saraswat, Rinard, Panangaden 1990).

Both entailment relations of constraint systems as well as as agent definitions of programs in cc languages can be seen as production rules of graph grammars. Hence, given a program in a cc language, the information necessary to determine its semantics can be encoded in the form of a single graph grammar. Montanari and Rossi have developed methods of deriving different true concurrency semantics of cc programs from their graph grammar representations. These are: partial order semantics (Montanari, Rossi 1991c; Montanari, Rossi 1993b), event structure semantics (Montanari, Rossi 1992), and contextual net semantics (Montanari, Rossi 1993a).

A logical semantics for the cc paradigm can be given using the *formulas-as-agents* and *proof-as-computation* interpretation of intuitionistic logic (Lincoln, Saraswat 1991). Indeterminacy can be properly handled by moving to the setting of linear logic (Lcc), and if one wants to allow process abstractions to be passed as messages in communications, higher-order logic is needed (HLcc) (Saraswat, Lincoln 1992).

An example of a cc language is Janus (Saraswat, Kahn, Levy 1989; Saraswat, Kahn, Levy 1990). Janus is a language for distributed programming, and enjoys the pleasant property that its computations cannot abort because of the store having become inconsistent as a result of a uncoordinated tells by several agents. This is achieved by severe syntactic restrictions on programs. A completely visual programming environment, called Pictorial Janus is under development (Kahn 1992), where exactly the same visual terms are used to depict a program, its execution states, and the whole history of these.(Saraswat 1992b) presents a thorough account of the state of the cc art.

The novel Oz (Smolka et al. 1990) language extends the cc model with object-orientation (higher-orderness), avoiding thereby the clumsiness of stream communication, which is the usual communication mechanism in the mergers of concurrent LP and object-orientation.

1.1.8.3 Constraint Imperative Programming

The constraint imperative paradigm (CIP), proposed by Borning and colleagues and implemented in the object oriented languages Kaleidoscope90, '91, and '93 (Borning et al. 1992; Freeman-Benson, Borning 1992; Lopez et al. 1994), is conservative in that it seeks to keep to traditional programming idioms. In particular, it remains faithful to the conventional understanding of stores as valuations, as opposed to the store-as-constraint approach of CLP and cc. As imperative variables are subject to destructive assignments and always possess values, the task of the constraint handler of a CIP system is not to find one set of permissible valuations of a program's variables, which is typical of declarative constraint programming, but to reinstate the permissibility of the store (by changing some values), whenever an assignment to some variable happens to have spoilt this. Different constraints may have different degrees of priority.

A variable can be blocked from automatic adjustments due to violation of its constraint and from potentially triggering adjustment of the other variables of its constraint by annotating it either read-only or write-only in the statement of the constraint.

Mentally, the idiom of dynamic variables-of-state can always be replaced with that of static variables-of-history (streams). Doing so, the relation between two successive states of the store can be semantically considered as determined by strong constraints of change and weak constraints of stay between old and new values, with old values read-only.

1.1.9 Conclusion

Despite the illusory freedom we experience from time to time, life is, in fact, pretty constrained. We have to fulfill expectations, obey regulations, stay alive... and all of that simultaneously. Luckily, in our daily doings, most of us manage to cope satisfactorily with the constraints that our wonderful world imposes on us. And in these days, we have even algorithms at our disposal to solve them "scientifically". So there is no reason for depression. What we need is a deeper insight into the nature and habits of these tiny tyrants and just some more algorithms—in order to make machines see our problems in the way we do, and have them helping us.

References

Aiba, A., Sakai, K., Sato, Y., Hawley, D. J., Hasegawa, R. 1988. Constraint logic programming language CAL. In Proc. Int'l Conf. on Fifth Generation Computer Systems, Tokyo, Japan, Dec 1988, 263–276. Tokyo: Ohmsha Publishers

Bibel, W. 1988. Constraint satisfaction from a deductive viewpoint. Artificial Intelligence **35**(3), 401–413

Borning, A., Duisberg, R., Freeman-Benson, B. N., Cramer, A., Woolf, M. 1987. Constraint hierarchies. In Proc. ACM Conf. on Object-Oriented Programming Systems, Languages and Applications, OOPSLA'87, Orlando, FL, USA, Oct 1987, 48–60. ACM

Borning, A., Freeman-Benson, B. N., Wilson, M. 1992. Constraint hierarchies. Lisp and Symbolic Computation **5**(3), 223–270

Buchberger, B. 1985. Gröbner bases: An algorithmic method in polynomial ideal theory. In Bose, N. K. (ed.), Multidimensional systems theory, 184–232. Dordrecht: D. Reidel

Cohen, J. 1990. Constraint logic programming languages. Communications of the ACM **33**(7), 52–68

Collins, G. E. 1975. Quantifier elimination for real closed fields by cylindrical algebraic decomposition. In Proc. 2nd GI Conf. on Automata Theory and Formal Languages, 515–532. LNCS 33 Berlin: Springer-Verlag.

Colmerauer, A. 1990. An introduction to Prolog-III. Communications of the ACM **33**(7), 69–90

Dechter, R. 1990. Enhancement schemes for constraint processing: Backjumping, learning and cutset decomposition. Artificial Intelligence **41**(3), 273–312

Dechter, R., Pearl, J. 1988. Network-based heuristics for constraint-satisfaction problems. Artificial Intelligence **34**(1), 1–38

Dechter, R., Pearl, J. 1989. Tree clustering for constraint networks. Artificial Intelligence **38**(3), 353–66

Dincbas, M., Van Hentenryck, P., Simonis, H., Aggoun, A., Graf, T., Berthier, F. 1988. The constraint logic programming language CHIP. In Proc. Int'l Conf. on Fifth Generation Computer Systems, Tokyo, Japan, Dec 1988, 693–702. Tokyo: Ohmsha Publishers

Franzén, T., Haridi, S., Janson, S. 1991. An overview of the Andorra Kernel Language. In Eriksson, L.-H., Hallnäs, L., Schroeder-Heister, P. (eds), Proc. 2nd Int'l Workshop on Extensions of Logic Programming, ELP'91, Stockholm, Sweden, Jan 1991, 163–179. LNAI 596 Berlin: Springer-Verlag.

Freeman-Benson, B., Borning, A. 1992. Integrating constraints with an object-oriented language. In Lehrmann Madsen, O.(ed), Proc. European Conf. on Object-Oriented Programming, ECOOP'92, Utrecht, The Netherlands, June/July 1992, 268–86. Berlin: Springer-Verlag. LNCS 615

Frühwirth, T., Herold, A., Küchenhoff, V., Le Provost, T., Lim, P., Monfroy, E., Wallace, M. 1992. Constraint logic programming: An informal introduction. In Comyn, G., Fuchs, N. E., Ratcliffe, M. J. (eds), Logic Programming in Action: Proc. 2nd Int'l Logic Programming Summer School, LPSS'92, Zürich, Switzerland, Sept 1992, 3–35. Berlin: Springer-Verlag. LNAI 636

Freuder, E. C., Wallace, R. J. 1992. Partial constraint satisfaction. Artificial Intelligence bf 58(1–3), 21–70

Guesgen, H. W., Hertzberg, J. 1992. A Perspective of Constraint-Based Reasoning: An Introductory Tutorial. Berlin: Springer-Verlag. LNAI 597

Hyvönen, E. 1992. Constraint reasoning based on interval arithmetic: The tolerance propagation approach. Artificial Intelligence 58(1–3), 71–112

Jaffar, J., Lassez, J.-L. 1987. Constraint logic programming. In Conf. Record 14th Annual ACM Symp. on Principles of Programming Languages, Munich, West Germany, Jan 1987, 111–119. ACM SIGACT/SIGPLAN

Jaffar, J., Lassez, J.-L. 1988. From unification to constraints. In Furukawa, K., Tanaka, H., Fujisaki, T. (eds), Logic Programming '87: Proc. 6th (Japanese) Conf. Tokyo, Japan, June 1987, 1–18. Berlin: Springer-Verlag. LNCS 315

Jaffar, J., Michaylov, S. 1987. Methodology and implementation of a constraint logic programming system. In Proc. 4th Int'l Conf. on Logic Programming, Melbourne, Australia, 1987, 196–218. The MIT Press

Kahn, K. M. 1992. Concurrent constraint programs to parse and animate pictures of concurrent constraint programs. In Proc. Int'l Conf. on Fifth Generation Computer Systems, Tokyo, Japan, June 1992. ICOT: Tokyo

Latombe, J.-C. (ed) 1978. Proc. IFIP Workshop on Artificial Intelligence and Pattern Recognition in CAD. Amsterdam: North-Holland

Lauriere, J.-L. 1978. A language and a program for stating and solving combinatorial problems. Artificial Intelligence 10(1), 29–127

Lincoln, P., Saraswat, V. A. 1991. Proofs as concurrent processes: A logical interpretation for concurrent constraint programming. Technical report, Systems Sciences Laboratory, Xerox PARC, Palo Alto, CA

Lopez, G., Freeman-Benson, B. N., Borning, A. 1994. Kaleidoscope: A constraint imperative programming language. In this volume

Mackworth, A. K. 1977. Consistency in networks of relations. Artificial Intelligence 8(1), 99–118

Mackworth, A. K. 1992. The logic of constraint satisfaction. Artificial Intelligence 58(1–3), 3–20

Mackworth, A. K., Freuder, E. C. 1985. The complexity of some polynomial network consistency algorithms for constraint satisfaction problem. Artificial Intelligence 25(1), 65–74

Martin, U., Nipkov, T. 1990. Boolean unification: The story so far. In Kirchner, C. (ed), Unification. Academic Press

Mints, G., Tyugu, E. 1983. Justification of the structural synthesis of programs. Science of Computer Programming 2, 215–240

Mohr, R., Henderson, T. C. 1986. Arc and path consistency revisited. Artificial Intelligence 28(2), 225–233

Montanari, U. 1974. Networks of constraints: Fundamental properties and application to picture processing. Information Sciences 7(2), 95–132

Montanari, U., Rossi, F. 1991a. Constraint relaxation may be perfect. Artificial Intelligence 48(2), 143–170

Montanari, U., Rossi, F. 1991b. Perfect relaxation in constraint logic programming. In Furukawa, K. (ed.), Proc. 8th Int'l Conf. on Logic Programming, Paris, France, June 1991, 223–237. Cambridge, MA: The MIT Press

Montanari, U., Rossi, F. 1991c. True concurrency in concurrent constraint logic programming. In Saraswat, V., Ueda, K. (eds), Proc. 1991 Symp. on Logic Programming, 694–713

Montanari, U., Rossi, F. 1992. An event structure semantics for concurrent constraint programming. Submitted for publication

Montanari, U., Rossi, F. 1993a. Contextual occurrence nets and concurrent constraint programming. In Proc. Dagstuhl Seminar on Graph Transformations in Computer Science, Jan 1993, Berlin: Springer-Verlag. LNCS

Montanari, U., Rossi, F. 1993b. Graph rewriting for a partial ordering semantics of concurrent constraint programming. Theoretical Computer Science 109, 225–56

Panangaden, P., Saraswat, V. A., Scott, P. J., Seely, R. A. G. 1991. What is a constraint system? Technical report, Xerox Parc, Palo Alto, CA

Saraswat, V. A. 1992a. The category of constraint systems is cartesian-closed. In Proc. 7th Annual IEEE Symposium on Logic in Computer Science, Santa Cruz, CA, USA, June 1992, 341–345. Los Alamitos, CA: IEEE Comp. Soc. Press

Saraswat, V. A. 1992b. Concurrent constraint programming: A survey. Technical report, Xerox PARC, Palo Alto, CA

Saraswat, V. A., Kahn, K. M., Levy, J. 1989. Programming in Janus. Technical report, Xerox PARC, Palo Alto, CA

Saraswat, V. A., Kahn, K. M., Levy, J. 1990. Janus: A step towards distributed constraint programming. In Proc. North American Conf. on Logic Programming, Austin, TX, USA, Oct 1990.

Saraswat, V. A., Lincoln, P. 1992. Higher-order, linear concurrent constraint programming. Technical report, Xerox PARC, Palo Alto, CA

Saraswat, V. A., Rinard, M. 1990. Concurrent constraint programming. In Conf. Record 17th Annual ACM Symp. on Principles of Programming Languages, San Fransisco, CA, USA, Jan 1990, 232–245. ACM SIGPLAN/SIGACT

Saraswat, V. A., Rinard, M., Panangaden, P. 1990. Semantic foundations of concurrent constraint programming. In Conf. Record 18th Annual ACM Symp. on Principles of Programming Languages, Orlando, FL, USA, 1991, 333–352. ACM SIGPLAN/SIGACT

Shapiro, E. 1989. The family of concurrent logic programming languages. ACM Computing Surveys **21**(3), 413–510

Smolka, G., Henz, M., Würtz, J. 1993. Object-oriented concurrent constraint programming in Oz. Research Report RR-93-16, DFKI, Saarbrücken

Sussman, G. J., Steele Jr. G. L. 1980. CONSTRAINTS—a language for expressing almost-hierarchical descriptions. Artificial Intelligence bf 14(1), 1–39

Sutherland, I. E. 1963. Sketchpad: A man-machine graphical communication system. In Proc. AFIPS Spring Joint Computer Conf., Detroit, MI, USA, 1963, 329–346

Tyugu, E. 1970. Solving problems on computational models. J. Computational Mathematics and Math. Phys. **10**, 716–33

Tyugu, E., Uustalu, T. 1994. Higher-order functional constraint networks. In this volume

Van Hentenryck, P., Deville, Y., Teng, C.-M. 1992. A generic arc-consistency algorithm and its specializations. Artificial Intelligence **57**(2–3), 291–321

Voda, P. 1988. The constraint language Trilogy: Semantics and computations. Technical report, Complete Logic Systems, North Vancouver, BC

Waltz, D. L. 1972. Generating semantic descriptions from drawings of scenes with shadows. Technical Report AI-TR-271, MIT

1.2 Constraint Programming and Artificial Intelligence

Brian Mayoh

Computer Science Department, Aarhus University
Ny Munkegade, Bldg. 540, 8000 Aarhus C, Denmark
brian@daimi.aau.dk

There is a symbiosis between artificial intelligence (AI) and constraint programming (CP). In this chapter we will describe both the relevance of many AI ideas on knowedge representation and reasoning to CP and the contribution new CP ideas and techniques can make to AI. It is a historic fact that many constraint programming techniques were developed by people primarily interested in artificial intelligence problems. In this chapter we shall look not only at the work of such pioneers, because they were explicit about the connections between AI and CP, but also at more recent work of AI-ers.

1.2.1 CP techniques emerge from AI

Why is AI such a potent source of inspiration for constraint programming?

It is characteristic for AI that one tries not to oversimplify problems. Flexible and powerful representation languages have been developed and they suggest ways of making existing constraint languages more expressive. Elaborate ways of dealing with partial, uncertain and imprecise data have been devised. Intuitively one feels that using more elaborate representations of problems should make them harder to solve. As we shall see in subsection 1.2.2.2 when we discuss the vision work of Waltz and Winston, this intuition is misleading. Usually the price for not oversimplifying is that general problems become NP-complete or undecidable and thereby "computationally infeasible" for conventional computer scientists. But we all solve NP-complete problems every day, so it is no surprise that the heuristics and constraints in most AI systems allow them to solve most of their problems most of the time.

What makes a problem hard to solve? The answer given by several recent papers is : most problems are easy to solve, the relatively rare hard problems lie near the phase transitions in the problem space. To quote (Cheeseman, Kanefsky, and Taylor 1991): " ⋯ for many NP problems one or more "order parameters" can be defined, and hard instances occur around particular critical values of these order parameters. In addition, such critical values form a boundary that separates the space of problems into two regions. One region is underconstrained, so the density of solutions is high, thus making it relatively easy to find a solution. The other region is overconstrained and very unlikely to contain a solution. If there are solutions in this overconstrained region, then they have such deep local minima (strong basin of attraction) that any reasonable algorithm is likely to find it.If there is no solution, then a backtrack search can usually establish this with ease, since potential solution paths are usually cut off early in the search. Really hard problems occur on the boundary between these two regions, where the probability of a solution is low but non-negligible. At this point there are typically many local minima corresponding to almost solutions separated by high "energy barriers". These almost solutions form deep local minima that may often trap search methods that rely on local information." Graph colouring, a classic CP problem, is one of the problems investigated in (Cheeseman, Kanefsky, and Taylor 1991) as evidence for this phase transition phenomenon. For 3-colouring {4-colouring} of random graphs there is a sharp transition when the average number of neighbours is 5 {8} and the sharpness of the transition increases with the number of the nodes in the graph. In (Huberman and Hogg 1987; Williams and Hogg 1993; Mitchell 1992; Musick and Russell 1992; Williams and Hogg 1992) such phase transition phenomena in various kinds of heuristic search are investigated and their results confirm the above answer to the question of why everyday, real-life CP problems are surprisingly easy to solve.

Most AI problems can be put in the form of searching in an enormous state graph, but straightforward solutions lead to a "combinatorial explosion". As constraint programs can also be considered as searching in a large space this is probably the main reason why CP techniques emerge from AI. Later we shall describe several ways of making the concept of "state" precise. One unusual way is to define a state as a solution of constraint satisfaction problem, so the state space (= nodes in search graph) is the set of solutions of the constraint satisfaction problem. If there is a variable for each attribute of each object and there are no constraints in the constraint satisfaction problem, then we get the popular definition of a state as a function from Features to Values (usually the features are attributes of objects so states are sets of object-attribute-value triples).

Perhaps we should explain how early planning systems are in essence searches in a large state graph. In the usual semantics for planning one has actions with pre- and post-conditions. An action A can be applied in a state S, if the precondition of A holds in S. If one chooses to apply A in state S, then the resulting state is (S - precondition[A]) + postcondition[A].

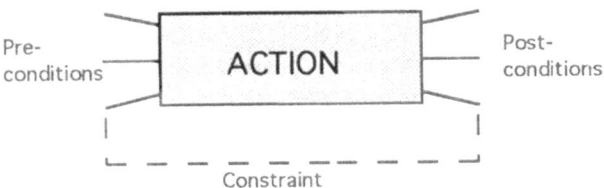

Fig. 1 Actions are binary constraints on states

In the state graph there is an edge from S_i to S_j labelled A, if action A can be applied to state S_i and it yields state S_j. An application of an action, an edge in the state graph, is just a binary constraint between two states; state graphs are no more than a particular kind of constraint net. A linear plan from state START to state GOAL is a sequence of actions $A_1, A_2 \cdots A_n$, such that

- A_1 can be applied in START

- A_k can be applied in the resulting state of the previous action for $1 < k <= n$

- GOAL is the result of action A_n

Thus a linear plan is a path from START to GOAL in the state graph. The

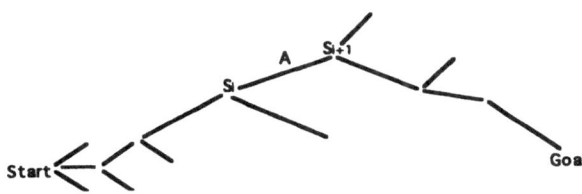

Fig. 2 A linear plan is a path from START to GOAL in the state graph

long pioneering paper of Stefik (Stefik 1981) emphasized the central role of constraints in planning. The paper describes the MOLGEN program, that planned a few experiments in molecular genetics. More importantly it introduced the idea of constraint posting .As Stefik says "this approach is a marriage of ideas from hierarchical planning and constraint satisfaction. It distinguishes three operations on constraints :

1. constraint formulation

2. constraint propagation

3. constraint satisfaction

All of these operations could be broadly characterised as inferences in problem solving ⋯ The power of constraint posting comes largely from two abilities: (1) the ability to plan hierarchically by introducing new constraints and variables, and (2) the ability to anticipate interference betweeen subproblems (using constraint propagation) and to eliminate the interfering solutions"(p130). We shall discuss hierarchical planning in section 1.2.2.4 and subproblem interference in section 1.2.3.

In his short survey at of the Japanese fifth generation project (Furukawa 1992) Koichi Furukawa stresses their various CP languages as the main result of the project, but he admits their origins in DNA sequencing and other AI problems. As a recent example of how CP techniques emerge from AI , let us look at (Codognet and Saraswat 1992). This paper proposes a notion of abduction for cc languages (see chapter by Saraswat or last chapter). But what is abduction? Consider

A)   Socrates was a man
I)   All men are mortal
D)   Socrates was mortal

Deduction is inferring D from A and I, induction is inferring I from A and D, and abduction is inferring A from I and D. Now consider a deadlocked cc program where all agents are suspended on ask operations (as explained in the last chapter). One could revive the program by abducing hypothetical constraints until some ask operation is satisfied and its agent resumes activity.

Several new developements of backtracking use explanation-based learning (described in section 1.2.6.1) - another example of CP techniques emerging from AI.

1.2.2 CP permeates every corner of AI

The pioneering papers of Stefik, Sussman and Waltz were in the AI areas of Planning, Design and Vision respectively. We shall also look at recent papers in these and other areas. It is somewhat surprising that constraint programming does not prevail in the natural language area, because constraint-based models for natural language analysis are becoming very popular. Theoretical linguists approve of them (Kaplan and Bresman 1982) and computational linguists use them frequently (Schreiber 1992). This is natural because constraints capture both syntactical restrictions like "adjectives must have the same gender as the nouns they modify" and semantic restrictions like "'I','my','mine' refer to the current speaker". However the computational linguists use methods that are more similar to attribute grammars than constraint programming. The only exception to this seems to be the knowledge representation and natural language groups in Novosibirsk, whose work is based on a particular form of constraint called a subdefinite set (Narinyani 1983).

1.2.2.1 CP permeates design Sussman and Stallman (Stallman and Sussman 1977) used constraints to design circuits. Three years later Sussman and Steele wrote another paper (Sussman and Steele Jr. 1980) on the subject. In it they introduced a constraint language which can describe "the simultaneous multiple views of a circuit that make the use of equivalences so powerful". The key idea of their paper is that experienced designers use "equivalent circuits" and these can be incorporated in a constraint language. Many later systems for helping designers have built on this idea of capturing expert intuitions as constraints.

Are there general intuitions about good design? Sussman & Steele describe two views of a designed object such as a watch, the structural view and the functional view.

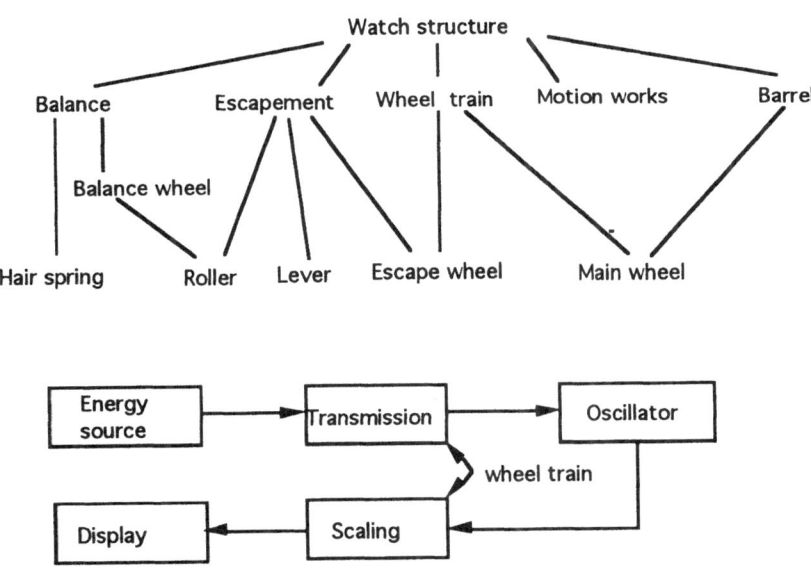

Fig. 3 Structural and functional views of wristwatch

Ideally such views should form a strict hierarchy, but for many well-designed objects they almost do, but not quite. Our structural view of a watch is not a hierarchy because the roller, the escape wheel and the main wheel have dual roles; our functional view of a watch is not a hierarchy because the wheel train is part of both "transmission" and "scaling". In section 1.2.3 we shall discuss such "almost hierarchies". If the computer is to help the human designer, it should provide constraint languages that are so expressive that they can handle multiple views and almost hierarchies.

1.2.2.2 CP permeates Vision The central role of constraints in vision was recognised as early as 1974. To quote (Montanari 1974) : "if the problem is to recognize human faces, we must, of course, limit the search for particular elements (eyes, nose, mouth, ears etc.) to the areas of the picture where they may ever be present ⋯ If for instance the position of one ear has already been determined, the area in which the mouth could be found is further restricted ⋯ if also an eye has been determined, the allowed area for the mouth can be considered the intersection of the constraints given by the ear and the eye". The algorithm in (Montanari 1974) uses relational operations to propagate constraints. In section 1.2.3 we describe a recent work (Lin, Tsao, and Chen 1992) on scene labelling.

As the paper (Mackworth 1977) which introduced node, arc and path inconsistency acknowledges Montanari and Waltz as major contributors to the development of these ideas, let us look at the pioneering work of Waltz and Winston (Winston 1975; Waltz 1975) on scene labelling. From it we learn the surprising fact that some CP problems become simpler if one makes the domains of values larger and allows more complicated constraints. This is so counter-intuitive that we should look at this work more closely. The problem is to determine the objects in a scene and their faces from the edges detected in the scene. This can be formulated as a CP problem: there is a variable for each edge in the scene, and a constraint for each vertex. In the early work of Waltz there were only 3 kinds of edges (concave, convex and boundary) and the 18 possible constraints shown in fig. 4.

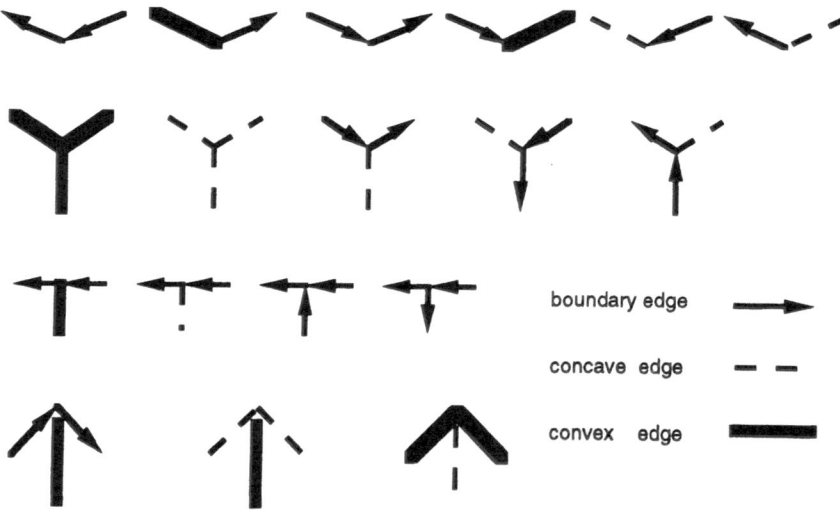

Fig. 4 18 possible constraints for simple scene analysis

The simplest version of the Waltz filtering algorithm is:

1. determine the boundary edges and make them into a cycle by putting arrows

2. use the constraints for vertices on marked edges to determine labels on adjacent edges

3. if some edges are still unlabelled, go to 2)

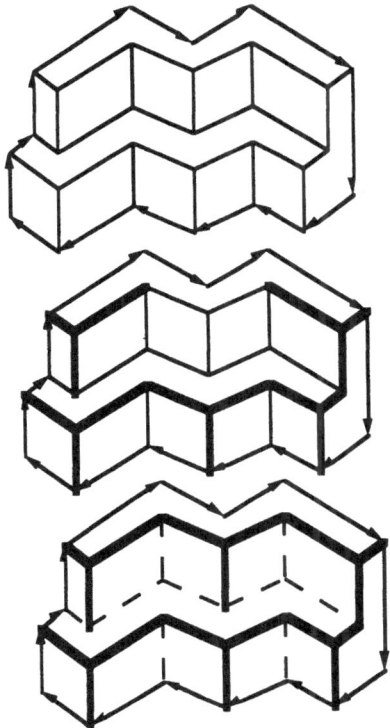

Fig. 5 Waltz filtering on a simple scene

In the later work of Winston there were about 50 kinds of edges and about 1800 kinds of vertices, but the results were much better – much more complicated scenes cold be analysed and simple scenes could be analysed much faster. The later work paid due attention to shadows, cracks and illumination. There is still only one form of convex edge, but there are four forms of concave edges and two forms of boundary, shadow and crack edges. As there are 3 kinds of face illumination (Illuminated, Shadow, and SelfShadowing), 11 edge forms, and edges separate 2 faces one has $3 \times 3 \times 11 = 99$ combinatorial possibilities for edges, but not all of these can occur in reality. The search space has become enormous, and one would expect the filtering algorithm to be unacceptably slow. However this is not so, because the search pruning given by the constraints is much, much more effective. Here our intuitions are misleading.

1.2.2.3 CP permeates Diagnosis and Decision Support Systems The dominant approach to diagnostic problems is "model based"; the system is treated as an idealised structure of components, whose local behaviours interact to produce overall system behaviour. One popular approach is first to assume the system is working, make predictions, compare with observations and repeat until the predicted behaviour does not conflict with the observations. Predictions are done by constraint propagation and adjustment of assumptions is done by some kind of Truth Maintenance method (Geffner and Pearl 1987).

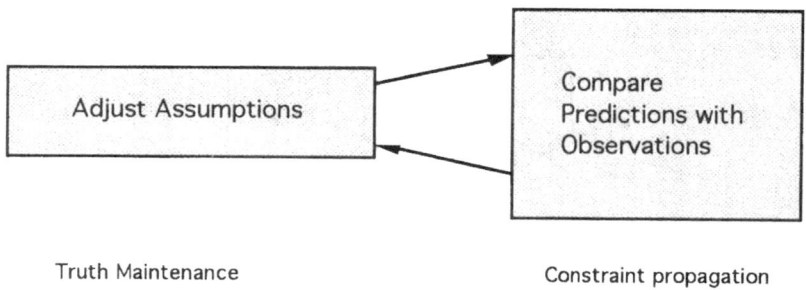

Truth Maintenance   Constraint propagation

Fig. 6 Model Based Diagnosis

Truth Maintenance systems are a popular way of handling incomplete knowledge. In the memory of such a system one has not only formulas—facts about the domain of interest—but also *justifications* of formulas by other formulas. Thus one has a labelled hypergraph with formulas as vertices and justifications as hyperedges. At any given time each of the formula-vertices is either IN (the belief set) or OUT, but subject to the constraint

> if there is a justification of B from $A_1, A_2 \cdots$ An
> and all of $A_1, A_2 \cdots$ An are IN, then B must be IN also

The NOGOODS in constraint programming (see chapter by Wallace) are the special case when B is the always false formula so at least one of $A_1, A_2 \cdots$ An must be OUT of the belief set. As formula/vertices can be considered as variables whose value is either IN or OUT and justifications can be considered as constraints, memory states are solutions of a Boolean valued constraint net, but the constraint nets are dynamic. When new information appears, one must add new formula-vertices and/or justification-edges and find a new belief set- i.e. solve a new constraint satisfaction problem.

Remember the discussion of deduction, induction and abduction in section 1.2. If the truth maintenance system is told one of the formulas A,I,or D, and it knows the other two formulas, then it can add both the new formula and the new justification of D from A and I. One should start solving the new CSP with the new formula IN, but the solution process may put it OUT. For abduction and induction this is obvious, but it is also true for deduction (D may conflict with other information in the truth maintenance system). However notice that we have a new, syntactic notion of state: a state is a set of justifications and IN formulas in a truth maintenance system. In section 1.2.4 we shall say more about syntactic states, but for now notice that our new states may be partial because some formulas are neither IN nor OUT.

Diagnosis is a particular kind of decision making in situations where one has incomplete and uncertain knowledge. As a recent example of constraint programming in decision making, let us look at (Benjamin, Viana, Corbett, and Silva 1993). This paper describes MDA, a decision support system currently being developed at the Naval Undersea Warfare Center. The goal of MDA is to generate the optimal next manoeuvre recommendation to support the submarine commander decision making process, "which includes absorbing an extensive amount of complex information in the short time interval between manoeuvres".

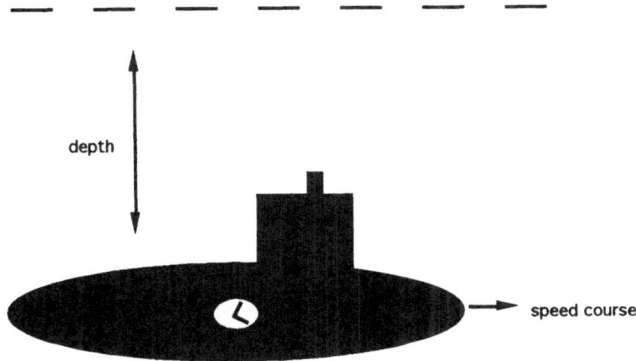

Fig. 7 MDA system for submarine manoeuvres

In a given situation MDA generates a set of constraints on the four motion variables: speed, depth, time. and course. The typically overconstrained nature of the resulting CSP is "countered by propagating the manoeuvre goals to produce rated constraints and choosing a feasible solution from a maximal subset of the original constraints". The author introduces a 4-dimensional discrete "Manoeuvre Space"

$$MAN = Speed * Depth * Time * Course$$

and "region areas" are subspaces of MAN given by taking intervals in the 4 dimensions. Although MDA uses blackboard techniques (as in Stefik's constraint posting), it is easier to explain as a sequence of four phases:

1. Every constraint is converted into a set of region areas, each with a rating (each constraint has an importance rating e.g. 50 for "avoid land obstacle", 5 for "maintain depth")

2. Constraints are combined – a new set of mutually exclusive region areas is computed, each with its priority

3. The midpoint of the region area with the highest priority is given as the recommended speed, depth, time and course

4. Various justifications of these recommendations are given to the user.

The authors write that integer programming and various other Operations Research techniques were tried, but constraint programming was much better.

However constraint programming is only one of many ways of handling uncertain, imprecise and incomplete knowledge. Among the alternatives are default logic, circumscription, fuzzy logic and belief nets. Dechter is one of the few constraint programmers who have tapped the goldmine in the alternative approaches to "non-monotonic logic".

1.2.2.4 CP permeates Planning Since the pioneering paper of Stefik (Stefik 1981) the constraint approach has dominated planning. In the subfield of scheduling, Operations Research scientists have developed sophisticated methods for handling scheduling constraints, but traditional constraint programming languages are beginning to be competitive (see chapter by Wallace).

Most recent planning systems are heirarchic planners. Stefik explains the basic idea "In hierarchical planning a solution is first sketched out in terms of abstract steps which are refined into specific plan steps during the planning process". Remember the description of a linear plan as a path in a state graph in fig. 2. If one abstracts the state graph by imposing an equivalence relation on states, then one expects that paths to become shorter and easier to find. One form of hierachic planning is to impose nested equivalence relations on states, to have a fixed plan for the coarsest equivalence, and to refine it as one progresses through ever finer equivalences.

To show that this way of building hierarchies is not restricted to planning problems, consider once again the submarine problem with its state space

MAN = Speed * Depth * Time * Course

We did not mention that MAN was made finite for pragmatic reasons-e.g. there are 36 possible values of Course because directions are partitioned into10 degree segments. Let MAN' be the state space given by choosing 20 degree segments. The obvious map from MAN to MAN' gives the hierarchical solution to the submarine problem:

Solve MAN' problem with 20 degree segments, then refine to solution of MAN problem.

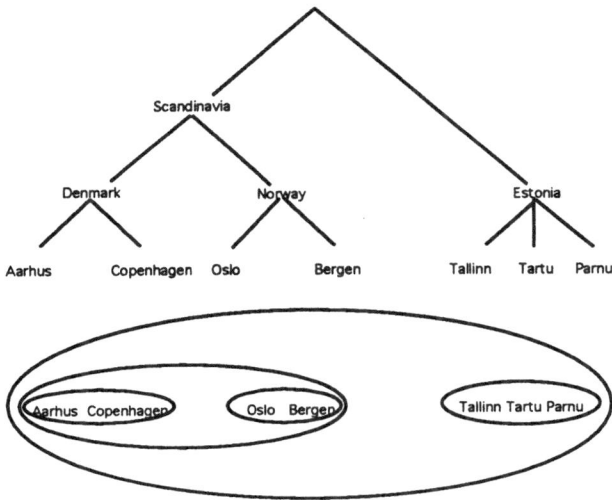

Fig. 8 Hierachical Planning

Believers in hierarchies claim that such abstracting away from detail gives an exponential decrease in complexity. Sometimes it indeed does, but not always; in section 1.2.2.2 we described a problem where careful attention to detail gave a large decrease in complexity.

As a recent example of constraint programming in planning, let us look at (Reece and Shafer 1993). This paper describes the tactical part of Ulysses, a system for driving an autonomous vehicle. There are many groups around the world working on the glamorous, but potentially useful problem of safe autonomous cars, ships, trains, planes etc., but most of them focus on either the strategic problems like route planning or operational problems like following a curving road. In (Reece and Shafer 1993) the focus is on tactical problems like overtaking another car or behaving properly at an intersection with traffic lights. To quote "Knowledge of driving is primarily encoded in Ulysses in the form of constraints. The constraints are based on implicit goals of driving lawfully and safely. Constraints limit the set of allowable actions based on the presence and characteristics of certain objects in the scene. These objects – signs, signals, vehicles, road markings, etc.– are generally identified by their relation to the corridor. Ulysses must look for all objects in the scene that could trigger a constraint. After all triggered constraints have been combined, Ulysses chooses an acceleration and lane-changing action from the available choices. This selection is based on the implicit goals of driving quickly and courteously." Traffic constraints are so complex that they can only be formulated in a very expressive language.

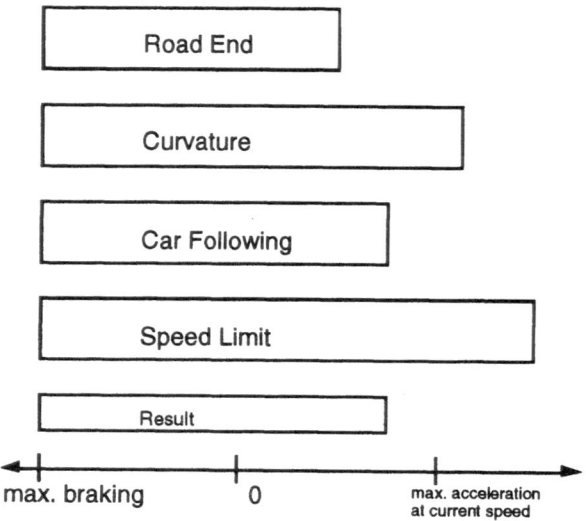

Fig. 9 Typical Ulysses constraints on accelerations

1.2.2.5 Semantics of Planning In section 1.2.1 we described linear planners, but most recent planners are non-linear. In a non-linear planner any partial ordered set of actions is a plan,

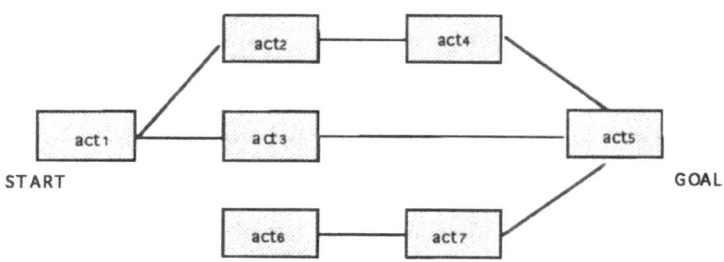

Fig. 10 Non-linear plans

but just as in concurrency studies graph grammars, event systems · · · have also been tried (see chapter by Rossi). Indeed planning systems have considered more subtle situations than concurrency studies. In concurrency studies until recently (Murphy 1993) (see chapter by Saraswat, Jagadeesan and College) one abstracted away from start and finish times of actions, whereas these are usually key factors in planning. In concurrency "A and B can happen simultaneously" almost always implies "A and B can happen in either order", but this is not true in planning or reality. We all can do things with two hands, which MUST be done simultaneously- clapping at a concert or lifting heavy furniture or

Fig. 11 A || B ↛ A; B + B; A

In planning this unrealistic implication is true if actions are of the simple type with just preconditions and postconditions, but it is not true in the Linköping approach (Backstrom 1992; Sandewall and Ronnquist 1986) where actions also have

> *keep conditions*- maintaining some environmental property throughout the action

> *prevail conditions*- requiring some environmental property throughout the action.

Keep and prevail conditions allow for the fact that actions take time and can overlap.

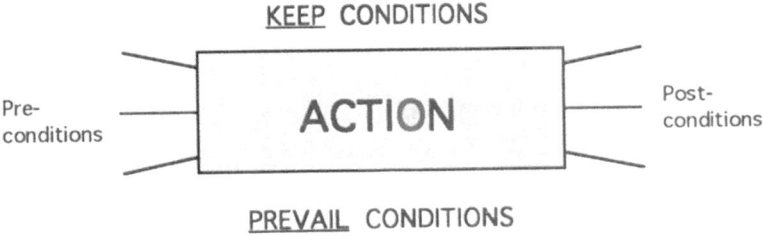

Fig. 12 Actions can have keep and prevail conditions

Furthermore CP can capture this fact because keep and prevail conditions can be expressed as (higher order?) constraints between actions, just as pre- and post-conditions can be expressed as constraints between (partial?) states.

In the Linköping approach they use an interesting variation of the usual "Features → Values" semantic notion of state; they let the domain Values be a complete lattice with "undefined" as its lowest element, so there are 4 truth values: True, False, Undefined, Contradiction. Once they have "undefined", states can be partial; pre- , post-, prevail and keep conditions can be identified with partial states and one can insist on constraints like:

pre- and post- condition of an action have the same features defined
features defined in the prevail condition of an action are undefined in its precondition
features defined in the keep condition of an action are also defined in its precondition.

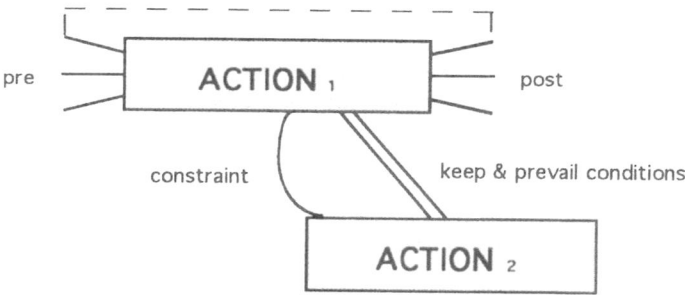

Fig. 13 Keep and prevail conditions captured by constraints on actions

1.2.3 Intelligent Behaviour and Constraint Programming

"The mind is a large constraint network" Andrei Mantsivoda
"To throw away all constraints would be to destroy the capacity for creative thinking" Margaret Boden

Many of those studying intelligent behaviour use the methodology first expounded by Marr (Marr 1982). He argued that there are three levels of investigation:

at the *computational* level one looks at what the behaviour is and the **constraints** that determine why the behaviour is as it is

at the *algorithmic* level one looks at the steps in the behaviour and how the behaviour develops at the *implementation* level one looks at the physical, chemical and biological mechanisms that underlie the behaviour.

As Marr was primarily interested in low level visual processes – how the brain develops "3D impressions" from the "2D images" presented by the eyes – his methodology is designed for subconscious, non-symbolic behaviour, but it is also appropriate for conscious, symbolic behaviour.

Notice the central role of constraints in the Marr methodology; students of intelligent behaviour should first hunt for sufficiently many constraints that they determine a unique behaviour. They can also consider constraint propagation and other mechanisms developed by the CP community as candidate algorithms for explaining how the behaviour develops. The Waltz filtering algorithm, described in the section 1.2.2.2, is an elegant example of this; the human and computer solutions of this visual problem differ only at the implementational level. Another elegant example has been described by Boden (Boden 1990). The intelligent (?) behaviour to be studied "hoverflies fly to their mates hovering nearby (so as to mate in mid-air)" is determined by the single constraint "if flylike object sensed, then turn towards it". We know the particular cells in the hoverfly's brain that fire when a flylike object is sensed, and we know that one of them is directly connected to a cell which sends a controlling signal to the "turning muscle" for the hoverfly's wings. If one wanted a robot with this behaviour, it could use the same algorithm as real hoverflies do and its behaviour would only differ from that of a real moth at the implementational level. Other examples of intelligent (?) behaviour can be found in (Resnikoff 1987).

The currently dominant belief among robot builders (Brookes 1991; Maes 1991) is : reactive behaviour is more crucial than rational behaviour; appropriate immediate reactions to anomalies in the environment are vital, slow directed intensional actions towards a goal are just desirable. Although it is customary to formulate appropriate reactions as rules, it is more proper to consider them as constraints enforced by the environment and the capabilities of the robot. For a natural analogue think of the intelligent(?) behaviour of a spider continually spinning new webs, or insects wandering in Estonian forests. Do insects follow rules, or do they react to constraints enforced by the environment? AI fans should remember Simon's ant (Simon 1969) wandering home across a stony beach, its complicated path determined by the pebbles and a few simple rules; they also should remember Kobrysinski's maxim "the best model of the world is the world itself".

As the complex behaviour of humans, insects and other biological organisms is generated quickly, nature obviously exploits parallelism. We do not know exactly how nature exploits parallelism, but some of the computer constraint systems that exploit parallelism seem closer to nature than others. Let us look at CSNNs, constraint satisfaction neural networks. The basic idea is that constraints are represented as weights on links in a neural network and the solution of a constraint problem is given by the firing neurons when the neural network has stabilised. One can take any binary constraint net and build a neural net by introducing a neuron for each value of each variable and setting the weight of a link between neuron $< x_i, v_i >$ and neuron $< x_j, v_j >$ from the constraint on variables x_i and x_j. As the simplest rule – if constraint on x_i and x_j rules out assignment $< v_i, v_j >$, then no link,else link of weight 1– leads to slow convergence, more complex rules are used in practice. One also has to ensure a suitable initial state of the neural network.

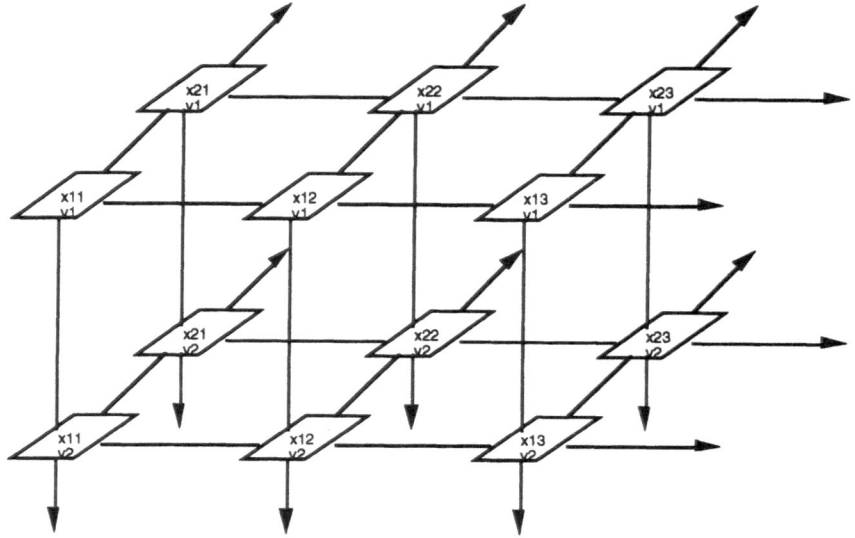

Fig. 14 Constraint satisfaction neural networks

In (Lin, Tsao, and Chen 1992) the problem of segmenting an image is considered. For every pixel in an n*n image there is a variable for each of m possible region labels, so there are n*n*m neurons in the network. There is a link between neuron $< x_{ij}, v_k >$ and neuron $< x_{pq}, v_r >$ iff pixels x_{ij} and x_{pq} are immediate neighbours; the weight of the link is positive if the region labels v_k and v_r are compatible, otherwise negative. The initial state of the network is determined by a completely separate Kohonen net. Although there is no guarantee that both these neural nets converge, the results in this and similar papers indicate that for medical and other realistic images, these neural net methods not only converge but also give better solutions than more conventional methods.

Earlier we asserted that the Marr methodology is also appropriate for conscious, symbolic behaviour. One reason for this is that such behaviour is often modular and there are implicit constraints between the modules. In any top-down, divide-and-conquer approach to a problem the ideal is that the problems are independent, but usually they are dependent–there are constraints on the solution of subproblems. This view of problem solving is old:

"Divide each problem that you examine into as many parts as you can and as you need to solve them more easily"
Descartes, *Oeuvres* vol. VI p.18, *Discours de la Methodes*

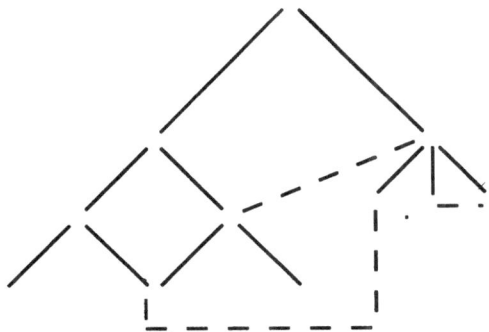

Fig. 15 Almost hierarchies

"This rule of Descartes is of little use as long as the art of dividing $\cdots$ remains unexplained $\cdots$ By dividing his problem into unsuitable parts, the inexperienced problem-solver may increase his difficulty"
Leibniz, *Philosophische Schriften*, ed. Gerhart, vol. IV p. 331

Leibniz's difficulty is that the parts of a problem may interact. Several AI pioneers suggested that such interactions can be captured by constraints. Remember the definition of heirarchical planning in section 1.2.2.4. At each level of the hierarchy every abstract step is a constraint on the abstract states before and after the abstract step. The hierarchy was built from nested equivalence relations on states, and most hierarchies for topdown problem solving (also CP problems) can be built in this way. But where do the nested equivalences on states come from? The general answer is: functions from finer state spaces to cruder state spaces. If one accepts that states are functions from Features to Values, then one has the simple answer: nested equivalences come by dropping features. This simple answer corresponds to the heuristic of ordering variables in CSP problems. The more general heuristic of grouping variables in CSP corresponds to replacing features $f_1, f_2 \cdots f_n$ with values in $V_1, V_2, \cdots V_n$ by a general feature f_0 with values in (maybe a subset of) $V_1 * V_2 * \cdots V_n$.

Leibniz's difficulty with Descartes rule is that the parts of a problem may interact. The AI solution of this difficulty is that such interactions can be captured by constraints. To check whether constraints do in fact have this central role in intelligent behaviour, the author made notes when solving a simplified version of the constraint benchmarks devised for the NATO Advanced Study Intitute (available from the archive ftp.daimi.aau.dk directory pub/CLP) . This analysis of minibenchmark solutions does not conflict with the belief that common sense and rules of thumb i.e. heuristics have a major role in intelligent, symbolic behaviour of humans. Furthermore many of these heuristics are constraints but some are not. Most of the heuristics that are not constraints, seem to be "algorithms for solving subproblems". Since biological contraints are the primary reason for the topdown division of problems into subproblems, our analysis does not conflict with the Marr methodology. One reason for the omnipresence of constraint programming in AI is that every partition of almost all problems has interacting parts. Constraints do seem to be one of the keys to intelligent behaviour.

1.2.4 Constraint nets and Semantic nets

In this section we show how constraint nets are a particular kind of semantic net, and that some of the AI techniques for manipulating semantic nets suggest extensions to CP. CP devotees know what constraint nets are : labelled hypergraphs with a vertex for each variable and a hyperedge for each constraint. They also know how arc consistency, path consistency, constraint propagation and other CP techniques relate to constraint nets; in particular how graph grammar semantics (see Rossi chapter) relate to constraint propagation. Fig. 16 shows the constraint net for the zebra problem, a well-known CP benchmark.

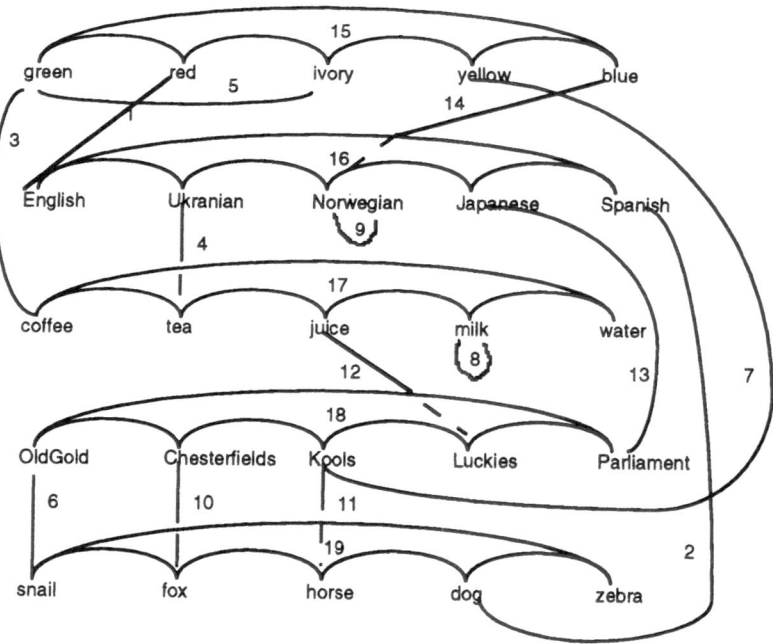

Fig. 16 Constraint net for zebra problem -
hyperedge labels refer to formulas in figure 17

What are the labels on the hyperedges in a constraint net? The simple answer is relations, but this is only a particular case of the proper answer: a logical formula with an assignment of its free variables to the vertices of the hyperedge. There are myriads of logics, but for almost all of them the wellformed formulas are given by a signature Σ. We shall only consider first order sorted logic where Σ gives the predicate, function and constant symbols. The signature Σ gives not only the Σ -terms and Σ -formulas of the language but also Σ -algebras as the structures in which the terms and formulas can be interpreted. In AI and CP there is usually a particular Σ -algebra (the intended interpretation) and a finite theory of this algebra. By Godel's theorem this theory is usually incomplete.

```
1: English      = red
2: Spanish      = dog             Signature Σ1 one sort
3; coffee       = green           pred.syms: Neighbour,Different
4: Ukranian     = tea             func.syms: Succ
5: green        = Succ(ivory)     cons.syms: 1,2,3,4,5
6: OldGold      = snail
7: Kools        = yellow
8: milk         = 3               Σ1–algebra has the domain
9: Norwegian    = 1               Five = {1,2,3,4,5} and the
10: Neighbour(Chesterfield,fox)   expected predicates,
11: Neighbour(Kools,horse)        functions and constants
12: Luckies     = juice
13: Japanese    = Parliament
14: Neighbour(Norwegian,blue)
15: Different(green,red,ivory,yellow,blue)
16: Different(English,Ukranian,Norwegian,Japanese,Spanish)
17: Different(coffee,tea,juice,milk,water)
18: Different(OldGold,Chesterfields,Kools,Luckies,Parliament)
19: Different(snail,fox,horse,dog,zebra)
20: Axioms for the intended domain Five
```

Fig. 17 Logical theory and algebra for Zebra constraint net

What are the labels on the vertices in a constraint net? The CP answer is a variable of the appropriate sort, but one could answer "a sort" or even a Σ -term of the appropriate sort. These answers give us four new syntactic notions of states as solutions of CP problems:

- a state is a set of equations, one for each variable

- a state is a set of Σ -formulas,one for each constraint, and a set of equations, one for each variable

- a state is a ground substitution, a Σ -term for each variable

- a state is a set of Σ -formulas, one for each constraint,
  and a ground substitution, a Σ -term for each variable.

This analysis suggests "logical theory and designated algebra" as an appropriate generalisation of CSP. Logical theories are no more than finite sets of formulas and the essence of CSP is finding substitutions for variables that makes the formulas true in the designated algebra. Usual CSP's have no quantifiers in the formulas and no structural function symbols.

One of the central problems of AI (and data base practitioners) is the representation of knowledge. Just as entity-relationship models are popular in the data base world, so semantic nets are popular in the AI world. Both ER models and semantic nets are hypergraphs with a vertex for each "object" and a hyperedge for each "relationship". Figure 1.2.4 shows an ER diagram for the zebra problem-the ellipses indicate the entities, the diamonds indicate the relationships. We see that some constraints are represented naturally, but others are not so easy to represent (so not in the figure). Even so, some argue for a symbiosis between CP and data base theory seduced by the similarity between constraint propagation and the various ways of "joining" data base relations.

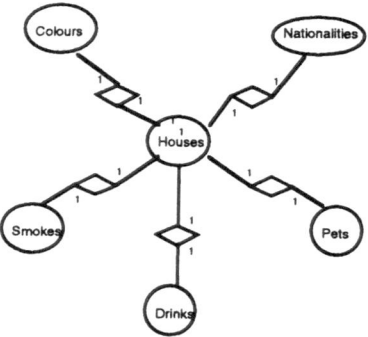

Fig. 18 Zebra Entity Relationship Diagram

ER models have a standard well-defined semantics, but this is not so for some of the many varieties of semantic nets in the literature. Conceptual graphs – a variety of semantic net introduced by Sowa (Sowa 1984; Sowa 1991) – do have a well-defined semantics, but it is based on a logic that is much more expressive than first ordered sorted logic. Instead we look at a simpler form of semantic net

VertexLabels = Σ-algebra A (so labels can be stored as Σ-terms in the computer)
EdgeLabels = Formulas in the first order logic for signature Σ

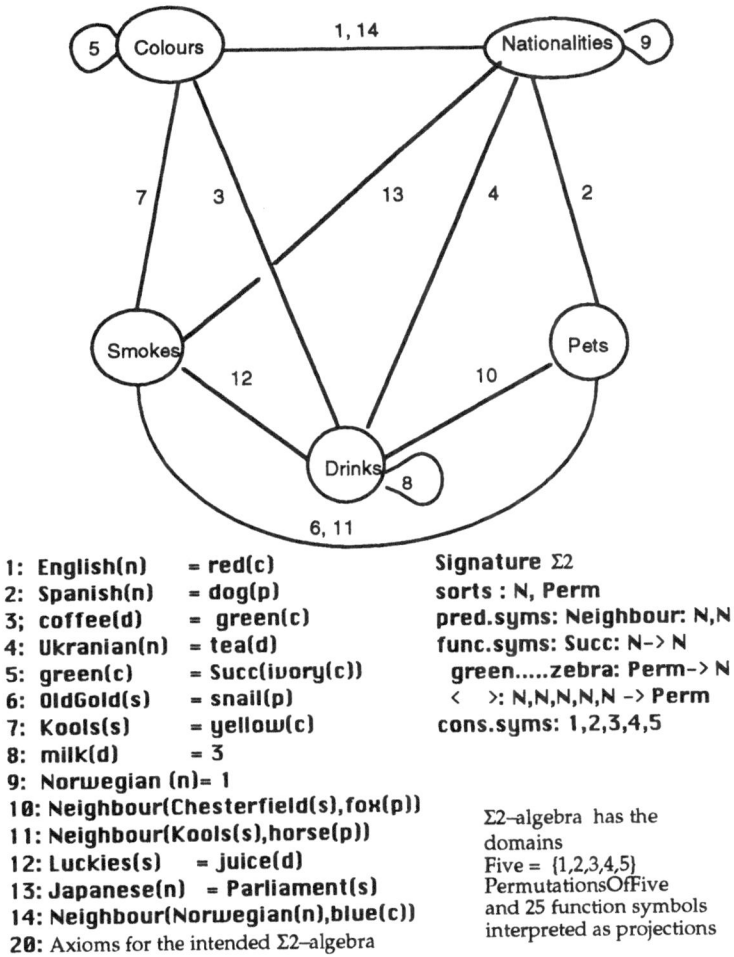

1: **English(n)   = red(c)**
2: **Spanish(n)   = dog(p)**
3; **coffee(d)   = green(c)**
4: **Ukranian(n)   = tea(d)**
5: **green(c)   = Succ(ivory(c))**
6: **OldGold(s)   = snail(p)**
7: **Kools(s)   = yellow(c)**
8: **milk(d)   = 3**
9: **Norwegian (n)= 1**
10: **Neighbour(Chesterfield(s),fox(p))**
11: **Neighbour(Kools(s),horse(p))**
12: **Luckies(s)   = juice(d)**
13: **Japanese(n)   = Parliament(s)**
14: **Neighbour(Norwegian(n),blue(c))**
20: Axioms for the intended Σ2-algebra

Signature Σ2
sorts : N, Perm
pred.syms: Neighbour: N,N
func.syms: Succ: N-> N
green.....zebra: Perm-> N
<   >: N,N,N,N,N -> Perm
cons.syms: 1,2,3,4,5

Σ2–algebra has the
domains
Five = {1,2,3,4,5}
PermutationsOfFive
and 25 function symbols
interpreted as projections

Fig. 19 Zebra Semantic Net and its 5 variable logical theory

If only variables are allowed as vertex labels and only quantifier free formulas are allowed as edge labels, then we get traditional constraint nets. The extension to CP suggested by this form of semantic net is : allow variables to range over structured domains. After all a Σ-algebra is no more than a domain for each sort in Σ and an interpretation for each constant, function and predicate symbols in Σ.; so a Σ-algebra A is just a structured domain.

Not only do semantic nets capture the grouping and structuring of constraint variables, but they also give a clean description of hierarchical solution of constraint problems. Simple transformations,that do not change the underlying signature, are given by Σ-morphisms from an algebra A to another Σ-algebra B. Although they do not change the Σ-formulas in a state or theory, they can be very useful when domains are finite and constraints/relations must be stored as tables (Remember the MAN to MAN' transform in section 1.2.2.4). But more complex transformations are more useful; one can transform a net over an algebra A into a net over algebra B with another signature Σ'. Indeed we have just seen an example of this when the constraint net for the Zebra problem in fig. 16 was transformed into the semantic net for the Zebra problem in fig. 19. We have described a hierarchical solution of the Zebra problem:

Solve the semantic net problem in fig. 19
then refine to solution of constraint problem in fig. 16.

Clearly the refinement step is trivial. In section 1.2.2 we described hierarchical plan refinement as a function sequence

$$A \to B \to C \to \cdots$$

In this section we showed how this idea gives a general hierarchical approach to CP and we gave a couple of examples. The use of Σ-terms for vertex labelling is closely related to various suggestions for using "structured variables" and "partial knowledge" in CP. The use of a particular Σ-algebra A suggests the use of the theory of A in directing constraint propagation $\cdots$

The form of semantic net in fig. 19 is a simple modification of the "graphics" studied in (Hess and Mayoh 1990), where edges are unlabelled and vertex labels can incorporate edge information. In the "graphics"-papers graph grammars are used to describe the transformation of one semantic net into another. In (Hess and Mayoh 1990) this generality was used to give a new approach to ANALOGIES, the theme of the next section. Readers interested in the category theory behind this generalisation of CP to semantic nets, Σ-algebras and logical theories can consult the "logics as institutions" literature started by (Goguen and Burstall 1984).

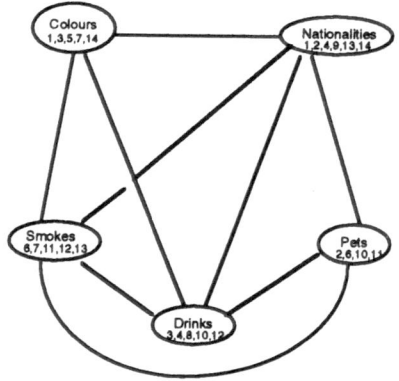

Fig. 20 Zebra graphic

1.2.5 CaseBased Reasoning and Analogy are CP

It has been said that rationality is 99% analogy and the remaining 1% logical reasoning is used for convincing ourselves and others that our immediate opinions and decisions are not totally idiotic. One argument for this is that the "common sense" solutions of everyday problems seem to "pop up" analogically – a solution of a similar earlier problem suggests the solution of a new problem.

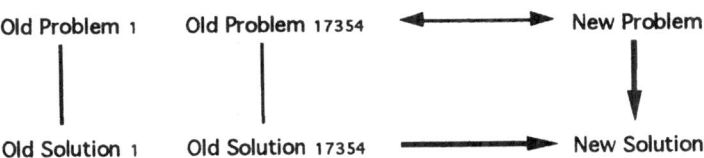

Fig. 21 Analogies and case based reasoning

Computers can also reason by analogy and they can use case-based reasoning. They have no difficulty in remembering early cases, but they are far inferior to us in

1. MATCHING new problems to similar old problems

2. RECALLING old problems that may besimilar to the current problem.

Most existing case-based reasoning programs use semantic nets (described in the last section) to represent old cases/problems but there is no consensus about the level of abstraction/schematization. Obviously no problem is identical to an earlier problem; many, many details should not be remembered and general solutions of abstract problem schemes should be "tweaked" to get detailed solutions of new problems.

There is also no consensus about "tweaking". In the next section we shall look at the popular "explanation based learning", which uses a logical theory of the problem domain. Other ways of finding and using analogies use less strict matching methods (Owen 1990; Gentner 1983). Just as semantic nets are generalisations of constraint nets, so analogical and case-based systems are generalisations of constraint programs.

One of the earliest AI papers (Evans 1968) was about using analogies to solve the once so popular IQ tests.

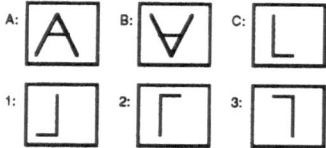

Fig. 22 Analogy problem A is to B as C is to ??

One of the latest AI books (Mitchell 1993) is about using analogies for pattern matching problems like:

"APC" is to "ABC" as "OPC" is to ???

Are those who answer OPQ more creative than those who answer OBC ? It would be interesting to apply modern constraint programming techniques first to this problem, then to Bongard's 100 visual concept problems (Bongard 1970) like

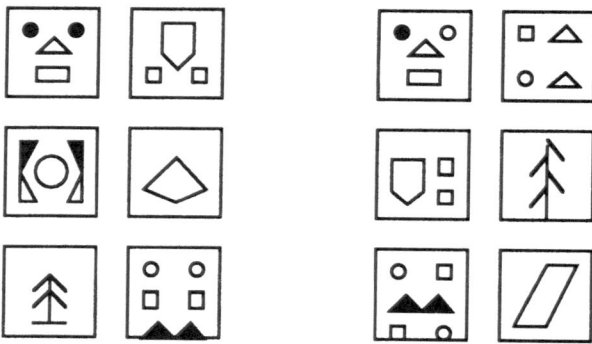

Fig. 23 Left pictures enjoy a common property, that no right picture enjoys (An old problem that is still rather difficult for computers).

Constraint programming and case-based reasoning have been combined in a recent paper (Townidnejad, Myler, and Gonzalez 1993). The objective of this research is "to construct a complete knowledge base for a diagnostic and control reasoning system that resides in Computer Aided Design databases". The paper describes the AKG system that captures the information from a CAD data base and identifies a unique component in its internal library of components that matches the properties of each output in the system.

The AKG internal library of components is the casebase and it contains the necessary information regarding their functionality, mostly in the form of strong, normal, weak and supporting constraints. The AKG algorithm for identifying components in a particular computer-aided design uses not only traditional CP

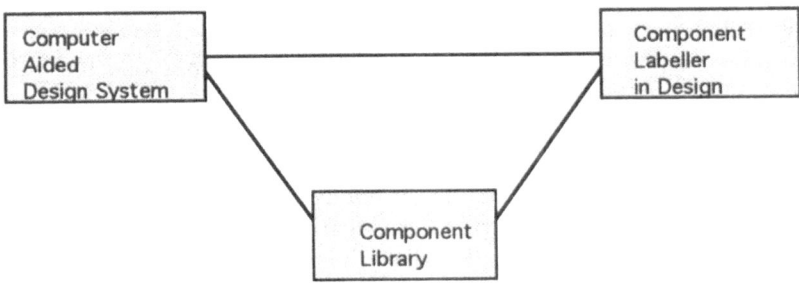

Fig. 24 AKG case based constraint system

methods like node, arc and path consistency but it also introduces "constraint stiffening", a method that exploits the fact that the AKG case base forms a hierarchy. The AKG system is not perfect, it asks its users for help from time to time. On the NASA Orbiter Maintenance and Refurbishment data the AKG system needed help for 24 of the 138 components to be identified. However it took two man-years to generate the knowledge base for the KATE diagnostic and control system from this data, whereas with the help of AKG the same knowledge base could be generated in the matter of a man-month.

1.2.6 Machine Learning and Constraint Programming

Thousands of computer scientists work in the area of Machine learning; there is a constant stream of journal articles, books and even applications in practice. Many of the techniques developed by these scientists are clearly applicable to constraint programming, so that it is extremely strange that there seem to be very few published applications. The journal "Machine Learning", published since 1986, has several articles on constraint programming, but none on the learning of constraints.

1.2.6.1 Learning while solving a single constraint problem
Rina Dechter (Dechter 1986) seems to have been the first to have noticed that dependency-directed backtracking and other constraint programming techniques are a form of machine learning. Earlier M. Bruynooghe and L.M. Pereira (Bruynooghe and Pereira 1984) suggested recording "conflict sets" when dead-ends occur (the similar idea of no-goods appeared earlier in the truth maintenance literature).

Dechter distinguishes between deep and shallow learning; shallow learning derives constraints from an easily computed approximation to the conflict set, deep learning derives constraints from the hard-to-compute conflict set. She shows that both forms of learning greatly help in the solution of the Zebra problem. Since 1984 there have been several impressive developments of backtracking using "Explanation based learning" and other powerful machine learning techniques.

The idea behind "Explanation based learning" is that one has a logical theory T and whenever one has an example E one can generalise the T-proof of E to get a whole family of examples. In the constraint programming application we look at, T is a theory of failure and "Explanation based learning" gives a "censor" that prevents a whole family of failures.

A pretty example of explanation based learning in constraint programming is (Bhatnagar 1990). The author describes the planning system FAILSAFE II , which uses censors to prevent plan steps that violate a constraint.

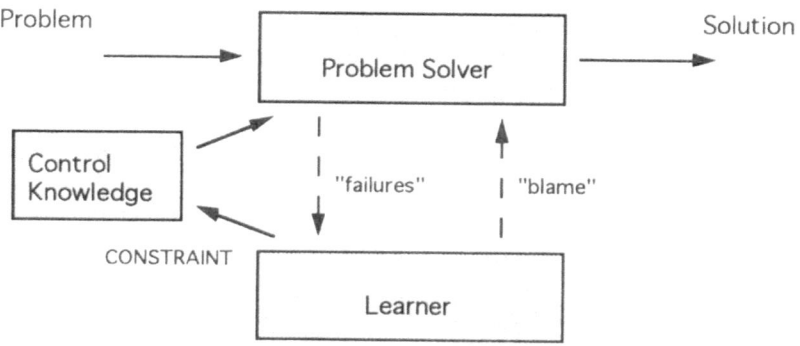

Fig. 25 Explanation based learning of constraints in FAILSAFE II

The system combines ideas from the well-known learning system PRODIGY (Minton 1991) with Stefik's planning ideas. A problem for FAILSAFE II is specified by an initial state and a goal. At every state FAILSAFE II has a current state and zero, one or more pending goals. To expand a state S the system uses an operator generator that returns an operator whose preconditions are satisfied in S. When the current goal is achieved it is protected and one of the pending goals is chosen to be the next current goal by the goal selection rules. Explanation based learning is used to cut down on backtracking by learning new censors and/or goal selection rules. The system does not call the learner module every time it backtracks. Problem solving heuristics gathered by the system indicate whether the search is under- or over-constrained. In either of these cases the system declares a failure and calls the learner.

1.2.6.2 Learning from one constraint program so similar constraint programs can be solved more efficiently As the discussion of case-based reasoning and analogy in section 1.2.5 suggests, one can find good ways of solving new problems by examining the solutions of similar old problems.

The impetus for the paper we shall discuss (Day 1992) is the extremely large size of the scheduling problems faced by the United States Transportation

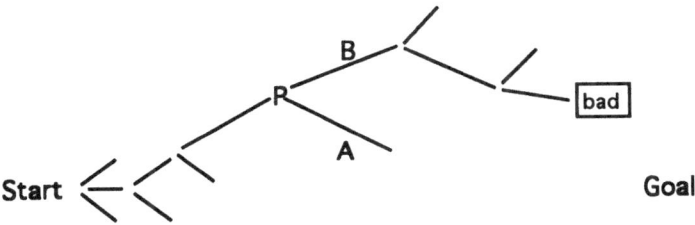

Fig. 26 Learner might suggest censoring step B

Command. Surely one can use the experience from one such problem (typically hundreds of thousands of movement orders) in solving the next. But how can one generalise from one constraint net to a quite different constraint net. Day focuses on ordering the values assigned to the variables (i.e. nodes in the constraint nets). He uses the machine learning technique of "conceptual clustering" to build a hierarchy of variable types. To get a suitable set of features for building this hierarchy, each variable in his system keeps information about its neighbouring variables. As one solves more and more CP's, this hierarchy grows and grows. When faced with a new constraint program, the system looks up each of the constrained variables in the classification hierarchy and finds suggestions of an order in which domain values should be assigned to the variable.

1.2.6.3 Other forms of learning and constraint programming In section 1.1.3 we gave an example of neural net and in section 1.1.5 we described case-based reasoning and analogy.

Inductive logic programming (Muggleton 1992; Lavrac and Dzeroski 1993) is a popular form of machine learning, but it does not as yet seem to have been applied to constraint programming. This is somewhat surprising as this form of learning produces a logic program and the changes needed to make it produce a constraint logic program seem rather minor.

Genetic algorithms have been applied to planning and scheduling problems, but apparently not to other constraint problems. Genetic algorithms have even been incorporated within constraint programs for scheduling (Uckun, Bagchi, Kawamura, and Miyabe 1993) (also see chapter by Wallace). Not only are genetic algorithms surprisingly successful with other search and optimisation problems, but – particularly in the form of genetic programming (Koza 1992) – they can also produce small constraint logic programs. One can also have a population of constraint programs for a particular type of constraint problem – try them all when a new problem arises – and from time to time use genetic operators to make a new population from the old. Another possibility is to use genetic algorithms to choose the appropriate constraint solving techniques for a particular type of problem – Prosser's recent paper (Prosser 1993) compares many "hybrid techniques" and one can easily devise appropriate genotypes.

1.2.6.4 Scientific discovery & constraint programming There has been much research recently for finding patterns in data (Piatersky and Frawley 1993; Margolis 1987). Automatic "goldmining of large databases- medical journals, astronomical data, genetic information and the like- has become popular. In (Freedman 1993) there is a brief description of various AI goldmining techniques in biology. Recently one of these "had puzzled out the rough structure of a protein that plays a role in the spread of a certain cancer". Sometimes these goldmining techniques go by the name of "Scientific Discovery" because some of them have been developed by those who believe that scientists develop new theories by "seeing" new patterns in data. Prominent among these developers is H.Simon who was responsible for the early Bacon system (Langley, Simon, and Bradshaw 1983; Prosser 1993). When given data such as

Moon	Distance D	Period P
A	5.67	1.769
B	8.67	3.571
C	14.00	7.155
D	24.67	16.689

BACON uses heuristics like "if variable X increases monotonically with variable Y, then look at X/Y" to discover patterns like Kepler's third law

Moon	Distance D	Period P	D/P	D^2/P	D^3/P^2
A	5.67	1.769	3.203	18.153	58.15
B	8.67	3.571	2.427	21.036	51.06
C	14.00	7.155	1.957	27.395	53.61
D	24.67	16.689	1.478	36.459	53.89

Fig. 27 Discovery of Kepler's law $D^3 = $ Constant* P^2

In this case the pattern discovered is an equation and equations are a simple form of constraints, Can one use these discovery techniques to find more complex constraints in interesting databases? Indeed one can- as (BharatRao and Lu 1993) shows. This paper describes the KEDS system for discovering statistical constructs of the form

$$y = f(x1, x2 \cdots xn) + mu(0, \Sigma)$$

where $mu(0, \Sigma)$ is the 0-mean Gaussian noise process with standard deviation Σ.

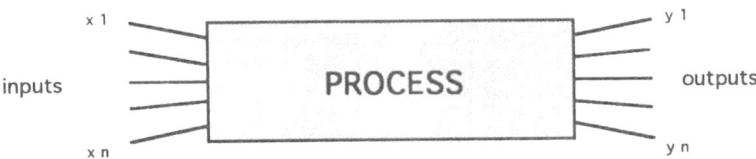

Fig. 28 KEDS learning constraints on processes

The user can specify several template functions to be considered as f in such constraints, e.g.

$f(x_1, x_2) = ax_1 * x_1 + bx_2 + c$ where a, b, c are real parameters

The major novelty of the KEDS system is that it allows for different constraints on the variable y to be discovered in different regions of the n-dimensional space spanned by the variables $x1, x2 \cdots xn$; indeed KEDS investigates different partitions of this space as it hunts for constraints that fit the data. As Rao and Lu write "The KEDS algorithm can be viewed as a two-phase process involving discovery and partitioning. Each invocation of the KEDS algorithm for a chosen template produces zero, one or more candidate region-equation pairs. The partitioning is model-driven and based on the relationships that are discovered in the data, while the discovery process is restricted within the boundaries of the regions created by the partitioning. This close interaction between the two processes enables KEDS to combine characteristics of both empirical discovery and conceptual clustering systems."

For those who distrust statistics, we describe a constraint learning system that is purely logical. In (Richards, Kraan, and Kuipers 1992) the authors describe the MISQ system for building constraint models from behavioural information; if the information provided by the user is complete and consistent, the generated models reproduce the input behaviours. The model generation process is broken into three major phases:

1. consistent qualitative behaviours are input directly; a qualitative value consists of a quantitative magnitude and a direction of change; quantitative behaviours are converted into consistent qualitative behaviours (e.g. only maxima, minima and zeroes are kept in high resolution data).

2. constraints consistent with the input behaviour are created by "generate and test" and are filtered by comparison with the input behaviours and by dimensional analysis; the constraint satisfaction criteria are based on magnitudes, signs, directions of change, and corresponding values of the variables.

3. these constraints are combined into a model using the "relational pathfinding" technique.

The current system implements the following constraint types:

- arithmetical constraints (add,mult,minus...)

- differential constraints (d/dt)

- functional constraints (steady, M+ or M- for constant, increasing or decreasing).

Users can supply dimensions for variables, so meaningless constraints are not generated. Once it has a consistent set of constraints MISQ checks to see if they form a connected graph. If they do not, it assumes that some variables are missing and it uses the relational path finding technique from the general purpose learning system FORTE to create new variables. Let us illustrate this technique with a simple example, the double-bath configuration in figure 1.2.6.4:

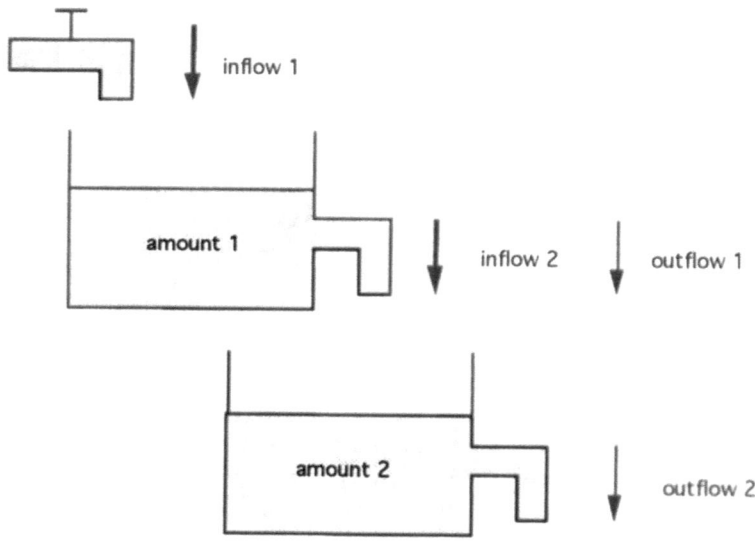

Fig. 29 Double bath system

Suppose the user measured all flows and amounts but did not realise that the calculated net flow for each bath would be important. With such data the first two phases of MISQ produce constraints:

outflow1 = inflow2
inflow1 is steady
outflow1 increases with amount1
outflow2 increases with amount2

As these constraints are not connected, relational pathfinding is used to find the missing two variables and the following six constraints:

$$\text{outflow1} + \text{netflow1} = \text{inflow1}$$
$$\text{outflow2} + \text{netflow2} = \text{inflow2}$$
$$\text{d amount1}/\text{dt} \quad = \text{netflow1}$$
$$\text{d amount2}/\text{dt} \quad = \text{netflow2}$$

This gives the model (a constraint network):

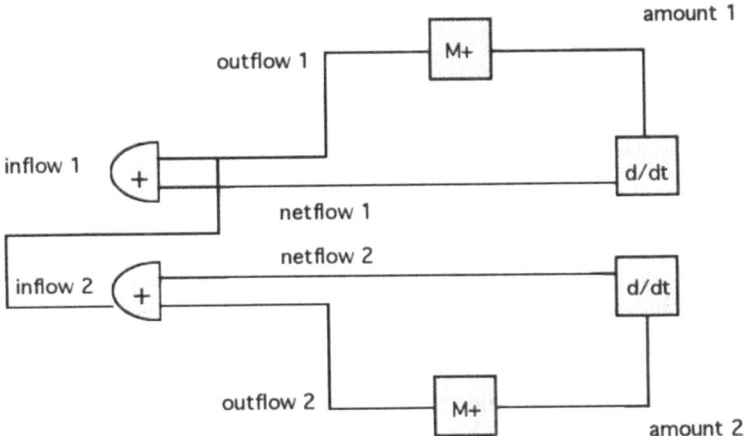

Fig. 30 Constraint net for double bath system

We can observe that Kuiper's functional constraints can be replaced by higher order constraints (see chapter by Tyugu), with the time variable explicitly represented. It would be extremely interesting to see whether models produced by MISQ on biological data (e.g. fish in the Baltic Sea, penguins in the Antarctic) are at all similar to those produced by ecologists.

1.2.7 Conclusion

Some conclusions for CP seem warranted by this foray into AI:

- Do not fear expressive constraint languages, not only may complex formulations give efficient solutions but instances of theoretically infeasable problems that arise in practice are usually easy to solve.

- Structuring the representation of a problem can help in solving it.

- Analogical, case-based and other approximate reasoning can help solving problems.

- Machine learning techniques can help in optimising the solution of costraint problems.

AI and CP are symbiotic. Constraints play a role in both artificial and natural intelligence. People seem to behave intelligently by

1. extracting constraints from sensual experience

2. using such constraints to interpret current situations and react appropriately.

In constraint programming people formulate constraints and incorporate them in constraint programs. A natural dream is that this can be done automatically. In this chapter we have looked at some papers that are a modest start in the fulfilment of this dream.

References

Backstrom, C. (1992). *Computational complexity of reasoning about plans*. Ph. D. thesis, Linkoping University, Linkoping, Sweden.

Benjamin, M., T. Viana, K. Corbett, and A. Silva (1993). Satisfying multiple rated constraints in a knowledge based decision aid. In *Proc. 9 Conf.Art.Int.Appl.*, pp. 277–283.

BharatRao, R. and S. C.-Y. Lu (1993). A knowledge based equation discovery system for engineering domains. *IEEE Expert 8*, 37–42.

Bhatnagar, N. (1990). Adaptive search by learning from incomplete examples. In *Proc. 8 Nat.Conf.AI*. MIT Press.

Boden, M. (1990). *The Creative Mind & Mechanisms*. George Weidenfeld and Nicholson.

Bongard, N. (1970). *Pattern Recognition*. Spartan Books.

Brookes, R. A. (1991). Intelligence without reason. In *Proc.12 IJCAI*, pp. 569–595. Morgan Kaufmann.

Bruynooghe, M. and L. M. Pereira (1984). Deduction revision by intelligent backtracking. In J. A. Campbell (Ed.), *Implementations of Prolog*. Ellis Horwood.

Cheeseman, P., B. Kanefsky, and W. M. Taylor (1991). Where the really hard problems are. In *Proc. 12 IJCAI*, pp. 331–337.

Codognet, P. and V. Saraswat (1992). Abduction in concurrent constraint programming. Technical report, Xerox Park.

Day, D. S. (1992). Acquiring search heuristics automatically for constraint-based planning and scheduling. In J. Hendler (Ed.), *Artificial intelligence planning systems*. Morgan Kaufmann.

Dechter, R. (1986). Learning while searching in constraint satisfaction problems. In *AAAI-86 Proceedings*. Morgan Kaufmann.

Evans, T. G. (1968). A heuristic program to solve geometric analogy problems. In M. Minsky (Ed.), *Semantic Information Processing*. MIT Press.

Freedman, D. (1993). Ai helps researchers find meaning in molecules. *Science 261*, 844–845.

Furukawa, K. (1992). Logic programming as the integrator of the fifth generation computer systems project. *Comm.ACM 35*, 82–92.

Geffner, H. and J. Pearl (1987). An improved constraint-propagation algorithm for diagnosis. In *Proc. 10 IJCAI*, Milan. Morgan Kaufman.

Gentner, D. (1983). Structure-mapping: a theoretical framework for analogy. *Cognitive Science 7*.

Goguen, J. A. and R. M. Burstall (1984). Introducing institutions. *LNCS 164*, 221–256, Springer–Verlag.

Hess, L. and B. Mayoh (1990). The four musicians: analogies and expert systems - a graphic approach. *LNCS 532*, 430–445, Springer–Verlag.

Huberman, B. A. and T. Hogg (1987). Phase transitions in artificial intelligence systems. *Art.Int. 33*, 155–171.

Kaplan, R. M. and J. Bresman (1982). *Lexical Functional Grammar: a formal system for grammatical representations*. MIT Press.

Koza, J. R. (1992). *Genetic Programming - on the programming of computers by means of natural selection*. MIT Press.

Langley, W., H. Simon, and G. Bradshaw (1983). Rediscovering chemistry with the bacon system. In R. Michalski, J. G. Carbonell, and T. M. Mitchell (Eds.), *Machine Learning, an artificial intelligence approach*. Tioga and Springer-Verlag.

Lavrac, N. and S. Dzeroski (Eds.) (1993). *Inductive Logic Programming: techniques and applications*. Ellis Horwood.

Lin, W. C., E. C. K. Tsao, and C. T. Chen (1992). Constraint satisfaction neural networks for image segmentation. *Pattern Recognition 25*, 679–693.

Mackworth, A. K. (1977). Consistency in networks of relations. *Art.Int. 8*, 99–118.

Maes, P. (Ed.) (1991). *Designing autonomous agents*. MIT Press.

Margolis, H. (1987). *Patterns, Thinking, and Cognition: a theory of justice*. University of Chicago Press.

Marr, D. (1982). *Vision*. W. H. Freeman.

Minton, S. (1991). Prodigy: an integrated architecture for planning and learning. In K. VanLehn (Ed.), *Architectures for Intelligence*. Lawrence Erlbaum.

Mitchell, D. (1992). Hard and easy distributions of sat problems. In *AAAI-92 Proceedings*, San Jose, California.

Mitchell, M. (1993). *Analogy-making as Perception: a computer model*. Bradford Book. MIT Press.

Montanari, U. (1974). Networks of constraints : fundamental properties and applications to picture processing. *Information Sciences 7*, 95–132.

Muggleton, S. (Ed.) (1992). *Inductive Logic Programming*. A.P.I.C. Academic Press.

Murphy, D. (1993). Time and duration in noninterleaving concurrency. *Fundamenta Informatica 5*, 403–416.

Musick, R. and S. Russell (1992). How long will it take? In *AAAI-92 Proceedings*, San Jose, California.

Narinyani, A. S. (1983). Subdefiniteness and basic means of knowledge representation. *Comp.Art.Int. 2*, 443–452.

Owen, S. (1990). *Analogy for Automated Reasoning*. Academic Press.

Piatersky, G. and W. J. Frawley (Eds.) (1993). *Knowledge Discovery in Databases*. AAAI Press.

Prosser, P. (1993). Hybrid algorithms for the constraint satisfaction problem. *Comp.Int. 9*, 268–299.

Reece, D. A. and S. A. Shafer (1993). A computational model of driving for autonomous vehicles. *Transport Research 27A*, 23–50.

Resnikoff, H. L. (1987). *The Illusion of Reality*. Springer-Verlag.

Richards, B., I. Kraan, and B. Kuipers (1992). Automatic abduction of qualitative models. In *AAAI-92 Proceedings*. Morgan Kaufmann.

Sandewall, S. and R. Ronnquist (1986). A representation of action structures. In *AAAI-86 Proceedings*. Morgan Kaufmann.

Schreiber, M. (1992). *Constraint-based grammar formalisms*. MIT press.

Simon, H. A. (1969). *The Sciences of the Artificial*. MIT Press.

Sowa, J. F. (1984). *Conceptual Structures: information processing in mind and machine*. Addison-Wesley.

Sowa, J. F. (Ed.) (1991). *Principles of Semantic Networks: explorations in the representation of knowledge*. Morgan Kaufman.

Stallman, R. and G. J. Sussman (1977). Forward reasoning and dependency-directed backtracking in a system for computer-aided circuit analysis. *Art.Int. 9*, 135–196.

Stefik, M. (1981). Planning with constraints. *Art.Int. 16*, 111–170.

Sussman, G. J. and G. L. Steele Jr. (1980). Constraints a language for expressing almost-hierarchical descriptions. *Art.Int. 14*, 1–39.

Townidnejad, M., H. R. Myler, and A. J. Gonzalez (1993). Constraint mechanisms in automated knowledge generation. *Applied Art. Int. 7*, 113–134.

Uckun, S., S. Bagchi, K. Kawamura, and Y. Miyabe (1993, oct). Managing genetic search in jobshop scheduling. *IEEE Expert 8*, 34–45.

Waltz, D. (1975). Understanding line drawings of scenes with shadows. In P. H. E. Winston (Ed.), *The Psychology of Computer Vision*. McGraw-Hill.

Williams, C. and T. Hogg (1992). Using deep structure to locate hard problems. In *AAAI-92 Proceedings*, San Jose, California.

Williams, C. and T. Hogg (1993). The typicality of phase transitions in search. *Comp.Int. 9*, 221–238.

Winston, P. H. (1975). *The Psychology of Computer Vision*. McGraw-Hill.

2. Constraint Solving Techniques

2.1 Exploiting Structure in Constraint Satisfaction Problems

Eugene C. Freuder

Department of Computer Science, University of New Hampshire
Durham, New Hampshire 03824, USA
ecf@cs.unh.edu

2.1.1 Introduction

Constraint satisfaction problems (CSPs) involve finding values for problem variables subject to restrictions on which combinations of values are allowed. Fig. 2.1a presents an example: color the graph shown such that no vertices joined by an edge have the same color. The small letters indicate the choice of colors available at each vertex (a stands for aquamarine if you like). Here the variables are the vertices, the values for each variable are the set of colors available at the vertex and the constraints all happen to be the same: "not same color". This is a *binary CSP* because all constraints involve two variables. For simplicity, we will assume here that our problems are presented as binary CSPs.

One *solution* would be a for W, b for X, c for Y and a for Z. Fig. 2.1b shows a *backtrack search tree* that finds that solution. We say that the variable X is *constrained* by the variable Y, but not by the variable Z. We say that a for X is *consistent* with b for Y, but *inconsistent* with a for Y. When we try the value c for Y during the search we need to check that it is consistent with the previous choices a for W and b for X. Each of these checks is called a constraint check.

Constraint satisfaction is NP-complete, so we do not expect to find an efficient general algorithm. However, by exploiting problem structure we can often obtain solutions relatively efficiently. This chapter provides an introduction to CSP structure, specifically to the work that I have done over the past decade, with colleagues and students, exploiting such structure.

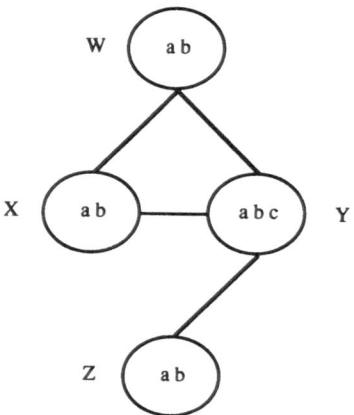

a. Graph coloring problem

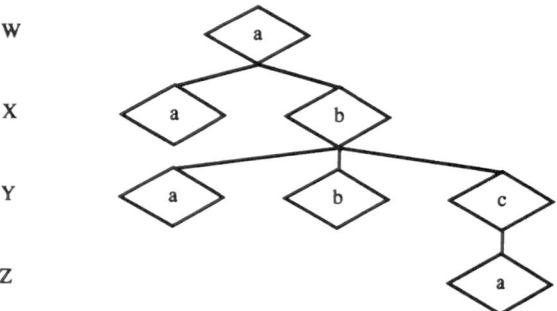

b. Search tree

Fig. 2.1. A constraint satisfaction problem

The references I provide are largely to this body of work. These references in turn provide many further pointers into the literature. I have taken the opportunity here to provide a few additional, mostly more recent references.

Structure can be studied on three levels: macro, micro and meta. The chapter will *informally* introduce three approaches to structure exploitation at each level. Simple coloring problems will be used throughout as examples.

At the *macro* level we are concerned with the pattern of constraints. This can be represented as a *constraint graph*, where the vertices correspond to problem variables, the vertex labels correspond to *domains* of values and the edges correspond to constraints. We can label the edges with the constraints, but will not do so here unless we wish to make a point about how the original coloring constraints have been modified. When we do specify a constraint here we will do so by listing the consistent pairs of values. The coloring problem in Fig. 2.1a is represented by the constraint graph in Fig. 2.2a.

It may be a bit confusing that the constraint graph for a graph coloring problem looks like the graph to be colored. Imagine instead, if you like, that this constraint graph represents the problem of coloring a map with four countries, where, for example, country X borders country W and country Y, and countries that share a common border must have different colors to distinguish them on the map.

At the *micro* level we areconcerned with the pattern of pairs of consistent values. This can be represented as a *consistency graph*, where the vertices represent values and an edge indicates that a pair of values is consistent. The consistency graph for the same coloring problem is shown in Fig. 2.2b.

At the *meta* level we are concerned with a decomposition into subproblems. Often we can view such a decomposition as a *metaproblem*, where the *metavariables* of the metaproblem correspond to subproblems of the original problem. Each subproblem includes a subset of the variables in the original problem, along with the values for these variables and the constraints between pairs of these variables. The set of *metavalues* for a metavariable is the set of solutions to the subproblem.

A *metaconstraint* in the metaproblem, between metavariables corresponding to subproblems S and T, enforces all the constraints in the original problem that involve one variable from S and one from T. If the same variable appears in both S and T, the metaconstraint must ensure that this variable receives the same value in the solution chosen as the metavalue for the S metavariable as it does in the solution chosen as the metavalue for the T metavariable.

Metaproblems can be represented by a *metaconstraint graph*, where vertices correspond to metavariables, i.e. subproblems, and edges correspond to metaconstraints. A metaconstraint graph corresponding to one possible division of our sample coloring problem is shown in Fig. 2.2c. A problem decomposition may be desirable because either the metaproblem or the metavariable subproblems have a desirable macro or micro structure.

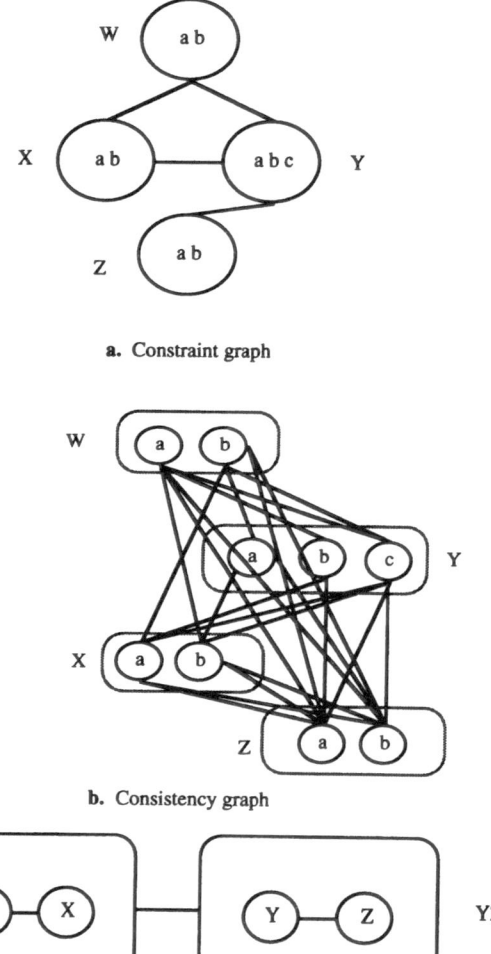

a. Constraint graph

b. Consistency graph

c. Metaconstraint graph

Fig. 2.2. Macro, micro and meta level representations

2.1.2 Macro Structure

2.1.2.1 Trees The constraint graph in Fig. 2.3a represents a simple coloring problem. If we choose a specific ordering for the vertices of a constraint graph we obtain a directed constraint graph. Fig. 2.3b is a *directed constraint graph* for this problem. The graph is directed top down, so, for example, X preceeds Y.

The constraint graph is tree-structured, i.e. there are no cycles in the graph. Given a tree-structured problem we can always choose an ordering for the variables in which no variable is constrained by more than one preceding variable, e.g. by a breadth-first traversal of the tree. Such an ordering gives rise to a directed constraint graph in which no vertex shares an edge with more than one preceding vertex. We say that the directed constraint graph, and the variable ordering, have *width 1* (unless there are no edges at all, which would be width 0). The directed constraint graph in Fig. 2.3b has width 1.

If we use a width 1 variable ordering, it is clear that when we choose a value for a variable we will only need to ensure that the value is consistent with at most one preceding choice. It is possible to *preprocess* a solvable problem in such a way that we can be assured that given any value for any one variable, it will be possible to find a value for any other variable consistent with it. This is called achieving *arc consistency*.

In Fig. 2.3b we have achieved arc consistency by eliminating the value a from the variable X. Any value remaining is consistent with at least one value at each other variable. Now the search tree is very simple (Fig. 2.3c). Since the preprocessing, and the variable ordering, ensure that we can always find a consistent value at the next level in the search tree, we have achieved *backtrack-free search*.

We now have a three step process for solving tree-structured problems:

1. Find a width 1 variable ordering.

2. Achieve arc consistency.

3. Conduct a backtrack-free search.

For tree-structured problems all three steps can be carried out in time linear in the number of variables, n, so we have a bound on the complexity of tree-structured CSPs that is linear rather than exponential in n.

Even when a CSP is not tree-structured, we may be able to use tree structures to help solve the problem. We may be able to reduce a problem to a tree-structured problem by removing redundant constraints, we can use tree-structured subproblems to provide search guidance, and we can obtain metaproblems in which the metaproblem or the metavariable subproblems are tree-structured.

See (Freuder 1982, 1988, Mackworth and Freuder 1985, 1993) also (Dechter 1990, Dechter and Pearl 1988, 1989, Jegou 1993, Meiri, Dechter and Pearl 1990).

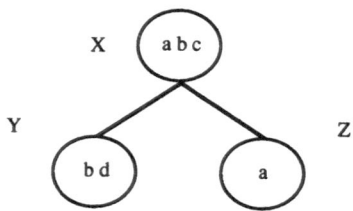

a. Constraint graph

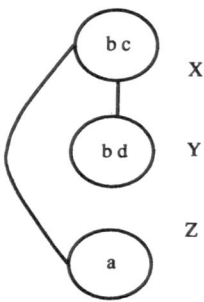

b. Arc consistent ordered constraint graph

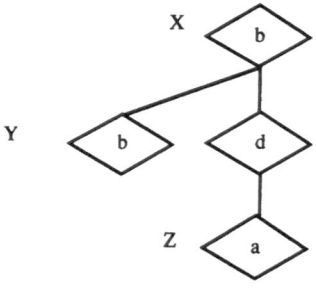

c. Search tree

Fig. 2.3. Backtrack-free search for a tree-structured problem

2.1.2.2 K-Trees Tree structure can be generalized to *k-tree* structures, where trees are 1-trees. A k-tree graph structure is formed starting with a clique of k vertices, i.e. a set of k vertices any pair of which is joined by an edge. Thereafter we add vertices by connecting them to a clique of k vertices that is already present in the graph. Fig. 2.4a shows a constraint graph that is a 2-tree. We could start with vertices W and X as a clique of two vertices, then add Y, joining it to W and X, and finally add Z, connecting it to W and X also. (If we connected Z to X and Y we would still have a 2-tree.)

The procedure we used to ensure backtrack-free search for trees generalizes:

1. Find a width k variable ordering.

2. Achieve strong directed k+1-consistency.

3. Conduct a backtrack-free search.

The result is a procedure for solving a k-tree-structured problems that is still linear in the number of problem variables. (However, the complexity bound is $O(d^{k+1})$ as a function of the maximum domain size, d.) Fig. 2.4b shows a width 2, strongly directed 3-consistent constraint graph, and Fig. 2.4c shows the search tree that results, using the variable search order corresponding to the directed constraint graph.

A *width k* directed constraint graph is simply one in which the maximum number of edges from a variable to preceeding variables is k. The definition of a k-tree makes it clear that a k-tree-structured constraint graph will have a width k variable ordering.

K+1-consistency is achieved by ensuring that given mutually consistent values for any k variables, we can find a value for any k+1st variable, such that all the values taken together are consistent. For example, in the original problem we can choose a for W and c for X; these choices are consistent with the constraint given between W and X. However, there is no value that can be chosen for Z that is consistent with these choices for W and X. We can eliminate this problem by strengthening the constraint between W and X so that it no longer allows the choice of a for W and c for X.

Directed k+1-consistency is a limited form of k+1-consistency. We only really need to be concerned that having chosen values for k variables in our search that we will be able to find a value for a k+1st variable further on in the variable search order. *Strong directed k+1-consistency* ensures that we also have directed j-consistency for j less than k+1. (Here it eliminates the value a from W.) Thus we will have no trouble beginning our search.

The concept of a partial k-tree allows us to extend this work to a broader class of problems. Indeed any constraint graph is a partial k-tree for some k. However, the minimum k that will work may be hard to find, and may indeed be n-1.

See (Freuder 1990) also (Cooper 1989, Dechter and Pearl 1990, Montanari and Rossi 1991, Seidel 1981, Zabith 1990).

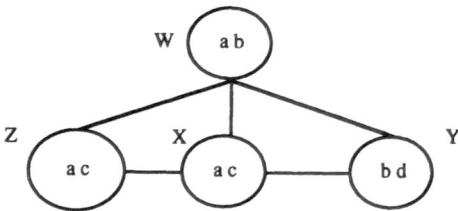

a. Constraint graph

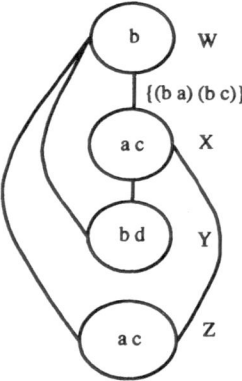

b. Strongly directed 3-consistent ordered constraint graph

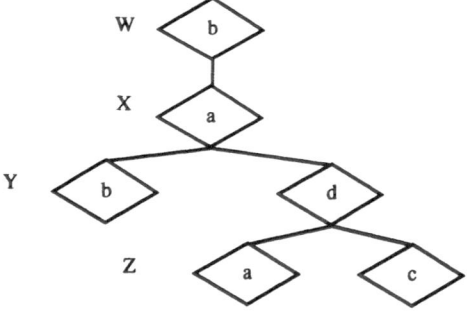

c. Search tree

Fig. 2.4. Backtrack-free search for a 2-tree-structured problem

2.1.2.3 Stable Sets If there is a set of variables in our problem that do not share any constraints, it would seem that we ought to be able to take advantage of that fact somehow to simplify the search for a solution. Fig. 2.5a is the constraint graph for a simple problem in which the variables Y and Z do not constrain each other. (The values a1 and a2 are shades of the same color; shades of the same color can not be used at vertices joined by an edge.) A set of vertices in a graph where there are no edges between any pair of vertices in the set is called a *stable set*.

Fig. 2.5b shows a conventional search tree for a solution to this problem. It involves 12 constraint checks. Fig. 2.5c represents a search tree that takes advantage of the independence of Y and Z. It only requires 6 constraint checks. Notice that we could construct an example that saved any number of checks.

Normally we have a "multiplicative effort" when instantiating a set of variables. The number of possibilities to consider is the product of the number of values available for each. Each combination of values has to be considered separately, because the values may not be consistent with each other. If there are 10 values for each of three variables, there could be 1000 combinations to consider. (However, this is only an upper bound. Normal backtrack search may avoid some of these combinations. See for example how the first choice of a1 for Y in Fig. 2.5b terminates search at that point.)

The second search seeks values for Y and Z "simultaneously" (indeed with a parallel machine this could be simultaneous). When we find that there is no value for Z that will work, we do not try to change Y. We have already found a value for Y that is consistent with the choice for X. Finding another one cannot affect the failure at Z. Thus we have a *conjunctive search* for Y and Z.

Knowledge of the independence of Y and Z permits an "additive effort". If there are 10 values for each of three independent variables we only need consider at most 30 possibilites. We can look independently for a value for each of the three variables consistent with other values already instantiated. There is no concern about whether the choices for the three variables are consistent with each other.

This example supports the general observation that the complexity of a CSP has a bound exponential in n-s+1, as opposed to n, where s is the size of the largest stable set. Of course for a complete graph s is 1. Finding the largest stable set in a graph is a hard problem; however, there are some good approximation methods, and for a given practical problem, the semantics of the problem may identify a stable set.

We can extend this approach to take advantage of multiple stable sets within a problem. This involves a structure called a pseudotree, which will be described further in Section 2.1.3.3. A depth-first traversal of a constraint graph will produce a pseudotree structure, so any CSP has such structure. The complexity of a CSP is exponential in the depth of a pseudotree representation of the CSP. Pseudotrees also support parallel processing.

See (Freuder and Quinn 1985) also (Collin, Dechter and Katz 1991).

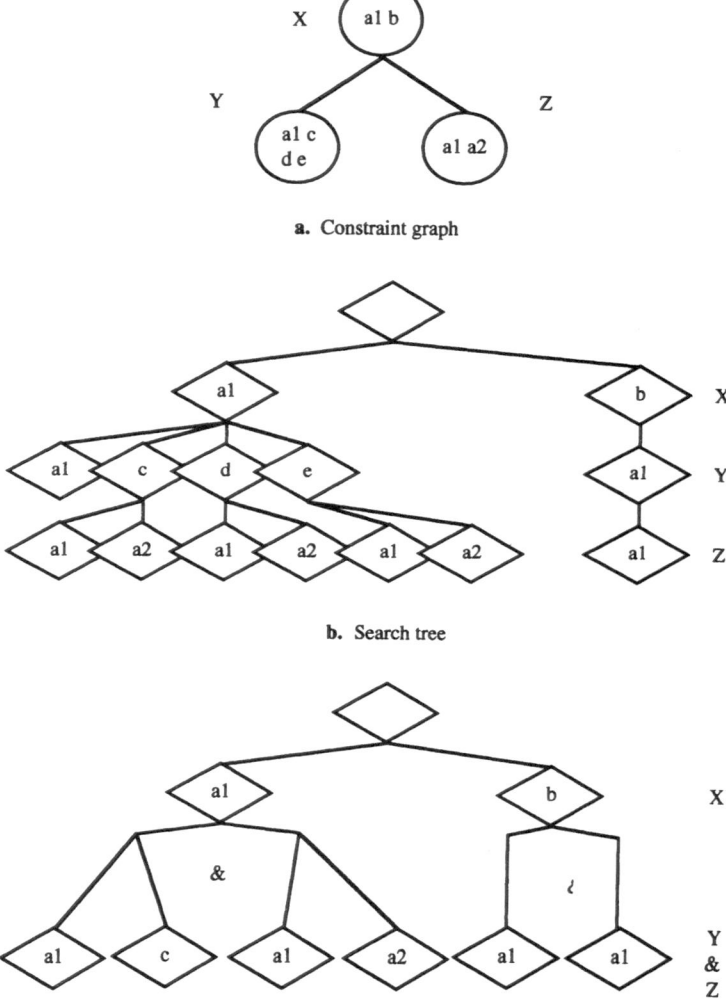

a. Constraint graph

b. Search tree

c. Conjunctive search tree

Fig. 2.5. Stable sets permit conjunctive search

2.1.3 Meta Structure

2.1.3.1 Biconnected Component Trees A graph is *biconnected* if removing any one vertex will not disconnect the graph, i.e. there will still be a sequence of edges going between any pair of vertices. The maximal biconnected subgraphs of a graph are called its *biconnected components*. In Fig. 2.6b we see a metaproblem where the two subproblems correspond to the biconnected components of the original constraint graph, given in Fig. 2.6a.

We will sketch a proof that any CSP can be solved in time exponential in the size of the maximal biconnected component. We can find the biconnected components in quadratic time. It turns out that the corresponding metaproblem, where the metavariables are the biconnected component subproblems and the metaconstraints enforce consistency on the single variables shared by pairs of subproblems, will always be tree-structured. We would like therefore to apply the preprocessing procedure for tree-structures of Section 2.1.2.1 to the metaproblem.

We need to find the set of metavalues for our metavariables. This involves solving subproblems with at most b variables; the effort required to solve each subproblem has a bound exponential in b.

Arc consistency preprocessing for trees is $O(nd^2)$, where n is the number of variables and d is the maximum domain size. Since we could have d^b solutions to a subproblem, if we simply applied arc consistency to the results, the effort could be exponential in 2b. However, we can actually ensure arc consistency in the metaproblem by achieving (1,b-1) consistency in the original problem, which can be done in time exponential in b. (1,b-1)-consistency ensures that if we choose a value for one variable, we can find values for any b-1 additional variables, such that all b values are consistent.

If we choose a metavalue for one metavariable, to find a consistent metavalue for another metavariable we only have to worry that the second metavalue assigns the same value as the first metavalue does to the one original problem variable that the two metavariables have in common. This is equivalent to saying that we fix a value for one of the variables in the second metavalue, and require values for the other variables be consistent with it. But (1,b-1)-consistency ensures that we can do precisely that.

(1,b-1)-consistency preprocessing removes the value a from variable X. If we chose a for X, we could not find values for Y and Z such that all three values were consistent. Once we remove this value and achieve (1,b-1)-consistency, we can go on to find the metavariable values, and solve the metaproblem with a backtrack-free search.

See (Freuder 1985, 1988) also (Dechter and Pearl 1988, Kirousis and Thilikos 1993, Schiex and Verfaillie 1993).

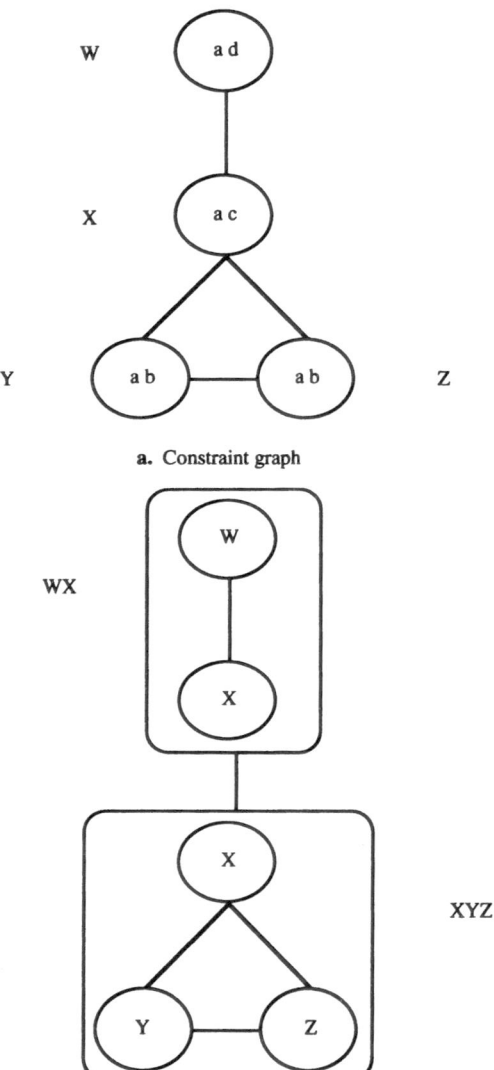

a. Constraint graph

b. Biconnected components metaconstraint graph

Fig. 2.6. Biconnected component tree

2.1.3.2 K-Tree Clique Trees Sometimes we may want to process constraint data in other ways than to simply obtain a solution. For example, we may want to process our representation so that any value for a variable is part of some complete solution to the problem, a form of *variable completability*. Consider the constraint graph in Fig. 2.7a. The value a for W is not part of any complete solution.

Of course we could simply find all the solutions and remove from W any variable that did not appear in one of them. We will outline an alternative approach that will accomplish our objective for any k-tree-structured problem in $O(nd^{k+2})$ time.

The constraint graph in Fig. 2.7a is a 2-tree. Fig. 2.7b is a metaconstraint graph where the metavariables correspond to the maximum cliques in the constraint graph. (A clique has an edge between any two pairs of vertices.) We show the metavariable metavalues, i.e. the solutions to the subproblems, and the metaconstraints.

Notice that all the constraints of the original problem are constraints within one or more of the subproblems, so the metaconstraints simply enforce the requirement that a solution to the metaproblem cannot require any original problem variable to take on two different values. Notice further that a constraint between the WXY and XVZ metavariables is unnecessary because the consistency of their shared variable, X, will be enforced by the "transitivity" of the two other constraints.

It turns out that the maximal cliques of any k-tree can be organized into a tree-structured metaproblem of this sort. Once we have such a *clique tree* we process it for arc consistency. Fig. 2.7c shows the result in this case. Several values have been eliminated. The metavalues for each metavariable represent a refined ternary constraint on three variables from the original problem.

At this point we can project these ternary constraints back down onto the original problem variables. Notice in particular that the value a for variable W will be eliminated because it does not appear in the WXY ternary constraint. Any values remaining appear in some complete solution to the problem.

The discussion of tree-structured problems in Section 2.1.2.1 suggests why this process assures variable completability. Suppose we are questioning whether a value v for variable V is part of some complete solution. We can make a metavariable that contains V the first metavariable in a width 1 metavariable search order. We can choose a metavalue that contains v. The arc consistency then assures us that we can complete a solution to the metaproblem, using that metavalue. The solution to the metaproblem will induce a solution to the original problem containing v.

We can identify many other forms of completability, and again extend results to partial k-trees. An interesting application is to bandwidth-k constraint graphs, those for which an ordering of the vertices exists where no vertex shares an edge with another more than k vertices distant in the ordering. See (Freuder 1991).

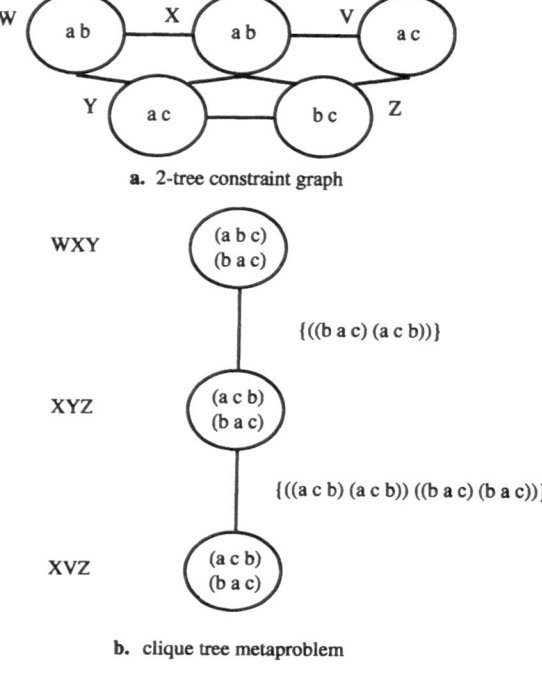

a. 2-tree constraint graph

WXY (a b c)
     (b a c)

          {((b a c) (a c b))}

XYZ (a c b)
     (b a c)

          {((a c b) (a c b)) ((b a c) (b a c))}

XVZ (a c b)
     (b a c)

b. clique tree metaproblem

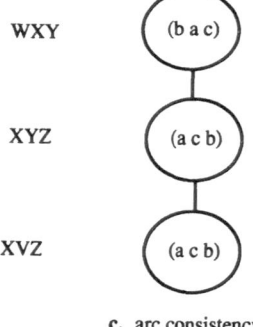

WXY (b a c)

XYZ (a c b)

XVZ (a c b)

c. arc consistency

Fig. 2.7. Using clique trees to obtain variable completeability

2.1.3.3 Separator Pseudotrees We discussed separating graphs into disconnected pieces in Section 2.1.3.1. In the constraint graph in Fig. 8a there is not any one vertex whose removal separates the graph into two pieces. The largest biconnected component of this graph is the graph itself. However, there are several ways in which we can separate the graph by removing two vertices, for example U and V. The subgraph with vertices U and V is a *separator*.

By recursively removing separators from the two separated components we can generate a metaproblem with the *pseudotree* structure alluded to in Section 2.1.2.3. Fig. 2.8b is an example. There is an underlying tree structure plus some additional edges that run between a vertex and an ancestor of that vertex in the tree. Notice, however, that there are no "cross edges" running between vertices in different branches of the tree.

In forming the tree the first separator provides the root of the tree. This is the a vertex representing the UV subproblem metavariable. The two separated components form the subtrees of the root. We use X and Y to further separate one of components. The XY separator subproblem will be one of the children of the UV vertex. The other is the unseparable T subproblem. Since W and Z do not separate further they themselves are the children of XY. Thus the underlying tree structure is formed.

An additional metaconstraint edge is needed between metavariables UV and W to reflect the constraint between original problem variables W and U and the constraint between original variables W and V. Similarly, we need a metaconstraint between metavariables UV and Z.

Because the tree was generated using the separation process, there can be no cross edges. For example, there is no constraint between the original problem variables W and T; if there was U and V could not have separated W and T.

Now we can try to instantiate the metavariables, level by level in the pseudotree. Within each level, the metavariables form a stable set; for example, XY and T, at the second level, have no metaconstraint between them. As we proceed through a level we can operate additively as in Section 2.1.2.3.

Notice further that when we back up, because we cannot find a suitable metavalue, the pseudo tree structure guarantees that there is at most one metavariable at each higher level that we need to reconsider as we back up. Suppose we have chosen (a c) for UV, (c a) for XY, and (b) for T. Now (a) will not work for X. As we back up we need to reconsider XY and eventually UV, but not T.

These observations support a search algorithm that has a bound exponential in the number of levels in the pseudotree. There is a body of work on graph separators that might be brought to bear on CSPs through this pseudotree metaproblem mechanism.

See (Freuder and Quinn 1985)

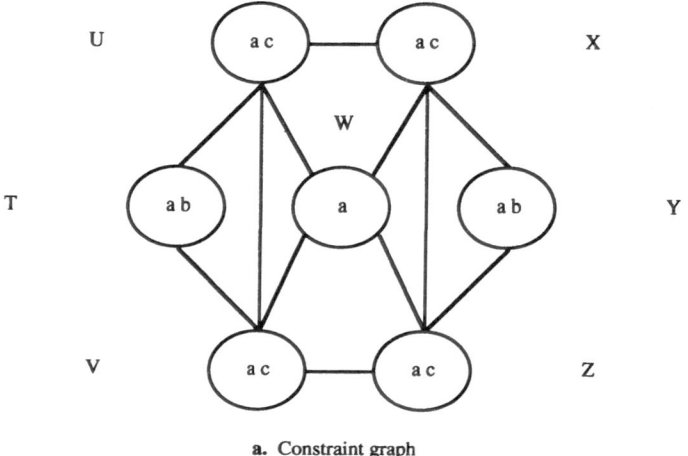

a. Constraint graph

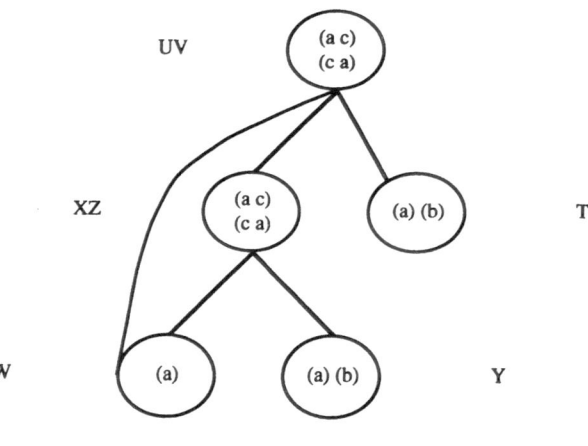

b. Pseudotree metaproblem

Fig. 2.8. Separator pseudotree metaproblem

2.1.4 Micro Structure

2.1.4.1 Interchangeability In the problem represented by the constraint graph in Fig. 2.9a, the values c and d for variable Y are *interchangeable* in the sense that they appear in the same solutions. Given a solution that involves c we can substitute d and still have a solution, and vice versa.

Thus we could simplify our search space by eliminating, say c, before searching for a solution, and be guaranteed not to have eliminated all the solutions. Indeed, if we want all solutions, we could find all that we could find without the c value, and then recover any solutions we had lost by substituting c for d in any solutions we found that used d.

Of course, there seems to be a circularity involved: we can try to make it easier to find *solutions* by eliminating values that appear in the same *solutions*. Fortunately, we can determine locally here that c and d are interchangeable.

Consider the portion of the consistency graph for this problem shown in Fig. 2.9b. Here we show all the values consistent with c and with d. Notice that the set of values consistent with c is the same as the set of values consistent with d. This means that c and d are *neighborhood interchangeable*, and that is sufficient to guarantee that they will be interchangeable.

It is possible, however, if a bit counterintuitive, for two values to be interchangeable without being neighborhood interchangeable. By the time we obtain complete solutions, the local differences may have ceased to matter.

A problem can be preprocessed to eliminate neighborhood interchangeable values, just as we can preprocess a problem to remove locally inconsistent values. Neighborhood interchangeability can be determined in quadratic time. One can prove the existence of problems for which even neighborhood interchangeable preprocessing will save exponential effort.

A number of variations on the theme of interchangeability can be considered. A particularly promising one is *substitutability*. Given values u and v for the same variable, value v is substitutable for a value u if we can substitute v for u in any solution. In this case we can eliminate u prior to search. There may be more substitutable values to eliminate than interchangeable ones.

Notice, however, that if we find all the solutions that we can without u, we cannot easily recover all the solutions that we may have thrown away. If we find a solution involving v, we cannot simply substitute u. We have no guarantee that all the solutions involving v will be solutions when u is substituted.

Once again we can determine a form of local substitutability. If the set of values consistent with u is a subset of those consistent with v, then v is substitutable for u.

See (Freuder 1991) also (Haselbock 1993).

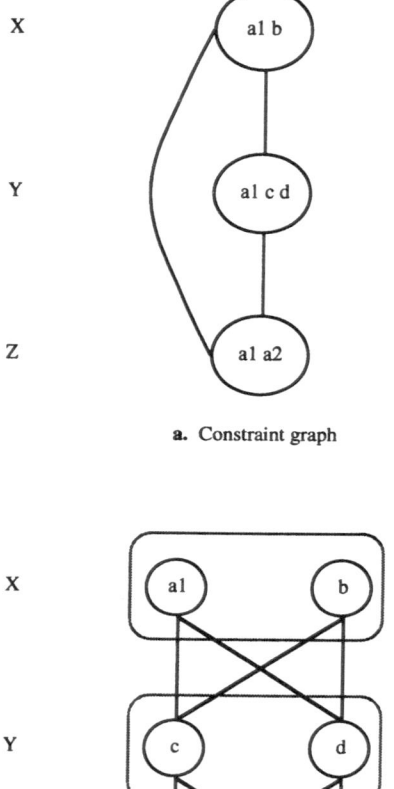

a. Constraint graph

b. Portion of consistency graph

Fig. 2.9. Identifying neighborhood interchangeable values

2.1.4.2 Cartesian Product Representation Consider the problem represented by the constraint graph in Fig. 2.10a. In Fig. 2.10b we see a portion of the consistency graph that demonstrates that all combinations of values a1, b, c for X with values d, e, f for Y are consistent. This set of consistent pairs can be represented compactly as a Cartesian product:

$$\{a1\, b\, c\}x\{d\, e\, f\}.$$

Furthermore we can check values for variable Z against these combinations in an efficient, additive manner, without considering each of the nine possible pairs individually. (It is interesting to note that in the subproblem where the values for X are limited to $\{a1\, b\, c\}$ and the values for Y are limited to $\{d\, e\, f\}$, X and Y become a stable set.) For example, to check the value a1 for variable Z against all the consistent combinations in the cross product, we just have to make 6 consistency checks, and we find that a1 is consistent with:

$$\{b\, c\}x\{d\, e\, f\}$$

If the nine consistent pairs were represented in a standard backtrack search tree, we would have to check a1 for Z against each pair. This would result in three constraint checks for the pairs where a1 for Z is found inconsistent with a1 for X plus twelve constraint checks for the pairs where a1 for Z is found consistent with the values for X and Y, for a total of eighteen constraint checks.

This insight can be embodied in an enhancement to standard backtracking that is guaranteed to reduce (or in extreme cases, simply not increase) the number of constraint checks required when searching for all solutions to a problem (and, in particular, when determining that none exist). The process is illustrated in Fig. 2.10c. This figure represents a complete search tree where each node contains a Cartesian product representation of a set of consistent tuples, and the leaves represent sets of solutions. Every solution appears at one of the leaves.

The leftmost leaf represents an extension of the set of pairs

$$\{b\, c\}x\{d\, e\, f\}$$

to a set of triples

$$\{b\, c\}x\{d\, e\, f\}x\{a1\, a2\}$$

that reflect that fact that not only is a1 consistent with each pair, but a2 is also. Each element in this enlarged Cartesian product represents a triple of mutually consistent values

When we check b for Z against the set of pairs

$$\{b\, c\}x\{d\, e\, f\}$$

we find that b for Z is only consistent with

$$\{c\}x\{d\, e\, f\}$$

resulting in the second leaf node of the search tree

$$\{c\}x\{def\}x\{b\}.$$

This Cartesian product representation can also be added to forward checking, one of the most successful CSP algorithms, again with a guarantee that it will not increase, and can reduce, the number of constraint checks required to find all solutions. (See Hubbe and Freuder 1992) also (Lesaint 1993).

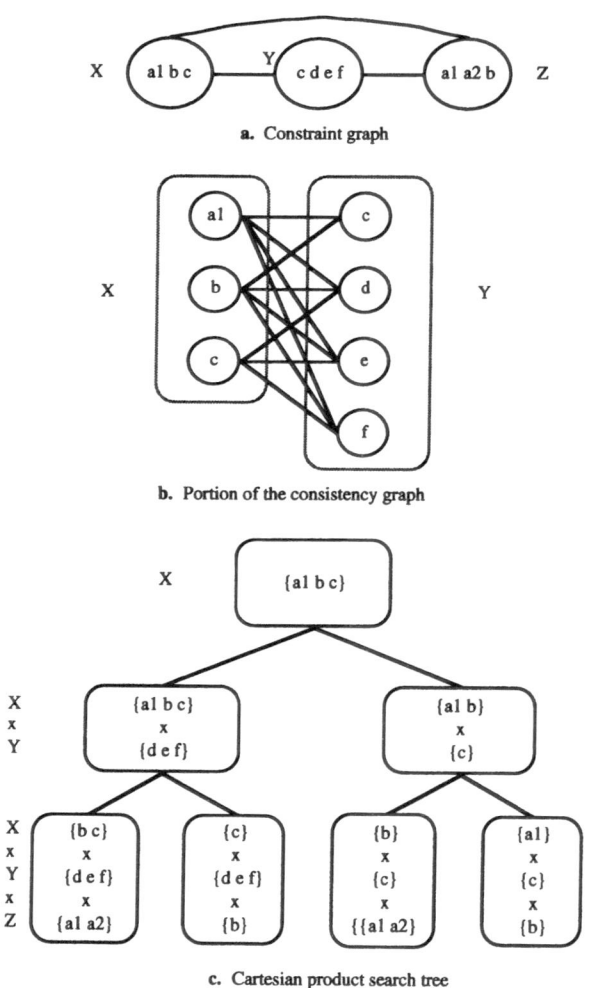

a. Constraint graph

b. Portion of the consistency graph

c. Cartesian product search tree

Fig. 2.10. Cartesian product representation

2.1.4.3 Consistent Subproblems Consider the problem represented by the constraint graph in Fig. 2.11a. The consistency graph for this problem would show that the value a for W is consistent with values b and c for X and Z and with all values for Y. Consider the subproblem represented by the constraint graph in Fig. 2.11b, where the domains of the variables X, Y and Z have been restricted to the values consistent with a for W, and the domain of W contains all values except a. Call this the *consistent subproblem* with respect to a for W. I claim that if we are only looking for one solution, we can throw away this subproblem!

First we need to understand why we can throw it away. Then we need to figure out exactly *how* to throw it away. If we "throw it away" what are we left with?

We can throw it away because if there is any solution to the original problem in this subproblem, there will be a solution not in this subproblem. Consider a solution to the subproblem. Now replace the W value in this solution with a, the W value missing in the subproblem. The result will still be a solution to the original problem, because the X, Y and Z values in the solution will all be consistent with a for W. We know that they are consistent with a because all the values for X, Y and Z in the consistent subproblem are consistent with a for W. That is why it is called the consistent subproblem (with respect to a for W).

How though can we take advantage of this insight? There are twenty-four possible combinations of values in the consistent subproblem, out of only eighty-one in the entire problem. We would like to be able to ignore those twenty-four. We would like a representation of the problem that includes only the remaining fifty-seven (eighty-one minus twenty-four) possibilities.

The decomposition tree in Fig. 2.11c provides the key. Each node represents a coloring problem with the same pattern of constraints as in our original problem, but with the values for the variables W, X, Y, Z listed in order as shown. At the root we have the original problem. At the lower right we have the consistent subproblem with respect to a for W.

We form the children of the root node by dividing the values for W into two pieces, leaving the other values unchanged. We put a for W in the left child and the other values for W in the right child. We form the children of the node that does not contain a by dividing the values for X into two pieces, those consistent with a for W and those inconsistent with a for W, and leaving the other values unchanged. The consistent values are in the right child. We continue this process along the right hand branch until we are left with the consistent subproblem.

The leaves of this decomposition tree will contain among them all the possible combinations of values in the original problem. (One leaf was discarded because it contained no values for Y.) If we throw away the consistent subproblem with respect to a for W, we are left with the remaining leaves as the problem representation we are seeking. This observation can be embodied in an algorithm that decomposes repeatedly in this manner while searching for a solution. See (Freuder and Hubbe 1993).

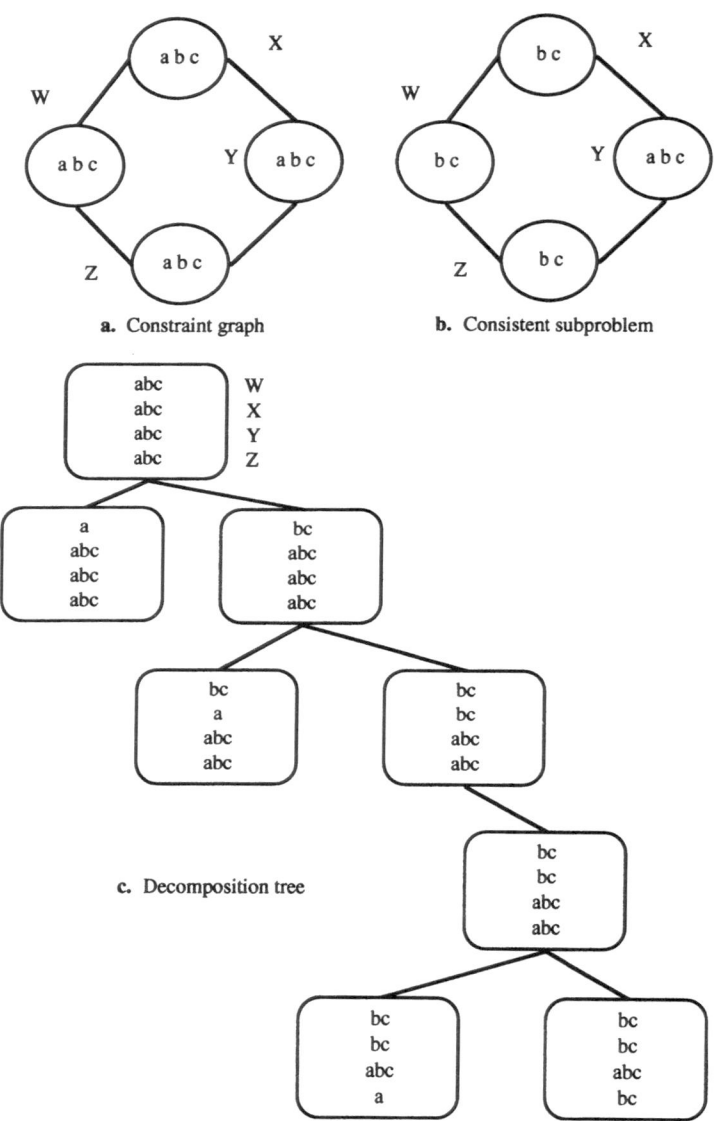

a. Constraint graph   b. Consistent subproblem

c. Decomposition tree

Fig. 2.11. Removing a consistent subproblem

2.1.5 Acknowledgements

This material is based upon work supported by the National Science Foundation under Grant No. IRI-9207633.

References

Collin, Z., Dechter, R. and Katz, S. (1991) On the feasability of distributed constraint satisfaction. *Proceedings of the Twelfth International Joint Conference on Artificial Intelligence*, 318-324

Cooper, M.C (1989) An optimal k-consistency algorithm. *Artificial Intelligence 41*, 89-95.

Dechter, R. (1990) Enhancement schemes for constraint processing: backjumping, learning and cutset decomposition. *Artificial Intelligence 41*, 273-312

Dechter, R. and Pearl, J. (1988) Network-based heuristics for constraint-satisfaction problems. *Artificial Intelligence 34*, 1-38

Dechter, R. and Pearl, J. (1989) Tree-clustering schemes for constraint-processing. *Artificial Intelligence 38*, 353-366

Freuder, E.C. (1982) A sufficient condition for backtrack-free search. *Journal of the ACM 29*, 24-32

Freuder, E.C. (1985) A sufficient condition for backtrack-bounded search. *Journal of the ACM 32*, 755-761

Freuder, E.C. (1988) Backtrack-free and backtrack-bounded search. In: L. Kanal, V. Kumar (eds.) *Search in Artificial Intelligence*, 343-369. New York, Springer-Verlag

Freuder, E.C. (1990) Complexity of k-tree structured constraint satisfaction problems. *Proceedings of the Eighth National Conference on Artificial Intelligence*, 4-9

Freuder, E.C. (1991) Completable representations of constraint satisfaction problems. *Proceedings of the Second International Conference on Principles of Knowledge Representation and Reasoning*, 186-195

Freuder, E.C. (1991). Eliminating interchangeable values in constraint satisfaction problems. *Proceedings of the Ninth National Conference on Artificial Intelligence*, 227-233

Freuder, E.C. and Hubbe, P.D. (1993) Using inferred disjunctive constraints to decompose constraint satisfaction problems. *Proceedings of the Thirteenth International Joint Conference on Artificial Intelligence*, 254-260

Freuder, E.C. and Quinn, M.J. (1985) Taking advantage of stable sets of variables in constraint satisfaction problems. *Proceedings of the Ninth International Joint Conference on Artificial Intelligence*, 1076-1078

Haselbock, A. (1993) Exploiting interchangeabilities in constraint satisfaction problems. *Proceedings of the Thirteenth International Joint Conference on Artificial Intelligence*, 282-287

Hubbe, P.D. and Freuder, E.C. (1992) An efficient cross product representation of the constraint satisfaction problem search space. *Proceedings of The Tenth National Conference on Artificial Intelligence*, 421-427

Jegou, P. (1993) On the consistency of general constraint satisfaction problems. *Proceedings of the Eleventh National Conference on Artificial Intelligence*, 114-119

Kirousis, L.M. and Thilikos, D.M. (1993) The linkage of a graph. Technical Report 93.04.16, Computer Technology Institute, P.O Box 1122, Patras, Greece

Lesaint, D. (1993) Specific sets of solutions for constraint satisfaction problems. *Thirteenth International Conference on Expert Systems and Natural Language, Avignon'93*, 255-264.

Mackworth, A.K. and Freuder, E.C. (1985) The complexity of some polynomial network consistency algorithms for constraint satisfaction problems. *Artificial Intelligence 25*, 65-74 & 247

Mackworth. A.K. and Freuder, E.C. (1993) The complexity of constraint satisfaction revisited. *Artificial Intelligence 59*, 57-62

Meiri. I., Dechter, R. and Pearl, J. (1990) Tree decomposition with applications to constraint processing. *Proceedings of the Eighth National Conference on Artificial Intelligence*, 10-16

Montanari, U. and Rossi, F. (1991) Constraint relaxation can be perfect. *Artificial Intelligence 48*, 143-170

Schiex, T. and Verfaillie, G (1993) Constraint relaxation can be perfect. *Artificial Intelligence 48*, 143-170.

Seidel, R. (1988) A new method for solving constraint satisfaction problems. *Proceedings of the Seventh International Joint Conference on Artificial Intelligence*, 338-342

Zabih, R. (1990) Some applications of graph bandwidth to constraint satisfaction problems. *Proceedings of the Eighth national Conference on Artificial Intelligence*, 46-51.

2.2 Constraint Hierarchies

Alan Borning, Bjorn Freeman-Benson and Molly Wilson

Dept. of Computer Science & Engineering, FR-35
University of Washington, Seattle,
Washington 98195, USA
borning@cs.washington.edu

This paper was originally published in *Lisp and Symbolic Computation*, Vol. 5
No. 3, (September 1992), pages 223–270.

Abstract

Constraints allow programmers and users to state declaratively a relation that
should be maintained, rather than requiring them to write procedures to maintain the relation themselves. They are thus useful in such applications as programming languages, user interface toolkits, and simulation packages. In many
situations, it is desirable to be able to state both *required* and *preferential* constraints. The required constraints must hold. Since the other constraints are
merely preferences, the system should try to satisfy them if possible, but no
error condition arises if it cannot. A *constraint hierarchy* consists of a set of
constraints, each labeled as either required or preferred at some strength. An
arbitrary number of different strengths is allowed. In the discussion of a theory
of constraint hierarchies, we present alternate ways of selecting among competing possible solutions, and prove a number of propositions about the relations
among these alternatives. We then outline algorithms for satisfying constraint
hierarchies, and ways in which we have used constraint hierarchies in a number
of programming languages and systems.

2.2.1 Introduction

A constraint describes a relation that should be satisfied. Examples of constraints include:

- a constraint that a resistor in a circuit simulation obey Ohm's Law

- a constraint that two views of the same data remain consistent (for example, bar graph and pie chart views)

- a default constraint that parts of an object being edited remain fixed,
  unless there is some stronger constraint that forces them to change.

Constraints are useful in programming languages, user interface toolkits, simulation packages, and other systems because they allow users to declare that a

relation is to be maintained, rather than requiring users to write, and invoke, procedures to do the maintenance. In general constraints are *multi-directional*. For example, a constraint that $A + B = C$ might be used to find a value for any of A, B, or C. In general there may be many interrelated constraints in a given application; it is left up to the system to sort out how they interact and to keep them all satisfied.

2.2.1.1 The Refinement Versus the Perturbation Model

We can roughly classify constraint-based languages and systems as using one of two approaches: the *refinement* model or the *perturbation* model. In both cases constraints restrict the values that variables may take on. In the refinement model, variables are initially unconstrained; constraints are added as the computation unfolds, progressively refining the permissible values of the variables. This approach is more or less universally adopted in the logic programming community, for example, in the Constraint Logic Programming language scheme (Cohen 1990; Jaffar and Lassez 1987) and in the cc (concurrent constraint) languages (Saraswat, Rinard, and Panangaden 1991; Saraswat 1989).

In contrast, in the perturbation model, at the beginning of an execution cycle variables have specific values associated with them that satisfy the constraints. The values of one or more variables are perturbed (usually by some outside influence, such as an edit request from the user), and the task of the system is to adjust the values of the variables so that the constraints are again satisfied. The perturbation model has often been used in constraint-based applications such as the interactive graphics systems Sketchpad (Sutherland 1963a), ThingLab I (Borning 1981), Magritte (Gosling 1983), and Juno (Nelson 1985), and user interface construction systems such as Garnet (Myers, Guise, Dannenberg, Vander Zanden, Kosbie, Marchal, Pervin, Mickish, and Kolojejchick 1990; Myers, Guise, Dannenberg, Vander Zanden, Kosbie, Marchal, and Pervin 1990). We can also view the ubiquitous spreadsheet as using the perturbation model: formulas are constraints relating the permissible values in cells. Before a user action, cells have values that satisfy the constraints (formulas). The user edits the value in a cell, or edits a formula, and the system must change the values of other cells as needed so that the constraints are again satisfied.

In the perturbation model, there will generally be many ways to update the current state so that the constraints are again satisfied. As a trivial example, suppose we have a constraint $A + B = C$, and edit the value of B. Should we change just A, change just C, change both A and C, undo the change to B, or what? At some cost in generality, we can use *read-only annotations* to limit this choice. A common special case is to use *one-way constraints*, that is, constraints in which all but one of the variables are declared to be read-only. For the $A + B = C$ constraint, if A and B are declared to be read-only, it is clear what to do when B is edited (change C), at least if there are no circularities in the constraint graph.

Except for systems that are restricted to non-circular one-way constraints, a problem with the perturbation model is that it is often unclear which variables to alter to re-satisfy the constraints. A variety of heuristics were used in earlier systems (see Section 2.2.6.1). However, none of these methods was entirely satisfactory: sometimes they gave counter-intuitive solutions. Worse, it was difficult to specify declaratively which solutions were preferred and to alter these preferences, since the heuristics were buried in the procedural code of the satisfier.

2.2.1.2 Requirements and Preferences Constraint hierarchies were originally devised to solve the problem of specifying declaratively what to change when perturbing a constraint system (Borning, Duisberg, Freeman-Benson, Kramer, and Woolf 1987). In a constraint hierarchy, the programmer or user can state both *required* and *preferential* constraints (also known as *hard* and *soft* constraints). The required constraints must hold. The system should try to satisfy the preferential constraints if possible, but no error condition arises if it can't. We allow an arbitrary number of levels of preference, each successive level being more weakly preferred than the previous one.

Thus, in the $A + B = C$ example, we could also include weak constraints that A and B remain unchanged, and a weaker constraint that C remain the same. Given this hierarchy, if we edit A, the system will change C rather than B to re-satisfy the constraints. One use, therefore, of constraint hierarchies is to take a problem for which the perturbation model is more natural, and turn it into a more declarative "refinement" problem.

However, constraint hierarchies have numerous other applications as well—anywhere that we would like to state preferences as well as requirements—for example, planning, scheduling, or layout. As a simple example, consider the problem of laying out a table in a document. We would like the table to fit on a single page while still leaving adequate white space between rows. This can be represented as the interaction of two constraints: a hard constraint that the height of the blank space between lines be greater than zero, and a soft constraint that the entire table fit on one page. As another example, suppose we are moving a part of a constrained geometric figure around on the display using the mouse. While the part moves, other parts may also need to move to keep all the constraints satisfied. However, if the locations of all parts aren't determined, we would prefer that they remain where they were, rather than flailing wildly about. Further, there may be choices about which parts to move and which to leave fixed; the user may have preferences in such cases. Again, constraint hierarchies provide a convenient way of stating these desires.

In the remainder of this paper, we first present a theory of constraint hierarchies; this theory is the paper's primary focus. As part of this presentation, we discuss a number of alternate ways of selecting among competing possible solutions, and prove several propositions about the relations among these alternatives. Following this, we outline several algorithms for satisfying constraint hierarchies, and describe how we have used constraint hierarchies in a number of programming languages and systems, including HCLP (a logic programming language scheme), CIP (a hybrid constraint-imperative language scheme), and

ThingLab II (a constraint-based simulation environment). Finally, we discuss some previous and related work in more detail; we describe in particular how these other systems handle problems involving defaults and preferences, and show how to classify their behavior in terms of the constraint hierarchy theory.

2.2.2 A Theory of Constraint Hierarchies

In this section we present a theory of constraint hierarchies. In later sections, we describe some extensions to this basic theory, and then how these notions have been embedded in a variety of systems and languages, including logic programming and object-oriented languages.

2.2.2.1 Definitions

A constraint is a relation over some domain $\mathcal{D}$. The domain $\mathcal{D}$ determines the constraint predicate symbols $\Pi_{\mathcal{D}}$ of the language, so that a constraint is an expression of the form $p(t_1, \ldots, t_n)$ where p is an n-ary symbol in $\Pi_{\mathcal{D}}$ and each t_i is a term.

A *labeled constraint* is a constraint labeled with a strength, written sc, where s is a strength and c is a constraint. For clarity in writing labeled constraints, we give symbolic names to the different strengths of constraints. In both the theory and in our implementations of languages and systems that include constraint hierarchies, we then map each of these names onto the integers $0 \ldots n$, where n is the number of non-required levels. Strength 0, with the symbolic name *required*, is always reserved for required constraints.

A *constraint hierarchy* is a multiset of labeled constraints. Given a constraint hierarchy H, H_0 denotes the required constraints in H, with their labels removed. In the same way, we define the sets $H_1, H_2, \ldots, H_n$ for levels $1, 2, \ldots, n$. We also define $H_k = \emptyset$ for $k n$.

A *solution* to a constraint hierarchy H is a valuation for the free variables in H, i.e., a function that maps the free variables in H to elements in the domain $\mathcal{D}$. We wish to define the set S of all solutions to H. Clearly, each valuation in S must be such that, after it is applied, all the required constraints hold. In addition, we desire each valuation in S to be such that it satisfies the non-required constraints as well as possible, respecting their relative strengths. To formalize this desire, we first define the set S_0 of valuations such that all the H_0 constraints hold. Then, using S_0, we define the desired set S by eliminating all potential valuations that are worse than some other potential valuation using the comparator predicate *better*. (In the definition, $c\theta$ denotes the boolean result of applying the valuation θ to c, and we say that "$c\theta$ holds" if $c\theta = \textbf{true}$.)

$$S_0 = \{\theta \mid \forall c \in H_0 \; c\theta \text{ holds}\}$$
$$S = \{\theta \mid \theta \in S_0 \wedge \forall \sigma \in S_0 \; \neg better(\sigma, \theta, H)\}$$

There are many plausible candidates for comparators. We insist that *better* be irreflexive and transitive:

$$\forall \theta \forall H \ \neg better(\theta, \theta, H)$$
$$\forall \theta, \sigma, \tau \forall H \ better(\theta, \sigma, H) \wedge better(\sigma, \tau, H) \rightarrow better(\theta, \tau, H)$$

However, in general, *better* will not provide a total ordering—there may exist θ and σ such that θ is not better than σ and σ is not better than θ. We also insist that *better* respect the hierarchy—if there is some valuation in S_0 that completely satisfies all the constraints through level k, then all valuations in S must satisfy all the constraints through level k:

if $\exists \theta \in S_0 \wedge \exists k0$ such that
$$\forall i \in 1 \ldots k \ \forall p \in H_i \ p\theta \text{ holds}$$
then $\forall \sigma \in S \ \forall i \in 1 \ldots k \ \forall p \in H_i \ p\sigma \text{ holds}$

We now define several different comparators. In the definitions, we will need an error function $e(c\theta)$ that returns a non-negative real number indicating how nearly constraint c is satisfied for a valuation θ. This function must have the property that $e(c\theta) = 0$ if and only if $c\theta$ holds. For any domain $\mathcal{D}$, we can use the trivial error function that returns 0 if the constraint is satisfied and 1 if it is not. A comparator that uses this error function is a *predicate* comparator. For a domain that is a metric space, we can use its metric in computing the error instead of the trivial error function. (For example, the error for $X = Y$ would be the distance between X and Y.) Such a comparator is a *metric* comparator.

The first of the comparators, *locally-better*, considers each constraint in H individually.

Definition. A valuation θ is *locally-better* than another valuation σ if, for each of the constraints through some level $k - 1$, the error after applying θ is equal to that after applying σ, and at level k the error is strictly less for at least one constraint and less than or equal for all the rest.

$locally\text{-}better(\theta, \sigma, H) \equiv$
$\quad \exists k0$ such that
$$\quad\quad \forall i \in 1 \ldots k - 1 \ \forall p \in H_i \ e(p\theta) = e(p\sigma)$$
$$\quad\quad \wedge \ \exists q \in H_k \ e(q\theta) < e(q\sigma)$$
$$\quad\quad \wedge \ \forall r \in H_k \ e(r\theta) \leq e(r\sigma)$$

Next, we define a schema *globally-better* for global comparators. The schema is parameterized by a function g that combines the errors of all the constraints H_i at a given level.

Definition. A valuation θ is *globally-better* than another valuation σ if, for each level through some level $k - 1$, the combined errors of the constraints after applying θ is equal to that after applying σ, and at level k it is strictly less.

$globally\text{-}better(\theta, \sigma, H, g) \equiv$
$\quad \exists k0$ such that
$$\quad\quad \forall i \in 1 \ldots k - 1 \ g(\theta, H_i) = g(\sigma, H_i)$$
$$\quad\quad \wedge \ g(\theta, H_k) < g(\sigma, H_k)$$

Using *globally-better*, we now define three global comparators, using different combining functions g. The weight for constraint p is denoted by w_p. Each weight is a positive real number.

$$weighted\text{-}sum\text{-}better(\theta, \sigma, H) \equiv globally\text{-}better(\theta, \sigma, H, g)$$
$$where \quad g(\tau, H_i) \equiv \sum_{p \in H_i} w_p e(p\tau)$$

$$worst\text{-}case\text{-}better(\theta, \sigma, H) \equiv globally\text{-}better(\theta, \sigma, H, g)$$
$$where \quad g(\tau, H_i) \equiv \max\{w_p e(p\tau) \mid p \in H_i\}$$

$$least\text{-}squares\text{-}better(\theta, \sigma, H) \equiv globally\text{-}better(\theta, \sigma, H, g)$$
$$where \quad g(\tau, H_i) \equiv \sum_{p \in H_i} w_p e(p\tau)^2$$

Orthogonal to the choice of *locally-better* or one of the instances of *globally-better*, we can choose an appropriate error function for the constraints. *Locally-predicate-better* is *locally-better* using the trivial error function that returns 0 if the constraint is satisfied and 1 if it is not. *Locally-metric-better* is *locally-better* using a domain metric in computing the constraint errors. *Weighted-sum-predicate-better*, *weighted-sum-metric-better*, and so forth, are all defined analogously.

Unsatisfied-count-better is a special case of *weighted-sum-predicate-better*, using weights of 1 on each constraint; it counts the number of unsatisfied constraints in making its comparisons. The predicate versions of the other two global comparators aren't particularly useful: *worst-case-predicate-better* has an all-or-nothing behavior which doesn't filter out solutions as well as one might like; and *least-squares-predicate-better* always gives the same results as *weighted-sum-predicate-better* (since $1^2 = 1$).

2.2.2.2 Illustrative Examples The first example in this subsection illustrates that constraints in stronger levels dominate those in weaker levels, while the second illustrates the various solutions that different comparators can produce.

First, consider the following constraint hierarchy, which includes the canonical Celsius–Fahrenheit constraint:

Level	Constraints
H_0	required Celsius $* 1.8$ = Fahrenheit $- 32.0$
H_1	strong Fahrenheit $= 212$
H_2	weak Celsius $= 0$

The set S_0 consists of all valuations such that the H_0 (required) constraints hold. For this hierarchy, the set S_0 is infinite, and consists of all valuations with valid temperature pairs $\langle C, F \rangle$, i.e.,

$$S_0 = \{\ldots,\ \langle\text{-}60,\text{-}76\rangle,\ \langle\text{-}40,\text{-}40\rangle,\ \langle 0,32\rangle,\ \langle 10,50\rangle,\ \langle 100,212\rangle,\ \ldots\}$$

while the set S consists of the single pair $\theta = \langle 100, 212\rangle$. For example, S does not contain the pair $\sigma = \langle 10, 50\rangle$ because θ satisfies the level H_1 constraint whereas σ does not. Thus, $\exists k0$ (namely $k = 1$) such that $\exists c \in H_k$ for which $e(c\theta) <$ $e(c\sigma)$. Therefore, *locally-better*(θ, σ, H). Further, S does not contain the pair $\rho = \langle 0, 32\rangle$ because although ρ satisfies the H_2 constraint that θ does not, θ satisfies the H_1 constraint that ρ does not. Intuitively, because θ satisfies the stronger H_1 constraint better than ρ, *locally-better*(θ, ρ, H). This example produces exactly the same answer whether *locally-predicate-better*, *locally-metric-better*, or one of the *globally-better* comparators is used. However, this would not be the case in general. (Some propositions concerning the relations between the comparators are discussed in Section 2.2.2.3.)

As a second example, consider the following constraint hierarchy H for the domain $\mathcal{R}$, and its solutions under each of the useful comparators. (Note that H_0 is empty for this hierarchy.)

Level	Constraint	Weight
H_1	weak $X = 0$	1.0
H_1	weak $X \geq 2$	1.0
H_1	weak $X = 4$	0.25

Comparator	Solutions
locally-predicate-better	$X = 0.0$ or $X = 4.0$
locally-metric-better	$0.0 \leq X \leq 4.0$
weighted-sum-predicate-better	$X = 4.0$
weighted-sum-metric-better	$X = 2.0$
worst-case-metric-better	$X = 1.0$
least-squares-metric-better	$X = 1.3333$

Using the *weighted-sum-metric-better* comparator, the solution consists of exactly one valuation: $\theta = \{X \mapsto 2.0\}$. Thus, θ is *weighted-sum-metric-better* than all other valuations including, for example, $\sigma = \{X \mapsto 0.46\}$. The following table summarizes the computation of $g(\theta, H_1)$ and $g(\sigma, H_1)$, verifying that $g(\theta, H_1) < g(\sigma, H_1)$.

Constraints	$\theta = \{X \mapsto 2.0\}$ Error	Weighted	$\sigma = \{X \mapsto 0.46\}$ Error	Weighted
$X = 0$	2.0	2.0	0.46	0.46
$X \geq 2$	0.0	0.0	1.54	1.54
$X = 4$	2.0	0.5	3.54	0.89
Weighted Sum		2.5		2.89

Using the *locally-predicate-better* comparator, the solution consists of two valuations: $\theta = \{X \mapsto 0.0\}$ and $\rho = \{X \mapsto 4.0\}$. Both valuations are better than all the other valuations (including $\sigma = \{X \mapsto 0.46\}$), but neither one is better than the other. For example, the first of the following two tables illustrates that *locally-predicate-better*(θ, σ) is true and thus $\sigma \notin S$.

Constraints	$\theta = \{X \mapsto 0.0\}$ Trivial Error	Comparison	$\sigma = \{X \mapsto 0.46\}$ Trivial Error
$X = 0$	0	$<$	1
$X \geq 2$	1	$\leq$	1
$X = 4$	1	$\leq$	1
	$\exists q \in H_1\ e(q\theta) < e(q\sigma)\ \wedge\ \forall r \in H_1\ e(r\theta) \leq e(r\sigma)$		

This second table illustrates that neither *locally-predicate-better*(θ, ρ) nor *locally-predicate-better*(ρ, θ) is true, and thus both $\rho \in S$ and $\theta \in S$.

Constraints	$\theta = \{X \mapsto 0\}$ Trivial Error	Comparison	$\rho = \{X \mapsto 4\}$ Trivial Error
$X = 0$	0	$<$	1
$X \geq 2$	1		0
$X = 4$	1		0
	$\neg\forall r \in H_1\ e(r\theta) \leq e(r\rho)\ \wedge\ \neg\forall r \in H_1\ e(r\theta) \geq e(r\rho)$		

2.2.2.3 Remarks on the Comparators The definitions of the global comparators include weights on the constraints. For the local comparators, adding weights would be futile, since the result would be the same with or without the weights.

One might argue that allowing an arbitrary number of constraint strengths is unnecessary: since soft constraints can have weights on them, one could make do with only two levels (required and one preferential level), and use appropriate weights to achieve the desired effects. There are three reasons we believe such an argument is not valid: two conceptual, and the other pragmatic. To illustrate the first reason, consider moving a line with a mouse in an interactive graphics application. The line has a strong constraint that it be horizontal, and another strong constraint that one endpoint follow the mouse. There is also a weaker constraint that the line be attached to some fixed point in the diagram. The user's expectations in this case are likely that the line will remain exactly horizontal and will precisely follow the mouse (letting the weaker attachment constraint be unsatisfied), rather than keeping the line nearly horizontal, or quite close to the mouse, but letting the weaker constraint have a bit of influence on the result. Second, since adding weights to constraints is futile for the local comparators, we would need to give up these comparators and use only global ones. Third, solutions to constraint hierarchies in which one level completely dominates the next can often be found much more efficiently than solutions to systems with only one preferential level and weights on the constraints—see Section 2.2.4.

Most of the concepts in constraint hierarchies derive from concepts in subfields of operations research such as linear programming (Murty 1983), multiobjective linear programming (Murty 1983), goal programming (Ignizio 1985), and generalized goal programming (Ignizio 1983). The domain of the constraints in operations research is usually the real numbers, or sometimes the integers (for integer programming problems). The notion of constraint hierarchies is preceded by the approach to multiobjective problems of placing the objective functions in a priority order. The concept of a *locally-better* solution is derived from the concept of a *vector minimum* (or *pareto optimal solution*, or *nondominated solution*) to a multiobjective linear programming problem. Similarly, the concepts of *weighted-sum-better* and *worst-case-better* solutions are both derived from analogous concepts in multiobjective linear programming problems and generalized goal programming.

There are a number of relations that hold between local and global comparators.

Proposition 2.1 *For a given error function e,*

$$\forall \theta \forall \sigma \forall H \; \text{locally-better}(\theta, \sigma, H) \rightarrow \text{weighted-sum-better}(\theta, \sigma, H)$$

Proof. Suppose *locally-better*(θ, σ, H) holds. Then there is some level $k0$ in H such that the error after applying θ to each of the constraints through levels $k-1$ is equal to that after applying σ. It then follows that the sum of the weighted errors after applying θ to the constraints through levels $k - 1$ is equal to that after applying σ. Furthermore, at level k the error after applying θ is strictly less for at least one constraint and less than or equal for all the rest. This implies that the weighted sum of the errors after applying θ to the constraints at level k is strictly less than that after applying σ. Therefore *weighted-sum-better*(θ, σ, H) also holds.

Corollary 2.2 *For a given constraint hierarchy, let S_{LB} denote the set of solutions found using the* locally-better *comparator, and S_{WSB} that for* weighted-sum-better. *Then $S_{\text{WSB}} \subseteq S_{\text{LB}}$.*

Proposition 2.3 *For a given error function e,*

$$\forall \theta \forall \sigma \forall H \; \text{locally-better}(\theta, \sigma, H) \rightarrow \text{least-squares-better}(\theta, \sigma, H)$$

The proof is similar to that for Proposition 2.1.

Corollary 2.4 *Let S_{LSQ} denote the set S of solutions found using the* least-squares-better *comparator. Then $S_{\text{LSQ}} \subseteq S_{\text{LB}}$.*

Propositions 2.1 and 2.3 concern particular instances of the *globally-better* schema. However, *locally-better* does not imply *globally-better* for an arbitrary combining function g. In particular, *locally-better* does not imply *worst-case-better*.

2.2.2.4 Errors for Inequalities A problem arises in connection with metric predicates and strict inequalities. For example, what should be the error function for the constraint XY, where X and Y are reals? If X is greater than Y, then the error must be 0. If X isn't greater than Y, we'd like the error to be smaller the closer X is to Y. Thus, an obvious error function is $e(XY) = 0$ if XY, otherwise $Y - X$. This isn't correct, however, since it gives an error of 0 if X and Y are equal. However, if the error when X and Y are equal is some positive number d, then we get a smaller error when Y is equal to $X + d/2$ than when Y is equal to X, thus violating our desire that the error become smaller as X gets closer to Y.

To solve this problem, we introduce an infinitesimal number ϵ (Robinson 1966), which is greater than 0 and less than any positive standard real number. Using ϵ we can then define

$$e(XY) = \begin{cases} Y - X & \text{if } X < Y \\ \epsilon & \text{if } X = Y \\ 0 & \text{if } XY \end{cases}$$

$$e(X \neq Y) = \begin{cases} 0 & \text{if } X \neq Y \\ \epsilon & \text{if } X = Y \end{cases}$$

$$e(X < Y) = \begin{cases} 0 & \text{if } X < Y \\ \epsilon & \text{if } X = Y \\ X - Y & \text{if } XY \end{cases}$$

Note that ϵ is only being added to the range of the error function, not to the domain $\mathcal{D}$. If we did try to change the domain itself to be the hyperreal numbers, we would end up with the same problem as before.[1]

2.2.2.5 Existence of Solutions If the set of solutions S_0 for the required constraints is non-empty, intuitively one might expect that the set of solutions S for the hierarchy would be non-empty as well. However, this is not always the case. Consider the hierarchy *required* $N0$, *strong* $N = 0$ for the domain of the real numbers, using a metric comparator. Then S_0 consists of all valuations mapping N to a positive number, but S is empty, since for any valuation $\{N \mapsto d\} \in S_0$, we can find another valuation, for example $\{N \mapsto d/2\}$, that better satisfies the soft constraint $N = 0$.

However, the following proposition, especially relevant for floating point numbers, does hold:

Proposition 2.5 *If S_0 is non-empty and finite, then S is non-empty.*

Proof. Suppose to the contrary that S is empty. Pick a valuation θ_1 from S_0. Since $\theta_1 \notin S$, there must be some $\theta_2 \in S_0$ such that $better(\theta_2, \theta_1, H)$. Similarly, since $\theta_2 \notin S$, there is an $\theta_3 \in S_0$ such that $better(\theta_3, \theta_2, H)$, and so forth for an infinite chain $\theta_4, \theta_5, \ldots$. Since $better$ is transitive, it follows by induction that $\forall i, j0 \; [ij \rightarrow better(\theta_i, \theta_j, H)]$. The irreflexivity property of $better$ requires that

---

[1] What would be the error for the constraint $0\epsilon/2$? According to the definition, the error would be $\epsilon/2$. But this is less than the error for 00, even though the 00 constraint is more nearly satisfied.

$\forall i0 \; \neg better(\theta_i, \theta_i, H)$. Thus all the θ_i are distinct, and so there are an infinite number of them. But, by hypothesis S_0 is finite, a contradiction.

For most (if not all) practical applications of constraint hierarchies, H will be finite. For example, for a CIP or HCLP program, if the program terminates, the resulting set of constraints will be finite. The next proposition tells us that in many cases of practical importance, if the required constraints can be satisfied, then solutions to the hierarchy exist.

Proposition 2.6 *If S_0 is non-empty, if H is finite, and if a predicate comparator is used, then S is non-empty.*

Proof. Suppose to the contrary that S is empty. Using the same argument as before, we show that there must be an infinite number of distinct valuations $\theta_i \in S_0$. However, if the comparator is predicate, one valuation cannot be better than another if both valuations satisfy exactly the same subset of constraints in H. Therefore each of the θ_i must satisfy a different subset of the constraints in H. However, this is a contradiction, since H is finite.

2.2.3 Extensions to the Constraint Hierarchy Theory

2.2.3.1 Read-only Annotations As noted in Section 2.2.1.1, perturbation-based constraint systems often use read-only annotations to help limit the choice of which variables should be updated to re-satisfy the constraints after some change to the system. Constraint hierarchies provide an alternative method for specifying this choice, without giving up the generality of multi-way constraints. However, even in a multi-way constraint system with hierarchies, read-only annotations can still be useful. One use is in constraints that reference an external input device or other outside source of information. If we have a constraint that a point follow the mouse, the constraint should be read-only on the mouse position (unless, of course, the mouse is equipped with a small computer-controlled motor). Another use is in constraints describing a change over time, where the constraint relates an old and a new state. Here, we may wish to make the old state read-only, so that the future can't alter the past.

Intuitively, when choosing the best solutions to a constraint hierarchy, constraints should not be allowed to affect the choice of values for their read-only variables, i.e., information can flow out of the read-only variables, but not into them. (Alternatively we can say that constraints are only allowed to affect the choice of values for their unannotated variables.) However, we still want the constraints to be satisfied if possible (respecting their strengths). In particular, required constraints must be satisfied, even if they contain read-only annotations.

We now give an informal outline of the definition. One way of preventing a constraint from affecting the choice of values for a variable is to replace that occurrence of the variable by a constant. Thus, we begin the definition of the set of solutions to a constraint hierarchy H by forming a set Q of constraint hierarchies, where each element of Q is a constraint hierarchy with arbitrary domain elements substituted for the read-only variables. (Note that the same variable v may have read-only occurrences and normal occurrences. Only the read-only occurrences are replaced when forming elements of Q.) Intuitively, we guess a valuation for v, and then form a hierarchy using that guess. After making all possible guesses, we weed out solutions arising from incorrect ones. (Note that this is purely a specification of the meaning of read-only annotations, not a reasonable algorithm for actually solving such constraint hierarchies! Algorithms are discussed in Section 2.2.4.)

Here is an example:

Original H	$q \in Q$ formed by replacing $Y?$ with $d \in \mathcal{D}$			
	$Y? \mapsto 9.83$	$Y? \mapsto 3$	$Y? \mapsto -6.2$	$\cdots$
required $X = Y?$	$X = \mathbf{9.83}$	$X = \mathbf{3}$	$X = \mathbf{-6.2}$	
strong $\quad X = 4$	$X = 4$	$X = 4$	$X = 4$	$\cdots$
weak $\quad\;\; Y = 3$	$Y = 3$	$Y = 3$	$Y = 3$	

Next we solve the constraint hierarchies in Q, discarding any valuations that map the remaining unannotated occurrences of a variable to something different from what was substituted for its read-only occurrences. (In other words, we discard all valuations in which we guessed incorrectly.) This ensures that the permissible values for a variable won't be affected by read-only occurrences of that variable, but that they will be consistent with the read-only occurrences. Continuing the example:

	$q \in Q$ formed by replacing $Y?$ with $d \in \mathcal{D}$		
replacement ρ	$Y? \mapsto 9.83$	$Y? \mapsto 3$	$\cdots$
hierarchy q	required $X = \mathbf{9.83}$ strong $\quad X = 4$ weak $\quad\;\; Y = 3$	required $X = \mathbf{3}$ strong $\quad X = 4$ weak $\quad\;\; Y = 3$	$\cdots$
valuation θ	$\{Y \mapsto 3, X \mapsto 9.83\}$	$\{Y \mapsto 3, X \mapsto 3\}$	$\cdots$
consistency	$Y\theta \neq Y?\rho$	$Y\theta = Y?\rho$	$\cdots$
outcome	Discard	Keep	$\cdots$

The valuation $\{Y \mapsto 3, X \mapsto 3\}$ is the only consistent solution, and thus is the solution to the original hierarchy.

We now give a formal definition of the meaning of read-only annotations. In the definition, we will introduce new variables w_i, which we will want to omit in the final solution. We therefore define an operator *omitting*.

Definition. Let θ be a valuation. Let the domain of θ be the variables $v_1, \ldots, v_n$. Then

$$\theta \text{ omitting } w_1, \ldots, w_m$$

is the valuation σ such that the domain of σ is $\{v_1, \ldots, v_n\} - \{w_1, \ldots, w_m\}$, and such that $\sigma v = \theta v$ for all v in the domain of σ. Similarly, if Θ is a set of valuations,

Θ omitting $w_1, \ldots, w_m$ = $\{\theta$ omitting $w_1, \ldots, w_m \mid \theta \in \Theta\}$

Definition. Let H be a constraint hierarchy, containing read-only annotations, and let $\mathcal{D}$ be the domain of the constraints. Let $v_1, \ldots, v_m$ be the variables in H that have one or more read-only occurrences. Let $w_1, \ldots, w_m$ be new variables not occurring in H, and let J be the hierarchy that results from substituting w_i for each read-only occurrence of the corresponding variable v_i. (The w_i are no longer annotated as read-only in J; also, occurrences of the variables v_i that aren't annotated as read-only are unaffected.) Define Q as the set of all hierarchies $J\rho$, where each ρ is formed by substituting arbitrary domain elements for the w_i:

$$Q = \{J\rho \mid d_1 \in \mathcal{D}, \ldots, d_m \in \mathcal{D}, \rho = \{w_1 \mapsto d_1, \ldots, w_m \mapsto d_m\}\}$$

Let $solutions(J\rho)$ be the set of solutions to $J\rho$. (Here we are using the definition of "solutions" given in the basic theory section (2.2.2), since J has no variables with read-only annotations.) Let the set of *consistent solutions* to $J\rho$ be defined as:

$$consistent(J\rho) = \{\theta \mid \theta \in solutions(J\rho) \wedge$$
$$w_1\rho = v_1\theta \wedge \ldots \wedge w_m\rho = v_m\theta\}$$

In English, to be a consistent solution, if ρ maps w_i to some domain element d_i, then θ must map the corresponding v_i to the same domain element d_i (i.e., we guessed correctly).

The desired set of solutions to H is the set of all consistent solutions, omitting the mappings for the newly introduced variables w_i:

$$solutions(H) = \left(\bigcup_{J\rho \in Q} consistent(J\rho)\right) \text{ omitting } w_1, \ldots w_m$$

Proposition 2.7 *For a constraint hierarchy H containing only required constraints, let H' be the same hierarchy, but with the read-only annotations removed. Then $solutions(H) = solutions(H')$.*

Proof.
$solutions(H) \supseteq solutions(H')$
Let $v_1, \ldots, v_m, w_1, \ldots, w_m$, and J be defined as above. Let θ be a solution for H'. Define $\rho = \{w_i \mapsto v_i\theta, \ldots, w_m \mapsto v_m\theta\}$. (In other words, if θ maps v_i to d_i, then ρ maps the corresponding w_i to d_i.) Then clearly $\theta \in solutions(J\rho)$ and θ is consistent. So $\theta \in solutions(H)$.
    $solutions(H) \subseteq solutions(H')$
Now assume θ is a solution for H. By definition, θ is a consistent solution to $J\rho$ for some ρ. As H consists only of required constraints and as θ is consistent with ρ, θ also satisfies all of the constraints in H'.

Blocked Hierarchies Even with this definition, it is possible for a constraint to restrict the values that its read-only annotated variables can take on. For example, consider the following constraint hierarchy for the domain $\mathcal{R}$:

required   V0
required   V? = 1

The $V0$ constraint contains the only unannotated occurrence of V, and thus only $V0$ is allowed to affect the choice of values for V, and not $V? = 1$. However, the solutions to the first constraint by itself, $V0$, includes $V \mapsto 0.3$, $V \mapsto 1.728$, and so forth, in addition to $V \mapsto 1$, while $solutions(H) = \{V \mapsto 1\}$. Thus, the choice of values for V is being affected by the $V? = 1$ constraint. We therefore impose an additional check, $blocked(H)$, that tests for this situation.

   The $blocked(H)$ predicate is true if any constraint in H limits the permissible values for one of its read-only annotated variables. In such a case, additional constraints can be added to the hierarchy so that the set of solutions can be found without any constraints limiting the permissible values for the read-only annotated variables.

   The definition of $blocked(H)$ is based on the following observation: if there is a domain element d such that there are no solutions when d replaces all occurrences of a variable (both annotated and unannotated), but there are solutions when d replaces only the unannotated occurrences, then the annotated (read-only) occurrences are eliminating d from $solutions(H)$. Thus, if such a d exists, the annotated occurrences are restricting the values that the variable can take on, and $blocked(H)$ is true.

   Definition.

$$blocked(H) \equiv \exists d \in \mathcal{D}\ \exists i \in [1\dots m]\ \text{such that}$$
$$solutions(J\rho\theta\sigma) = \emptyset \wedge solutions(J\theta\sigma) \neq \emptyset$$
$$\text{where } \rho = \{w_i \mapsto d\}\,,\ \theta = \{v_i \mapsto d\}\,,\ \text{and}$$
$$\sigma = \{w_1 \mapsto v_1, \dots, w_{i-1} \mapsto v_{i-1},$$
$$w_{i+1} \mapsto v_{i+1}, \dots, w_m \mapsto v_m\}$$

If there are no read-only annotations on the variables in H, then clearly $blocked(H)$ is false.

   Within the logic programming community, read-only annotations were originally introduced in Concurrent Prolog (Shapiro 1986) for an entirely different purpose than ours, namely for the control of communication and synchronization among networks of processes. In our work, having a blocked solution is an unusual and undesirable state, which would arise only if a design or other error had been made in specifying the constraints. In contrast, in concurrent logic programming, blocking caused by read-only annotations is ubiquitous and essential in controlling program execution.

   There were problems with the original formulation of read-only annotations in Concurrent Prolog (see (Saraswat 1985) for a discussion), and a number of alternatives have been proposed. For example, Maher (Maher 1987) describes

ALPS, a class of languages that incorporates constraints into a flat committed-choice logic language. The definition of *blocked* was directly inspired by the ALPS work.

Illustrative Examples of Using Read-only Annotations Consider the hierarchy H for the domain $\mathcal{R}$:

required $C * 1.8 = F? - 32.0$
strong $\qquad C = 0.0$
weak $\qquad F = 212.0$

Without the read-only annotation on F, the solution to this hierarchy would be $\{\{C \mapsto 0.0, F \mapsto 32.0\}\}$.

However, to find the solution while accommodating the read-only annotation, the hierarchy J is formed by replacing $F?$ by a newly introduced variable W:

required $C * 1.8 = W - 32.0$
strong $\qquad C = 0.0$
weak $\qquad F = 212.0$

Q is the set of all hierarchies resulting from substituting an arbitrary real number for W. For example, the hierarchy resulting from the substitution $\rho = \{W \mapsto 14.0\}$ is:

required $C * 1.8 = 14.0 - 32.0$
strong $\qquad C = 0.0$
weak $\qquad F = 212.0$

which has the singleton set of solutions $\{\theta = \{C \mapsto -10.0, F \mapsto 212.0\}\}$, but is not consistent because $W\rho \neq F\theta$ ($14.0 \neq 212.0$).

The only hierarchy in Q with a consistent solution results from $\rho = \{W \mapsto 212.0\}$:

required $C * 1.8 = 212.0 - 32.0$
strong $\qquad C = 0.0$
weak $\qquad F = 212.0$

and so the set of solutions to the original hierarchy H is $\{\{C \mapsto 100.0, F \mapsto 212.0\}\}$. (Note that the *strong* $C = 0.0$ constraint is not satisfied because there is no consistent solution that satisfies it.)

Now consider the motivating example in Section 2.2.3.1 for which *blocked* is true:

required $V0$
required $V? = 1$

To illustrate the definition of *blocked*, form the new hierarchy J by replacing $V?$ with W:

required V0
required W = 1

There exists a $d \in \mathcal{R}$, for example $d = 6$, such that, for the substitutions $\rho = \{W \mapsto 6\}$, $\theta = \{V \mapsto 6\}$, and $\sigma = \{\}$, $J\rho\theta\sigma$ has no solutions, but $J\theta\sigma$ does have a solution:

$J\rho\theta\sigma$	$J\theta\sigma$
required 60	*required* 60
required 6 = 1	*required W* = 1
no solutions	$\{\{W \mapsto 1\}\}$

Hence *blocked* is true for this hierarchy. However, if we added the additional constraint *required V* = 1 to the original hierarchy, then *blocked* would become false.

Practical Examples of Using Read-only Annotations A trivial but useful example is a spreadsheet-like constraint that $A? + B? + C? = Sum$. The read-only annotations prevent the user from editing *Sum* and having the change propagate back to A, B, or C, but still allow the user to edit A, B, or C.

As noted in the introduction, an important use of read-only annotations is in constraints that reference an external input device or other outside source of information. For example, if we have a constraint that a point P follow the mouse, the constraint should be read-only on the mouse position:

$$P \;=\; mouse.position?$$

As another example, suppose we have a simple scrollbar displayed on the screen. When the "thumb" is dragged up and down, we want the top and bottom of the scrollbar to remain fixed. However, we want to be able to reposition the scrollbar as a whole, so simply anchoring the top and bottom isn't the correct solution.[2] To handle this problem cleanly, we define a constraint relating the position of the thumb, the top, the bottom, and a number *percent*, in which the the top and bottom are annotated as read-only:

$$percent \;=\; \frac{thumb - bottom?}{top? - bottom?}$$

The read-only annotations on *top* and *bottom* are specific to this constraint, so the whole scrollbar can be repositioned by some other "move" constraint.

---

[2]We could almost achieve the desired result by putting strong (but not required) anchors on the top and bottom of the mouse. However, if other constraints on the output value from the slider became too strong, then the top or bottom would move; we would prefer a more robust object.

Circularities While the sets of solutions to many hierarchies are intuitively clear, this clarity often vanishes when the hierarchy contains cycles. We present two such examples here. These are pathological cases that would not arise in realistic applications—but nevertheless the theory should and does specify how they are to be handled.

The following two hierarchies both contain a cycle through variables annotated as read-only. In the first hierarchy, none of the constraints in the cycle is more restrictive than the others and so, intuitively, information can flow properly and still yield a solution.

required $X? = Y + 1$
required $X = Y? + 1$

For this hierarchy, *blocked* is false and the set of solutions is the infinite set $\{\{X \mapsto d + 1, Y \mapsto d\} \mid d \in \mathcal{R}\}$.

In the second hierarchy, however, the *required* $X? = Y + 1$ constraint is more restrictive than the *required* $X \geq Y?$ one. Thus the "unequal" information flow results in *blocked* being true.

required $X? = Y + 1$
required $Y = 20$
required $X \geq Y?$

For this hierarchy, the set of solutions is $\{\{X \mapsto 21, Y \mapsto 20\}\}$; however, *blocked* is true.

2.2.3.2 Write-only Annotations

In addition to read-only annotations, it is also convenient if *write-only annotations* are available. Intuitively, if a variable is annotated as write-only in a constraint, we only want information to be able to flow from the constraint into that variable, and not back. We could define the effect of write-only annotations from first principles, in a manner analogous to the definition for read-only annotations. However, it is simpler to define write-only annotations in terms of read-only annotations.

Definition. Let H be a constraint hierarchy containing write-only annotations (it may contain read-only annotations as well), and let $\mathcal{D}$ be the domain of the constraints. Let $v_1, \ldots, v_m$ be the variables in H that have one or more write-only occurrences. Let $w_1, \ldots, w_m$ be new variables not occurring in H, and let J be the hierarchy that results from substituting w_i for each write-only occurrence of the corresponding variable v_i. Let J' be the hierarchy formed by augmenting J with the additional required constraints $v_i = w_i?$ for $1 \leq i \leq m$. The desired set of solutions to H is the the set of solutions to J', with the mappings for the w_i omitted:

$$solutions(H) \;\;=\;\; solutions(J') \text{ omitting } w_1, \ldots w_m$$

The definition of the set $solutions(J')$ used above is, of course, that given in Section 2.2.3.1.

For example, let H be:

required $X! = Y$
strong $X = 4$
weak $Y = 3$

Intuitively, even though the constraint $X = 4$ is stronger than the constraint $Y = 3$, information will only be allowed to flow from Y to X in the $X! = Y$ constraint, since X is annotated as write-only. Tracing through the definition, the hierarchy J' is formed by replacing $X!$ by a newly introduced variable W, and adding the required constraint $X = W?$.

required $W = Y$
required $X = W?$
strong $X = 4$
weak $Y = 3$

The set of solutions to J' is $\{\{W \mapsto 3, X \mapsto 3, Y \mapsto 3\}\}$. The desired set of solutions to H is the same, but with the mapping for W omitted: $\{\{X \mapsto 3, Y \mapsto 3\}\}$.

2.2.3.3 Partially Ordered Hierarchies In some applications, imposing a total order on the constraint strengths may be over-specifying the problem. We therefore also define the set of solutions to a *partially ordered* constraint hierarchy. A partially ordered hierarchy must still have a distinguished *required* strength. However, the other constraint strengths need only be placed in a partial order, rather than a total order.

Informally, we define the set of solutions to a partially ordered constraint hierarchy by forming the set of all totally ordered hierarchies that are *consistent* with the original one. These totally ordered hierarchies are formed by adding any additional, permissible orderings between the partially ordered strengths: less than, greater than, or equal. The desired set of solutions is then the union of the sets of solutions to the totally ordered hierarchies.

Definition. If P is a partially ordered hierarchy, a totally ordered hierarchy H is *consistent* with P if (1) both hierarchies contain the same constraints, and (2) there is a mapping m from the strengths of P to the strengths of H such that if $s_1 < s_2$ in P then $m(s_1) < m(s_2)$ in H, and (3) $\forall i, s_i c_i \in P$ iff $m(s_i) c_i \in H$.

Definition. Let P be a partially ordered hierarchy. Then

$$solutions(P) \quad = \quad \bigcup_{H \in \mathcal{H}} solutions(H)$$

where $\mathcal{H}$ is the set of all totally ordered hierarchies consistent with P.

As a trivial example, consider the following hierarchy:

wimpy $X = 3$
indecisive $X = 4$

Strengths *wimpy* and *indecisive* are both non-required, but no ordering is specified between them. The total orders that are consistent with this partial order make *wimpy* stronger than *indecisive*, *wimpy* weaker than *indecisive*, and *wimpy* the same strength as *indecisive*. The *locally-predicate-better* solutions to these hierarchies are $\{\{X \mapsto 3\}\}$, $\{\{X \mapsto 4\}\}$, and $\{\{X \mapsto 3\}, \{X \mapsto 4\}\}$ respectively. Therefore, the set of *locally-predicate-better* solutions to the original partially ordered hierarchy is $\{\{X \mapsto 3\}, \{X \mapsto 4\}\}$.

The definition involves adding all possible orderings between the strengths, including equality. For the local comparators, equality is unnecessary—any solution for a totally ordered hierarchy formed using an equality relation will also be a solution for one of the other totally ordered hierarchies formed using just inequality. This is, however, not the case for the global comparators. For example, if the *least-squares-better* comparator is used, the solutions to the totally ordered hierarchies are $\{\{X \mapsto 3\}\}$, $\{\{X \mapsto 4\}\}$, and $\{\{X \mapsto 3.5\}\}$ respectively, so that the set of *least-squares-better* solutions to the original partially ordered hierarchy is $\{\{X \mapsto 3\}, \{X \mapsto 3.5\}, \{X \mapsto 4\}\}$.

We have also considered a variant definition for the solutions to partially ordered hierarchies. In the variant, not only would the constraints from two partially ordered strengths be combined into a single strength (i.e., the equality ordering), but also all possible weightings between the constraints would be used. In the above example, for *least-squares-better*, the following infinite set of totally ordered hierarchies would be considered:

strong $X = 3$
weak $X = 4$

strong $X = 4$
weak $X = 3$

$medium[w_1] \; X = 3$
$medium[w_2] \; X = 4$
    for all positive numbers (weights) w_1 and w_2.

The set of solutions in this case would map X to all numbers between 3 and 4 inclusive, i.e. $\{\{X \mapsto a\} \mid a \in [3 \ldots 4]\}$.

2.2.3.4 Objective Functions

In a standard linear programming problem (Murty 1983), we wish to minimize (or maximize) the value of a linear function $z(x_1, \ldots, x_k) = a_1 x_1 + \ldots + a_k x_k$ in k real-valued variables $x_1, \ldots, x_k$, subject to the non-negativity constraints $x_1 \geq 0, \ldots, x_k \geq 0$, and also subject to m additional linear equality or inequality constraints on $x_1, \ldots, x_k$. The function to be minimized or maximized is called the *objective function*.

If the objective function is to be minimized, and if its coefficients z_i are all non-negative, then we can easily represent the linear programming problem as a constraint hierarchy. The k non-negativity constraints and the m additional linear equality and inequality constraints can be represented as required constraints, and the objective function can be represented as a soft constraint $z(x_1, \ldots, x_k) = 0$, since we know *a priori* a lower bound (namely 0) on the value of the objective function. However, if a lower bound isn't known *a priori*, then this transformation would not be appropriate. We could instead set a goal g for the objective function, and decide that we would be completely satisfied if we reach or exceed the goal. (This is the goal programming approach.) In this case, we can represent the objective function as the soft constraint $z(x_1, \ldots, x_k) \leq g$. Another approach would be to represent the objective function as the soft constraint $z'(x_1, \ldots, x_k) = 0$ where

$$z'(x_1, \ldots, x_k) = \begin{cases} -1/z(x_1, \ldots, x_k) & \text{if } z(x_1, \ldots, x_k) < \text{-1} \\ z(x_1, \ldots, x_k) + 2 & \text{if } z(x_1, \ldots, x_k) \geq \text{-1} \end{cases}$$

However, this approach has the disadvantage that it has converted a linear problem into a nonlinear one, making it much harder to solve.

Similar arguments apply for the case of maximizing an objective function.

To overcome these difficulties, we can again extend the basic constraint hierarchy theory to include objective functions explicitly. A *constraint hierarchy with objective functions* is a constraint hierarchy, along with a set of objective functions, also labeled with strengths (which must all be non-required). To simplify the definition, we first replace any objective function $z(x_1, \ldots, x_k)$ to be maximized by $0 - z(x_1, \ldots, x_k)$, which should be minimized. Let Z_i be the set of objective functions at the ith level of the hierarchy. We can then extend the definition of *locally-better* as follows. (The expression $z\theta$ denotes the value of $z(x_1\theta, \ldots, x_k\theta)$, i.e. the value of z when applied to the values for $x_1, \ldots, x_k$ defined by θ.)

$locally\text{-}better(\theta, \sigma, H) \equiv$
  $\exists k0$ such that
    $\forall i \in 1 \ldots k - 1 \ (\forall p \in H_i \ e(p\theta) = e(p\sigma) \ \wedge \ \forall z \in Z_i \ z\theta = z\sigma)$
    $\wedge \ (\exists q \in H_k \ e(q\theta) < e(q\sigma) \ \vee \ \exists z \in Z_k \ z\theta < z\sigma)$
    $\wedge \ \forall r \in H_k \ e(r\theta) \leq e(r\sigma)$
    $\wedge \ \forall z \in Z_k \ z\theta \leq z\sigma$

In other words, for θ to be *locally-better* than σ, θ must do exactly as well as σ on both the constraints and objective functions through level $k - 1$; at level k, θ must do as well or better on all the constraints and objective functions, and it must do strictly better for at least one constraint or objective function.

In keeping with its nature, *locally-better* considers constraints and objective functions individually. The *globally-better* comparators combine the errors for the constraints at a given level of the hierarchy. The constraint errors are bounded below by 0, while in general the objective function has no definite minimum value—so combining these values into one composite value seems unwise. For the global comparators, therefore, we restrict the constraint hierarchy with objective functions to have at each level either just constraints, or just a single objective function. (Multiple objective functions at a given level should be replaced by a single function that combines the values appropriately.)

The extended *globally-better* schema is:

$$globally\text{-}better(\theta, \sigma, H, g) \equiv$$
$$\exists k0 \ \text{such that}$$
$$\forall i \in 1 \ldots k-1 \ (\ g(\theta, H_i) = g(\sigma, H_i) \ \wedge \ z_i\theta = z_i\sigma\ )$$
$$\wedge \ (\ g(\theta, H_k) < g(\sigma, H_k) \ \vee \ z_k\theta < z_k\sigma\ )$$

Here, if i is a level containing constraints, $g(\tau, H_i)$ is defined in the usual way and $z_i\tau$ is 0; if i is a level containing an objective function, $g(\tau, H_i)$ is defined to be 0, and $z_i\tau$ is the value of the objective function at that level.

2.2.3.5 Comparing Solutions Arising from Different Hierarchies In some applications—in particular, in many HCLP($\mathcal{R}$) programs that we have written—to rule out unintuitive solutions, it is useful to compare not just solutions to a given constraint hierarchy, but also solutions from several different hierarchies. (In logic programming, these different hierarchies are generated by alternate choices of rules.) We have extended the theory described above to include such comparisons (Wilson and Borning 1989), but, for the sake of brevity, we don't discuss this extension here.

2.2.4 Constraint Satisfaction Algorithms

Searching for an efficient constraint satisfaction algorithm that works for all domains, comparators, and kinds of constraints would be a futile endeavor. Rather, we need to look for algorithms specialized by one or more attributes. In (Freeman-Benson, Maloney, and Borning 1990) we outline a number of algorithms for solving constraint hierarchies, each of which makes a different engineering trade-off between generality and efficiency. Much of our research so far has used the *locally-predicate-better* comparator over arbitrary domains. When there are no circularities in the constraint graph, we have an efficient incremental algorithm for this comparator. For arbitrary linear constraints, we also have an efficient algorithm based on linear programming techniques. In the following sections, we briefly discuss these two algorithms. For more details on the incremental acyclic algorithm, the reader is referred to (Freeman-Benson and Maloney 1989; Freeman-Benson, Maloney, and Borning 1989; Freeman-Benson, Maloney, and Borning 1990; Maloney 1991); (Freeman-Benson, Maloney, and Borning 1990) and (Maloney 1991) include proofs of correctness and complexity results. References (Freeman-Benson and Wilson 1990; Freeman-Benson, Wilson, and Borning 1992; Wilson 1992) discuss the linear programming algorithm.

2.2.4.1 Blue and DeltaBlue: Algorithms for Acyclic Hierarchies Among the most common techniques for satisfying constraints is *local propagation*.

In local propagation, a constraint can be used to determine the value of one of its variables whenever the values of the other $n - 1$ of its variables are known. This may then allow some other constraint to determine another variable's value, and so forth. Local propagation is similar in this respect to propagating values through a dataflow network. The difference is that while a dataflow network has a single (partially ordered) propagation path, a set of multi-way constraints typically has many potential propagation paths. Thus the constraint solver must in general decide which path to use, and in the case of a constraint hierarchy solver, ensure that this is a path that computes a "best" solution.

For local propagation, each constraint supplies one or more *methods*: procedures that, if executed, will cause the constraint to be satisfied. Each method determines a value for one or more variables (outputs) from its other variables (inputs). For example, the plus constraint $A + B = C$ has three methods: $A \leftarrow C - B$, $B \leftarrow C - A$, and $C \leftarrow A + B$. A local propagation constraint solver produces a propagation path by selecting, and perhaps executing, a method for each constraint in the hierarchy (or, if the constraint cannot be satisfied, no method).

Because local propagation solutions are based on these "all or nothing" methods rather than on some error metric, local propagation constraint solvers are restricted to the predicate comparators from Section 2.2.2.1. Similarly, because local propagation paths utilize at most one method (i.e., at most one constraint) per output variable, they are unable to solve cyclic constraints such as those produced by a set of simultaneous equations.

We christened our local propagation algorithm for constraint hierarchies "Blue". Subsequently, to improve response time for large constraint graphs, we developed an incremental version of the algorithm which we named DeltaBlue. The Blue algorithm is $O(N^2)$ in the total number of constraints, whereas the DeltaBlue algorithm is $O(cN)$ in the number of affected constraints (Gangnet and Rosenberg 1992).

Local propagation algorithms, such as Blue and DeltaBlue, can easily accommodate read-only and write-only annotations as well as partially ordered hierarchies. The read-only and write-only annotations are handled by not including certain methods. For example, $A? + B = C$ would have two, instead of three, methods: $B \leftarrow C - A$ and $C \leftarrow A + B$, but not $A \leftarrow C - B$. Similarly, $A + B! = C$ would have just one method: $B \leftarrow C - A$. Partially ordered hierarchies are easily handled as well by the basic Blue and DeltaBlue algorithms. The basic Blue and DeltaBlue algorithms find a single *locally-predicate-better* solution to the constraint hierarchy. However, both algorithms can be modified to return all solutions, as in the ThingLab I Multiple Solutions Browser (Freeman-Benson 1988).

We have implemented and used both Blue and DeltaBlue in Smalltalk, C, C++, Object Pascal, and Common Lisp. All of these implementations support read-only and write-only annotations, but only the Smalltalk implementation accommodates partially ordered hierarchies.

2.2.4.2 Algorithms for Linear Equality and Inequality Constraints
One disadvantage of local propagation algorithms is that they cannot reliably
handle cycles in the constraint graph. In some cases these algorithms will find
an acyclic solution to a cyclic graph, but this behavior is not guaranteed; the algorithms often halt with a "cyclic constraint graph" error message instead. Further, if the constraints are truly simultaneous, then local propagation algorithms
simply cannot find a solution. Therefore, we designed another set of algorithms
that can solve constraint hierarchies consisting of arbitrary collections of linear
equality and inequality constraints using the *weighted-sum-metric-better*, *worst-
case-metric-better*, and *locally-metric-better* comparators. These algorithms are
instances of our general DeltaStar (Freeman-Benson and Wilson 1990; Freeman-
Benson, Wilson, and Borning 1992) framework and are collectively referred to
as the Orange algorithms.

The DeltaStar framework is an algorithm for incrementally solving a constraint hierarchy, based on an alternate, but provably equivalent, description of
the constraint hierarchy theory (Freeman-Benson and Wilson 1990; Freeman-
Benson 1991; Wilson 1992). Whereas the basic constraint hierarchy theory in
Section 2.2.2 emphasizes the dichotomy between the hard and soft levels, the
alternative theory emphasizes the hierarchical refinement of the set of solutions.

The Orange algorithms use the basic DeltaStar framework by transforming the constraint hierarchy into a series of linear programming problems—one
problem for each level in the hierarchy. All three Orange algorithms have been
implemented in Smalltalk and Common Lisp. However, none of these implementations supports partially ordered hierarchies or read-only and write-only
annotations.

2.2.4.3 Other Algorithms Although not designed for solving constraint hierarchies, many other constraint solving techniques are available, including augmented term rewriting (Leler 1987), relaxation (Borning 1981; Konopasek and
Jayaraman 1984; Sutherland 1963a), and searching for a solution over a finite
domain. Augmented term rewriting is an equation rewriting technique bor-
rowed from functional programming languages, with added support for objects
and multi-directional constraints. Relaxation is an iterative numerical technique, in which the value of each real-valued variable is repeatedly adjusted
to minimize the error in satisfying its constraints. Relaxation will converge on
a *least-squares-better* solution, unless it gets trapped in a local but suboptimal
minimum. Mackworth (Mackworth 1977), Van Hentenryck (Van Hentenryck
1989), and others describe efficient algorithms for solving sets of constraints on
variables ranging over finite domains.

2.2.5 Using Constraint Hierarchies

In the following sections, we discuss four systems in which we have used constraint hierarchies: ThingLab, ThingLab II, HCLP($\mathcal{R}$) (a language that integrates constraint hierarchies with logic programming), and Kaleidoscope (a hy-

brid constraint-imperative programming language); we also list a number of systems built by other researchers that have applied this theory as well.

2.2.5.1 Systems for Building Simulations and User Interfaces ThingLab
(Borning 1981) was a constraint-based laboratory that allowed a user to construct simulations of such things as electrical circuits, mechanical linkages, demonstrations of geometric theorems, and graphical calculators using interactive direct-manipulation techniques. ThingLab used two kinds of local propagation, as well as relaxation, to solve constraints. It would propagate known values "forward" and degrees of freedom "backward" through the graph. Later versions of ThingLab incorporated such features as explicit constraint hierarchies (as described here), incremental compilation, and a graphical facility for defining new kinds of constraints (Borning 1986; Borning, Duisberg, Freeman-Benson, Kramer, and Woolf 1987; Freeman-Benson 1989). The Animus system (Borning and Duisberg 1986; Duisberg 1986) was an animation system implemented on top of ThingLab. Animus added *temporal constraints* to ThingLab where a temporal constraint is a relation that is required to hold between the existence of a stimulus event and a response in the form of a stream of new events. ThingLab II is a complete rewrite of the original ThingLab, oriented toward building user interfaces (Maloney 1991; Maloney, Borning, and Freeman-Benson 1989). ThingLab II supports constraint hierarchies, and includes an implementation of the DeltaBlue incremental constraint satisfaction algorithm. ThingLab II also includes a compiler that optimizes structured, constrained objects by discarding unnecessary structure and compiling the constraints into native code (Freeman-Benson 1989).

In other research on using constraint hierarchies in user interfaces, Epstein and LaLonde (Epstein and LaLonde 1988) used our constraint hierarchy theory in implementing a layout system for Smalltalk windows. They used constraints to define the relation between the canvas size, window size, and scale factors. By default, all parameters were variable. However, the user could add a stronger constraint that one or more of the parameters stayed fixed, thus creating a fixed canvas, fixed size, or fixed scale window. TRIP and TRIP II (Kamada and Kawai 1991; Takahashi, Matsuoka, and Yonezawa 1991) also use constraint hierarchies for user interfaces, with a two-level constraint hierarchy consisting of required constraints and one level of soft constraints, with weights on each soft constraint. Delta TRIP is a version of TRIP II using the DeltaBlue algorithm as its constraint satisfier. Finally, constraint hierarchies were used to simulate the physiological affects of open-heart surgery in a system for supporting anesthesiologists in the operating room (Rotterdam 1989).

2.2.5.2 Constraint Hierarchies in Logic Programming Languages In
standard logic programming, as exemplified by Prolog, rules are of the form

$$p(\mathbf{t}) \; :- \; q_1(\mathbf{t}), \ldots, q_m(\mathbf{t}).$$

where $p, q_1, \ldots, q_m$ are predicate symbols, and t denotes a list of terms. The Constraint Logic Programming (CLP) scheme (Jaffar and Lassez 1987) is a general scheme for extending logic programming to include constraints, and is parameterized by $\mathcal{D}$, the domain of the constraints. In a CLP language, rules are of the form

$$p(t) :- q_1(t), \ldots, q_m(t), c_1(t), \ldots, c_n(t).$$

where $p, q_1, \ldots, q_m$ are as before, and $c_1, \ldots, c_n$ are constraints over the domain $\mathcal{D}$.

Operationally, in a CLP language we can think of executing the Prolog part of the program in the usual way, accumulating constraints on logic variables as we go, and either verifying that the constraints are solvable or else backtracking if they are not. The program can terminate with substitutions being found for all variables in the input, or with some constrained variables still unbound, in which case the output would include the remaining constraints on these variables.

Hierarchical Constraint Logic Programming (HCLP) (Borning, Maher, Martindale, and Wilson 1989; Wilson 1992; Wilson and Borning 1989) is a generalization of the CLP scheme, and is again parameterized by the domain $\mathcal{D}$ of the constraints. In HCLP rules are of the form

$$p(t) :- q_1(t), \ldots, q_m(t), s_1 c_1(t), \ldots, s_n c_n(t).$$

where each s_i is a symbolic name indicating the strength of the corresponding constraint c_i.

Operationally, goals are satisfied as in CLP, temporarily ignoring the non-required constraints, except to accumulate them. After a goal has been successfully reduced, there may still be non-ground variables in the solution. In this event, the accumulated hierarchy of non-required constraints is solved, using a method appropriate for the domain and comparator, thus further refining the values of these variables. Additional answers may be produced by backtracking. As with CLP, constraints can be used multi-directionally, and the scheme can accommodate collections of constraints that cannot be solved by simple forward propagation methods.

To test our ideas, and to allow us to experiment with HCLP programs, we have written two different HCLP interpreters. Our first interpreter is written in CLP($\mathcal{R}$), allowing it to take advantage of the underlying CLP($\mathcal{R}$) constraint solver and backtracking facility. As a result, it is small (2 pages of code) and clean. However, it is not incremental—rather, it recomputes all the *locally-predicate-better* answers for each derivation, instead of incrementally updating its answers as constraints are added and deleted due to backtracking, and thus the interpreter is not particularly efficient. Our second HCLP interpreter is again for the domain of the real numbers, but supports the *weighted-sum-metric-better*, *worst-case-metric-better*, and *locally-metric-better* comparators instead. The comparator to be used in a given program is indicated by a declaration at the beginning of an HCLP program. The second interpreter is implemented in

Common Lisp, and uses the DeltaStar algorithm mentioned in Section 2.2.4.2. The second interpreter includes some evaluable predicates for performing input and graphical output, so that we can use HCLP for interactive graphics applications. Further details regarding both implementations may be found in (Wilson 1992).

2.2.5.3 Constraint Hierarchies in Imperative Languages and Systems
Imperative languages, such as those in the Algol family, have the standard notions of state and destructive assignment. Pure constraint languages, on the other hand, are declarative, without state and assignment. Constraint imperative programming languages, such as Kaleidoscope'90 and '91, are an attempt to merge these two apparently incompatible paradigms.

In CIP (Constraint Imperative Programming), the two paradigms are reconciled by using imperative statements to provide control flow and constraint expressions to provide computation. Imperative assignment statements are translated into constraints between the previous and current states of the object. In other words, X:=X+1 is defined as the constraint $X_t = X_{t-1}? + 1$. (The read-only annotation is used to prevent any computations in the present from changing the past.) Objects are represented as a stream of values over time, as in Lucid (Wadge and Ashcroft 1985), where time is defined by the execution of subsequent imperative statements. A weak equality constraint between each pair of values ensures that the object does not change randomly: $\forall t \; weak \; X_t = X_{t-1}?$. When a variable is assigned to, the stronger "assignment" constraint will override the weaker stay constraint, and the object's state will change. The new value will be propagated forward via the weak stay constraints until the variable is assigned to again.

Constraints do not typically refer to time, whereas time (or rather, sequencing) is crucial to an imperative language. Thus the Kaleidoscope languages use *constraint templates* to create constraints over a variety of intervals, including: just once (e.g., an assignment constraint), until some condition is false (e.g., asserting a constraint while the mouse button is held down), or always (e.g., a data invariant).

Additionally, the Kaleidoscope languages are object-oriented, supporting both user defined objects and user defined constraints over those objects. These latter constraints are defined using *constraint constructors*: side-effect-free procedures that define the meaning of complex constraints over objects in terms of more primitive constraints over the objects' component parts.

Further details regarding the semantics and implementations of both Kaleidoscope'90 and '91 can be found in (Freeman-Benson 1990; Freeman-Benson and Borning 1992a; Freeman-Benson and Borning 1992b).

2.2.5.4 User Interface Issues
There are a number of user interface issues that arise in supporting constraint hierarchies, three of which are discussed here: how to express constraints, how to show alternate solutions to the constraint

hierarchy, and how to achieve good performance in an interactive graphical constraint-based system.

Expressing Constraints Expressing constraint hierarchies in a textual language presents no particular difficulty; once we have a syntax for the constraints themselves, we can annotate them with strengths. In ThingLab, our approach has been to manipulate graphical objects that carry the constraints, rather than graphically representing the constraints themselves. For example, when constructing a graphical calculator, we insert *Plus*, *Times*, *Printer*, and other sorts of objects, each of which holds state, icon, and constraint information. This approach carries over naturally to constraint hierarchies: objects can carry both required and preferential constraints. Objects will normally have weak stay constraints on their parts to give stability to them and to any larger containing object, in addition to any other constraints they may have.

Showing Alternate Solutions A given constraint hierarchy may have several solutions (even infinitely many). The technique used in HCLP($\mathcal{R}$) to present multiple solutions is the same as in other logic programming languages such as Prolog and CLP($\mathcal{R}$). A single *answer* may represent one or more solutions. For example, the answer $X5$ compactly represents the infinite set of solutions mapping X to each real number greater than 5. Answers are presented, one at a time. The user can reject an answer, and backtracking will produce a new one (if one exists). As in CLP($\mathcal{R}$), a given answer can contain variables, perhaps with constraints on them. For example, consider the following short HCLP($\mathcal{R}$) program:

(a) `banana(X)  :- artichoke(X), weak X 6.`
(b) `artichoke(X)  :- strong X=1.`
(c) `artichoke(X)  :- required X 0, required X<10, weak X<4.`

Given the goal `?- banana(A)`, the first answer would be produced using the `banana` clause (a) and the first of the `artichoke` clauses (b), yielding the hierarchy *strong* $X = 1$, *weak* $X6$. There is a single answer to this hierarchy, namely $X = 1$, which would then be displayed. Upon backtracking, the second `artichoke` clause (c) is selected, resulting in the hierarchy *required* $X0$, *required* $X < 10$, *weak* $X < 4$, *weak* $X6$. Using the *locally-predicate-better* comparator, this hierarchy has two answers. The first answer to this hierarchy, but the second to the goal, is $X0, X < 4$. Upon further backtracking the third and final answer to the goal, namely $X6, X < 10$, would be displayed. Thus, this program produces two constraint hierarchies and three answers:

Clauses	Hierarchies	Answers	
a, b	strong $X = 1$ weak $X6$	$X = 1$	
a, c	required $X0$ required $X < 10$ weak $X < 4$ weak $X6$	$0 < X < 4$	$6 < X < 10$

Both of our HCLP($\mathcal{R}$) implementations have primarily textual interfaces. In a system with a graphical interface, presenting multiple solutions raises some interesting problems. ThingLab II adopts the simple strategy of just picking one solution. In a previous version of ThingLab (Freeman-Benson 1988), we did allow the user to browse through multiple solutions graphically. For overconstrained problems (i.e., cases in which HCLP would return additional answers on backtracking), the multiple solution browser would pop up a menu of alternate solutions, so that the user could browse through the different alternatives. For underconstrained problems (i.e., cases where HCLP would return an answer with one or more variables not bound to a unique value), the multiple solution browser would allow the user to move interactively through the space of possible solutions. The user would select an underconstrained part, and the system would respond by displaying a control icon in a new pane and by setting up constraints relating the position of the icon to underconstrained variables in the selected part. The user could then move the control icon in either one or two dimensions, depending on how many degrees of freedom remained for the underconstrained part. (Our implementation didn't support manipulating parts with more than two degrees of freedom, although it could be so extended.) Based on the position of the icon, the system would satisfy the constraints and display the solution. Both techniques (for overconstrained and underconstrained problems) would be used simultaneously if needed.

Performance Issues In an interactive application, keeping the perceived response time low is perhaps more important than achieving the fastest speed. We use two terms in discussing response time: latency, the delay between the input event and the first time the constraints are satisfied; and repetition time, the time it takes to re-satisfy the constraints each time the screen image is updated.

In a naive implementation of constraint hierarchies, the system, in response to each new input event, would first remove any old constraints from previous input events, and then add one or more constraints to the constraint hierarchy. Thus, each new input event would result in a new constraint hierarchy, a new invocation of the constraint solver, and a new set of solutions. The latency and repetition time would be identical. For example, if the scroll bar of a window is being moved by the mouse, the mouse motion events remove and add a sequence of individual constraints: $ScrollBar = 15$, $ScrollBar = 16$, ..., $ScrollBar = 25$, etc.

The implementations of the DeltaBlue algorithm in ThingLab and ThingLab II divide the task of solving the constraints into two parts: structure-directed solving, and data-directed solving. The structure solver, or planner, finds one or more solutions to a constraint hierarchy based only on the structure of the constraints (which variables they constrain, whether or not they constrain their variables uniquely, and so forth). The data solver uses the structure solution to satisfy the constraint hierarchy for specific data values. The structure solution is known as a "plan" because it embodies the procedure for solving the hierarchy. The same plan can be used to solve for multiple data values, until the hierarchy is altered by adding or removing constraints.

Because the data solver is much faster than the structure solver, an "active" (or "edit") constraint is used to modify data values without changing the hierarchy. In the scroll bar example, this means that rather than adding and removing the sequence of constraints, the single active constraint $ScrollBar = Mouse$ is used. The $Mouse$ variable injects the current position of the mouse into the constraint hierarchy, and the data-driven solver can use the existing plan to produce a new solution. The run-time of this technique is $1S + nD$ (1 Structure solution + n Data solutions) whereas the run time if constraints are added and removed for each new value is $n(S + D)$—substantially slower.

ThingLab II has two techniques for executing the plan. The first is interpretation; the second is compilation into native code, followed by execution of that code. When the plan is interpreted, the latency is moderate and the repetition time is moderate. When the plan is compiled, the latency is very high and the repetition time is low. Thus, if the same plan will be used repeatedly, the average run-time will be decreased by compiling the plan. However, during prototyping and development, the constraint hierarchy is in a constant state of flux, causing compiled plans to become obsolete and be discarded. Thus, to decrease the variability of response time, our ThingLab II work has emphasized fast interpretation. Once the constraint hierarchy for an object has been designed, implemented, and tested, the ThingLab II compiler (Freeman-Benson 1989) can be used to compile the constraints into efficient native code.

2.2.6 Other Related Work

Much of the previous and related work on constraint-based languages and systems can be grouped into the following areas: geometric layout, spreadsheets and similar systems, user interface support, general-purpose programming languages, and artificial intelligence applications. In this section we discuss a number of these related efforts. Since this body of related work is very large, here we concentrate on work, in addition to that described in Section 2.2.5, involving combinations of hard and soft constraints. Other bibliographies and discussions may be found in (Freeman-Benson, Maloney, and Borning 1990), (Freeman-Benson 1991), and (Leler 1987).

2.2.6.1 Geometric Layout Geometric layout is a natural application for constraints, and was also their first area of application, in the venerable Sketchpad system (Sutherland 1963a; Sutherland 1963b). Sketchpad allowed the user to build up geometric figures using primitive graphical entities and constraints, such as point-on-line, point-on-circle, collinear, and so forth. When possible, constraints were solved using local propagation. When this technique was not applicable, Sketchpad would resort to relaxation. Although the primitive constraints were hard-coded into the system, new primitive constraints could be added by programming an error function in the underlying implementation language. In addition to its geometric applications, Sketchpad was used for simulating mechanical linkages. Sketchpad was a pioneering system in interactive graphics and object-oriented programming as well as in constraints. Its requirements for CPU cycles and display bandwidth were such that the full use of its techniques had to await cheaper hardware years later.

Juno (Nelson 1985) is a constraint based system for geometric layout similar to ThingLab. The major innovation of Juno was its dual presentation of the constraints: one window contained the graphical layout defined by the constraints while the other window contained the textual definition of the same constraints. Both representations were editable, and the results were reflected in both windows simultaneously. Other constraint-based geometric layout systems include IDEAL (van Wyk 1980; van Wyk 1982), Magritte (Gosling 1983), COOL (Kamada and Kawai 1991), Converge (Sistare 1990) for 3-d geometric modeling, and (Böhringer 1990) for laying out cyclic graphs.

All of the interactive geometric layout systems had to deal in some way with the problem of default constraints. As discussed in Section 2.2.1.1, given a collection of geometric objects with constraints on them, if a part is moved, in general there are many ways to readjust the objects so that the constraints are satisfied. For example, if we move one endpoint of a horizontal line, we don't expect that it will suddenly triple in length (even though the constraint that it be horizontal would still be satisfied). In Sketchpad, the old x and y locations of points are the starting values for the iterative relaxation routine. Even when using local propagation, Sketchpad would solve for values using an individual constraint by considering the constraint error and finding a new value that would make the error go to zero. Thus, if one views the old values as "stay" constraints, and the user's input as a required constraint, Sketchpad would find a *locally-metric-better* solution to the constraints. If only relaxation were used and not local propagation, the solution would also be close to a *least-squares-better* solution. Sketchpad also supported read-only annotations on variables (Sutherland called them "reference-only variables"). Sutherland notes that misusing reference-only variables can lead to instabilities in the relaxation algorithm.

The original version of ThingLab followed Sketchpad's lead, and added local propagation methods to constraints, and constraints over arbitrary domains (not just the real numbers). All the explicit constraints were required; the user's edit requests were implicitly treated as strong preferences rather than requirements, so that if the edit conflicted with a required constraint, the user's constraint would be overridden. In addition, there were implicit weak or very weak constraints that parts of an object keep their old values as the object was being manipulated by the user, unless it was necessary for them to change to satisfy the user's edit or the explicit required constraints. Some of these implicit weak constraints needed to be stronger than others to achieve intuitive behavior. For example, suppose that we have a simple graphical calculator, which includes a constraint $A + B = C$. Now suppose the user edits the value of A. We expect that the system will re-satisfy the plus constraint by changing C, rather than by changing B. To achieve this, the local propagation methods of a constraint were ordered to indicate which ones should be used in preference to others. (For $A + B = C$, the method for updating C would be listed first.) This (usually) gave the same effect as making the stay constraint on C weaker than the ones on A and B. Also, the user's input—for example, moving something with the mouse—was considered as a preference rather than a requirement, so that an anchor or constant could cause it to be overridden. Thus ThingLab would usually also find a *locally-metric-better* solution.

Neither Sketchpad nor ThingLab used a separate, declarative theory of constraints; these choices were embedded in the procedural code of the constraint satisfier. This situation became increasingly troublesome when we tried to improve on ThingLab's constraint satisfier, since there was no declarative specification that we could use to decide whether a particular optimization would lead to a correct answer. In response, the constraint hierarchy theory described in this paper was developed, and was used in later versions of the system.

Similar considerations obtain for the other interactive geometric layout systems. In Magritte (Gosling 1983), the system performed a breadth-first search to change as few variables as possible. This often gives similar answers to *unsatisfied-count-better*, but without too much trouble one can come up with problems where it doesn't give a reasonable answer. For example, consider the constraint $X_1 + \ldots + X_n = Sum$, which is represented as a chain of three-argument plus constraints. If X_i is changed, the breadth-first search solution would be to update either X_{i-1} or X_{i+1}; but the user might well intend that plus have its normal directional bias, so that Sum would be updated instead. Constraint hierarchies allow either of these solutions to be preferred by suitable choice of comparator and strength of the stays. Vander Zanden's algorithm (Vander Zanden 1988) uses a heuristic that attempts to minimize the number of equations that must be solved; again, this is related to *unsatisfied-count-better*, but the exact choice is embedded procedurally in the satisfier.

2.2.6.2 Spreadsheets and Related Systems

Spreadsheets, such as Lotus 1-2-3 or Microsoft EXCEL, are constraint systems in that the user specifies relations to hold between values in cells, although these constraints are usually unidirectional. Spreadsheets in effect trivially implement stay constraints on unedited cells by their update algorithm. The most recent spreadsheet implementations include built-in solver and optimization packages, and thus have much of the power of the other constraint systems. TK!Solver (Konopasek and Jayaraman 1984) is a commercially available system that uses constraints in a "general purpose problem solving environment" targeted at mechanical and electrical engineers. It uses local propagation and relaxation as solution techniques, but when relaxation is required, it asks the user to make initial guesses of the variable's values, thus greatly improving the chances of convergence.

2.2.6.3 User Interface Toolkits Another frequent application of constraints is in user interface toolkits, where they are used for such tasks as maintaining consistency between underlying data and a graphical depiction of that data, maintaining consistency among multiple views, specifying formatting requirements and preferences, and specifying animation events and attributes. The constraint-based user interface system with the largest user base is Garnet (Myers, Guise, Dannenberg, Vander Zanden, Kosbie, Marchal, Pervin, Mickish, and Kolojejchick 1990; Myers, Guise, Dannenberg, Vander Zanden, Kosbie, Marchal, and Pervin 1990). This system is a full-fledged user interface construction set, written in Common Lisp, which provides considerable functionality beyond just a constraint system. The standard constraint portion of Garnet supports only unidirectional constraints and not multidirectional ones, but does include support for constraints containing arbitrary pointer variables (Vander Zanden, Myers, Guise, and Szekely 1991). We recently extended Garnet to Multi-Garnet, which supports multi-way constraints, constraint hierarchies, and pointer variables in an integrated framework (Sannella and Borning 1992). A precursor to Garnet is the Peridot system (Myers 1987a; Myers 1987b); an interesting feature of Peridot is its mechanism for inferring constraints from a widget's layout. Reference (Carter and LaLonde 1984) discusses the design of a syntax-based program editor using constraints. References (Cohen, Smith, and Iverson 1986) and (Epstein and LaLonde 1988) describe using constraint hierarchies to define the inter- and intra-window relations in a window system. Other user interface toolkits that use constraints include GROW (Barth 1986), MEL (Hill 1990), GITS (Olsen 1990), the FilterBrowser user interface construction tool (Ege, Maier, and Borning 1987), and the Cactus statistics exploration environment (McDonald, Stuetzle, and Buja 1990).

2.2.6.4 General-Purpose Programming Languages A number of researchers have investigated general-purpose languages that use constraints, in addition to those mentioned in Section 2.2.5. Steele's Ph.D. dissertation (Steele 1980) is one of the first such efforts. Leler (Leler 1987) describes Bertrand, a constraint language based on augmented term rewriting. Both Steele and Leler's languages use the refinement rather than the perturbation model and don't deal with the issues of soft constraints or the stability of an existing solution when editing it. (Steele's implementation maintains dependency information to decide which deductions should be invalidated when editing the constraint graph, as well as to aid in generating explanations. However, when such edits are made, the old values are simply erased, rather than being used as defaults for the new values.) Siri (Horn 1992a; Horn 1992b) and RENDEZVOUS (Hill 1992) are other recent languages that combine constraints with imperative programming. Siri uses a

graph rewriting model of execution, derived from Bertrand's. Unlike Kaleidoscope, Siri requires the programmer to state explicitly which parts of an object
remain the same after a change. In addition, Siri uses a single abstraction mechanism, a *constraint pattern*, for object description, modification, and evaluation,
rather than separate mechanisms for these tasks. (This uniform use of patterns
is derived from BETA (Kristensen, Madsen, ller Pederson, and Nygaard 1983).)
RENDEZVOUS includes extensive support for processes and multiple users; its
intended domain of use is multi-user, multi-media systems.

Much of the recent research on general-purpose languages with constraints
has used logic programming as a base. Several instances of the CLP scheme
(see Section 2.2.5.2) have now been implemented, including CLP($\mathcal{R}$) (Jaffar and Michaylov 1987; Jaffar, Michaylov, Stuckey, and Yap 1992), Prolog
III (Colmerauer 1990), CHIP (Dincbas, Hentenryck, Simonis, Aggoun, Graf,
and Bertheir 1988; Van Hentenryck 1989), CAL (Satoh and Aiba 1990), and
CLP(Σ^*) (Walinsky 1989). The cc family of languages (Saraswat, Rinard, and
Panangaden 1991; Saraswat 1989) generalizes the CLP scheme to include such
features as concurrency, atomic tell, and blocking ask. Work on logic programming and constraint hierarchies other than HCLP includes that of Maher and
Stuckey (Maher and Stuckey 1989), who give a definition of constraint hierarchies similar to the one in this paper. In their definition, pre-solutions for
hierarchies perform the same function as the set S_0 in our formulation. Maher
and Stuckey define a pre-measure that maps pre-solutions and sets of constraints to some scale, so that they can then be compared via a lexicographic
ordering. Satoh (Satoh 1990) proposes a theory for constraint hierarchies using a meta-language to specify an ordering on the interpretations that satisfy
the required constraints. The theory is quite general, and can accommodate
all of the comparators described in Section 2.2.2.1. However, since it is defined
by second-order formulae, it is not in general computable. In subsequent work
(Satoh and Aiba 1991a; Satoh and Aiba 1991b), Satoh and Aiba present an
alternative theory that restricts the constraints to a single domain $\mathcal{D}$, so that
they can be expressed in a first-order formula. This theory is similar to the one
presented here, with the following differences: first, only the *locally-predicate-
better* comparator is supported; second, the semantics of constraint hierarchies
is described model theoretically rather than set theoretically; and third, the
class of constraints is generalized from atomic constraints to disjunctions of
conjunctions of atomic constraints. Satoh and Aiba embed such constraints in
the CLP language CAL (Satoh and Aiba 1990), to yield an HCLP language
CHAL (Satoh and Aiba 1991a; Satoh and Aiba 1991b).

Ohwada and Mizoguchi (Ohwada and Mizoguchi 1990) discuss the use of
logic programming for building graphical user interfaces, including the use of default constraints. Their constraint hierarchy is implemented using the negation-
as-failure rule, i.e., if the negation of a constraint is not known to hold, then
the constraint can be assumed to hold. A problem with this approach is that it
then becomes necessary to list all possible conflicts when a rule is being written
in order to avoid inconsistencies. In contrast, in HCLP the need for consistency

is assumed and there is no need to enumerate specifically those constraints that might conflict with the goal.

2.2.6.5 Artificial Intelligence Applications

There is a substantial body of research in the artificial intelligence community using constraints in planning, simulation, computer vision, and other areas. Constraints can, for example, improve the performance of an inferencing system by early pruning of the search space, i.e., by using the constraint system as a faster, but less general, inferencer that runs as a subtask of the more general system. Again, since this body of related work is very large, here we concentrate on work involving combinations of required and preferential constraints.

Descotte and Latombe (Descotte and Latombe 1985) use required and preferential constraints in a system, Gari, for generating plans for machining parts. For example, there might be a required constraint that a particular cut be made with either a surface grinding machine or a lathe, and a preference that such cuts not be made with a lathe. Production rules are used to encode Gari's knowledge: on the left hand side of the rule are conditions that must be satisfied for the rule to be used; on the right hand side are labeled constraints that are added if the rule's conditions are satisfied. Gari supports ten levels of constraints (required and nine preferential levels). The solver finds (close to) a *locally-predicate-better* solution to the collection of constraints using an iterative search.[3] Fox (Fox 1987) discusses the problem of constraint-directed reasoning for job-shop scheduling, and allows the relaxation of constraints when conflicts occur, as well as context-sensitive selection and weighted interpretation of constraints. In Fox's system, ISIS, non-required constraints include a *relaxation specification* that specifies procedurally how to generate alternative, less restrictive, versions of the constraint. ISIS searches for a solution to the soft constraints that meets a minimum *weighted-sum-better* threshold. (Due to the complexity of the search space for this domain, the system doesn't attempt to find an optimal solution, just an acceptable one.) Constraints in ISIS have a number of other attributes, such as duration and context, which in the formalism described in this paper would be handled outside the constraint system (for example, in HCLP rules or a Kaleidoscope procedure).

The constraint systems in many AI applications solve systems of constraints over finite domains (Mackworth 1977). Three typical applications of such CSPs (constraint satisfaction problems) are scene labeling, map interpretation, and computer system configuration. Freuder (Freuder 1989) gives a general model for partial constraint satisfaction problems (PCSPs) for variables ranging over finite domains, extending the standard CSP model. In Freuder's model, alternate CSPs are compared with the original problem using a metric on the

---

[3]The definition of a correct solution in Gari is actually a bit weaker than *locally-predicate-better*: in the terminology used in this paper, a Gari solution must simply respect the hierarchy (see Section 2.2.2.1). Equivalently, one can view Gari as using a two-level constraint hierarchy (required and one preferential level), with integral weights between 1 and 9 on the preferential constraints; taking this view, it finds *worst-case-better* solutions.

problem space (as opposed to a metric on the solution space, as in our work). An optimal solution s to the original PCSP would be one in which the distance between the original problem and the new problem (for which s is an exact solution) is minimal. In an earlier CSP extension, Shapiro and Haralick (Shapiro and Haralick 1981) define the concepts of exact and inexact matching of two structural descriptions of objects, and show that inexact matching is a special case of the inexact consistent labeling problem.

A classic problem in AI is the *frame problem*: the need to infer that state will not change across events.[4] In response to this problem, a substantial body of research has been done on *nonmonotonic reasoning*; reference (Ginsberg 1987) is a collection of many of the classic papers in the area. Brewka (Brewka 1989) describes an approach to representing default information with multiple levels of preference. In this framework, there are many levels of theories, some of which are more preferred than others. A preferred subtheory is obtained by taking a maximally consistent subset of the strongest level, and then adding as many formulas as possible from the next strongest level, and so on, without introducing any inconsistencies. Reference (Wilson and Borning 1989) discusses some additional aspects of the relationship between constraint hierarchies and nonmonotonic logic.

2.2.7 Conclusion

The primary contribution of this paper has been a complete presentation of the theory of constraint hierarchies: both the basic form, and a number of useful extensions. We have also outlined a number of applications and algorithms to demonstrate that constraint hierarchies are useful and practical, and have shown how the operation of a number of other systems can be categorized using the constraint hierarchy theory.

We are continuing to investigate various aspects of constraint hierarchies, including fully integrated programming languages and additional solver algorithms. One of our primary goals in this work is to support user interfaces and interactive graphics, both of which require highly efficient constraint solvers. Thus, with Michael Sannella, we are extending the DeltaBlue algorithm to accommodate cycles, simultaneous equations, and other complex constraint graphs. Additionally, we believe that there are significant benefits that arise when constraint hierarchies are fully integrated into programming languages. Thus we are further refining our second HCLP($\mathcal{R}$) implementation and, with Gus Lopez, are implementing a second generation CIP language, Kaleidoscope'91.

---

[4]The use of weak stay constraints to assert that parts of a graphical object being manipulated should remain in the same place is in fact a way of addressing the frame problem in the context of interactive graphics.

Acknowledgements

Thanks for many useful discussions, and comments on drafts of this paper, to John Maloney, Michael Sannella, and Dan Weld. John Maloney has done much of the work on ThingLab II, and Amy Martindale and Michael Maher worked with us on HCLP. Thanks to the anonymous referees for useful comments, in particular for pointing out a problem in one of the definitions and certain parts of the exposition that needed to be clarified. This project was supported in part by the National Science Foundation under Grants CCR-9107395 and IRI-9102938, by the Canadian National Science and Engineering Research Council under Grant OGP0121431, by the University of Victoria, and by graduate fellowships from the National Science Foundation and Apple Computer for Bjorn Freeman-Benson and Molly Wilson respectively.

References

Barth, P. (1986, April). An Object-Oriented Approach to Graphical Interfaces. *ACM Transactions on Graphics 5*(2), 142–172.

Böhringer, K.-F. (1990, April). Using Constraints to Achieve Stability in Automatic Graph Layout Algorithms. In *CHI'90 Conference Proceedings*, Seattle, Washington, pp. 43–52. ACM SIGCHI.

Borning, A. (1981, October). The Programming Language Aspects of ThingLab, A Constraint-Oriented Simulation Laboratory. *ACM Transactions on Programming Languages and Systems 3*(4), 353–387.

Borning, A. (1986). Graphically Defining New Building Blocks in ThingLab. *Human-Computer Interaction 2*(4), 269–295.

Borning, A. and R. Duisberg (1986, October). Constraint-Based Tools for Building User Interfaces. *ACM Transactions on Graphics 5*(4).

Borning, A., R. Duisberg, B. Freeman-Benson, A. Kramer, and M. Woolf (1987, October). Constraint Hierarchies. In *Proceedings of the 1987 ACM Conference on Object-Oriented Programming Systems, Languages, and Applications*, pp. 48–60. ACM.

Borning, A., M. Maher, A. Martindale, and M. Wilson (1989, June). Constraint Hierarchies and Logic Programming. In *Proceedings of the Sixth International Conference on Logic Programming*, Lisbon, pp. 149–164.

Brewka, G. (1989, August). Preferred Subtheories: An Extended Logical Framework for Default Reasoning. In *Proceedings of the Eleventh International Joint Conference on Artificial Intelligence*, pp. 1043–1048.

Carter, C. A. and W. R. LaLonde (1984, May). The Design of a Program Editor Based on Constraints. Technical Report CS TR 50, Carleton University.

Cohen, E. S., E. T. Smith, and L. A. Iverson (1986, May). Constraint-Based Tiled Windows. *IEEE Computer Graphics and Applications*, 35–45.

Cohen, J. (1990, July). Constraint Logic Programming Languages. *Communications of the ACM 33*(7), 52–68.

Colmerauer, A. (1990, July). An Introduction to Prolog III. *Communications of the ACM*, 69–90.

Descotte, Y. and J.-C. Latombe (1985, November). Making Compromises among Antagonist Constraints in a Planner. *Artificial Intelligence 27*(2), 183–217.

Dincbas, M., P. V. Hentenryck, H. Simonis, A. Aggoun, T. Graf, and F. Bertheir (1988). The Constraint Logic Programming Language CHIP. In *Proceedings Fifth Generation Computer Systems-88.*

Duisberg, R. A. (1986). *Constraint-Based Animation: The Implementation of Temporal Constraints in the Animus System.* Ph. D. thesis, University of Washington. Published as UW Computer Science Department Technical Report No. 86-09-01.

Ege, R., D. Maier, and A. Borning (1987, June). The Filter Browser—Defining Interfaces Graphically. In *Proceedings of the European Conference on Object-Oriented Programming*, Paris, pp. 155–165. Association Française pour la Cybernétique Économique et Technique.

Epstein, D. and W. LaLonde (1988, September). A Smalltalk Window System Based on Constraints. In *Proceedings of the 1988 ACM Conference on Object-Oriented Programming Systems, Languages and Applications*, San Diego, pp. 83–94. ACM.

Fox, M. S. (1987). *Constraint-Directed Search: A Case Study of Job-Shop Scheduling.* Los Altos, California: Morgan Kaufmann.

Freeman-Benson, B. (1989, October). A Module Compiler for ThingLab II. In *Proceedings of the 1989 ACM Conference on Object-Oriented Programming Systems, Languages and Applications*, New Orleans, pp. 389–396. ACM.

Freeman-Benson, B. (1990, October). Kaleidoscope: Mixing Objects, Constraints, and Imperative Programming. In *Proceedings of the 1990 Conference on Object-Oriented Programming Systems, Languages, and Applications, and European Conference on Object-Oriented Programming*, Ottawa, Canada, pp. 77–88. ACM.

Freeman-Benson, B. and A. Borning (1992a, June). Integrating Constraints with an Object-Oriented Language. In *Proceedings of the 1992 European Conference on Object-Oriented Programming*, pp. 268–286.

Freeman-Benson, B. and A. Borning (1992b, April). The Design and Implementation of Kaleidoscope'90, A Constraint Imperative Programming Language. In *Proceedings of the IEEE Computer Society International Conference on Computer Languages*, pp. 174–180.

Freeman-Benson, B. and J. Maloney (1989, March). The DeltaBlue Algorithm: An Incremental Constraint Hierarchy Solver. In *Proceedings of the Eighth Annual IEEE Phoenix Conference on Computers and Communications*, Scottsdale, Arizona. IEEE.

Freeman-Benson, B., J. Maloney, and A. Borning (1989, August). The DeltaBlue Algorithm: An Incremental Constraint Hierarchy Solver. Technical Report 89-08-06, Department of Computer Science and Engineering, University of Washington.

Freeman-Benson, B., J. Maloney, and A. Borning (1990, January). An Incremental Constraint Solver. *Communications of the ACM 33*(1), 54–63.

Freeman-Benson, B. and M. Wilson (1990, May). DeltaStar, How I Wonder What You Are: A General Algorithm for Incremental Satisfaction of Constraint Hierarchies. Technical Report 90-05-02, Department of Computer Science and Engineering, University of Washington.

Freeman-Benson, B., M. Wilson, and A. Borning (1992, March). DeltaStar: A General Algorithm for Incremental Satisfaction of Constraint Hierarchies. In *Proceedings of the Eleventh Annual IEEE Phoenix Conference on Computers and Communications*, Scottsdale, Arizona, pp. 561–568. IEEE.

Freeman-Benson, B. N. (1988, April). Multiple Solutions from Constraint Hierarchies. Technical Report 88-04-02, University of Washington, Seattle, WA.

Freeman-Benson, B. N. (1991, July). *Constraint Imperative Programming.* Ph. D. thesis, University of Washington, Department of Computer Science and Engineering. Published as Department of Computer Science and Engineering Technical Report 91-07-02.

Freuder, E. (1989, August). Partial Constraint Satisfaction. In *Proceedings of the Eleventh International Joint Conference on Artificial Intelligence*, pp. 278–283.

Gangnet, M. and B. Rosenberg (1992, January). Constraint Programming and Graph Algorithms. In *Second International Symposium on Artificial Intelligence and Mathematics*.

Ginsberg, M. L. (Ed.) (1987). *Readings in Nonmonotonic Reasoning.* Los Altos, California: Morgan Kaufmann.

Gosling, J. A. (1983, May). *Algebraic Constraints.* Ph. D. thesis, Carnegie-Mellon University. Published as CMU Computer Science Department Technical Report CMU-CS-83-132.

Hill, R. D. (1990). A 2-D Graphics System for Multi-User Interactive Graphics Based on Objects and Constraints. In E. H. Blake and P. Wisskirchen (Eds.), *Advances in Object Oriented Graphics I*, pp. 67–91. Berlin: Springer-Verlag.

Hill, R. D. (1992). Languages for the Construction of Multi-User Multi-Media Synchronous (MUMMS) Applications. In B. Myers (Ed.), *Languages for Developing User Interfaces*, pp. 125–143. Boston: Jones and Bartlett.

Horn, B. (1992a, October). Constraint Patterns as a Basis for Object-Oriented Constraint Programming. In *Proceedings of the 1992 ACM Conference on Object-Oriented Programming Systems, Languages, and Applications*, Vancouver, British Columbia.

Horn, B. (1992b). Properties of User Interface Systems and the Siri Programming Language. In B. Myers (Ed.), *Languages for Developing User Interfaces*, pp. 211–236. Boston: Jones and Bartlett.

Ignizio, J. P. (1983). Generalized Goal Programming. *Computers and Operations Research 10*(4), 277–290.

Ignizio, J. P. (1985). *Introduction to Linear Goal Programming.* Beverly Hills: Sage Publications. Sage University Paper Series on Qualitative Applications in the Social Sciences, 07-056.

Jaffar, J. and J.-L. Lassez (1987, January). Constraint Logic Programming. In *Proceedings of the Fourteenth ACM Principles of Programming Languages Conference*, Munich.

Jaffar, J. and S. Michaylov (1987, May). Methodology and Implementation of a CLP System. In *Proceedings of the Fourth International Conference on Logic Programming*, Melbourne, pp. 196–218.

Jaffar, J., S. Michaylov, P. Stuckey, and R. Yap (1992, July). The CLP($\mathcal{R}$) Language and System. *ACM Transactions on Programming Languages and Systems 14*(3), 339–395.

Kamada, T. and S. Kawai (1991, January). A General Framework for Visualizing Abstract Objects and Relations. *ACM Transactions on Graphics 10*(1), 1–39.

Konopasek, M. and S. Jayaraman (1984). *The TK!Solver Book.* Berkeley, CA: Osborne/McGraw-Hill.

Kristensen, B. B., O. L. Madsen, B. Moeller-Pederson, and K. Nygaard (1983, January). Abstraction Mechanisms in the BETA Programming Language. In *Proceedings of the Tenth Annual Principles of Programming Languages Symposium*, Austin, Texas. ACM.

Leler, W. (1987). *Constraint Programming Languages*. Addison-Wesley.

Mackworth, A. K. (1977). Consistency in Networks of Relations. *Artificial Intelligence 8*(1), 99–118.

Maher, M. J. (1987, May). Logic Semantics for a Class of Committed-choice Programs. In *Proceedings of the Fourth International Conference on Logic Programming*, Melbourne, pp. 858–876.

Maher, M. J. and P. J. Stuckey (1989, October). Expanding Query Power in Constraint Logic Programming. In *Proceedings of the North American Conference on Logic Programming*, Cleveland.

Maloney, J. (1991, August). *Using Constraints for User Interface Construction*. Ph. D. thesis, Department of Computer Science and Engineering, University of Washington. Published as Department of Computer Science and Engineering Technical Report 91-08-12.

Maloney, J., A. Borning, and B. Freeman-Benson (1989, October). Constraint Technology for User-Interface Construction in ThingLab II. In *Proceedings of the 1989 ACM Conference on Object-Oriented Programming Systems, Languages and Applications*, New Orleans, pp. 381–388. ACM.

McDonald, J. A., W. Stuetzle, and A. Buja (1990, October). Painting Multiple Views of Complex Objects. In *Proceedings of the 1990 ACM Conference on Object-Oriented Programming: Systems, Languages, and Applications and the European Conference on Object-Oriented Programming*, Ottawa, Canada, pp. 245–257.

Murty, K. G. (1983). *Linear Programming*. Wiley.

Myers, B. (1987a). *Creating User Interfaces by Demonstration*. Ph. D. thesis, University of Toronto.

Myers, B. A. (1987b, April). Creating Dynamic Interaction Techniques by Demonstration. In *CHI+GI 1987 Conference Proceedings*, pp. 271–278.

Myers, B. A., D. Guise, R. B. Dannenberg, B. Vander Zanden, D. Kosbie, P. Marchal, and E. Pervin (1990, November). Comprehensive Support for Graphical, Highly-Interactive User Interfaces: The Garnet User Interface Development Environment. *IEEE Computer 23*(11), 71–85.

Myers, B. A., D. Guise, R. B. Dannenberg, B. Vander Zanden, D. Kosbie, P. Marchal, E. Pervin, A. Mickish, and J. A. Kolojejchick (1990, March). The Garnet Toolkit Reference Manuals: Support for Highly-Interactive Graphical User Interfaces in Lisp. Technical Report CMU-CS-90-117, Computer Science Dept, Carnegie Mellon University.

Nelson, G. (1985, July). Juno, A Constraint-Based Graphics System. In *SIGGRAPH '85 Conference Proceedings*, San Francisco, pp. 235–243. ACM.

Ohwada, H. and F. Mizoguchi (1990, October). A Constraint Logic Programming Approach for Maintaining Consistency in User-Interface Design. In *Proceedings of the 1990 North American Conference on Logic Programming*, pp. 139–153. MIT Press.

Olsen, Jr., D. R. (1990, October). Creating Interactive Techniques by Symbolically Solving Geometric Constraints. In *Proceedings of the ACM SIGGRAPH Symposium on User Interface Software and Technology,* Snowbird, Utah, pp. 102–107. ACM SIGGRAPH and SIGCHI.

Robinson, A. (1966). *Non-Standard Analysis.* Amsterdam: North-Holland Publishing Company.

Rotterdam, E. (1989, June). Physiological Modeling and Simulation with Constraints. Technical Report R89001, Medical Information Science, Department of Anesthesiology, Oostersingel 59, 9713 E2 Groningen.

Sannella, M. and A. Borning (1992, September). Multi-Garnet: Integrating Multi-Way Constraints with Garnet. Technical Report 92-07-01, Department of Computer Science and Engineering, University of Washington.

Saraswat, V. A. (1985, May). Problems with Concurrent Prolog. Technical Report CS-86-100, Carnegie-Mellon University. Revised January 1986.

Saraswat, V. A. (1989, January). *Concurrent Constraint Programming Languages.* Ph. D. thesis, Carnegie-Mellon University, Computer Science Department.

Saraswat, V. A., M. Rinard, and P. Panangaden (1991). Semantic Foundations of Concurrent Constraint Programming. In *Proceedings of the Eighteenth Annual Principles of Programming Languages Symposium.* ACM.

Satoh, K. (1990). Formalizing Soft Constraints by Interpretation Ordering. In *Proceedings of the European Conference on Artificial Intelligence.*

Satoh, K. and A. Aiba (1990, February). CAL: A Theoretical Background of Constraint Logic Programming and its Applications (Revised). Technical Report TR-537, Institute for New Generation Computer Technology, Tokyo.

Satoh, K. and A. Aiba (1991a, January). Computing Soft Constraints by Hierarchical Constraint Logic Programming. Technical Report TR-610, Institute for New Generation Computer Technology, Tokyo.

Satoh, K. and A. Aiba (1991b, September). The Hierarchical Constraint Logic Language CHAL. Technical Report TR-592, Institute for New Generation Computer Technology, Tokyo.

Shapiro, E. (1986, August). Concurrent Prolog: A Progress Report. *IEEE Computer 19*(8), 44–58.

Shapiro, L. and R. Haralick (1981, September). Structural Descriptions and Inexact Matching. *IEEE Transactions on Pattern Analysis and Machine Intelligence PAMI-3*(5), 504–519.

Sistare, S. (1990, December). *A Graphical Editor for Constraint-Based Geometric Modeling.* Ph. D. thesis, Department of Computer Science, Harvard. Published as Technical Report TR-06-9.

Steele, G. L. (1980, August). *The Definition and Implementation of a Computer Programming Language Based on Constraints.* Ph. D. thesis, MIT. Published as MIT-AI TR 595, August 1980.

Sutherland, I. (1963a). Sketchpad: A Man-Machine Graphical Communication System. In *Proceedings of the Spring Joint Computer Conference.* IFIPS.

Sutherland, I. (1963b, January). *Sketchpad: A Man-Machine Graphical Communication System.* Ph. D. thesis, Department of Electrical Engineering, MIT.

Takahashi, S., S. Matsuoka, and A. Yonezawa (1991, November). A General Framework for Bi-Directional Translation between Abstract and Pictorial Data. In *Proceedings of the ACM SIGGRAPH Symposium on User Interface Software and Technology,* Hilton Head, South Carolina, pp. 165–174.

Van Hentenryck, P. (1989). *Constraint Satisfaction in Logic Programming*. Cambridge, MA: MIT Press.

van Wyk, C. J. (1980, June). *A Language for Typesetting Graphics*. Ph. D. thesis, Department of Computer Science, Stanford.

van Wyk, C. J. (1982, April). A High-level Language for Specifying Pictures. *ACM Transactions on Graphics 1*(2).

Vander Zanden, B., B. Myers, D. Guise, and P. Szekely (1991, November). The Importance of Pointer Variables in Constraint Models. In *Proceedings of the ACM SIGGRAPH Symposium on User Interface Software and Technology*, Hilton Head, South Carolina, pp. 155–164.

Vander Zanden, B. T. (1988, April). *An Incremental Planning Algorithm for Ordering Equations in a Multilinear system of Constraints*. Ph. D. thesis, Department of Computer Science, Cornell University.

Wadge, W. W. and E. A. Ashcroft (1985). *Lucid, the Dataflow Programming Language*. London: Academic Press.

Walinsky, C. (1989, June). CLP(Σ^*): Constraint Logic Programming with Regular Sets. In *Proceedings of the Sixth International Conference on Logic Programming*, Lisbon, pp. 181–196.

Wilson, M. (1992). *Hierarchical Constraint Logic Programming*. Ph. D. thesis, Department of Computer Science and Engineering, University of Washington. Forthcoming.

Wilson, M. and A. Borning (1989, October). Extending Hierarchical Constraint Logic Programming: Nonmonotonicity and Inter-Hierarchy Comparison. In *Proceedings of the North American Conference on Logic Programming*, Cleveland, pp. 3–19.

2.3 Higher-Order Functional Constraint Networks

Enn Tyugu and Tarmo Uustalu

The Royal Institute of Technology, Dept. of Teleinformatics
Electrum 204, S-164 40 Kista, Sweden
tyugu | tarmo@it.kth.se

This paper discusses value propagation on functional constraint networks. We first focus on conventional "first-order" networks, and then show how the technique generalizes for what we call higher-order networks. Value propagation is attractive because of its simplicity and efficiency. Although it cannot solve all satisfiable networks (since it cannot break loops of constraints) and it may suggest solutions to unsatisfiable networks (since it does not discover inconsistency), it is of significant practical value. We describe several algorithms for planning value propagation, and point out that planning can be regarded as proof search in intuitionistic propositional logic.

2.3.1 Introduction

One of the oldest and still most common constraint solving techniques is value propagation along a constraint network. This technique is based on the direct usage of constraints as functional dependencies. The technique is very simple and efficient (Borning 1981). Efficiency is largely due to the technique's inherent "impatience" in deciding variable values, which sets limits to its applicability. As soon as, after having studied some chain of constraints in the given network, it is established that a variable X cannot take a value else than x, it is decided that X shall be x, without checking whether that is consistent with the other constraints. Thus, value propagation may in general produce wrong solutions. Nevertheless, if a network is known to be satisfiable in advance, the answers produced by the technique are surely correct, and such cases are not rare. Typical examples are constraint networks one uses for analyzing real-life situations, where constraints state the laws governing a situation and the values of known parameters. Such networks are obviously solvable, as the values are all "out there"; the problem is just how to get to know (derive) the values that cannot be measured directly. Also, clearly satisfiable are networks where any variable is the output of at most one constraint.

Value propagation is a way of gradually making constraint networks more explicit, and thus just a particular case of consistency propagation, such that propagation is interrupted as soon as non-trivial information is derived about each of the asked variables. Various consistency propagation algorithms for non-functional networks can be regarded as generalizations of value propagation, if one considers entities like sets or intervals as primitive values (e.g. tolerance propagation in interval arithmetic (Hyvönen 1992)). This is especially true in the case when a constraint network schema can be transformed into a tree (Dechter, Pearl 1989; Dechter 1992; Montanari, Rossi 1991).

In the present paper, we first discuss value propagation on "first-order" functional constraint networks. Thereafter, we define a form of higher-order constraint networks and show how value propagation can be generalized to work on such networks. Algorithms are presented for planning value propagation on different classes of functional constraint networks.

Finding values for variables of higher-order functional constraints leads us to a concept of subproblem. Surprisingly enough, constraint satisfaction on certain classes of higher-order constraint networks has precise meaning in terms of propositional logics. These classes have been investigated in computer science in relation with automatic program construction by several authors (Mints, Tyugu 1983; Kanovich 1991).

2.3.2 Constraint Networks

2.3.2.1 Basic Definitions Throughout the paper, we will use underscored letters to denote either finite sets or finite lists (tuples). The set of all finite lists over a given set $\mathcal{M}$ will be denoted $\mathcal{M}^*$. The concatenation of two lists will be denoted by an infix comma, a list containing just one element will be identified with this element.

Definition 2.1 (Constraint network schema (CNS)) *A constraint network schema (CNS) is a triple $\langle \mathcal{X}, \mathcal{R}, C \rangle$, where $\mathcal{X}$ is a finite non-empty set of variables, $\mathcal{R}$ is a finite non-empty set of constraints, $\mathcal{X} \cap \mathcal{R} = \emptyset$, and C is a function from $\mathcal{R}$ into finite lists over $\mathcal{X}$. For any constraint $R \in \mathcal{R}$, $C(R)$ is called its var-list.*

Definition 2.2 (Constraint network (CN)) *A constraint network (CN) is a quintuple $\langle \mathcal{X}, \mathcal{R}, C, \mathcal{D}, \mathcal{I} \rangle$, where $\langle \mathcal{X}, \mathcal{R}, C \rangle$ is a constraint network schema, D is a function from $\mathcal{X}$ into non-empty sets, and I is a function from $\mathcal{R}$ into relations on $D(C(R))$. For any variable $X \in \mathcal{X}$, $D(X)$ is called its domain. For any constraint $R \in \mathcal{R}$, $I(R)$ is called its interpretation.*

Relations can be defined either extensionally (by enumerating all the tuples in the relation), or intensionally, in general case in the form $\{\underline{x} \mid \phi[\underline{x}]\}$, where $\phi[\underline{x}]$ is a formula in an interpreted language whose all free variables appear in $\underline{x}$ (equivalently, in the form $\{\underline{x} \mid \phi(\underline{x})\}$, where ϕ is a closed predicate abstraction in an interpreted language). Relations with infinite extensions can only be defined intensionally.

Definition 2.3 (Valuation, solution of CN, equivalence of CNs) *Given a constraint network $\langle \mathcal{X}, \mathcal{R}, C, \mathcal{D}, \mathcal{I} \rangle$. A valuation is a function defined on $\mathcal{X}$, such that, for any variable $X \in \mathcal{X}$, $V(X) \in D(X)$. The set of all valuations is denoted $\mathcal{V}$. A valuation V satisfies the network, and is called its solution, if the* *interpretations of its constraints hold at the values of their var-lists, i.e.*

$$\bigwedge_{R \in \mathcal{R}} I(R)(V(C(R))).$$

Two constraint networks are called equivalent, *if they have the same solutions.*

Definition 2.4 (Constraint satisfaction problem (CSP), solution of CSP) *A constraint satisfaction problem (CSP) is given by a constraint network* $\langle \mathcal{X}, \mathcal{R}, C, \mathcal{D}, \mathcal{I} \rangle$ *and a non-empty set* $\mathcal{X}_a \subseteq \mathcal{X}$ *of asked variables. The restriction of* $\mathcal{X}_a$ *of a solution of the constraint network onto* $\mathcal{X}_a$ *is called a* solution *of the CSP.*

It is convenient to represent constraint network schemas in the form of bipartite graphs, where nodes of one sort correspond to variables, nodes of the other sort correspond to constraints, and edges correspond to bindings between variables and constraints. (Given a schema, *bindings* are (unordered) variable-constraint pairs $\langle X, R \rangle$, such that $X \in C(R)$.) For an illustration of this representation, see Fig. 2.1. The information about the order of the variables in the var-list of a constraint is lost in the graph representation.

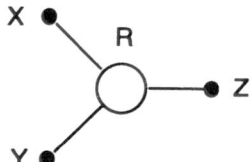

Fig. 2.1. Graph representation of CNSs.
The picture expresses that $C(R) = X, Y, Z$.

Alternatively, constraint network schemas can be represented as hypergraphs, where nodes correspond to variables and hyperedges correspond to constraints, and the incidence function of hyperedges corresponds to the var-list function of the network schema.

2.3.2.2 Equivalent Transformations Transforming a CN into an equivalent CN that meets certain requirements is a constituent of many CSP solving techniques. Typical equivalent transformations can be regarded as being built of augmentation and absorption steps, defined below.

Definition 2.5 (Augmentation step) *Given a constraint network* $\langle \mathcal{X}, \mathcal{R}, C, \mathcal{D}, \mathcal{I} \rangle$. *Any set of its constraints $\underline{R}$, and any finite list of its variables $\underline{X}$ determine an* augmentation step *which amounts to augmenting $\mathcal{R}$ with a new constraint R', and defining C and I at R' as follows:*

- $C(R') = \underline{X}$,

- $I(R') = \{\underline{x} \mid \exists V \in \mathcal{V}. \mathcal{V}(\underline{\mathcal{X}}) = \S \wedge \bigwedge_{\mathcal{R} \in \underline{\mathcal{R}}} \mathcal{I}(\mathcal{R})(\mathcal{V}(\mathcal{C}(\mathcal{R})))\}.$

We say that, $\underline{R}$ induces R' on $\underline{X}$.

Proposition 2.6 *Given a constraint network, applying any of its augmentation steps yields an equivalent constraint network.*

Proof. For any $V \in \mathcal{VX}$,

$$\bigwedge_{R \in \mathcal{R}} I(R)(V(C(R))) \equiv$$
$$\equiv \bigwedge_{R \in \mathcal{R}} I(R)(V(C(R)) \wedge \bigwedge_{R \in \underline{R}} I(R)(V(C(R))$$
$$\equiv \bigwedge_{R \in \mathcal{R} \cup \{\mathcal{R'}\}} I(R)(V(C(R)),$$

and hence the original and the modified CN have the same solutions.

Definition 2.7 (Absorption step) *Given a constraint network $\langle \mathcal{X}, \mathcal{R}, \mathcal{C}, \mathcal{D}, \mathcal{I} \rangle$. Any two of its constraints R_0, R', with var-lists $\underline{X_0}, \underline{X'}$, such that:*

- $\underline{X_0} \subseteq \underline{X'}$,

- $I(R') \subseteq \{\underline{x} \mid \exists V \in \mathcal{V}. \mathcal{V}(\underline{\mathcal{X}}) = \S \wedge \mathcal{I}(\mathcal{R}_,)(\mathcal{V}(\underline{\mathcal{X}}_,))\},$

determine an absorption step. *This step amounts to deleting R_0 from $\mathcal{R}$. We say that R' subsumes R_0.*

Proposition 2.8 *Given a constraint network, applying any of its absorption steps yields an equivalent constraint network.*

Proof. Omitted.

Example 2.9 Given a CN and two of its constraints R_1, R_2 with a common var-list $\underline{X}$. The interpretation of the constraint R' that R_1, R_2 induce on $\underline{X}$ is $I(R') = I(R_1) \cap I(R_2)$. R' subsumes both R_1 and R_2. Replacing R_1, R_2 with R' yields an equivalent CN.

Example 2.10 Given a CN and a finite list of its variables $\underline{X} \in \mathcal{X}^*$, the interpretation of the constraint R' induced by the empty set of constraints on $\underline{X}$ is $I(R') = D(\underline{X})$ (the total relation). Adding R yields an equivalent CN.

Often, it is assumed about a constraint network that, for any finite list of variables $\underline{X} \in \mathcal{X}^*$ (or, for any set of variables $\underline{X} \subseteq \mathcal{X}$), there is at most one (or even exactly one) constraint $R \in \mathcal{R}$ with list $\underline{X}$ (or a fixed listing of set $\underline{X}$) as its var-list. Modifications in the spirit of the previous examples allow to transform any constraint network into such a form.

Example 2.11 Given a CN and a non-empty set of its constraints $\underline{R} \cup \{R_0\} \subseteq \mathcal{R}$, with the var-list of R_0 being $\underline{X_0}$. Let R' be a name for the constraint these constraints induce on $\underline{X_0}$. Then

$$I(R') = I(R_0) \cap \{\underline{x} \mid \exists V \in \mathcal{V}. \mathcal{V}(\underline{X_l}) = \S \wedge \bigwedge_{\mathcal{R} \in \underline{R}} \mathcal{I}(\mathcal{R})(\mathcal{V}(\mathcal{C}(\mathcal{R})))\}.$$

R' subsumes R_0. Replacing R_0 with R' yields an equivalent CN.

In the previous example, R_0 is replaced with a constraint R', whose interpretation takes into account the restrictions that constraints $\underline{R}$ impose on variables in $\underline{X_0}$, and is, therefore, tighter than the interpretation of R_0. Such explication transformation might be called a *consistency-enforcement step*, and it is the basic instrument of the numerous consistency techniques. Their underlying idea is to bring an original network into a shape from which the solutions of a problem can be read off with the least pain. This is accomplished by gradually explicating the network by a series of consistency-enforcement steps.

Example 2.12 Given a CN. Let R' be a name for the constraint that the set $\mathcal{R}$ of all constraints of the CN induces on an enumeration $\underline{X}$ of the set $\mathcal{X}$ of all variables of the CN. Then

$$I(R') = \{\underline{x} \mid \exists V \in \mathcal{V}. \mathcal{V}(\underline{X}) = \S \wedge \bigwedge_{\mathcal{R} \in \mathcal{R}} \mathcal{I}(\mathcal{R})(\mathcal{V}(\mathcal{C}(\mathcal{R})))\}.$$

R' subsumes all the constraints in $\mathcal{R}$. Replacing $\mathcal{R}$ with R' yields an equivalent CN which has exactly one constraint R'. R' *represents* the solutions of the CN.

2.3.3 Functional Constraint Networks

2.3.3.1 Basic Definitions Functional constraint networks are a specialization of constraint networks, where constraints can only be interpreted as functional relations.

Definition 2.13 (Functional relation) *A $(n+m)$-ary relation P on $D_1 \times D_2$ is functional if it is a graph of a (total) function from D_1 into D_2, i.e. if*

$$\forall \underline{x} \in D_1. \exists! \underline{y} \in D_2. P(\underline{x}, \underline{y}).$$

Functional relations are typically defined intensionally, generally in the form $\{\underline{x}, \underline{y} \in \mid f[\underline{x}] = \underline{y}\}$, where $f[\underline{x}]$ is a term in an interpreted language whose all free variables appear in $\underline{x}$ (equivalently, in the form $\{\underline{x}, \underline{y} \in \mid f(\underline{x}) = \underline{y}\}$, where f is a closed function abstraction in an interpreted language).

For any function f, let us denote its graph by $\lceil f \rceil$.

The definitions of CNS and CN are specialized in the following way.

Definition 2.14 (Functional constraint network schema (FCNS)) *A functional constraint network schema (FCNS) is a triple* $\langle \mathcal{X}, \mathcal{R}, \mathcal{C} \rangle$, *where* $\mathcal{X}$ *is a finite non-empty set of variables,* $\mathcal{R}$ *is a finite non-empty set of constraints,* $\mathcal{X} \cap \mathcal{R} = \emptyset$, *and* C *is a pair of functions* $\langle C_{\mathrm{in}}, C_{\mathrm{out}} \rangle$, *both from* $\mathcal{R}$ *into finite lists over* $\mathcal{X}$. *For any constraint* $R \in \mathcal{R}$, $C_{\mathrm{in}}(R)$ *is called its* input-var-list, *and* $C_{\mathrm{out}}(R)$ *is called its* output-var-list.

Below, a writing $C(R) = \underline{X} \to \underline{Y}$ will be often used as a shortcut notation for stating that $C_{\mathrm{in}}(R) = \underline{X}$ and $C_{\mathrm{out}}(R) = \underline{Y}$.

Definition 2.15 (Functional constraint network (FCN)) *A functional constraint network (FCN) is a quintuple* $\langle \mathcal{X}, \mathcal{R}, \mathcal{C}, \mathcal{D}, \mathcal{I} \rangle$, *where* $\langle \mathcal{X}, \mathcal{R}, \mathcal{C} \rangle$ *is a functional constraint network schema,* D *is a function from* $\mathcal{X}$ *into non-empty sets, and* I *is a function from* $\mathcal{R}$ *into functional relations on* $D(C_{\mathrm{in}}(R), C_{\mathrm{out}}(R))$. *For any variable* $X \in \mathcal{X}$, $D(X)$ *is called its* domain. *For any constraint* $R \in \mathcal{R}$, $I(R)$ *is called its* interpretation.

Functional constraint network schemas are best represented in the form of directed bipartite graphs, where arcs correspond to directed bindings between variables and constraints. (Given a schema, *directed bindings* are variable-constraint pairs $\langle X, R \rangle$, where $X \in C_{\mathrm{in}}(R)$, and constraint-variable pairs $\langle R, X \rangle$, where $X \in C_{\mathrm{out}}(R)$). For an illustration of this representation, see Fig. 2.2.

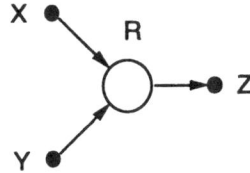

Fig. 2.2. Graph representation of FCNSs.
The picture expresses that $C(R) = X, Y \to Z$.

2.3.3.2 Equivalent Transformations Normally, functional relations are "implemented" as functions, which means that they are meant to be used "in one direction" — for producing an output value for given input values —, and not for producing input values for a given output value, for checking where a tuple values belongs to the graph of the function, or for anything else.

When solving a FCN whose constraints are efficiently implemented in one direction, we want to take advantage of it. Therefore, we are interested in equivalent transformations of FCNs that preserve efficiently implemented functionality of constraints. Not all augmentation and absorption steps do so. E.g. the transformation of Example 2.9 need not necessarily preserve functionality, since the intersection of the graphs of two functions need not generally be the graph of a function. The constraint R' induced on X by two functional constraints R_1, R_2 with $C(R_1) = X \to Y, I(R_1) = \lceil f \rceil$, $C(R_2) =\to Y, I(R_2) = \lceil g \rceil$, may be a non-functional relation (if f is not one-to-one), and even if it is a functional relation (constant $\lceil f^{-1}(g) \rceil$), its implementation may not be directly derivable from those of R_1, R_2.

The following proposition concerns five important types of augmentation steps of FCNs, and demonstrates that they preserve efficiently implemented functionality. They are illustrated in Fig. 2.3.

Proposition 2.16 *Given a functional constraint network* $\langle \mathcal{X}, \mathcal{R}, \mathcal{C}, \mathcal{D}, \mathcal{I} \rangle$.

1. *For any two constraints* R_1, R_2 *with* $C(R_1) = \underline{Z} \to \underline{X}$, $C(R_2) = \underline{X} \to \underline{Y}$, *and* $I(R_1) = \lceil f \rceil$, $I(R_2) = \lceil g \rceil$, *the interpretation of the constraint* R' *induced by* $\{R_1, R_2\}$ *on* $\underline{Z} \to \underline{Y}$ *is*

$$I(R') = \lceil g \circ f \rceil.$$

2. *For any constraint* R *with* $C(R) = \underline{Z} \to \underline{X}, \underline{Y}$, *where* $\#\underline{X} = m_1, \#\underline{Y} = m_2$, *and* $I(R) = \lceil f \rceil$, *the interpretation of the constraint* R' *induced by* $\{R\}$ *on* $\underline{Z} \to \underline{X}$ *is*

$$I(R') = \lceil \text{select}_{1...m_1}^{m_1+m_2} \circ f \rceil.$$

3. *For any two constraints* R_1, R_2 *with* $C(R_1) = \underline{Z} \to \underline{X}$, $C(R_2) = \underline{Z} \to \underline{Y}$, *and* $I(R_1) = \lceil f \rceil$, $I(R_2) = \lceil g \rceil$, *the interpretation of the constraint* R' *induced by* $\{R_1, R_2\}$ *on* $\underline{Z} \to \underline{X}, \underline{Y}$ *is*

$$I(R') = \lceil (f, g) \rceil.$$

4. *For any constraint* R *with* $C(R) = \underline{Z} \to \underline{X}$, *where* $\#\underline{Z} = n_1$ *and* $I(R) = \lceil f \rceil$, *and any finite list of variables* $\underline{W}$, *where* $\#\underline{W} = n_2$, *the interpretation of the constraint* R' *induced by* $\{R\}$ *on* $\underline{Z}, \underline{W} \to \underline{X}$ *is*

$$I(R') = \lceil f \circ \text{select}_{1...n_1}^{n_1+n_2} \rceil.$$

5. *For any finite list of variables* $\underline{Z}$, *where* $\#\underline{W} = n$, *the interpretation of the constraint* R' *which the empty set of constraints induces on* $\underline{Z} \to \underline{Z}$ *is*

$$I(R') = \lceil \text{id}^n \rceil.$$

Proof.

1.

$$I(R') =$$
$$= \{\underline{z}, \underline{y} \mid \exists x. I(R_1)(\underline{z}, \underline{x}) \wedge I(R_2)(\underline{x}, \underline{y})\}$$
$$= \{\underline{z}, \underline{y} \mid \exists x. f(\underline{z}) = \underline{x} \wedge g(\underline{x}) = \underline{y}\}$$
$$= \{\underline{z}, \underline{y} \mid g(f(\underline{z})) = \underline{y}\}$$
$$= \lceil g \circ f \rceil.$$

Proof of (2–4) omitted.

The following two examples show that, on a FCN, the augmentation sub-steps of the traditional arc- and path-consistency-enforcement steps computationally amount to application of a function on a constant and to composition of two functions, respectively. This is illustrated in Fig. 2.4.

Example 2.17 Given a FCN and two of its constraints R_1, R_2 with $C(R_1) = \to X$, $C(R_2) = X \to Y$, and $I(R_1) = \lceil f \rceil$, $I(R_2) = \lceil g \rceil$ (where f is a 0-ary function, i.e. constant, and g is a unary function). The interpretation of the constraint R' which R_1, R_2 induce on $\to Y$ is

$$I(R') = \lceil g(f) \rceil.$$

Example 2.18 Given a FCN and two of its constraints R_1, R_2 with $C(R_1) = Z \to X$, $C(R_2) = X \to Y$, and $I(R_1) = \lceil f \rceil$, $I(R_2) = \lceil g \rceil$ (where f and g are unary functions). The interpretation of the constraint R' which R_1, R_2 induce on $Z \to Y$ is

$$I(R') = \lceil g \circ f \rceil.$$

2.3.3.3 Relation to Logic Constraint networks have various logical interpretations (Mackworth 1992). Value propagation on functional constraint networks has a good explanation in terms of constructive logic. All augmentation steps of Proposition 2.16 can be regarded as valid proof rules of intuitionistic propositional logic annotated with realizations of formulae (I/O-var-lists correspond to formulae, interpretations correspond to realizations) :

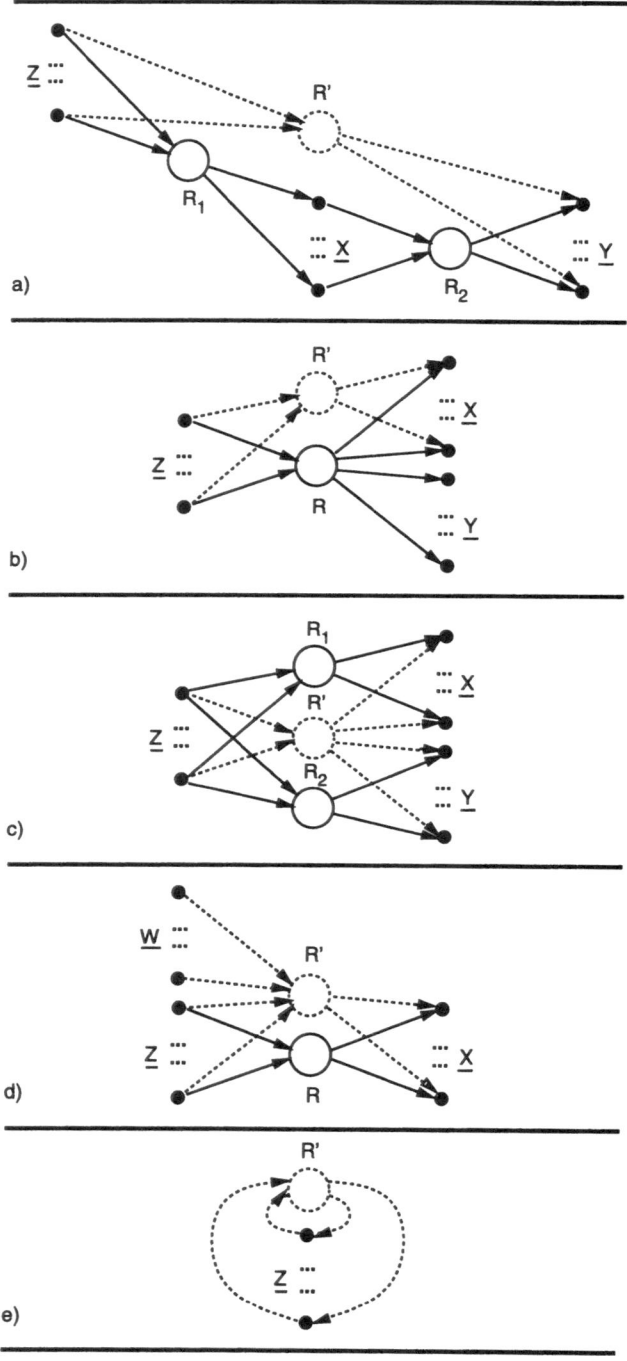

Fig. 2.3. Augmentation steps for FCNs.

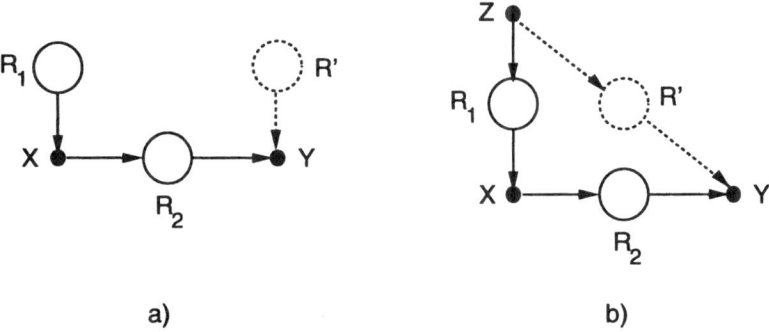

Fig. 2.4. Arc- and path-augmentation steps for FCNs.

$$I1: \quad \frac{f \ \mathbf{r} \ \underline{Z} \to \underline{X} \qquad g \ \mathbf{r} \ \underline{X} \to \underline{Y}}{g \circ f \ \mathbf{r} \ \underline{Z} \to \underline{Y}}$$

$$I2: \quad \frac{f \ \mathbf{r} \ \underline{Z} \to \underline{X}, \underline{Y}}{\mathrm{select}_{1...m_1}^{m_1+m_2} \circ f \ \mathbf{r} \ \underline{Z} \to \underline{X}}$$

$$I3: \quad \frac{f \ \mathbf{r} \ \underline{Z} \to \underline{X} \qquad g \ \mathbf{r} \ \underline{Z} \to \underline{Y}}{(f,g) \ \mathbf{r} \ \underline{Z} \to \underline{X}, \underline{Y}}$$

$$I4: \quad \frac{f \ \mathbf{r} \ \underline{Z} \to \underline{X}}{f \circ \mathrm{select}_{1...n_1}^{n_1+n_2} \ \mathbf{r} \ \underline{W}, \underline{Z} \to \underline{X}}$$

$$I5: \qquad \overline{\mathrm{id}^n \ \mathbf{r} \ \underline{Z} \to \underline{Z}}$$

Rule (I1) is a version of implication elimination, (I2–3) are elimination and introduction rules of conjunction, (I4) is a weakening rule on the left, and (I6) is an identity axiom.

2.3.3.4 Value Propagation The underlying idea of value propagation is in finding an induced (0+1)-ary functional constraint on $\to X$ for as many asked variables X of a given CSP as possible. These constraints would tell what values the variables necessarily have to have in every solution of the CSP (if there are any solutions at all).

Proposition 2.19 *Given a FCN* $\langle \mathcal{X}, \mathcal{R}, \mathcal{C}, \mathcal{D}, \mathcal{I} \rangle$ *with a constraint* R', *such that* $C(R') = \to X$ *and* $I(R') = \lceil v \rceil$ *(v is a constant), then in every solution* V *of the FCN,* $V(X) = v$.

Proof. If V is a solution, then $I(R')(V(X))$ must hold, and this is equivalent to $V(X) = v$.

Only augmentation steps of Proposition 2.16 are used in value propagation. Since their applicability depends only on the I/O-var-lists of the inducing constraints and not on their interpretation, value propagation can be pre-planned on a FCNS. We shall soon see that various efficient algorithms exist for value propagation planning. But, first, we will point out the important limitations of the technique.

If the value of a certain variable X is not uniquely determined by the constraints in a network, then no functional constraint can be induced on $\rightarrow X$, and value propagation yields no information about that particular variable. The same can happen, if the value is uniquely determined just due to a particular interpretation of constraints, since the purely schema-based planning of value propagation uses no information about the interpretation of constraints. (Example: equation systems.)

If two or more functional constraints with different interpretations are induced on $\rightarrow X$, then the FCN is clearly unsatisfiable. Most value propagation algorithms find just one induced constraint for each asked variable, and do not thus detect unsatisfiablity.

It is sufficient to use only the rules (I1–I3) with empty $\underline{Z}$ in "first-order" value propagation, augmenting the original network only with constraints whose input-var-lists are empty. Production of any such new constraint means that its output variables have become "known".

The following is the naive algorithm for value propagation planning of FCNs.

Algorithm 2.20 (Value propagation planning on FCNSs, ver 1)

```
proc naive-propag(X, R, C, Xa, plan, succeeded) is
    Xk := ∅;
    initlist(plan);
    succeeded := false;
    changes := true;
    while changes and not succeeded do
        changes := false;
        for R ∈ R do
            if Cin(R) ⊆ Xk and Cout(R) ⊄ Xk then
                changes := true;
                plan := addto(plan, R);
                Xk := Xk ∪ Cout(R);
                if Xa ⊆ Xk then
                    succeeded := true
                endif
            endif
        endfor
    endwhile
endproc
```

The time-complexity of Algorithm 2.20 is $O(N^2)$, where N is the number of constraints of a FCNS.

Search for appropriate inducing constraints can be guided by counters which show the number of still unknown input variables of a constraint, as done in the following algorithm.

Algorithm 2.21 (Value propagation planning on FCNSs, ver 2)

---

proc propag($\mathcal{X}, \mathcal{R}, \mathcal{C}, \mathcal{X}_a$, plan, succeeded) is
   $\mathcal{X}_k := \emptyset$;
   initqueue(beam);
   initlist(plan);
   succeeded := false;
   for $R \in \mathcal{R}$ do
      $c[R] := \#C_{in}(R)$;
      if $c[R] = 0$ then
         enqueue(R, beam)
      endif
   endfor;
   while not emptyqueue(beam) and not succeeded do
      $R :=$ dequeue(beam);
      if $C_{out}(R) \not\subseteq \mathcal{X}_k$ then
         for $X \in C_{out}(R) - \mathcal{X}_k$ do
            for $R' \in C_{in}^{-1}(X)$ do
               $c[R'] := c[R'] - 1$;
               if $c[R'] = 0$ then
                  enqueue(R, beam)
               endif
            endfor;
            $\mathcal{X}_k := \mathcal{X}_k \cup \{X\}$;
         endfor;
         plan := addto(plan, R);
         if $\mathcal{X}_a \subseteq \mathcal{X}_k$ then
            succeeded := true
         endif
      endif
   endwhile
endproc

Proposition 2.22 *The time-complexity of Algorithm 2.21 is $O(L)$, where L is the number of bindings in a given FCNS.*

Proof. For any problem, all operations in the algorithm are performed at most once either per binding of type variable-constraint, or per binding of type constraint-variable, or per constraint, according to the following division:

Binding $\langle X, R \rangle$: During initializations: check if $X \notin \mathcal{X}_k$, increase $c[R]$ by one. During search: decrease $c[R]$ by one, check if $c[R] = 0$, set $X \in \mathcal{X}_k$.

Binding $\langle R, X \rangle$: During search: check if $X \notin \mathcal{X}_k$.

Constraint R : During initializations or search: enqueue R. During search: dequeue R, add R to plan, check if $\mathcal{X}_a \subseteq \mathcal{X}_k$.

The key observations to be made are that every constraint is enqueued at most once, and that every variable is marked as having become known at most once.

Value propagation planning algorithms with time-complexity linear in the number of bindings that make use of counters have been proposed independently by several people. The idea for Algorithm 2.21 originated from (Dikovski 1985).

2.3.4 Higher-Order Functional Constraint Networks

2.3.4.1 Basic Definitions We shall now make the following generalization: we will allow variables to take higher-order (relational) values. Higher-order variables will behave like ordinary variables in that they are uninterpreted in a network. From the other side, they will behave like constraints in that they will have var-lists. Their values are functional relations. Conceptually, higher-order variables will serve as names for constraints inducible by the network.

Definition 2.23 (Higher-order functional constraint network schema (HFCNS)) *A higher-order functional constraint network schema (HFCNS) is a triple $\langle \mathcal{X}, \mathcal{R}, \mathcal{C} \rangle$, where $\mathcal{X}$ is a finite non-empty set of variables, with a distinguished subset $\mathcal{S}$ of higher-order variables, $\mathcal{R}$ is a finite non-empty set of constraints, $\mathcal{X} \cap \mathcal{R} = \emptyset$, and C is a pair of functions $\langle C_{in}, C_{out} \rangle$, both from $\mathcal{R} \cup \mathcal{S}$ into finite lists over $\mathcal{X}$. For any constraint $R \in \mathcal{R}$ (any higher-order variable $S \in \mathcal{S}$), $C_{in}(R)$ ($C_{in}(S)$) is called its* input-var-list, *and $C_{out}(R)$ ($C_{out}(S)$) is called its* output-var-list.

Definition 2.24 (Functional constraint network (HFCN)) *A higher-order functional constraint network (HFCN) is a quintuple $\langle \mathcal{X}, \mathcal{R}, \mathcal{C}, \mathcal{D}, \mathcal{I} \rangle$, where $\langle \mathcal{X}, \mathcal{R}, \mathcal{C} \rangle$ is a HFCNS, D is a function from $\mathcal{X}$ into non-empty sets, satisfying the condition that, for any $S \in \mathcal{S}$, $D(S)$ is the set of all functional relations on $D(C_{in}(S), C_{out}(S))$, and I is a function from $\mathcal{R}$ into functional relations on $D(C_{in}(R), C_{out}(R))$. For any variable $X \in \mathcal{X}$, $D(X)$ is called its* domain. *For any constraint $R \in \mathcal{R}$, $I(R)$ is called its* interpretation.

Definition 2.25 (Solution of HFCN) *A valuation V satisfies the network, and is called its* solution, *if*

$$\bigwedge_{R \in \mathcal{R}} I(R)(V(C(R)) \wedge \bigwedge_{S \in \mathcal{S}} V(S)(V(C(S)).$$

In fact, we look only for constructive solutions in which the values of higher-order variables are induced by the network. This means that whenever a functional constraint R' with $I(R') = \lceil f \rceil$ is inducible on $\underline{Z}, \underline{X} \to \underline{Y}$ and $C(S) = X \to Y$, then $V(S) = \lceil \lambda \underline{x}.f(V(\underline{Z}, \underline{x})) \rceil$. This is conceptually and logically motivated, and in concert with the principle of efficient implementability of functional relations.

Similarly to ordinary FCNSs, HFCNSs can be represented graphically, but the graphs are not bipartite in general. An example of a HFCN can be found in the calculus, where higher-order variables are connected by various constraints. Fig. 2.5 shows a HFCNS, where functions $\boldsymbol{x}, \boldsymbol{y}, \boldsymbol{x}', \boldsymbol{y}', \boldsymbol{f}', \boldsymbol{f}_{xy}$ are connected by superposition, integration, and differentiation constraints, and these functions themselves connect first-order variables t, x, y, f. As before, arrows show directions of bindings.

Below, we will restrict our study to HFCNs, where the var-lists of higher-order variables may only contain first-order variables (i.e. they are, in fact, second-order), and they themselves cannot appear in the output-var-lists of constraints. This does not restrict generality. Any HFCN can be transformed into this form by using abstraction and application operators as additional constraints. When we solve a CSP on a HFCN, and a second-order variable S has to be computed, we have to solve a problem of finding $C_{\text{out}}(S)$ from given $C_{\text{in}}(S)$. This is a CSP in its own right. Therefore, in our restricted HFCNs, second-order variables are also called *subproblems*.

There is an alternative notation for subproblem nodes in graphs shown in Fig. 2.6, where the direction of arcs is motivated by dataflow of computations. The dataflow direction for a subproblem S is from S to $C_{\text{in}}(S)$, and from $C_{\text{out}}(S)$ to S. The value of S in a solution to the network in Fig. 2.7 represents the constraint induced on $U \to V$ by constraints $\{R_1, R_2\}$. The interpretation of constraint R represents a functional, which uses the value of S for producing Y from X. In this process, the value of V is computed for as many values of U as needed, i.e. the sequence R_1, R_2 may be called several times.

Under the stipulation that we are only interested in constructive solutions, the following holds on HFCNs. Given a constraint R with $C(R) = \underline{Z}, \underline{X} \to \underline{Y}$ and $I(R) = \lceil f \rceil$, and a second-order variable S with $C(S) = \underline{X} \to \underline{Y}$, the interpretation of the constraint R' induced by $\{R\}$ on $\to S$ is $I(R') = \lceil \lambda \underline{z}.(\lambda \underline{x}.f(\underline{z}, \underline{x})) \rceil$. This augmentation step is illustrated in Fig. 2.8,a.

2.3.4.2 Relation to Logic The augmentation step for subproblems can be regarded as the following valid proof rule of intuitionistic propositional logic annotated with realizations of formulae.

$$\text{I6:} \quad \frac{f \ \text{r} \ ZX, \to Y}{\lambda \underline{z}.(\lambda \underline{x}.f(\underline{z}, \underline{x})) \ \text{r} \ \underline{Z} \to S} \quad \text{if } S \text{ is definitionally equivalent to } \underline{X} \to \underline{Y}$$

The proof rules (I1–I6) form a complete set of rules for the intuitionistic propositional logic in the following sense. Any finite set of propositional formulae can be translated into an intuitionistically deductively equivalent set of formulae in our (implicative) language (Mints, Tyugu 1983).

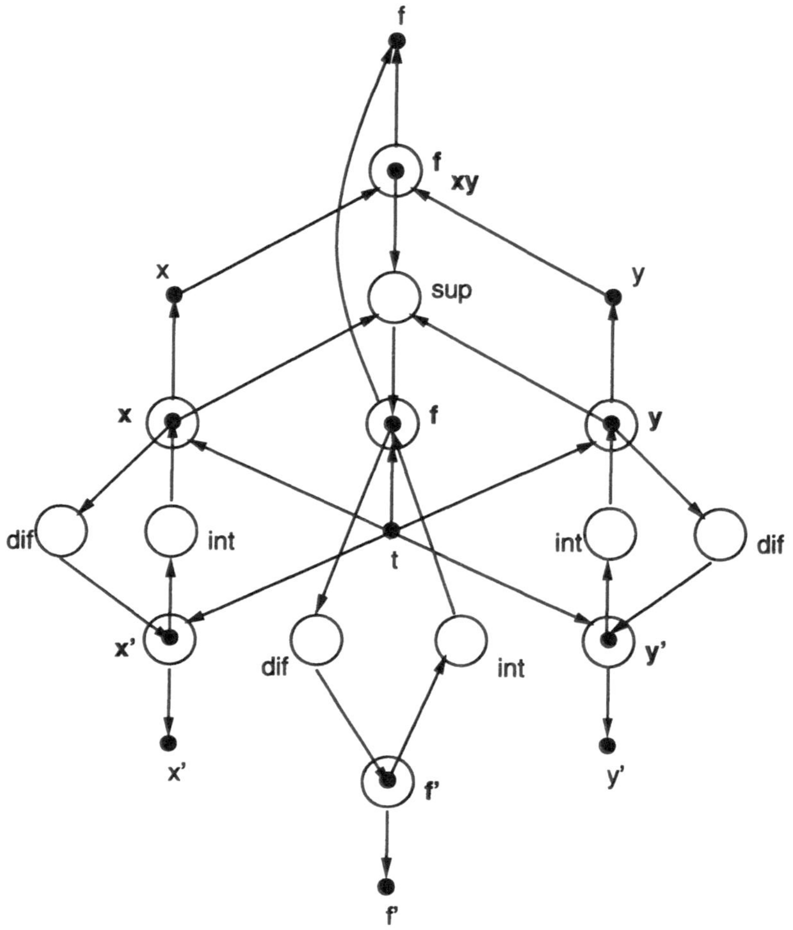

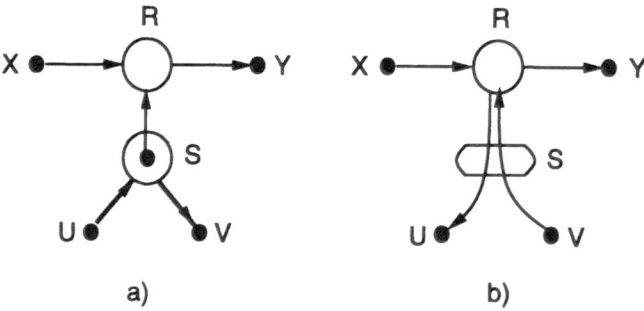

Fig. 2.5. The schema of a HFCN from the calculus.

Fig. 2.6. A constraint with a subproblem $(C(R) = S, X \to Y, C(S) = U \to V)$. Two graphical notations.

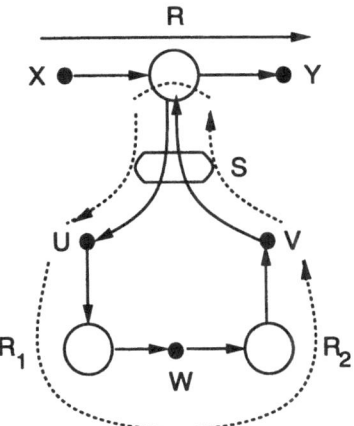

Fig. 2.7. Dataflow through a constraint with a subproblem.

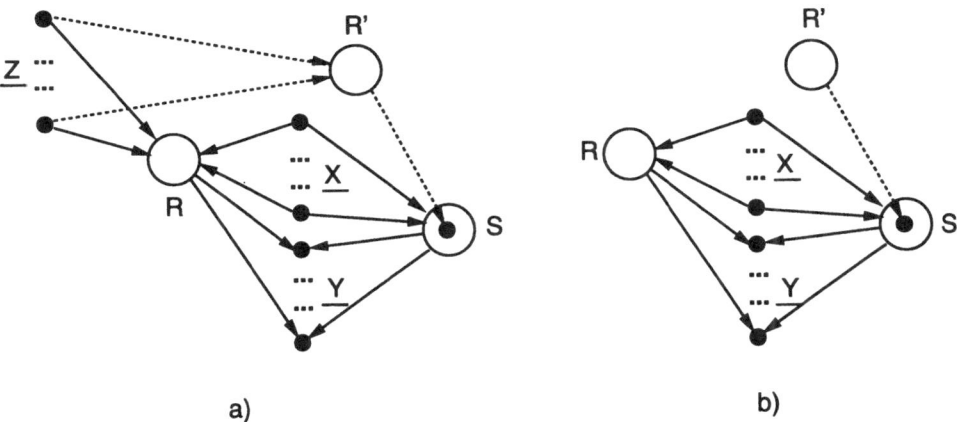

Fig. 2.8. The augmentation step for subproblems. *a)* general case, *b)* independent subproblems.

2.3.4.3 Value propagation Value propagation on HFCNSs is based on rules (I1-I6). The general problem of propagation planning on HFCNSs is PSPACE-complete, as it will be stated later.

Let us define the degree of subproblem dependence as the largest number of other subproblems whose inputs may be used when solving a subproblem. Fortunately, in the constraint networks which turn up in practice there are usually few subproblems and these do not interact very deeply. Thus, algorithms that work just for a fixed small degree of dependence of subproblems are practically meaningful and applicable.

If the degree of subproblem dependence is 0, then we talk about independent subproblems. In case of independent subproblems, rule (I6) can be applied with empty list $\underline{Z}$ only (see Fig. 2.8,b). Search for a propagation plan for a problem with M independent subproblems can be organized in the following way. We construct the main plan in parallel with construction of M subplans, each for one subproblem, with the following interactions between these parallel processes. If a subproblem is completed, the corresponding variable is marked as known in the process of the main problem. Whenever some variable becomes known for the main problem, it is also marked as known in the processes of all the subproblems. If the search fails, no plan for the problem can exist.

The following is the formal description of the algorithm.

Algorithm 2.26 Value propagation planning on HFCNSs, independent subproblems

---

```
proc initialize(𝒳, ℛ, 𝒞, 𝒳ₖ, ⌋, beam, plan, succeeded) is
    initqueue(beam);
    initlist(plan);
    succeeded := false;
    for R ∈ ℛ do
        c[R] := #(Cᵢₙ(R) − 𝒳ₖ);
        if c[R] = 0 then
            enqueue(R, beam)
        endif
    endfor
endproc
```

```
proc recordnew(𝒳, ℛ, 𝒞, 𝒳ₖ, ⌋, beam, X) is
    for R′ ∈ Cᵢₙ⁻¹(X) do
        c[R′] := c[R′] − 1;
        if c[R′] = 0 then
            enqueue(R′, beam)
        endif
    endfor;
    𝒳ₖ := 𝒳ₖ ∪ {X}
endproc
```

```
proc search(𝒳,ℛ,𝒞,𝒳ₐ,𝒳ₖ,⌋, beam, plan, changes, succeeded) is
   while not empty(beam) and not succeeded do
      R := dequeue(beam);
      if C_out(R) ⊄ 𝒳ₖ then
         for X ∈ C_out(R) − 𝒳ₖ do
            recordnew(𝒳,ℛ,𝒞,𝒳ₖ,⌋, beam, X)
         endfor;
         plan := addto(plan, R);
         changes := true;
         if 𝒳ₐ ⊆ 𝒳ₖ then
            succeeded := true
         endif
      endif
   endwhile
endproc
```

```
proc propag-indep(𝒳,ℛ,𝒞,𝒳ₐ, plan, succeeded) is
   𝒳ₖ := ∅;
   initialize(𝒳,ℛ,𝒞,𝒳ₖ,⌋, beam, plan, succeeded);
   for S ∈ 𝒮 do
      𝒳_{aS} := C_out(S);
      𝒳_{kS} := C_in(S);
      initialize(𝒳,ℛ,𝒞,𝒳_{kS},⌋_S, beam_S, plan_S, succeeded_S)
   endfor;
   changes := true;
   while changes and not succeeded do
      changes := false;
      search(𝒳,ℛ,𝒞,𝒳ₐ,𝒳ₖ,⌋, beam, plan, changes, succeeded);
      if not succeeded then
         for S ∈ 𝒮 do
            for X ∈ 𝒳ₖ − 𝒳_{kS} do
               recordnew(𝒳,ℛ,𝒞,𝒳_{kS},⌋_S, beam_S, X)
            endfor;
            search(𝒳,ℛ,𝒞,𝒳_{aS},𝒳_{kS},⌋_S, beam_S, plan_S, changes, succeeded_S); if succeeded_S
            then
               recordnew(𝒳,ℛ,𝒞,𝒳ₖ,⌋, beam, S);
               plan := addto(plan, plan_S)
            endif
         endfor
      endif
   endwhile
endproc
```

Proposition 2.27 *The time-complexity of Algorithm 2.26 is $O(ML)$, where M is the number of subproblems and L is the number of bindings of a HFCNS.*

Proof. In this algorithm, $1 + M$ plans are built pseudoparallelly: one main plan plus, for every $S \in \mathcal{S}$, a plan for finding $C_{\text{out}}(S)$ from $C_{\text{in}}(S)$. Each individual plan is formed on a separate copy of the network schema, essentially in the same way as in Algorithm 2.21.

Proposition 2.28 *Given d, a problem on a HFCNS with M subproblems and L bindings can be planned/detected to be unsolvable with the degree of subproblem dependence d in time $O(M^{d+1}L)$.*

Proof. For any given d, there is a suitable generalization of Algorithm 2.26: The following plans have to be built pseudoparallelly on separate copies of the network schema: one main plan plus, for every $S \in \mathcal{S}$ and every set $\{S_1, \ldots, S_k\} \subseteq \mathcal{S} - \{S\}$, where $k \leq d$, a plan for finding $C_{\text{out}}(S)$ from $C_{\text{in}}(S_1), \ldots, C_{\text{in}}(S_k), C_{\text{in}}(S)$. The total number of plans involved in the algorithm is $1 + M(\binom{M}{0} + \ldots + \binom{M}{d})) = O(M^{d+1})$.

Remark. Solvable problems with M subproblems are solvable with the degree of subproblem dependence $d = M - 1$.

Proposition 2.29 *The (general) problem of planning on HFCNSs is PSPACE-complete.*

Proof. The problem of derivability in intuitionistic propositional calculus is PSPACE-complete, and is polynomially reducible to the problem of planning on HFCNSs, as shown in (Mints, Tyugu 1983).

Kanovich (1991) has described and thoroughly analyzed a number of algorithms for what he calls program synthesis on relational knowledge bases, and what is essentially the same as propagation planning on HFCNSs. In particular, he has shown that linear space is sufficient for the general planning problem (with no limit on the dependence of subproblems).

2.3.4.4 Examples Let us study two examples of value propagation on HFCNs with dependent subproblems.

Example 2.30 ("Double integration") Consider the HFCNS with five first-order variables X, Y, A, B, D, two second-order variables S_1, S_2, and three constraints R_1, R_2, R_3, presented in Fig. 2.9. The var-lists of the constraints and second-order variables are as follows:

$$
\begin{aligned}
C(R_1) &= S_1 \rightarrow D, \\
C(S_1) &= Y \rightarrow B, \\
C(R_2) &= S_2 \rightarrow B, \\
C(S_2) &= X \rightarrow A, \\
C(R_3) &= X, Y \rightarrow A.
\end{aligned}
$$

This network can have several simple interpretations. For instance, it can embody a scenario of double integration in bounds $0 \ldots 1$ of a binary function on reals, if its constraints are interpreted as follows:

$$
\begin{aligned}
I(R_1) = I(R_2) &= \lceil \lambda \phi. \int_0^1 \phi \rceil, \\
I(R_3) &= \lceil f \rceil.
\end{aligned}
$$

A reasonable CSP to be solved on this HFCN is to ask the value of the double integral, i.e. D.

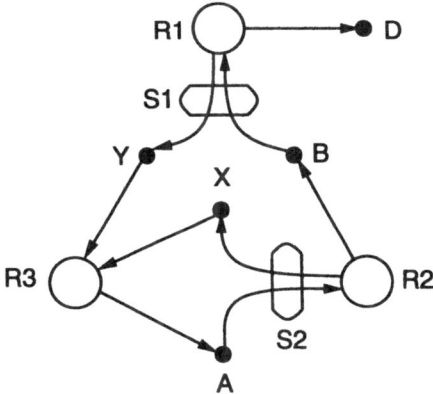

Fig. 2.9. The constraint network schema to Example "Double integration".

This HFCNS contains a dependent subproblem of finding A, given X. It can be solved only when solving of the other subproblem has started, because the value of Y is needed for producing the A. However, it is not hard to find the proper order of propagations on this constraint network for finding the value of D.

Value propagation plans for HFCSPs are labelled trees. One value propagation plan tree for this problem is presented in Fig. 2.10.

Every constructive solution V of this network has the following form:

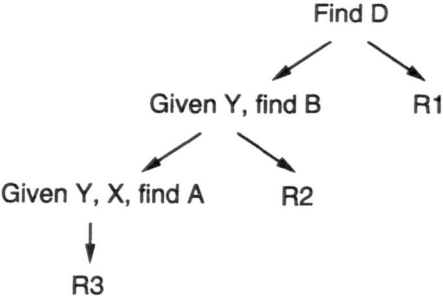

Fig. 2.10. A plan tree for Example "Double integration".

$$
\begin{aligned}
V(X) &= x_0, \\
V(Y) &= y_0, \\
V(A) &= f(x_0, y_0), \\
V(S_2) &= \lceil \lambda x. f(x, y_0) \rceil, \\
V(B) &= \int_0^1 f(x, y_0)\mathrm{d}x, \\
V(S_1) &= \lceil \lambda y. \int_0^1 f(x, y)\mathrm{d}x \rceil, \\
V(D) &= \int_0^1 \int_0^1 f(x, y)\mathrm{d}x\mathrm{d}y.
\end{aligned}
$$

Only S_1, D are uniquely determined. And they are the only variables for whom values can be found using value propagation.

Example 2.31 ("Kripke") Consider the HFCNS with four first-order variables X, Y, A, B, two second-order variables S_1, S_2, and three constraints R_1, R_2, R_3, presented in Figure 2.11. The var-lists of the constraints are as follows:

$$
\begin{aligned}
C(R_1) &= S_1 \to B, \\
C(S_1) &= Y \to A, \\
C(R_2) &= S_2 \to X, \\
C(S_2) &= A \to B, \\
C(R_3) &= X, Y \to A.
\end{aligned}
$$

The intended domain for X, Y, A, B is the set of reals. The constraints are meant to be interpreted as follows:

$$
\begin{aligned}
I(R_1) = I(R_2) &= \lceil \lambda \phi. \sum_{i=1}^3 \phi(i) \rceil, \\
I(R_3) &= \lceil \lambda x, y. x \cdot y \rceil.
\end{aligned}
$$

The problem is to find a value for B.

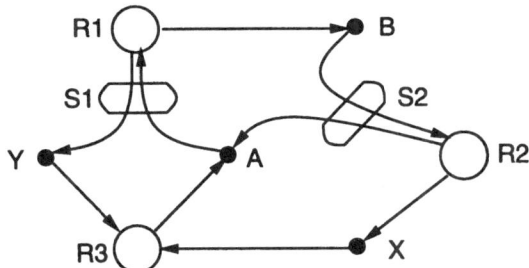

Fig. 2.11. The constraint network schema for Example "Kripke".

At the first glance, it may seem that this problem is unsolvable. However, this intuition is wrong. One possible plan tree for this problem is presented in Fig. 2.12. Executing the plan, we derive that B must be 108. The corresponding proof tree in our variant of intuitonistic propositional logic is in Fig. 2.13. The trick is that the constraint R_1 has to be used twice, first only for helping to solve a subproblem of the constraint R_2, and, second, for solving the main problem.

We have to note that there are other, alternative plans for solving this problem, and they produce other "only possible" values of B than 108. This shows that the HFCN is, in fact, inconsistent. Value propagation techniques do not detect that, and are not supposed to do so either.

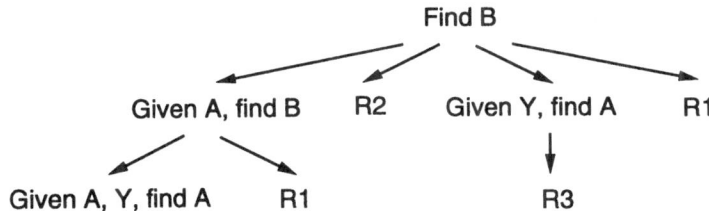

Fig. 2.12. A plan tree to Example "Kripke".

2.3.5 Conclusions

In this paper, we have shown that value propagation is a sufficient and efficiently implementable constraint satisfaction technique for a certain class of CSPs (namely, finding the values of the uniquely determined variables on satisfiable functional constraint networks). Remarkably, it not only works on constraint networks that are "first-order", but also on higher-order constraint networks. Unlike the "complete" consistency techniques, value propagation can be pre-planned on the constraint network schemas, abstracting away from the concrete interpretations of constraints at the planning stage. The time-efficient planning algorithms are forward-oriented (the idea being: "produce all that you can until you get what you are striving for, and, in the end, find what was really needed"), and suitable for parallel implementation. Planning can be regarded as proof search in intuitionistic propositional logic.

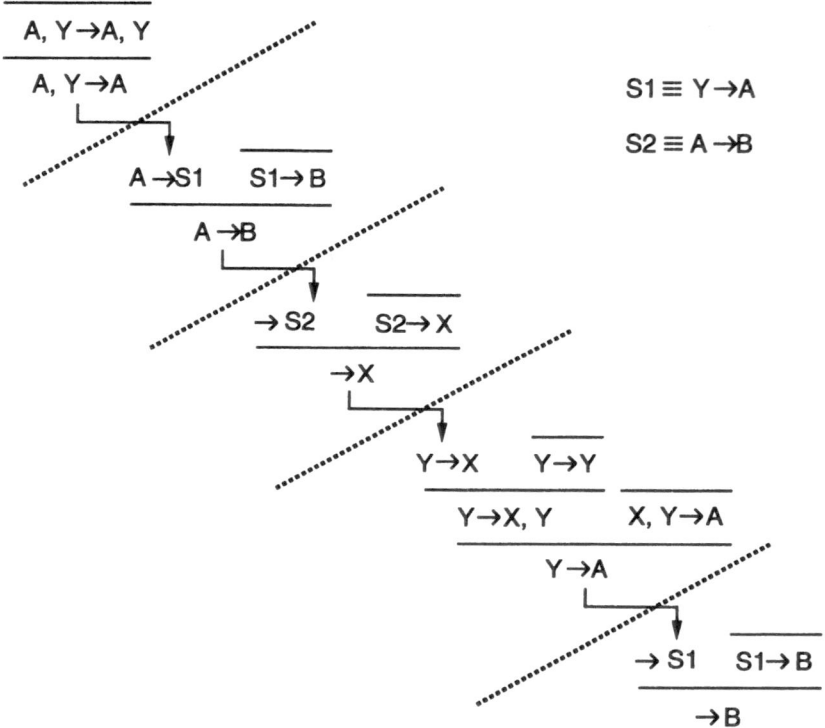

Fig. 2.13. A proof tree for Example "Kripke".

Acknowledgements

We are very thankful to Grigori Mints for his interest in the problems of propagation planning on computational models and his explanation of the propagation planning in terms of intuitionistic propositional logic and modal logic.

References

Borning, A. H. 1981. Programming language aspect of ThingLab: A constraint-oriented simulation laboratory. In ACM Transactions on Programming Languages and Systems 3(4), 353–387

Dechter, R. Pearl, J. 1989. Tree clustering for constraint networks. Artificial Intelligence 38, 353–366

Dechter, R. 1992. From local to global consistency. Artificial Intelligence 55(1), 87–107

Dikovski, A. 1985. Solving algorithmic problems of synthesis of programs without loops in linear time. System Programming and Computer Software 3, 38–49

Hyvönen, E. 1992. Constraint reasoning based on interval arithmetic: the tolerance propagation approach. Artificial Intelligence 581–3, 71–112

Kanovich, M. 1991. Efficient program synthesis: semantics, logic, complexity. In Proc. Int'l Conf. on Theoretical Aspects of Computer Software, 615–632. LNCS 526 Berlin: Springer-Verlag.

Mackworth, A. 1992. The logic of constraint satisfaction. Artificial Intelligence 58(1–3), 3–20

Mints, G., Tyugu, E. 1983. Justification of the structural synthesis of programs. Science of Computer Programming 2(3), 215–240

Montanari, U., Rossi, F. 1991. Constraint relaxation may be perfect. Artificial Intelligence 48, 143–170

2.4 Interval Computations as Propagation of Constraints

Yuri Matiyasevich

Steklov Institute of Mathematics of Russian Academy of Sciences
Saint-Petersburg Branch (POMI RAN) 27 Fontanka, Saint-Petersburg,
191011, Russia
yuma@Lomi.spb.su

2.4.1 The Problem

Suppose that we have a program $\mathcal{P}$ written in some ordinary (i.e. non-constraint) programming language which for given real inputs $x_1, \ldots, x_n$ computes some real output y. To simplify presentation, we will consider the case of a simple linear program of the form

$$
\begin{aligned}
x_{n+1} &:= x_{i_{n+1}} \; \circ_{n+1} \; x_{j_{n+1}}; \\
&\;\;\vdots \\
x_m &:= x_{i_m} \; \circ_m \; x_{j_m}; \\
y &:= x_m
\end{aligned}
\tag{2.1}
$$

where $i_k < k$, $j_k < k$, and $\circ_k$ is one of the signs $+$, $-$, $\times$ or $/$; we admit non-positive subscripts treating $x_0, x_{-1}, \ldots$ as constants.

In typical situation the computed value y is only an approximation to the genuine quantity ψ we wanted to calculate. There may be several sources contributing to this approximative nature of y. They can be separated into the following three groups.

1. *Mathematical errors.* As an example here one can think about computing a definite integral by some quadrature formula or solving a differential equation by considering corresponding difference equation.

2. *Arithmetical errors.* Typically, performing arithmetical operations in (2.1) includes some roundoffs caused by the finite precision of machine numbers.

3. *Initial errors.* The input values of $x_1, \ldots, x_n$ may be themselves only approximations to some unknown genuine quantities $\chi_1, \ldots, \chi_n$. There may be several reasons for using the x's instead of the χ's:

   (a) χ may be a transcendental number having no exact representation by a machine number.

   (b) χ may be the result of a previous approximative calculation.

(c) χ may be the result of a physical measument performed with limited accuracy.

(d) χ may have no value at the present; its value may depend on future events which we cannot predict now, a typical example here is weather forcasting.

In this paper we are going to concentrate on the third source of errors, i.e. on the influence of errors in the input data on the error in the output. To simplify the presentation we start by considering a modelling situation in which the first two sources of errors are elliminated. Respectively, we will suppose that

1. our goal is to calculate the value of the rational function $Y(x_1, \ldots, x_n) = y$ defined by (2.1), so $\psi = Y(\chi_1, \ldots, \chi_n)$;

2. the constants and input values are rational numbers and our computer is capable to perform exact rational arithmetic.

Clearly, taking into accout mathematical errors requires specific considerations and cannot be treated in general setting. However, the assumption of exact rational arithmetic is temporary, at the end of the paper we shall outline a standard way to eliminate this assumption using only machine numbers.

To take into account the third source of errors, we shall suppose that we have additional rational inputs $e_1, \ldots, e_n$ such that the unknown quantities $\chi_1, \ldots, \chi_n$ satisfy constraints

$$|\chi_i - x_i| \leq e_i, \qquad i = 1, \ldots, n. \tag{2.2}$$

The problem which is of interest for us is as follows: *How could one transform (2.1) into a new program $\mathcal{P}^*$ with rational inputs $x_1, e_1, \ldots, x_n, e_n$ which would produce two outputs y, e satisfying the constraint*

$$|Y(\chi_1, \ldots, \chi_n) - y| \leq e \tag{2.3}$$

provided that constraints (2.2) are satisfied? It should be emphasized that here we have only the problem of propagation of constraints; in this setting we cannot consider the problem of satisfaction of constraints because they include $\chi_1, \ldots, \chi_n$, the quatities that belong to the enviroment (for example, real world) and which we cannot control in any way.

Three techniques for constructing such a program $\mathcal{P}^*$ will be described below, and their advantages and disadvantages will be compared.

2.4.2 First Technique

The first technique is known as *interval arithmetic*. It is rather natural and straightforward, and it is difficult to pinpoint the one who was the first to use it. The beginning of systematical study of interval arithmetic is usually attributed to monograph of Moore (1966). The name of the technique is due to the possibility of rewriting constraints (2.2) as

$$\chi_i \in [x_i - e_i, x_i + e_i], \qquad i = 1, \ldots, n. \tag{2.4}$$

The main idea of interval arithmetic is to calculate constraints for all intermediate values similar to (2.3) . In modern high-level programming languages this can be easily accomplished by leaving the text of program (2.1) unmodified but interpreting the x's and y as objects of new type **interval** and redefining the arithmetical operations on objects of this type to include calculations of the constraints as well. However, we will continue to consider the x's and y as rational variables and describe the new program as the result of inserting new lines corresponding to lines in (2.1). Namely, after each line of the form

$$x_k := x_i + x_j \tag{2.5}$$

we insert line

$$e_k := e_i + e_j; \tag{2.6}$$

after each line of the form

$$x_k := x_i - x_j \tag{2.7}$$

we insert line

$$e_k := e_i + e_j; \tag{2.8}$$

after each line of the form

$$x_k := x_i * x_j \tag{2.9}$$

we insert line

$$e_k := e_i * |x_j| + |x_i| * e_j + e_i * e_j; \tag{2.10}$$

before each line of the form

$$x_k := x_i / x_j \tag{2.11}$$

we insert line

$$\textbf{if } |x_j| \leq e_j \textbf{ then ABNORMAL\_TERMINATION}$$

and after each line of the form (2.11) we insert line

$$e_k := (e_i + |x_k| * e_j) / (|x_j| - e_j); \tag{2.12}$$

At last, we add the final line

$$e := e_m$$

corresponding to the last line in (2.1). In the added lines values $e_0, e_{-1}, \ldots$ may be treated as zeros with corresponding simplifications. The resulting program will be denoted $\mathcal{P}^{\text{interval}}$. It is easy to show by induction that

$$|X_k(\chi_1, \ldots, \chi_n) - x_k| \leq e_k \tag{2.13}$$

where $X_k(x_1, \ldots, x_n) = x_k$ is the rational function defined by (2.1). In particular, constraint (2.3) holds, so program $\mathcal{P}^{\text{interval}}$ can be used as program $\mathcal{P}^*$.

There are many industrial implementation of interval arithmetic, however interval computations have not become everyday routine. One obvious shortcoming of interval computations consists in the increase in time and space required, but this is not the main obstacle. There is a less evident and more drastic shortcoming preventing widespreading use of interval computations. The values of y and e produced by program $\mathcal{P}^{\text{interval}}$ may give a very weak constraint (2.3), very far from the strongest possible one. To be able to decide what is a weak and what is a strong constraint, let us consider the ratio

$$\frac{E^*(x_1, e_1, \ldots, x_n, e_n)}{\Delta(x_1, e_1, \ldots, x_n, e_n)} \tag{2.14}$$

where $E^*(x_1, e_1, \ldots, x_n, e_n) = e$ is the function defined by program $\mathcal{P}^*$, and $\Delta(x_1, e_1, \ldots, x_n, e_n)$ is the least possible value of e still satisfying (2.3), i.e.

$$\Delta(x_1, e_1, \ldots, x_n, e_n) = \sup_{\chi_i \in [x_i - e_i, x_i + e_i]} |Y(\chi_1, \ldots, \chi_n) - Y(x_1, \ldots, x_n)|.$$

In the case $\mathcal{P}^* = \mathcal{P}^{\text{interval}}$ ratio (2.14) can be arbitrary large. To see how this can happen let us consider the following example of a program with one input x_1 and some positive constant x_0:

$$
\begin{aligned}
x_2 &:= 1 + x_0; \\
x_3 &:= x_2 * x_1; \\
x_4 &:= x_0 * x_1; \\
x_5 &:= 1 + x_4; \\
x_6 &:= 1/x_5; \\
x_7 &:= x_3 + x_6; \\
y &:= x_7.
\end{aligned}
$$

This program computes function

$$y = Y(x_1) = (1 + x_0)x_1 + \frac{1}{1 + x_0 x_1}.$$

Corresponding program $\mathcal{P}^{\text{interval}}$ (with simplifications due to treating x_0 as exact positive value) looks like

$$x_2 \;\; := \;\; 1 + x_0;$$
$$e_2 \;\; := \;\; 0;$$
$$x_3 \;\; := \;\; x_2 * x_1;$$
$$e_3 \;\; := \;\; |x_2| * e_1;$$
$$x_4 \;\; := \;\; x_0 * x_1;$$
$$e_4 \;\; := \;\; x_0 * e_1;$$
$$x_5 \;\; := \;\; 1 + x_4$$
$$e_5 \;\; := \;\; e_4;$$

$$\textbf{if } |x_5| \le e_5$$
$$\textbf{then } \text{ABNORMAL\_TERMINATION};$$

$$x_6 \;\; := \;\; 1/x_5;$$
$$e_6 \;\; := \;\; |x_6| * e_5/(|x_5| - e_5);$$
$$x_7 \;\; := \;\; x_3 + x_6;$$
$$e_8 \;\; := \;\; e_3 + e_6;$$
$$y \;\; := \;\; x_7;$$
$$e \;\; := \;\; e_7.$$

Computations by this program in the case $x_1 = 0$ would give the following values:

$$x_2 \;=\; 1 + x_0, \tag{2.15}$$
$$e_2 \;=\; 0, \tag{2.16}$$
$$x_3 \;=\; 0, \tag{2.17}$$
$$e_3 \;=\; (1 + x_0)e_1, \tag{2.18}$$
$$x_4 \;=\; 0, \tag{2.19}$$
$$e_4 \;=\; x_0 e_1, \tag{2.20}$$
$$x_5 \;=\; 1, \tag{2.21}$$
$$e_5 \;=\; x_0 e_1, \tag{2.22}$$
$$x_6 \;=\; 1 \tag{2.23}$$
$$e_6 \;=\; \frac{x_0 e_1}{(1 - x_0 e_1)}, \tag{2.24}$$
$$y = x_7 \;=\; 1, \tag{2.25}$$
$$e = e_7 \;=\; x_0 * e_1 + \frac{x_0 * e_1}{(1 - x_0 * e_1)}, \tag{2.26}$$

so

$$E^{\text{interval}}(0, e_1) \;=\; x_0 e_1 \left(1 + \frac{1}{1 - x_0 e_1}\right) = 2x_0 e_1 + o(e_1).$$

On the other hand,

$$Y(\chi_1) - Y(0) = \chi_1 + \frac{x_0^2 \chi_1^2}{1 + x_0 \chi_1}, \tag{2.27}$$

hence

$$\Delta(0, e_1) \;=\; e_1 + o(e_1)$$

and

$$\lim_{e_1 \to 0} \frac{E^{\text{interval}}(0, e_1)}{\Delta(0, e_1)} = 2x_0.$$

It seems attractive to try to write program $\mathcal{P}^*$ in such a way that the value of e calculated by it be equal to $\Delta(x_1, e_1, \ldots, x_n, e_n)$, the best possible value. However, it is easy to show (and this was actually done by Gaganov (1985)) that the problem to decide, given values of $x_1, e_1, \ldots, x_n, e_n, y$ and e whether constraint (2.3) holds for all $\chi_1, \ldots, \chi_n$ satisfying constraints (2.2), is NP-hard. Thus, at our present level of knowledge we cannot calculate $\Delta(x_1, e_1, \ldots, x_n, e_n)$ in reasonable time.

We could weaken the condition $E^*(x_1, e_1, \ldots, x_n, e_n) = \Delta(x_1, e_1, \ldots, x_n, e_n)$ to the condition

$$\lim_{e_1, \ldots, e_n \to 0} \frac{E^*(x_1, e_1, \ldots, x_n, e_n)}{\Delta(x_1, e_1, \ldots, x_n, e_n)} = 1. \tag{2.28}$$

However, it seems that this requirement is also difficult to fulfill for all values of $x_1, \ldots, x_n$.

We have:

$$X_k(\chi_1, \ldots, \chi_n) - X_k(x_1, \ldots, x_n) \approx \sum_{i=1}^{n} \frac{\partial X_k}{\partial x_i} * (\chi_i - x_i) \tag{2.29}$$

in particular,

$$Y(\chi_1, \ldots, \chi_n) - Y(x_1, \ldots, x_n) \approx \sum_{i=1}^{n} \frac{\partial Y}{\partial x_i} * (\chi_i - x_i), \tag{2.30}$$

and hence

$$\Delta(x_1, e_1, \ldots, x_n, e_n) \approx \delta(x_1, e_1, \ldots, x_n, e_n) = \sum_{i=1}^{n} \left| \frac{\partial Y}{\partial x_i} \right| * e_i$$

because the difference $\chi_i - x_i$ can have have absolute value equal to e_i and be of the same sign as the corresponding partial derivative. We shall say that point $\langle x_1, \ldots, x_n \rangle$ is *non-degenerate* if

$$\frac{\partial Y}{\partial x_i} \neq 0, \qquad i = 1, \ldots, n.$$

At a non-degerate point

$$\lim_{e_1, \ldots, e_n \to 0} \frac{\Delta(x_1, e_1, \ldots, x_n, e_n)}{\delta(x_1, e_1, \ldots, x_n, e_n)} = 1$$

and we can use $\delta(x_1, e_1, \ldots, x_n, e_n)$ rather than $\Delta(x_1, e_1, \ldots, x_n, e_n)$ for deciding whether $E^*(x_1, e_1, \ldots, x_n, e_n)$ produces a good constraint or not. Namely, we shall say a that program $\mathcal{P}^*$ computes on *asymptotically optimal constraint* if

$$\lim_{e_1, \ldots, e_n \to 0} \frac{E^*(x_1, e_1, \ldots, x_n, e_n)}{\delta(x_1, e_1, \ldots, x_n, e_n)} = 1 \qquad (2.31)$$

for every non-degenerate point $x_1, \ldots, x_n$.

As it was shown before, program $\mathcal{P}^{\text{interval}}$ does not produce an asymptotically optimal solution. However, it can be verified that

$$\frac{E^{\text{interval}}(x_1, e_1, \ldots, x_n, e_n)}{\delta(x_1, e_1, \ldots, x_n, e_n)} = O_{x_1, \ldots, x_n}(1) \qquad (2.32)$$

for every non-degenerate point $x_1, \ldots, x_n$.

The next two techniques will give us programs computing asymptotically optimal constraints.

2.4.3 Second Technique

To see why program $\mathcal{P}^{\text{interval}}$ does not produce asymptotically optimal constraint, let us analyze the above example a bit further. If calculations were performed for $x_1 = \chi_1$, they would give the following genuine values for the intermediate quantities:

$$
\begin{aligned}
\chi_2 &= 1 + x_0, \\
\chi_3 &= (1 + x_0)\chi_1, \\
\chi_4 &= x_0\chi_1, \\
\chi_5 &= 1 + x_0\chi_1, \\
\chi_6 &= \frac{1}{1 + x_0\chi_1} = 1 - x_0\chi_1 + o(\chi_1), \\
\psi = \chi_7 &= (1 + x_0)\chi_1 + \frac{1}{1 - x_0\chi_1} = \chi_1 + o(\chi_1).
\end{aligned}
$$

It is easy to check that the intermediate constraints

$$|\chi_3 - x_3| \leq (1 + x_0)e_1$$

and

$$|\chi_6 - x_6| \leq \frac{x_0 e_1}{(1 - x_0 e_1)}$$

given by (2.18) and (2.24) are asymptotically optimal, nevertheless, they do not produce corresponding asymptotically optimal constraint for ψ and $y = x_7$. This happens so because line (2.8) was based on the assumption that the constraints on x_i and x_j were independent and the actual differences $\chi_i - x_i$ and $\chi_j - x_i$ could have the extreme values $\pm e_i$ and $\pm e_j$ simultaneously. In our case χ_3 and χ_6 are evidently correlated.

We cannot make any improvements by local means, line (2.8) is the best possible in the worst case. An improvement can be achived only by some global mechanism which would take into account the history of previous calculations. The problem is in what way the history should be described.

The second technique is due to Hansen (1975). A partial history of previous computations is taken into account by using constraints of more sophisticated form than (2.13). Namely, formula (2.29) suggests using constraints of the form

$$|X_k(\chi_1,\ldots,\chi_n) - x_k - \sum_{i=1}^{n} d_{k,i} * (\chi_i - x_i)| \le h_i \qquad (2.33)$$

where

$$d_{k,i} = \frac{\partial X_k}{\partial x_i}.$$

Thus, in Hansen's approach the linear influence of initial errors is taken into account by exact values of d's, and quantities h's bound only to the contribution of second and higher derivatives in Taylor's expansion. To implement calculation of these more sophisticated constraints, one can insert, after each line in program (2.1), n new lines for calculating corresponding partial derivatives $d_{k,1},\ldots,d_{k,n}$ and an extra line for calculating h_k. For example, after a line of the form (2.5) one has to add lines

$$d_{k,1} \quad := \quad d_{i,1} + d_{j,1};$$
$$\vdots$$
$$d_{k,n} \quad := \quad d_{i,n} + d_{j,n};$$
$$h_k \quad := \quad h_i + h_j$$

(for cases of other arithmetical operations see (Hansen 1975)). The program should start with initialization of the form

> **for** $k := 1$ **to** n **do**
> > **for** $l := 1$ **to** n **do**
> > > $d_{k,l} :=$ **if** $k = l$ **then** 1 **else** 0 **od**;
> > $h_k := 0$ **od**

and the last line should be

$$e \quad := \quad \sum_{l=1}^{n} |d_{m,l}| * e_l + h_m \qquad (2.34)$$

(this line transforms constraint of the form (2.33) imposed on x_m into into constaint of the desired form (2.3)).

It can be verifyed that the h's are values of second order of magnitude compared to the e's and thus Hansen's *generelized interval arithmetic* does produce an asymptotically optimal constraint.

Hansen's technique is rather special one but nevertheless it can serve as an illustration of more general rule: in order to entail strong constraints, sometimes it may be useful to use intermediate constraints of the form different from the initial ones and desired final one. Such improved constraints may include some sort of history of the computation in order to take into account the dependences between different conmstraints.

There have been several experimental implementations of Hansen's generalized interval arithmetic, which showed that it may produce much stronger constraints than standard interval arithmetic in the case of sufficiently small e's. However, the author does not know any industrial implementation of generalized interval arithmetic. In this case the increase in required time is the main obstacle. In ordinary interval arithmetic one has to perform a bounded number of additional arithmetical operations for each arithmetical operation in the original program, which results in only *linear slowdown*. In generalized interval arithmetic the increase of required time depends on the number of input values and hence is not bounded at all.

2.4.4 Third Technique

The third technique described below combines the best features of the two techniques described above, i.e. the asymptotic optimality and linear slowdown. The two previous techniques were *total* in the sence that constraints were calculated for every intermediate value. In the third technique we shall compute asymptotically optimal constraint only for the output value $y = x_m$.

The main idea is suggested by formula (2.30). Note that line (2.34) contains only partial derivatives of function $Y(x_1, \ldots, x_n) = X_m(x_1, \ldots, x_n)$ but no partial derivatives of X_k with $k < m$. It turns out that all required partial derivatives can be calculated quickly, i.e. with linear slowdown. Such technique for fast calculation of many partial derivatives was known for a long time; in fact, it has been rediscovered by several researchers, ignorant of the works of their predecessors. The last rediscovery known to the author was done in (Kim et al 1984). The author has learnt about that technique from (Baur, Strassen 1983) and later found an earlier paper (Linnainmaa 1976). For further historical data see survey (Iri 1991).

The underlying idea of fast calculation of partial derivatives can be explained in the following way. Suppose that the x's are functions of some independent variables t rather than fixed numbers, and we are intrested in calculation of $Y(x_1(0), \ldots, x_n(0))$. In such a case all the values of $x_{n+1}, \ldots, x_m, y$ also became functions of t.

The partial derivatives $d_{m,1}, \ldots, d_{m,n}$ we want to calculate come into the following formula:

$$\frac{dy}{dt} = \sum_{i=1}^{n} d_{m,i} \frac{dx_i}{dt}. \tag{2.35}$$

We shall consider more general equations of the form

$$\frac{dy}{dt} = \sum_{i=1}^{l} z_i \frac{dx_i}{dt} \tag{2.36}$$

where $n \leq l \leq m$ and the z's are numbers. According to (2.35) in the case $l = n$ equation (2.36) has the solution

$$z_i = d_{m,i}, \qquad i = 1, \ldots, n. \tag{2.37}$$

This solution is in fact unique if we consider (2.36) as an identity valid at point $t = 0$ for every choice of functions $x_1(t), \ldots, x_n(t)$. (To see it take all functions but one constant.)

Solution (2.37) can be extended to solution of (2.36) for l greater than n by putting $z_i = 0$ for $i > n$ but this solution need not be unique any longer. In fact, in the case $l = m$ equation (2.36) has another solution

$$z_1 = \ldots = z_{m-1} = 0, \qquad z_m = 1$$

because y is nothing else than x_m.

If we have a solution of (2.36) for some $l = k$ and $k > n$, then we can easily transform it into a solution of (2.36) for $l = k - 1$. Namely, according to (2.1)

$$x_k(t) = x_i(t) \circ_k x_j(t) \tag{2.38}$$

for some i and j which are less than k. Differentiation of (2.38) gives us

$$\frac{dx_k}{dt} = \alpha_{i,j,k} \frac{dx_i}{dt} + \beta_{i,j,k} \frac{dx_i}{dt} \tag{2.39}$$

where exact form of $\alpha_{i,j,k}$ and $\beta_{i,j,k}$ depends on which arithmetical operation $\circ_k$ was. Now we can use (2.39) to eliminate $\frac{dx_k}{dt}$ from (2.36). In other words, in order to transform a solution of (2.36) for $l = k$ into a solution of (2.36) for $l = k - 1$ it is sufficient to change the values of only z_i and z_j.

Namely, to each line of the form (2.5) the two corresponding assignments are

$$\begin{aligned} z_i &:= z_i + z_k; \\ z_j &:= z_j + z_k; \end{aligned} \tag{2.40}$$

to each line of the form (2.7) they are

$$\begin{aligned} z_i &:= z_i + z_k; \\ z_j &:= z_j - z_k; \end{aligned} \tag{2.41}$$

to each line of the form (2.9) they are

$$
\begin{aligned}
z_i &:= z_i + x_j * z_k; \\
z_j &:= z_j + x_i * z_k;
\end{aligned}
\qquad (2.42)
$$

at last, to each line of the form (2.11) they are

$$
\begin{aligned}
z_i &:= z_i + z_k/x_j; \\
z_j &:= z_j + x_k/x_j * z_k.
\end{aligned}
\qquad (2.43)
$$

Program $\mathcal{D}$ calculating partial derivatives $d_{m,1}, \ldots, d_{m,n}$ consists of initialization

$$
z_1 := 0
$$
$$
\vdots
$$
$$
z_{m-1} := 0
$$
$$
z_m := 1
$$

and $2(m - n)$ lines of the forms (2.40), (2.41), (2.42) and (2.43) *written in the order opposite to the order of coresponding lines in the original program* (2.1). The values of $z_1, \ldots, z_n$ calculated by this program are the desired partial derivatives (2.37) because they give the unique solution of (2.36) for $l = n$.

At this point we cannot easily calculate a value of e satisfying (2.3) because we have no value of h_m which in (2.34) takes into account the contribution of higher derivatives. Furthermore we cannot calculate h_m quickly, because program $\mathcal{D}$ calculates only partial derivative of X_m. To overcome this difficulty let us rewrite the approximate equality (2.30) as an exact equality

$$
Y(\chi_1, \ldots, \chi_n) - Y(x_1, \ldots, x_n) = \sum_{i=1}^{n} \frac{\partial Y}{\partial x_i}(\eta_1, \ldots, \eta_n) * (\chi_i - x_i) \qquad (2.44)
$$

where $\eta_1, \ldots, \eta_n$ are some quantities about which we know only that they satisfy constraints analogous to those satisfied by $\chi_1, \ldots, \chi_n$:

$$
|\eta_i - x_i| \le e_i, \qquad i = 1, \ldots, n.
$$

At first sight, we seem to be in a vicious circle to find a constraint (2.3) at some unknown point $\langle \chi_1, \ldots, \chi_n \rangle$ according to (2.44) we need to calculate n similar constraints for partial derivatives at another unknown point $\langle \eta_1, \ldots, \eta_n \rangle$. Luckily, we can break this circle thanks to the fact that the partial derivatives in (2.44) are multiplied by the e's which in the definition of asymptotical optimality (2.31) approach zero. Thus, the constraints for the partial derivative need not be themselves asymptotically optimal, and we may use standard interval arithmetic for calculating them.

More specifically, we append program $\mathcal{D}$ to program $\mathcal{P}$ and apply the first technique described above to the combined program. (Strictly speaking, program $\mathcal{D}$ is not of the simple form (2.1) but evidently lines (2.42) and (2.43) can be split into several lines each containing only one arithmetical operation.) The resulting program $[\mathcal{PD}]^{\text{interval}}$ computes with linear slowdowm numbers $z_1, f_1, \ldots, z_n, f_n$ satisfying constraints

$$\left| \frac{\partial Y}{\partial x_i}(\eta_1, \ldots, \eta_n) - z_i \right| \le f_i, \qquad i = 1, \ldots, n. \tag{2.45}$$

These numbers allow us to calculate

$$e := \sum_{i=1}^{n} (|z_i| + f_i) * e_i. \tag{2.46}$$

Thanks to (2.45) this number satisfies constraint (2.3) and thanks to (2.32) this constraint is asymptotically optimal.

Formula (2.46) gives us an upper bound to $\Delta(x_1, e_1, \ldots, x_n, e_n)$. To see how excessive it can be, we can easily calculate a lower bound

$$\sum_{i=1}^{n} (|z_i| - f_i) e_i \le \Delta(x_1, e_1, \ldots, x_n, e_n).$$

The above described method for calculating asymptotically optimal constraint with linear slowdown, called *a posteriori interval analysis*, was proposed by the author in (Matiyasevich 1985), more detailed presentation is given in (Matiyasevich 1986). For a further development see (Kaishev 1989).

Above we imposed the assumption of exact rational arithmetic. A way to eliminate that assumption is well known. Namely, we can use alternative representation (2.4) and use *directed rounding* when performing arithmetical operations on interval constraints. For example, the sum $[a_1, b_1] + [a_2, b_2]$ can be calculated as $[a_1 \overset{\triangledown}{+} a_2, b_1 \overset{\triangle}{+} b_2]$ where $\overset{\triangledown}{+}$ and $\overset{\triangle}{+}$ are operations which adds two machine numbers with roundings to the nearest machine numbers in the directions to $-\infty$ and $+\infty$ respectively.

Ordinary interval arithmetic and Hansen's generalized interval arithmetics can be easily implemented for programs with all standard constructions such as loops and branches. Such an extension is possible also for a posteriori interval analysis with linear slowdown in time but it is much more costly with respect to memory requirements. The simplest way to do it is to consider linear program (2.1) as an intermediate byproduct of running a program with loops and branches. The main shortcoming of aposteriori interval analysis is caused by the fact that the lines of program $\mathcal{D}$ go in the order opposite to the that of the progran (2.1) and thus all intermediate values should be kept in memory during the run of program $\mathcal{P}$. However, in some cases it is possible to write a more sophisticated program $\mathcal{D}$ with loops and branches that does not require all the intermediate values to be kept.

There have been several experimental implementations of a posteriori interval analysis (see,. e.g. (Iri 1991)). They show that it produces constraints of strength similar to those produced by generalized interval arithmetic but, of course, much faster.

References

Baur W., Strassen V. (1983) The complexity of partial derivatives. Theor. Computer Sci. **22**, 317–330

Hansen E. (1975) A generalized interval arithmetic. Lecture Notes Computer Sci. **29**, 7–18, Springer-Verlag, Berlin.

Gaganov A. A. (1985) O slozhnosti vychisleniya intervala znachenii polynoma ot mnogikh peremennykh. Kibernetika (Kiev) 4, (1985) 6-8; translation: Computational complexity of the range of a polynomial in several variables. Cybernetics **21**, 418–421

Iri M. (1991) History of automatic differentiation and rounding error estimation. In: A. Griewank, G. F. Corliss (eds.) Automatic Differentiation of Algorithms: Theory, Implementation, and Application, 3-16; common Automated Differentiation Bibliography collected by G. F. Corliss, 331-353. Philadelphia, SIAM

Kaishev A.I. (1989) Updated scheme for construction of a posteriori interval extensions for elementary functions (in Russian). Voprosy Kibernetiki (Academy of Sciences of the USSR, Moscow) **149**, 14–18

Kim K. V., Nesterov Yu. E., Cherkasskiĭ B.V. (1984) Otsenka trudoemkosti vychisleniya gradienta. Doklady AN SSSR **275** (1984) 1306–1309; translation: An estimate of the efforts in computing the gradient. Sov. Math. Dokl. **29**, 384–387

Linnaimaa S. (1976) Taylor expansion of the accumulated rounding error. Bit **16**, 146-160

Matijasevich Yu. (1985) A posteriori interval analysis. Lecture Notes Computer Sci. **204**, 328–334, Springer-Verlag, Berlin

Matiyasevich Yu. (1986) Vetschestvennye chisla i ÉVM. In: V.A.Mel'nikov (ed.) Kibernetika i Vychislitel'naya technika 2, Nauka, Moscow, 104–133

Moore R. E. (1966) Interval Analysis. Prentice Hall, Englewood Cliffs

2.5 Applying Constraints for Scheduling

Mark Wallace
Institute European Computer-Industry Research Centre
Arabellastr. 17, 81925 München
Germany
Mark.Wallace@ecrc.de

2.5.1 Introduction

Scheduling problems come in all shapes and sizes, and no two problems are alike. However it is possible to abstract certain features which are common to whole classes of problems. Some of the features can be expressed as logical requirements on the solution, and can be mapped directly to constraints in logic programming. Even within the logical framework there are features, like symmetry, and sheer problem size, which require some extension of the standard CLP approach to be solved in practice. Most scheduling problems, however, are not amenable to a precise, correct logical specification. For longer term scheduling only approximate times are required: to the nearest day or month perhaps. Moreover for both long term and short term scheduling the data input to the scheduler often turns out to be incorrect in practice due to unpredictable events like cancelled orders and machine breakdowns. Finally it is rarely possible, or sufficient, to find a single feasible schedule which satisfies a set of requirements. Instead an optimal schedule is sought, which may perhaps omit some jobs, but on balance meets the most possible requirements at the least overall cost.

In the next section we analyse the job shop scheduling problem highlighting the features listed above and the difficulties they cause for the CLP approach. In section 3 we describe solutions that have been proposed in the literature and examine how they can be accommodated in CLP.

2.5.2 Features of the Job Shop Scheduling Problem

2.5.2.1 Requirements Expressible As Constraints

Job Due Date and Task Sequencing Requirements The fundamental aim of scheduling in a factory is to complete each order by its due date. Simplistically this means that each production job J must be started in time to finish before its due date. The resulting constraint is

$$\forall J, Start.assign(J, Start) \rightarrow (Start \leq dueDate(J) - duration(J))$$

Throughout this paper we shall use functions, such as $dueDate(J)$ in our examples rather than relations, such as $dueDate(J, Date)$, for simplicity and clarity, even though the syntax of logic programming requires us to use relations in practical programs.

Each production job comprises a set of tasks, and the duration of a job is (at least) the minimum duration of all the tasks it involves. Some of the tasks must be completed before others can start. Other temporal constraints on tasks can also arise. For example in an application of CHIP to wafer fabrication (Baues 1989) the next task had to start as soon as the previous one finished, since the wafers would be damaged by any waiting between two stages of the production. Each individual task runs for a certain duration, which can be viewed as a temporal interval, so the temporal constraints between tasks can be represented as constraints on these intervals. Seven such interval constraints have been identified (Allen 1984), of which we have encountered two, *before* and *meets*, in the examples above. The minimum duration of two tasks is the duration of the longest one, if they can run in parallel, or the sum of their durations if one is constrained not to start until the other is completed. For larger groups of tasks, under interval constraints, a minimum duration can be easily calculated. The set of non-overlapping tasks in a job with the largest minimum duration make up a *critical path*, and clearly $duration(J)$ is the sum of the durations of the tasks on the critical path of each job J.

The scheduling problem characterised above is quite simple. All the constraints satisfy a monotonicity condition, which allows them to be solved by a polynomial propagation algorithm (Van Hentenryck, Deville, and Teng 1992).

Resource Contention We now introduce the problem of resource contention, when we consider that tasks must be run on machines and there is a limited number of machines available. Suddenly the problem become dramatically harder. The reason is that if two tasks $T1$ and $T2$ need the same machine then they are constrained such that *either* $T1$ runs before $T2$ *or* vice versa. The introduction of two alternatives makes it much harder to decide which tasks lie on the critical path for a job: each alternative might lead to a different critical path. The problem of disjunctive constraints, in this sense, is the first reason why scheduling is such a hard problem. Complete algorithms for reasoning about time, in this case, are exponential, whether expressed in terms of $(T1[before, after]T2)$ (Allen 1983), or in terms of points (Vilain and Kautz 1986) are known, but their cost is exponential.

We have now reached the "pure" job shop scheduling problem. In this problem there are several jobs to be scheduled, each job comprising several tasks. The tasks in a job are constrained to run in sequential order (effectively we simplify the problem by only considering tasks lying on the critical path). Each task runs on a separate machine. In the pure job shop scheduling problem each job comprises the same number of tasks, equivalent tasks in separate jobs running on the same machine. The only difference between jobs are the task durations.

When there are three machines or less, the jobs can always be run in the same sequence on all three machines (Ignall and Schrage 1965).[1] However if

---

[1]The problem therefore reduces to the "flow shop" problem.

there are four or more machines it is easy to construct examples where the "best" solution has jobs running in different sequences on different machines. A simple example has two jobs A and B with tasks $t_{A1}, t_{A2}, t_{A3}, t_{A4}$ running on four different machines and tasks $t_{B1}, t_{B2}, t_{B3}, t_{B4}$ also running on the same four machines. Their durations are

$duration(t_{A1}) = duration(t_{A4}) = duration(t_{B2}) = duration(t_{B3}) = 4$ and
$duration(t_{A2}) = duration(t_{A3}) = duration(t_{B1}) = duration(t_{B4}) = 1.$

The shortest overall schedule for these jobs, which takes 12 units of time, has A running before B on some machines and B running before A on others.

Symmetry A difficulty with solving the job shop scheduling problem is the multiplicative increase in choices when the number of jobs and machines increases. Nevertheless many of the choices often lead to the same intermediate, or final, completion time. An obvious case is when two jobs have tasks of the same length: any schedule can be changed by replacing all the tasks in one job consistently by those in the other job without affecting the completion times of the other jobs. The two schedules are symmetrical in the sense that there is an isomorphic mapping of one to the other which leaves the important properties of the schedules unchanged. To reduce the search space of possible schedules, it is vitally important to recognise such symmetries and avoid repetitive search through alternatives that differ only in that they have symmetrical subschedules.

Setup Times In practice, tasks which run on a single machine are rarely independent. A scheduling problem where this dependence is crucial is in the scheduling of disk accesses on a computer. Movement of the disk head are minimised if successive disk accesses are on nearby tracks. A similar dependence arises in the scheduling of cloth weaving. When scheduling work on a loom it is important to sequence tasks involving cloth of the same colour together. Each time a colour change is required, the setup time for the next task is very significant. The constraint reflecting setup times can be expressed in logical form as follows:

$assign(T1, M, ST1) \land assign(T2, M, ST2) \land (ST2 > ST1)$
$\land setupTime(colour(T1), colour(T2), Setup) \rightarrow$
$ST2 \geq ST1 + duration(T1) + Setup,$

where $assign(T, M, ST)$ denotes the assignment of a task T to a machine M at start time ST; $colour(T)$ denotes the colour involved in task T; and $setupTime(C1, C2, T)$ relates the setup time T needed to change from a task with colour $C1$ to one with colour $C2$.

   If setup times are significant, the scheduling problem for a set of tasks which need to run on the same machine becomes isomorphic to a travelling salesman problem. The minimum time between the start of one task $T1$ and the start of the next $T2$ is the duration of $T1$ plus the time to setup between tasks $T1$

and $T2$. Mapping each task to a location in the TSP problem, we map this minimum time to the distance between the two locations. A schedule which optimises setup times now corresponds to a TSP solution that minimises the total distance travelled. Additionally there is a choice of different machines and also a due date for each task. This extended problem maps to an extended TSP called the "vehicle scheduling problem" (VSP) with multiple delivery vehicles and time windows for visiting locations (Christodoulou and Assimakopoulos 1992).

Optimisation A typical feature of scheduling problems is the requirement for optimisation. This is a major challenge even for pure job-shop scheduling problems; for example proof of optimality has been obtained for a 10 job/10 machine problem only in 1988 (Pinson 1988). The size of general TSP problems for which an optimum can be guaranteed to be found is around 30 locations. The number of machines in a real scheduling application can be in the order of hundreds, with tasks in the order of thousands! Such numbers prevent the problem from being amenable to any complete search technique, even when the search space is pruned by constraint handling and recognition of symmetries.

For such problems approximation algorithms are a good alternative to optimisation. Approximation algorithms do not guarantee to find an optimal solution, but only to find a good solution with a high probability by exploring only a part of the solution space. The successful application of approximation to a scheduling problem is described in (Minton, Johnston, Philips, and Laird 1992).

2.5.2.2 Requirements Based on Probabilistic Information and on Preferences

A logical formulation of the scheduling problem is only possible on the assumption of complete precise information. A solution is a complete precise schedule satisfying the logical requirements. However real life scheduling is not based on complete precise information, and nor is a complete precise schedule always required. Practical experience with a completed scheduling program showed that "the level of temporal granularity and the imperative nature of the schedules" were "too stringent for human operators".

Granularity One approach to this difficulty is based on a notion of granularity. A more precise schedule based on more precise information is obtained by dividing time into smaller units, such as hours; a looser schedule based on looser data is obtained by dividing time into larger units, such as months. For many practical applications it is necessary to perform both long term scheduling (at a coarser level of granularity) and short term planning (at a finer granularity). The results of mid-term planning are fed into the short term planner as constraints. Another example is the scheduling of the Hubble Space Telescope (Minton, Johnston, Philips, and Laird 1992), which has been divided into two parts: a long term scheduling problem which assigns a year's work to a set of time segments of several days length, and a short term scheduling problem which produces a detailed sequence of commands for the telescope.

In case two schedulers working at different granularities are integrated, there is a need to map events specified at one level of granularity to a higher or lower granularity. This problem is being tackled in the EQUATOR project (Montanari, Maim, Ciapessoni, and Ratto 1992).

Scheduling and Rescheduling The data input to long term planning and scheduling systems is subject to change. Customers cancel or modify their orders, or change their due dates. Production processes and tools change, affecting task durations and setup times. Even in the case of short term scheduling, the data input to the scheduler is of uncertain quality. Tasks exceed their expected durations, people go ill or absent, and machines break down without notice.

For this reason two kinds of scheduler exist: predictive schedulers and reactive schedulers. A predictive scheduler makes a schedule based on (probabilistic) input about jobs and task durations. A reactive schedule takes a global schedule as input together with information about the actual state of affairs. Each time that something unexpected happens, the reactive scheduler makes local changes to the schedule to accommodate the new information.

Predictive scheduling is in a sense a harder problem, for which more processing time is available and in which it is possible to abstract away from the details of the factory. Reactive scheduling needs input that reflects precisely the current situation in the factory, but has less processing time available, and must therefore solve only simpler local problems.

An archetypal reactive scheduling problem is the scheduling of processes on a multi-processor computer system. On the assumption that the communication between processes is not a significant factor, a very naive approach can show a very good performance (Blake 1992). It suffices, in this case, for each new process to be queued on the processor which spawned it; whenever a processor becomes free it takes a process from the processor with the longest queue.

A naive reactive scheduler is one which simply postpones tasks without any attempt to try moving them to another machine, or reordering them on the same machine. However if computation time can be controlled, a more sophisticated reactive scheduler would improve the chances of localising the disruption to the global schedule. A goal of current research is to design algorithms which behave reactively when given a small processing time, but behave predictively when more time is available (Dean and Boddy 1987).

Optimisation with "Soft" and Probabilistic Constraints Optimisation is already difficult in case all the constraints have a logical semantics: true or false. It becomes even harder when some of the constraints are *hard* (eg. two tasks cannot run on one machine at the same time), and some are *soft* (eg. job J must be completed by date D or as soon as possible afterwards). Soft constraints can be handled by associating a cost with violated constraints, but this leads to optimisation conflicts. Consider a scheduling problem where missed due dates have an associated cost. Suppose there is another cost associated with setting up machines between certain tasks. Then there are conflicting optimisation requirements.

The maximum number of due dates may be met by a schedule which involves a large number of costly and labour intensive changes of colour on the looms. The experience of Braghenti shows that a solution which maximises the number of jobs scheduled in time for their due date, is quite different from a solution which minimises colour changes. No method has yet been found of moving from an "optimal" solution in the first sense to an "optimal" solution in the second sense.

Moreover in the case of uncertainty about machine breakdowns, etc., it is unclear what should be optimised. The tightest schedule will very probably be impossible to stick to in the factory, so the "optimal" schedule must provide the best balance between robustness and efficiency.

2.5.3 Solving Scheduling Problems in CLP

2.5.3.1 The CLP Paradigm Scheduling problems are solved within the CLP paradigm by constraint handling and search. In this paragraph we summarise the different ways of handling constraints: solving, propagation and simplification. The CLP Scheme (Jaffar and Lassez 1987) is a generalisation of logic programming where constraints are handled by a *solver* for a specific class of constraints: each instance of the scheme deals with a different constraint class. Essentially the role of the solver is to detect inconsistency. CHIP, and more generally cc(FD) (Van Hentenryck, Simonis, and Dincbas 1992), provides another way of handling constraints over finite domains: constraint *propagation*. Constraint propagation can be less powerful but more efficient than constraint solving. Propagation does not always detect inconsistency amongst the current constraints, but when augmented by a (program defined) variable labelling procedure, completeness is restored in the sense that any inconsistency will be eventually detected. Generalised propagation (Le Provost and Wallace 1993) supports propagation without finite domains. Generalised propagation can produce new constraints of the specific class which can be treated by the constraint solver. Constraint *simplification* is a technique that improves the efficiency of constraint solving, however the same technique can be adapted to provide program-defined constraint propagation. Constraint simplification rules (Frühwirth 1992) allow the programmer to encode specific simplification and propagation steps, giving him precise control over the handling of constraints.

In this paragraph we focus on the search component of CLP. Firstly, the control of the search is program defined: both the order in which choices are made, and the order in which alternatives are chosen, are specified by the programmer. In CHIP (Dincbas, Van Hentenryck, Simonis, Aggoun, Graf, and Berthier 1988) new constraints can even be added during the search process. The classic form of a CLP program, however, separates the posting of the constraints from the search procedure. The search procedure is classically a simple labelling procedure which selects each problem variable in turn and assigns to it a possible value. The decision of what variable to label next, and with what variable to label it, can be done either in advance, by defining an ordering on variables and values, or dynamically at runtime by routines that examine the current state of the computation before deciding which variable to choose next and what value to label it with. If the current choices prove to have been incorrect, or non-optimal, the CLP system offers the programmer no dynamic control over the subsequent behaviour of the program: it backtracks to the next value or variable after the choice that proved wrong.

2.5.4 Disjunctive Constraints

For the simplest sheduling problems, where there is no contention for resources, CHIP's constraint handling techniques are sufficient to guide the search so the problem can be solved without backtracking. The cost of such powerful constraint handling for such problems is not prohibitive since the constraint problem is polynomial (Van Hentenryck, Deville, and Teng 1992).

Contention for resources, as in the case that two tasks require the same machine, introduces a new difficulty. Either one task must run first - imposing one constraint on the final schedule - or the other runs first - in which case a different constraint must be imposed.

Such disjunctive constraints have been dealt with in CHIP by simply choosing one disjunct during the search process (Dincbas, Simonis, and Van Hentenryck 1990). In this case the disjunctive constraint is expressed as a rule with two clauses, one for each constraint.[2]

$$contention(Task1, Task2) \leftarrow start(Task1) + duration(Task1) < start(Task2)$$
$$contention(Task1, Task2) \leftarrow start(Task2) + duration(Task2) < start(Task1)$$

However for many problems such an approach introduces too many choice points and yields an unsatisfactory performance (Chamard and Fischler 1993).

Disjunctive constraints can be used completely passively, by simply checking them for consistency. In this case the constraint is not used to prune the domains of any problem variables, it merely causes failure if, at any point in the search, all the disjuncts are inconsistent. However a more active use is possible if the system can detect when all but one alternative is excluded, and then impose the remaining alternative as an active constraint. In this case the individual disjuncts are checked for consistency, instead of the whole disjunctive constraint. When only one consistent disjunct remains, it is imposed as an active constraint, and can be used for pruning the domains of the remaining variables.

The simplest way to achieve this behaviour is to introduce an auxiliary variable with a binary domain (Chamard and Fischler 1993). In fact it has proved effective to include the auxiliary variable in the labelling routine. This

---

[2]Our syntax for rules is not the CHIP compiler syntax

gives the effect of setting the constraint at a choice point, as discussed earlier, but in this case the labelling routine can select the variable for labelling at the best point in the search.

Although one binary variable suffices for a choice point with just two choices, the solution with auxiliary variables becomes more complicated and less efficient for processing when there are multiple choices. Multiple choices arise naturally, for example, when there are multiple tasks in contention for one, or even several, machines. To avoid an increasing number of auxiliary variables, it is possible to obtain a similar constraint behaviour by using simplification rules (CHR's) (Frühwirth and Hanschke 1993). An example simplification rule for the contention problem is:

$$contention(Task1, Task2) \Leftrightarrow start(Task1) + duration(Task1) > start(Task2) \mid$$
$$start(Task1) \geq start(Task2) + duration(Task2)$$
$$contention(Task1, Task2) \Leftrightarrow start(Task2) + duration(Task2) > start(Task1) \mid$$
$$start(Task2) \geq start(Task1) + duration(Task1)$$

These rules yield the following behaviour. If $contention(Task1, Task2)$ is a current goal then the system continually checks the conditions

$$start(Task1) + duration(Task1) > start(Task2) \text{ and}$$
$$start(Task2) + duration(Task2) > start(Task1).$$

As soon as one of the conditions is entailed by the scheduling choices made so far (say the first one for example) the system immediately replaces the goal $contention(Task1, Task2)$ with the body of the rule (in this case $start(Task1) \geq start(Task2) + duration(Task2)$).

Of course the number and complexity of such CHR's also increases with the number of contending tasks. However the power of multi-headed CHR's can be used to avoid adding each pair of contending tasks as an explicit constraint. If any two tasks run on the same machine, they are in contention. Therefore we simply need two CHR's for all contending tasks:

$$assign(T1, M, ST1), assign(T2, M, ST2) \Leftrightarrow start(T1)$$
$$+duration(T1) > start(T2) \mid start(T1) \geq start(T2) + duration(T2)$$
$$assign(T1, M, ST1), assign(T2, M, ST2) \Leftrightarrow start(T2)$$
$$+duration(T2) > start(T1) \mid start(T2) \geq start(T1) + duration(T1)$$

In this case it is the CHR processor that detects all the contending tasks and enforces the constraint on each of them instead of the programmer.

The amount of propagation invested in a disjunctive constraint has a significant effect on overall performance. In (Dincbas, Simonis, and Van Hentenryck 1990) various ways of using disjunctive constraints for a scheduling problem were investigated. The constraints were used for lookahead – a powerful form of propagation – for forward checking – which corresponds approximately to the weak form of propagation proposed by (Chamard and Fischler 1993) – and as choice points. For the particular scheduling application at hand, the use of disjunctive constraints as choice points proved to be most efficient!

Generalised propagation (Le Provost and Wallace 1993) allows the disjunctive constraints to be expressed as ordinary Prolog rules (as in the first example above). When the constraint is invoked as a goal it is then possible to specify how it should be used - for propagation, or for search. A way of experimenting with different amounts of propagation is offered by *approximate* generalised propagation (Le Provost 1993). The advantage is that different amounts of propagation can be achieved by modifying a single parameter. The change has no effect on program semantics and is a small syntactic change, which makes experimentation and program support and maintenance much easier.

2.5.4.1 The Pure Job-Shop Scheduling Problem
We now consider more complex disjunctive scheduling problems where many tasks are in contention for a machine. In this case rather than treating the contention between each pair of tasks as a constraint, it proves more effective to define a single "global" constraint on the whole set of contending tasks. The use of global constraints for solving complex tasks has been explored within the CHIP context by devising and hard wiring specific constraints (Beldiceanu 1990). A hard wired global constraint for scheduling has been built into CHIP (Aggoun and Beldiceanu 1992), and used for finding an optimal solution to the 10X10 job-shop scheduling problem.

A global constraint can be as complex as required. From a purely theoretical point of view the whole job-shop scheduling problem could be "wrapped up" as a global constraint. If the problem is chopped up into a few large global constraints, constraint-solving then becomes equivalent to solving large chunks of the scheduling problem, which could require a lot of computation. For making efficient use of global constraints, therefore, it is necessary to deliberately reduce the power of the constraints handler. The subtlety of global constraints is to extract useful information while limiting the amount of constraint propagation so that it does not become too computationally expensive.

Simplification rules provide the necessary control to experiment with appropriate global constraint behaviour for scheduling problems. We now give some examples of global constraint behaviour expressed as CHR's. Assume a set of tasks is in contention for a machine. We impose a constraint $global(T)$, where T is the set of tasks. We define a function $minstart$ that finds the earliest possible start time for any of the tasks, by analysing the domains of the variables denoting the start times. Similarly we define a function $maxend$ which finds the latest possible end time. Finally we define a function $duration$ which sums the durations of all the tasks. Now the following CHR detects as soon as a set of tasks will no longer fit into the available time on a machine:

$$global(T) \leftrightarrow duration(T) > maxend(T) - minstart(T) \mid fail$$

Active propagation is possible by detecting local ordering choices that would violate the global condition on T. For example if there was one task $T1$ in T with an earlier possible start time than any other, the system could check whether $duration(T) > maxend(T) - minstart(T \setminus \{T1\})$. If not, then $T1$ would become constrained to start before all the other tasks. It is still too early to predict whether CHRs alone will provide a sufficiently powerful and efficient framework for solving complex scheduling problems.

2.5.4.2 Eliminating Symmetries We detour briefly to look at a cutting stock problem which provides a good example of a technique for avoiding repeated search of symmetrical configurations. A problem which had been solved with CHIP (Dincbas, Simonis, and Van Hentenryck 1988) was solved even more efficiently by the new approach which used dynamically generated *nogood* assertions to prune branches of the search tree (Maruyama, Minoda, S., and Takizawa 1992). The idea is based on the concept of *nogood* environments introduced by Assumption-Based Truth Maintenance Systems (de Kleer 1986).

As an example, suppose a customer requires 200 thin boards and 300 fat ones. The raw material comes in large sheets which can be cut in a fixed number of different ways. Each alternative way C of cutting the sheet produces $t(C)$ thin boards and $f(C)$ fat boards. The problem is to satisfy the customers requirement with (say) 10 sheets. We encode the problem by introducing 10 variables $C1 \ldots C10$ to represent the chosen cutting of each sheet. Thus each Ci has a finite number of possible values reflecting the different possible cuttings. The constraints on the problem are two:

$$t(C1) + \ldots + t(C10) \geq 200$$
$$f(C1) + \ldots + f(C10) \geq 300$$

Now suppose a labelling starts with $C1 = a, C2 = b, C3 = c, C4 = d, C5 = e$, but that no labelling of the remaining variables can be found that satisfies the constraints. Consequently the above partial labelling is, effectively, a *nogood*. Clearly any other ordering of the choices a, b, c, d, e for $C1, C2, C3, C4, C5$ is also *nogood*. The cause of the failure is that the sums $t(a) + t(b) + t(c) + t(d) + t(e) = thinsum5$ and $f(a) + f(b) + f(c) + f(d) + f(e) = fatsum5$ are too small.

Moreover from the point of view of solving the problem, even the choices a, b, c, d, e are irrelevent: if any five boards are chosen which yield $thinsum5$ (or less) thin boards and $fatsum5$ (or less) fat boards, the partial labelling will be *nogood*. This follows because the failed search for a labelling of $C6, C7, C8, C9, C10$ shows that there is no labelling which makes

$$t(C6) + t(C7) + t(C8) + t(C9) + t(C10) \geq (200 - thinsum5) \quad \wedge$$
$$f(C6) + f(C7) + f(C8) + f(C9) + f(C10) \geq (300 - fatsum5).$$

Thus any labelling of $C1, \ldots, C5$ which makes

$$t(C1) + t(C2) + t(C3) + t(C4) + t(C5) \leq thinsum5 \quad \wedge$$
$$f(C1) + f(C2) + f(C3) + f(C4) + f(C5) \leq fatsum5$$

is also *nogood.*

By adding this last conjunction as a *nogood* assertion to be checked by the program after each labelling of the first five variables, the system can prune large subparts of the subtree. The symmetrical assignments of the values a, b, c, d, e to $C1, C2, C3, C4, C5$ are immediately pruned by this approach, together with possibly many other partial labellings.

Effectively the approach is complementary to constraint propagation: propagation is performed before search, whilst *nogoods* are extracted after the search has failed. Both propagation and *nogoods* are used to prune the search tree subsequently. Indeed the information captured in a *nogood* could equally be extracted by propagation. In the above example, the kernel information extracted from the failed search is that

$$t(C6) + t(C7) + t(C8) + t(C9) + t(C10) \leq (200 - thinsum5) \vee$$
$$f(C6) + f(C7) + f(C8) + f(C9) + f(C10) \leq (300 - fatsum5)$$

Theoretically, such information could also be extracted by propagation, but the difficulty is in choosing what propagation information is worth extracting. In the *nogood* approach there is no need to make such a decision, since the information is extracted as a side-effect of a failed search that had to be done anyway.

We have experimented with this approach using CHIP augmented with nogoods. We used it to tackle a real application concerned with shift timetabling. The improved backtrack behaviour enabled the whole search space to be explored and an optimum timetable to be found. The application is still being further developed.

2.5.4.3 Heuristics for Large Scheduling Problems For many large practical problems, it is not possible to search all possible schedules, even using sophisticated constraint techniques to prune impossible schedules from the search tree. Consequently much of the research on scheduling is about heuristics to focus the search on promising parts of the search tree, without any attempt to cover all possibilities. In this section we will concentrate on heuristics that guide both the order in which variables are labelled, and the order in which values are chosen with which to label the chosen variables. Even though completeness is not guaranteed, heuristic approaches often admit some local backtracking in case a previous choice proves to have been wrong. We therefore also discuss techniques that guide backtracking.[3]

Variable Selection Many scheduling problems have parts that are relatively easy to satisfy and other parts which are much harder. The hard parts of a schedule - where many tasks need to be run on few machines within a short time period in order to meet due dates - are termed "bottlenecks" of the schedule. When

---

[3]In subsection 2.5.4.7 below we shall examine another heuristic approach to scheduling which starts with a complete schedule and attempts to improve it by making successive small changes.

searching for a solution, if the bottlenecks are left till last, then they may be unsolvable because of certain choices made earlier which could have easily been changed. Therefore it is best to try and deal with the bottlenecks first, since each choice is important. The other parts of the schedule can then be fitted around the bottlenecks. This is often known as the "first fail" principle.

To identify bottlenecks the concept of variable "tightness" was introduced in (Fox, Sadeh, and Baycan 1989). A tight variable is one that eliminates lots of possible solutions. Specifically "the tightness of a variable is the probability that an assignment consistent with all the problem constraints that do not involve the variable does not result in a solution". The first fail principle requires the search routine to label tighter variables first. However variable tightness is not a fixed measure. A certain choice for one variable may leave very few options for another variable. Essentially the influence of variables on each other is dictated by the problem constraints. Therefore another measure which helps select which variables to label next is based on the constraints, called "constraint tightness" (Fox, Sadeh, and Baycan 1989).

In a job-shop scheduling problem there are essentially two kinds of constraints relating different tasks. For tasks belonging to the same job there are ordering constraints on the tasks. For tasks in contention for the same machine there are disjunctive constraints on the tasks. Constraint tightness is a measure of which machines look like being heavily loaded in an emerging schedule, or which jobs look like breaching their due dates. Clearly the next variables to label are the ones associated with the currently tightest constraint.

2.5.4.4 Value Selection Given that a certain variable is to be labelled, the next requirement is to label it in a way that allows the maximum freedom in labelling the remaining variables. A direct measure of the total reduction in the domains of the remaining task variables may not be very useful if the real difficulty is with one or two other particular variables. A better way to control the labelling of variable is to measure "variable contention" which records the extent to which a number of constraints on the variable conflict with each other. Two variables constrained by a common set of constraints should be labelled in such a way as to minimise this contention.

2.5.4.5 Preference Propagation In order to use the measures of tightness and contention outlined above, some technique of estimating them is required. The techniques described in (Lepape and Smith 1987) and (Sadeh and Fox 1989) are based on constraint propagation. In this context, the purpose of propagation is not to eliminate impossible values from the domains of variables, but rather to identify degrees of freedom for variables and sources of contention.

A simple motivating example of preference propagation is in (Sycara, Roth, Sadeh, and Fox 1991). Consider a schedule involving four jobs, A, B, C and D which all have to run in a time period $0 - 15$. Each job has a few tasks, each of which lasts 3 units of time, and which must be run in sequence. Job A has tasks AL, AM, AN, which run on machines L, M and N respectively. Job B has tasks BL, BM, job C has tasks CN, CL, CM and job D has tasks DK, DM, where the task name also reflects which machine it should run on.

Preference propagation can be used to build up a measure of the contention for each machine by simply summing possibilities. For example task AL can start at times 0..6, which makes 6 alternative start times. For only one of those start times is AL running on machine L in the time period $0-1$. However it is running in time period $1-2$ for two of the start times, it is running in the period $3-7$ for three of the possible start times, and so on. Propagation concludes that task AL makes a contribution of $1/6$ to the activity of machine L in the period $0-1$, $2/6$ in the period $1-2$ and $3/6$ in the period $3-7$, $2/6$ in the period $7-8$ and $1/6$ in the period $8-9$.

Propagation on tasks BL and CL yield further contributions, which are summed to produce the estimated contention for machine L. The estimated contention for the four machines is shown in the figure on the next page.

The greatest contention is for machine M, and therefore tasks running on this machine should be scheduled first. Moreover the maximum contention is in the time period $8-10$, so the start times should be chosen for the tasks so as to avoid this peak.

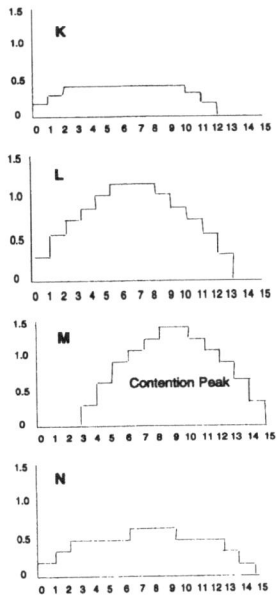

Implementation in CLP CLP offers the appropriate control to support variable and value selection. Moreover the modification required to generalised propagation to support preference propagation is not dramatic. The requirement is to retreat all the alternatives and combine them into a set of preferences. Generalised propagation already provides the facility to extract information from the set of alternative answers to a goal: the difference is merely in the operations that build the result from the answers as they are extracted.

The general problem of assessing tightness and contention by preference propagation is by no means a solved problem. The example illustrated above was artificially simple. However it seems likely that as new forms of preference propagation are devised, it will be possible to incorporate them into the CLP propagation framework.

The amount of propagation which should be performed to obtain the best overall scheduling performance is not fixed for all scheduling problems - nor even for the whole scheduling process for a single problem. Experiments described in (Lepape 1991) show that the amount of propagation should be tailored to the current requirements of the scheduler. For example more propagation should be performed while scheduling bottlenecks, where all choices affect each other and it is important to make the correct decision, than while scheduling the "looser" tasks, where propagation produces little valuable information. Approximate generalised propagation is designed to provide just such control over the propagation, and would appear to fit this requirement for efficient scheduling. It remains a subject of investigation, whether approximate generalised propagation can provide sufficient control to obtain the best amount of propagation for this application.

Backtracking The other area of intense investigation in the scheduling world is how to control backtracking. One approach that has been proposed recently (Sycara, Roth, Sadeh, and Fox 1991) is to distribute the search into separate processes. Each search process has access to global information, about tightness and contention and, later, resource consumption. However, it can only backtrack locally and the information it has contributed to the other processes is not removed. Thus future local solutions must respect the same global restrictions.

If the total search space has 5^{10} alternatives but it is divided into ten separate search processes, each process explores only a search space of around 5 alternatives. Thus only a global total of $5 * 10 = 50$ backtracks are possible instead of 5^{10}. Such a backtracking behaviour is obtained very easily within the CLP paradigm.

2.5.4.6 Predictive and Reactive Scheduling The requirement for both predictive and reactive scheduling is a feature of many, if not most, real scheduling applications. A technique which is possible using finite domains is to produce, as output from the predictive scheduler, not just the chosen start time for each task, but a finite set of possible start times.

The reactive scheduler associates a variable with each task, as usual, and labels it with the start time when it starts. As long as every task starts on time (i.e. at the start time chosen by the predictive scheduler), then no constraint checking is necessary, since that has already been done during the predictive schedule.

However as soon as a task is labelled with an unpredicted start time, all the constraints on this variable are woken. Propagation on these constraints may remove the predicted start time from the domains of other tasks. The constraints on these tasks are then also woken. Thus the effect of an unexpected event are allowed to ripple through the constraint network, waking up all constraints that are affected - but no other constraints.

A typical example of such a reactive behaviour occurs in train timetabling. When one train is late it is necessary to modify the timetables for trains which must wait for it, but not for other trains. The challenge is to identify the affected part of the railway network and reschedule it, with the aim of achieving minimal disruption.

The tools necessary for such a reactive scheduling mechanism in CLP are provided by CHR's. For each task there is a rule; for example

$$react(T) \Leftrightarrow start(T) = 25 \mid true.$$
$$react(T) \Leftrightarrow start(T) \neq 25 \mid C1(T, T2), C2(T, T3) \ldots$$

where 25 is the start time for T chosen by the predictive scheduler, $C1(T, T1)$, $C2(T, T3), \ldots$ are the constraints on task T. This rule does nothing until $start(T)$ either becomes equal to 25, or becomes constrained not to equal 25. In the second case all the constraints on T are awoken, and used during the subsequent propagation and labelling. This approach is still in its infancy, and much further work will be required to make it mature and useable in practice.

2.5.4.7 Optimisation by Constrained Approximation

Optimisation Problems Constraint logic programming supports search over a solution space structured into a tree, some of whose leaves are feasible solutions. The constraints allow some of the branches, whose leaves include no feasible solutions, to be pruned away in advance during the search. Many problems require not just a feasible solution but an optimal one, assuming some function associating a cost with each solution. To find the optimum some kind of enumeration of the feasible solutions is required. The enumeration efficiency can be improved by pruning away in advance branches whose leaves include no *optimal* feasible solutions (branch and bound), or by other well-known techniques such as cutting planes, or dynamic programming. Unfortunately for large problems even the pruned search tree is often too large too explore in realistic timescales; thus the enumeration method is computationally impractible.

Approximation Algorithms In case it is impractible to find the actual optimum by enumeration, approximation algorithms can be used to find, with a high probability, a good solution, by exploring only a part of the solution space. For many hard search problems, such as the travelling salesman problem, assembly-line sequencing, and scheduling, approximation algorithms have been used very successfully (Mühlenbein 1992; Chew, David, Nguyen, and Tourbier 1992; Minton, Johnston, Philips, and Laird 1992).

Such methods are often viewed as an alternative to constrained search. In fact constraints can be used with approximation algorithms in exactly the same way they are used with enumeration algorithms: the choice of approximation or enumeration is independent of the use of constraints. Experiments we have carried out show that constraints bring the same benefits of simplicity and efficiency when used with approximation algorithms that they do with enumeration algorithms (Küchenhoff 1992).

Intuitively, approximation algorithms such as hill-climbing, simulated annealing and genetic algorithms, work when solutions which are similar have a broadly similar cost: the cost function is in a loose sense continuous. When there is no relationship between the costs of similar solutions, then there is no reason why an approximation method should perform any better than standard backtracking. In this case, both approximation algorithms and standard backtracking just pick one solution after another, recording the best solution found so far.

The notion of "similarity" between solutions is captured by operators defined for the problem at hand. For hill-climbing and simulated annealing these are "neighbourhood" operators which produce new solutions similar to a given one; for genetic algorithms they are "recombination" operators which produce a new solution which is an appropriate mixture of two existing ones.

The Need for Constrained Approximation Unconstrained approximation algorithms make no distinction between feasible solutions and others. Therefore the elimination of infeasible solutions has to be achieved by a kind of trick. Violated constraints have an associated cost. For example in a hill-climbing algorithm for the n-queens problem (Minton, Johnston, Philips, and Laird 1992) the cost of a solution is simply the number of pairs of queens which can take each other - the number of violated constraints. For problems which involve both *hard* constraints (eg. two tasks cannot run on one machine at the same time), and *soft* constraints (eg. job J must be completed by date D or as soon as possible afterwards), it is important to ensure that solutions violating the hard constraints are eliminated. This is achieved by associating with them a very high cost, so that solutions with a reasonably low overall cost are ones that don't violate hard constraints.

The immediate consequence of this approach is that "similar" solutions, as defined in terms of the operators described above, no longer necessarily have a similar cost. Thus the graph of solutions against their costs is no longer broadly continuous, but full of spikes. When applied to problems whose solution space has such an irregular cost function, the intuitive basis for the effectiveness of the approximation algorithm is no longer satisfied. Constrained approximation avoids this difficulty. It works by constraining the search for an initial solution and constraining the operators that produce new (similar) solutions from old ones. The consequence is that the spikes in the graph of solutions against their costs are smoothed out. Notice that the infeasible solutions cannot simply be dropped from the solution space. This would leave gaps in the solution space in place of spikes. It could prevent certain "good" solutions being recombined during the genetic algorithm, and for hill-climbing and simulated annealing it could leave some solutions without any neighbours at all. Rather than the constraints being used passively, therefore, they are used actively to guide the neighbourhood or recombination operator to a feasible solution (see below).

Experiments and Conclusions Our experiments have focussed on the travelling salesman problem (TSP), using a constrained genetic algorithm. We studied three problems: a small TSP and a larger TSP without specific constraints, and the larger TSP with a number of specific constraints of different kinds (eg. a constraint on the distance travelled from a certain location to the subsequent one). For a simple TSP problem without constraints, branch and bound is an effective technique. However a larger problem without constraints is better solved using the genetic algorithm. The larger problem was then modified by the inclusion of constraints. These - declaratively specified - constraints were used by the constrained genetic algorithm during generation of an initial set of solution, and during the recombination of pairs of descendants. The effect of constraints during recombination is to enforce some variables to take certain values, and to preclude other variables from taking the value proposed by the recombination operator. The latter variables are subsequently labelled under the constraints in the usual CLP manner. The constrained TSP problem was too large too be solved by enumeration techniques, but very good solutions were found by the constrained genetic algorithm. These experiments are described in more detail in another paper (Küchenhoff 1992).

Our experiments and our work on the theoretical foundations of constrained approximation are still in progress. Based on early results we are optimistic that the technique will be effective for a broad range of problems. We believe that the incorporation of constrained approximation algorithms into CLP, as an alternative to branch and bound, will enable the technology to be scaled up to larger real world problems.

2.5.5 Conclusion

The scheduling problem is not yet fully understood, let alone solved. However because it is so important and pervasive, the problem is heavily researched by many different research communities. This paper has not, therefore, begun to cover all the techniques which have been used for solving scheduling problems.

Instead, a number of difficult features of scheduling problems have been identified, and solutions proposed in the literature have been explained. A very satisfactory result has been the ease with which it is possible to capture these solutions in CLP. Moreover the CLP framework has suggested new ways of combining these techniques.

Acknowledgements

This work was partly supported by the ESPRIT Project 5291 CHIC. Thanks to the CHIC user group for lots of great discussions, and to Thom Frühwirth for corrections and suggestions.

References

Aggoun, A. and N. Beldiceanu (1992). Extending CHIP in order to solve complex scheduling problems. In *Proc. JFPL*, Lille.

Allen, J. F. (1983). Maintaining knowledge about temporal intervals. *Communications of the ACM 26*, 832–843.

Allen, J. F. (1984). Towards a general theory of action and time. *Artificial Intelligence 23*, 123–154.

Baues, G. (1989). Einsatz der Constraint-Logic-Programming-Sprache CHIP bei der Lösung eines Job-Shop-Scheduling-Problems. Master's thesis, Technische Universität München, Germany.

Beldiceanu, N. (1990). An example of introduction of global constraints in CHIP: Application to block theory problems. Technical Report TR-LP-49, ECRC.

Blake, B. (1992). Assignment of independent tasks to minimize completion time. *Software Practice and Experience 22*(9).

Chamard, A. and A. Fischler (1993). Applying CHIP to a complex scheduling problem. Technical Report D3.1.2, Dassault Aviation. CHIC report.

Chew, T.-L., J.-M. David, L. Nguyen, and Y. Tourbier (1992). Le car sequencing problem revisité: analyse d'une utilisation du recuit simulé. Technical report, RENAULT, Service Systèmes Experts.

Christodoulou, N. and V. Assimakopoulos (1992). Constraint handling in vehicle-fleet scheduling: Modelization and formulation using CHIP. Technical Report doc-1.2, CMSU. CHIC report.

de Kleer, J. (1986). An assumption-based TMS. *Artificial Intelligence 28*, 127–162.

Dean, T. and M. Boddy (1987). An analysis of time-dependent planning. In *Proc. IJCAI*.

Dincbas, M., H. Simonis, and P. Van Hentenryck (1988, August). Solving a cutting-stock problem in constraint programming. In M. Press (Ed.), *Fifth International Conference on Logic Programming (ICLP'88)*, Seattle, USA.

Dincbas, M., H. Simonis, and P. Van Hentenryck (1990). Solving large combinatorial problems in logic programming. *Journal of Logic Programming 8*.

Dincbas, M., P. Van Hentenryck, H. Simonis, A. Aggoun, T. Graf, and F. Berthier (1988, December). The constraint logic programming language chip. In *Proceedings of the International Conference on Fifth Generation Computer Systems (FGCS'88)*, Tokyo, Japan, pp. 693–702.

Fox, M., N. Sadeh, and C. Baycan (1989). Constrained heuristic search. In *Proc. IJCAI*, pp. 309–316.

Frühwirth, T. (1992). Constraint simplification rules. Technical Report ECRC-92-18, ECRC.

Frühwirth, T. and P. Hanschke (1993). Terminological reasoning with constraint handling rules. In *First Workshop on the Principles and Practice of Constraint Programming*, Newport, RI, USA.

Ignall, E. and L. Schrage (1965). Application of the branch and bound technique to some flow-shop scheduling problems. *Operations Research Quarterly 13*(3).

Jaffar, J. and J.-L. Lassez (1987). Constraint logic programming. In *Proceedings of the Fourteenth ACM Symposium on Principles of Programming Languages (POPL'87)*, Munich, Germany.

Küchenhoff, V. (1992). Novel search and constraints - an integration. Technical report, ECRC. CHIC deliverable.

Le Provost, T. (1993). Approximation in the framework of generalised propagation. Technical report, ECRC. Presented at the CLP workshop, FGCS'92, Tokyo, Japan.

Le Provost, T. and M. G. Wallace (1993). Generalised constraint propagation over the CLP scheme. *Journal of Logic Programming 16*.

Lepape, C. (1991, Jan). Constraint propagation in planning and scheduling. Technical report, Robotics Lab., Stanford Univ.

Lepape, C. and S. F. Smith (1987). Management of temporal constraints for factory scheduling. In *IFIP Working Conf. on Temporal Aspects in Information Systems*.

Maruyama, F., Y. Minoda, S. S., and Y. Takizawa (1992). Constraint satisfaction and optimisation using nogood justifications. In *Proc. 2nd Pacific Rim Conf. on AI*.

Minton, S., M. D. Johnston, A. B. Philips, and P. Laird (1992). Minimizing conflicts: a heuristic repair method for constraint satisfaction and scheduling problems. *Artificial Intelligence 58*.

Montanari, A., E. Maim, E. Ciapessoni, and E. Ratto (1992). Dealing with time granularity in the event calculus. In *Proceedings of the International Conference on Fifth Generation Computer Systems (FGCS '92)*, Tokyo, Japan.

Mühlenbein, H. (1992). Parallel genetic algorithms and combinatorial optimization. *SIAM J. on Optimization*.

Pinson, E. (1988). *Le Probleme de Job Shop*. Ph. D. thesis, Univ. Paris VI.

Sadeh, N. and M. S. Fox (1989). Preference propagation in temporal/capacity constraint graphs. Technical Report CMU-RI-TR-89-2, Robotics Institute, Carnegie Mellon Univ.

Sycara, K. P., S. Roth, N. Sadeh, and M. Fox (1991). Resource allocation in distributed factory scheduling. *IEEE Expert*.

Van Hentenryck, P., Y. Deville, and C.-M. Teng (1992). A generic arc-consistency algorithm and its specialisations. *Artificial Intelligence 57*.

Van Hentenryck, P., H. Simonis, and M. Dincbas (1992). Constraint satisfaction using constraint logic programming. *Artificial Intelligence 58*.

Vilain, M. and H. Kautz (1986). Constraint propagation algorithms for temporal reasoning. In *Proc. AAAI-86*, pp. 377–382.

3. Foundations of Constraint Programming Approaches

3.1 Concurrent Semantics for Concurrent Constraint Programs

Francesca Rossi and Ugo Montanari

University of Pisa, Computer Science Department
Corso Italia 40, I-56125 Pisa, Italy
{ugo,rossi}@di.unipi.it

Abstract. A concurrent semantics is a semantics where concurrency can be realistically represented and naturally described. Therefore we believe that every concurrent language should be provided with a formal concurrent semantics. Here we describe three concurrent semantics for concurrent constraint (cc) programs. They are all based on partial order structures relating the various objects involved in the program computations, so that objects not related by the partial order are concurrent, and those related are instead dependent on each other and thus need to be sequentialized. Furthermore, they all employ a distributed representation of the constraint system, so that several sources of useless sequentializations are avoided. The first one is based on a graph-rewriting description of the operational behaviour of cc programs, and consists of a partial order involving all objects of each (equivalence class of) computation(s). The second one uses a simpler notion of context-dependent rewriting for the operational semantics, and consists of an event structure, which is able to represent both the concurrency and the non-determinism present in a cc program but which relates only the computation steps, and not the objects. The last one, instead, consists of a contextual net (that is, a Petri net extended with context condidities), which again represents both concurrency and nondeterminism and furthermore relates all objects and steps of the computations. The three semantics are compared and it is argued that the last one is the most suitable concurrent semantics for cc programs, since 1) contextual items are a general and elegant way of formalizing ask operations and avoiding their useless sequentialization, 2) nets allow a direct representation of concurrent information, as well as dependency and mutual exclusion (that is, nondeterminism). The information contained in any one of these semantics, possibly abstracted, can be of great help to a scheduler, in order to obtain an efficient execution of the program, or also to a compile-time optimizer.

3.1.1 Introduction

A concurrent semantics is a semantics where concurrency can be realistically represented and naturally described. We believe that every concurrent language should be provided with a formal concurrent semantics. In fact, this would allow a deeper understanding of the way concurrent agents interact, and such understanding could then be fruithfully used by a scheduler or a compile-time optimizer in order to make program execution more efficient.

Instead, concurrent languages are usually provided with a formal sequential semantics and an informal concurrent semantics. This allows to reason about simple properties of the programs, but usually not about complex ones. For example, semantics based on input-output relations or sequences of agent operations (like the ones already proposed for cc programs (Saraswat and Rinard 1990; Saraswat, Rinard, and Panangaden 1991; Boer and Palamidessi 1991)) are not able to provide enough knowledge about agent interaction, and therefore identify too many programs. We believe that two programs, one exhibiting intrinsic parallelism and the other one employing a sequentialization of the same operations should not be identified in any semantics which aims to being useful for the understanding, as well as the compile- and run-time optimization, of a given concurrent program.

Here we describe three concurrent semantics for concurrent constraint (cc) programs (Saraswat 1993). Such programs are based on a very simple model, consisting of a collection of concurrent agents sharing a set of variables which are subject to some constraints. Each agent may perform two basic operations over the common constraint: either add a new constraint (*tell* operation), or test whether a new constraint is entailed (*ask* operation). The constraints are defined and handled by an underlying constraint system, which can be described very generally as a set of primitive constraints and an entailment relation among subsets of them. This framework appears to be very general, in that it is able to express and encompass all the features of logic programming (Lloyd 1987), constraint logic programming (Jaffar and Lassez 1987), concurrent logic programming (Shapiro 1989), Linda-like programming, actor-based programming, and others.

The basic point, which all the semantics we describe in this paper rely on, is that a non-monolithic model of the shared store and of its communication with the agents is necessary if one wants to give a semantics to the cc framework which is both faithful and able to explicitly describe the maximal level of concurrency contained in any cc program. This consideration is the result of a study of the existing approaches to the semantics of cc programs and of the analysis of different approaches to the specification of concurrent systems.

More precisely, consider the previously proposed semantics for concurrent constraint programs. As far as we know, most of them are defined operationally, by adapting some of the classical techniques already used for process description languages like CCS and CSP. Some examples are the use of sequences of ask and tell operations ((Saraswat and Rinard 1990)), or also sequences of "assume" and tell ((Boer and Palamidessi 1991)) to describe a computation. All these attempts to give a formal semantics to the *cc* paradigm follow the SOS-style operational semantics ((Plotkin 1981)) and thus, while being successful in describing computation results or deadlock properties of a program, suffer of the typical pathologies of an interleaving semantics, i.e., of a semantics where concurrency is modelled by nondeterminism. It is easy to see that this approach is somewhat unrealistic, since processes which can be executed simultaneously are instead forced to be executed in a(ny) sequence, thus representing them exactly in the same way as two processes which could not be executed simultaneously. Therefore, some of the independency information among the parallel processes is lost, and thus there is no way to derive the real causal dependencies among the processes of a system. Furthermore, in concurrent systems where processes interact through a shared memory, the interleaving approach does not permit to derive information concerning the maximal parallelism in the use of such a memory. Thus any intelligent implementation which wants to exploit this information in order to increase efficiency cannot get it from the semantic analysis but instead has to obtain it from some other level of static or dynamic analysis. On the contrary, in the so-called "true-concurrency" approach, (which in the following we will simply refer to as the "concurrent" approach) interleaving is abandoned and the description of the simultaneous execution of parallel processes is formally allowed. Thus information about the maximal memory parallelism and the causal dependencies among processes can be formally obtained from the semantic analysis of a program. Moreover, it has been noted that a concurrent approach is also convenient when interested in fairness properties of a distributed system ((Peled and Pnueli 1990)). For these reasons we believe that a concurrent semantics for any concurrent paradigm, and for the cc paradigm in particular, would be very convenient and interesting.

Our approach to define a concurrent semantics for cc programs consists of the following. First we define the operational behaviour of the cc languages via a context-dependent rewriting system which is inherently concurrent and which treats uniformly the agents and the constraints, thus giving a non-monolithic interpretation of the underlying constraint system. This allows to avoid useless sequentializations and thus, in the concurrent semantics, to express a greater amount of concurrency. The operational semantics is then defined as the set of all sequences of rewriting steps starting from a given initial agent. Finally, we obtain the concurrent semantics from the operational semantics, or from the set of rewrite rules. Such concurrent semantics associates a structure, based on a partial order, to a class of computations. The partial order is essential, since it is used to model concurrency and dependency: objects related by the partial order are dependent and thus need to be sequentialized, while objects not related by the partial order are independent and thus can be executed (or can appear) simultaneously in a computation. Summarizing, the main common features of the three semantics are: 1) a uniform and non-monolithic representation of the the behaviour of the agents and the constraints, 2) a context-dependent rewriting formalism, and 3) a partial order structure for the concurrent semantics.

The first of the three concurrent semantics we present here employs the graph rewriting formalism (Ehrig 1978) to express the operational behaviour of cc programs. More precisely, the shared store is represented as a (hyper)graph, where nodes are variables and arcs are constraints or agents. Then, both the entailment relation of the underlying constraint system and the local behaviour of agents is expressed by suitable sets of graph productions, which transform the current global state of the system into a new one. Graph productions are a very useful tool, since they allow to represent realistically the ask operation, which is very important in cc programming, and which consists of checking that some constraint is entailed by the current store. Asked constraints, in fact, are represented by items which are needed for a production to take place but which are not affected (and that are called context items). Finally, each computation is represented by a graph derivation, form which then a partial order can be derived. Such partial order represents all those computations which differ only from the order in which concurrent steps are executed. This first semantics is a significant step forward from the usual SOS-style semantics for cc languages, and it has the merit of being the first attempt to give a concurrent semantics to cc programs (and also to graph grammars). However, it is not entirely satisfactory from the expressivity point of view. In fact, cc programs may contain several nondeterministic choices, but such choices cannot be seen in the partial order semantics. Instead, the ability to see them is crucial if one wants, for example, to reason about the level of or-parallelism contained in a program.

The second semantics extends the first one in order to capture not only the concurrency implicitly contained in a cc program, but also its nondeterminism. We start by defining in a novel way the operational behaviour of cc programs. Instead of using graph rewriting, we adopt simpler context-dependent rewrite rules, which however maintain those features of graph rewriting which are very useful for our purposes. As before, the evolution of each of the agents in a cc program, as well as the declarations of the program and its underlying constraint system, are all expressible by sets of such rules. In this way each computation step, i.e., the application of one of such rules, represents either the evolution of an agent, or the expansion of a declaration, or the entailment of some new token. Then, from each computation, an event structure (Winskel 1986) (and not a partial order) is associated to each program. Such event structure is simply a set of events together with a causal dependency and a mutual exclusion relation among them. Each event in the event structure represents a single computation step in a cc program, while the causal dependency relation induces a partial order among events in the same computation (to be interpreted as in the first semantics), and the mutual exclusion relation provides a way of expressing nondeterministic information (and thus different computations). In this way, a structure alone (and not a set of structures) is able to represent all possible deterministic computations of the given cc program. This is a significant advance over the first concurrent semantics, since this semantics is able to represent in a unique structure the maximal level of both nondeterminism and concurrency available in the given program and in its underlying constraint system.

The third semantics increases the expressive power of the second one by adopting not event structures, but nondeterministic contextual nets. The advantage is that the three relations (concurrency, dependency, and mutual exclusion) involve now not only the computation steps but also the objects involved in the computations. The operational behaviour is represented as in the second semantics (that is, via context-dependent rewrite rules). However, the construction which allowed to pass from such rules to the event structure is now modified in order to get a contextual net. A contextual net ((Montanari and Rossi 1993a)) is just a Petri net ((Reisig 1985)) where each event may have context conditions, besides the usual pre- and post-conditions. In this way a context object is an object which is checked for presence (or, in some sense, read), but which is not consumed, and represent faithfully the context items used in the rewriting formalism adopted for describing the operational behaviour. As in event structures, also from a contextual occurrence net it is possible to derive three relations among its objects (either conditions or events), describing respectively the causal dependency, the mutual exclusion, and the concurrency among such objects, which can then be interpreted as describing, respectively, the temporal precedence, the possible simultaneity, and the nondeterministic choices among both steps and objects of cc computations.

From this last semantics it is possible to obtain the first two. In fact, by restricting the obtained contextual net to subnets without mutual exclusion, we get essentially the partial orders defined in the first semantics. Instead, by restricting its relations to the events only (and forgetting the objects of the net), we get the event structure defined in the second semantics. The second and the third semantics are very close in spirit, since both of them are based on an unfolding construction which generates the semantics structure (event structure or contextual net) from a cc program. However, the second semantics is in some sense easier to understand, since it does not need the additional concept of contextual nets in order to be developed.

We have started applying our concurrent semantics to various optimization tasks. In particular, we have used the semantics based on contextual nets to improve the analysis needed in order to parallelize (C)LP goals in a way which is both correct and efficient (Bueno, de la Banda, Hermenegildo, Rossi, and Montanari 1993). The advantage of using our approach consists of 1) a formal description of the parallel execution model, and 2) the possibility of recognizing much more parallelism. In fact, our semantics describes the parallelism at the smallest level of granularity. Therefore goals which appeared to be not parallelizable at all in the usual approach (Hermenegildo and Rossi 1990; de la Banda, Hermenegildo, and Marriott 1993) because of conflicts in small subparts of their execution trees, here they can be partially parallelizable.

The paper is organized as follows. Section 3.1.2 describes the cc framework. Then Section 3.1.3 presents the partial order semantics Section 3.1.4 defines the event structure semantics, and Section 3.1.5 gives the contextual net semantics. Finally, Section 3.1.6 concludes the paper by pointing at possible future developments of our concurrent semantics approach.

Subparts of this paper appeared already. The partial order semantics has been described in (Montanari and Rossi 1991) and in (Montanari and Rossi 1992), contextual nets have been proposed in (Montanari and Rossi 1993a), and the contextual net semantics has been written in (Montanari and Rossi 1993b). Moreover, the partial order and the event structure semantics are also contained in (Rossi 1993).

3.1.2 Concurrent Constraint Programming

A cc program (Saraswat 1993; Saraswat and Rinard 1990; Saraswat, Rinard, and Panangaden 1991) consists of a set of agents interacting through a shared store, which is a set of constraints on some variables. The framework is parametric w.r.t. the kind of constraints that can be handled. The concurrent agents do not communicate with each other, but only with the shared store, by either checking if it entails a given constraint (ask operation) or adding a new constraint to it (tell operation). Therefore computations proceed by monotonically accumulating information (that is, constraints) to the shared store. The following grammar describes the cc language we consider:

$P ::= F.A$
$F ::= p(\mathbf{x}) :: A \mid F.F$
$A ::= success \mid failure \mid tell(c) \rightarrow A \mid \sum_{i=1,\ldots,n} ask(c_i) \rightarrow A_i \mid A \parallel A \mid \exists \mathbf{x}.A \mid$
$p(\mathbf{x})$

where P is the class of programs, F is the class of sequences of procedure declarations, A is the class of agents, c ranges over constraints, and $\mathbf{x}$ is a tuple of variables. Each procedure is defined once, thus nondeterminism is expressed via the + combinator only (which is here denoted by $\sum$). We also assume that, in $p(\mathbf{x}) :: A$, $vars(A) \subseteq \mathbf{x}$, where $vars(A)$ is the set of all variables occurring free in agent A. In a program $P = F.A$, A is called initial agent, to be executed in the context of the set of declarations F.

Agent "$\sum_{i=1,...,n} ask(c_i) \rightarrow A_i$" behaves as a set of guarded agents A_i, where the success of the guard $ask(c_i)$ coincides with the entailment of the constraint c_i by the current store. If instead c_i is inconsistent with the current store, then the guard fails. Lastly, if c_i is not entailed but it is consistent with the current store, then the guarded agent gets suspended. No particular order of selection of the guarded agents is assumed, and only one of the choices is taken. In an "atomic" interpretation of the tell operation, agent "tell(c) $\rightarrow$ A" adds constraint c to the current store and then, if the resulting store is consistent, behaves like A, otherwise it fails; in an "eventual" interpretation of the tell, this same agent adds c to the store (without any consistency check) and then behaves like A (if the resulting store is inconsistent this will result in an uncontrolled behaviour of the system, since from now on all ask operations will succeed). In this paper we adopt the eventual interpretation of the tell operation. This choice is related to the way the underlying constraint system is modelled, as we will see later. Agent $A_1 \parallel A_2$ behaves like A_1 and A_2 executing in parallel, agent $\exists x.A$ behaves like agent A, except that the variables in x are local to A, and agent $p(x)$ is a call of procedure p.

Given a program P, in the following we will refer to $Ag(P)$ as the set of all agents (and subagents) occurring in P, i.e., all the elements of type A occurring in a derivation of P according to the above grammar.

In the cc paradigm, the underlying constraint system can be described ((Saraswat, Rinard, and Panangaden 1991)) as a *system of partial information* (derived from the *information system* introduced in (Scott 1982)) of the form $\langle D, \vdash \rangle$ where D is a set of *tokens* (or primitive constraints) and $\vdash \subseteq \wp(D) \times D$ is the entailment relation which states which tokens are entailed by which sets of other tokens. The relation $\vdash$ has to satisfy the following axioms:

$u \vdash x$ if $x \in u$ (reflexivity), and
$u \vdash x$ if $v \vdash x$ and, for all $y \in v$, $u \vdash y$ (transitivity).

Given D, $\mid D \mid$ is the set of all subsets of D closed under entailment. Then, a constraint in a constraint system $\langle D, \vdash \rangle$ is simply an element of $\mid D \mid$ (that is, a set of tokens).

Each pair $\langle S, t \rangle$ of the entailment relation $\vdash$ can be seen as an ask agent of the form $ask(S) \rightarrow tell(t) \rightarrow success$ (although we should assure that such agent is executed atomically; however, we do not deal with atomicity issues in this paper). This uniformity of agents and pairs of the entailment relation will be rather useful in the next section, where we will model both of them within the same formalism.

Note also that there is no notion of consistency in a system of partial information. This means that inconsistency has to be modelled through entailment. More precisely, the convention is that D contains a $\perp$ element which is entailed by any inconsistent set of tokens. We will see later that this implies that adding a constraint inconsistent with the current store means that "sooner or later" $\perp$

will be generated by the entailment relation. This is the reason why we consider the eventual interpretation of the tell operation.

3.1.3 The Partial Order Semantics

In the *cc* framework, the global state can be described by the current set of active agents and of already generated tokens which are contained in the shared store. Both processes and tokens involve (and possibly share) some variables, thus the idea is to consider a (hyper)graph where nodes represent the current variables and (hyper)arcs represent the current tokens and agents. Notice that both agents and tokens are here uniformly expressed as arcs in such a graph, and this makes clear that they are in fact very similar in nature. In fact, they both can be thought of as constraints which are defined by the user (via the program) or by the system (via the entailment relation) respectively.

Then, each computation step, which may involve either the evolution of an agent or the generation of (entailed) constraints by the entailment relation, is represented by a graph production, which rewrites a part of the current graph into another graph. A computation is therefore any finite or infinite sequence of graphs and graph rewriting steps. Notice again that usually the evolution of the store via the entailment relation is not observed at all, or it is considered at a lower level w.r.t. the agents' description. The fact that both can instead be represented at the same level is important, since it means that part of the entailment relation, which is usually defined at the constraint system level, can be described at the program level, and viceversa, that some programs can be built-in in the constraint system. Or, in other words, that the constraint system is not fixed once and for all, but can be tailored to the needs of the user.

From each computation it is possible to derive a suitable partial ordering among agents and tokens which have been generated and used in the program. Such a partial ordering is exactly what describes the causal dependencies among the agents (via the tokens), and thus gives the basis to obtain the desired knowledge about the degree of parallelism. The way we obtain such a partial ordering is by defining an occurrence net (Reisig 1985) corresponding to each computation. In fact, occurrence nets automatically induce a corresponding partial ordering.

Graph rewriting is not simply one among many formalisms that we could possibly choose to describe the behaviour of agents and tokens in a *cc* program. On the contrary, we feel that it allows us to describe in a very natural and elegant way all the main ingredients of *cc* programming and thus can be regarded as a powerful "abstract machine" for the execution of such programs. In fact, hypergraphs are a natural way to describe objects sharing variables (i.e., nodes), like agents and constraints are. Also, hyperarcs are able to describe in a uniform way both agents and tokens, and graph productions can express, again uniformly, their behaviour. Furthermore, the possibility of checking elements without consuming them and of performing a generalized read (i.e., an ask), which are fundamental issues in cc programming, can easily be expressed in the algebraic representation of graph productions (Ehrig 1978).

3.1.3.1 Operational Semantics The global state in a cc program can be described by the current set of active processes and of already generated tokens, which are contained in the shared store. Both processes and tokens involve (and possibly share) some variables, thus a a state will be represented by a graph where nodes represent the current variables and arcs the current tokens and agents.

Definition 1 (graph) *A labelled (hyper)graph $H = (N, A, c, l)$ consists of*

- *a set of nodes N,*

- *a set of (hyper)arcs A,*

- *a connection function $c : A \to \cup_k N^k$, and*

- *a labelling function $l : A \to L$, where L is a set of labels.*

Given a graph G, we will write $arcs(G)$ to denote the set of its (hyper)arcs. ∎

Graphs are defined here up to isomorphism, i.e., two graphs are not distinguishable if they are isomorphic to each other. The labelling function is needed, since, intuitively, arc labels represent agents and arcs represent instances of agents, i.e. processes. Thus we need to distinguish between different instances of the same agent. This problem already occurs for logic programming, where we may have to faithfully model two or more copies of the same atomic formulas in the same goal. In the setting of a concurrent semantics of cc programming, this situation is even more evident, since different instances of tokens and agents may have different causes and thus have to be kept distinct. Thus, in the following definition of a state, we need both agents and agent instances (the same applies also to tokens).

Definition 2 (state) *Given a set of variables X, a set of agents $Ag = \{ag_1, \ldots, ag_n\}$, a set of occurrences of each of such agents, i.e., $\{ag_{i1}, \ldots, ag_{il(i)}\}$ for $i = 1, \ldots, n$, and a set of tokens $T = \{t_1, \ldots, t_m\}$ with their occurrences $\{t_{i1}, \ldots, t_{ik(i)}\}$ for $i = 1, \ldots, m$, (where all the above occurrences of tokens and agents involve subsets of X), a state is a graph (N, A, c, l) where*

- $N = X$,

- $A = \bigcup_{i=1,\ldots,n} \{ag_{i1}, \ldots, ag_{il(i)}\} \cup \bigcup_{j=1,\ldots,m} \{t_{i1}, \ldots, t_{ik(i)}\}$,

- $c(ag_{ih}) = vars(ag_i)$ *for $i = 1, \ldots, n$ and $h = 1, \ldots, l(i)$, and*
  $c(t_{ih}) = vars(t_i)$ *for $i = 1, \ldots, m$ and $h = 1, \ldots, k(i)$, where $vars(e)$ is the tuple (not the set) of variables occurring free in e,*

- $l(ag_{ih}) = ag_i$ for $i \leq n$, $h = 1, \ldots, l(i)$, $l(t_{ij}) = t_i$
  for $i \leq n$, $h = 1, \ldots, k(i)$. ∎

In the following, we will always consider occurrences of agents and tokens, but for the sake of brevity we will call them agents and tokens respectively.

Note that a state, as defined above, can contain sets of tokens which are not closed under entailment and thus cannot be called constraints. Instead, the *cc* store is typically defined as containing, at any moment, only constraints and not arbitrary sets of tokens. The reason for this apparent discrepancy is that our model of the entailment relation is "lazy", in the sense that, as we will see in detail later, the entailment relation is represented by a set of productions which possibly will, in a finite number of steps, generate all entailed tokens which are needed by any other production to be applicable. In fact, any production needs only a finite number of arcs in order to be applicable (those arcs in its left side), and each of such arcs is generated by a finite number of applications of the entailment productions. Our approach eliminates the need to give higher priority to the productions for the entailment relation, and thus is preferable in distributed frameworks. Note, however, that the two approaches are equivalent in settings, like ours, where only causal dependency information is important.

As an example, let us consider a state where the store contains $\{x = 3, y = 3, x = y\}$, and there are two agents: $a_1 = p(x, z)$ and $a_2 = q(z, y)$. Then the state can be represented by the graph in Figure 3.1, where nodes are circles and arcs are lines connecting all the involved variables. Note that hyperarcs are directed, according to their connection function. However, we will usually draw them without a direction to simplify the pictures. Also, note that unary arcs are drawn as a loop around the only connected node.

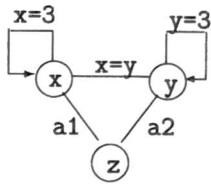

Fig. 3.1. A graph representing a state of a *cc* computation.

This representation of the global state of a *cc* system highlights the fact that tokens and agents are very similar. However, we will see that they are very different in one important respect: tokens, once generated, are never removed, while agents evolve only by disappearing and creating new agents.

At each moment of a computation, new constraints may be generated and added to the current store because of the accomplishment of some operation by one or more of the active agents. In particular, let us consider the two basic operations in the *cc* framework: ask and tell.

If an active agent (i.e., an agent occurring in the current state) wants to tell a constraint c to the store, it will add the tokens in c to the current store (assuming that the current store is consistent with c), and will transform itself into another agent. This can be modelled by changing the graph representing the current state in such a way that the arc representing the active agent is deleted, and the arcs representing the tokens in c are added, together with an arc representing the new active agent.

On the other hand, if an active agent asks the constraint c, then this can be modelled by checking if the tokens in c occur in the current state, and, if so, by deleting the arc representing such an agent and adding the new arc representing a new active agent.

An important observation is the following: the entailment check involved in the accomplishment of an ask operation can be modelled by a change in the graph as well. In fact, each entailment pair $< s, t >$, where s is a set of tokens and t is a token, and which means that $s \vdash t$, can be represented by the addition of the token t to the current graph if the tokens in s are already there. Thus entailment check and agent operations are both modelled by graph changes, which may be formally described by graph productions.

The following definitions are based on the algebraic approach to graph rewriting, as summarized for example in (Ehrig 1978). Such approach is able to provide a satisfactory, elegant, and convenient formal description of graph productions and all their properties. In our setting, its power is clear in many respects. Among the others, it has the possibility of elegantly representing arcs which are tested for existence but not rewritten (like those representing asked constraints).

Definition 3 (graph production) *A graph production p is a pair of graph morphisms $l : K \to L$ and $r : K \to R$, such that l is a isomorphism over nodes and both l and r are injective. L, R, and K are called left side, right side, and interface of p, respectively.*∎

In the above definition, given two graphs G and H, a graph morphism f from G to H, written $f : G \to H$, consists of a pair of functions, mapping nodes and arcs repectively, which are compatible with the connection and labelling functions. Graph productions may be defined in a more general way by not restricting l and r to be injective. However, the above definition is not restrictive for our purposes, since we always have such properties when modelling cc agents as graph productions.

Definition 4 (direct derivation) *Given a production $p = (L \xleftarrow{l} K \xrightarrow{r} R)$, a graph G, and a graph morphism $g : L \to G$, called an occurrence of L in G, there exists a direct derivation from G to G' iff the diagram in Figure 3.2 can be built, where both squares are pushouts. In the following we will represent a double pushout construction by the tuple of all the objects involved, i.e., we will* *write:* $PO =< p, g, k, h, h_1, h_2, G, H, G' >$, *where* $p = (L \xleftarrow{l} K \xrightarrow{r} R)$ *and the names correspond to those in Figure 3.2.*∎

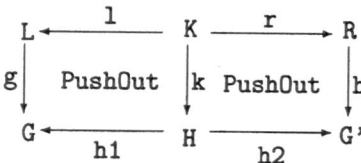

Fig. 3.2. The double pushout construction.

The formal definition of a pushout can be found in (Lane 1971). However, we may informally describe the application of a production p to G as follows: in the pushout to the left, the occurrence of L in G identified by g is removed (except for the image of K in L) to produce H; in the pushout to the right, G' is built as the disjoint union of R and H, where the nodes and arcs in $r(K)$ and in $k(K)$ are identified. Thus, while K represents the part of G which is rewritten but remains unchanged (i.e. the nodes and the arcs which are not deleted), H represents the part of G which is not rewritten at all.

Definition 5 (entailment as graph productions) *Given a constraint system* $< D, \vdash >$, *the set of graph productions associated to it, written* $Prod(< D, \vdash >)$, *is the set of all productions* $p_i = (L_i \xleftarrow{l_i} K_i \xrightarrow{r_i} R_i)$ *such that* $< s_i, t_i >\in\vdash$, L_i *and* K_i *are both the state representing* s_i *and* l_i *is its identity morphism,* R_i *is the state representing* s_i *and* t_i *together, and* r_i *is the obvious injection of* K_i *into* R_i.∎

In words, each production representing a pair $< s, t >$ of the entailment relation adds token t if all tokens in s are already in the current graph. Note that the tokens in s are not deleted, and this is simply modelled by the fact that the interface K of the production contains them.

For example, the production representing the entailment pair $< \{x = 3, x = y\}, y = 3 >$ and its application to a graph H to produce a new graph H' is given in Figure 3.3.

Definition 6 (tell as a graph production)
Given an agent $ag = tell(c) \rightarrow ag'$, *the graph production associated to it, called* $prod(ag)$, *is defined as* $p = (L \xleftarrow{l} K \xrightarrow{r} R)$, *where* L *is the state representing* ag, R *is the state representing* ag' *and* c, K *is iso to the set of nodes in* L, *and* l *and* r *are the obvious injections of* K *into* L *and* R *respectively.*∎

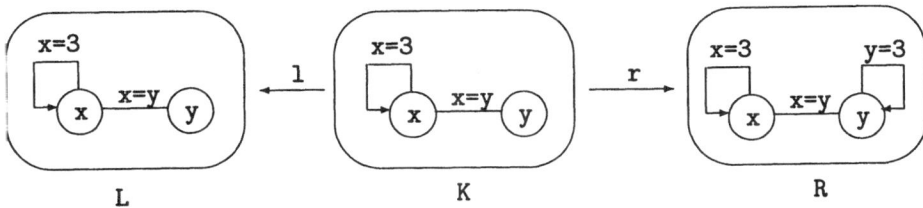

Fig. 3.3. A production for the pair $< \{x = 3, x = y\}, y = 3 >$ of the entailment relation.

Notice that the production associated to a tell agent, by itself, "implements" the eventual interpretation of a tell operation, since the constraint is added to the store even though it may lead to an inconsistency. However, it is important to stress that the atomic interpretation of the tell operation can be expressed by simply associating a suitable applicability condition to this same production. The production representing the agent $ag = tell(x = 3) \rightarrow ag'(x, z)$ is given in Figure 3.4.

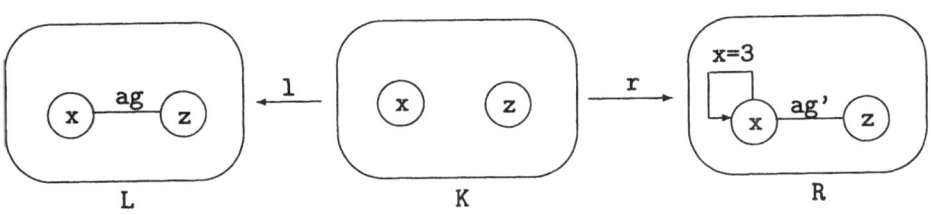

Fig. 3.4. A production for the agent $ag = tell(x = 3) \rightarrow ag'(x, z)$.

Definition 7 (nondeterministic composition as graph productions)
Given an agent $ag = \sum_{i=1}^{n} ask(c_i) \rightarrow ag_i$, n graph productions $prod_1, \ldots, prod_n$ are associated to it. If $prod_i = (L_i \xleftarrow{l_i} K_i \xrightarrow{r_i} R_i)$, then L_i is the state representing ag and c_i, R_i is the state representing ag_i, c_i, and all the nodes in L_i, K_i is the state representing c_i and all the nodes in L_i, and l_i and r_i are the obvious injections of K_i into L_i and R_i.∎

As the above definition formally says, to model the nondeterministic composition of agents we create a graph production for each branch of the nondeterministic choice. At the language level, nondeterminism arises whenever different branches are enabled (i.e., their ask constraints are all entailed by the current store). Such situation is represented in our setting by the fact that all the productions corresponding to such branches are appliable. Note that, contrarily to the Prolog underlying interpreter, which is deterministic and thus needs a precise selection rule to resolve the language level nondeterminism, our graph rewriting abstract machine is nondeterministic, and therefore implements directly the nondeterministic operator of the cc framework. This means that when several productions are applicable, one of them will be nondeterministically chosen and applied.

An example of the productions associated to the nondeterministic agent $ag(x, y, z) = ask(x = 3) \rightarrow ag_1(x, y) + ask(y = 3) \rightarrow ag_2(y, z)$ is given in Figure 3.5.

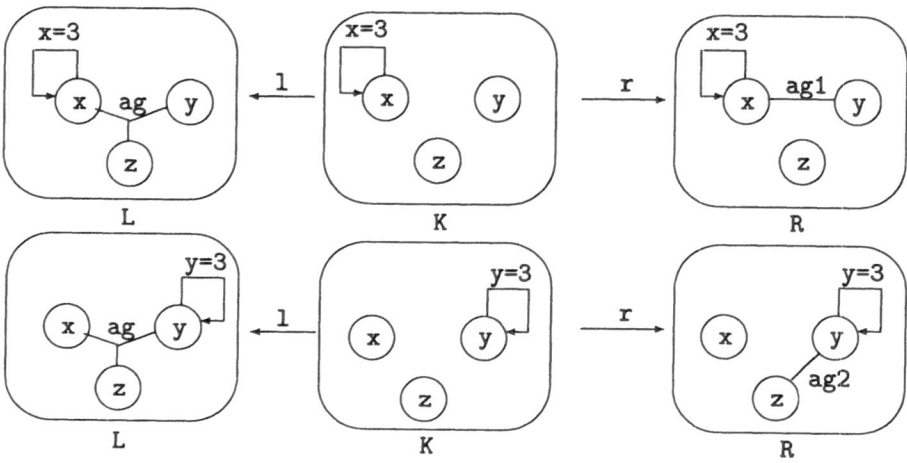

Fig. 3.5. The productions for the agent $ag(x, y, z) = ask(x = 3) \rightarrow ag_1(x, y) + ask(y = 3) \rightarrow ag_2(y, z)$.

Definition 8 (parallel composition as a graph production)
Given an agent $ag = ag_1 \parallel ag_2$, the graph production associated to it, called $prod(ag)$, is defined as $p = (L \xleftarrow{l} K \xrightarrow{r} R)$, where L is the state representing ag, R is the state representing ag_1 and ag_2, K is iso to the set of nodes in L, and l and r are the obvious injections of K into L and R.∎

An example of a production associated to the parallel agent $ag(x, y, z) = ag_1(x, y) \parallel ag_2(y, z)$ is given in Figure 3.6.

Definition 9 (hiding as a graph production) *Given an agent $ag = \exists X.ag'$, the graph production associated to it, called $prod(ag)$, is defined as*

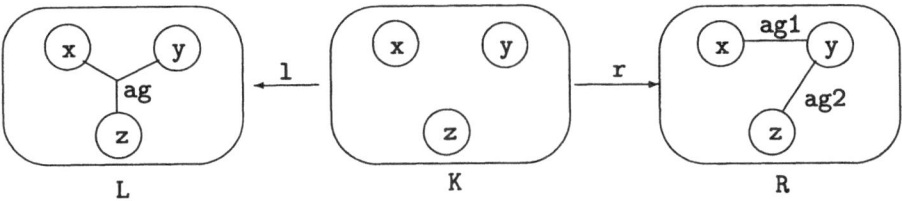

Fig. 3.6. A production for the agent $ag(x, y, z) = ag_1(x, y) \parallel ag_2(y, z)$.

$p = (L \xleftarrow{l} K \xrightarrow{r} R)$, where L is the state representing ag, R is the state representing ag', K is iso to the set of nodes in L, and l and r are the obvious injections of K into L and R.■

Note that the production associated to the hiding combinator is the only one which can add nodes, which are then considered as local variables of the generated subgraph. All the other productions leave the set of nodes unchanged. An example of a production associated to the agent $ag(x) = \exists v.ag'(x, v)$ is given in Figure 3.7.

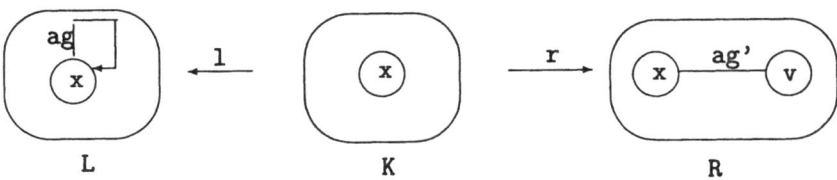

Fig. 3.7. A production for the agent $ag(x, y, z) = \exists v.ag'(x, v)$.

Note that not all agents have one or more associated productions. In fact, the agents of the form $p(X)$ do not generate any production. It is their declaration, if any, which generates the appropriate productions for their evolution.

Definition 10 (clause as a graph production) *Given a clause* $C = (H :: ag)$, *the graph production associated to it, called* $prod(C)$, *is defined as* $p = (L \xleftarrow{l} K \xrightarrow{r} R)$, *where* L *is the state representing* H, R *is the state representing* ag *and all the variables in* H, K *is iso to the set of nodes in* L, *and* l *and* r *are the obvious injections of* K *into* L *and* R.■

An example of a production associated to the clause $p(x, y, z) :: ag(x, z)$ is given in Figure 3.8.

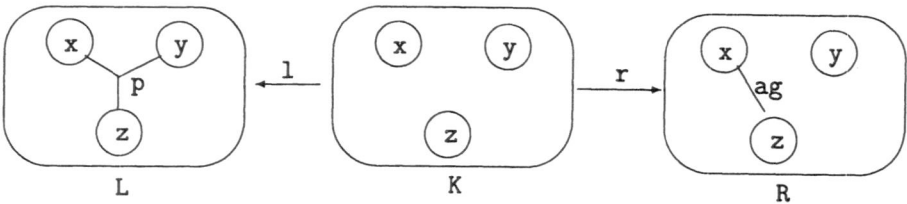

Fig. 3.8. A production for the clause $p(x, y, z) :: ag(x, z)$.

Given a *cc* program, together with the underlying constraint system, we can consider the set of all productions associated to all agents occurring in the program and to the entailment relation, as described in the previous sections. This set can be formalized in a more structured way by the concept of a graph rewriting system.

Definition 11 (graph rewriting systems and derivations) *A graph rewriting system $GG = (G_0, PP, V)$ consists of an initial graph G_0, a set of productions PP, and an alphabet V. A derivation (of length n) for GG is a finite sequence of double pushout constructions $(PO_1, PO_2, \dots, PO_n)$, where $PO_i = < p_i, g_i, k_i, h_i, h_{i1}, h_{i2}, G_{i-1}, H_i, G_i >$ (and $p_i = (L_i \xleftarrow{l_i} K_i \xrightarrow{r_i} R_i)$), thus such that PO_i is a direct derivation from G_{i-1} to G_i, for $i = 1, \dots, n$.∎*

Definition 12 (*cc* programs as graph rewriting systems) *Given a cc program $P = Decl.A$, and a constraint system $< D, \vdash >$, the graph rewriting system associated to them is $GG = (G_0, PP, V)$, where*

- *G_0 is the state representing A,*

- *$PP = Prod(\vdash) \cup \{prod(ag) \text{ for all } ag \in Ag(P)\} \cup \{prod(d) \text{ for all procedure declarations } d \text{ in } P\}$, and*

- *$V = D \cup Ag(P)$.∎*

Notice that the set of productions associated to a program is always finite, since the program contains a finite number of agents and declarations. However, the set of productions representing the entailment relation of the underlying constraint system can in general be infinite.

3.1.3.2 The Concurrent Semantics Given a *cc* program and its constraint system, the operational meaning of such a program is thus described by all the derivations of the associated graph rewriting system. Depending on what we are interested in, we may choose to observe only some of such derivations.

For example, we may choose to disregard all those derivations whose last graph represents an inconsistent set of tokens, or also all infinite derivations. Or, which is very natural in the cc setting, we may decide to observe only those derivations leading to a state with no agents.

A naive way to give a semantics to the program from the selected set of derivations is to consider the set of all their result graphs, which represents the set of all possible final stores in cc computations. However, this formalization does not give any knowledge about the possible parallelism degree in successful derivations, even though such information is implicitly contained in them. This is the reason why we propose to associate a suitable occurrence net which is the simplest kind of Petri net) to each derivation. This occurrence net relates agents and tokens and represents the causal dependencies among them. From such a net, different partial orderings can automatically be derived, depending, again, on what we want to observe.

In general, having a causal dependency structure (like both occurrence nets and partial orders are) as the semantics of a given program is important for several reasons. First of all, as we already said, such structure allows to derive information about the maximal degree of parallelism in the program and thus to efficiently allocate processes to processors. Furthermore, debugging or testing the program becomes much more efficient, since performing the test with the information in the causal dependency structure coincides with performing the same test over all its linearizations. As an example, a specific application of such efficient testing methodology is the use of an intelligent backtracking technique in logic programming ((Codognet, Codognet, and Filé 1988)). Such technique consists in backtracking not to the last refuted goal, but to the closest one which the failing goal is dependent on. Thus, it is evident that having a structure containing the causal dependencies among the goals allows to eliminate many redundant refutation steps and thus to speed up the execution of any non-deterministic logic program.

For a formal and comprehensive treatment of Petri nets and occurrence nets see (Reisig 1985). Here we will only give the definitions necessary for our approach.

Definition 13 ((Petri) nets) *A net N is a triple (S, T, F) where*

- $S \cap T = \emptyset$;

- $F \subseteq (S \times T) \cup (T \times S)$. ∎

Definition 14 (pre-set and post-set) *Given a net $N = (S, T, F)$ and an element $x \in S \cup T$, its pre-set if the set ${}^\bullet x = \{y \mid F(y, x)\}$, and its post-set is the set $x^\bullet = \{y \mid F(x, y)\}$.* ∎

A traditional interpretation of a net is the following: the elements of S are considered as being "conditions", and the elements of T are instead "events".

A set of conditions, called *case*, represents the global state of the net. If a case c *enables* a transition t, i.e., ${}^{\bullet}t \subseteq c$, then *firing* t brings the net from case c to case $(c - {}^{\bullet}t) \cup t^{\bullet}$. Note that, by the definition of F, there is no possibility to relate two events or two conditions, but only one event and one condition, or viceversa. This refers to the classical interpretation of nets, which, assuming to move upon a continue time domain, associates a closed interval to each event and an open one to each condition. In this way, a computation is a sequence of closed and open intervals, where two open (or closed) intervals are never adjacent.

Definition 15 (occurrence nets) *A net $N = (S, T, F)$ is an occurrence net iff*

- F^+ *(i.e., the transitive closure of F) is irreflexive;*

- $\forall s \in S, \mid {}^{\bullet}s \mid \leq 1$ *and* $\mid s^{\bullet} \mid \leq 1.$ ∎

That is, an occurrence net is a Petri net without cycles and such that each event can be enabled by (and can enable) at most one condition. That is, an occurrence net can be seen as the unfolding of a Petri net computation, where every choice has already been done.

Theorem 1 (from occurrence nets to partial orderings ((Reisig 1985))) *Given an occurrence net $N = (S, T, F)$, we have that $P(N) = (T, (F^*)_{|_T})$, where $(F^*)_{|_T}$ is the reflexive and transitive closure of F restricted to T, is a partial ordering.* ∎

The construction of this partial ordering which relates only events is very common in concurrency theory, since it is very important to know when two or more events are independent from each other, and thus can occur concurrently. Intuitively, two events are considered to be concurrent if none of them causes the other one. The formal definition follows.

Definition 16 (concurrent events) *Given a partial ordering $P(N) = (T, \leq)$, two distinct events e and e' in T are said to be concurrent iff neither $e \leq e'$ nor $e' \leq e$ holds.* ∎

Definition 17 (from derivations to occurrence nets) *Given a finite derivation $D = (PO_1, PO_2, \ldots, PO_n)$, where $PO_i = <p_i, g_i, k_i, h_i, h_{i1}, h_{i2}, G_{i-1}, H_i, G_i>$ and $p_i = (L_i \xleftarrow{l_i} K_i \xrightarrow{r_i} R_i)$, for $i = 1, \ldots, n$, let us set $E = \{e_1, \ldots, e_n\}$, $B = \{<a, i>, a \in arcs(G_i)\}$, for $i = 0, \ldots, n$, and $C = \{[a, i], a \in arcs(K_i)\}$. Then, let us define the relation F by using the following inference rules (where $i = 1, \ldots, n$):*

- $a \in arcs(H_i),\ a \notin arcs(k_i(K_i))$ **implies** $<h_{i1}(a), i-1> \equiv <h_{i2}(a), i>;$

- $a \in arcs(L_i),\ a \notin arcs(l_i(K_i))$ **implies** $<g_i(a), i-1> F e_i;$

- $a \in arcs(R_i)$, $a \notin arcs(r_i(K_i))$ **implies** $e_i F < h_i(a), i >$;

- $a \in arcs(K_i)$ **implies**

  - $< h_{i1}(k_i(a)), i - 1 > \equiv < h_{i2}(k_i(a)), i >$;
  - $[a, i] F e_i$;
  - $bF < h_{i1}(k_i(a)), i - 1 >$ **implies** $bF[a, i]$;

- $a \equiv b$ **implies**

  - $a' F a$ **implies** $a' F b$;
  - $a F a'$ **implies** $b F a'$.

Then, the occurrence net associated to D is $N(D) = (B_{|_\equiv} \cup C, E, F)$.∎

First we will explain informally the above definition, and then we will show that $N(D)$ is indeed an occurrence net.

There are different kinds of arcs in a graph which is being rewritten by the application of a production: those which are not involved in the production (i.e, all the arcs a such that $a \in arcs(H_i)$ and $a \notin arcs(k_i(K_i))$), those which are consumed by the production ($a \in arcs(L_i)$ but $a \notin arcs(l_i(K_i))$), those which are generated by the production ($a \in arcs(R_i)$ and $a \notin arcs(r_i(K_i))$), and finally those which are checked for presence but not consumed ($a \in arcs(K_i)$). Each of these kinds of arcs interact in a different way with the event associated to the applied production. The above definition has one item for each of these kinds of arcs. Now we will try to explain informally what they mean. First we have to say that the intuitive understanding of aFb is that b depends on a, or, alternatively, that a causes b.

The first item ($a \in arcs(H_i)$, $a \notin arcs(k_i(K_i))$ implies $< h_{i1}(a), i - 1 > \equiv < h_{i2}(a), i >$) simply states that all those arcs of G_{i-1} which are left unchanged by the application of the production ($a \in arcs(H_i)$), and which do not appear in its left hand side ($a \notin arcs(k_i(K_i))$), should be identified with the corresponding arcs of G_i. This means that such arcs do not generate any dependency with the event e_i and/or with the other arcs involved in the production application. Note that, as the last item says, the identification of two arcs implies that each of them inherits the dependencies of the other one.

The second item ($a \in arcs(L_i)$, $a \notin arcs(l_i(K_i))$ implies $< g_i(a), i-1 > F e_i$) generates a dependency of the event e_i on all those arcs in its left hand side ($a \in arcs(L_i)$) which are consumed by the production ($a \notin arcs(l_i(K_i))$). In fact, these arcs are necessary in order to apply such a production.

The third item ($a \in arcs(R_i)$, $a \notin arcs(r_i(K_i))$ implies $e_i F < h_i(a), i >$) means that the event e_i causes all those arcs which are in G_i but which were not in G_{i-1}. In fact, the presence of such arcs in G_i is only due to the application of the production corresponding to e_i.

The fourth item concerns all those arcs which are checked for presence by the production but are not consumed (since they appear in K_i, and thus they also have to appear in R_i). Intuitively, these arcs are necessary for the application of the production (and thus e_i should be dependent on them), but at the same time they should be maintained in G_i (and thus there should be corresponding arcs in G_i which are identified with those in G_{i-1}). The identification is accomplished by "$< h_{i1}(k_i(a)), i-1 > \equiv < h_{i2}(k_i(a)), i >$". Then, to model the dependency of the event e_i on such arcs, but not on the events which already used them, we consider a copy of the arc, called $[a, i]$, and we set $[a, i]Fe_i$. Lastly, to propagate the dependencies of the original arc to its copies, we have that $bF < h_{i1}(k_i(a)), i - 1 >$ implies $bF[a, i]$.

Note that other sets of inference rules could give a correct set of dependencies. However, our choice was guided by the desire to obtain an occurrence net, and not only a partial ordering, since occurrence nets (and in general Petri nets) are the classical way of giving a true-concurrency description of the behaviour of a distributed system.

Given a derivation of length n, the construction of the relation F is accomplished by following the derivation step by step, that is by adding elements to the relation at each of the n steps. This means that, considering the first i steps, we already know all the causal dependencies among elements (arcs and events) appearing in such steps, i.e., no later step can add dependencies involving only elements in previous steps.

Consider a simple example where we have the agent
$ag(x, y, z) = tell(x = 3) \rightarrow (ask(x = 3) \rightarrow p(x, y)) \| (ask(x = 3) \rightarrow q(x, z))$.
This agent can be defined in terms of its subagents
$ag_1(x, y, z) = tell(x = 3) \rightarrow ag_2(x, y, z)$
$ag_2(x, y, z) = ag_3(x, y) \| ag_4(x, z)$
$ag_3(x, y) = ask(x = 3) \rightarrow p(x, y)$
$ag_4(x, z) = ask(x = 3) \rightarrow q(x, z)$
such that one production is associated to each of the above subagents.

Let us assume that the initial graph represents $ag_1(x, y, z)$ (and no constraints), and that the production corresponding to ag_1 is applied first, then the one for ag_2, then the one for ag_3, and finally the one for ag_4. Then we have $E = \{e_1, e_2, e_3, e_4\}$, and by considering the first step (i.e., the application of the production for ag_1) we have that $< ag_1, 0 > Fe_1$, $e_1F < (x = 3), 1 >$, and $e_1F < ag_2, 1 >$. Then the application of the second production will add the following elements to the relation F: $< ag_2, 1 > Fe_2$, $e_2F < ag_3, 2 >$, $e_2F < ag_4, 2 >$, and $< (x = 3), 1 > \equiv < (x = 3), 2 >$ (that is, $e_1F < (x = 3), 2 >$). Then we apply the production for ag_3 and we get $< ag_3, 2 > Fe_3$, $< ag_4, 2 > \equiv < ag_4, 3 >$ (that is, $e_2F < ag_4, 3 >$), $e_3F < p, 3 >$, $[x = 3, 3]Fe_3$, $e_1F[x = 3, 3]$, and $< (x = 3), 2 > \equiv < (x = 3), 3 >$ (that is, $e_1F < (x = 3), 3 >$). Finally, the production for ag_4 will generate $< (x = 3), 3 > \equiv < (x = 3), 4 >$ (that is, $e_1F < (x = 3), 4 >$), $< p, 3 > \equiv < p, 4 >$ (that is, $e_3F < p, 4 >$), $< ag_4, 3 > Fe_4$, $e_4F < q, 4 >$, $[x = 3, 4]Fe_4$, and $e_1F[x = 3, 4]$.

The resulting F relation can be seen in Figure 3.9, where an arc between cbjects a and b is intended to mean aFb if a is above b in the picture, and a double arc between a and b stands for $a \equiv b$. The picture is drawn such that, for all $i = 0, \ldots, 4$, all elements in $arcs(G_i)$ are at the same level.

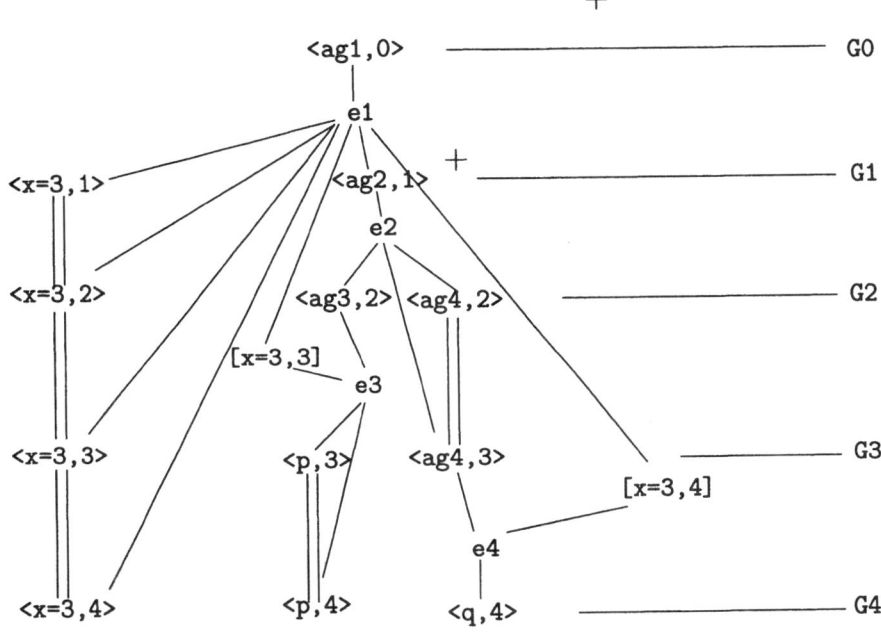

Fig. 3.9. The F relation.

In Figure 3.9, it is easy to see that the final state contains the token $(x = 3)$, together with the two agents p and q. Also, and most important, e_4 depends on the agent ag_4, on the token $(x = 3)$, and (by closing transitively) on the events e_1 and e_2. However, it does not depend on e_3, even though both e_3 and e_4 use the token $(x = 3)$ which has been generated by e_1. Therefore e_1 and e_2 can be considered to be independent, and may thus evolve concurrently.

The occurrence net associated to the above derivation can be seen in Figure 3.10. As usual in Petri nets, places are drawn as circles and transitions as boxes.

Theorem 2 ($N(D)$ is an occurrence net) *Given a finite derivation D, $N(D)$ is an occurrence net.*

Proof: By Definition 17, it is easy to see that $(B_{|_{\equiv}} \cup C) \cap E = \emptyset$ and that $F \subseteq ((B_{|_{\equiv}} \cup C) \times E) \cup (E \times (B_{|_{\equiv}} \cup C))$. Thus $N(D)$ is a net. In order it to be an occurrence net, by Definition 15, we have to prove that F^+ is irreflexive, and also that $\forall s \in (B_{|_{\equiv}} \cup C)$, $| \ ^{\bullet}s | \leq 1$ and $| \ s^{\bullet} | \leq 1$.

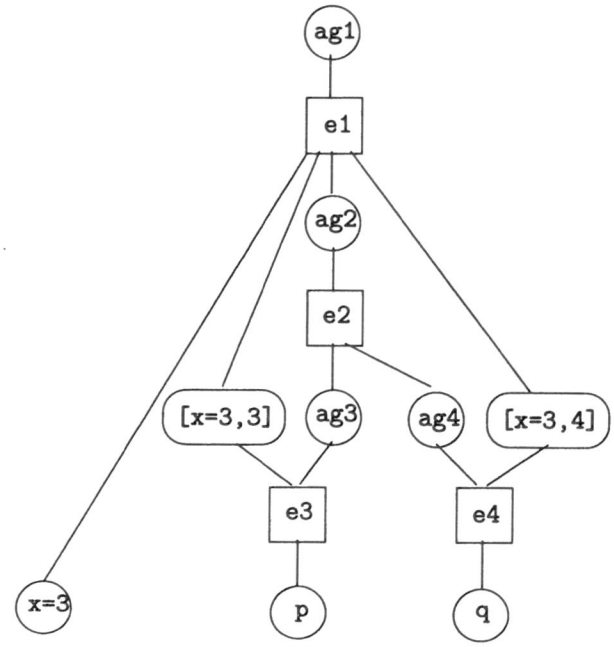

Fig. 3.10. The occurrence net.

Proving that F^+ is irreflexive means showing that there is no pair of distinct elements a and b in $(B_{|_\equiv} \cup C)$ such that both aF^+b and bF^+a hold. We may consider different kinds of elements in $(B_{|_\equiv} \cup C)$, since this set contains both the arcs, labelled by the level in which they are present (in $B_{|_\equiv}$), and the "copies" of tokens (in C). Also, we have to consider the events in E. In a topological view of such a domain, an event e_i and the copies of elements in level $i-1$ can be considered to be between level $i-1$ and level i (as depicted in Figure 3.9). We will show now that, given two elements a and b such that a is "topologically higher" than b, aF^+b cannot hold. This is obviously enough to ensure the not-reflexivity of the relation F^+. We may first note that, given a and b such that $a =< a', i$ and $b =< b', j$ with $i < j$, then bF^+a does not hold. In fact, the only inference rules in Definition 17 which may generate a dependency of b on a are the first and the fourth one, but in both cases they identify the two elements, thus implying that a and b would be not distinct in $B_{|_\equiv} \cup C$. Another possibility concerns copies of tokens, as involved in the last inference rule. However, e_i is always set to be caused by elements on level $i-1$ (see the second inference rule), to cause elements on level i (see the third inference rule), and to cause the copies (see the fourth inference rule). Also, a copy of an element in level i is never set to cause elements on any level, but only events e_j with $i < j$.

The second condition is easy to prove, since the items in Definition 17 are "guarderd" by mutual exclusive conditions (and each one of them generates at most one dependency for each elements of S), and thus they cannot generate more than one dependency for each $s \in S$.∎

We can extract many kinds of information from the above occurrence net $N(D)$. One possible choice is to label only tokens and to forget all processes (or to give the same name to all of them). In this way the occurrence net would show the concurrency pattern of the derivation and the evolution of the store, but not the identity of the agents. Another possibility is to forget the events and to maintain all tokens and agents, thus showing the names of which agents are dependent (or not) on which others. A third choice, which is the one we will adopt in the rest of this section instead, is to consider only the events and to forget both tokens and agents. That is, we will consider the partial ordering induced by $N(D)$, i.e., $(E, (F^*)_{|E})$. The following corollary, which follows directly from Theorem 1, states that $(E, (F^*)_{|E})$ is a partial ordering.

Corollary 1 (derivations and associated partial orderings) *Given a finite derivation D and the corresponding occurrence net $N(D) = (B_{|\equiv} \cup C, E, F)$, $P(N(D)) = (E, (F^*)_{|E})$ is a partial ordering.*∎

For the example considered in this section, the Hasse diagram of the associated partial ordering $(E, (F^*)_{|E})$ is depicted in Figure 3.11, where it is immediate to see that events e_3 and e_4 are concurrent.

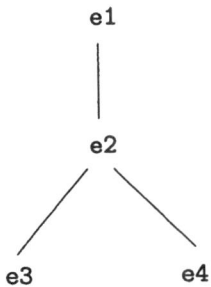

Fig. 3.11. The partial ordering relating events.

We will now introduce a compatibility relationship between the total ordering on events given directly by the sequential derivations (and called generation ordering) and the partial ordering associated to the same derivation. In words, these two orderings are said to be compatible if the partial ordering does not introduce dependencies which are not in the total ordering. From another point of view, this means that the partial ordering can be linearized to yield the given total ordering, or equivalently that the partial ordering is a sound parallelization of the total ordering. We will then show that such compatibility relationship holds when the partial ordering is obtained through the construction of this section.

Definition 18 (generation ordering) *Given a (finite) derivation* $D = (PO_1, \ldots, PO_n)$, *and the associated partial ordering on events* $P(N(D)) = (E, \sqsubseteq)$, *where* $E = \{e_1, \ldots, e_n\}$, *its generation ordering is the total ordering* $O(D) = (E, \leq)$ *on the events in* E *where* $e_i \leq e_j$ *if* $i \leq j$.∎

Definition 19 (compatibility of total and partial orderings) *Given a total ordering* $O = (S, \leq)$ *and a partial ordering on the same set* $P = (S, \sqsubseteq)$, *we say that* O *is compatible with* P *whenever* $\sqsubseteq$ *(as a set)* $\subseteq \leq$ *(as a set)*.∎

Theorem 3 (compatibility of generation and partial orderings) *Given a derivation* D, *consider its associated partial ordering* $P(N(D)) = (E, \sqsubseteq)$ *and its generation ordering* $O(D) = (E, \leq)$. *Then we have that* $O(D)$ *is compatible with* $P(N(D))$, *i.e.,* $\sqsubseteq \subseteq \leq$.

Proof: It is enough to notice that $\leq$ contains all pairs of the form $< e_i, e_j$ where $i \leq j$, and that $\sqsubseteq$ cannot contain pairs of the form $< e_i, e_j$ where $j \leq i$ (by Definition 17). Thus $\sqsubseteq$ is either smaller than or equal to $\leq$.∎

3.1.3.3 An Example Consider the logic program (adapted from a program in (Shapiro 1989)):

```
treesum(tree(l,r),s) := treesum(l,s1), treesum(r,s2), sum(s1,s2,s).
treesum(leaf(x),x).
```

which computes the sum of the values contained in the leaves of a tree. The corresponding cc program is then:

```
treesum(t,s) ::

      ask(t = tree(l,r)) → ∃ s1 s2. (treesum(l,s1) ‖ treesum(r,s2) ‖
      sum(s1,s2,s))
      +
      ask(t = leaf(x)) → (tell(s=x) → success).
```

This program generates a tree-like net of **treesum** processes down the given term and then computes the sum of the leaf values by computing partial sums for each pair of adjacent leaves and "adjacent" **treesum** processes. Note that, even though the + combinator is used, in reality this is a deterministic program, since the "guards" in the two branches of the choice are mutually exclusive. We assume **sum** to be defined by a declaration whose body is a nondeterministic agent with an infinite number of choices, where each choice involves asking for the value of the first two arguments and then telling the corresponding value of the third. This way, it would be represented by an infinite number of productions. On the other hand, another choice would be to define it by induction, thus obtaining only two choices (and corresponding productions).

Being the program under consideration a *cc* representation of a logic program, it is obvious that the underlying constraint system $< D, \vdash$ has to represent the Herbrand universe of terms and implement unification over them.

We choose to include in D all equations of the form $x = f(Y)$, where x is a variable, Y is a vector of variables (as many as the arity of f), and f is a function symbol. Then $\vdash$ contains pairs of the form $< \{x = f(Y), z = f(V), x = z\}, Y = V >$ (which is a shorthand for as many pairs as the arity of f) or $< \{x = f(Y), z = f(V), Y = V\}, x = z >$, and also the pairs necessary to define Clark's equality theory.

It is important to notice that such a formalization of the Herbrand constraint system as a partial information system is finite. Also, while not being the only possible one, it is sufficient to capture unification. Another choice would be to have tokens of the form $x = t$ where t is any Herbrand term, but then $\vdash$ would have to make more complex deductions.

Suppose we are given the goal

```
:-treesum(tree(tree(leaf(10),leaf(15)),tree(leaf(3),leaf(34))),s).
```

According to the *cc* syntax given previously, this has to be represented as an agent, which in this case is:

```
tell({t=tree(l,r), l=tree(l1,r1), r=tree(l2,r2), l1=leaf(x), x=10,
r1=leaf(y), y=15, l2=leaf(z), z=3, r2=leaf(v), v=34}) → treesum(t,s)
```

Now, the set of agents occurring in the *cc* program are:
$ag_1 = \text{tell}(\{t=tree(l,r), l=tree(l1,r1), r=tree(l2,r2), l1=leaf(x), x=10, r1=leaf(y), y=15, l2=leaf(z), z=3, r2=leaf(v), v=34\}) \to treesum(t,s)$
$ag_2 = \text{ask}(t = tree(l,r)) \to ag_3 + \text{ask}(t = leaf(x)) \to ag_4$
$ag_3 = \exists \, s1 \, s2. \, ag_5$
$ag_4 = \text{tell}(s=x) \to success$
$ag_5 = treesum(l,s1) \parallel treesum(r,s2) \parallel sum(s1,s2,s)$

We now show the productions associated to such a *cc* program. Note, however, that for brevity sake we omit the (schema of the) productions for the definition of sum. We also use some other obvious shorthands in order to keep the presentation of reasonable length.

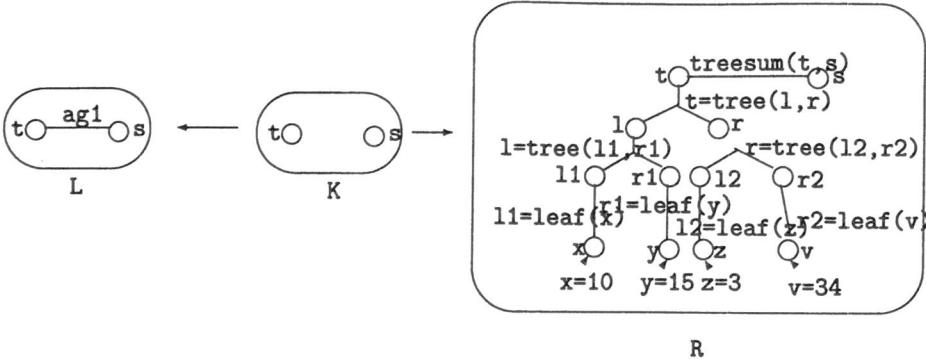

Fig. 3.12. The production for ag_1.

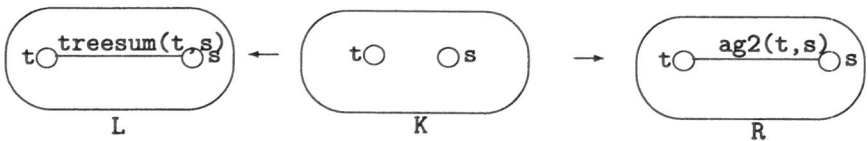

Fig. 3.13. The production for the procedure declaration.

The production for ag_1 builds the term representing the given tree, as a set of tokens, and activates the process **treesum**[1]. It is given in Figure 3.12. The production for the declaration of **treesum**, which has to transform **treesum** into the agent ag_2, is given in Figure 3.13. The two productions for ag_2 have to activate either ag_3 or ag_4 depending on whether t is either a tree or a leaf. They can be seen in Figure 3.14 and 3.15. The production for ag_3, which adds two new nodes and then becomes ag_5, can be seen in Figure 3.16. The production for ag_5 activates in parallel two processes **treesum** (on different variables) and a **sum** process. It can be seen in Figure 3.17. The production for ag_4 adds the constraint $s = x$ to the current store and is given in Figure 3.18. The pairs of the entailment relation which are needed for this program are all of the form $< \{x = a, s = x\}, s = a$, that is, the constraint $\{x = a, s = x\}$ entails the token $s = a$, for any constant a. The production schema associated to such pairs is given in Figure 3.19.

---

[1]There should be a hiding combinator for the addition of all the nodes in the right hand side of this production which are not in its left hand side (i.e., all except t and s), but we omit it for not adding another production.

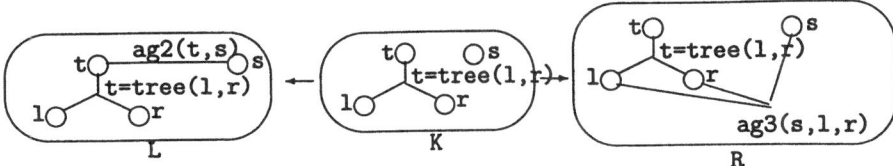

Fig. 3.14. The first production for ag_2.

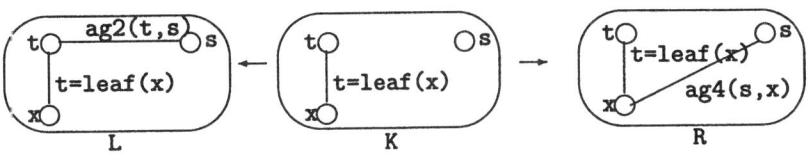

Fig. 3.15. The second production for ag_2.

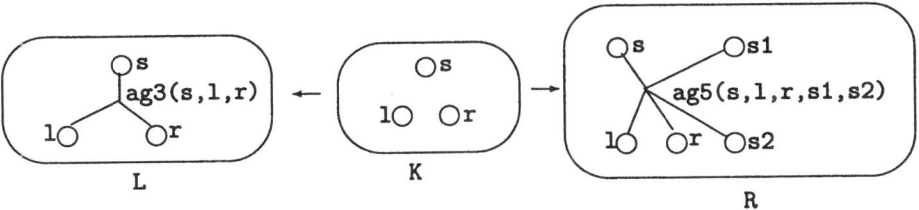

Fig. 3.16. The production for ag_3.

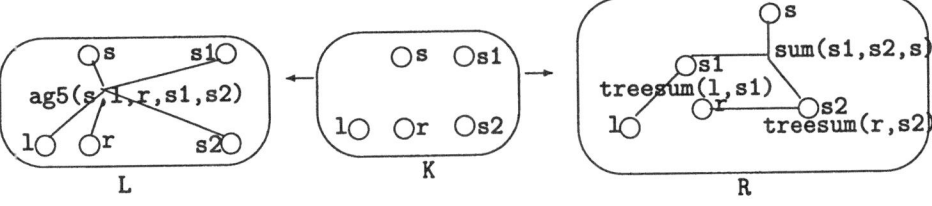

Fig. 3.17. The production for ag_5.

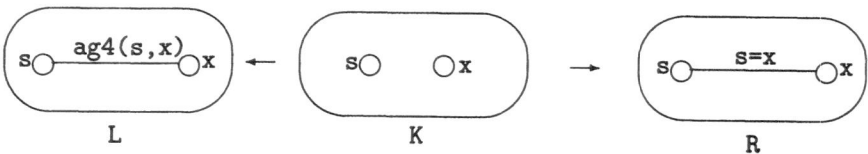

Fig. 3.18. The production for ag_4.

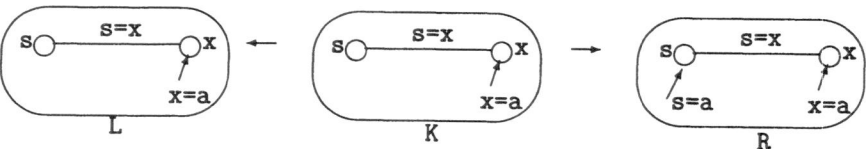

Fig. 3.19. The production schema for the entailment relation pairs.

As we noticed above, this is a deterministic program, since the only occurrence of the $+$ operator is used for choosing between two mutually exclusive conditions ($t = tree(l, r)$ or $t = leaf(x)$). Thus, given any ground goal, it is easy to see that there is only one partial ordering associated to all derivations of the grammar. A version of such partial ordering, where agents and tokens are shown but events are canceled, is given in Figure 3.20.

Many considerations can be made by exploiting the knowledge contained in such a partial ordering. Here are only two of them.

By considering the causal dependencies expressed by the partial ordering, it is possible to see that the maximal parallelism degree of the program is represented by the simultaneous execution of four processes, and in particular it is exploited by the concurrent execution of agents $treesum(l_1, s_{11})$, $treesum(r_1, s_{12})$, $treesum(l_2, s_{21})$, $treesum(r_2, s_{22})$, which are mutually independent (since they do not depend on each other in the partial order).

Notice also that the tokens representing the tree-like term contained in the initial goal are not used all at once but only some at a time, even though they are all generated at the beginning of the computation by the production for agent ag_1. Such term could instead be generated in a "lazy" way without increasing the waiting time of any agent.

3.1.4 The Event Structure Semantics

In the previous section, states of computations were represented by graphs, computation steps were seen as graph production applications, and each computation had an associated partial order, which was able to express the causal

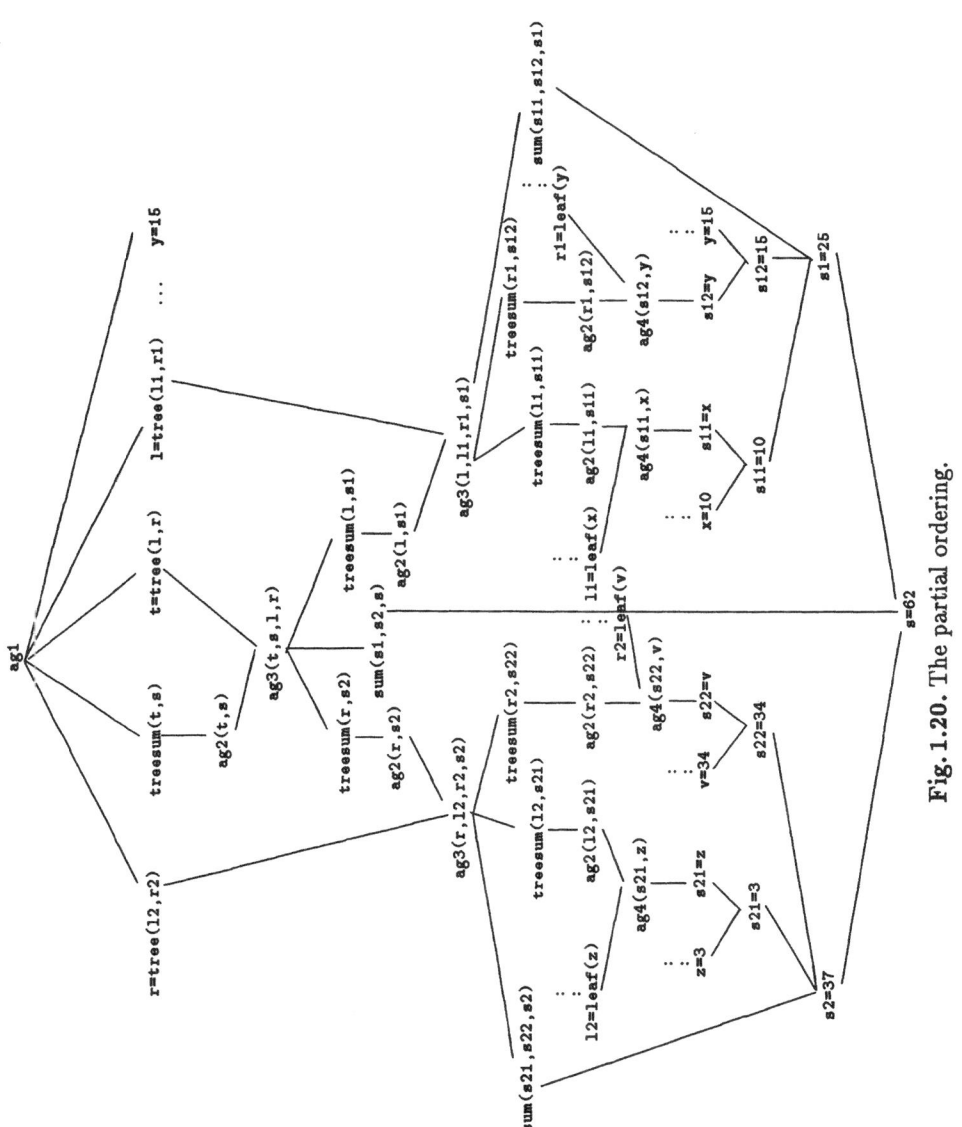

Fig. 1.20. The partial ordering.

dependencies among the steps of such computation. However, that semantics, though rather interesting and itself original for the uniform treatment of tokens and agents, as well as for the analysis of a cc program from the true-concurrency approach, was not entirely satisfactory, for two main reasons. First, the use of graph grammars and their categorical description to model cc computations allowed an elegant formalization of all the basic cc features, but even a simpler structure can have the same essential features. Second, a partial order was associated to each deterministic computation, but no unique structure was associated to a (possibly nondeterministic) cc program. Therefore we could analyze the concurrency available in a cc program, but not its nondeterminism. Here we try to eliminate such unsatisfactory points of the approach of Section 3.1.3 by giving an adequate solution to both problems.

Graph grammars are here replaced by significantly simpler rewrite rules, which however maintain all the properties of graph grammars which are fundamental for the true-concurrency approach. In particular, one of the most important features is the possibility of expressing formally what we call "context objects", i.e., objects which are needed for a computation step to take place, but which are not affected by such step. In fact, these objects allow to model faithfully the concept of asked constraints, which is necessary if we want to model simultaneous ask operations. Therefore, our rewrite rules are context-dependent, i.e., they have a left hand side, a right hand side, and a context. A rule is applicable if both its left hand side and its context are present in the current state of the computation, and its application removes the left hand side (but not the context) and adds the right hand side. The evolution of each of the agents in a cc program, as well as the declarations of the program and its underlying constraint system, are all expressible by sets of such rules. In this way each computation step, i.e., the application of one of such rules, represents either the evolution of an agent, or the expansion of a declaration, or the entailment of some new token. In such view of a computation, we adopt the eventual interpretation of the tell operation, where a constraint is added to the current store without any consistency check.

In this way, a set of rules is obtained from a cc program. Such a set provides an operational semantics of the given cc program. In addition, for us it is the starting point of our concurrent semantics. The idea is to construct a set of terms from the rules, by starting from the initial agent and by unfolding it applying the rules in all possible ways. Each of such terms contains both the object it represents (i.e., a constraint or an agent or a rule application), and also its history (i.e., the part of the computation it depends on). The latter allows to distinguish between different occurrences of the same object which are possibly generated in different computation paths. Relations of concurrency, mutual exclusion, and dependency among such terms can be easily defined: two terms are concurrent if they represent objects which may appear together in a computation state, while they are mutually exclusive if they represent objects which may not appear in the same computation (thus they have to appear in different computations), and they are dependent if they represent objects which may appear in the same computation but at different computation states.

This set of terms, together with the three relations just described, is able to represent all the (deterministic) computations of a given cc program, as defined by its operational semantics, and for each of such computations it provides a partial order expressing the dependency pattern among the events of the computation. The partial orders are the same we proposed in Section 3.1.3, thus making our new proposal a conservative extension of the old one. The most important and original trait of our present approach is that all such computations are represented in a unique structure, where it is possible to see the maximal degree of both concurrency (via the concurrency relation) and nondeterminism (via the mutual eclusion relation) available both at the program level and in the underlying constraint system.

Note that the fact of being able to express the concurrency and the nondeterminism also of the constraint system is convenient not only for an efficient implementation of the constraint solver, but also because a non-monolithic view of the constraint system provides a greater level of concurrency and nondeterminism at the language level as well.

The semantics presented in this section can be referred to as an "event structure semantics" because the set of terms associated to a cc program, restricted to those terms representing rule applications, yields what is called an event structure in (Winskel 1986).

3.1.4.1 The operational semantics Each state of a cc computation consists of the active agents and of the already generated tokens. However, a state consists of a *multiset* of agents and tokens, rather than a set, since the same agent (and also the same token) may occur in a state with multiplicity higher than one (just think to the computations of $A \parallel A$). Both agents and tokens will have associated the variables they involve. Then, each computation step will model either the evolution of a single agent, or the entailment of a new token through the $\vdash$ relation (in its operational interpretation given above). Such a change in the state of the computation will be performed via the application of a rewrite rule. There will be as many rewrite rules as the number of agents and declarations in a program (which is finite), plus the number of pairs of the entailment relation (which can be infinite). The role of such rewrite rules coincides with that of the graph productions used before. However, in this section we choose to use a formalism which is simpler, while still retaining all the features of graph grammars which are necessary for our approach.

Definition 20 (computation state) *Given a program $P = F.A$ with a constraint system $\langle D, \vdash \rangle$, a state is a multiset of elements of $Ag(P) \cup D$.* ∎

Each item in a state involves some variables, and usually we will explicitly write these variables. For example, if t involves variables $x_1, \ldots, x_n$, then we will write $t(x_1, \ldots, x_n)$. Since each state of the computation is a multiset, when in the following we will use the operations of union and difference, as well as the inclusion predicate, we will always consider their multiset interpretation. In a multiset, the multiplicity of each item is the natural number associated to it. For example, if an item A appears n times in the multiset, then its multiplicity is n and we will write nA.

Definition 21 (rewrite rules) *A rewrite rule has the form*

$$r : L(r)(\mathbf{x}) \stackrel{c(r)(\mathbf{x})}{\rightsquigarrow} R(r)(\mathbf{xy})$$

where $L(r)$ is an agent, $c(r)$ is a constraint, and $R(r)$ is a state. Moreover, $\mathbf{x}$ is the tuple of variables appearing both in $L(r) \cup c(r)$ and in $R(r)$, while $\mathbf{y}$ is the tuple of variables appearing only in $R(r)$. ∎

The intuitive meaning of a rule is that $L(r)$, which is called the left hand side of the rule, is rewritten into (or replaced by) $R(r)$, i.e., the right hand side, if $c(r)$ is present in the current state. $R(r)$ could contain some variables not appearing in $L(r)$ nor in $c(r)$ (i.e., the tuple $\mathbf{y}$). The application of r would then rename such variables to constants which are different from all the others already in use.

The items in $c(r)$ have to be interpreted as a context, since it is necessary for the application of the rule but it is not affected by such application. The possibility of having a context-dependent formalism is very significant if we are interested in the causal dependencies among the objects involved in a computation. In fact, consider for example two rule applications with overlapping contexts but with disjoint left hand sides. Then, in a context-dependent formalism they can be applied independently. On the other hand, a context-independent formalism would simulate a context object by first cancelling it and then generating it again, and thus would not be able to express the simultaneous execution of the same rules, but only their sequential execution in any order. The cc framework is obviously context-dependent, since a constraint to be asked to the store is naturally interpreted as an object which is needed for the computation to evolve but which is not affected by such evolution. Therefore, the modelling of cc computations via a context-dependent formalism provides a more faithful description of this framework.

Note that the variables appearing in a rule are "really" variables, since they can be instantiated and aliased whenever the rule is applied. However, the variables appearing in a computation state can never be aliased via substitutions (although a constraint could state that they are equal). Thus they can be treated as constants without loss of generality. This is what we will do in the rest of the paper. More precisely, a rule r will be considered to involve a tuple of variables $\mathbf{x}$, while a state of the computation S will involve a tuple of constants $\mathbf{a}$.

Definition 22 (computation steps) *Consider a computation state $S_1(\mathbf{a})$ and a rule $r : L(r)(\mathbf{x}) \overset{c(r)(\mathbf{x})}{\rightsquigarrow} R(r)(\mathbf{xy})$. Suppose also that $(L(r) \cup c(r))[\mathbf{a}/\mathbf{x}] \subseteq S_1(\mathbf{a})$. Then the application of r to S_1 is a computation step which yields a new computation state $S_2 = (S_1 - L(r)[\mathbf{a}/\mathbf{x}]) \cup R(r)[\mathbf{a}/\mathbf{x}][\mathbf{b}/\mathbf{y}]$, where the constants in $\mathbf{b}$ are fresh, i.e. they do not appear in S_1. We will write[2] $S_1 \overset{r[\mathbf{a}/\mathbf{x}][\mathbf{b}/\mathbf{y}]}{\Longrightarrow} S_2$.* ∎

In words, a rule r can be applied to a state S_1 if both the left hand side of the rule and its context can be found (via a suitable substitution) in S_1. Then, the application of r removes from S_1 the left hand side of r and adds its right hand side.

Definition 23 (from programs to rules) *The rules corresponding to agents, declarations, and entailment pairs are given as follows:*

$(tell(c) \to A) \rightsquigarrow c, A$

$A_1 \parallel A_2 \rightsquigarrow A_1, A_2$

$\exists \mathbf{x}.A \rightsquigarrow A$

$(\sum_{i=1,\dots,n} ask(c_i) \to A_i) \overset{c_i}{\rightsquigarrow} A_i$ *for all* $i = 1, \dots, n$

$p(\mathbf{x}) \rightsquigarrow A$ *for all* $p(\mathbf{x}) :: A$

$\overset{S}{\rightsquigarrow} t$ *for all* $S \vdash t$

Given a cc program $P = F.A$ and its underlying constraint system $\langle D, \vdash \rangle$, we will call $RR(P)$ the set of rewrite rules associated to P, which consists of the rules corresponding to all agents in $Ag(P)$, plus the rules representing the declarations in F, plus those rules representing the pairs of the entailment relation $\vdash$. ∎

That is, if the agent $(tell(c) \to A)$ is found in the current state, then such agent can be replaced by the agent A together with the constraint c. In other words, $(tell(c) \to A)$ is cancelled by the current state, while both c and A are added.

Agent $A_1 \parallel A_2$ is instead replaced by the multiset containing the two agents A_1 and A_2. Note that if $A_1 = A_2 = A$ we would still have two distinct elements, since a state is a multiset of elements. Therefore, in that case we would denote by $2A$ the new computation state.

Agent $\exists \mathbf{x}.A$ is replaced by agent A. This is the only rule where the right hand side has more variables than the left hand side.

---

[2]The application of a substitution θ to a rule r, written $r\theta$, is a new rule whose left hand side, right hand side, and context are obtained by applying θ to the corresponding constituents of r.

Agent $\sum_{i=1,\ldots,n} ask(c_i) \rightarrow A_i$ gives rise to as many rewrite rules as the number of possible nondeterministic choices. In each of such branches, say branch i, the whole agent is replaced by agent A_i only if c_i is present already in the store. Note that only this rule, which corresponds to an ask agent, needs a context. In fact, as noted before, asked constraints in cc programming are directly related to context objects in a context-dependent formalism.

The other rules are needed for describing the environment in which agents evolve. Such environment is made up of the declarations in the given program and of the underlying constraint system. For declarations, the head of the clause (if declarations are seen as clauses in the logic programming sense) is replaced by its body. This is an unfolding rule which allows to pass from the agent $p(\mathbf{x})$ to the agent A, which will then evolve via the rules given above. For entailment pairs, the rules have an empty left hand side. In fact, the presence of the context S is enough to add the token t to the current store.

Example (computation step): Consider a computation state containing agent

$$A(a_1, a_2) = ask(t_1(a_1, a_2)) \rightarrow A'(a_2)$$

and tokens $t_1(a_1, a_2)$ and $t_2(a_2, a_3)$. Consider also the rewrite rule

$$(ask(t_1(x_1, x_2)) \rightarrow A'(x_2)) \overset{t_1(x_1, x_2)}{\rightsquigarrow} A'(x_2).$$

Then, since there exists a matching between the left hand side of the rule and (a subset of) the state (via the substitution $\{a_1/x_1, a_2/x_2\}$), the rule can be applied, yielding the new state containing agent $A'(a_2)$ and tokens $t_1(a_1, a_2)$ and $t_2(a_2, a_3)$. Note that token $t_1(a_1, a_2)$ has not been cancelled by the rewrite rule, since it was in its context part. ∎

Definition 24 (computations) *Consider a cc program $P = F.A$. A computation for P is any sequence of computation steps*

$$S_1 \overset{r_1[\mathbf{a_1}/\mathbf{x_1}]}{\Longrightarrow} S_2 \overset{r_2[\mathbf{a_2}/\mathbf{x_2}]}{\Longrightarrow} S_3 \ldots$$

such that $S_1 = \{A\}$ and $r_i \in RR(P)$, $i = 1, 2, \ldots$. Two computations which are the same except that different fresh constants are employed in the various steps, are called α-equivalent. ∎

3.1.4.2 The Concurrent Semantics computation.

The idea is to take the set of rewrite rules $RR(P)$ associated to a given cc program P, to construct a set of terms representing the elements involved in each possible computation via these rules, and then to relate such terms via some causality relation (and others), in order to know which elements are causally related to which others. Such terms should be able to represent all possible (deterministic) computations of a cc program P in a unique structure.

Definition 25 (from rewrite rules to terms) *Given a cc program P, the set $ST(P) = S \cup T$ of terms is constructed by means of the following two inference rules:*

- $A(\mathbf{x})$ *initial agent of* P
  implies
  $< \emptyset, A(\mathbf{a}), 1 \in S;$

- $\{s_1, \ldots, s_n\} \subseteq S$, *where* $s_i =< e_i, B_i(\mathbf{a_i}), k_i$ *for all* $i = 1, \ldots, n$, $r \in RR(P)$ *such that*
  $(L(r) \cup c(r)) = \{B_1(\mathbf{x_1}), \ldots, B_n(\mathbf{x_n})\}$, $\exists$ *a substitution* $[\mathbf{a}/\mathbf{x}]$ *such that* $B_i(\mathbf{x_i})[\mathbf{a}/\mathbf{x}] = B_i(\mathbf{a_i})$, *and* $s_i \underline{co} \; s_j$ *for all* i, j, $i \neq j$, $i, j = 1, \ldots, n$
  implies

  - $e =< \{s_1, \ldots, s_n\}, r[\mathbf{a}/\mathbf{x}], 1 \in T$ *and*

  - *let* h *be the multiplicity of* $B(\mathbf{x}, y_1, \ldots, y_m)$ *in* $R(r)$. *Then for all* $l = 1, \ldots, h$,
    $< \{e\}, B[\mathbf{a}/\mathbf{x}][< e, y_1/y_1] \ldots > [< e, y_m/y_m], l >\in S.\blacksquare$

We will now try to explain informally but in great detail the above definition, since it represents the core of this semantics. The idea is to unfold the rewrite rules, starting from the initial agent, in any possible way, so that different occurrences of the same rule are represented by different terms and generate different objects. The technique used to achieve that consists into denoting each term by a triple, and by embedding the whole history of the term (i.e., the set of terms it depends on) as the first element of the triple. The second element of the triple is instead the element represented (i.e., type and involved variables), and the third one is a number which is needed to distinguish different occurrences of the same element in a state (which, we recall, is a multiset, while we are generating a set of terms). If there is only one of such occurrences, then the number will be 1, otherwise, the k-th occurrence will have number k. Note that, for the language we consider, k is always either 1 or 2, since there cannot be more than two occurrences of the same element. In fact, the only rule which may generate a multiset containing different occurrences of the same element is the one associated to the agent $A_1 \parallel A_2$. However, our approach can also handle languages where an agent may fork into more than two agents. Finally, note that we don't have to handle the problem of different rules generating different occurrences of the same agent, since the identity of such occurrences is automatically made distinct by the fact that they will appear in terms having different histories.

The first inference rule creates one term which represents the initial agent A of the given program P. Such term, $< \emptyset, A, 1 >$, has the empty set as the first element of the triple, the agent as the second element, and the number 1 as the third element. This means that this agent A has no element it depends on, which is reasonable since it is the first agent of each computation. Moreover, it also means that it is the first (and only) occurrence of agent A.

The second inference rule creates the terms representing the application of a rewrite rule r, as well as the objects in the right hand side of r. To apply r, we have to find a set of elements, already in $ST(P)$, which match the left hand side and the context of r. These are the terms s_i, each of which is the triple $< e_i, B_i(\mathbf{a_i}), k_i >$. This means that each s_i represents the object B_i, which can be either an agent or a token, involves constants $\mathbf{a_i}$, depends on term e_i, and it is the k_i-th occurrence of B_i. The matching condition is expressed by the substitution $[\mathbf{a}/\mathbf{x}]$, which is able to make the left hand side and the context of a rule to coincide with a subset of terms already generated. Note that if agents B_i contain different sets of constants, we assume that tuple $\mathbf{a}$ contains their union. Furthermore, such terms must be concurrent (i.e., $s_i \underline{co} s_j$). Informally, this means that they have the possibility of being all together simultaneously in a computation. The formal meaning of the concurrency relation among terms will be given later in this section. With these preconditions satisfied, the inference rule creates new terms. One of them, $e = < \{s_1, \ldots, s_n\}, r[\mathbf{a}/\mathbf{x}], 1 >$, represents the application of r, which depends on its left hand side and its context (this is why the first element of the triple contains the set $\{s_1, \ldots, s_n\}$). The other terms represent all the objects (either tokens or agents) in the right hand side of r. Thus, for each of such objects, say B, which involves the variables in the left hand side of r (i.e., $\mathbf{x}$) and possibly some other variables (i.e., $y_1, \ldots, y_m$), we create the term $< e, B[\mathbf{a}/\mathbf{x}][< e, y_1 > /y_1] \ldots [< e, y_m > /y_m], l >$. This term represents the l-th occurrence of object B with variables $\mathbf{x}$ suitably substituted by the constants $\mathbf{a}$ (which is the matching needed for the application of the rule), plus the other variables, which have been renamed to contain term e, which is the term representing the rule application. In this way, such variables are different from any other variable ever used in the computation. It is worthwhile to notice that the technique of embedding the history of an object in the term representing the object, applied to the variables y_i, allows a formal handling of the so-called "standardization apart" step in logic programming ((Lloyd 1987)), which informally says that all existential variables found in a clause should be renamed to be "fresh variables". The first element of the term representing B is the set $\{e\}$, because B obviously depends only on the rule application (and thus on the term representing such application).

The elements of $ST(P)$ have been partitioned into two sets, i.e., S and T. The idea is that terms in T represent rule applications, while terms in S represents objects in computation states, i.e., either tokens or agents. This will be useful later when we will restrict our attention to the elements in T, so to understand the causal dependencies among all rule applications in a cc computation.

Due to the way terms are constructed, the notion of concurrency among terms, which we described above only informally, is easily definable as follows.

Definition 26 (causal dependency, mutual exclusion, concurrency)
Given any two terms $t_1, t_2 \in ST(P)$, we may define three relations between them:

- causal dependency: *t_1 is causally dependent on t_2 if t_2 appears as a subterm of t_1;*

- mutual exclusion: *t_1 and t_2 are mutually exclusive if at least one of the maximal terms they share represents an agent (i.e., there is one of such maximal terms which is of the form $< e, B, n >$, where B is an agent);*

- concurrency: *t_1 and t_2 are concurrent if they are not causally dependent on each other nor mutually exclusive. In other words, they either do not share any term, or, if they do, then all the maximal terms they share represent tokens.∎*

The intuitive reason why terms sharing an agent are not concurrent, while terms sharing only tokens are so, is that tokens are context objects, i.e., they are read but not consumed, and thus computation steps reading (or asking) the same token should result to be concurrent. Therefore it should be possible to have such (concurrent) steps simultaneously in the same computation. On the other hand, two steps which both depend on the same agent should not appear in the same computation, but instead in two different (and alternative) computation branches. Another way to see that is to think of agents as consumable resources (which thus can be used by one step only) and of tokens as non-consumable resources (which therefore can be used by any number of steps). Note that the notion of mutual exclusion is what allows us to embed nondeterministic information in the set of terms.

It is important to notice that the construction of set $ST(P)$, as described in Definition 25, is completely deterministic. That is, given a cc program P, a unique set $ST(P)$ is obtained, independently of the order in which the rules in $RR(P)$ are selected to create new terms. In fact, it is possible that a set of terms matching the left hand side and the context of more than one rule are present in the current set of terms, and thus more rules can be used for the second inference rule in Definition 25. The reason why the order does not matter is that the concurrency, or mutual exclusion, or dependency relations among terms already generated are not changed by the addition of new terms. In fact such relations, by the way they are defined in Definition 26, rely only on the set of elements such terms depend on. Therefore, two terms which are causally dependent (resp., mutually exclusive, concurrent) in the current set of terms will remain causally dependent (resp., mutually exclusive, concurrent) if new terms are generated.

The above construction of the set $ST(P)$ of terms resembles the one proposed in (Winskel 1986) to obtain a (possibly nondeterministic) occurrence net from a Petri net. Furthermore, the aim coincides, since in both cases the idea is to find a structure which represents all possible computations (of the Petri net in the case of (Winskel 1986), and of the given cc program in our case). However, there are four main differences. First, we do not start from a given net, but from a set of rules. Second, our definition of the mutual exclusion and dependency relations, as noted above, has to take into account the two types of resources in a cc program (i.e., agents and tokens), while Petri net computations only involve consumable resources. In fact, as we noted above, Petri nets in their classical formulation are a context-independent formalism, and therefore they cannot express non-consumable resources. Third, variables are not present in the Petri net formalism, while we have to consider them for a faithful description of the cc framework. In this respect, it is therefore original the extension to the existential variables of the technique which puts together each element and its history. Finally, our terms are triples and not pairs, since we have to deal with the possibility of having different instances of the same object in a computation state, and thus we have to use a numbering technique to distinguish among such different occurrences. A by-product of the strong relationship between the construction in (Winskel 1986) and ours is that, in both cases, the set $ST(P)_{|_T}$ (i.e., the restriction of $ST(P)$ to the set T), together with the dependency and mutual exclusion relations, corresponds to what is called an "event structure" in (Winskel 1986).

Definition 27 *(event structures and deterministic sequential configurations (Winskel 1986))* *An event structure is a triple $(E, \#, \sqsubseteq)$ where E is a set of events, $\#$ (i.e., the conflict relation) is a binary, symmetric, irreflexive, and hereditary (i.e., if $e_1 \# e_2$ and $e_1 \sqsubseteq e_3$, then $e_3 \# e_2$) relation among events, and $\sqsubseteq$ (i.e., the dependency relation) is a partial order. A deterministic sequential configuration for an event structure $(E, \#, \sqsubseteq)$ is a sequence $E' = e_1 e_2 \ldots$ such that*

- *$e_i \sqsubseteq e_j$ implies $i \leq j$;*

- *$E' \subseteq E$;*

- *$e, e' \in E'$ implies $\neg(e \# e')$;*

- *$e \in E'$ and $e' \sqsubseteq e$ implies $e' \in E'$.* ∎

That is, a deterministic sequential configuration for an event structure is a sequence of events which is left closed w.r.t. the dependency relation and such that no two events are mutually exclusive. This means that they can all appear in the same deterministic computation. In fact, as we will see later, deterministic sequential configurations can be assumed to represent deterministic computations.

Theorem 4 *($(ST(P)_{|_T}, \#, \sqsubseteq)$ is an event structure)* *$(ST(P)_{|_T}, \#, \sqsubseteq)$, where $\#$ and $\sqsubseteq$ are respectively the mutual exclusion and causal dependency relations as defined in Definition 26, is an event structure.*

Proof: The causal dependency relation $\sqsubseteq$ is, by Definition 26, subterm containment. Therefore it is reflexive, antisymmetric, and transitive, that is, a partial order. Also, the mutual exclusion relation $\#$ is, again by Definition 26, defined as the sharing, between two terms, of a maximal subterm which represents an agent. Therefore it is binary, symmetric, and irreflexive (because terms of $ST(P)_{|_T}$ do not represent agents). Let us now check whether it is hereditary. Suppose $e_1 \# e_2$ and $e_1 \sqsubseteq e_3$. This means that e_1 and e_2 share a maximal subterm, say t, which represents an agent, and that e_1 appears as a subterm of e_3. Then e_3 contains, among others, the subterms of e_1, and thus also t. Therefore e_2 and e_3 share t, and t is still maximal for them.∎

Definition 28 (event structure semantics) *Given a cc program P,*
$(ST(P)_{|_T}, \#, \sqsubseteq) = ES(P)$ *is its event structure semantics.*∎

$ES(P)$ is able to represent all deterministic computations possible for the given cc program P. The above theorem formalizes this claim. In fact, it proves that for each computation there is a corresponding deterministic sequential configuration, and viceversa.

Theorem 5 (soundness and completeness of $ES(P)$) *Given a cc program P and its event structure semantics $ES(P)$, consider a computation of P*

$$S_1 \xrightarrow{S_1', r_1[\mathbf{a_1}/\mathbf{x_1}]} S_2 \xrightarrow{S_2', r_2[\mathbf{a_2}/\mathbf{x_2}]} S_3 \ldots$$

Then there is a deterministic sequential configuration of $ES(P)$

$$e_1 e_2 e_3 \ldots$$

where $e_i = < e_i1, e_i2, e_i3 >$ such that $r_i[\mathbf{a_i}/\mathbf{x_i}] = e_i2$ for all $i = 1, \ldots$. Also, for any deterministic sequential configuration of $ES(P)$

$$e_1 e_2 e_3 \ldots$$

there is a computation of P

$$S_1 \xrightarrow{S_1', r_1[\mathbf{a_1}/\mathbf{x_1}]} S_2 \xrightarrow{S_2', r_2[\mathbf{a_2}/\mathbf{x_2}]} S_3 \ldots$$

such that, if $e_i = < e_i1, e_i2, e_i3 >$, then $r_i[\mathbf{a_i}/\mathbf{x_i}] = e_i2$ for all $i = 1, \ldots$.

Proof: Given the above computation, which is deterministic, we have that $r_i[\mathbf{a_i}/\mathbf{x_i}]$ and $r_j[\mathbf{a_j}/\mathbf{x_j}]$ cannot be mutually exclusive (otherwise they would be in the same computation). Therefore they are either concurrent or causally dependent on each other. However, it is not possible that $r_i[\mathbf{a_i}/\mathbf{x_i}]$ causally depends on $r_j[\mathbf{a_j}/\mathbf{x_j}]$ if $j > i$, due to the way terms are constructed from the set of rules. Therefore it is always possible to construct the written deterministic sequential configuration. Consider now a deterministic sequential configuration. Then of course it is possible to construct the computation which follows exactly configuration. i.e, where step i of the computation corresponds to the element i of the configuration.∎

Note that the above theorem implies that the set $ST(P)_{|_T}$ is in general infinite, since among all possible computations there may be also infinite ones.

Note also that we cannot prove the stronger claim that there is a bijective correspondence between computations of P and deterministic sequential configurations of $ES(P)$, since there may be different deterministic sequential configurations which represent the same computation. This depends on the fact that the definition of computation given by Definition 24, and usually used in the literature, is not able to distinguish computations which use the same sequence of rules and where the intermediate states have non-identity endomorphisms. This problem could be solved by adopting a different notion of computation which is based on the idea os "standard representatives" of computation states. This approach has been introduced in (Corradini, Ehrig, Lowe, Montanari, and Rossi 1992) for a correct handling of graph derivations, and we believe that it can also be successfully used for cc computations, due to the strong relationship existing between cc programs and graph grammars (see Section 3.1.3).

Furthermore, $ES(P)$ is also able to express the causal dependency among all the computation steps involved in each deterministic computation, in a way which is compatible to the partial order approach in Section 3.1.3. More precisely, if we consider a computation C for a cc program P, it is possible to construct an associated partial order, following the approach in Section 3.1.3. Let us call it $PO(C)$. On the other hand, let us consider the deterministic sequential configuration E' of $ES(P) = (ST(P)_{|_T}, \#, \sqsubseteq)$ corresponding to C in the sense of the above theorem. Then the restriction of relation $\sqsubseteq$ to E' is a partial order, which we call $PO'(C)$. Then we have that $PO(C) = PO'(C)$.

Example (cc programs and sets of terms): Consider the cc program P consisting of the initial agent $IA = tell(c_1, c_2, c) \rightarrow A$, where
$A = (ask(c_1) \rightarrow A_1 + ask(c_2) \rightarrow success)$,
$A_1 = A_3 \parallel A_4$,
$A_3 = A_4 = ask(c) \rightarrow success$,
and no declarations. The rules corresponding to such agent and all its subagents are:
$r_1 : IA \rightsquigarrow c_1, c_2, c, A$
$r_2 : A \overset{c_1}{\rightsquigarrow} A_1$
$r_3 : A \overset{c_2}{\rightsquigarrow} A_2$
$r_4 : A_1 \rightsquigarrow A_3, A_4$
$r_5 : A_3 \overset{c}{\rightsquigarrow} success$.
For simplicity sake, we assume the entailment relation to be empty (or not relevant to the constraints involved in such program). Furthermore, the variables are not taken into consideration. This program has two alternative finite computations, depending on how agent A evolves. In one case, we have the parallel evolution of two occurrences of A_3 (even though they both ask for the same constraint

c), and in the other case we have one computation step generating the success agent. The terms which are generated for this program are as follows. First, term $s_1 =< \emptyset, IA, 1 >$ is generated for the initial agent IA. At this point, rule r_1 can be applied, and thus we generate term $e_1 =< s_1, r_1, 1 >$ to represent the rule application and terms $s_2 =< e_1, A, 1 >$, $s_3 =< e_1, c_1, 1 >$, $s_4 =< e_1, c_2, 1 >$, and $s_5 =< e_1, c, 1 >$ to represent its right hand side. Since there are terms representing A, c_1, and c_2 (i.e., s_2, s_3, and s_4), rules r_2 and r_3 can now be applied, and thus we have $e_2 =< \{s_2, s_3\}, r_2, 1 >$ and $e_3 =< \{s_2, s_4\}, r_3, 1 >$, as well as $s_6 =< e_2, A_1, 1 >$ and $s_7 =< e_3, A_2, 2 >$. Now there is a term representing A_1, thus rule r_4 can be applied, and we have $e_4 =< \{s_6\}, r_4, 1 >$, $s_8 =< e_4, A_3, 1 >$, $s_9 =< e_4, A_3, 2 >$. Now both s_8 and s_9 match the left hand side of rule r_5, and there is a term representing c (i.e., s_5), therefore we can apply twice rule r_5, obtaining $e_5 =< \{s_5, s_8\}, r_5, 1 >$ and $s_{10} =< e_5, success, 1 >$ for the first application, and $e_6 =< \{s_5, s_9\}, r_5, 1 >$ and $s_{11} =< e_6, success, 1 >$ for the second application. Thus we obtained the set of terms $ST(P) = S \cup T$, where $S = \{s_1, \ldots, s_{11}\}$ and $T = \{e_1 \ldots, e_6\}$. Thus the event structure semantics of P is the set $\{e_1 \ldots, e_6\}$, together with the causal dependency and mutual exclusion, relations among elements of such set. It is easy to see that e_2 causally depends on e_1, since $e_2 =< \{s_2, s_3\}, r_2, 1 >=< \{< e_1, A, 1 >, s_3\}, r_2, 1 >$ and thus contains e_1 as a subterm. Similarly, e_3 depends on e_1. However, e_3 and e_2 are mutually exclusive, since $e_3 =< \{s_2, s_4\}, r_3, 1 >=< \{< e_1, A, 1 >, < e_1, c_2, 1 >\}, r_3, 1 >$ and $e_2 =< \{< e_1, A, 1 >, < e_1, c_1, 1 >\}, r_2, 1 >$, and thus the maximal term they share (i.e., $< e_1, A, 1 >$) represents an agent. This means the the rules represented by e_2 and e_3, i.e., r_2 and r_3, cannot be applied in the same computation, but only in two alternative computations. Then, we have that $e_4 =< \{s_6\}, r_4, 1 >=< \{< e_2, A_1, 1 >\}, r_4, 1 >$, thus it depends on e_2. Also, $e_5 =< \{s_5, s_8\}, r_5, 1 >=< \{< e_1, c, 1 >, < e_4, A_3, 1 >\}, r_5 >$, and thus it depends on e_4. Finally, $e_6 =< \{s_5, s_9\}, r_5, 1 >=< \{< e_1, c, 1 >, < e_4, A_3, 2 >\}, r_5, 1 >$ and thus it depends on e_4 as well. However, e_5 and e_6 are concurrent, since they only share one maximal subterm, i.e., $< e_1, c >$, which represents a token. Figure 3.21 shows the dependency pattern among all the terms e_is. Arrows denote causal dependency, while the $\#$ sign denotes mutual exclusion. For sake of semplicity neither the transitive closure nor the hereditary closure of such relations have been drawn in the picture.

We believe that there are many areas of research, either related or not to the cc programming area, which could possibly gain from an analysis of a given program via a method based on our event structure semantics. In fact, all those areas which need some information on concurrency and/or nondeterminism, and which now obtain it through some informal methodology, could use our semantics and have 1) a much cleaner way of stating their results, and 2) the possibility of expressing more concurrency and non-determinism than before. In particular, we are thinking at two areas, which are both strongly related to the logic programming framework and thus to the cc framework as well: independent and-parallelism ((Hermenegildo and Rossi 1990)) and intelligent

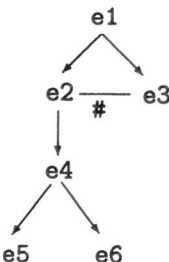

Fig. 3.21. The dependency and mutual exclusion relations among events.

backtracking ((Codognet, Codognet, and Filé 1988)). In fact, both of them need a precise understanding of the dependencies between goals, in order to decide, respectively, whether to run them in parallel or not, or to which search step go back.

3.1.5 The Contextual Net Semantics

The main difference between the event structure semantics described in the previous section and the contextual net semantics we are going to describe now is that event structures are replaced by contextual nets (Montanari and Rossi 1993a). In fact, the operational behaviour of cc programs is still expressed by using the context-dependent rewrite rules described in the previous section. However, the construction which obtains the event structure is modified in order to obtain instead a contextual net.

3.1.5.1 Contextual nets In classical nets, as defined for example in (Reisig 1985), each element of the set of conditions can be a precondition (if it belongs to the pre-set of an event) or a postcondition (if it belongs to the post-set of an event). We now add the possibility, for a condition, to be considered as a *context* for an event. Informally, a context is something which is necessary for the event to be enabled, but which is not affected by the firing of that event. In other words, a context condition can be interpreted as an item which is *read without being consumed* by the event, in the same sense as preconditions can be considered being *read and consumed* and postconditions being instead simply *written*.

The formal technique which we use to introduce contexts consists of adding a new relation, beside the usual flow relation, which we call the *context relation*. Such relations state which conditions are to be considered as a context for which event. Nets with such contexts will be called *context-dependent nets*.

In the following, we assume the reader to be familiar with the classical notions of nets, C/E systems, occurrence nets, and relatives. For the formal definitions missing here we refer to (Reisig 1985). Moreover, a longer and more detailed treatment of contextual nets and their process-based semantics can be found in (Montanari and Rossi 1993a).

Definition 29 (context-dependent nets) *A context-dependent net CN is a quadruple $(B, E; F_1, F_2)$ where*

- $B \cap E = \emptyset$, *where elements of B are called conditions and elements of E are called events;*

- $F_1 \subseteq (B \times E) \cup (E \times B)$ *and it is called the flow relation;*

- $F_2 \subseteq (B \times E)$ *and it is called the context relation;*

- $(F_1 \cup F_1^{-1}) \cap F_2 = \emptyset.$ ∎

The last conditions assures that a condition, which is a context for an event, be not also a precondition for that same event, and not even a postcondition. However, a condition which is a context for an event can be a precondition, a postcondition, or even a context for another event.

It is immediate to see that context-dependent nets are more general than nets. In fact, a net is simply a context-dependent net where $F_2 = \emptyset$.

Example: Context-dependent nets will be graphically represented in the same way as nets. I.e., conditions are circles, events are boxes, and the flow relation is represented by directed arcs from circles to boxes or viceversa. We choose to represent the context relation by undirected arcs (since the direction of such relation is unambiguous, i.e., from elements of B to elements of E). An example of a context-dependent net can be found in Figure 3.22, where there are five events $e_1, \ldots, e_5$ and nine conditions $b_1, \ldots, b_9$. In particular, event e_2 has b_2 and b_3 as preconditions, b_5 as postcondition, and b_7 as a context. Note, however, that b_7 is not a context for all events. In fact, it is a precondition for e_4 and a context for e_3, for which b_6 is a context as well, while b_4 is a precondition and b_8 is a postcondition. ∎

Definition 30 (pre-set, post-set, and context) *Given a context-dependent net $CN = (B, E; F_1, F_2)$ and an element $x \in B \cup E$,*

- *the pre-set of x is the set $^\bullet x = \{y \mid F_1(y, x)\}$,*

- *the post-set of x is the set $x^\bullet = \{y \mid F_1(x, y)\}$, and*

- *the context of x is defined if $x \in E$ and it is the set $\hat{x} = \{y \mid F_2(y, x)\}$.* ∎

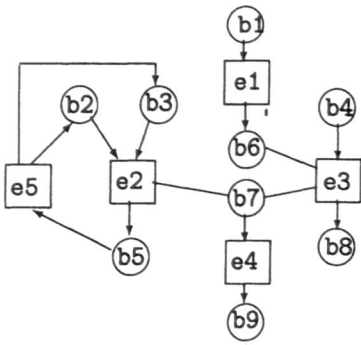

Fig. 3.22. A context-dependent net.

It has been recognized that the possibility of having an event where some of its pre- and postconditions coincide (thus if the preconditions are in the case, then some postconditions are in the case as well) is of great practical interest, since it allows to model in a faithful way the operation of "atomic rewriting", where an item is first read and then written, all in one step. The modelling is the following: the event, say e, represents the operation, while the conditions $\bullet e \cap e \bullet$ (i.e., the items which are both preconditions and postconditions of e) represent the rewritten items. For this reason, we will use nets where such situations are allowed. The definition of enabling for such nets is the following: an event is enabled by a case if 1) both its preconditions and its context conditions are in the case, and 3) its postconditions are either not in the case or, if they are, then they are also preconditions. Note, however, that such definition forbids the enabling of an event whose postcondition is in the case while not being a precondition of the same event.

Definition 31 (enabling) *A case $c \subseteq B$ enables an event $e \in E$ iff $\bullet e \cup \hat{e} \subseteq c$ and $e \bullet \subseteq \bullet e \cup (B - c)$.* ∎

Example: Consider again the context-dependent net in Figure 3.22 and the case $c = \{b_2, b_3, b_4, b_7\}$. Then e_2 and e_4 are the only enabled events. In fact, for example, e_3 is not enabled due to the absence of its context condition b_6 in the considered case. ∎

Similarly to the classical case, a step consists of the taking place of enabled events. However, due to the presence of context conditions, there is an additional requirement: if an item is a context for one event and a precondition or a postcondition for another event, then such two events cannot belong to the same step.

Definition 32 (step) *Given a context-dependent net $CN = (B, E; F_1, F_2)$, if $c_1, c_2 \subseteq B$ and $G \subseteq E$, then the step $c_1[G\rangle c_2$ is defined if:*

- $\forall e \in G$, e is enabled by c_1;

- $\forall e_1, e_2 \in G$, if $e_1 \neq e_2$, then ${}^\bullet e_1 \cap {}^\bullet e_2 = e_1^\bullet \cap e_2^\bullet = \emptyset$, $\widehat{e_1} \cap {}^\bullet e_2 = \widehat{e_1} \cap e_2^\bullet = \emptyset$;

- $c_2 = (c_1 - {}^\bullet G) \cup G^\bullet$.   ∎

Definition 33 ((finite) computations) *Given a context-dependent net* $(B, E; F_1, F_2)$, *a computation is a finite sequence of steps such that each step ends with a case which is the starting case of the subsequent step. I.e. a computation (of length n) is a sequence of the form* $c_0[G_1\rangle c_1[G_2\rangle \ldots [G_n\rangle c_n$.   ∎

The concept which we will use to give a truly concurrent semantics to cc programs is the notion of a contextual process, which is a contextual occurrence net together with a suitable mapping of the events onto the rewrite rules. Informally, a contextual occurrence net is just an acyclic context dependent net. More precisely, the main feature of a contextual occurrence net is the following: given a context dependent net, it is possible to derive an associated dependency relation among its items (events and conditions); then, in a contextual occurrence net such associated relation is a partial order.

The idea is that such relation (seen as a set of pairs) contains all pairs in F_1, plus other pairs, derived by the combination of F_1 and F_2. In fact, if an element b is a postcondition of $e1$ and a context condition of $e2$, then $e2$ depends on $e1$ and this has to be reflected in the partial order. The same holds when b is a context condition of $e1$ and a precondition of $e2$. In fact, in this last case, in any computation where both e_1 and e_2 are present, e_1 must happen before e_2 (that is, b cannot be cancelled before being read).

Definition 34 (dependency) *Consider a context-dependent net* $N = (B, E; F_1, F_2)$. *Then we define a corresponding structure* $(B \cup E, \leq_N)$, *where the dependency relation* $\leq_N$ *is the minimal relation which is reflexive, transitive, and which satisfies the following conditions:*

- $x F_1 y$ *implies* $x \leq_N y$;

- $e1 F_1 b$ *and* $b F_2 e2$ *implies* $e1 \leq_N e2$;

- $b F_2 e1$ *and* $b F_1 e2$ *implies* $e1 \leq_N e2$.   ∎

Therefore in the following we will say that x depends on y whenever $y \leq_N x$. However, a context-dependent net not only gives information about dependency of events and conditions, but also about their mutual exclusion (or conflict). In fact, given one such net, it is possible to derive two relations, besides the dependency relation just defined, all of which are sets of pairs of elements of $(B \cup E)$, which express 1) concurrency and 2) mutual exclusion.

Definition 35 (mutual exclusion and concurrency) *Consider a context-dependent net* $N = (B, E; F_1, F_2)$ *and the associated dependency relation* $\leq_N$. *Assume also that* $\leq$ *is antisymmetric. Then*

- *The mutual exclusion relation $\#_N \subseteq ((B \cup E) \times (B \cup E))$ is defined as follows. First we define $x\#'y$ iff $x, y \in E$ and $\exists z \in B$ such that zF_1x and zF_1y. Then, $\#_N$ is the minimal relation which includes $\#'$ and which is symmetric and hereditary (i.e., if $x\#_Ny$ and $x \leq z$, then $z\#_Ny$).*

- *The concurrency relation co_N is just $((B \cup E) \times (B \cup E)) - (\leq_N \cup \leq_N^{-1} \cup \#_N)$.* ∎

In words, the mutual exclusion is originated by the existence of conditions which cause more than one event, and then it is propagated downwards via the partial order. Finally, two items are concurrent if they are not dependent on each other nor mutually exclusive.

We now come to the notion of a contextual occurrence net, which is just a context-dependent net where the dependency relation is a partial order, there are no "forwards conflicts" (i.e., different conditions with a common precondition), and $\#_N$ is irreflexive. The latter requirement forbids events with mutually exclusive preconditions.

Definition 36 (contextual occurrence net) *A contextual occurrence net is a context-dependent net $N = (B, E; F_1, F_2)$ where*

- $\leq_N$ *is antisymmetric;*

- $b \in B$ *implies $| \ ^\bullet b | \leq_N 1$;*

- $\#_N$ *is irreflexive.* ∎

A useful special case of a contextual occurrence net occurs when the mutual exclusion relation is empty. This means that, taken any two items in the net, they are either concurrent or dependent. Since no conflict is expressed in such nets, they represent a completely deterministic behaviour. For this reason they are called deterministic occurrence nets.

Definition 37 (deterministic contextual occurrence net) *A deterministic contextual occurrence net is a quadruple $N = (B, E; F_1, F_2)$ such that N is a contextual occurrence net with $\#_N = \emptyset$.* ∎

Example: Consider for example the deterministic contextual occurrence net in Figure 3.23 a). Then its dependency partial order can be seen in Figure 3.23 b). ∎

Given a (nondeterministic) contextual occurrence net, it is easy to derive the set of all its subnets which are deterministic.

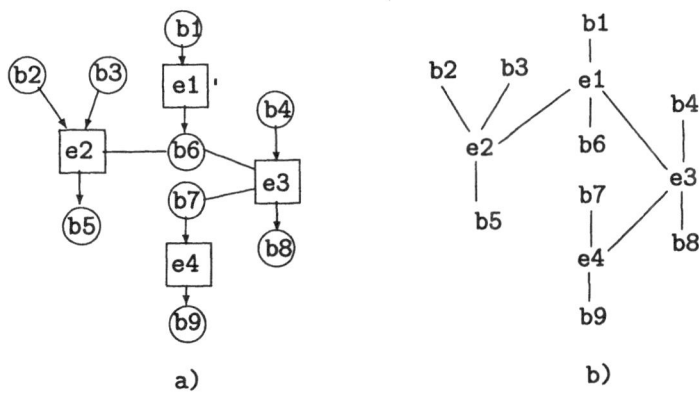

Fig. 3.23. A deterministic contextual occurrence net and the associated partial order.

Definition 38 (from contextual occ. nets to deterministic contextual occ. nets) *Consider a contextual occurrence net $N = (B, E; F_1, F_2)$ and the associated relations $\leq$, $\#$, and co. Then a deterministic contextual occurrence net of N is a deterministic contextual occurrence net $N' = (B', E'; F_1', F_2')$ where*

- $B' \subseteq B$ *and* $E' \subseteq E'$;

- F_1' *and* F_2' *are the restrictions to* B' *and* E' *of* F_1 *and* F_2 *respectively ;*

- $x \in (B' \cup E')$ *and* $y \in (B \cup E)$ *such that* $y \leq x$ *implies that* $y \in (B' \cup E')$.

∎

The last condition states that the set $B' \cup E'$ is left-closed w.r.t. relation $\leq_N$. That is, the causes of the elements in $B' \cup E'$ are in $B' \cup E'$ as well. The intuition behind this condition is that deterministic nets which are not left-closed represent meaningless computations, since there are objects which are causally inconsistent.

Let us now try to relate (nondeterministic) contextual occurrence nets to cc programs. We will do that by defining a contextual process, which is just a contextual occurrence net plus a suitable mapping from the items of the net (i.e., conditions and events) to the agents of the cc program and the rules representing it.

Definition 39 (contextual process) *Given a cc program P with initial agent A, and the associated sets of rewrite rules $RR(P)$, of agents $Ag(P)$, and of constraints D, consider the sets $RB = \{b\theta\}$ and $RE = \{r\theta\}$, with $b \in (Ag(P) \cup D)$, $r \in RR(P)$ and θ any substitution. Then a contextual process is a pair $\langle N, \pi \rangle$, where*

- $N = (B, E; F_1, F_2)$ *is a nondeterministic contextual occurrence net;*

- $\pi : (B \cup E) \to (RB \cup RE)$ *is a mapping with*

  - $b \in B$ *implies* $\pi(b) \in RB$;

  - $e \in E$ *implies* $\pi(e) \in RE$;

  - *consider* $^\circ N = \{x \in B \mid \nexists y \in (B \cup E) \mid y \leq_N x\}$. *Then* $\pi(^\circ N) = A$;

  - *let* $\pi(e) = r\theta$, *with* $r = L \overset{c}{\leadsto} R$. *Then we have* $\pi(^\bullet e) = L\theta$, $\pi(\hat{e}) = c\theta$, *and* $\pi(e^\bullet) = R\theta$. *Notice that here and in the previous definition we homomorphically extended* π *to a function from sets to multisets: the multiplicity of an item in the result is simply the cardinality of its inverse image;*

  - *for each* $e \in E$, *consider* $\pi(e) = r\theta'_e \theta''_e$, *where* θ''_e *replaces the variables which are in* R *but not in* L *nor in* c. *Then for all events* e *and* e' *and variables* x *and* x' *we have:*

    * *let constant* a *occur in the initial agent* A. *Then* $x\theta''_e \neq a$
    * $x\theta''_e = x'\theta''_{e'}$ *implies* $x = x'$ *and* $e = e'$

    i.e. the constants introduced by the rewrite rule instantiations associated to events must be fresh, namely they must be all different and different from the constants in the initial state.   ∎

In the following we will show how to obtain a contextual process from any given cc program, and we will prove that such contextual process contains the information necessary to represent all possible computations of the given program.

3.1.5.2 The Concurrent Semantics The idea is to take the set of rewrite rules $RR(P)$ associated to a given cc program P and to incrementally construct a corresponding contextual process. Such process is able to represent all possible computations of the cc program P in a unique structure.

Definition 40 (from rewrite rules to a contextual process) *Given a cc program* P, *the pair* $CP(P) = \langle (B, E; F_1, F_2), \pi \rangle$ *is constructed by means of the following two inference rules:*

- $A(\mathbf{a})$ *initial agent of* P
  implies
  $\langle A(\mathbf{a}), \emptyset, 1 \rangle \in B$;

- $\{s_1, \ldots, s_n\} \subseteq B$, *where* s_i co s_j *for all* i, j, $i \neq j$, $i, j = 1, \ldots, n$, *and* $s_i = \langle e_i, B_i(\mathbf{a_i}), k_i \rangle$ *for all* $i = 1, \ldots, n$, $r \in RR(P)$ *such that* $L(r) = \{B_1(\mathbf{x_1}), \ldots, B_j(\mathbf{x_j})\}$, *and* $c(r) = \{B_{j+1}(\mathbf{x_{j+1}}), \ldots, B_n(\mathbf{x_n})\}$, *and* $\exists$ *a substitution* $[\mathbf{a/x}]$ *such that* $B_i(\mathbf{x_i})[\mathbf{a/x}] = B_i(\mathbf{a_i})$
  implies

- $e = \langle r[\mathbf{a}/\mathbf{x}], \{s_1, \ldots, s_n\}, 1 \rangle \in E$,
- $s_i F_1 e$ for all $i = 1, \ldots, j$,
- $s_i F_2 e$ for all $i = j+1, \ldots, n$,
- let h be the multiplicity of $B(\mathbf{x}, y_1, \ldots, y_m)$ in $R(r)$. Then for all $l = 1, \ldots, h$,
   $b_l = \langle B[\mathbf{a}/\mathbf{x}][\langle e, y_1 \rangle / y_1] \ldots [\langle e, y_m \rangle / y_m], e, l \rangle \in B$, and $e F_1 b_l$.

Moreover, for any item $x = \langle x_1, x_2, x_3 \rangle \in (B \cup E)$, $\pi(x) = x_1$.   ∎

It is easy to see that this construction is very similar to that in Definition 25. In fact, the basic idea is the same: to apply the rewrite rules, starting from the initial agent, in any possible way, so to obtain a set of terms which represent all possible objects and steps involved in the computations of the program.

While in the previous section (a subset of) such terms was then used to model the events of an event structure, here they model the conditions and the events of a contextual net. Moreover, while before the three relations of concurrency, dependency, and mutual exclusion were defined over the terms, now a flow and context relation are defined (from which the same three relations can be derived). Note however that only the terms representing the rule applications appeared in the event structure, while now the contextual net contains also those representing the constraints and the agents.

Even the technique used to distinguish different occurrences of the same object is the same: we generate a new event for each rule application and new conditions representing the right hand side of the rule, and we structure each event or condition as a triple, where the first element contains the object being represented (either an agent, or a token, or a rule application), the second element contains the whole history of the event or condition, and the third element is a number which allows us to distinguish different occurrences with the same history (we recall that a state is a multiset, while here we are generating a set of conditions).

To use the notion of a contextual process, a mapping π is here needed, which tells us either the rule or the object represented (with the applied substitution) by the item of the net. However, such mapping always maps the triple representing a term to its first element. Therefore in the following we will often omit it.

Due to the difference between the three relations and the F_1 and F_2 relation of the net, this construction has to distinguish between the conditions (already created) which match the left hand side of the rule under consideration, and those which match its context. In fact, the first ones have to be connected through the F_1 relation to the event representing the rule application, while the second ones need the F_2 relation.

Example (cc programs and contextual processes): Consider the cc program P consisting of the initial agent $IA = tell(c_1, c_2, c) \to A$, where

$A = (ask(c_1) \to A_1 + ask(c_2) \to success)$,
$A_1 = A_2 \parallel A_2$,
$A_2 = ask(c) \to success$,

and no declarations. The rules corresponding to such agent and all its subagents are:

$r_1 : IA \rightsquigarrow c_1, c_2, c, A$
$r_2 : A \overset{c_1}{\rightsquigarrow} A_1$
$r_3 : A \overset{c_2}{\rightsquigarrow} success$
$r_4 : A_1 \rightsquigarrow 2A_2$
$r_5 : A_2 \overset{c}{\rightsquigarrow} success$.

For simplicity sake, we assume the entailment relation to be empty (or not relevant to the constraints involved in such program). Furthermore, the variables are not taken into consideration. This program has two alternative finite computations, depending on how agent A evolves. In one case, we have the parallel evolution of two occurrences of A_2 (even though they both ask for the same constraint c), and in the other case we have one computation step generating the success agent.

The process that is generated for this program is as follows (again, we will not explicitly write the mapping π, since each triple is mapped by π to its first element). First, condition $s_1 = \langle IA, \emptyset, 1 \rangle$ is generated for the initial agent IA. At this point, rule r_1 can be applied, and thus we generate event $e_1 = \langle r_1, \{s_1\}, 1 \rangle$ to represent the rule application, and conditions $s_2 = \langle A, e_1, 1 \rangle$, $s_3 = \langle c_1, e_1, 1 \rangle$, $s_4 = \langle c_2, e_1, 1 \rangle$, and $s_5 = \langle c, e_1, 1 \rangle$ to represent its right hand side. Moreover, we set $s_1 F_1 e_1$, and $e_1 F_1 s_i$ for $i = 2, \ldots, 5$.

Since there are conditions representing A, c_1, and c_2 (i.e., s_2, s_3, and s_4), rules r_2 and r_3 can now be applied, and thus we have events $e_2 = \langle r_2, \{s_2, s_3\}, 1 \rangle$ and $e_3 = \langle r_3, \{s_2, s_4\}, 1 \rangle$, as well as conditions $s_6 = \langle A_1, e_2, 1 \rangle$ and $s_7 = \langle success, e_3, 2 \rangle$. Moreover, we also have $s_2 F_1 e_2$, $s_3 F_2 e_2$, $e_2 F_1 s_6$, $s_2 F_1 e_3$, $s_4 F_2 e_3$, $e_3 F_1 s_7$.

Now there is a condition representing A_1, thus rule r_4 can be applied, and we have the event $e_4 = \langle r_4, \{s_6\}, 1 \rangle$, and the conditions $s_8 = \langle A_2, e_4, 1 \rangle$ and $s_9 = \langle A_2, e_4, 2 \rangle$. Moreover, $s_6 F_1 e_4$, $e_4 F_1 s_8$, and $e_4 F_1 s_9$.

Now both s_8 and s_9 match the left hand side of rule r_5, and there is a condition representing c (i.e., s_5), therefore we can apply twice rule r_5, obtaining $e_5 = \langle r_5, \{s_5, s_8\}, 1 \rangle$, $s_{10} = \langle success, e_5, 1 \rangle$, $s_8 F_1 e_5$, $s_5 F_2 e_5$, and $e_5 F_1 s_{10}$ for the first application, and $e_6 = \langle r_5, \{s_5, s_9\}, 1 \rangle$, $s_{11} = \langle success, e_6, 1 \rangle$, $s_9 F_1 e_6$, $s_5 F_2 e_6$, and $e_6 F_1 s_{11}$ for the second application.

Thus we obtained the contextual process $\langle N, \pi \rangle$, where $N = (B, E; F_1, F_2)$, and $B = \{s_1, \ldots, s_{11}\}$, $E = \{e_1 \ldots, e_6\}$, and F_1 and F_2 are as defined above. Figure 3.24 shows such a net N. In N, it is easy to see that e_2 causally depends on e_1, since they are related by a chain of F_1 pairs. Similarly, e_3 depends on e_1. However, e_3 and e_2 do not depend on each other, and they are not even concurrent. In fact, thet are mutually exclusive, since they have a common precondition. This means the the rules represented by e_2 and e_3, i.e., r_2 and

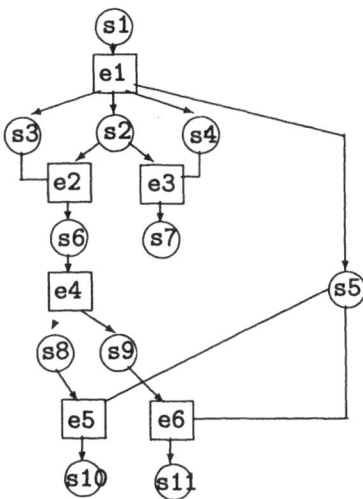

Fig. 3.24. The contextual occurrence net corresponding to a cc program.

r_3, cannot be applied in the same computation, but only in two alternative computations. Then, we have that e_4 depends on e_2 because of a chain of F_1 pairs. Also, e_5 depends on e_4. Finally, e_6 depends on e_4 as well. However, e_5 and e_6 are concurrent, since they do not depend on each other and they are not mutually exclusive. Note that e_5 and e_6 have a common context condition. However, this does not generate any dependency, as desired. ∎

Theorem 3.1 $CP(P)$ **is a contextual process** *Given a cc program P, consider the structure $CP(P)$ as defined above. Then, $CP(P)$ is a contextual process.* ∎

The process $CP(P)$ is able to represent all deterministic computations possible for the given cc program P. The following theorem formalizes this claim.

Theorem 3.2 soundness and completeness of $CP(P)$ *Let P be a cc program and let $CP(P) = \langle N, \pi \rangle$ be the corresponding contextual process. Given a computation of P, there is:*

- *an α-equivalent computation*

$$S_1 \stackrel{r_1[\mathbf{a_1}/\mathbf{x_1}]}{\Longrightarrow} S_2 \stackrel{r_2[\mathbf{a_2}/\mathbf{x_2}]}{\Longrightarrow} S_3 \ldots$$

- *a deterministic contextual occurrence net of N, say N', with associated partial order $\leq'$, and one of its linearizations (restricted to events), say $e_1 e_2, \ldots$,*

such that $\pi(e_i) = r_i[\mathbf{a_i}/\mathbf{x_i}]$ for all $i = 1, 2, \ldots$.
Also, for any linearization $e_1 e_2 \ldots$ of the partial order associated to a determin-
istic contextual occurrence net of N, there is a computation of P

$$S_1 \overset{r_1[\mathbf{a_1}/\mathbf{x_1}]}{\Longrightarrow} S_2 \overset{r_2[\mathbf{a_2}/\mathbf{x_2}]}{\Longrightarrow} S_3 \ldots$$

such that, if $e_i = \langle e_{i1}, e_{i2}, e_{i3} \rangle$ and $\pi(e_i) = r$, then $r_i[\mathbf{a_i}/\mathbf{x_i}] = r$ for all $i = 1, \ldots$.

∎

3.1.6 Further Work and Applications

The concurrent semantics we have described in this paper have to be considered only as a formal basis upon which to reason about cc programs. In fact, the explicit presence of the information about concurrency, dependency, and mutual exclusion, can be useful in order to understand better the behaviour of cc programs with respect to such concepts. However, it is only a basis in the sense that, once a particular application had been chosen, it would be necessary to tailor the semantics for that application, possibly simplifying the partial order, or the event structure, or the contextual net by some sort of abstraction, which allows either to forget some elements of the contextual net, or to identify several nets, or both.

It is easy to see that the last semantics is the most informative, among the three we presented in this paper. In fact, the contextual net contains all the information about both the concurrency (which is present also in the other two semantics) and the nondeterminism (which is instead present only in the event structure semantics). Moreover, it provides a representation of both computation steps (and this holds also for the other two semantics) and of the agents and constraints (and this hold only for the partial order semantics. Therefore it can be said to combine the information of both previous semantics in one unique structure, the contextual process. While it is true that all such information can be very useful for some tasks, it is reasonable to think that some of this information is not relevant for the particular application in mind.

For example, if we want to know the maximal level of concurrency of a given program, then such information can be obtained by just looking at the events of the contextual net, and by computing the maximum number of concurrent events. Another way of saying this is that the event structure is enough for this application. If instead we want to know which agent depends on which constraint, then events can be forgotten. The restriction to only some kind of elements can possibly be done after the net has been generated, by first obtaining the three relations of the net (concurrency, dependency, and mutual exclusion), and then deleting from them all the pairs which involve some element of the non-desired sort.

Moreover, several nets can be identified, if we feel that the programs which correspond to such nets should be identified. For example, if we wish to recover the input-output semantics for cc programs, then we would identify all those nets which "produce" the same set of constraints. A formal way of saying that a net produces a set of constraints $S = \{c_1, \ldots, c_n\}$ is that such a net has n maximal deterministic subnets, say $N_1, \ldots, N_n$, such that the set of tokens appearing in N_i is logically equivalent to c_i. Our semantics, as it is now, makes no identifications at all, since the syntax of the program itself is contained in the semantics, via the mapping π of the process.

To make a concrete example where our semantics can be a useful tool, let us consider the automatic parallelization of logic programs (Lloyd 1987) or constraint logic programs (CLP) (Jaffar and Lassez 1987), which is a typical task where the concepts of dependency and concurrency are essential. In fact, the aim is to run in parallel, independently, as many goals as possible while of course not loosing any solution (soundness) nor taking a longer time (efficiency) w.r.t. the sequential execution of the same program (Hermenegildo and Rossi 1990; de la Banda, Hermenegildo, and Marriott 1993). The restriction to only sound and efficient parallelizations means that only goals which do not affect each other, that is, which are independent, can be run in parallel. Therefore any tool that can help understand whether two goals are independent or not would be of great help to such parallelization task. Our semantics can be used with profit to this extent. In fact, suppose we consider a CLP program as a cc program (it would just be a cc program without any ask agent, and with nondeterminism intended as don't know nondeterminism). Then the contextual net associated to such program would contain all the dependency and concurrency information needed to decide which goals to run in parallel safely. In fact, if two agents turn out to be concurrent in the net, then it means that they do not need each other during the computations of the program, and thus are independent. Note however that some adjustment has to be made to our semantics, since we must be able to model the conflicting situation in which different agents attempt to accomplish inconsistent tells. This can be done by adding one more relation to the three already there, called the inconsistency relation, which contains those pairs of elements (agents, events, or tokens) which are inconsistent with each other, or generate inconsistency if run together. The existence of this relation can then be used to add some more dependency links (besides those generated during the construction phase) in order to force, only for the inconsistent pairs, the left-to-right execution order given by the CLP programmer in the clauses. In this way, the events that can be safely executed in parallel are all those which are still concurrent after the addition of such new links. By adopting our semantics, not only goals, i.e., entire computation trees, can be run in parallel, but also parts of computation trees. In fact, our semantics gives the independence information at the smallest level of granularity. A more detailed description of how to use our concurrent semantics to help the automatic parallelization of CLP programs can be found in (Bueno, de la Banda, Hermenegildo, Rossi, and Montanari 1993).

We plan to enrich even more our semantic approach via the possibility of providing a structured representation of the computation states. In fact, in any of the three semantics we have presented here, a computation state is always a set or a multiset of items (representing agents and constraints). This is true also in the first semantics, even though the operational semantics in that case represents the state as a graph. This is not very realistic, since agents and constraints often share variables, and such sharing is not expressed in the actual semantics. Therefore our idea is to represent a state as a graph even in the concurrent semantics. Starting from the contextual net semantics, this development would lead us to the definition of a *graph process*, which differs from a contextual process just in the structure of the underlying set of conditions: a graph instead of a set.

Acknowledgments

This research has been partially supported by the GRAGRA Basic Research Esprit Working Group n.7183, the ACCLAIM Basic Research Esprit Working Group n.7195 and Alenia S.p.A.

References

Boer, F. D. de and C. Palamidessi (1991). A fully abstract model for concurrent constraint programming. In *Proc. CAAP*. LNCS 493, Springer-Verlag, pp. 296-319.

Bueno, F., M. J. G. de la Banda, M. Hermenegildo, F. Rossi, and U. Montanari (1993). Towards true concurrency semantics based transformation between clp and cc. Technical Report TR CLP 2/93.1, Universidad Politecnica de Madrid, Facultad de Informatica.

Codognet, C., P. Codognet, and G. Filé (1988). Yet another intelligent backtracking method. In *Proc. 5th International Conference and Symposium on Logic Programming*. MIT Press.

Corradini, A., H. Ehrig, M. Lowe, U. Montanari, and F. Rossi (1992). Standard representation of graphs and graph derivations. Technical report, TU Berlin.

de la Banda, M. G., M. Hermenegildo, and K. Marriott (1993). Independence in constraint logic programs. In *Proc. International Logic Programming Symposium*. MIT Press.

Ehrig, H. (1978). Introduction to the algebraic theory of graph grammars. In *Proc. International Workshop on Graph Grammars*. LNCS 73, Springer-Verlag, pp. 1-69.

Hermenegildo, M. and F. Rossi (1990). Non strict independent and-parallelism. In *Proc. ICLP90*. MIT Press.

Jaffar, J. and J. Lassez (1987). Constraint logic programming. In *Proc. POPL*. ACM.

Lloyd, J. W. (1987). *Foundations of Logic Programming*. Springer Verlag.

MacLane, S. (1971). *Categories for the Working Mathematician*. Springer-Verlag.

Montanari, U. and F. Rossi (1991). True concurrency in concurrent constraint programming. In *Proc. ILPS91*. MIT Press.

Montanari, U. and F. Rossi (1992). Graph rewriting for a partial ordering semantics of concurrent constraint programming. *Theoretical Computer Science*. Special issue on graph grammars, Courcelle B. and Rozenberg eds.

Montanari, U. and F. Rossi (1993a). Contextual nets. Technical Report TR-4/93, CS Department, University of Pisa, Italy.

Montanari, U. and F. Rossi (1993b). Contextual occurrence nets and concurrent constraint programming. In *Proc. Dagstuhl Seminar on Graph Transformations in Computer Science*. LNCS 776, Springer-Verlag, pp. 280-295.

Peled, D. and A. Pnueli (1990). Proving partial order liveness properties. In *Proc. ICALP*. LNCS 443, Springer-Verlag, pp. 553-571.

Plotkin, G. (1981). A structural approach to operational semantics. Technical Report TR DAIMI FN-19, Aarhus University, CS Department.

Reisig, W. (1985). *Petri Nets: An Introduction*. EATCS Monographs on Theoretical Computer Science. Springer-Verlag.

Rossi, F. (1993). *Constraints and Concurrency*. Ph. D. thesis, University of Pisa, TD-14/93.

Saraswat, V. (1993). *Concurrent Constraint Programming*. MIT Press.

Saraswat, V. A. and M. Rinard (1990). Concurrent constraint programming. In *Proc. POPL*. ACM.

Saraswat, V. A., M. Rinard, and P. Panangaden (1991). Semantic foundations of concurrent constraint programming. In *Proc. POPL*. ACM.

Scott, D. S. (1982). Domains for denotational semantics. In *Proc. ICALP*, LNCS 140. Springer-Verlag, pp. 325-392.

Shapiro, E. (1989). The family of concurrent logic programming languages. *ACM Computing Surveys 21*(3).

Winskel, G. (1986). Event structures. In *Petri nets: applications and relationships to other models of concurrency*. LNCS 255, Springer-Verlag, pp. 325-392.

3.2 Abstract Interpretation for (Constraint) Logic Programming

M. Bruynooghe and D. Boulanger

Katholieke Universiteit Leuven
Celestijnenlaan 200, AB 3001 Heverlee, Belgium
Maurice.Bouynooghe
@@cs.kuleuven.ac.be

The theory of abstract interpretation, initially developed by the Cousot's for imperative languages has been adapted to logic programming where it has become a very active area of research, illustrated by the list of references in the survey paper (CoC92b). It has reached a level of maturity where it is included as an optimisation tool in some prototype implementations of Prolog. In recent years, also abstract interpretation of constraint logic programming has been studied. Abstract interpretation is an area where the majority of publications is very technical in nature. This tutorial aims at making the topic more accessible to newcomers. Therefore, we have tried to present the main intuitions in a rather informal way. We have preferred informal accounts above very precise but rigid and hard to penetrate formalism. The paper is not a survey, so although we give some entry points to the literature, we have not aimed at completeness.

A first part discusses the framework of abstract interpretation in very general terms, as a way to approximate the semantics which has to be formulated as a fixpoint of some function. A second part applies this theory to logic programming, at the same time showing general examples of the theory, and explaining some of the major approaches towards abstract interpretation of logic programs. A third and a final part tries to explain that the step from logic programming to constraint logic programming is a small one and that frameworks developed for abstract interpretation of logic programs carry over to constraint logic programming.

This chapter assumes some familiarity with the basic notions of logic programming and with the concept of fixpoint. The reader can find material concerning these in (Llo87).

3.2.1 Basic Principles

3.2.1.1 Abstracting computations As part of our education we have learned to compute properties of the results of calculations by performing approximate or abstract computations. The general idea is to abstract the operands, apply an abstract operator and to obtain a result which is the abstraction of the result of the concrete operation.

A typical example mastered in the first years of school, is the multiplication of multidigit numbers. To check against silly errors, due to a slip of our mind, we have learned to perform an independent abstract computation: take the operands modulo 9^1 and multiply them modulo 9. The result should be equal to the result, modulo 9, of the original multiplication. Although this check cannot reveal deviations from the correct result which are multiples of 9, it is so good at catching errors, that it is known as the nine proof.

Similarly, in our physics course, we learned to check the dimensions of formulas retrieved from our unreliable human memory before applying them in solving a problem. For example, when in doubt whether $2\pi r$, or πr^2 is the right formula for computing the area of a circle, we compute their dimensions. Using L for dimension of length, we obtain L^1 for the former and L^2 for the latter. Comparing these results with the dimension of an area, L^2, we can make the proper choice.

These simple examples suggest the notion of an abstraction function, a total function mapping elements from a concrete domain into elements of an abstract domain and the following definition for (exact) abstraction:

Definition 3.1 *Exact Abstraction*
Let $f : D_1 \times D_2 \times \cdots \times D_n \rightarrow D$ be a function over concrete domains $D_1, D_2, \cdots, D_n$ and D;   let $\alpha_i : D_i \rightarrow D_i{}^{\alpha}$, $(i = 1, \cdots, n)$ and $\alpha : D \rightarrow D^{\alpha}$ be abstraction functions and $f^{\alpha} : D_1{}^{\alpha} \times D_2{}^{\alpha} \times \cdots \times D_n{}^{\alpha} \rightarrow D^{\alpha}$ a function over the abstract domains. f^{α} is the exact abstraction of f iff for all $i_1 \in D_1, \cdots, i_n \in D_n$ holds: $\alpha(f(i_1, \cdots, i_n)) = f^{\alpha}(\alpha_1(i_1), \ldots, \alpha_n(i_n))$.   □

Example 3.2 *Abstraction of Multiplication*

$$f = mult : N \times N \rightarrow N \qquad\qquad \alpha_1 = \alpha_2 = \alpha = mod_9 : N \rightarrow N_9$$
$$mult(x, y) = x * y \qquad\qquad\qquad mod_9(x) = x \, modulo \, 9$$

where the abstract domain N_9 is the set $\{0, 1, \cdots, 8\}$; elements are denoted x^{α} and y^{α}.

$$f^{\alpha} = mult^{\alpha} : N_9 \times N_9 \rightarrow N_9$$
$$mult^{\alpha}(x^{\alpha}, y^{\alpha}) = mod_9(x^{\alpha} * y^{\alpha})$$

$mult^{\alpha}$ is an exact abstraction of $mult$.   □

However, this definition is too stringent. A first problem is with partial functions. Consider division and the use of the $modulo_9$ function as abstraction function for the division. While division by 0 is undefined, division by 9, or multipliers of 9 are defined. But 0 and 9 are indistinguishable after abstraction, so exact abstraction of the division operation is not achievable. A first step towards a solution consists of extending the partial function to be abstracted into a total function. We add an element $\perp$ (undefined) to the concrete domain. The question arises how to abstract $\perp$. By a new element $\perp^{\alpha}$ in the abstract domain D^{α}? Doing so would make the goal of exact abstraction unachievable as $\perp^{\alpha}$ cannot be the exact abstraction of the result of a division by 9. The problem

---

[1] which we implement by taking, modulo 9, the sum of the digits

has nothing to do with the element $\perp$ but points to a second problem with the notion of exact abstraction.

Consider sign abstraction (abstract domain $\{+, 0^\alpha, -\}$) for numbers. While exact abstraction of multiplication is straightforward, it is not achievable for addition: $+ +^\alpha -$ should be $+$ if we consider abstraction of $7 + (-5)$, but 0^α if we consider the abstraction of $7 + (-7)$ and $-$ if we consider the abstraction of $5 + (-7)$. To get out of this impasse, we introduce a new element e.g. $\top$ which is not the abstraction of any number, but a safe approximation of the abstraction of any number, i.e. a safe approximation of $+$, 0^α and $-$. In addition we replace the notion of exact abstraction by the notion of approximate abstraction or safe abstraction.

Similar, in the division example, one has to be satisfied with a result which approximates as well the abstraction of $\perp$ as the result of division by multiples of 9.

Definition 3.3 *Safe Approximation*
Given domain D equipped with a partial order $\subseteq$; an element d_1 is safe approximation of an element d_2 iff $d_2 \subseteq d_1$.   □

Definition 3.4 *Safe Abstraction*
Let $f : D_1 \times D_2 \times \cdots \times D_n \rightarrow D$ be a total function over the concrete domains $D_1, D_2, \cdots, D_n$ and D; let $\alpha_i : D_i \rightarrow D_i{}^\alpha$, $(i = 1, \cdots, n)$ and $\alpha : D \rightarrow D^\alpha$ be abstraction functions, $f^\alpha : D_1{}^\alpha \times D_2{}^\alpha \times \cdots \times D_n{}^\alpha \rightarrow D^\alpha$ a total function over the abstract domains and $\subseteq$ a partial order over D^α. f^α is a safe abstraction of f iff for all $i_1 \in D_1, \cdots, i_n \in D_n$ holds: $\alpha(f(i_1, \cdots, i_n)) \subseteq f^\alpha(\alpha_1(i_1), \ldots, \alpha_n(i_n))$.   □

Example 3.5 *Abstraction of Addition*

$$f = add : Z \times Z \rightarrow Z \qquad \alpha_1 = \alpha_2 = \quad \alpha = sign : Z \rightarrow Z^\alpha$$
$$add(x, y) = x + y \qquad sign(x) = \quad \text{if } x > 0 \text{ then } +$$
$$\text{else} \quad \text{if } x = 0 \text{ then } 0^\alpha$$
$$\text{else} \quad -$$

where the abstract domain Z^α is the set $\{+, 0^\alpha, -, \top\}$ and is ordered as follows: $+ \subseteq \top, 0^\alpha \subseteq \top$ and $- \subseteq \top$.

$$f^\alpha = add^\alpha : Z^\alpha \times Z^\alpha \rightarrow Z^\alpha$$

add^α	$+$	0^α	$-$	$\top$
$+$	$+$	$+$	$\top$	$\top$
0^α	$+$	0^α	$-$	$\top$
$-$	$\top$	$-$	$-$	$\top$
$\top$	$\top$	$\top$	$\top$	$\top$

add^α is a safe abstraction of add.   □

Example 3.6

As more elaborate example, to be used later, we consider the safe abstraction of a reduction step in the Martelli-Montanari unification algorithm (MaM82). The domain of the reduction step is an equation system; this is a set of equations over terms constructed from function symbols and variables. Also $\perp$ is an equation system, it denotes failure. We use the notation $e :: Eqs$ for the multiset[2] Eqs extended with element e, we use X, Y, Z to denote variables, T and S to denote terms, $var(e)$ to denote the set of variables in expression e and X/T to denote a substitution. This allows us to formulate the reduction step as the following set of reduction rules:

$$X = X :: Eqs \xrightarrow{remove} Eqs$$
$$X = T :: Eqs \xrightarrow{substitute} \text{ if } X \in var(T) \text{ then } \perp$$
$$\text{else if } X \in var(Eqs) \text{ then } X = T :: Eqs[X/T]$$

$$f(T_1, \cdots, T_n) = X :: Eqs \xrightarrow{switch} X = f(T_1, \cdots, T_n) :: Eqs$$
$$f(T_1, \cdots, T_n) = g(S_1, \cdots, S_m) :: Eqs \xrightarrow{peel}$$
$$\text{if } f/n = g/m \text{ then } T_1 = S_1 :: \cdots :: T_n = S_n :: Eqs \text{ else } \perp$$

Consider the following abstraction function over terms ($\mathcal{G}$ is a new 0-arity function symbol)

$$\alpha(T) = \text{ if } ground(T) \text{ then } \mathcal{G} \text{ else } T$$

This can be extended into an abstraction function over equation systems:

$$\alpha(\perp) = \perp^\alpha$$
$$\alpha(\emptyset) = (\mathcal{G} = \mathcal{G})$$
$$\alpha(T = S :: Eqs) = \text{ if ground } (T = S) \text{ then } \alpha(Eqs)$$
$$\text{else } \alpha(T) = \alpha(S) :: \alpha(Eqs)$$

The idea is to have a one-to-one mapping between the non-groud equations of the concrete and the abstract system and to abstract the zero or more ground equations of the concrete system by single equations $\mathcal{G} = \mathcal{G}$. In the abstract reduction step below, α is also applied on abstract equation systems. In this trivial extension of α, $\mathcal{G}$ is considered as a ground term.

Now we can formulate the following abstract reduction step (T and S can also denote $\mathcal{G}$):

$$X = X :: Eqs^\alpha \xrightarrow{remove} Eqs^\alpha$$
$$X = T :: Eqs^\alpha \xrightarrow{substitute} \text{ if } X \in var(T) \text{ then } \perp^\alpha$$
$$\text{else if } X \in var(Eqs^\alpha) \text{ then } X = T :: \alpha(Eqs^\alpha[X/T])$$

---

[2]A multiset can have several occurrences of the same element.

$$f(T_1, \cdots, T_n) = X :: Eqs^\alpha \xrightarrow{switch} X = f(T_1, \cdots, T_n) :: Eqs^\alpha$$
$$f(T_1, \cdots, T_n) = g(S_1, \cdots, S_m) :: Eqs^\alpha \xrightarrow{peel}$$

if $f/n = g/m = \mathcal{G}($ so $n = m = 0)$ then $\mathcal{G} = \mathcal{G} :: Eqs^\alpha$
else if $f/n = g/m$ then $\alpha(T_1 = S_1 :: \cdots :: T_n = S_n :: Eqs^\alpha)$
else if $f/n = \mathcal{G}$ then $\alpha(\mathcal{G} = S_1 :: \cdots :: \mathcal{G} = S_n :: Eqs^\alpha)$
else if $g/n = \mathcal{G}$ then $\alpha(T_1 = \mathcal{G} :: \cdots :: T_n = \mathcal{G} :: Eqs^\alpha)$
else $\bot^\alpha$

Equipped with the partial order $\bot^\alpha \sqsubseteq Eqs^\alpha$ for any abstract equation system Eqs^α, the abstract reduction step is a safe abstraction of the concrete reduction step. However, it is not an exact reduction step. Indeed, consider for example, the concrete system $h(a) = g(a, b) :: Eqs$, assume abstracted as $\mathcal{G} = \mathcal{G} :: Eqs^\alpha$ and a reduction step on the first equation. Concrete reduction yields $\bot$, abstract reduction yields $\mathcal{G} = \mathcal{G} :: Eqs^\alpha$ which is a safe approximation of $\bot$. Notice that one could obtain an exact abstraction by restricting the concrete domain to solvable systems, then $\bot$ and $\bot^\alpha$ are not needed.   □

A simpler approach would have been to have no equations $\mathcal{G} = \mathcal{G}$ in the abstract system and to have sets instead of multisets as representation of concrete and abstract systems. However, the close correspondence between a concrete and abstract reduction step would be lost. Indeed, a peel step on a concrete ground equation corresponds to a no-operation on the abstract system. Also, when several non-ground equations are abstracted by the same abstract equation, then a reduction step on that abstract equation corresponds to a number of reduction steps in the concrete system.

3.2.1.2 Abstracting programs

While manual computations are usually abstracted to catch some of the errors produced by their unreliable implementation in our brains, programs are usually abstracted with a different purpose. One is interested in properties of (intermediate) results which are produced during execution of the program. A well known application is in compiler optimisation. For example, knowing that a predicate in a logic program is always called with its first argument ground allows to specialise the code.

Programs have two features which distinguish them from simple manual computations. Firstly, nontrivial programs have either iterative or recursive constructs, which allow to perform long sequences of primitive operations. Abstracting such a sequence by abstracting each operation in the sequence is problematic. The concrete sequence can be very long, even worse, it can be infinite. As an example consider the well known append predicate (see example 3.11 in section 3.2.2.1), called with all arguments variables; it produces through backtracking, an infinite number of solutions. Secondly, programs are usually intended to be executed for many different inputs, while a manual computation is performed for a particular input. It is usually impractical to perform the abstract computation for every allowed input.

A plausible solution for the second problem is to lift f, the operation to be abstracted, to an operation f' between power domains. As will be seen in section 3.2.1.5, this approach also contains the germ for solving the termination problem.

Example 3.7
Consider the sign abstraction of multiplication. The input of a multiplication consist of a tuple of numbers. The purpose of lifting is to consider a set of tuples. Therefore, we define multiplication as an operation on the domain of tuples of numbers.

$$mult : Z^2 \to Z$$
$$mult(<x,y>) = x * y$$

The abstract domain $Sign$ is the set $\{+, 0^\alpha, -\}$. We need two abstraction functions:

$$\begin{aligned}
\alpha_1 : Z &\to Sign & \alpha_2 : Z^2 &\to Sign^2 \\
\alpha_1(n) = &\quad \text{if } n > 0 \text{ then } + & \alpha_2(<x,y>) &= <\alpha_1(x), \alpha_1(y)> \\
&\quad \text{else if } n = 0 \text{ then } 0^\alpha \\
&\quad \text{else } -
\end{aligned}$$

Lifting $mult$ to power-domains, we obtain ($\mathcal{P}D$ denotes the powerdomain of D):

$$mult' : \mathcal{P}Z^2 \to \mathcal{P}Z$$
$$mult'(S) = \{mult(<x,y>) \,|<x,y> \in S\}$$

Lifting the abstraction function we obtain:

$$\begin{aligned}
\alpha_1' : \mathcal{P}Z &\to \mathcal{P}Sign & \alpha_2' : \mathcal{P}Z^2 &\to \mathcal{P}Sign^2 \\
\alpha_1'(S) &= \{\alpha_1(n) \,|\, n \in S\} & \alpha_2'(S) &= \{\alpha_2(<x,y>) \,|<x,y> \in S\}
\end{aligned}$$

The abstraction of $mult'$ is:

$$mult'^\alpha : \mathcal{P}Sign^2 \to \mathcal{P}Sign$$
$$mult'^\alpha(S) = \{mult^\alpha(<x,y>) \,|<x,y> \in S\}$$

where $mult^\alpha : Sign^2 \to Sign$ is defined by the following table:

$mult^\alpha$	$+$	0^α	$-$
$+$	$+$	0^α	$-$
0^α	0^α	0^α	0^α
$-$	$-$	0^α	$+$

□

Power domains are partially ordered by the subset ordering. Even stronger, they are complete lattices. So the lifted abstraction function $\alpha' : \mathcal{P}D \to \mathcal{P}D^\alpha$ maps elements from a lattice into a lattice (see fig.3.1 for the lattice of $\mathcal{P}Sign$).

One can make a lot of interesting observations:

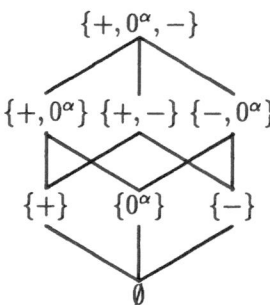

Fig. 3.1. Lattice for $\mathcal{P}Sign$

- every element d of $\mathcal{P}D$ has an abstraction $d^\alpha = \alpha'(d)$ in $\mathcal{P}D^\alpha$.

- elements $d_2{}^\alpha \supseteq d_1{}^\alpha = \alpha'(d_1)$ are *safe* approximations of the abstraction of d_1.

- elements $d_1{}^\alpha = \alpha'(d_1)$ are *safe* approximations of the abstractions of $d_2 \subseteq d_1$.

- safe approximations $d_2{}^\alpha$ of an abstraction $d_1{}^\alpha$ of an element d_1 can also be seen as correct abstractions of d_1, however, they are not as precise. Every element d_1 has a *best* abstraction $d_1{}^\alpha = \alpha'(d_1)$.

- one can also consider a function γ from $\mathcal{P}D^\alpha$ to $\mathcal{P}D$, the concretization function, mapping an element d^α to d, the largest set it abstracts. This set is uniquely defined as it is the union of all sets abstracted by d^α.

However, in many cases, it is undesirable to have the full power domain, i.e. the abstract domain could be too big, or could contain too much irrelevant detail. So requesting that the abstract domain is a power domain, or even a subset of a power domain is too rigid. For example, it might be preferable to restrict the domain $\mathcal{P}Sign$ to the elements $\perp(=\emptyset)$, $+$, $-$, 0^α $\top = \{+, -, 0^\alpha\}$.

Also, there is an interest in considering several layers of abstraction where the abstract domain of some layer is the concrete domain of the next layer (an example will be mentioned in section 3.2.2.1). Consequently, requiring the concrete domain to be a power domain is also too restrictive. However a number of properties are quite essential:

- An order relation between the elements of the concrete domain D. In the sequel, this order relation will be denoted by $\subseteq$ as it is a quite natural case that the concrete domain consists of sets.

- An order relation between the elements of the abstract domain D^α. In the sequel, this order relation will be denoted by $\sqsubseteq$, to distinguish it from the order relation in the concrete domain, and as the elements of the abstract domain are often not sets.

- The abstraction function α is total, i.e. every element of D has an abstraction in D^α.

- Elements $d^\alpha \sqsupseteq \alpha(d)$ are safe approximations of $\alpha(d)$.

- Elements $\alpha(d_1)$ are safe approximations of $\alpha(d_2)$ with $d_2 \subseteq d_1$.

Others, such as the existence of a *best* abstraction for each element of the concrete domain, and a *best* concretization for each element of the abstract domain, while not essential, are often desirable. An algebraic structure which enforces all the above properties is the Galois connection. Before having a closer look at it, we sum up the basic issues and ideas underlying abstract interpretation of programs.

3.2.1.3 Basic Issues and Ideas The theory of abstract interpretation has been developed with the aim of providing a systematic approach to the problem of extracting properties from programs. The basic idea is that the properties of interest are properties of some mathematical function which correctly characterises (certain aspects of) the program. This mathematical function can be a definition of the meaning of the program, independent of a particular execution mechanism, i.e. the declarative semantics such as T_P semantics for logic programs. It can also be a function which characterises substantial aspects of the execution mechanism of the programming language, for example, the SLD semantics of logic programs equipped with the depth-first left-to-right computation rule. One could argue that this function is the definition of the language, or a specification of an implementation. Alternatively, one can see it as an abstraction of an implementation.

As computing this mathematical function for the arguments of interest is in general as infeasible as running the program for the inputs of interest, the goal of abstract interpretation is to approximate this function in a systematic way (in accordance with the intuitions described in the previous sections). Given the programming language and the properties of interest, the idea is to select appropriate abstract domains and to define an abstract function[3] which safely approximates the concrete function. Then, given a particular program, the abstract function is computed and this yields correct information regarding the properties of interest. The framework for abstract interpretation gives requirements for the abstract domains, and the abstract function which guarantee that the computation of the abstract function terminates and provides sound information. Choosing abstract domains and abstract functions such that the computation is efficient and provides sufficiently precise information belongs to

---

[3]The *abstraction* function is a mapping from the concrete to the abstract domain; the *abstract* function is a function over the abstract domain intended to approximate a function over the concrete domain.

the art of abstract interpretation, and explains why this is such a lively research area. Selecting an abstract domain and defining an abstraction function
can be seen as choosing a non-standard domain of data descriptions and defining a non-standard semantics. Computing the abstract function for a particular
program can be seen as executing the program over the non-standard domain,
using non-standard operations.

3.2.1.4 Galois connections As explained above, the concrete domain D is
equipped with an order relation $\subseteq$ such that, if $d_1 \subseteq d_2$, then d_2 is a safe approximation of d_1, i.e. d_2 represents more states than d_1. Similarly, the abstract
domain D^α is equipped with an order relation $\sqsubseteq$ with a similar approximation
property: if $d_1{}^\alpha \sqsubseteq d_2{}^\alpha$ then $d_2{}^\alpha$ is a safe approximation of $d_1{}^\alpha$, i.e. $d^\alpha{}_2$ abstracts
more states than $d_1{}^\alpha$. Both domains are linked to each other by the abstraction
and concretization functions. Both are total functions, the former from D to
D^α gives the *best* abstraction of elements of D, the latter, from D^α to D gives
the *largest* element from D abstracted by a given element from D^α.

Definition 3.8 *Galois connection*
Given $(D, \subseteq)$, a domain D equipped with a partial order $\subseteq$ and, $(D^\alpha, \sqsubseteq)$, a
domain D^α equipped with a partial order $\sqsubseteq$, a Galois connection is a pair of
functions α and γ satisfying:

- α is a total function from D to D^α (the abstraction function)

- γ is a total function from D^α to D (the concretization function)

- $\forall d \in D : \forall d^\alpha \in D^\alpha : \alpha(d) \sqsubseteq d^\alpha \text{ iff } d \subseteq \gamma(d^\alpha)$

$\square$

The condition expresses the relationship between both orders and constrains
α and γ:

- If d^α approximates the best abstraction of d then the largest set abstracted
  by d^α is an approximation of d.

- If d is approximated by the largest set abstracted by d^α, then d^α approximates the best abstraction of d.

An alternative definition is often used. The conditions expressed by it can
be proven from the conditions expressed by the first definition and vice-versa,
so both definitions are equivalent.

Definition 3.9 *Galois connection*
Given $(D, \subseteq)$, a domain D equipped with a partial order $\subseteq$ and, $(D^\alpha, \sqsubseteq)$, a
domain D^α equipped with a partial order $\sqsubseteq$, a Galois connection is a pair of
functions α and γ satisfying:

- α is a total and monotone function from D to D^α

- γ is a total and monotone function from D^α to D

- $\forall d \in D : d \subseteq \gamma(\alpha(d))$

- $\forall d^\alpha \in D^\alpha : \alpha(\gamma(d^\alpha)) \sqsubseteq d^\alpha$

□

This definition requires α and γ to be monotone functions. In addition the third condition requires that the largest concretization of the best abstraction of an element of the concrete domain D is at least as large as the element, i.e. the loss of information due to abstraction is sound, and the fourth condition that the best abstraction of the largest concretization of an element of the abstract domain D^α is at most as large as the element, i.e. concretization introduces no loss of information.

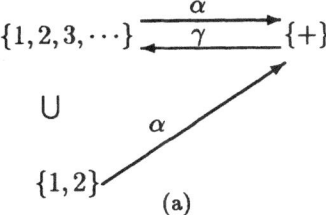

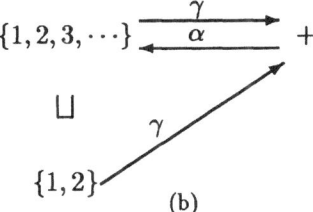

Sign abstraction fragment of the Galois connection between the powerset of the numbers and the powerset of $\{+, -, 0^\alpha\}$	Not a Galois connection after reversing the roles of abstract and concrete domain. The requirement $\alpha(\gamma(\{1,2\})) \sqsubseteq \{1,2\}$ is violated.

Fig. 3.2. Asymmetry of Galois connections

Notice the asymmetry in the definitions (see fig.3.2 for an illustration). In general, one does not obtain a Galois connection when reversing D and D^α. Typically α^{-1} is not a function, so it cannot be chosen as abstraction function. Taking γ as abstraction function and α as concretization function usually violates the last condition of definition 3.9 as illustrated in fig.3.2. To obtain a Galois connection one also has to invert the order relation.

Many other observations can be made about Galois connections. We list some of them:

- $\gamma(\alpha(\gamma(d^\alpha))) = \gamma(d^\alpha)$ and $\alpha(\gamma(\alpha(d))) = \alpha(d)$. The former indicates that no information is lost by abstracting the concretization of an abstract element, the latter that all information lost by abstraction is lost at once.

- The choice of α determines the choice of γ and vice-versa. So the definition of the second function can be left implicit.

- α preserves arbitrary many least upper bounds, i.e.

$$\alpha(\mathsf{lub}(d_1, \ldots, d_n)) = \mathsf{lub}(\alpha(d_1), \ldots, \alpha(d_n))$$

and γ preserves arbitrary many greatest lower bounds, i.e.

$$\gamma(\mathsf{glb}(d_1{}^\alpha, \ldots, d_n{}^\alpha)) = \mathsf{glb}(\gamma(d_1{}^\alpha), \ldots, \gamma(d_n{}^\alpha))$$

- Elements d^α in D^α such that $\alpha(\gamma(d^\alpha)) \sqsubset d^\alpha$ can be considered as superfluous elements of the abstract domain, as they represent the same element in the concrete domain as a strictly smaller element. In the absence of such superfluous elements, i.e. if for all d^α holds that $\alpha(\gamma(d^\alpha)) = d^\alpha$, we have a Galois surjection, sometimes also called a Galois insertion (γ is one-to-one and α is onto).

- In a Galois surjection, the order of the concrete domain is induced in the abstract domain. For example, if the concrete domain is a complete lattice (e.g. a power domain ordered by the subset relation then the abstract domain is also a complete lattice.

It is not impossible to compute safe approximations by means of an algebraic structure that is weaker than a Galois connection, but it will not have all the elegant properties. However, in some cases, it may be more precise, i.e. computing over domains D and D^α which are not linked by a Galois connection can be more precise than computing over subdomains $D_1 \subset D$ and $D^\alpha{}_1 \subset D^\alpha$ which are linked by a Galois connection.

3.2.1.5 Approximating the semantics of programming languages

The standard approach to perform abstract interpretation of programs is to define the behaviour of the program as the least fixpoint of a monotone function over some domain of program properties equipped with a partial order. This function must capture those parts of the behaviour which are of interest and either can be a definition of the semantics of the program or has to be proven correct with regard to the semantics of the program. Developing an abstract interpretation consists of choosing a second non-standard domain, defining a Galois connection between both domains, and a monotone function over the non-standard domain approximating the original function. In this way, the steps performed in computing the fixpoint of the original function are approximated by the function computing over the non-standard domain. Computing (safe approximations of) the fixpoint is easier when the function is also continuous. We will make this assumption in the remainder of the text.

Example 3.10 $\mathsf{T_P}$ *semantics*
Let P be a definite logic program, B_p its Herbrand base and ground(P) the set

of all ground instances of clauses in P. Then $\mathsf{T_P}$ is a function from the powerset of the Herbrand base to the powerset of the Herbrand base and is defined as: $\mathsf{T_P}(S) = \{A \mid A \leftarrow B_1, \ldots, B_n \in \text{ground }(P) \text{ and } \forall i \in [1, n] : B_i \in S\}$. The $\mathsf{T_P}$ semantics gives the least Herbrand model of the program and is the least fixpoint of the $\mathsf{T_P}$ function: $\mathsf{lfp} \ \mathsf{T_P} = \cup_{n \geq 0} \mathsf{T_P}^n(\emptyset)$. $\square$

Having a concrete domain D, an abstract domain D^α, a Galois connection between them and a concrete semantics defined as the least fixpoint of a function F over D, the purpose of abstract interpretation is to compute $\alpha(\mathsf{lfp} \ F)$, or short of that, a safe approximation of it.

The simplest and most accurate way is to compute $\mathsf{lfp} \ F$ and to abstract it. Unfortunately, in most cases, computing the least fixpoint requires an unbounded number of steps. So, a different approach has to be followed. Assuming the least fixpoint of F is given by $\mathsf{lub}_{n \geq 0}(F^n(\bot))$, with $\bot$ the infimum of D, we will approximate the least fixpoint by the least fixpoint of a monotone function F^α over the abstract domain.

The most precise approach is to have an infimum $\bot^\alpha$ in the abstract domain with $\bot^\alpha = \alpha(\bot)$ and to define F^α as $F^\alpha(d^\alpha) = \alpha(F(\gamma(d^\alpha)))$. As F^α is monotonic, it has a least fixpoint. Unfortunately, the least fixpoint of F^α is not necessarily the abstraction of the least fixpoint of F. Indeed, it is possible that $\gamma(\alpha(\mathsf{lfp} \ F)) \supset \mathsf{lfp} \ F$ and thus that $\alpha(F(\gamma(\alpha(\mathsf{lfp} \ F)))) = F^\alpha(\alpha(\mathsf{lfp} \ F)) \sqsupset \alpha(\mathsf{lfp} \ F)$, i.e. $\alpha(\mathsf{lfp} \ F)$, is not a fixpoint of F^α. However the least fixpoint of F^α is the abstraction of some fixpoint of F; in the worst case, it is the abstraction of the greatest fixpoint (see fig.3.3 for an illustration).

This approach can still be impractical. In the common case where the concrete domain is a power domain, $\gamma(d^\alpha)$ is a set which can be infinite. If $F(\gamma(d^\alpha))$ is defined by applying some function F' on each element of $\gamma(d^\alpha)$, then it is impossible to compute $F(\gamma(d^\alpha))$. In such a situation, it is necessary to define F^α directly over D^α. The ideal is to have: $\forall d^\alpha : F^\alpha(d^\alpha) = \alpha(F(\gamma(d^\alpha)))$, however, a safe approximation is sufficient, i.e. $\forall d^\alpha : F^\alpha(d^\alpha) \sqsupseteq \alpha(F(\gamma(d^\alpha)))$.

Having replaced the problem of approximating the least fixpoint of the concrete semantic function F over the concrete domain D by the problem of finding the least fixpoint of the abstract semantic function F^α over the abstract domain D^α has not solved by itself the termination problem. However, termination is assured if the abstract domain has no infinite ascending chains. i.e. if D^α has no infinite sequence of elements $d^\alpha_0 \sqsubset d^\alpha_1 \sqsubset d^\alpha_2 \sqsubset \ldots$. Indeed, the number of steps in computing a fixpoint is bounded by the length of the longest chain. In the presence of infinite ascending chains, termination can still be enforced by so-called widening. The idea is to replace $F^\alpha(d^\alpha)$ by $F^\alpha(d^\alpha)\nabla d^\alpha \sqsupseteq F^\alpha(d^\alpha)$ where ∇ is a so-called widening operator which assures that in a finite number of steps a post fixpoint is reached, i.e. a point d^α for which $F^\alpha(d^\alpha) \sqsubseteq d^\alpha$ and which is a safe approximation of the fixpoint. (The simplest way is to define ∇ as: $F^\alpha(d^\alpha)\nabla d^\alpha = $ if number of iteration below threshold then $F^\alpha(d^\alpha)$ else $\top$ with $\top$ the supremum of D^α). Widening can also be used in case of finite ascending chains to further reduce the number of steps in the fixpoint computation.

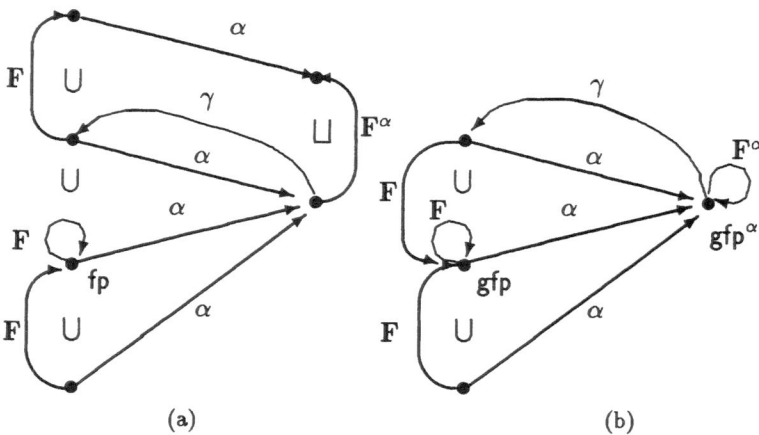

(a)   (b)

The abstraction of a fixpoint of   The abstraction of the greatest
F is not necessarily a fixpoint   fixpoint of F is necessarily a fix-
of F^α. The node labelled fp is a   point of F^α. The nodes labelled
fixpoint of F.   gfp and gfp$^\alpha$ are fixpoints of re-
                                           spectively F and F^α.

Fig. 3.3. F^α defined as $\alpha \circ F \circ \gamma$

Applying widening can overshoot the fixpoint of F^α, it is possible to reach
a point d^α where $F^\alpha(d^\alpha) \sqsubset d^\alpha$. A better approximation can be obtained by
applying so-called narrowing on the monotone F^α. Roughly speaking, the idea
is to apply F^α a finite number of times to obtain a better approximation of the
fixpoint of F^α.

Widening and narrowing enforce termination by ensuring that only a finite
subspace of the infinite abstract domain is explored. This is in general better
than starting with a finite abstract domain as each program being analysed can
explore a different finite part of the infinite abstract domain and the union of
all finite parts for all possible programs can easily be infinite (CoC92c).

Patrick and Radhia Cousot have pioneered the formal development of abstract interpretation. The recent papers (CoC92a) and (CoC92b) summarise the
results and contain an extensive list of references to the original papers (and
were the main source of inspiration for the material in this section).

3.2.2 Abstract interpretation for logic programs

3.2.2.1 Abstracting T$_P$ semantics The least Herbrand model of a program
P is given by the least fixpoint of the T$_P$ function as defined in example 3.10.
In this section we illustrate the ideas by developing an abstraction of the T$_P$
semantics. The purpose of the abstraction is to derive so-called size relations.
Size relations express relationships between arguments of atoms in the least

Herbrand model. For example, using the length of a list as its size, and considering append (see example 3.11 below) atoms in the least Herbrand model, we have that $size(arg_1) + size(arg_2) = size(arg_3)$.

Size relations are of interest in proving termination of programs (VDS91,VDS92), they can also be interesting for compiler optimisations, for example, a list of known length can be implemented as an array. In constraint logic programming, they can be used to make implicit constraints explicit. However, the main point here is that they are an elegant abstraction of T_P semantics.

In what follows, we discuss the abstract domain for a single predicate. It is straightforward to generalise the introduced notions to a vector whose elements are the domain elements of individual predicates.

First we define a function $size$ which maps a term in the Herbrand Universe into a natural number. Assuming the size of interest is $listlength$ (another possibility is the number of function symbols), we define:

$$size : \text{Herbrand Universe} \rightarrow N$$
$$size(t) = \text{ if } (t = [x|y]) \text{ then } 1 + size(y) \text{ else } 0$$

The function can be extended in a function mapping atoms from the Herbrand Base of a predicate p/m into m-tuples:

$$size : \text{Herbrand Base of } p/m \rightarrow N^m$$
$$size(p(t_1, \ldots, t_m)) = < size(t_1), \ldots, size(t_m) >$$

In this way, a Herbrand interpretation of predicate p/m is mapped into a set of m-dimensional points. These sets of m-dimensional points make up a complete lattice ordered by the subset relation. As abstract domain we choose systems of linear equations. Such a system consists of sets of equations of the form $a_1 x_1 + \cdots + a_m x_m = b$. They define *affine subspaces*, also called *linear varieties* of the m-dimensional space. Given a system E^p for predicate p/m, its concretization is the set of ground atoms whose size tuple is a solution of E^p. Formally:

$$\gamma(E^p) = \{p(t_1, \ldots, t_m) \mid < size(t_1), \ldots, size(t_m) > \text{ is a solution for the equations in } E^p\}$$

This concretization function induces a preorder relation (reflexive and transitive) over the systems of equations E^p:

$$E_1^p \sqsubseteq E_2^p \text{ iff } \gamma(E_1^p) \subseteq \gamma(E_2^p)$$

Defining equivalence as:

$$E_1^p \approx E_2^p \text{ iff } \gamma(E_1^p) \sqsubseteq \gamma(E_2^p) \text{ and } \gamma(E_2^p) \sqsubseteq \gamma(E_1^p)$$

we obtain a partial order between equivalence classes. For convenience, we introduce $\bot$ with $\gamma(\bot) = \emptyset$, i.e. an unsolvable system and $\top$ with $\gamma(\top) = \{p(t_1, \ldots, t_m)\}$, i.e. the system representing the complete Herbrand Base of the predicate. This abstract domain is infinite, however, the length of ascending

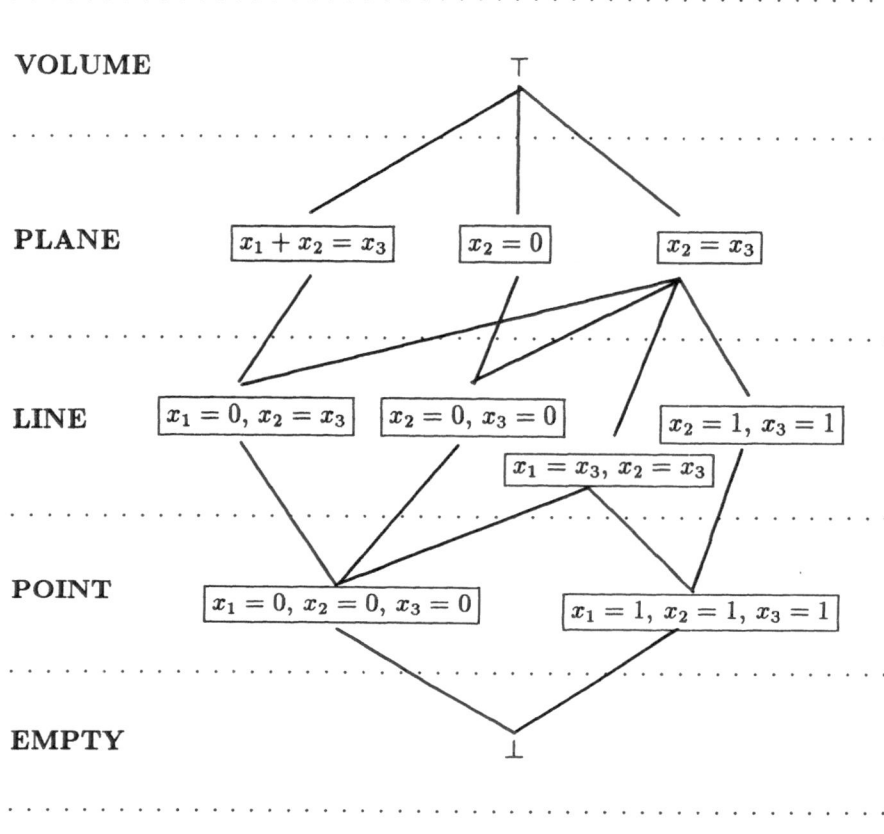

Fig. 3.4. Part of the Infinite Abstract Domain

chains is bounded by the arity of the predicate. A fragment of the abstract domain for a 3-argument predicate is shown in fig.3.4.

We have a Galois connection. The order relations together with the concretization function, induce the abstraction function. Given a set of ground atoms $p(t_1,\ldots,t_m)$, the abstraction is a representative from the least equivalence class E^p having the points $< size(t_1),\ldots,size(t_m) >$ as a solution. A representative of the **glb** of two systems of equations is given by the system containing the equations of both systems. Computing the **lub** of two systems is less trivial. The **lub** of two different points is the line connecting the points, the **lub** of a line and a point outside the line is a plane, ... An algorithm for computing a representative of the **lub** class is given in (Karr76).

Notice that we could have formulated our construction as a two layered abstraction. At the concrete level we have sets of atoms from the Herbrand Base of p/m, at the first level of abstraction we have sets of points in a m-

dimensional space and at the second level, we have the systems of equations. All levels can be connected to each other by Galois connections.

To perform a manual analysis as in the next example, we define $\mathsf{T_P}^\alpha$ as $\alpha \circ \mathsf{T_P} \circ \gamma$.

Example 3.11 *Size Relation for Append*
The program for *append/3* is:

$$append([\,], X, X) \leftarrow$$
$$append([X|U], V, [X|W] \leftarrow append(U, V, W)$$

As initialisation, we have:

$$\mathsf{T_P} \uparrow 0 = \emptyset$$
$$\mathsf{T_P}^\alpha \uparrow 0 = \bot^\alpha$$

while $\alpha(\emptyset) = \bot^\alpha$ and $\gamma(\bot^\alpha) = \emptyset$.

$$\begin{aligned}\mathsf{T_P}^\alpha \uparrow 1 \ &= \alpha(\mathsf{T_P}(\gamma(\bot^\alpha))) \\ &= \alpha(\mathsf{T_P}(\emptyset)) \\ &= \alpha(\{append([\,], t, t)\})\end{aligned}$$

The function *size* maps these atoms into the points $< 0, 0, 0 >$, $< 0, 1, 1 >$, $< 0, 2, 2 >, \ldots, < 0, n, n >, \ldots$. The minimal system of equations having these points as solutions describes a line going through the points, so

$$\begin{aligned}\mathsf{T_P}^\alpha \uparrow 1 \ &= \{x_1 = 0, x_2 = x_3\} \\ \mathsf{T_P}^\alpha \uparrow 2 \ &= \alpha(\mathsf{T_P}(\gamma(\{x_1 = 0, x_2 = x_3\}))) \\ &= \alpha(\mathsf{T_P}(\{append(t_1, t_2, t_3) \mid size(t_1) = 0, size(t_2) = size(t_3)\})) \end{aligned}$$

Notice that $\gamma(\{x_1 = 0, x_2 = x_3\}) \supseteq \{append([\,], t, t)\}$.

$$\begin{aligned}\mathsf{T_P}^\alpha \uparrow 2 = \alpha(\ &\{append([\,], t, t)\} \cup \\ &\{append([t_X|t_U], t_V, [t_X|t_W]) \mid size(t_U) = 0, size(t_V) = size(t_W)\}\ )\end{aligned}$$

Because we have a Galois connection, we can perform the **lub** in the abstract domain ($\alpha(a \cup b) = \mathsf{lub}(\alpha(a), \alpha(b))$):

$$\begin{aligned}\mathsf{T_P}^\alpha \uparrow 2 = \mathsf{lub}(\ &\alpha(\{append([\,], t, t)\}), \\ &\alpha(\{append([t_X|t_U], t_V, [t_X|t_W]) \mid size(t_U) = 0, size(t_V) = size(t_W)\}\ ))\end{aligned}$$

The atoms contributed by the second clause are mapped by the function *size* into the points $(1, 0, 1)$, $(1, 1, 2), \ldots, (1, n, n+1), \ldots$. The abstraction of this set of points is the equation of the line going through them, so

$$\mathsf{T_P}^\alpha \uparrow 2 = \mathsf{lub}(\ \{x_1 = 0, x_2 = x_3\}, \{x_1 = 1, x_2 + 1 = x_3\}\ )$$

The upper bound of these two parallel lines is a plane:

$\mathsf{T_P}^\alpha \uparrow 2 = \{x_1 + x_2 = x_3\}$

$$\begin{aligned}
\mathsf{T_P}^\alpha \uparrow 3 \ &= \alpha(\mathsf{T_P}(\gamma(\{x_1 + x_2 = x_3\}))) \\
&= \alpha(\mathsf{T_P}(\{append(t_1, t_2, t_3) \mid size(t_1) + size(t_2) = size(t_3)\})) \\
&= \alpha(\ \{append([], t, t)\} \ \cup \\
&\quad \{append([t_X|t_U], t_V, [t_X|t_W]) \mid size(t_U) + size(t_V) = size(t_W)\} \ ) \\
&= \mathsf{lub} \ (\alpha(\ \{append([], t, t)\}), \\
&\quad \alpha(\{append([t_X|t_U], t_V, [t_X|t_W]) \mid size(t_U) + size(t_V) = size(t_W)\} \ ))
\end{aligned}$$

Observe that atoms contributed by the second clause are mapped into points of the same plane $x_1 + x_2 = x_3$, so

$$\begin{aligned}
\mathsf{T_P}^\alpha \uparrow 3 \ &= \mathsf{lub} \ (\ \{x_1 = 0, x_2 = x_3\}, \{x_1 + x_2 = x_3\} \ ) \\
&= \{x_1 + x_2 = x_3\}
\end{aligned}$$

So a fixpoint is reached. Notice that computing the fixpoint of $\mathsf{T_P}$ requires an infinite number of steps.   □

The analysis can be automated without much difficulty. A key step is to make unification explicit by calls to the equality predicate $=/2$ which is interpreted as syntactical identity. Then $\mathsf{T_P}^\alpha$ can be defined directly on the abstract domain, as a function mapping a vector of systems of equations — one for each predicate — into a vector of systems of equations. The abstraction of calls to predicates different from equality are obtained by renaming the system in the given vector. Full details can be found in (VDS91,VDS92) (although in a top-down setting). We sketch the idea by some examples.

The first clause of $append/3$ is rewritten as:

$$append(X_1, X_2, X_3) \leftarrow X_1 = [], X_2 = X_3$$

The calls to $=/2$ are abstracted respectively as $\{x_1 = 0\}$ and $\{x_2 = x_3\}$. The **glb** of both systems is given by their conjunction, i.e. $\{x_1 = 0, x_2 = x_3\}$ which is the abstraction of the atoms contributed by the clause.

The second clause is rewritten as:

$$append(X_1, X_2, X_3) \leftarrow X_1 = [X|U], X_3 = [X|W], append(U, X_2, W)$$

At the beginning of the second iteration, the current abstraction of $append/3$ in the vector is $\{x_1 = 0, x_2 = x_3\}$. The recursive call is abstracted by a renaming of this, i.e. $\{u = 0, x_2 = w\}$. The calls to $=/2$ are abstracted respectively by $\{x_1 = 1 + u\}$ and $\{x_3 = 1 + w\}$. The **glb** of these systems is

$$\{u = 0, x_2 = w, x_1 = 1 + u, x_3 = 1 + w\}$$

which is equivalent to

$$\{u = 0, x_2 = w, x_1 = 1, x_3 = 1 + x_2\},$$

projection upon x_1, x_2, x_3 gives $\{x_1 = 1, x_3 = 1 + x_2\}$ which is the abstraction of the atoms contributed by the second clause during the second iteration.

Observe that one could take an alternative view where the abstract domain consists of sets of affine subspaces and where widening is used to limit the cardinality of the computed abstract elements. By limiting cardinality to 1, we obtain exactly the computations described above. This illustrates that computing in a richer domain need not be more expensive when widening is used.

Finally, it is interesting to remark that one could use a richer abstract domain containing also inequalities $a_1 x_1 + \cdots + a_m x_m \geq b$. Such systems define solution spaces which are convex hulls. The abstract domain becomes of infinite height and widening is needed to ensure termination. Such an abstract domain has been used in (CoH78) for deriving properties of imperative programs.

3.2.2.2 OLD Semantics T_P semantics captures only information about the least Herbrand model of the program, about the result of a computation. To obtain information about intermediate states in the computation, i.e. information about the calls in a Prolog program, a different semantics is needed. Here we study OLD semantics. OLD, introduced by Sato (TaS86), is SLD where the computation rule is restricted to select always the leftmost literal (as Prolog does). Concepts such as OLD derivation, OLD refutation and OLD tree are obvious adaptations from the similar concepts for SLD (Llo87).

To define the semantics as the fixpoint of an operator mapping partial OLD trees into partial OLD trees, we introduce the notion of a (partial) OLD tree.

Definition 3.12 *Partial OLD tree*
Let P be a definite program and G a definite goal. A partial OLD tree for $P \cup \{G\}$ is a tree satisfying the following:

- Each node of the tree is a (possibly empty) definite goal.

- The root node (if any) is G.

- Let $\leftarrow A_1, \ldots, A_m (m \geq 1)$ be a node in the tree that is not a leaf. Then for each program clause $A \leftarrow B_1, \ldots, B_k$ such that A_1 and A unify with *mgu* θ, the node has a child $\leftarrow (B_1, \ldots, B_k, A_2, \ldots, A_m)\theta$ (these children are the result of expanding the node).

- Nodes which are empty goals are leaves.

A leaf node $\leftarrow A_1, \ldots, A_m$ such that there exists a program clause $A \leftarrow B_1, \ldots, B_k$ such that A_1 and A unify is called an unexpanded leaf.   □

Now we can define a monotone operator $F_{P,SG}$ for a program P and a set of goals SG which maps a set of partial OLD trees into a set of partial OLD trees as follows:

$$F_{P,SG}(ST) = \begin{aligned}&\{t \mid t \text{ has a single node consisting of a goal from } SG\} \cup \\ &\{t \mid t' \in ST \text{ and } t \text{ is derived from } t' \\ &\qquad \text{by expanding all unexpanded leaves }\}\end{aligned}$$

The OLD semantics consists of the least fixpoint of the operator $F_{P,SG}$. It computes information about all goal statements which are processed while executing a query from the set SG, in particular it shows all instances of called predicates.

A simple minded abstraction of the domain of OLD trees would keep the tree structure and abstract the goals. It is obvious that this suffers from termination problems as the depth of the trees can be unbounded. Therefore, it is more convenient to first modify the OLD execution mechanism before abstracting it.

3.2.2.3 OLDT Resolution

OLDT resolution stands for OLD resolution with tabulation and has been introduced by Tamaki and Sato (TaS86) as a run-time engine to improve standard Prolog interpreters. A little later it was also introduced by Vieille as the SLD-AL method for execution of deductive database queries (Vie89). Recently OLDT resolution is widely used as an abstract interpretation engine (KaK93,CoF92).

OLD resolution is SLD resolution with a restricted computation rule: only the first atom of the current goal can be selected. This restriction upon the computation rule is a crucial point for the correctness of tabulation (in general, tabulation is not applicable to SLD resolution – certain restrictions upon the computation rule are necessary).

The idea of tabulation is very simple. All call patterns of the selected atoms of the goals met so far in the derivation are collected in a table. Also (different) answers to the calls are stored in the table. When a call has to be performed and its pattern is already in the table, then instead of using the clauses of the program, the answers stored in the table are used as facts defining the called predicate. So entries of the table consist of two parts: a call pattern and a list of corresponding answers which are instances of the call pattern.

Example 3.13

Given the definite logic program

$$c_1 : \quad path(X,Y) \leftarrow p(X,Y)$$
$$c_2 : \quad path(X,Y) \leftarrow path(X,Z), p(Z,Y)$$

$$c_3 : \quad p(a,b).$$
$$c_4 : \quad p(b,c).$$
$$c_5 : \quad p(c,a).$$

and the initial goal $\leftarrow path(a,Y)$. The corresponding OLDT tree is shown in fig.3.5. The argument i in $lookup(i)$ refers to the number of the first node with the same call pattern. The indices (i,j) in $\mathcal{A}_{ij}$ refer to the position in the table of answers below.

The table entries created during execution are:

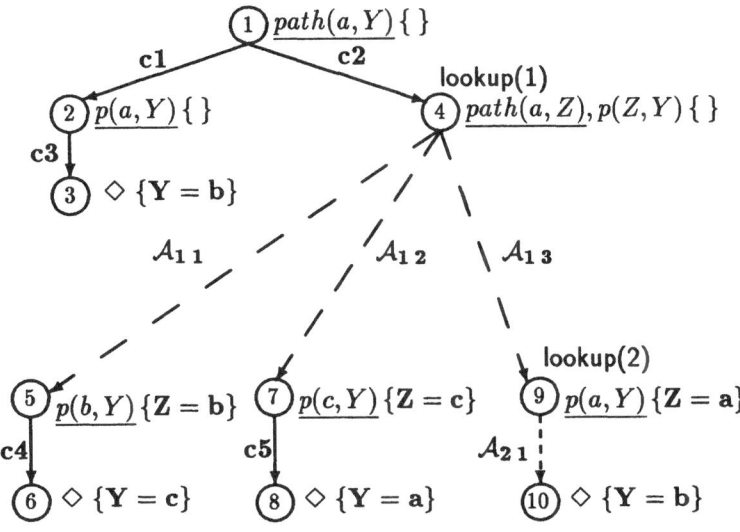

Fig. 3.5. OLDT Tree

	call	\multicolumn{3}{c}{answers}		
		1	2	3
1	$path(a, U)$	$path(a, b)$	$path(a, c)$	$path(a, a)$
2	$p(a, U)$	$p(a, b)$		
5	$p(b, U)$	$p(b, c)$		
7	$p(c, U)$	$p(c, a)$		

□

The calls resolved with the facts in the table are called *lookup* calls (e.g nodes 4 and 9 in fig. 3.5). The most important property of OLDT resolution is that it is sound and complete. Moreover, given an OLD tree, the corresponding OLDT tree has exactly the same call/answer patterns. The latter is very important when applying OLDT resolution for abstract interpretation. It is intuitively obvious that an OLDT tree can be expanded into a full OLD tree by replacing *lookup* extensions by the corresponding properly renamed subrefutations. In general, this process can be infinite as the replacement can introduce again *lookup* nodes. This is the case for the above example 3.13.

An OLDT tree can also be infinite. However, it can rather easily be abstracted in a finite structure. A generic abstraction scheme for OLDT resolution should specify at least the following components:

- **Goal abstraction:** whenever a new goal is obtained, it is abstracted. The abstraction must be such that the concretization includes the original goal. The next *OLDT* step uses the abstracted goal. In particular, the abstracted call either becomes a new entry in the table or is used to locate the appropriate entry to be used in a *lookup* step. Another requirement on the abstraction is that only a finite number of table entries are created.

- **Answer abstraction:** Whenever an answer has been obtained, it is abstracted before storing it in the table. Again, the abstraction must be such that the concretization includes the original answer and that only a finite number of answers are possible.

Having a Galois connection linking sets of concrete goals/answers with abstract goals/answers, we can obtain $AOLDT$, the abstract counterpart of $OLDT$.

Example 3.14

Using the abstract equation systems of example 3.6, we can represent abstract goals and answers by a pair consisting of a concrete goal/answer and an abstract equation system. For example the pair $append(X, Y, Z), \{X = \mathcal{G}, Y = \mathcal{G}\}$ represents $append(X, Y, Z)\{X \leftarrow t_1, Y \leftarrow t_2\}$ where t_1, t_2 are ground terms. (To obtain a Galois connection between the domains of concrete and abstract terms, we should introduce an abstract term Any representing the whole Herbrand universe; a widening operator should introduce Any when terms are too deeply nested and abstract unification, as defined in example 3.6, has to be extended with rules coping with Any. However, in the examples we consider here, widening and Any are not needed).

Starting from an abstract goal $\leftarrow append(X, Y, Z), \{X = \mathcal{G}, Y = \mathcal{G}\}$, one can work out an abstract $OLDT$ tree and one can observe that it is finite (see fig.3.6). The boxes labelling the branches are either the clauses used in node expansion or answers used in *lookup*. The table has only a single entry: $append(X, Y, Z)\{X = \mathcal{G}, Y = \mathcal{G}\}$ $[\{X = \mathcal{G}, Y = \mathcal{G}, Z = \mathcal{G}\}]$ (The second abstract equation system specifies how the calls are instantiated by the answers).

□

An abstract $OLDT$ tree can be expanded into an abstract OLD tree, in the same way as an $OLDT$ tree can be expanded into an OLD tree. Doing this for the tree of the *append* program will result in an infinite tree which abstracts any OLD tree obtained from a query $\leftarrow append(X, Y, Z), \{X = t_1, Y = t_2\}$ where t_1, t_2 are ground terms.

Abstract $OLDT$ has the inconvenience that it somehow computes too detailed information. Consider a goal $\leftarrow A_1, A_2$ somewhere in an $AOLDT$ tree such that it is the body of some program clause. Due to the non-determinism of logic programs, the subtree rooted at this node will usually have different branches. Once A_1 is refuted, one finds the goal $\leftarrow A_2$ on different branches. Usually, these goals will have been instantiated differently. $AOLDT$ will perform an analysis for each of them. However, in many applications, i.e. compilation, one wants to have a single analysis for A_2, starting from a call pattern which is general enough to describe the calls to A_2 on the different branches. It is more

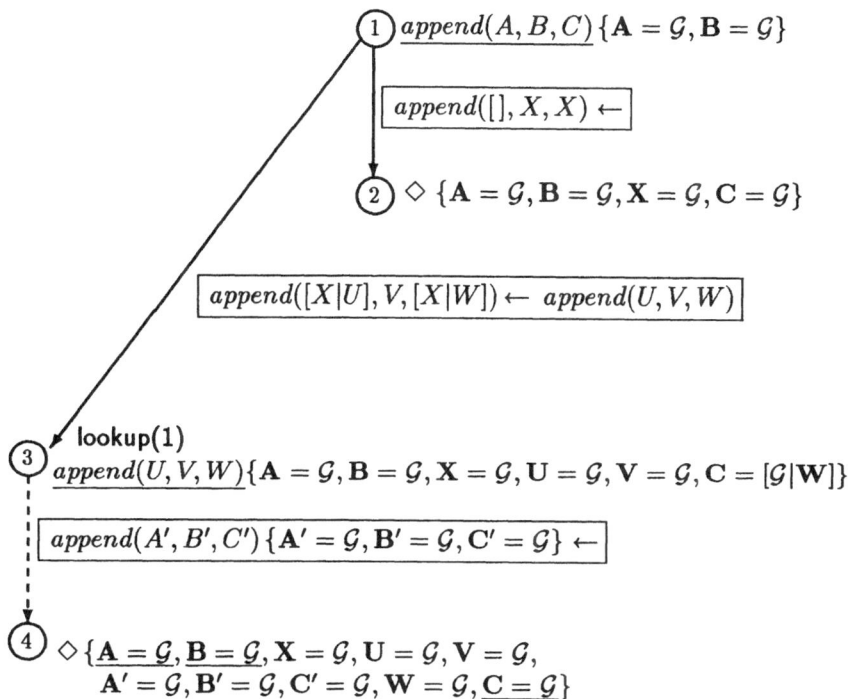

Fig. 3.6. Abstract OLDT Tree

economical to do a single analysis for the more general pattern than to perform an analysis for each pattern and then to combine the results. While one could modify *AOLDT* to handle the situation, there is another approach which avoids this problem in a more natural way.

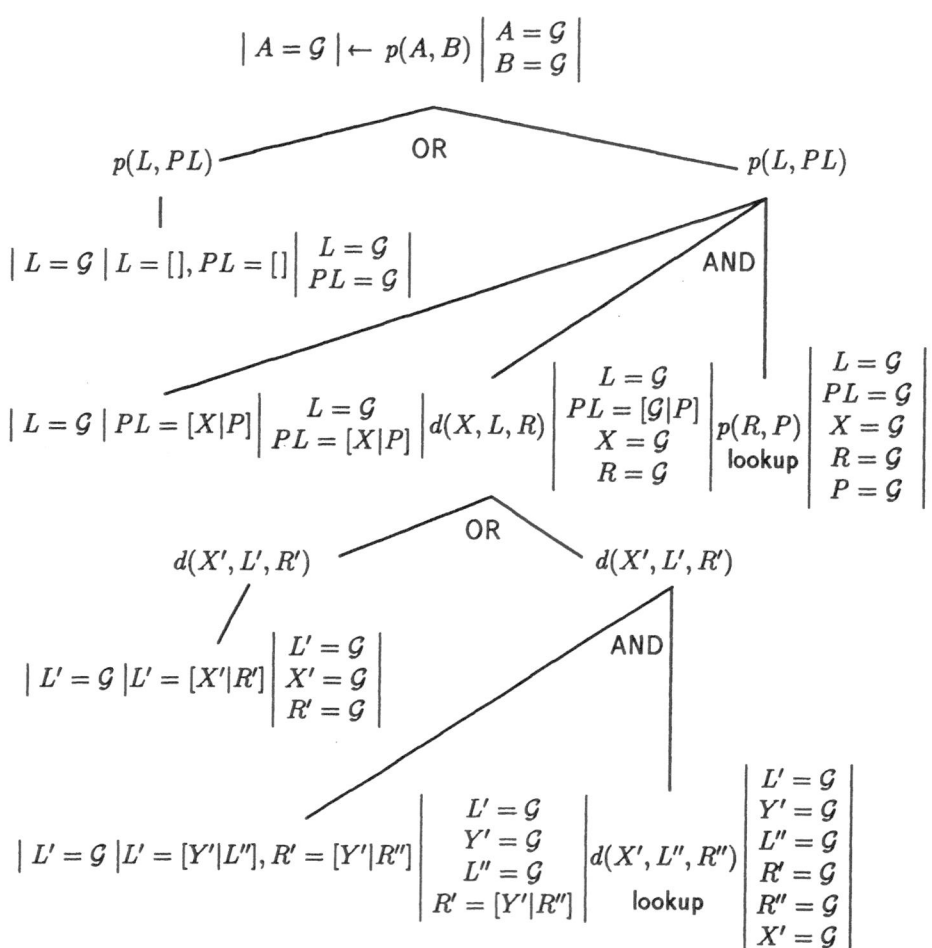

Fig. 3.7. $AND - OR$ graph

3.2.2.4 Local SLD with tabulation: $LSLDT$

The basic step of SLD is to select a literal in a goal and a clause in the program, to replace the literal by the clause body and to apply the mgu of the literal and the clause head. Here we define a variant of SLD which we call local $SLD(LSLD)$. Given a goal $\leftarrow A_1, \ldots, A_n$, a literal A_i is selected and for each clause $H \leftarrow B_1, \ldots, B_m$ such that A_i and H have mgu θ, a subrefutation $\leftarrow (B_1, \ldots, B_m)\theta$ is initiated. Eventually, this subderivation computes an answer τ (through backtracking several ones). By soundness of SLD, $H\tau$ is a logical consequence of the program, i.e. it can be considered as a lemma. Now, one returns to the main computation with the goal $\leftarrow A_1, \ldots, A_n$. The call A_i is selected and the lemma $H\tau$ is used to resolve it.

Notice that we restrict the computation rule in a way very similar to OLD. Indeed we divide the computation into many subcomputations one for each call, and return to the caller's computation only when the subcomputation has completed by computing an answer. This corresponds to SLD where the computation rule always selects one of the most recently introduced literals. In the sequel we will for simplicity assume always the leftmost literal is selected, as in OLD.

We call the resulting mechanism $LSLD$ because the computation is splitted into many local parts. A subderivation corresponds closely to the viewpoint of a compiler writer generating code for a predicate definition: different clauses defining the predicate are tried, and the clause bodies are executed by initiating calls to the different body literals. Each of them creates another subderivation. So it is no surprise that $LSLD$ is a good starting point for an analysis aimed at providing compiler writers with useful information.

To avoid the problem of an unbounded number of different subderivations, $LSLD$ can be enhanced with tabulation, in the same way as OLD was. The call patterns in the table are the goals which are at the roots of the subderivations. Similar as for $OLDT$, each entry has a list of answers, the lemmas. When a new subderivation is created, the table entries are checked. If the created subderivation is in the table, then it is cancelled and the stored lemmas are used to resolve the call; if not, a new table entry is created and the subderivation is solved[4].

Now abstraction of $LSLDT$ is very similar to abstraction of $OLDT$, i.e. goal statements and answers are abstracted. As the table can have different answers for a particular call, at first glance we still suffer from the same inconvenience as $AOLDT$, that we have different continuations for the same residual part of clause bodies (the $LSLD$ tree branches, one branch for each answer). However, this branching can be avoided in a very natural way. The abstract domain of answers for a given literal form a partial order, and each set of answers has an upper bound. So, in executing a goal statement $\leftarrow A_1, A_2, \ldots$, the upper bound of all answers to A_1 is used as a single lemma, this assures there is a single continuation $\leftarrow A_2, \ldots$.

However, there is still a subtle problem when performing an analysis based on this scheme: it is possible one first uses a lemma for solving the literal A_1 in $\leftarrow A_1, A_2, \ldots$, derives a new goal $\leftarrow A_2, \ldots$, and next, creates a new subcomputation for $\leftarrow A_2$. At a later point, another solution for the goal $\leftarrow A_1$ can be obtained, which is not smaller than the lemma which has been used. At this point a new least upper bound for solutions to A_1 is obtained and the derivation starting from $\leftarrow A_1, A_2$ has to be redone. Notice that this implies that the

---

[4]In practice it is more convenient to table the literal which triggered the creation of a subderivation; the information showing which clause contributed which lemma is lost, but this information is not needed. However, the overhead of creating subderivations is avoided in a case of a *lookup*.

original entry in the table for A_2 becomes useless, as well as the subderivation it was initiating (and may have created other table entries).

A high level data structure which integrates all subderivations into a single structure and, at a high level, addresses the problem of avoiding useless table entries and useless subcomputations is the $AND - OR$ graph used in the framework of Bruynooghe (Bru91). The unexpanded calls at the leaves of the graph are nothing else than calls resolved by table look-up. Somewhere else in the tree, there is an equivalent call which has been expanded by entering all defining clauses and whose answers have been collected into a single upper bound. The $AND-OR$ graph structure is instrumental in (1) allowing different specialised versions of the same clause and indicating which version has to be called at which point, (2) avoiding useless table entries and useless subderivations, (3) organising the computation of safe approximations (fixpoints) in an optimal way, (4) providing a high level interface with the compiler.

Example 3.15

$$c_1 : \quad delete(X, L, R) \leftarrow L = [X|R].$$
$$c_2 : \quad delete(X, L, R) \leftarrow L = [Y|L'], \, R = [Y|R'], \, delete(X, L', R').$$
$$c_3 : \quad perm(L, PL) \leftarrow L = [], \, PL = [].$$
$$c_4 : \quad perm(L, PL) \leftarrow PL = [X|P], \, delete(X, L, R), perm(R, P).$$

Query : $\leftarrow perm(A, B), \{\mathbf{A} = \mathcal{G}\}$

creation of subrefutations (a) and (b)

$$\leftarrow \Diamond \{\mathbf{A} = \mathcal{G}, \mathbf{B} = \mathcal{G}\} \text{ (using L1 below)}$$

(a) subderivation body c_3

$$\leftarrow L = [], PL = []\{\mathbf{L} = \mathcal{G}\}$$
$$\leftarrow PL = []\{\mathbf{L} = \mathcal{G}\}$$
$$\leftarrow \Diamond \{\mathbf{L} = \mathcal{G}, \mathbf{PL} = \mathcal{G}\}$$
Lemma : $perm(L, PL)\{\mathbf{L} = \mathcal{G}, \mathbf{PL} = \mathcal{G}\}$ (L1)

(b) subderivation body c_4

$$\leftarrow PL = [X|P], delete(X, L, R), perm(R, P)\{\mathbf{L} = \mathcal{G}\}$$
$$\leftarrow delete(X, L, R), perm(R, P)\{\mathbf{L} = \mathcal{G}, \mathbf{PL} = [\mathbf{X}|\mathbf{P}]\}$$

creation of subrefutations (c) and (d)

$$\leftarrow perm(R, P)\{\mathbf{L} = \mathcal{G}, \mathbf{PL} = [\mathcal{G}|\mathbf{P}], \mathbf{X} = \mathcal{G}, \mathbf{R} = \mathcal{G}\} \text{ (using L2)}$$
$$\leftarrow \Diamond \{\mathbf{L} = \mathcal{G}, \mathbf{PL} = \mathcal{G}, \mathbf{X} = \mathcal{G}, \mathbf{R} = \mathcal{G}, \mathbf{P} = \mathcal{G}\} \text{ (using L1)}$$

Same lemma as L1
(c) subderivation body c_1

$$\leftarrow L = [X|R] \ \{\mathbf{L} = \mathcal{G}\}$$
$$\leftarrow \Diamond\{\mathbf{L} = \mathcal{G}, \mathbf{X} = \mathcal{G}, \mathbf{R} = \mathcal{G}\}$$
Lemma : $delete(X, L, R)\{\mathbf{X} = \mathcal{G}, \mathbf{L} = \mathcal{G}, \mathbf{R} = \mathcal{G}\}$ **(L2)**

(d) subderivation body c_2

$$\leftarrow L = [Y|L'], R = [Y|R'], delete(X, L', R')\{\mathbf{L} = \mathcal{G}\}$$
$$\leftarrow R = [Y|R'], delete(X, L', R')\{\mathbf{L} = \mathcal{G}, \mathbf{Y} = \mathcal{G}, \mathbf{L}' = \mathcal{G}\}$$
$$\leftarrow delete(X, L', R')\{\mathbf{L} = \mathcal{G}, \mathbf{Y} = \mathcal{G}, \mathbf{L}' = \mathcal{G}, \mathbf{R} = [\mathcal{G}|\mathbf{R}']\}$$
$$\leftarrow \Diamond\{\mathbf{L} = \mathcal{G}, \mathbf{Y} = \mathcal{G}, \mathbf{L}' = \mathcal{G}, \mathbf{R} = \mathcal{G}, \mathbf{X} = \mathcal{G}, \mathbf{R}' = \mathcal{G}\} \ (\text{using L2})$$

Same lemma as L2

The $AND-OR$ graph summarising the computation is shown in fig.3.7. The structure is called a graph because the *lookup* nodes can be considered as arcs pointing to the nodes with the same call pattern. Between | | one can observe the abstract states as computed in the subderivations. The nodes $p(R, P)$ and $d(X', L'', R'')$ are leaves as they are solved by table *lookup* (use of lemmas). □

The $AND - OR$ graphs represent, via the concretization function, a set of $LSLDT$ derivations. These derivations in turn represent OLD derivations. The $AND - OR$ graph is the fixpoint of a function mapping partial $AND - OR$ graphs into partial $AND - OR$ graphs. It can be shown this fixpoint represents a fixpoint of the function $F_{P,SG}$ introduced in section 3.2.2.2, which maps sets of partial OLD trees into sets of partial OLD trees (Bru91). The $AND - OR$ graph is the conceptual basis for several implemented frameworks such as PLAI (MuH92) and GAIA (CVH91,CVH92).

In abstracting $OLDT$ and abstracting $LSLDT$, we can distinguish a couple of crucial operations. To bring them more to the foreground and in view of the extension to constraint logic programming, it is useful to separate goals and literals in two parts: a skeleton and a substitution. A skeleton is of the form $p(X_1, \cdots, X_n)$ with the X_i different variables. The substitution can be written as a solved form of a system of equations (LMM88). We use $eq(\theta)$ to denote the solved form corresponding to the substitution θ.

A first crucial operation is unification. In both $OLDT$ and $LSLDT$, one has to unify a call $< A, eq(\theta) >$ with a clause head H. It means one has to bring into solved form the system $\{eq(\theta), A = H\}$. In both $OLDT$ and $LSLDT$, one has also lemma application (*lookup*), i.e. a call $< A, eq(\theta) >$ and a lemma $< A', eq(\tau) >$ have to be unified. So, abstracting unification in the most general setting, one has a literal A with associated abstract system of equations E_A, and a literal B with associated system E_B (no sharing of variables), and the purpose is to compute a new system E which approximates the system $\{\mathsf{E}_A, A = B, \mathsf{E}_B\}$. More formally, one can formulate a correctness condition as follows: $\forall eq(\theta) \in \gamma(\mathsf{E}_A), \forall eq(\sigma) \in \gamma(\mathsf{E}_B)$: if $vars(A\theta) \cap vars(B\sigma) = \emptyset$ and $\{eq(\theta), A = B, eq(\sigma)\}$ has $eq(\tau)$ as solved form then $eq(\tau) \in \gamma(\mathsf{E})$.

Another operation is concerned with restricting the domain of substitutions. While we have pairs $< A, eq(\theta) >$, what is really important is the instance of

A, i.e. $A\theta$. So one can drop those components of θ that do not affect $A\theta$, in other words, the substitution can be restricted to the variables of A. While this operation passes almost unnoticed at the concrete level, it is not unimportant when considering the table entries. When separating the table entries also in pairs skeleton-solved form, it is crucial that the solved form is restricted to the variables of the skeleton, otherwise, matches of new calls with existing table entries will go unnoticed. The operation becomes more prominent at the abstract level, not only to avoid mismatches when checking new calls, but also to restrict the size of the abstract equation systems, i.e. the number of elements in the abstract domain. Notice that this restriction can also be seen as existential quantification, indeed in a component $X = t$ in a solved form one can hide the X by existential quantification $\exists X : X = t$ which reduces to true. A formal condition for abstract restriction/projection/existential quantification is as follows: for a pair $< A, \mathsf{E} >$ being restricted to $< A, \mathsf{E}_R >$, one requires: $\forall eq(\theta) \in \gamma(\mathsf{E}) : \exists eq(\sigma) \in \gamma(\mathsf{E}_R)$ such that $A\theta = A\sigma$.

Several researchers, with a background in denotational semantics, have formulated the semantics of logic programs as a function mapping call substitutions of predicates into their success substitutions (JoS87). In this setting, a top down analysis aims at computing that part of the function which is relevant for a given set of initial goals (Win92). The thus obtained information corresponds closely with the information derived by the approaches using OLD semantics.

3.2.3 From Logic Programming to Constraint Logic Programming

3.2.3.1 Constraint Logic Programming Constraint Logic Programming (CLP) is the extension of the Logic Programming paradigm with the constraint solving paradigm. The integration of both paradigms yields a paradigm which is more flexible and more expressive.

Syntactically, the extension introduces constraints in the goal statements and in the bodies of clauses. These constraints are constructed from a so-called signature Σ defining a set of function and predicate symbols and including the $= /2$ predicate. These function and predicate symbols are given a fixed interpretation by means of a so called Σ-structure consisting of a domain $\mathcal{D}$ and an assignment linking the symbols of Σ with the elements of $\mathcal{D}$. The $= /2$ predicate is interpreted as syntactical identity; the other symbols of Σ typically have an interpretation different from the Herbrand interpretation. Constraints are formulas in some first order language over Σ which contains at least all primitive constraints of Σ and is closed under renaming, conjunction and existential quantification.

The simplest example is standard logic programming. Besides the predicate symbol $= /2$, Σ contains a collection of constants and function symbols. The domain $\mathcal{D}$ is the Herbrand universe H, i.e. the set of finite trees and the function symbols are interpreted as tree constructors. The primitive constraints in L are equations between terms.

Example 3.16 *Append in $CLP(H)$*
The definition for append is written as[5]:

$$append(X, Y, Z) \leftarrow X = nil, Y = Z \; \square.$$
$$append(X, Y, Z) \leftarrow X = [X' \mid U], Z = [X' \mid W] \; \square \; append(U, Y, W).$$

Notice that X' is local to the constraint part, so it is existentially quantified. The explicit constraint is $\exists X' : (X = [X'|U], Z = [X'|W])$. □

Another well known example is $CLP(R)$. Σ contains the binary predicate symbols $=$, $<$ and $\leq$, the binary function symbols $+$ and $*$ and the constants 0 and 1. $\mathcal{D}$ is the set of real numbers and the symbols of Σ are interpreted as usual when doing arithmetic. Both domains can be combined, yielding CLP(H,R).

Example 3.17 *Listlength in $CLP(H, R)$*
listlength can be defined as:

$$listlength(L, N) \leftarrow L = nil, N = 0 \; \square.$$
$$listlength(L, N) \leftarrow L = [X \mid L'], N = N' + 1 \; \square \; listlength(L', N').$$

Also here, there is a variable local to the constraint part of the body, and a more explicit representation of the constraint is : $\exists X : L = [X|L'], N = N' + 1$. □

For more details, the reader is referred to (JaM93) and (Hen91).

3.2.3.2 Abstracting semantics of CLP Looking back at the different ways we performed abstract interpretation of logic programs, we observe that the basic entities being abstracted are sets of atoms. In the case of OLD semantics, these sets include non ground atoms. It means we are working with observables similar to computed answer substitutions as formalised in the S-semantics of (FLM89,BGL93). There it is shown that the sets of atoms representing the meaning of a program are closed under variable renaming. Intuitively, computed answers $X \leftarrow f(Z)$ and $X \leftarrow f(Y)$ for a query $\leftarrow P(X)$ are equivalent. The name of the variable (Z or Y) in the answer depends on the arbitrary renaming of the clauses used in the refutation (on arbitrary addresses in the real implementation). So, back to abstract interpretation one can say that it is advantageous to have that the set of states computed by the concretization function is closed under variable renaming. Failure to do so might cause extra iterations in fixpoint computations.

Example 3.18
Consider a table entry $< p(X, Y), \{X = \mathcal{G}, Y = f(Z)\} >$ in abstract $OLDT$ or abstract $LSLDT$. A formulation of the concretization function which is more

---

[5]In this section, the symbol □ is used as a separator between the constraint part and the logic part of a clause.

useful than the concretization function following naturally from the setting of example 3.6:

$$\gamma(< p(X,Y), \{X = \mathcal{G}, Y = f(Z)\} >) =$$
$$\{< p(X,Y), \{X = t, Y = f(Z)\}\rho > | \ t \text{ is ground },$$
$$\rho \text{ is a renaming of the variables in the right hand side of the equations } \}$$

$\square$

The S-semantics have been extended to CLP in (GaL91); in this extension, the basic entities being manipulated become unit CLP clauses (constrained atoms) of the form $p(X) \leftarrow \mathbf{c} \,\square$. Two constrained atoms $p(X) \leftarrow \mathbf{c_1} \,\square$ and $p(X) \leftarrow \mathbf{c_2} \,\square$ are equivalent if they have the same solutions for the variable X.

Example 3.19

$$p(X,Y) \leftarrow X + Y = Z, X - Y = Z, Z = 2\,\square$$
$$p(X,Y) \leftarrow X + Y = 2, X - Y = 2\,\square$$
$$p(X,Y) \leftarrow X = 2, Y = 0\,\square$$

These three constrained atoms are equivalent with regard to X and Y. $\square$

The different semantics for LP can easily be reformulated for CLP : one can formulate an operator for the classical fixpoint semantics, or for the S-semantics. Also $OLDT$ and $LSLDT$ can be reformulated. In the latter case, table entries become constrained atoms. While one can consider these constrained atoms as syntactical objects, it is, as in the case of LP, advantageous to consider the equivalence class of semantically equivalent constrained atoms (an implementation freely chooses one of them). This will substantially reduce the number of table entries. Certainly for the elements of the abstract domain, it is recommended to have elements which, under the concretization function, yield sets of constrained atoms which are closed under semantical equivalence.

So, the semantics and frameworks we described in section 3.2.2 for LP carry over rather straightforwardly to CLP. The main difference being that constraints play the role of substitutions. Typically, one defines a Galois connection between sets of constrained atoms and their abstraction. The order relation on the concrete domain is the subset relation. As explained above, the concretization function should yield a set which is closed under constraint equivalence. The main difficulty in developing applications is that this is harder to achieve than for LP where one only has to cope with variable renaming. For example, in a freeness analysis for solvable systems of linear equations (DJB93), abstraction is conceptually performed on the infinite set of all linear combinations of the given equations. An equation $a_1 X_1 + \cdots + a_n X_n = b \ (a_1 \neq 0, \cdots, a_n \neq 0)$ is abstracted as $\{X_1, \cdots, X_n\}$; so, a system of equations is abstracted as a finite set of sets of variables. Freeness, whether a variable X_i can still range over the whole set of reals, is indicated by the absence of the singleton $\{X_i\}$ in the abstraction. The concretization function of an abstract element yields a set of solvable systems. Every solvable system in the set is such that its abstraction is a subset of the abstract element.

In some applications, one can use a concretization function which yields sets which are closed under the inverse of entailment, i.e. if a constrained atom $p(X) \leftarrow c\,\square$ is included, than also all more constrained atoms are included. In LP such domains are known as substitution closed. An example for LP and CLP is definiteness: whether a variable is constrained to at most one value. It is quite obvious that, when a variable is definite for some constraint system $\mathcal{C}$, then it is also definite in stronger systems $\mathcal{C}'$ which entail $\mathcal{C}$.

Many authors contributed to the insight regarding the relationship between abstract interpretation for LP and for CLP. A first contribution was by (MaS90); others are (GBH93,CoF92,GDL92,GDL93).

To finish, we take a closer look at the CLP case of abstract $LSLDT$ and formulate the correctness conditions of the abstract operations. Without loss of generality, we assume that clauses are of the form $h \leftarrow b_1, \cdots, b_n$[6] where the b_i are either constraints or predicates; moreover, all predicates of the clause are of the form $p(\overline{X})$ where $\overline{X}$ is a shorthand for a sequence of different variables, its length corresponds to the arity of the predicate.

$LSLDT$ consists of subderivations which find their origin either in the initial query or in a program clause. A subderivation is a sequence of goals. In the abstract space, a goal is represented as $<\leftarrow b_1, \cdots, b_n; \mathbf{c}^{\alpha}_{\overline{X}}>$ where $b_1, \cdots, b_n$ are the operations to be performed (predicates to be called or constraints to be added) and $\mathbf{c}^{\alpha}_{\overline{X}}$ is an abstract constraint system over the variables $\overline{X}$ (the abstraction of the constraint store)[7]. The vector $\overline{X}$ contains the variables from the context in which the subderivation is performed, i.e. either the variables from the initial query or from the clause which initiated the subderivation[8]. The abstract goal represents the set of concrete goals $<\leftarrow b_1, \cdots, b_n; \mathbf{c}_{\overline{X}}>$ such that $\mathbf{c}_{\overline{X}} \in \gamma(\mathbf{c}^{\alpha}_{\overline{X}})$. Here $\mathbf{c}_{\overline{X}}$, the constraint store, is a conjunction of constraints whose free variables are a subset of $\overline{X}$.

The simplest derivation step is when b_1 is a constraint. In this case, the concrete derivation adds b_1 to the constraint store. The new state in the abstract derivation is of the form $<\leftarrow b_2, \cdots, b_n; \mathbf{c}^{\alpha'}_{\overline{X}}>$ and the correctness condition for $\mathbf{c}^{\alpha'}_{\overline{X}}$ is:

$$\text{if } \mathbf{c}_{\overline{X}} \in \gamma(\mathbf{c}^{\alpha}_{\overline{X}}) \text{ then } \mathbf{c}_{\overline{X}} \wedge b_1 \in \gamma(\mathbf{c}^{\alpha'}_{\overline{X}}).$$

As this operation is abstracting conjunction, it is called abstract conjunction.

With b_1 a predicate of the form $p(\overline{Y})$ with $\overline{Y} \subseteq \overline{X}$ the step is more involved. In the concrete case, we consider the call $p(\overline{Y})$ with constraint store $\tilde{\exists}_{\overline{Y}}\mathbf{c}_{\overline{X}}$[9]. If it is in the table, then the lemmas describing the answers are used to resolve the call, if not, then subderivations are created: for each clause $p(\overline{Z}) \leftarrow d_1, \cdots, d_n$ with variables $\overline{U} \supseteq \overline{Z}$, a subderivation $<\leftarrow d_1, \cdots, d_n; \tilde{\exists}_{\overline{U}}((\tilde{\exists}_{\overline{Y}}\mathbf{c}_{\overline{X}}) \wedge (\overline{Z} =$

---

[6]So we stop using $\square$ as a separator between constraint and logic part.

[7]so ; is not a separator between constraint part and logic part but between a goal statement and a constraint store; $\square$ will be used for the empty goal statement.

[8]Careful reading will reveal that this is an invariant of the computation scheme.

[9]$\tilde{\exists}_{\overline{Y}}\mathbf{e}$ stands for $\exists_{X_1, \cdots, X_n}\mathbf{e}$ with $\{X_1, \cdots, X_n\} = var(\mathbf{e}) - \overline{Y}$.

$\overline{Y}$)) $>$ is created. Successful subderivations give rise to lemmas $p(\overline{Z}) \leftarrow \mathbf{c}_{\overline{Z}}$ which are then used to solve $p(\overline{Y})$ by *lookup*. Table *lookup* derives the state $<\leftarrow b_2, \cdots, b_n; \mathbf{c}_{\overline{X}} \wedge \tilde{\exists}_{\overline{X}}(\overline{Z} = \overline{Y} \wedge \mathbf{c}_{\overline{Z}}) >$.

The abstract computation mimics these operations. The constraint store $\mathbf{c}^{\alpha}{}_{\overline{Y}}$ associated with the call $p(\overline{Y})$ is computed; the correctness condition for $\mathbf{c}^{\alpha}{}_{\overline{Y}}$ is:

$$\text{if } \mathbf{c}_{\overline{X}} \in \gamma(\mathbf{c}^{\alpha}{}_{\overline{X}}) \text{ then } \tilde{\exists}_{\overline{Y}} \mathbf{c}_{\overline{X}} \in \gamma(\mathbf{c}^{\alpha}{}_{\overline{Y}}).$$

If this pattern is not in the table then subderivations are created: for each clause $p(\overline{Z}) \leftarrow d_1, \cdots, d_n$ with variables $\overline{U} \supseteq \overline{Z}$, a subderivation $<\leftarrow d_1, \cdots, d_n; \mathbf{c}^{\alpha}{}_{\overline{U}} >$ is created. The correctness condition for $\mathbf{c}^{\alpha}{}_{\overline{U}}$ is:

$$\text{if } \mathbf{c}_{\overline{Y}} \in \gamma(\mathbf{c}^{\alpha}{}_{\overline{Y}}) \text{ then } \tilde{\exists}_{\overline{U}}(\overline{Z} = \overline{Y} \wedge \mathbf{c}_{\overline{Y}}) \in \gamma(\mathbf{c}^{\alpha}{}_{\overline{U}}).$$

Lookup uses a lemma $p(\overline{Z}) \leftarrow \mathbf{c}^{\alpha}{}_{\overline{Z}}$ and derives $<\leftarrow b_2, \cdots, b_n; \mathbf{c}^{\alpha\prime}{}_{\overline{X}} >$. The correctness condition for $\mathbf{c}^{\alpha\prime}{}_{\overline{X}}$ is:

$$\text{if } \mathbf{c}_{\overline{X}} \in \gamma(\mathbf{c}^{\alpha}{}_{\overline{X}}) \text{ and } \mathbf{c}_{\overline{Z}} \in \gamma(\mathbf{c}^{\alpha}{}_{\overline{Z}}) \text{ then } \mathbf{c}_{\overline{X}} \wedge \tilde{\exists}_{\overline{X}}(\mathbf{c}_{\overline{Z}} \wedge \overline{Z} = \overline{Y}) \in \gamma(\mathbf{c}^{\alpha\prime}{}_{\overline{X}}).$$

Finally, there is the case of a successful subderivation. Let $p(\overline{Z}) \leftarrow d_1, \cdots, d_n$ be the clause activated for a call $p(\overline{Y})$ with constraint store $\mathbf{c}_{\overline{Y}}$ and let the answer be $< \square; \mathbf{c}_{\overline{U}} >$. The lemma stored as answer for the call pattern is $p(\overline{Z}) \leftarrow \tilde{\exists}_{\overline{Z}} \mathbf{c}_{\overline{U}}$. The abstract computation mimics this. We have a call $p(\overline{Y})$ with constraint store $\mathbf{c}^{\alpha}{}_{\overline{Y}}$ and answer $< \square; \mathbf{c}^{\alpha}{}_{\overline{U}} >$. The obtained lemma is $p(\overline{Z}) \leftarrow \mathbf{c}^{\alpha}{}_{\overline{Z}}$. The correctness condition for $\mathbf{c}^{\alpha}{}_{\overline{Z}}$ is:

$$\text{if } \mathbf{c}_{\overline{U}} \in \gamma(\mathbf{c}^{\alpha}{}_{\overline{U}}) \text{ then } \tilde{\exists}_{\overline{Z}} \mathbf{c}_{\overline{U}} \in \gamma(\mathbf{c}^{\alpha}{}_{\overline{Z}}).$$

However, only one lemma is allowed for each call pattern; so if there was already a lemma $p(\overline{Z}) \leftarrow \mathbf{c}^{\alpha\prime}{}_{\overline{Z}}$, then the lub of both lemma's, i.e. $p(\overline{Z}) \leftarrow \text{lub}(\mathbf{c}^{\alpha}{}_{\overline{Z}}, \mathbf{c}^{\alpha\prime}{}_{\overline{Z}})$ is replacing it. Moreover, all subderivations which were using the old lemma have to be redone, starting from the point where the old lemma was used.

Notice that the top-level derivation terminates with $< \square, \mathbf{c}_{\overline{X}} >$ in the concrete computation and with $< \square, \mathbf{c}^{\alpha}{}_{\overline{X}} >$ in the abstract computation, with $\overline{X}$ the variables of the initial goal and that $\mathbf{c}_{\overline{X}} \in \gamma(\mathbf{c}^{\alpha}{}_{\overline{X}})$.

3.2.4 Acknowledgements

We are indebted to Anne Mulkers, Veroniek Dumortier, Gerda Janssens, Roberto Giacobazzi and Panagiotis Tsarchopoulos for discussions and comments on drafts.

This work was supported by the "Belgian National Fund for Scientific Research", the "Research Council" of the Katholieke Universiteit Leuven and by the ESPRIT project 5246 PRINCE.

References

Bruynooghe, M. A Practical Framework for the Abstract Interpretation of Logic Programs J. Logic Programming, **10** (1991), 91–124

Bossi, A., Gabrielli, M., Levi G., Martelli, M. The S-semantics Approach: Theory and Applications Draft, submitted

Cousot, P., Cousot, R. Abstract Interpretation Frameworks J. Logic and Computations, **2**, (1992) 511–547

Cousot, P., Cousot, R. Abstract Interpretation and Application to Logic Programs J. Logic Programming, **13**, (1992) 103–180

Cousot, P., Cousot, R. Comparing the Galois Connection and Widening/Narrowing Approaches to Abstract Interpretation Proc. 5th Int. Symp. Programming Language Implementation and Logic Programming, LNCS 631, Springer-Verlag, (1992) 269–295

Codognet,P., Filé, G. Computations, Abstractions and Constraints in Logic Programs Proc. 4th Int. Conf. on Programming Languages, Oakland, 1992

Cousot, P., Halbwachs, N. Automatic Discovery of Linear Restraints among Variables of a Program Conference Record of the 5th ACM Symp. on Principles of Programming Languages, ACM Press, 1978, 84–97

Le Charlier, B., Van Hentenryck, P. A Generic Abstract Interpretation Algorithm and its Complexity Analysis (Extended Abstract) Proc. 8th Int. Conf. on Logic Programming, MIT Press, 1991, 64–78

Le Charlier, B., Van Hentenryck, P. Experimental Evaluation of a Generic Abstract Interpretation Algorithm for Prolog Proc. 4th IEEE International Conference on Computer Languages, San Francisco, 1992

Dumortier, V., Janssens, G., Bruynooghe, M., Codish, M. Freeness Analysis in the Presence of Numerical Constraints Proc. 5th Int. Conf. on Logic Programming, MIT Press, 1993, 100–115

Falaschi,M., Levi,G., Martelli,M., Palamidessi,C. Declarative Modelling of the Operational Behaviour of Logic Languages Theoretical Computer Science, **69** (1989), 289–318

Gabrielli, M., Levi, G. Modelling Answer Constraints in Constraint Logic Programs Proc. 8th Int. Conf. Logic Programming, MIT Press, 1991, 301–315

Garcia de la Banda, M., Hermenegildo, M. A Practical Approach to the Global Analysis of CLP Programs Proc. 1993 Int. Logic Programming Symp., MIT Press, 1993

Giacobazzi, R., Debray, S.,Levi, G. Generalised Semantics and Abstract Interpretation for Constraint Logic Programs Proc. Int. Conf. on Fifth Generation Computer Systems, Tokyo, 1992

Giacobazzi, R., Debray, S.,Levi, G. Generalised Semantics and Abstract Interpretation for Constraint Logic Programs Preliminary Report, April 1993

Van Hentenryck, P. Constraint Logic Programming Knowledge Engineering Review, **6** (1991), 151-194

Kanamori, T., Kawamura, T. Abstract Interpretation Based on OLDT Resolution J. Logic Programming **15** (1993), 1–30

Jaffar, J., Maher, M. Constraint Logic Programming, a Survey IBM T.J. Watson Research Center, Draft, submitted

Jones, N., Sondergaard, H. A Semantics-Based Framework for the Abstract Interpretation of PROLOG In S.Abramsky and C.Hankin (eds.), Abstract Interpretation for Declarative Languages, Ellis Horwood, 1987, 123–142

Karr, M. Affine Relationships among Variables of a Program Acta Inform., 6 (1976), 133–151

Lloyd, L. Foundations of Logic Programming Springer-Verlag, Berlin, 1987

Lassez, J.-L., Maher, M., Marriott, K. Unification Revisited In J. Minker (ed.), Foundations of Deductive Databases and Logic Programming, Morgan Kaufmann, 1988, 587–625

Martelli, A., Montanari, U. An Efficient Unification Algorithm ACM Transactions on Programming Languages and Systems, 4 (1982), 258–282

Marriott, K., Sondergaard, H. Analysis of Constraint Logic Programs Proc. 1990 North American Conference on Logic Programming, MIT Press, 1990, 532–547

Muthukumar, K., Hermenegildo, M. Compile-time Derivation of Variable Dependency Using Abstract Interpretation J. Logic Programming, 13 (1992), 315–374

Tamaki,H., Sato,T. OLD Resolution with Tabulation Proc. 3rd Int. Conf. on Logic Programming

Verschaetse, K., De Schreye, D. Deriving Termination Proofs for Logic Programs Proc. 8th Int. Conf. Logic Programming, MIT Press, 1991, 301–315

Verschaetse, K., De Schreye, D. Derivation of Linear Size Relations by Abstract Interpretation Proc. 5th Int. Symp. Programming Language Implementation and Logic Programming'92, LNCS 631, Springer-Verlag, (1992) 296–310

Vieille, L. Recursive Query Processing: The power of Logic Theoretical Computer Science, 69 (1989), 1–53

Winsborough, W. Multiple Specialisation Using Minimal-Function Graph Semantics J. Logic Programming, 13 (1992), 259–290

3.3 Denotational Semantics of Constraint Logic Programming – A Nonstandard Approach

Erik Palmgren[1]

Department of Mathematics, Uppsala University
PO Box 480, S-751 06 Uppsala, Sweden
palmgrem@bellatrix.tdt.uu.se

3.3.1 Introduction

Ideas and results from logic are continually put to use within the field of logic programming. In this paper we hope to contribute to this flow, by presenting a semantics of infinite computations in constraint logic programming (CLP), which uses the reduced power construction known from the model theory of nonstandard analysis.

If infinite computations are to be understood using ordinary model theory, this requires that infinite objects can be represented in the domain of interpretation. Consider the simplest possible example, the logic program P: $I(s(x)) \leftarrow I(x)$. The call $\leftarrow I(x_0)$ yields (under a suitable lazy computation scheme) a sequence of substitutions:

$$x_0 = s(x_1) \quad x_1 = s(x_2) \quad x_2 = s(x_3) \quad \cdots \quad (3.1)$$

In case the domain of interpretation $\mathcal{D}$ is the natural numbers, or equivalently, the terms built up by the successor symbol s and the constant 0, no solution to such a sequence can exist. One natural and well-known approach, due to Andreka, Nait Abdallah, Nemeti, Tiuryn and van Emden, is to base the models on infinite terms or trees (Lloyd 1984). In the example above this amounts to adding an infinite term s^ω with the property $s(s^\omega) = s^\omega$. The resulting semantics has the drawback that it does not reflect the occur check of the operational semantics, precisely because the equation $s(x) = x$ is solvable. (A radical approach in this particular case is of course to exclude occur check and develop semantics from this starting point (Weijland 1990).) What we request of $\mathcal{D}$ is not primarily topological completeness, as for the infinite terms, but rather *saturation,* which means, roughly speaking, that for each given set of 'constraints', if each finite subset is jointly solvable in $\mathcal{D}$, then the whole set is jointly solvable in $\mathcal{D}$. In nonstandard analysis one considers saturated structures, such as *ultra powers* of the real numbers, in order to get infinite and infinitesimal numbers (Lindstrøm 1988; Laugwitz 1973). The ultra powers are special instances of the

---

[1]The author gratefully acknowledges support from the Swedish Research Council for Engineering Sciences (TFR).

reduced power construction. The *Fréchet power* (see Sect. 3.3.5) is another instance, which shares many of the properties of the ultra power. In this paper we use mainly Fréchet powers, which gives rise to more fine grained models. In the Fréchet power, or the ultra power, of the natural numbers, $x_0, x_1, x_2, \ldots$ of (3.1) can be interpreted as a descending sequence of infinite numbers.

More generally, we consider constraint logic programs w.r.t. a given standard contraint structure $\mathcal{A}$, such as the finite trees or the real numbers. The declarative semantics for infinite computations is obtained by using an extended structure $\mathcal{A}^+$ (the Fréchet power of $\mathcal{A}$). By a transfer principle the same (finite) constraints are solvable in $\mathcal{A}$ and in $\mathcal{A}^+$. The difference appears when it comes to limit objects computed at infinity, i.e. objects given by infinite constraints. Moreover $\mathcal{A}^+$ inherits first order properties, expressible by Horn formulas, from $\mathcal{A}$. In particular, if $\mathcal{A}$ models Clark's equality theory, so does $\mathcal{A}^+$.

Infinite computations of logic programs are usually modelled using greatest fixed point semantics (see Lloyd (1984) for background), and we follow this route here too. A critical property for the adequacy of such a semantics is that the greatest fixed point of the immediate consequence operator, $T_P^{\mathcal{A}}$, can be reached after ω iterations downward. Algebras, or more generally, structures for which the $T_P^{\mathcal{A}}$-operator has this property for any program P, are called *canonical*. The problem of finding canonical structures for *logic programs,* which models Clark's equality theory, have been addressed by several authors, Blair and Brown (ta), Doets (1992) and Maher (1992).

One of the main results of the present paper is that the Fréchet power of any structure is a canonical structure. When $\mathcal{A}$ is a Fréchet power, we can in fact view $T_P^{\mathcal{A}}$ also as a continuous operator on (products of) Smyth power domains. Thereby the greatest fixed point is the least fixed point when seen domain-theoretically! Thus the traditional T_P-semantics can be related to the denotational semantics of Carlson (1991) and Jagadeesan et al. (1991). This explains the first part of the title.

3.3.1.1 Outline of This Paper. In Sect. 3.3.2 basic definitions concerning CLP are given; its declarative semantics is given in Sect. 3.3.3. The notion of saturation and how it gives a sufficient condition for canonicity is studied in Sect. 3.3.4. It is also shown that the infinite terms form canonical structures by using this condition. Section 3.3.5 is mainly concerned with the reduced power construction as a uniform method of extending structures to canonical structures. In Sect. 3.3.6 we relate the greatest fixed point semantics to domain theoretic least fixed point semantics.

3.3.2 Constraint Logic Programming

This is not the proper place for an extensive introduction to constraint logic programming, or its standard semantics; for this the reader is refered to Jaffar and Lassez (1986, 1987). Some background is also given in Mayoh et al. (199-) and Bruynooghe and Boulanger (199-). In comparison to pure logic programs, basic relations are allowed and functions need not be term formers. One has in mind a specific first order structure in which the formulas are interpreted, such as the real numbers with basic functions and relations. Another important difference, is that the result of a computation is in general not simply a set of substitutions, but may be a conjunction of any atomic formulas in the constraint language, e.g. $x < 2y + z \wedge 1 + y = z \cdot z$; quantifiers may also be allowed. Unification of terms is replaced by a test for solvability of a certain constraint in the resolution step (see Sect. 3.3.2.3).

It is important to note that we are not considering the full CLP scheme proposed by Jaffar and Lassez (1986). Their scheme consists of two parts for each problem domain: one model-theoretic and one proof-theoretic (also called algebraic and logical, respectively). They put certain restrictions (solution compactness) as to which constraint structures can be allowed, to maintain a close correspondence between the parts. By having these complementary aspects it possible is to preserve properties of logic programming, such as completeness of negation as failure. We are however mainly interested in infinite computations and shall therefore in the present paper ignore the proof-theoretic part. We are hence free to consider arbitrary constraint structures.

3.3.2.1 Logical Preliminaries and Notation

We recall and introduce some notation for later use. Let L be a first order language, where $\alpha(S)$ is the arity of $S \in L$. A structure $\mathcal{A}$ for L (an L-structure) consists in a universe of objects $|\mathcal{A}|$; for each relation symbol R of L, a relation $R_\mathcal{A} \subseteq |\mathcal{A}|^{\alpha(R)}$; for each function symbol f of L, a function $f_\mathcal{A} : |\mathcal{A}|^{\alpha(f)} \to |\mathcal{A}|$; and for each constant symbol c of L, a constant $c_\mathcal{A} \in |\mathcal{A}|$. By abuse of language, L is also called the *signature* of $\mathcal{A}$. The interpretation of a closed term t in a structure $\mathcal{A}$ is denoted $t_\mathcal{A}$. We apply the convention of using the same symbol for an element of $\mathcal{A}$ and for the constant corresponding to this element in the extended language $L(\mathcal{A})$. Writing an expression e as $e(x_1, \ldots, x_n)$ means that its free variables, $FV(e)$, are among $x_1, \ldots, x_n$. $\Delta(x_1, \ldots, x_n)$ denotes a set of formulas, with all their free variables among $x_1, \ldots, x_n$. Such a set is called a *type*. The closing of the formula φ by existentially quantifying its free variables is denoted $\exists(\varphi)$.

We take constants for truth ($\top$) and absurdity ($\bot$) as basic atomic formulas. A formula built from atomic formulas using only $\forall, \exists, \wedge$ and $\vee$ is called *positive*. Let φ be positive; if it lacks disjunctions it is called *positive definite*; if it lacks $\forall$ it is called *geometric*; if it lacks both $\forall$ and $\vee$ it is said to be *subgeometric*.

3.3.2.2 Constraint Logic Programs

We shall consider only definite clause CLP, but allow constraints from a wider class than usual. We will mainly consider constraints from the class of subgeometric formulas or from the more extensive class of *essentially positive definite* formulas in connection with reduced powers.

Let L be a fixed first order language – *the constraint language*; let K_L be a class of L-formulas, containing all equations, and closed under conjunction – these are the *constraint formulas*. A *constraint* is a formula in K_L. Let

$\mathbf{R} = R_1, \ldots, R_M$ be predicate symbols not in L – *the program predicates*. A *program atom* is an atomic formula $R_i(t_1, \ldots, t_n)$. A *constraint program clause* is a formula of $L(\mathbf{R})$:

$$R_i(t_1, \ldots, t_n) \leftarrow \sigma \wedge A_1 \wedge \cdots \wedge A_k \qquad (3.2)$$

where σ is a constraint and each A_j is a program atom. A *constraint logic program* P is a finite set of constraint program clauses. Sometimes we want to emphasise that the constraints in P come from K_L, in which case we say that P is a K_L-program. Note that (3.2) is equivalent to

$$R_i(x_1, \ldots, x_n) \leftarrow \exists y_1 \cdots \exists y_q [x_1 = t_1 \wedge \cdots \wedge x_n = t_n \wedge \sigma \wedge A_1 \wedge \cdots \wedge A_k]$$

where $x_1, \ldots, x_n$ are new variables and $y_1, \ldots, y_q$ are the free variables of (3.2). A conjunction of ℓ clauses (3.2) can therefore be written as $R_i(x_1, \ldots, x_n) \leftarrow \varphi_1 \vee \cdots \vee \varphi_\ell$ where each φ_j is an existentially quantified K_L-formula. This disjunction, ψ_{R_i}, is called the *defining formula* for R_i. Let Θ be a set of formulas. A *geometric combination* of Θ-formulas is built up from Θ-formulas using only $\exists$, $\wedge$ and $\vee$. The fact that the defining formula above is a geometric combination of K_L-constraints and program atoms will be important later on.

3.3.2.3 Operational semantics. To describe the operational semantics precisely we introduce a *goal language*. For each program predicate R_i, there is an infinite sequence of predicates $R_i^0, R_i^1, R_i^2, \ldots$ of the same arity. The superscripts are intended to signify the depth of rule application at which the program atom was introduced. Thus the *depth* of $R_i^m(t_1, \ldots, t_n)$ is m. By convention the depth of any other atomic formula is ∞. If A is a formula, $\mu(A)$ denotes the minimum depth of atomic subformulas of A. Let $L_\omega(\mathbf{R})$ be the extension of the language L by the predicates R_i^j, $i = 1, \ldots, M$, $j \in \omega$. For a formula A of $L(\mathbf{R})$, $A^{(j)}$ is the result of replacing each R_i by R_i^j.

The operational semantics is defined w.r.t. a particular *constraint L-structure* $\mathcal{A}$, also known as a *constraint system*. A goal G (or more fully: a K_L-*goal*) is a conjunction in $L_\omega(\mathbf{R})$,

$$\psi \wedge B_1 \wedge \cdots \wedge B_m,$$

where ψ is a constraint in K_L, and each B_i is a program atom. The constraint part, ψ, of G is denoted G_c. The goal

$$G' \equiv \theta \wedge B_1 \wedge \cdots \wedge B_{i-1} \wedge A_1^{(\nu+1)} \wedge \cdots \wedge A_k^{(\nu+1)} \wedge B_{i+1} \wedge \cdots \wedge B_m$$

is an $\mathcal{A}$-*resolvent* of G and the clause $H \equiv R_j(t_1, \ldots, t_n) \leftarrow \varphi \wedge A_1 \wedge \cdots \wedge A_k$, *selecting* the atom B_i, if the following holds

1. $B_i \equiv R_j^\nu(s_1, \ldots, s_n)$,

2. the constraint $\theta \equiv ((\bigwedge_{i=1}^n s_i = t_i) \wedge \varphi \wedge \psi)$ is solvable in $\mathcal{A}$, i.e. $\mathcal{A} \models \exists(\theta)$,

3. H is a variant of a clause in P (the *input clause*) with variables chosen to be distinct from the variables of G, and this choice should depend only on the form of G.

In this case we write $G \succ_{\mathcal{A}} G'$. If only the solvability condition 2 fails, G' is called a *pseudo resolvent of G*.

Clearly, by condition 3 there can be only finitely many different G'.

An $\mathcal{A}$-*derivation* is a finite or infinite sequence of goals $\{G_i\}_{i<\alpha}$, $\alpha \leq \omega$, where $G_i \succ_{\mathcal{A}} G_{i+1}$ for $i + 1 < \alpha$. A finite $\mathcal{A}$-derivation $G_0 \succ_{\mathcal{A}} \cdots \succ_{\mathcal{A}} G_m$ is *successful* if G_m has no program atoms, i.e. if it is a constraint; G_m is the *result*, or the *answer constraint*. An infinite $\mathcal{A}$-derivation $G_0 \succ_{\mathcal{A}} G_1 \succ_{\mathcal{A}} G_2 \succ_{\mathcal{A}} \cdots$ is *fair* if $\mu(G_i) \to \infty$, as $i \to \infty$. This means that, eventually, every atom is selected.

The result, or partial result, of a computation is simply a constraint. To see what it means in a structure we define, the $\mathcal{A}$-*denotation* of a goal G in the variables $\mathbf{x} = x_1, \ldots, x_n$ to be the set

$$\llbracket G \rrbracket_{\mathbf{x}}^{\mathcal{A}} = \{\mathbf{a} \in |\mathcal{A}|^n : \mathcal{A} \models \exists (G'[\mathbf{a}/\mathbf{x}])\},$$

where G' is G when every program atom has been replaced by $\top$. (This definition makes sense for any $L(\mathbf{R})$-formula.) In case G is a constraint, $\mathbf{a} \in \llbracket G \rrbracket_{\mathbf{x}}^{\mathcal{A}}$ if, and only if, $G[\mathbf{a}/\mathbf{x}]$ is solvable in $\mathcal{A}$. Otherwise, the denotation is just an approximation, since all program predicates of G are then treated as if they were universally true. The $\mathcal{A}$-*success set* of a goal G_0 for the variables $\mathbf{x}$ (w.r.t P) is the union of all sets $\llbracket G \rrbracket_{\mathbf{x}}^{\mathcal{A}}$, where G is the result of a sucessful $\mathcal{A}$-derivation starting with G_0. We denote this set by $S_P^{\mathcal{A}}(G_0; \mathbf{x})$. We turn to general fair derivations. The tuple $\mathbf{a} = (a_1, \ldots, a_n)$ is said to be $\mathcal{A}$-*computed fairly* on the call G_0 for the variables $\mathbf{x} = x_1, \ldots, x_n$ if either $\mathbf{a} \in S_P^{\mathcal{A}}(G, \mathbf{x})$, or there is an infinite fair derivation

$$G_0 \succ_{\mathcal{A}} G_1 \succ_{\mathcal{A}} G_2 \succ_{\mathcal{A}} \cdots$$

such that $\mathbf{a} \in \llbracket G_m \rrbracket_{\mathbf{x}}^{\mathcal{A}}$ for all m. Let $C_P^{\mathcal{A}}(G_0; \mathbf{x})$ denote the set of these tuples.

Proposition 3.1 *Let* $G = G_1 \wedge G_2$ *be a goal with* $FV(G) \subseteq \mathbf{x}$. *Then:*

(i) $S_P^{\mathcal{A}}(G; \mathbf{x}) = S_P^{\mathcal{A}}(G_1; \mathbf{x}) \cap S_P^{\mathcal{A}}(G_2; \mathbf{x})$,

(ii) $C_P^{\mathcal{A}}(G; \mathbf{x}) = C_P^{\mathcal{A}}(G_1; \mathbf{x}) \cap C_P^{\mathcal{A}}(G_2; \mathbf{x})$.

Proof. Straightforward. □

Proposition 3.2 *Let* $G \equiv R(t_1, \ldots, t_n)$ *be a program atom with free variables among* $\mathbf{x}$. *Let* $\mathbf{y} = y_1, \ldots, y_n$ *be distinct variables. Then:*

(i) $\mathbf{a} \in S_P^{\mathcal{A}}(G; \mathbf{x}) \iff (t_1[\mathbf{a}/\mathbf{x}]_{\mathcal{A}}, \ldots, t_n[\mathbf{a}/\mathbf{x}]_{\mathcal{A}}) \in S_P^{\mathcal{A}}(R(\mathbf{y}); \mathbf{y})$,

(ii) $\mathbf{a} \in C_P^{\mathcal{A}}(G; \mathbf{x}) \iff (t_1[\mathbf{a}/\mathbf{x}]_{\mathcal{A}}, \ldots, t_n[\mathbf{a}/\mathbf{x}]_{\mathcal{A}}) \in C_P^{\mathcal{A}}(R(\mathbf{y}); \mathbf{y})$.

Proof. Easy. □

From these results it follows that the operational semantics of complex goals are completely determined by the *pure calls*, i.e. program atoms of the form $R(y_1, \ldots, y_n)$, with distinct variables $y_1, \ldots, y_n$.

3.3.3 Declarative Semantics

A definite clause program P with program predicates $\mathbf{R} = R_1, \ldots, R_M$ over the constraint structure $\mathcal{A}$ can be considered as an inductive definition of the relations $\mathbf{R}$. To generate the relations we start out assuming that the relations are empty. Then we apply the clauses of P repeatedly to see what must be thrown in, until no further objects can be added. The program can also be regarded as a *coinductive definition*. In this case we start out assuming that the relations contain everything (in their domain of definition) and then apply the clauses to see what must be left out. This process is repeated until it stabilises.

The operator at work in both cases is the so called *immediate consequence operator*. We give a formal definition. Let P be a constraint logic program in the language $L(\mathbf{R})$, and let $\mathcal{A}$ be a constraint L-structure. Put $A = |\mathcal{A}|$, $\alpha_i = \alpha(R_i)$ and

$$\hat{A} = \mathcal{P}(A^{\alpha_1}) \times \cdots \times \mathcal{P}(A^{\alpha_M})$$

– the set of all possible interpretations of $\mathbf{R}$. We impose coordinatewise inclusion $\leq$ as an ordering on $\hat{A}$:

$$(G_1, \ldots, G_M) \leq (H_1, \ldots, H_M) \iff G_1 \subseteq H_1 \wedge \cdots \wedge G_M \subseteq H_M.$$

This gives a complete lattice, where $\wedge_n(G_1^n, \ldots, G_M^n) = (\cap_n G_1^n, \ldots, \cap_n G_M^n)$, and analogously for supremum ($\vee$). A formula $\varphi(x_1, \ldots, x_n)$ in $L(\mathbf{R})$ defines a set function $\Gamma^{\mathcal{A}}_{\varphi(x_1, \ldots, x_n)} : \hat{A} \to \mathcal{P}(A^n)$

$$\Gamma^{\mathcal{A}}_{\varphi(x_1, \ldots, x_n)}(\mathbf{G}) = \{(a_1, \ldots, a_n) : \mathcal{A}(\mathbf{G}) \models \varphi[a_1, \ldots, a_n]\}$$

by interpreting R_i as $(\mathbf{G})_i$ (the i:th component of $\mathbf{G}$) in the $L(\mathbf{R})$-expansion $\mathcal{A}(\mathbf{G})$ of $\mathcal{A}$. Let $\psi_{R_i}(x_1, \ldots, x_{\alpha_i})$ be the defining formula for R_i in the program P. The *immediate consequence operator* $T_P^{\mathcal{A}} : \hat{A} \to \hat{A}$ for P is given by

$$T_P^{\mathcal{A}}(\mathbf{G}) = (\Gamma^{\mathcal{A}}_{\psi_{R_1}(x_1, \ldots, x_{\alpha_1})}(\mathbf{G}), \ldots, \Gamma^{\mathcal{A}}_{\psi_{R_M}(x_1, \ldots, x_{\alpha_M})}(\mathbf{G})).$$

This is a slightly uncustomary phrasing of the well-known T_P-operator (Jaffar and Lassez 1986), but which is closer to the practice in logic. The program predicates occur only positively in the defining formulas. It follows that the operator is monotone. The *upwards iterations* of $T_P^{\mathcal{A}}$ are given by

- $T_P^{\mathcal{A}} \uparrow 0 = (\emptyset, \ldots, \emptyset)$,

- $T_P^{\mathcal{A}} \uparrow (n+1) = T_P^{\mathcal{A}}(T_P^{\mathcal{A}} \uparrow n)$,

- $T_P^{\mathcal{A}} \uparrow \omega = \vee_n(T_P^{\mathcal{A}} \uparrow n)$.

By the monotonicity of the operator this is an increasing sequence. Since only existential quantification is used over the program atoms in the defining formulas, we have the following.

Theorem 3.3 $T_P^{\mathcal{A}} \uparrow \omega$ *is the least fixed point of* $T_P^{\mathcal{A}}$. $\square$

The components of the least fixed point are the predicates on $\mathcal{A}$ *inductively defined* by P. The downward iterations of $T_P^{\mathcal{A}}$ is a decreasing sequence:

- $T_P^{\mathcal{A}} \downarrow 0 = (A^{\alpha_1}, \ldots, A^{\alpha_M})$,

- $T_P^{\mathcal{A}} \downarrow (\alpha + 1) = T_P^{\mathcal{A}}(T_P^{\mathcal{A}} \downarrow \alpha)$,

- $T_P^{\mathcal{A}} \downarrow \beta = \wedge_{\alpha < \beta}(T_P^{\mathcal{A}} \downarrow \alpha)$, if β is a limit ordinal.

Similarly, the components of the greatest fixed point of $T_P^{\mathcal{A}}$, gfp $T_P^{\mathcal{A}}$, is what is *coinductively defined* by P. This fixed point always exists too, since for cardinality reasons we must have $T_P \downarrow \alpha = T_P \downarrow \alpha + 1$ for some ordinal α. However, α may have to be greater than ω (Lloyd 1984), as in the following example.

Example 3.4 We consider constraint logic programming for the real numbers $\mathbb{R}$. Let P be the program:

$$\begin{cases} R_1(0) & \leftarrow R_2(x), \\ R_2(y/2) & \leftarrow 0 < y \wedge y < 1 \wedge R_2(y). \end{cases}$$

Put $T_P = T_P^{\mathbb{R}}$. We have $T_P \downarrow 0 = (\mathbb{R}, \mathbb{R})$, and for $n \geq 1$

$$T_P \downarrow n = (\{0\}, (0, 2^{-n})).$$

Thus $T_P \downarrow \omega = (\{0\}, \emptyset)$, but

$$T_P \downarrow \omega + 1 = (\emptyset, \emptyset) = T_P \downarrow \omega + 2.$$

Supposing that we instead considered nonstandard real numbers with infinitesimals the fixed point would have occured at ω! This is a clue to the general extension method in Sect. 3.3.5.

The importance of fixed points $\mathbf{F}$ of $T_P^{\mathcal{A}}$ is that they provide a declarative semantics. They are models of the *completion of the program P*, i.e.

$$\mathcal{A}(\mathbf{F}) \models R_i(\mathbf{x}) \leftrightarrow \psi_{R_i}(\mathbf{x}) \qquad (i = 1, \ldots, M)$$

where $\psi_{R_i}(\mathbf{x})$ is the defining formula of R_i in P, and R_j is interpreted as $(\mathbf{F})_j$.

3.3.3.1 Relation to Operational Semantics In this subsection we consider the relation between operational and declarative semantics for CLP. The results could probably be extracted from (Jaffar and Lassez 1986) by close inspection of their arguments to see where the dependence of solution compactness is essential. However, at least to the author, it seems easier to prove the results directly.

Theorem 3.5 *Let G_i be the goal $R_i^0(\mathbf{x_i})$, where $\mathbf{x_i} = x_{i,1}, \ldots, x_{i,\alpha_i}$ are distinct variables. Then:*

(i) $T_P^{\mathcal{A}} \uparrow \omega = (S_P^{\mathcal{A}}(G_1; \mathbf{x_1}), \dots, S_P^{\mathcal{A}}(G_M; \mathbf{x_M})),$

(ii) $T_P^{\mathcal{A}} \downarrow \omega = (C_P^{\mathcal{A}}(G_1; \mathbf{x_1}), \dots, C_P^{\mathcal{A}}(G_M; \mathbf{x_M})).$

The theorem thus states that $T_P^{\mathcal{A}} \uparrow \omega$ is exactly what is computed by finite derivations on pure calls. This is also the least fixed point, so we have a perfect match between operational and declarative semantics in this case. For general fair computations there is not necessarily a perfect match, since $T_P^{\mathcal{A}} \downarrow \omega$ need not be the greatest fixed point.

To prove the theorem we use auxiliary models of finite approximations to $T_P^{\mathcal{A}} \uparrow \omega$ and $T_P^{\mathcal{A}} \downarrow \omega$. For each $\mathbf{S}$, let $\mathcal{M}_n[\mathbf{S}]$ be the $L_\omega(\mathbf{R})$-structure obtained by expanding $\mathcal{A}$ such that

- R_i^j is interpreted as $(T_P^{n-j}(\mathbf{S}))_i$ if $j \leq n$,

- R_i^j is interpreted as $(\mathbf{S})_i$ otherwise.

Lemma 3.6 *Let G be a goal. If $\mathcal{M}_n[T_P^{\mathcal{A}} \uparrow 0] \models \exists(G)$, then: either there are no program atoms in G or their superscripts are all less than n.*

Proof. Immediate from the definition of the model. $\square$

Lemma 3.7 *Let G be a goal with at least one program atom. Suppose that λ is the largest superscript that occurs in G. Then for all $n\lambda$ and all $\mathbf{S} \in \hat{A}$,*

$$\mathcal{M}_n[\mathbf{S}] \models G \leftrightarrow \exists \mathbf{y_1} G_1 \vee \cdots \vee \exists \mathbf{y_k} G_k,$$

where $G_1, \dots, G_k$ are the pseudo resolvents of G, and $\{\mathbf{y_i}\} = FV(G_i) - FV(G)$. $G_1, \dots, G_k$ may also be choosen to be the pseudo resolvents when selecting a particular atom. For $\mathbf{S} = T_P \downarrow 0$, the $(\leftarrow)$-direction hold without restrictions on the superscripts.

Proof. By considering the defining formulas of the program predicates. $\square$

Proof. (of Theorem 3.5). We start by making the simple observation that if G' is a pseudo resolvent of G and $\mathcal{M}_n[\mathbf{S}] \models \exists(G')$, then in fact $G \succ G'$.

Let $T_P = T_P^{\mathcal{A}}$. Suppose $\mathbf{a} \in (T_P \uparrow n)_i$. Thus

$$\mathcal{M}_n[T_P \uparrow 0] \models R_i^0(\mathbf{a}).$$

By Lemma 3.6, $n0$. We can apply Lemma 3.7 (and the observation) to get $R_i^0(\mathbf{x_i}) \succ G^1$ and $\mathbf{b_1}$ so that

$$\mathcal{M}_n[T_P \uparrow 0] \models G^1(\mathbf{a}, \mathbf{b_1}).$$

If G^1 contains no program atoms, we are done. Otherwise Lemma 3.7 can be applied again. We get $G^1 \succ G^2$ and $\mathbf{b_2}$ such that

$$\mathcal{M}_n[T_P \uparrow 0] \models G^2(\mathbf{a}, \mathbf{b_1}, \mathbf{b_2}).$$

Eventually this process must stop, and we get a successful derivation

$$R_i^0(\mathbf{x_i}) \succ \cdots \succ G^m$$

with $\mathcal{M}_n[T_P \uparrow 0] \models G^m(\mathbf{a}, \mathbf{b_1}, \ldots, \mathbf{b_m})$. Hence: $\mathbf{a} \in S_P(R_i^0(\mathbf{x_i}); \mathbf{x_i})$.

To prove the converse ($\supseteq$), suppose that $\mathbf{a} \in S_P(R_i^0(\mathbf{x_i}); \mathbf{x_i})$ is witnessed by

$$R_i^0(\mathbf{x_i}) \succ \cdots \succ G^m. \tag{3.3}$$

Choose nm, which is thus greater than all superscripts in (3.3). Hence:

$$\mathcal{M}_n[T_P \uparrow 0] \models \exists(G^m(\mathbf{a}/\mathbf{x_i})).$$

Working backwards using Lemma 3.7 we get

$$\mathcal{M}_n[T_P \uparrow 0] \models R_i^0(\mathbf{a}),$$

i.e. $\mathbf{a} \in (T_P \uparrow n)_i$.

We now prove the second part (ii). Suppose $\mathbf{a} \in C_P(R_i^0(\mathbf{x_i}); \mathbf{x_i}) \backslash S_P(R_i^0(\mathbf{x_i}); \mathbf{x_i})$, with

$$R_i^0(\mathbf{x}) \equiv G_0 \succ G_1 \succ G_2 \succ \cdots$$

as the associated infinite fair derivation.

Let n be fixed. Choose m large enough that $\mu(G_m) \geq n$, where $G_m = \sigma \wedge B$. We have $\mathcal{A} \models \exists(\sigma[\mathbf{a}/\mathbf{x}])$, so by the definition of the model M_n,

$$\mathcal{M}_n[T_P \downarrow 0] \models \exists(G_m[\mathbf{a}/\mathbf{x}]).$$

Using the unrestricted ($\leftarrow$) direction of Lemma 3.7, we get

$$\mathcal{M}_n[T_P \downarrow 0] \models R_i^0(\mathbf{a}).$$

Since n was arbitrary, $\mathbf{a} \in (T_P \downarrow \omega)_i$.

For the converse, suppose $\mathbf{a} \in (T_P \downarrow \omega)_i$, and that $\mathbf{a} \notin S_P(R_i^0(\mathbf{x_i}); \mathbf{x_i})$. Consider the set $\mathcal{T}$ of sequences $\langle G_0, \ldots, G_m \rangle$ with

1. $G_0 \equiv R_i^0(\mathbf{x_i})$,

2. $G_0 \succ \cdots \succ G_m$ by selecting program atoms with minimal superscripts,

3. $(\forall \ell)\mathcal{M}_\ell[T_P \downarrow 0] \models \exists(G_m[\mathbf{a}/\mathbf{x_i}])$.

With the sequence extension order, $\mathcal{T}$ defines a finitely branching tree. Suppose that $\mathcal{T}$ is finite. Let $G_0 \succ \cdots \succ G_m$ be a maximal branch. By the assumption that $\mathbf{a}$ is not computed finitely, G_m must contain a program atom. Let N be greater than all the superscripts of program atoms in G_m. Thus by Lemma 3.7 and condition 3 there is a resolvent $G_m \succ G'$ (selecting a program atom with minimal superscript) such that for infinitely many $\ell(\geq N)$, $\mathcal{M}_\ell[T_P \downarrow 0] \models \exists(G'[\mathbf{a}/\mathbf{x_i}])$. By monotonicity,

$$(\forall \ell)\mathcal{M}_\ell[T_P \downarrow 0] \models \exists(G'[\mathbf{a}/\mathbf{x_i}]).$$

The branch is extended in contradiction to the assumption. Thus $\mathcal{T}$ must be infinite, and hence contain an infinite branch. By condition 3 with $\ell = 0$, this branch is the infinite fair derivation we are looking for. $\square$

3.3.4 Saturation

Saturation is a kind of completeness property of first order structures, which plays an important rôle in model theory. We will see that it provides a sufficient condition for canonicity of constraint structures.

Let $\Delta(x_1, \ldots, x_n)$ be a type of L-formulas. Given an L-structure $\mathcal{A}$, this set is said to be *realisable in* $\mathcal{A}$ if there exist $a_1, \ldots, a_n \in |\mathcal{A}|$ such that $\mathcal{A} \models \varphi(a_1, \ldots, a_n)$ for all $\varphi(x_1, \ldots, x_n) \in \Delta$. Δ is said to be *finitely realisable in* $\mathcal{A}$, if each of its finite subsets is realisable in $\mathcal{A}$.

Let Γ be a set of L-formulas, and let C be a set of new constants, i.e. $L \cap C = \emptyset$. Then $L[C]$ denotes the expansion of L with these new constants; $\Gamma[C]$ is the least set of $L[C]$-formulas containing Γ and such that for all variables x and all constants $c \in C$: $\varphi \in \Gamma[C] \Longrightarrow \varphi(c/x) \in \Gamma[C]$.

Definition 3.8 *Let Γ be a set of L-formulas. An L-structure $\mathcal{A}$ is ω-saturated (ω_1-saturated) for Γ-formulas, if for each finite (countable) set of new constants C, and each expansion $\mathcal{A}'$ of $\mathcal{A}$ to $L[C]$, and each $\Delta(\mathbf{x}) \subseteq \Gamma[C]$, the following implication holds: if $\Delta(\mathbf{x})$ is finitely realisable in $\mathcal{A}'$, then it is realisable in $\mathcal{A}'$.*

The expansion by constants allows for parameters in the formulas. Usually saturation is only considered when Γ is the set of *all L-formulas*. In this case we drop the qualification "for Γ-formulas". Some of the structures of interest in CLP are however saturated only for restricted classes of formulas, such as the algebra of infinite trees (Sect. 3.3.4.2).

We draw on some examples from Chang and Keisler (1990).

Example 3.9 Any finite structure is ω-saturated.

Note that the rational numbers $(\mathbb{Q}, <)$ are not ω_1-saturated in the language $L = \{<\}$. Consider the type $\Delta(x) = \{0 < x \wedge x < 2^{-n} : n \in \omega\}$, where 0, 2^{-n} are constants. While it is, in fact, ω-saturated in the same language. If we extend $\mathbb{Q}$ with the arithmetical operations then it is no longer ω-saturated. In Sect. 3.3.5 we encounter a systematic method for extending structures (with countable signatures) to saturated structures.

3.3.4.1 A Sufficient Condition for Canonicity There is a syntactic counterpart to the T_P-operator, which we call the *unfolding operator U_P*. Let φ be a formula in $L' = L(\mathbf{R})$; the L'-formula $unf_P(\varphi)$ results from unfolding the definitions one step, i.e. replacing all occurences $R_i(t_1, \ldots, t_n)$ in φ by $\psi_{R_i}(t_1, \ldots, t_n)$. It is assumed that the bound variables of the defining formulas are renamed to be different from the free variables of $t_1, \ldots, t_n$. Define

$$U_P(\varphi_1, \ldots, \varphi_M) = (unf_P(\varphi_1), \ldots, unf_P(\varphi_M)).$$

U_P thus operates on M-tuples of L'-formulas. Note that $FV(unf_P(\varphi)) \subseteq FV(\varphi)$. Define $U_P \downarrow 0 = (R_1(\mathbf{z}_1), \ldots, R_M(\mathbf{z}_M))$ (where $\mathbf{z}_1, \ldots, \mathbf{z}_M$ are all distinct) and put $U_P \downarrow (n+1) = U_P(U_P \downarrow n)$.

This is not the 'proof-theoretic' T_P-operator of Jaffar and Lassez (1986) since we do not have their satisfiability condition. Nevertheless there is the following connection to $T_P \downarrow n$.

Proposition 3.10 *Let P be a K_L-program, and let $\mathcal{A}$ be an L-structure.*

(i) *Every component of $(U_P \downarrow n)$ is a geometric combination of K_L-constraints and program atoms.*

(ii) *Let $\theta_{n,i}$ be the i:th component of $U_P \downarrow n$, where the program atoms have been replaced by $\top$. Then*

$$T_P^{\mathcal{A}} \downarrow n = ([\![\theta_{n,1}]\!]_{\mathbf{z}_1}^{\mathcal{A}}, \ldots, [\![\theta_{n,M}]\!]_{\mathbf{z}_M}^{\mathcal{A}}).\square$$

The following sufficiency condition is more or less explicit already in Doets (1992). It is possible to trace this condition further back by first noting that coinductive definitions can be defined in terms of inductive definitions, and then refer to (Moschovakis 1974, Exercise 4.7).

Theorem 3.11 *Suppose that $\mathcal{A}$ is an L-structure which is ω-saturated for geometric combinations of K_L-constraints. Then $T_P^{\mathcal{A}} \downarrow \omega$ is the greatest fixed point of $T_P^{\mathcal{A}}$, for every K_L-program P; i.e. $\mathcal{A}$ is canonical.*

Proof. It is easily shown by induction on n that, if $\mathbf{F}$ is a fixed point of $T_P^{\mathcal{A}}$, then $\mathbf{F} \leq T_P^{\mathcal{A}} \downarrow n$. Thus $\mathbf{F} \leq T_P^{\mathcal{A}} \downarrow \omega$, so it suffices to show that $T_P^{\mathcal{A}} \downarrow \omega$ is a fixed point. And to prove this it is by the monotonicity of T_P, sufficient to prove that $T_P^{\mathcal{A}} \downarrow \omega \leq T_P^{\mathcal{A}}(T_P^{\mathcal{A}} \downarrow \omega)$.

The components of $T_P^{\mathcal{A}}$ are $\Gamma_j = \Gamma_{\psi_{R_j}(x_1, \ldots, x_{\alpha(R_j)})}$, where $j = 1, \ldots, M$, so

$$T_P^{\mathcal{A}}(T_P^{\mathcal{A}} \downarrow \omega) = (\Gamma_1(T_P^{\mathcal{A}} \downarrow \omega), \ldots, \Gamma_M(T_P^{\mathcal{A}} \downarrow \omega)).$$

Now $T_P^{\mathcal{A}} \downarrow \omega = (\cap_n \Gamma_1(T_P^{\mathcal{A}} \downarrow n), \ldots, \cap_n \Gamma_M(T_P^{\mathcal{A}} \downarrow n))$, so we are done if we can prove

$$\cap_n \Gamma_j(T_P^{\mathcal{A}} \downarrow n) \subseteq \Gamma_j(\wedge_n T_P^{\mathcal{A}} \downarrow n). \tag{3.4}$$

The defining formula $\psi_{R_j}(\mathbf{x})$ can be written as

$$\exists \mathbf{y} \mathbf{z}_1 \cdots \mathbf{z}_M [\sigma(\mathbf{x}, \mathbf{y}, \mathbf{z}_1, \ldots, \mathbf{z}_M) \wedge R_1(\mathbf{z}_1) \wedge \cdots \wedge R_M(\mathbf{z}_M)]$$

with σ as a disjunction of K_L-constraints. Using Proposition 3.10 one finds that $\mathbf{a} \in \Gamma_j(T_P^{\mathcal{A}} \downarrow n)$ is equivalent to

$$\mathcal{A} \models \exists \mathbf{y} \mathbf{z}_1 \cdots \mathbf{z}_M [\sigma(\mathbf{a}, \mathbf{y}, \mathbf{z}_1, \ldots, \mathbf{z}_M) \wedge \theta_{n,1}(\mathbf{z}_1) \wedge \cdots \wedge \theta_{n,M}(\mathbf{z}_M)]. \tag{3.5}$$

Let $\varphi_n(\mathbf{y}, \mathbf{z}_1, \ldots, \mathbf{z}_M)$ be the $L[\mathbf{a}]$-formula within brackets in (3.5). This formula is a geometric combination of K_L-constraints. Assume that $\mathbf{a} \in \Gamma_j(T_P^{\mathcal{A}} \downarrow n)$ for all n. By monotonicity, this implies that $\Sigma = \{\varphi_n(\mathbf{y}, \mathbf{z}_1, \ldots, \mathbf{z}_M) : n \in \omega\}$ is finitely realisable in $\mathcal{A}$. Since $\mathcal{A}$ is ω-saturated for geometric combinations of K_L-constraints, Σ is realisable. Thus $\mathbf{a} \in \Gamma_j(\wedge_n T_P^{\mathcal{A}} \downarrow n)$. $\square$

Remark. With Doets (1992) we may observe that it is only necessary to consider recursive types. In fact, the gödel-number of φ_n (in the proof) is a recursive function of n.

Example 3.12 Let $L = \emptyset$, and let $\mathcal{A}$ be an infinite L-structure, i.e. $\mathcal{A}$ is just an infinite set. $\mathcal{A}$ can be proven to be ω-saturated using quantifier elimination. Hence $\mathcal{A}$ is canonical for any L-program. This is a (fancy) way of realising why logic programs without function symbols are canonical.

Some helpful results when trying to satisfy the sufficiency condition are the following. In the definition of saturation we considered types with arbitrary finitely many free variables. This is not necessary if Γ is closed under conjunction and existential quantification. In this case one need only to consider one free variable (Chang and Keisler 1990, Proposition 2.3.6).

Lemma 3.13 *Suppose that $\mathcal{A}$ is an L-structure, where L is countable. Let Γ be a set of formulas in L, and let $\Gamma_\vee$ be the closure of the Γ-formulas under disjunction. If $\mathcal{A}$ is ω-saturated (ω_1-saturated) for Γ-formulas, then it is also ω-saturated (ω_1-saturated) for $\Gamma_\vee$-formulas.*

Proof. Suppose that $\mathcal{A}$ is ω_1-saturated for Γ-formulas. Let C be a countable set of constants, new to L, and suppose that $\mathcal{A}'$ is an expansion of $\mathcal{A}$ to $L[C]$.

Let $\Phi(\mathbf{x}) \subseteq \Gamma_\vee[C]$ be any set of formulas

$$\{\varphi_{i,1}(\mathbf{x}) \vee \cdots \vee \varphi_{i,n_i}(\mathbf{x}) : i \in \omega\}$$

finitely realisable in $\mathcal{A}'$ (where $\varphi_{i,j} \in \Gamma[C]$). Then the following set of sequences defines a finitely branching, infinite tree under the usual extension order

$$\{\langle m_1, \ldots, m_k \rangle : 1 \le m_i \le n_i, \mathcal{A}' \models (\exists \mathbf{x})[\varphi_{1,m_1}(\mathbf{x}) \wedge \cdots \wedge \varphi_{k,m_k}(\mathbf{x})]\}.$$

Hence, by König's lemma, there is an infinite branch $\langle m_1, m_2, \ldots \rangle$ in this tree. Thus $\Theta = \{\varphi_{1,m_1}(\mathbf{x}), \varphi_{2,m_2}(\mathbf{x}), \ldots\}$ is finitely realisable. By saturation, Θ is realisable in $\mathcal{A}'$. The same realising tuple realises also Φ in $\mathcal{A}'$.

The proof is completely analogous for ω-saturation. $\square$

3.3.4.2 Infinite trees We now give a more substantial application of Theorem 3.11. Let Σ be a signature of function and constant symbols. Following Courcelle (1983) we denote the algebra of infinite trees (or terms) built from Σ by $M^\infty(\Sigma)$. In (Lloyd 1984, Theorem 18.9) it is shown, by topological methods, that this algebra is canonical for definite clause logic programs. We give an alternative proof applying Theorem 3.11. The logic programs correspond to CLP over the structure $M^\infty(\Sigma)$ where the constraints are conjunctions of atomic Σ-formulas. Thus we need to prove that $M^\infty(\Sigma)$ is ω-saturated for geometric Σ-formulas. First we observe that such structures are not ω-saturated (for all formulas). Consider, namely, $\Sigma' = \{0, s(\cdot)\}$ and the formulas

$$\varphi_n(x) \equiv \exists y[x \neq y \wedge x = s^n(y)].$$

The set $\{\varphi_1(x), \ldots, \varphi_m(x)\}$ has the solution $S^m(0)$ in x, but there is no solution in x common to all $\varphi_n(x)$.

The reader is invited to find a program with unequations which demonstrates that this structure indeed is not canonical (Jaffar and Stuckey 1986).

Nevertheless, we can prove the following

Theorem 3.14 $M^\infty(\Sigma)$ *is ω_1-saturated for geometric Σ-formulas.*

First we note that any geometric formula can be written as a disjunction of subgeometric formulas. Thus by Lemma 3.13 it is sufficient to prove the theorem for the latter class of formulas. Further, since this class is closed under $\exists$ and $\wedge$, it is enough to consider types with only one free variable. Next we prove, following Weijland (1990), a result on normal forms of subgeometric formulas, which is obtained by using a unification algorithm of Colmerauer (1982). However, here we encounter some extra complication by allowing external constants from $M^\infty(\Sigma)$.

Lemma 3.15 *Let $\mathcal{A}_W = M^\infty(\Sigma \cup W)$ where W are fresh constants. Suppose that $\varphi(x)$ is an arbitrary subgeometric formula in $L(M^\infty(\Sigma))$. Then, if this formula is satisfiable in $\mathcal{A}_W$, it can be written as*

$$\mathcal{A}_W \models \varphi(x) \leftrightarrow \exists u_2 \cdots u_n \mathbf{v}[u_1 = t_1(\mathbf{u}, \mathbf{v}) \wedge \cdots \wedge u_n = t_n(\mathbf{u}, \mathbf{v})], \qquad (3.6)$$

where $x \equiv u_1$ and $t_1, \ldots, t_n \in L(M^\infty(\Sigma))$ are non variables. For $n = 0$, the righthand side of (3.6) is $\top$.

Proof. Denote the (external) constants from $M^\infty(\Sigma)$ by $\alpha, \beta, \gamma, \ldots$. Note that for any such α, there are $f \in \Sigma$ and constants $\alpha_1, \ldots, \alpha_n$ with $M^\infty(\Sigma) \models \alpha = f(\alpha_1, \ldots, \alpha_n)$. Suppose that $\varphi(x)$ is satisfiable. First move the quantifiers outmost. The quantifier free part is now a conjunction

$$r_1 = s_1 \wedge \cdots \wedge r_m = s_m. \qquad (3.7)$$

Our object is now to transform this to a conjunct of the form in the lemma, which is said to be on *solved form*. Define $|t|$ to be the number of occurences of symbols *from Σ* in the term t; thus $|t| = 0$ if t is a variable or an external constant. The possible transformations are the following. Let u and v range over variables.

1. An equation $u = u$ can be removed.

2. If u and v are distinct and $u = v$ is an equation is the conjunct, we substitute v for u in the entire conjunct, except if $u \equiv x$, in which case we substitute the other way around. (This is to preserve x as a free variable.)

3. Replace any equation $t = u$ by $u = t$, if t is not a variable.

4. Two distinct equations $u = t_1$ and $u = t_2$ may be replaced by $u = t_1 \wedge t_1 = t_2$ if t_1, t_2 are not variables and $|t_1| \leq |t_2|$.

5. An equation $f(s_1, \ldots, s_n) = f(t_1, \ldots, t_n)$ may be replaced by the conjunction $s_1 = t_1 \wedge \cdots \wedge s_n = t_n$.

6. $f(t_1, \ldots, t_n) = \alpha$ can be replaced by $t_1 = \alpha_1 \wedge \cdots \wedge t_n = \alpha_n$, if $\mathcal{A}_W \models \alpha = f(\alpha_1, \ldots, \alpha_n)$.

7. $\alpha = f(t_1, \ldots, t_n)$ can be replaced by $\alpha_1 = t_1 \wedge \cdots \wedge \alpha_n = t_n$, if $\mathcal{A}_W \models \alpha = f(\alpha_1, \ldots, \alpha_n)$.

8. The equation $\alpha = \beta$ can be removed if it holds in $\mathcal{A}_W$.

We note that all transformations preserve logical equivalence.

The transformations 6 - 8 are not present in (Colmerauer 1982). To prove termination we need a norm. The following is a variant of the norm given in his paper:

$$||s_1 = t_1 \wedge \cdots \wedge s_n = t_n|| = k^{\max(|s_1|, |t_1|)} + \cdots + k^{\max(|s_n|, |t_n|)}$$

where k is a fixed number, greater than the arity of any function symbol that occurs in the conjunct. (We note that no transformation introduce new Σ-symbols.) Observe that variables and external constants are not counted. Nevertheless it can easily be proven that this norm is not increased by any transformation, and in fact decreased by the transformations 1, 5 - 8. Clearly, 2 - 4 cannot be applied indefinitely. From this it easily follows that

- any chain of transformations starting out with (3.7) ends after finitely many steps in a conjunct ψ, to which no further transformations are applicable.

Such a ψ is necessarily on solved form. Suppose otherwise. Then ψ would contain an equation of one of the following four forms 1) $\beta = \gamma$, where the constants have different interpretations, 2) $f(\mathbf{s}) = g(\mathbf{t})$ where $f \neq g$, 3) $f(\mathbf{s}) = \alpha$ or 4) $\alpha = f(\mathbf{s})$ where $\alpha = g(\alpha_1, \ldots, \alpha_n)$ and $f \neq g$. This contradicts that $\varphi(x)$ is satisfiable! Hence we arrive at the equivalence (3.6). $\square$

There is a natural notion of substitution associated with (infinite) tree algebras (Courcelle 1983): certain constants can at will be treated as variables.

Lemma 3.16 *For each subgeometric formula* $\varphi(x) \in L(M^\infty(\Sigma))$ *which is satisfiable in* $M^\infty(\Sigma)$, *there is a finite set of constants* V *and a term* $t \in \mathcal{A}_V$ *with* $\mathcal{A}_V \models \varphi(t)$ *which is the least solution in the following sense. If* $s \in \mathcal{A}_W$ *with* $\mathcal{A}_W \models \varphi(s)$, *then there is a substitution* $\sigma : V \to \mathcal{A}_W$ *such that* $s = t\sigma$.

Proof. Write using Lemma 3.15,

$$\mathcal{A}_\emptyset \models \varphi(x) \leftrightarrow (\exists u_2 \cdots u_n \mathbf{v}) \psi(\mathbf{u}, \mathbf{v}),$$

where $u_1 \equiv x$ and $\psi(\mathbf{u}, \mathbf{v}) \equiv \wedge_{i=1}^n (u_i = t_i(\mathbf{u}, \mathbf{v}))$. Let $V = \{\mathbf{v}\}$ and consider them as constants. We use the wellknown result (Courcelle 1983) that $\psi(\mathbf{u}, \mathbf{v})$ has a (unique) solution $\hat{u}_1, \ldots, \hat{u}_n$ in $\mathcal{A}_V$. Put $t \equiv \hat{u}_1$, so that $\mathcal{A}_V \models \varphi(t)$. Suppose that $\mathcal{A}_W \models \varphi(s)$. Hence there are $\hat{s}_1, \ldots, \hat{s}_n, \hat{r}_1, \ldots, \hat{r}_m$ with $s = \hat{s}_1$ and

$$\mathcal{A}_W \models \psi(\hat{s}_1, \ldots, \hat{s}_n, \hat{r}_1, \ldots, \hat{r}_m).$$

Let σ be the substitution $[\hat{r}_1, \ldots, \hat{r}_m / v_1, \ldots, v_m]$. It is easy to prove by induction on the depth of trees that $\hat{t}_i \sigma = \hat{s}_i$, so in particular $s = t\sigma$. $\square$

Proof. (of Theorem 3.14.) Let $\Delta(x) = \{\varphi_n(x) : n = 1, 2, 3, \ldots\}$ be a countable set of subgeometric formulas in $L(M^\infty(\Sigma))$, which is finitely satisfiable in $M^\infty(\Sigma)$. Let $\psi_n(x) \equiv \varphi_1(x) \wedge \cdots \wedge \varphi_n(x)$. For each n, Lemma 3.16 yields a least solution $t_n \in L(\mathcal{A}_{V_n})$ to this formula. We may assume that $V_n \cap V_m = \emptyset$ for $n \neq m$. Since t_{n+1} is also a solution to ψ_n, we get substitutions

$$\sigma_n : V_n \to \mathcal{A}_{V_{n+1}}$$

with $t_{n+1} = t_n \sigma_n$. Let Ω be a fresh constant and define a substitution $\eta_n : V_n \to V_n \cup \{\Omega\}$ by

$$\eta_n(x) = \begin{cases} \Omega & \text{if } (\forall k \geq n) x \sigma_n \cdots \sigma_k \in V_{k+1} \\ x & \text{otherwise.} \end{cases}$$

Thus $\eta_n(x) = \Omega$ if $x\sigma_n, x\sigma_n\sigma_{n+1}, \ldots$ never produces a term starting with a constructor from Σ. Now one can easily see that

$$t_1 \eta_1 \quad t_2 \eta_2 \quad t_3 \eta_3 \quad \cdots$$

is a Cauchy sequence in $M^\infty(\Sigma \cup (\cup_n V_n) \cup \{\Omega\})$ which tends to some $t_\infty \in \mathcal{A}_{\{\Omega\}}$. Hence for every k there exists θ_k with $t_k \eta_k \theta_k = t_\infty$. Hence for all k

$$\mathcal{A}_{\{\Omega\}} \models \varphi_k(t_\infty).$$

Replacing Ω by some arbitrary $r \in M^\infty(\Sigma)$, it follows that $M^\infty(\Sigma) \models \Delta(t_\infty[r/\Omega])$. $\square$

3.3.5 Extending Constraint Structures

Constraint structures are only rarely canonical. In this section we consider uniform methods for extending structures to canonical structures. But first some general considerations about extensions.

Definition 3.17 *Let $\mathcal{A}$ be an L-structure. The L-structure $\mathcal{A}^e$ is called a K_L-conservative extension of $\mathcal{A}$, if there exists a mapping $d : \mathcal{A} \to \mathcal{A}^e$ such that for all K_L-goals G, G' and all tuples of distinct variables $\mathbf{x}$:*

(i) $G \succ_\mathcal{A} G'$ if, and only if, $G \succ_{\mathcal{A}^e} G'$,

(ii) $\mathbf{a} \in [\![G]\!]_{\mathbf{x}}^{\mathcal{A}}$ if, and only if, $d(\mathbf{a}) \in [\![G]\!]_{\mathbf{x}}^{\mathcal{A}^e}$.

Where we write $d(\mathbf{a})$ for $(d(a_1), \ldots, d(a_n))$, when $\mathbf{a} = (a_1, \ldots, a_n)$.

Clearly, a sufficient condition for K_L-conservativity, is that d is an *elementary embedding* for K_L-formulas, i.e. for $\varphi(\mathbf{x}) \in K_L$:

$$\mathcal{A} \models \varphi(\mathbf{a}) \iff \mathcal{A}^e \models \varphi(d(\mathbf{a})).$$

Proposition 3.18 *Assume that $d : \mathcal{A} \to \mathcal{A}^e$ is a K_L-conservative extension. Then for all K_L-programs P and all K_L-goals G:*

(i) $\mathbf{a} \in S_P^{\mathcal{A}}(G; \mathbf{x})$ if, and only if, $d(\mathbf{a}) \in S_P^{\mathcal{A}^e}(G; \mathbf{x})$,

(ii) $\mathbf{a} \in C_P^{\mathcal{A}}(G; \mathbf{x})$ if, and only if, $d(\mathbf{a}) \in C_P^{\mathcal{A}^e}(G; \mathbf{x})$. $\square$

Proof. Immediate. $\square$

Remark. We note that albeit $M^\infty(\Sigma)$ is canonical, it is not a K_L-conservative extension of the finite terms $M(\Sigma)$. Consider $\Sigma = \{0, s(\cdot)\}$ and $G \equiv x = 0 \wedge y = s(y)$. Then $0 \in [\![G]\!]_x^{M^\infty(\Sigma)}$, but $0 \notin [\![G]\!]_x^{M(\Sigma)}$. Nevertheless, the $(\Rightarrow)$-halves of the definition hold when K_L is the set of subgeometric formulas.

In the first subsection we give some basic properties of a well-known model-theoretic construction, the reduced product construction (Chang and Keisler 1990). In the second subsection we explore the special cases of Fréchet powers and ultra powers as extensions.

3.3.5.1 Reduced Products We limit our attention to countably indexed products. Let $\langle \mathcal{A}_i : i \in \omega \rangle$ be a sequence of L-structures. The *direct product* of these structures, denoted $\Pi_{i \in \omega} \mathcal{A}_i$, has the universe $\Pi_{i \in \omega} |\mathcal{A}_i|$ (i.e. functions $f : \omega \to \cup_{i \in \omega} |\mathcal{A}_i|$ with $f(i) \in |\mathcal{A}_i|$). Let $\mathcal{A} = \Pi_{i \in \omega} \mathcal{A}_i$. The relations, functions and constants are defined pointwise, so that $R_\mathcal{A}(f_1, \ldots, f_n)$ iff $(\forall i) R_{\mathcal{A}_i}(f_1(i), \ldots, f_n(i))$ and $f_\mathcal{A}(f_1, \ldots, f_n) = \lambda i. f_{\mathcal{A}_i}(f_1(i), \ldots, f_n(i))$ and

$c_{\mathcal{A}} = \lambda i.c_{\mathcal{A}_i}$. A reduced product is a *quotient* of the direct product. Let $\mathcal{G}$ be a filter on ω, i.e. a set of subsets of natural numbers not containing the empty set, closed under intersection and upwards closed w.r.t. inclusion. Define the *reduced (direct) product* $\mathcal{A}'$ *of* $\langle \mathcal{A}_i : i \in \omega \rangle$, *modulo the filter* $\mathcal{G}$, as follows. The universe of $\mathcal{A}'$ is $\Pi_{i \in \omega} |\mathcal{A}_i| / \simeq$, where $\simeq$ is the equivalence relation given by

$$f \simeq g \iff \{i \in \omega : f(i) = g(i)\} \in \mathcal{G}.$$

Let $[f]$ denote the equivalence class containing f. The relations, functions and constants are now defined to respect the equivalence relation:

$$R_{\mathcal{A}'}([f_1], \ldots, [f_n]) \iff \{i \in \omega : R_{\mathcal{A}_i}(f_1(i), \ldots, f_n(i))\} \in \mathcal{G}$$

and

$$f_{\mathcal{A}'}([f_1], \ldots, [f_n]) = [\lambda i.f_{\mathcal{A}_i}(f_1(i), \ldots, f_n(i))]$$

and $c_{\mathcal{A}'} = [\lambda i.c_{\mathcal{A}_i}]$. A notation for $\mathcal{A}'$ is $\Pi_{\mathcal{G}} \mathcal{A}_i$. If the factors $\mathcal{A}_i$ are constantly $\mathcal{B}$, then $\mathcal{A}'$ is called the *reduced power* of $\mathcal{B}$ (notation: $\mathcal{B}^\omega/\mathcal{G}$). In the sequel we shall be interested mostly in reduced products modulo the *Fréchet filter* $\mathcal{F}$. This filter consists of the subsets of ω which have finite complements, i.e. for all $U \subseteq \omega$

$$U \in \mathcal{F} \iff (\exists k)(\forall n \geq k)n \in U.$$

The constructions $\Pi_{\mathcal{F}}\mathcal{A}_i$ and $\mathcal{B}^\omega/\mathcal{F}$ are called *Fréchet product* and *Fréchet power*, respectively. The latter is also denoted $\mathcal{B}^+$.

Example 3.19 Let $\mathcal{N} = (\mathbb{N}; \leq, 0, s)$ be the natural number structure with order relation and successor. Form the Fréchet power $\mathcal{N}^+$; each of its equivalence classes consists of sequences which are eventually equal when considered in pairs. We show how to satisfy the infinite constraint (3.1) in the introduction. Let $x_n = [f_n]$ where

$$f_n(i) = \begin{cases} i - n & \text{if } i \geq n \\ 0 & \text{otherwise} \end{cases}$$

Keeping the definition of equality on a Fréchet power in mind one easily sees that

$$x_n = s_{\mathcal{N}^+}(x_{n+1}).$$

The original structure is embedded by mapping objects to constant sequences in the Fréchet power. Note that each x_n is 'infinite', since for each constant sequence $[\lambda i.k]$ we have by definition

$$x_n \geq_{\mathcal{N}^+} [\lambda i.k] \iff \{i : f_n(i) \geq k\} \in \mathcal{F}.$$

Clearly $f_n(i) \geq k$, when $i \geq n + k$.

An *ultrafilter* $\mathcal{U}$ on ω is a filter such that for every subset $U \subseteq \omega$, either $U \in \mathcal{U}$ or $\omega \setminus U \in \mathcal{U}$. Since $\emptyset$ is not allowed in filters, $\mathcal{U}$ is maximal (cannot be extended). If $\mathcal{U} \supset \mathcal{F}$, the filter is called *non principal*. Such a filter can be shown to exist using Zorn's lemma. The corresponding reduced product and power are called *ultra product* and *ultra power*. For ultra products we have the following wellknown result (Chang and Keisler 1990).

Theorem 3.20 (Łos) *Let* $\mathcal{A} = \Pi_\mathcal{U} \mathcal{A}_i$ *be an ultra product of L-structures, and let* $\varphi(x_1, \ldots, x_n)$ *be any L-formula. Then for all* $[f_1], \ldots, [f_n] \in |\mathcal{A}|$,

$$\mathcal{A} \models \varphi([f_1], \ldots, [f_n]) \iff \{i \in \omega : \mathcal{A}_i \models \varphi(f_1(i), \ldots, f_n(i))\} \in \mathcal{U}. \square$$

When the maximality condition on $\mathcal{U}$ is dropped, the theorem does not hold for all formulas. In fact, the implications ($\Rightarrow$) and ($\Leftarrow$) are valid for different classes of formulas, as will be seen below. By an easy induction on the complexity of terms we can prove the following preparatory lemma.

Lemma 3.21 *Let* $\mathcal{A} = \Pi_\mathcal{G} \mathcal{A}_i$ *be a reduced product. For terms* $t(x_1, \ldots, x_n)$ *in L, and for all* $[f_1], \ldots, [f_n] \in |\mathcal{A}|$

$$t([f_1], \ldots, [f_n])_\mathcal{A} = [\lambda i.t(f_1(i), \ldots, f_n(i))]_{\mathcal{A}_i}. \square$$

Definition 3.22 *The set of Horn formulas,* $\mathcal{H}$, *is the least such that:*

(i) *If* φ *is an atomic L-formula, then* $\varphi \in \mathcal{H}$.

(ii) *If* $\varphi, \psi \in \mathcal{H}$, *then* $\varphi \wedge \psi, (\forall x)\varphi, (\exists x)\varphi \in \mathcal{H}$.

(iii) *If* φ *is a positive L-formula and* $\psi \in \mathcal{H}$, *then* $\varphi \to \psi \in \mathcal{H}$.

It is left to the reader to verify that the given definition of Horn formulas is logically equivalent to the usual one. Note that $\perp$ is atomic.

The fundamental theorem for reduced products can now be stated. The second part is familiar from model theory, see Chang and Keisler (1990, Proposition 6.2.2) or Mal'cev (1973, Chap. IV).

Theorem 3.23 *Let* $\varphi(x_1, \ldots, x_n)$ *be a formula in L. Suppose that* $\mathcal{A} = \Pi_\mathcal{G} \mathcal{A}_i$ *is a reduced product of L-structures.*

(i) *If* φ *is positive, then for all* $[f_1], \ldots, [f_n] \in |\mathcal{A}|$

$$\mathcal{A} \models \varphi([f_1], \ldots, [f_n]) \implies \{i \in \omega : \mathcal{A}_i \models \varphi(f_1(i), \ldots, f_n(i))\} \in \mathcal{G}$$

(ii) *If* φ *is a Horn formula, then for all* $[f_1], \ldots, [f_n] \in |\mathcal{A}|$

$$\{i \in \omega : \mathcal{A}_i \models \varphi(f_1(i), \ldots, f_n(i))\} \in \mathcal{G} \implies \mathcal{A} \models \varphi([f_1], \ldots, [f_n]).$$

Proof. By induction on the formulas. Note that $\mathcal{A} \models \bot \iff \{i \in \omega : \mathcal{A}_i \models \bot\} \in \mathcal{G}$, since $\emptyset \notin \mathcal{G}$. The other cases for atomic formulas φ, follows by definition and Lemma 3.21.

The non-atomic cases are proved by an essentially straightforward formula induction. The slightly problematic cases are the $\forall$-case for (i) and the $\exists$-case for (ii), which uses the axiom of choice. $\square$

The theorem does not hold for all φ; the formula $\forall x (x = 0 \vee x0)$ holds in $\mathcal{N}$, while it is false in the Fréchet power $\mathcal{N}^+$. We may note that the implications in the theorem goes both ways for positive definite formulas. Indeed an even stronger result can be obtained. Define the *essentially positive definite formulas* by closing atomic formulas under $\forall$, $\exists$, $\wedge$ and the construction $(\exists x \varphi) \wedge \forall x [\varphi \rightarrow \psi]$. Note that these include bounded universal quantifications, such as $\exists x [x \leq y] \wedge (\forall x \leq y) \psi$.

Theorem 3.24 (Palyutin 1980) *Let $\mathcal{A} = \Pi_{\mathcal{G}} \mathcal{A}_i$ be a reduced product. For each essentially positive definite formula $\varphi(x_1, \ldots, x_n)$ and for all $[f_1], \ldots, [f_n] \in |\mathcal{A}|$:*

$$\mathcal{A} \models \varphi([f_1], \ldots, [f_n]) \iff \{i \in \omega : \mathcal{A}_i \models \varphi(f_1(i), \ldots, f_n(i))\} \in \mathcal{G}. \square$$

Proof. By induction on the formula. $\square$

As already indicated in Example 3.19 there is a natural embedding $d : \mathcal{B} \rightarrow \mathcal{B}^\omega / \mathcal{G}$ mapping an element a of $\mathcal{B}$ to a constant sequence $d(a) = [\lambda i.a]$; $d(a)$ is called a *standard element*.

Corollary 3.25 *Let $\varphi(x_1, \ldots, x_n)$ be a formula, and let $a_1, \ldots, a_n \in |\mathcal{B}|$.*

(i) (Lifting principle) If φ is a Horn formula,

$$\mathcal{B} \models \varphi(a_1, \ldots, a_n) \Longrightarrow \mathcal{B}^\omega / \mathcal{G} \models \varphi(d(a_1), \ldots, d(a_n)).$$

(ii) (Transfer principle) If φ is essentially positive definite,

$$\mathcal{B} \models \varphi(a_1, \ldots, a_n) \iff \mathcal{B}^\omega / \mathcal{G} \models \varphi(d(a_1), \ldots, d(a_n)). \square$$

In case we let $\mathcal{G} = \mathcal{U}$, the embedding d is elementary *for all formulas*, due to Łos' theorem. While in general, such as when $\mathcal{G}$ is the Fréchet filter, the embedding is elementary merely w.r.t. essentially positive definite formulas, by the corollary. By the observation in the beginning of this section, any reduced power $\mathcal{B}^\omega / \mathcal{G}$ is thus a K_L-conservative extension of its base structure $\mathcal{B}$, where K_L is the set of essentially positive definite L-formulas. Further, these powers are in some cases ω_1-saturated, viz. $\mathcal{B}^+$ and $\mathcal{B}^* = \mathcal{B}^\omega / \mathcal{U}$ (for a non-principal ultra filter $\mathcal{U}$), and thereby *canonical structures*. This is a consequence of the following theorems.

Theorem 3.26 (Keisler) *Any ultra product $\Pi_{\mathcal{U}} \mathcal{A}_i$, with a countable signature, modulo a non-principal ultra filter is ω_1-saturated.*

Proof. See Chang and Keisler (1990). □

Theorem 3.27 (Jónsson-Olin 1968) *Any Fréchet product $\Pi_{\mathcal{F}} \mathcal{A}_i$ with a countable signature is ω_1-saturated.* □

Remark. Restricting the types to subgeometric formulas, a constructive version of Jónsson and Olin's theorem can be given (Palmgren 1992).

Ultra power constructions are not new in semantics of logic programming. Kunen (1987) uses ultralimits of three-valued structures to prove a completeness theorem for general logic programs.

3.3.5.2 Properties of the Extensions We take a closer look at the extensions $d : \mathcal{A} \to \mathcal{A}^*$ and $d : \mathcal{A} \to \mathcal{A}^+$, and give an example where they give different semantics (Example 3.29). By Los' theorem $\mathcal{A}^*$ and $\mathcal{A}$ have the same true first order formulas. As is clear from the upwards transfer principle, $\mathcal{A}^+$ inherits certain first order properties from $\mathcal{A}$. In particular note the following.

- If an equation $s = t$ holds universally in $\mathcal{A}$, then it holds universally also in $\mathcal{A}^+$; moreover if $\mathcal{A}$ is a ring, then $\mathcal{A}^+$ is a ring. However, not all of the field axioms can be expressed as Horn formulas, and indeed the Fréchet power of the reals is not a field (it has zero divisors).

- Clark's equality theory (CET) for a language L (see, e.g., Lloyd (1984)) is intended to capture unification aspects of a free term algebra. CET can be expressed by Horn formulas. Thus if $\mathcal{A}$ models CET, so does $\mathcal{A}^+$.

A Fréchet power is in general not *solution compact*, in the terminology of Jaffar and Lassez (1986) and Maher (1992). This is due to the following result (see remark below).

Proposition 3.28 *Let $\mathcal{A}$ be an L-structure. Then $F_\sigma([f]) = [f \circ \sigma]$ defines an automorphism $F_\sigma : \mathcal{A}^+ \to \mathcal{A}^+$ of L-structures, for every permutation $\sigma : \omega \to \omega$.*

Proof. Straightforward. □

Remark. Suppose $\mathcal{A}$ is an L-structure with at least two elements. Let $[f]$ be any nonstandard element of $\mathcal{A}^+$, i.e. $[f] \neq d(a)$ for all $a \in \mathcal{A}$. Hence there is a permutation $\sigma : \omega \to \omega$ such that $[f] \neq F_\sigma([f])$. By Proposition 3.28 any L-formula $\varphi(x)$ which is satisfied by $[f]$ must also be satisfied by $F_\sigma([f])$. Thus $[f]$ is not definable by any collection of L-formulas. We conclude that $\mathcal{A}^+$ is not solution compact, since its first condition thereby fails. (This is Blair and Brown's observation cited in (Maher 1992).)

Suppose, in addition, that $\mathcal{A}$ is countable. If we agree to restrict the possible constraints K_L to the essentially positive definite formulas, the second condition of solution compactness: for every K_L-constraint $\varphi(\mathbf{x})$, and every $\mathbf{a}$, there is a K_L-constraint $\psi(\mathbf{x})$ such that

$$\mathcal{A}^+ \models \psi(\mathbf{a}) \wedge [\varphi(\mathbf{a}) \leftrightarrow \exists \mathbf{x}(\varphi(\mathbf{x}) \wedge \psi(\mathbf{x}))],$$

fails as well. Let, namely, g be a sequence where each element of $\mathcal{A}$ occurs infinitely often. It is easy to see using Theorem 3.24, that if $\varphi(x)$ is an K_L-constraint, then $\mathcal{A}^+ \models \varphi([g])$ implies $\mathcal{A}^+ \models \forall x \varphi(x)$. Now, to violate the second condition, take $\varphi(x) \equiv (x = 0)$ and $\mathbf{a} = [g]$.

To find interesting constraint structures which are both solution compact and canonical seems to be a challenging problem. We refer to Maher (1992) for results about term algebras.

Example 3.29 *Infinite numbers.* We return to the program P of the introduction. Let $N^+ = |\mathcal{N}^+|$. The operator of P for the Fréchet power $\mathcal{N}^+$ is

$$T_P^{\mathcal{N}^+}(G) = \{a \in N^+ : \mathcal{N}^+(G) \models \exists x(s(x) = a \wedge I(x))\} = s_{\mathcal{N}^+}[G].$$

Let $F = T_P^{\mathcal{N}^+} \downarrow \omega = \cap_n (s_{\mathcal{N}^+})^n[N^+]$. The following statement is equivalent to $a \in F$:

$$\forall n \exists b_n \in N^+ (a = (s_{\mathcal{N}^+})^n(b_n)) \tag{3.8}$$

Another characterisation of $a \in F$ is that for all standard $n \in N$: $a \geq_{\mathcal{N}^+} d(n)$, i.e. a is *infinite*. Clearly this follows from (3.8). The converse is seen by noting that $\mathcal{N} \models \forall x(x \geq n \rightarrow \exists y(x = s^n(y)))$, and thus by Corollary 3.25, $\mathcal{N}^+ \models \forall x(x \geq d(n) \rightarrow \exists y(x = s^n(y)))$. Thus $a \geq_{\mathcal{N}^+} d(n)$, implies $(\exists b \in N^+)a = (s_{\mathcal{N}^+})^n(b)$.

Note that we do not have $a = s_{\mathcal{N}^+}(a)$, since this would imply $\mathcal{N} \models \exists x(x = s(x))$, by Corollary 3.25. This is to be contrasted to interpretations of P in infinite term models (Lloyd 1984), where the equation $x = s(x)$ is solved by an infinite s^ω, and thus $s^\omega \in F$.

Another example, illustrating the difference, is given by extending the program P to P_1 by adding the clause $I(0) \leftarrow \top$. Let P_2 be the program $I(x) \leftarrow \top$. It is easily seen that

$$T_{P_1}^{\mathcal{N}^+} \downarrow \omega = F \cup \{d(n) : n \in N\} \subset T_{P_2}^{\mathcal{N}^+} \downarrow \omega = N^+,$$

while in infinite term semantics the fixed points are the same.

If we had used the ultra power $\mathcal{N}^*$ instead of $\mathcal{N}^+$ we would have gotten an identification of the fixed points too, since in $\mathcal{N}^*$ every number is either standard or infinite. *This shows that the Fréchet power model is more fine grained than the ultra power model.*

Example 3.30 *Occurs check.* Consider the program $P: R(x, s(x)) \leftarrow R(x, x)$ (Lloyd 1984, p. 110). Again the denotation of the program is calculated in $\mathcal{N}^+$. The operator of the program is

$$T(G) = T_P^{\mathcal{N}^+}(G) = \{(c, s_{\mathcal{N}^+}(c)) : (c, c) \in G\}.$$

Thus $T \downarrow 1 = \{(c, s_{\mathcal{N}^+}(c)) : c \in N^+\}$; but $T \downarrow 2 = \emptyset$, since if $(d, d) \in T \downarrow 1$, then $d = s_{\mathcal{N}^+}(d)$ which is impossible. So $T \downarrow \omega = \emptyset$. This is in accordance with the operational semantics, since the call $\leftarrow R(x, y)$ fails by occur check, or rather by not solving $x = u, x = s(u)$, in the second step. However in infinite term semantics we have $s^\omega = s(s^\omega)$, so $T \downarrow \omega \neq \emptyset$.

3.3.6 Denotational Semantics

Carlson (1991) gave a domain-theoretic semantics of CLP. Jagadeesan et al. (1991) applied similar basic ideas for their modelling of concurrent constraint programming. A Smyth power domain built from the constraints were used in both cases. What is essentially this domain can be recovered in our approach by using saturation, and another special property of Fréchet products, namely *strong compactness*. The connection between the domain-theoretic least fixed point semantics and greatest fixed point semantics will become apparent. First we prove a general result about how formulas generate domains on ω-saturated structures.

Let $\mathcal{A}$ be any L-structure with countable signature. Consider sets of L-formulas $\Delta(\mathbf{x})$ where all free variables are among $\mathbf{x}$. Let $\mathrm{Com}^{\mathcal{A}}(\Delta(\mathbf{x}))$ be the set of denotations $\{[\![\varphi]\!]_{\mathbf{x}}^{\mathcal{A}} : \varphi \in \Delta(\mathbf{x})\}$, and order it by reverse inclusion:

$$S \sqsubseteq T \iff T \subseteq S.$$

The set $\Delta(\mathbf{x})$ is called a *conditional conjunctive system (cc-system) for $\mathcal{A}$* if $(\mathrm{Com}^{\mathcal{A}}(\Delta(\mathbf{x})), \sqsubseteq)$ is a conditional upper semilattice (*cusl*). I.e., if it is a partial order with least element $\bot$, such that if $a \sqsubseteq c$ and $b \sqsubseteq c$, for some c, then the supremum $a \sqcup b$ exists.

Example 3.31 Let $\Delta(\mathbf{x})$ be a set of L-formulas, containing $\top$ and closed under conjunction. This set is a cc-system for any L-structure.

As is wellknown from domain theory (Stoltenberg-Hansen et al. 199-) any cusl can be (ideal) completed to a Scott domain; a Smyth power domain can then be obtained from this domain, or directly from the cusl. In the domain-theoretic model by Carlson (1991) the cusl is $\mathcal{C}(\mathcal{A}, \Delta) = \{[\varphi] : \varphi \in \Delta\}$ where Δ is a set of constraints and $[\varphi]$ is the equivalence class of formulas ψ such that $\mathcal{A} \models \varphi \leftrightarrow \psi$. The order is given by $[\varphi] \lesssim [\psi]$ if, and only if, $\mathcal{A} \models \psi \rightarrow \varphi$. Thus when restricting to constraints with particular free variables $\mathbf{x}$ the cusls $(\mathcal{C}(\mathcal{A}, \Delta(\mathbf{x})), \lesssim)$ and $(\mathrm{Com}^{\mathcal{A}}(\Delta(\mathbf{x})), \sqsubseteq)$ are isomorphic.

We can construct such completions set-theoretically if we consider ω-saturated structures. Define $\text{Dom}^{\mathcal{A}}(\Delta(\mathbf{x}))$ to be the set of decreasing intersections

$$\cap_n \, [\![\varphi_n]\!]_{\mathbf{x}}^{\mathcal{A}} \tag{3.9}$$

where $\varphi_n \in \Delta(\mathbf{x})$ and $[\![\varphi_n]\!]_{\mathbf{x}}^{\mathcal{A}} \supseteq [\![\varphi_{n+1}]\!]_{\mathbf{x}}^{\mathcal{A}}$. Order this set by $\sqsubseteq$ too.

Theorem 3.32 *If $\Delta(\mathbf{x})$ is a cc-system for an ω-saturated structure $\mathcal{A}$, then $(\text{Dom}^{\mathcal{A}}(\Delta(\mathbf{x})), \sqsubseteq)$ is a Scott domain, with $\text{Com}^{\mathcal{A}}(\Delta(\mathbf{x}))$ as the set of compact elements.*

Proof. Obviously, $D = \text{Dom}^{\mathcal{A}}(\Delta(\mathbf{x}))$ is partially ordered with a least element. Write $[\![\varphi]\!] = [\![\varphi]\!]_{\mathbf{x}}^{\mathcal{A}}$. The following property is crucial. Let $\{[\![\varphi_n]\!] : n \in \omega\}$ be decreasing. Then:

$$[\![\varphi]\!] \supseteq \cap_{n \in \omega} [\![\varphi_n]\!] \implies (\exists n) \, [\![\varphi]\!] \supseteq [\![\varphi_n]\!]. \tag{3.10}$$

To prove this, suppose that $[\![\varphi]\!] \not\supseteq [\![\varphi_n]\!]$ for all n. Then the type

$$\Sigma(\mathbf{x}) = \{\neg\varphi, \varphi_n : n \in \omega\}$$

is finitely realisable in $\mathcal{A}$. Since $\mathcal{A}$ is assumed to ω-saturated, the type is indeed realisable, i.e $[\![\varphi]\!] \not\supseteq \cap_{n \in \omega} [\![\varphi_n]\!]$.
We now check the completeness condition. Let

$$\cap_n \, [\![\varphi_n^0]\!] \supseteq \cap_n [\![\varphi_n^1]\!] \supseteq \cap_n [\![\varphi_n^2]\!] \supseteq \cdots \tag{3.11}$$

be a decreasing ω-chain in D. We have to show that its intersection S is in D. It is enough to find a sequence $\{n_k\}$ such that $S \supseteq \cap_k [\![\varphi_{n_k}^k]\!] \in D$. Let $n_0 = 0$. Suppose $n_0, \ldots, n_k$ have been constructed such that

1. $[\![\varphi_k^0]\!], [\![\varphi_{k-1}^1]\!], \ldots, [\![\varphi_0^k]\!] \supseteq [\![\varphi_{n_k}^k]\!]$,

2. $[\![\varphi_{n_0}^0]\!] \supseteq \cdots \supseteq [\![\varphi_{n_k}^k]\!]$.

From (3.11) it is clear that

$$[\![\varphi_{k+1}^0]\!], [\![\varphi_k^1]\!], \ldots, [\![\varphi_0^{k+1}]\!], [\![\varphi_{n_k}^k]\!] \supseteq \cap_n [\![\varphi_n^{k+1}]\!], \tag{3.12}$$

so by (3.10) there exists an m such that $[\![\varphi_m^{k+1}]\!]$ is included in each of the sets on the lefthand side of (3.12). Let $n_{k+1} = m$. This defines the required sequence.

Using (3.10) and the above it is easy to prove that $\text{Com}^{\mathcal{A}}(\Delta(\mathbf{x}))$ is the set of compact elements. The other conditions are left to the reader to check. $\square$

The 'set-theoretic' power domain construction depends, on the other hand, on the following very special property of Fréchet products. A structure with this property is sometimes said to be *strongly compact*. For a discussion of this notion, see Lassez (1991) and Lassez and MacAloon (1990).

Theorem 3.33 *Let $\mathcal{A}$ be a Fréchet product, and suppose that $\varphi(\mathbf{x}), \psi_0(\mathbf{x}), \ldots, \psi_n(\mathbf{x})$ are essentially positive definite formulas. Assume*

$$\mathcal{A} \models \forall \mathbf{x}(\varphi(\mathbf{x}) \to \psi_0(\mathbf{x}) \vee \cdots \vee \psi_n(\mathbf{x})).$$

Then for some $i = 0, \ldots, n$,

$$\mathcal{A} \models \forall \mathbf{x}(\varphi(\mathbf{x}) \to \psi_i(\mathbf{x})).$$

Proof. Let $\mathcal{A} = \Pi_{\mathcal{F}} \mathcal{A}_k$. Suppose that the conclusion of the theorem is false. Thus there are $\mathbf{b}_i = [b_{i,1}], \ldots, [b_{i,m}]$, $i = 0, \ldots, n$ such that

$$\mathcal{A} \models \varphi(\mathbf{b}_i) \wedge \neg \psi_i(\mathbf{b}_i).$$

By Theorem 3.24, we can construct a sequence $k_0 < k_1 < k_2 < \cdots$ such that $\forall i = 0, \ldots, n, \forall j \geq 0$ there exists a $q \in B_j = \{k_j, \ldots, k_{j+1} - 1\}$ with

$$\mathcal{A}_q \models \neg \psi_i(b_{i,1}(q), \ldots, b_{i,m}(q)).$$

Define new sequences $c_1, \ldots, c_m$ by letting c_ℓ coincide with $b_{i,\ell}$ on the sets B_j, where $j \equiv i \bmod (n+1)$. Let $\mathbf{c} = [c_1], \ldots, [c_m]$. Clearly $\mathcal{A} \models \varphi(\mathbf{c})$, but $\mathcal{A} \models \neg \psi_0(\mathbf{c}) \wedge \cdots \wedge \neg \psi_n(\mathbf{c})$, contrary to the assumption of the theorem. $\square$

Theorem 3.34 *Let $\mathcal{A}$ be a Fréchet product with countable signature. Let $\Delta(\mathbf{x})$ be a cc-system for $\mathcal{A}$, consisting of essentially positive definite formulas. Then $\mathrm{Dom}^{\mathcal{A}}(\Delta_\vee(\mathbf{x}))$ is a Smyth power domain of $\mathrm{Dom}^{\mathcal{A}}(\Delta(\mathbf{x}))$.*

Proof. Let $\varphi \equiv \varphi_1 \vee \cdots \vee \varphi_m, \psi \equiv \psi_1 \vee \cdots \vee \psi_n \in \Delta_\vee(\mathbf{x})$, where $m, n \geq 1$ and $\varphi_i, \psi_j \in \Delta(\mathbf{x})$. An interesting consequence of Theorem 3.33 is the following. Make the abbreviation $[\![\theta]\!] = [\![\theta]\!]_{\mathbf{x}}^{\mathcal{A}}$. Then:

$$[\![\varphi]\!] \sqsubseteq [\![\psi]\!] \iff (\forall j)(\exists i)[\![\varphi_i]\!] \sqsubseteq [\![\psi_j]\!]. \tag{3.13}$$

This means that $(\mathrm{Com}^{\mathcal{A}}(\Delta_\vee(\mathbf{x})), \sqsubseteq)$ is the Smyth order of $(\mathrm{Com}^{\mathcal{A}}(\Delta(\mathbf{x})), \sqsubseteq)$. Thus if we can show that $\Delta_\vee(\mathbf{x})$ is a cc-system, we have proved the theorem.

We check the non-trivial condition. Let φ, ψ be as above, and suppose that

$$[\![\varphi \wedge \psi]\!] = [\![\varphi]\!] \cap [\![\psi]\!] \sqsubseteq [\![\theta]\!],$$

for some $\theta \equiv \theta_1 \vee \cdots \vee \theta_\ell$, where $\theta_i \in \Delta(\mathbf{x})$. Hence by the property (3.13) there exists i, j, k such that

$$[\![\varphi_i]\!] \cap [\![\psi_j]\!] = [\![\varphi_i \wedge \psi_j]\!] \sqsubseteq [\![\theta_k]\!].$$

Thus the set

$$S = \{(i, j) : (\exists \theta \in \Delta(\mathbf{x}))[\![\varphi_i]\!] \cap [\![\psi_j]\!] \sqsubseteq [\![\theta]\!]\}$$

is nonempty. For each $(i, j) \in S$, let $\tau_{i,j} \in \Delta(\mathbf{x})$ be so that $[\![\tau_{i,j}]\!]$ is the supremum of $[\![\varphi_i]\!]$ and $[\![\psi_j]\!]$. We claim that $[\![\vee_{(i,j) \in S} \tau_{i,j}]\!]$ is the supremum of $[\![\varphi]\!]$ and $[\![\psi]\!]$. It is clearly an upper bound. Suppose that $[\![\varphi]\!], [\![\psi]\!] \sqsubseteq [\![\sigma]\!]$, for $\sigma \equiv \sigma_1 \vee \cdots \vee \sigma_k$. Again by (3.13), for every ℓ, there exists i, j:

$$[\![\varphi_i \wedge \psi_j]\!] \sqsubseteq [\![\sigma_\ell]\!].$$

Thus $[\![\tau_{i,j}]\!] \sqsubseteq [\![\sigma_\ell]\!]$. Whence $[\![\vee_{(i,j) \in S} \tau_{i,j}]\!] \sqsubseteq [\![\sigma]\!].$ $\square$

Proposition 3.35 *Let $\mathcal{A}$ be an L-structure. Suppose that $\Delta(\mathbf{x})$ is a cc-system for $\mathcal{A}$, consisting of essentially positive definite L-formulas. Then*

$$(\mathrm{Com}^{\mathcal{A}}(\Delta(\mathbf{x})), \sqsubseteq) \ \text{and} \ (\mathrm{Com}^{\mathcal{A}^+}(\Delta(\mathbf{x})), \sqsubseteq)$$

are isomorphic.

Proof. We need only to check that for $\varphi, \psi \in \Delta(\mathbf{x})$:

$$\mathcal{A} \models \forall \mathbf{x}(\varphi(\mathbf{x}) \rightarrow \psi(\mathbf{x})) \iff \mathcal{A}^+ \models \forall \mathbf{x}(\varphi(\mathbf{x}) \rightarrow \psi(\mathbf{x})).$$

The direction $(\Rightarrow)$ follows by two applications of Theorem 3.24. As for the converse: for $\mathbf{a} \in \mathcal{A}$ we have $\mathcal{A}^+ \models \varphi(d(\mathbf{a})) \rightarrow \psi(d(\mathbf{a}))$. Hence by Corollary 3.25, $\mathcal{A} \models \varphi(\mathbf{a}) \rightarrow \psi(\mathbf{a})$. $\square$

We conclude that $\mathrm{Dom}^{\mathcal{A}^+}(\Delta(\mathbf{x}))$ is isomorphic to the ideal completion of $\mathrm{Com}^{\mathcal{A}}(\Delta(\mathbf{x}))$ when the signature of $\mathcal{A}$ is countable. (Recall that for a countable cusl the ideal completion and the ω-chain completion are equivalent.) Moreover $\mathrm{Dom}^{\mathcal{A}^+}(\Delta_\vee(\mathbf{x}))$ is isomorphic to the completion of $\mathrm{Com}^{\mathcal{A}}(\Delta(\mathbf{x}))$ to a Smyth power domain. The final theorem establish the relation between greatest fixed point semantics and domain-theoretic least fixed point semantics. (Again we prove the result for more general products.)

Theorem 3.36 *Let $\mathcal{A}$ be a Fréchet product of countable signature L. Let K_L be the set of essentially positive definite L-formulas, and $\Delta(\mathbf{x})$ the formulas in K_L with free variables among $\mathbf{x}$. Suppose that P is a K_L-program with program predicates $R_1, \ldots, R_M$. Then the immediate consequence operator $T_P^{\mathcal{A}}$ is a well defined, Scott continuous operator on*

$$\mathrm{Dom}^{\mathcal{A}}(\Delta_\vee(\mathbf{z_1})) \times \cdots \times \mathrm{Dom}^{\mathcal{A}}(\Delta_\vee(\mathbf{z_M})),$$

where $\mathbf{z_i} = z_{i,1}, \ldots, z_{i,\alpha_i}$ and α_i is the arity of R_i. Moreover, the least fixed point of this operator is exactly $\mathrm{gfp}\, T_P^{\mathcal{A}}$.

Proof. Write $[\![\varphi]\!] = [\![\varphi]\!]_{\mathbf{z}}^{\mathcal{A}}$ and $T = T_P^{\mathcal{A}}$. First of all we note that the operator is well defined on compact elements. Let $\varphi_i(\mathbf{z_i}) \in \Delta_\vee(\mathbf{z_i})$. Then

$$T([\![\varphi_1]\!]_1, \ldots, [\![\varphi_M]\!]_M) = ([\![\sigma_1]\!]_1, \ldots, [\![\sigma_M]\!]_M),$$

where σ_i is the result of first replacing each occurence $R_i(\mathbf{t})$ in the defining formula $\psi_{R_i}(\mathbf{z_i})$ by $\varphi_i(\mathbf{t})$, and then put the formula on disjunctive form. Clearly

$\sigma_i \in \Delta_\vee(\mathbf{z_i})$. To prove it is well defined on all elements it thus suffices to establish:

$$T(\cap_n[\![\varphi_1^n]\!]_1, \ldots, \cap_n[\![\varphi_M^n]\!]_M) = \wedge_n T([\![\varphi_1^n]\!]_1, \ldots, [\![\varphi_M^n]\!]_M), \qquad (3.14)$$

for $\cap_n[\![\varphi_i^n]\!]_i \in \mathrm{Dom}^{\mathcal{A}}(\Delta_\vee(\mathbf{z_i}))$. This in turn follows from the ω_1-saturation of $\mathcal{A}$, analogously to Theorem 3.11.

Now since T is monotone and (3.14) holds, it follows by domain theory that T is continuous. The least fixed point of T is by Tarski's familiar proof

$$\sqcup_n T^n(\bot),$$

where $\bot = ([\![\top]\!]_1, \ldots, [\![\top]\!]_M)$. But this is on closer inspection $T \downarrow \omega$. I.e. $\mathrm{gfp}\, T$ since $\mathcal{A}$ is canonical. $\square$

Acknowledgements A precursor to this paper (Palmgren 1992) was written while staying at the University of Amsterdam. I am grateful to A.S. Troelstra for making this visit possible and to K. Doets and K.R. Apt for discussions. Thanks goes also to B. Carlson and V. Stoltenberg-Hansen at Uppsala University for useful conversations. I thank J. Väänänen for drawing my attention to the result by Jónsson and Olin.

Finally, I should mention the lectures by P. Martin-Löf and his paper 'Mathematics of Infinity' as the prime inspiration to look for applications of nonstandard structures to infinite computations.

References

Apt, K.R., Logic Programming, In: *Handbook of Theoretical Computer Science (ed. J. van Leeuwen)*, 493 – 574, North-Holland, Amsterdam, 1990.

Blair, H.A., Brown, A.L., Definite Clause Programs are Canonical (over a Suitable Domain), *Annals of Mathematics in Artificial Intelligence*, to appear.

Bruynooghe, M., Boulanger, D., Abstract Interpretation for (Constraint) Logic Programming, *this volume*.

Carlson, B., A Characterisation of Logic Programming in Domain Theory, Master Thesis, Department of Computing Science, Uppsala University, 1989.

Carlson, B., An Approximation Theory for Constraint Logic Programs, Licentiate Thesis, Department of Computing Science, Uppsala University, 1991.

Chang, C.C., Keisler, H.J., *Model Theory, 3rd ed.*, North-Holland, Amsterdam, 1990.

Colmerauer, A., Prolog and Infinite Trees, In: *Logic Programming (eds. K.L. Clark and S.-Å. Tärnlund)*, 231 – 251, Academic Press, 1982.

Courcelle, B., Fundamental Properties of Infinite Trees, *Theoretical Computer Science*, 25 (1983) 95 – 169.

Doets, K., Levationis Laus, manuscript, University of Amsterdam, 1992.

Doets, K., *From Logic to Logic Programming*, MIT Press, to appear.

Golson, W., Toward a Declarative Semantics for Infinite Objects in Logic Programming, *Journal of Logic Programming*, 5(1988) 151 – 164.

Jaffar, J., Lassez, J.-L., Constraint Logic Programming, Technical Report, Department of Computer Science, Monash University, 1986.

Jaffar, J., Lassez, J.-L., From Unification to Constraints, In: *Logic Programming '87 (eds. K. Furukawa, H. Tanaka and T. Fujisaki)*, 1 – 18, Lecture Notes in Computer Science vol. 315, Springer, Berlin, 1987.

Jaffar, J., Stuckey, P., Semantics of Infinite Tree Logic Programming, *Theoretical Computer Science*, 46(1986) 141 – 158.

Jagadeesan, R., Shanbhogue, V., Saraswat, V.A., Angelic Non-determinism in Concurrent Constraint Programming, Xerox Parc Report 1991.

Jónsson, B., Olin, P., Almost Direct Products and Saturation, *Compositio Mathematica*, 20(1968) 125 – 132.

Kunen, K., Negation in Logic Programming, *Journal of Logic Programming*, 4(1987) 289 – 308.

Lassez, J.-L., From LP to LP: Programming with Constraints, In: *Theoretical Aspects of Computer Software '91 (eds. T. Ito and A.R. Meyer)*, 420 – 446, Lecture Notes in Computer Science, vol. 526, Springer, Berlin, 1991.

Lassez, J.-L., McAloon, K., A Constraint Sequent Calculus, In: *Proceedings of the 1990 Symposium on Logic in Computer Science*, IEEE Computer Society Press, Washington D.C., 1990.

Laugwitz, D., Ein Weg zur Nonstandard-Analysis, *Jahresbericht der Deutsche Mathematiker Verein*, 1973(75) 66–93.

Levi, G., Martelli, M., Palamidessi, C., A New Success and Finite Failure Semantics of Positive Logic Programs, manuscript, 1990.

Lindstrøm, T., An Invitation to Nonstandard Analysis, In: *Nonstandard Analysis and its Applications (ed. N. Cutland)*, Cambridge University Press, Cambridge, 1988.

Lloyd, J.W., *Foundations of Logic Programming*, Springer, Berlin, 1984.

Maher, M.J., A CLP View of Logic Programming, In: Algebraic and Logic Programming (eds. H. Kirchner and G. Levi), 364 – 383, Lecture Notes in Computer Science, vol. 632, Springer, Berlin, 1992.

Mal'cev, A.I., *Algebraic Systems*, Springer, Berlin, 1973.

Martin-Löf, P., Mathematics of Infinity, In: *COLOG-88 Computer Logic (eds. P. Martin-Löf and G.E. Mints)*, Lecture Notes in Computer Science, vol. 417, Springer, Berlin, 1989.

Mayoh, B., Tyugu, E., Uustalu, T., Constraint Satisfaction and Constraint Programming : A Brief Lead-in, *this volume.*

Moschovakis, Y.N., *Elementary Induction on Abstract Structures*, North-Holland, Amsterdam, 1974.

Naït Abdallah, M.A., On the Interpretation of Infinite Computations in Logic Programming, In: *Proceedings of ICALP '84, (ed. J. Paradaens)*, 358 – 370, Lecture Notes in Computer Science, vol. 172, Springer, Berlin, 1984.

Palmgren, E., Nonstandard Models of Constraint Logic Programs, Department of Mathematics Report 1992:10, Uppsala University.

Palyutin, E.A., *Algebra and Logic*, 19 (1980).

Saraswat, V.A., Rinard, M., Panangaden, P. Semantic Foundation for Concurrent Constraint Programming, In: Proc. ACM symposium on principles of programming languages, 1991.

Stoltenberg-Hansen, V., Griffor, E., Lindström, I., *Mathematical Theory of Domains*, Cambridge University Press, to appear.

Weijland, W.F., Semantics for Logic Programs without Occur Check, *Theoretical Computer Science,* 1990(71) 155–174.

3.4 Resolution Strategies for the Intuitionistic Logic

Grigori Mints

Department of Philosophy, Stanford University, Stanford, CA 94305
mints@csli.stanford.edu

This paper presents a general scheme of transforming a cutfree Gentzen-type system into a resolution type system, preserving the structure of derivations. This is a direct extension of the method introduced by Maslov for classical predicate logic. Ideas of the author and Zamov are used to avoid skolemization. Completeness of strategies is first established for the Gentzen-type system, and then transferred to resolution. The method is illustrated for the intuitionistic propositional and predicate calculus.

Introduction

This paper presents a general scheme (Mints 1990, Mints 1993) of transforming a cutfree Gentzen-type system into a resolution type system, preserving the structure of derivations. This is a direct extension of the method introduced by (Maslov 1969) for classical predicate logic. Ideas of the author and Zamov are used to avoid skolemization. Completeness of strategies is first established for the Gentzen-type system, and then transferred to resolution. The method is illustrated for the intuitionistic propositional and predicate calculus. Girard's linear logic (Girard 1987) is treated in (Mints 1993a, Tammet 1993). Adaptation of the Maslov's method to S4 is presented in (Voronkov 1992). Let us recapitulate some material from (Mints 1990, Mints 1993, Mints 1993a).

The main idea of Maslov's method can be summarized as follows:

A resolution derivation of the goal clause g from a list Γ of input clauses can be obtained as the result of deleting Γ from the Gentzen-type cutfree derivation of the sequent $\Gamma \Rightarrow g$.

Recall (Mints 1990) what we mean by a resolution method for a formal system $\mathbf{C}$. Such a method is determined by specifying:

1. A class of formulas called clauses.

2. A method of reduction of any formula F of the system $\mathbf{C}$ to a finite list Γ_F of clauses.

3. An inference rule R called the resolution rule for deriving clauses.

4. The derivation process by forward chaining so that all derivable objects are consequences of initial clauses, and garbage removal from the search space is possible.

The resolution method is sound and complete iff for any formula F the derivability of F in $\mathbf{C}$ is equivalent to derivability of the goal clause g from Γ_F using the rule R. For systems sufficiently similar to classical logic, the goal clause can be taken to be the empty clause $\emptyset$(constant false). Indeed, derivability of a goal variable g can be reduced to the derivability of $\emptyset$ from the negation $\neg g$. There are several important features of the standard resolution method for classical logic which are highly desirable for any extension to the non-classical case deserving of the name 'resolution'.

(i) Clauses should be much simpler than formulas in general with respect to complexity measure suitable for a given system $\mathbf{C}$. In the classical case standard clauses are quantifier free (with implicit universal quantification) disjunctions of literals. So there is neither nesting of boolean connectives (in the propositional case) nor alternating quantifiers. Clauses for the intuitionistic logic were defined (Mints 1985) as formulas of depth at most 2.

(ii) Reduction of an arbitrary formula F to the form $\Gamma_F \Rightarrow g$ where Γ_F is a finite set of clauses and g is a goal (variable or $\emptyset$) is based on the familiar depth-reducing transformation by introduction of new variables (cf. section 3 below). It is linear in time, universally applicable, and preserves the structure of the original formula. The list of relations defining new variables can be considered as a new encoding of the original formula or as a presentation of the data structure of its subformulas.

(iii) It is natural to require that the resolution rule R for a given system would be as close as possible to the standard resolution rule for classical propositional calculus. For systems based on classical logic (like modal systems), it is possible to preserve this rule completely. Differences between various modal systems are expressed by special rules for handling modalities, which can be used only together with the resolution rule, and so can be considered to be analogues of factorization or unification for classical resolution. Rules for handling linear logic modalities ?,! (exponentials) have a similar character. Our rules for special connectives of linear logic (Mints 1993a) are similar to rules for intuitionistic logic in (Mints 1985) , (Mints 1990) . The main difference from classical resolution is that a resolved term can be of complexity greater than 1; that is, it can have the form $L \circ L'$ where L, L' are literals, and $\circ$ is a non-classical connective.

(iv) Our requirement that the inference process should proceed by forward chaining corresponds to Maslov's (Maslov 1968, Maslov and Mints 1983) distinction between local methods (like resolution or his inverse method) and global methods (like semantic tableau methods with the introduction of dummy variables and finding their values by searching through closure conditions for all branches of the semantic tableau).

Local methods generate possible initial parts (close to axioms) of the derivation of the goal formula, until the whole derivation is generated. Global methods begin with the goal formula and construct final part of its derivation by searching through possible subgoals. The problem of combining these approaches for pruning the search space has not yet been sufficiently investigated.

Immediate extension of resolution to non-classical predicate logics is difficult because skolemization is usually non-available. We use ideas of the author (Mints 1985), (Mints 1985), (Mints 1993) and (Zamov 1987) that allow one to avoid skolemization.

Acknowledgment. Remarks by J. van Benthem, S. Feferman, A. Troelstra and N. Zamov influenced the form and content of this paper.

3.4.1 Gentzen-type Formulations of the Intuitionistic Predicate Logic

3.4.1.1 Standard Formulation GJ with Structural Rules As the first stage we consider a formulation GJ of the intuitionistic predicate calculus with structural rules which is close to Gentzen's system LJ (Gentzen 1934) and is even closer to Kleene's system G (Kleene 1952). Our language contains constant $\perp$, but no negation, and sequents have the form $\Gamma \Rightarrow D$ where Γ is a list of formulas and D is a formula. The main differences between GJ and LJ are that in GJ:

(a) Permutation rule is included into the formulations of all other rules.

(b) Parametric (non-active) formulas in all premises of two-premise rules are the same.

(c) We do not have negation or inference rules for the constant $\perp$ (false), and the only axiom for $\perp$ has atomic succedent.

(d) There is no rule for weakening in the succedent.

One of main reasons of interest to GJ in computer science is the possibility of extracting programs from the derivations in the intuitionistic logic. This is done by assigning λ-terms to derivations (cf. for example (Troelstra and van Dalen 1988)). Let us list the axioms and inference rules of the system GJ.

Axioms: $A \Rightarrow A \quad \perp \Rightarrow A$;

Inference rules:

$$\Rightarrow \& \quad \frac{\Gamma \Rightarrow A \quad \Gamma \Rightarrow B}{\Gamma \Rightarrow A\&B} \qquad \& \Rightarrow \quad \frac{A, \Gamma \Rightarrow D}{A\&B, \Gamma \Rightarrow D} \qquad \& \Rightarrow \quad \frac{B, \Gamma \Rightarrow D}{A\&B, \Gamma \Rightarrow D}$$

$$\rightarrow \Rightarrow \quad \frac{\Gamma \Rightarrow A \quad B, \Gamma \Rightarrow D}{(A \rightarrow B), \Gamma \Rightarrow D} \qquad \Rightarrow \rightarrow \quad \frac{A, \Gamma \Rightarrow B}{\Gamma \Rightarrow (A \rightarrow B)}$$

$$\Rightarrow \vee \quad \frac{\Gamma \Rightarrow A}{\Gamma \Rightarrow (A \vee B)} \qquad \Rightarrow \vee \quad \frac{\Gamma \Rightarrow B}{\Gamma \Rightarrow (A \vee B)}$$

$$\vee \Rightarrow \quad \frac{A, \Gamma \Rightarrow D \quad B, \Gamma \Rightarrow D}{A \vee B, \Gamma \Rightarrow D}$$

$$\Rightarrow \exists \quad \frac{\Gamma \Rightarrow A[t]}{\Gamma \Rightarrow \exists x A} \qquad \exists \Rightarrow \quad \frac{A[y], \Gamma \Rightarrow D}{\exists x A[x], \Gamma \Rightarrow D}$$

$$\Rightarrow \forall \quad \frac{\Gamma \Rightarrow A[y]}{\Gamma \Rightarrow \forall x A[x]} \qquad \forall \Rightarrow \quad \frac{A[t], \Gamma \Rightarrow D}{\forall x A[x], \Gamma \Rightarrow D}$$

$$Weakening \quad \frac{\Gamma \Rightarrow D}{A, \Gamma \Rightarrow D} \qquad Contraction \quad \frac{A, A, \Gamma \Rightarrow D}{A, \Gamma \Rightarrow D}$$

Rules $\exists \Rightarrow, \Rightarrow \forall$ have standard *proviso for variables*: variable y (the *eigenvariable*) does not appear in the conclusion, i.e. under the line.

All inference rules are by the definition invariant under permutation of formulas in the sequents. For example,

$$\frac{G, F, A, E \Rightarrow D}{E, A\&B, F, G \Rightarrow D}$$

is the application of the rule $\& \Rightarrow$. Equivalence to more standard (Hilbert-type) formulations of the intuitionistic logic is given by Gentzen's Hauptsatz (Gentzen 1934): the cut rule

$$\frac{\Gamma \Rightarrow C \quad C, \Sigma \Rightarrow D}{\Gamma, \Sigma \Rightarrow D}$$

is admissible in GJ.

3.4.1.2 Formulation GJ′ without structural rules We base our system on several formulations in the literature, especially (Vorob'ev 1970, Pliuskevicius 1965, Dyckoff 1992, Hudelmaier 1992). We present modifications of the standard logical LJ-rules such that every intuitionistically derivable sequent is derivable by these rules (without any structural rules). Recall that the sequents are treated up to the permutation of the formulas to the left of $\Rightarrow$. If Γ, Σ are lists of formulas, then (Γ, Σ) is the result of concatenating them and contracting repetitions.

Axioms. $A \Rightarrow A,$ $\bot \Rightarrow A$ for arbitrary formula A.
Inference rules.

$$\Rightarrow \& \quad \frac{\Gamma \Rightarrow A \quad \Sigma \Rightarrow B}{(\Gamma, \Sigma) \Rightarrow A\&B}$$

$$\& \Rightarrow \quad \frac{A, \Gamma \Rightarrow D}{(A\&B, \Gamma) \Rightarrow D} \qquad \frac{B, \Gamma \Rightarrow D}{(A\&B, \Gamma) \Rightarrow D} \qquad \frac{A, B, \Gamma \Rightarrow D}{(A\&B, \Gamma) \Rightarrow D}$$

$$\forall \Rightarrow \quad \frac{A[t], \Gamma \Rightarrow D}{(\forall x A[x], \Gamma) \Rightarrow D} \qquad \frac{A[t], \forall x A[x], \Gamma \Rightarrow D}{(\forall x A[x], \Gamma) \Rightarrow D}$$

$$\rightarrow \Rightarrow \quad \frac{\Gamma \Rightarrow A \quad B, \Sigma \Rightarrow D}{(A \rightarrow B, \Gamma, \Sigma) \Rightarrow D} \qquad \frac{A \rightarrow B, \Gamma \Rightarrow A \quad B, \Sigma \Rightarrow D}{(A \rightarrow B, \Gamma, \Sigma) \Rightarrow D}$$

$$\Rightarrow \rightarrow \quad \frac{A, \Gamma \Rightarrow B}{\Gamma \Rightarrow (A \rightarrow B)} \qquad \frac{\Gamma \Rightarrow B}{\Gamma \Rightarrow (A \rightarrow B)}$$

$$\Rightarrow \vee \quad \frac{\Gamma \Rightarrow A}{\Gamma \Rightarrow (A \vee B)} \qquad \Rightarrow \vee \quad \frac{\Gamma \Rightarrow B}{\Gamma \Rightarrow (A \vee B)}$$

$$\lor\Rightarrow \quad \frac{A,\Gamma \Rightarrow D \quad B,\Sigma \Rightarrow D}{(\,A\lor B,\Gamma,\Sigma)\Rightarrow D}$$

$$\exists\Rightarrow \quad \frac{A[y],\Gamma \Rightarrow D}{(\,\exists x A[x],\Gamma)\Rightarrow D}$$

$$\Rightarrow\exists \quad \frac{\Gamma \Rightarrow A[t]}{\Gamma \Rightarrow \exists x A} \qquad \Rightarrow\forall \quad \frac{\Gamma \Rightarrow A[y]}{\Gamma \Rightarrow \forall x A[x]}$$

with the standard proviso for eigenvariables.

Note. Admissibility of the permutation rule

$$\frac{\Gamma, A, B, \Delta \Rightarrow C}{\Gamma, B, A, \Delta \Rightarrow C}$$

follows from the stipulation: all rules are invariant under permutation. Admissibility of the weakening rule is ensured by the inclusion of the "weakened" forms of other rules, especially of $\&\Rightarrow, \Rightarrow\to$. Admissibility of the contraction rule is ensured by preservation of the main formula in the premises of the rules $\forall\Rightarrow, \to\Rightarrow$.

Theorem 1 *Sequent $\Gamma \Rightarrow D$ is derivable in GJ iff some sequent $\Gamma' \Rightarrow D$ with $\Gamma' \subseteq \Gamma$ is derivable in GJ*.

In particular the same formulas are derivable in GJ and GJ.

Proof. Consider equivalent formulation of GJ by Pliuskevicius 1965 reproduced by Dyckoff 1992.

System GJ1.

Axioms. $\quad A,\Gamma \Rightarrow A, \qquad \bot,\Gamma \Rightarrow A$ for arbitrary formula A.

Inference Rules

$$\Rightarrow\& \quad \frac{\Gamma \Rightarrow A \quad \Gamma \Rightarrow B}{\Gamma \Rightarrow A\&B}$$

$$\&\Rightarrow \quad \frac{A,B,\Gamma \Rightarrow D}{A\&B,\Gamma \Rightarrow D}$$

$$\forall\Rightarrow \quad \frac{A[t],\forall x A[x],\Gamma \Rightarrow D}{\forall x A[x],\Gamma \Rightarrow D}$$

$$\to\Rightarrow \quad \frac{(A\to B),\Gamma \Rightarrow A \quad B,\Gamma \Rightarrow D}{(A\to B),\Gamma \Rightarrow D}$$

$$\Rightarrow\to \quad \frac{A,\Gamma \Rightarrow B}{\Gamma \Rightarrow (A\to B)}$$

$$\Rightarrow\lor \quad \frac{\Gamma \Rightarrow A}{\Gamma \Rightarrow (A\lor B)} \qquad \Rightarrow\lor \quad \frac{\Gamma \Rightarrow B}{\Gamma \Rightarrow (A\lor B)}$$

$$\lor\Rightarrow \quad \frac{A,\Gamma \Rightarrow D \quad B,\Gamma \Rightarrow D}{A\lor B,\Gamma \Rightarrow D}$$

$$\exists\Rightarrow \quad \frac{A[y],\Gamma \Rightarrow D}{\exists x A[x],\Gamma \Rightarrow D}$$

$$\Rightarrow \exists \quad \frac{\Gamma \Rightarrow A[t]}{\Gamma \Rightarrow \exists x A} \qquad \Rightarrow \forall \quad \frac{\Gamma \Rightarrow A[y]}{\Gamma \Rightarrow \forall x A[x]}$$

with the standard proviso for eigenvariables.

Take arbitrary derivation d of a sequent $\Gamma \Rightarrow D$ according to the rules above and prune d: eliminate parametric formulas Γ from the axioms and propagate this down the derivation d deleting whole branches if necessary. (This corresponds to moving weakening rule downward (Kleene 1952)). Then eliminate repetitions from all sequents. The result is a derivation in GJ'. □

Note. System GJ' admits inferences like

$$\frac{A, A\&B, \Delta \Rightarrow D}{A\&B, \Delta \Rightarrow D} \qquad \frac{A \to B, \Delta \Rightarrow A \quad A \to B, B, \Delta \Rightarrow D}{A \to B, \Delta \Rightarrow D}$$

where the *main formula* $A\&B$ or $A \to B$ in the antecedent is preserved in all premises. In fact the following restriction is still complete:

neither of the lists Γ, Σ in the premises of an antecedent rule contains the main formula of the rule.

Completeness of this restriction is first proved for GJ1 and then transferred to GJ'. Proof for GJ1 using Kripke models can be given along the lines of (Mints 1969). Syntactic proof will use inversion of the rules.

3.4.1.3 Bottom-up Proof Search Cut-free systems like GJ or GJ' suggest proof search from goal to subgoals. Initially one has goal formula (or sequent). Each subsequent step replaces some of the current goals by subgoals from which it can be derived until all leaves are axioms. Subgoals are written on the top of the goal, so the whole procedure is working *bottom up*.

Example 0. Here are stages of proof search in GJ using the strategy: weakening is attempted only for testing axioms.

Goal	*Step 1*	*Step 2*	*Step 3*
			$a \Rightarrow a$
	$a \Rightarrow b \to a$	$a, b \Rightarrow a$	$\overline{a, b \Rightarrow a}$
$\Rightarrow a \to (b \to a)$	$\overline{\Rightarrow a \to (b \to a)}$	$\overline{a \Rightarrow b \to a}$	$\overline{a \Rightarrow b \to a}$
		$\overline{\Rightarrow a \to (b \to a)}$	$\overline{\Rightarrow a \to (b \to a)}$

3.4.2 Inverse Method. Propositional Case.

3.4.2.1 System I_F Consider first propositional case, when formulas are constructed from the propositional variables and $\bot$ by $\&, \vee, \to$. Instead of the bottom-up proof search described in the previous section, we consider here, following Maslov 1968, *top-down* proof search by direct chaining.

We begin with axioms, derive everything possible by one inference (application of an inference rule), then derive everything possible by two inferences etc. until the goal formula appears. Thus the proof search proceeds in the direction opposed to bottom-up search described in the previous section, which was used in most advanced programs during the first period of automated deduction. That is why Maslov used the term *inverse method* . Both the language and rules of the present formulation are determined by the goal formula F. Introduce new distinct propositional variables called *labels* l_A for all non-atomic subformulas A of F. For atomic formulas (propositional variables and constant $\perp$) put $l_a = a$.

Derivable objects are sequents $\Gamma \Rightarrow \Delta$ where Γ is a list of labels , and Δ is a label.

Axioms and inference rules of the system I_F

are obtained from the axioms and inference rules of GJ' by replacing all formulas by their labels.

Example 1. Let $F = a \rightarrow (b \rightarrow a)$.

Here is a derivation of $\Rightarrow F$ in the system I_F .

$$\frac{\dfrac{a \Rightarrow a}{a \Rightarrow l_{b \rightarrow a}}}{\Rightarrow l_{a \rightarrow (b \rightarrow a)}}$$

Definition 1 *Notation* $d : A_1, \ldots, A_n \Rightarrow B$ *means that* d *is a derivation of the sequent* $A_1, \ldots, A_n \Rightarrow B$.

If $A_1, \ldots, A_n, B$ *are subformulas of* F, *and* $d : A_1, \ldots, A_n \Rightarrow B$ *then* l_d *denotes the result of replacing all formulas (sequent members) in* d *by their labels.*

Example 2. Let d be the derivation in GJ' of the formula F from Example 1:

$$\frac{\dfrac{a \Rightarrow a}{a \Rightarrow b \rightarrow a}}{\Rightarrow a \rightarrow (b \rightarrow a)}$$

Then l_d is a derivation from Example 1.

Theorem 2 *If* $d : A_1, \ldots, A_n \Rightarrow B$ *is a derivation in* GJ', *then it is isomorphic to* $l_d : l_{A_1}, \ldots, l_{A_n} \Rightarrow l_B$ *as a labelled tree.*

Proof is obvious. $\square$

Corollary 1 $GJ' \vdash F$ *iff* $I_F \vdash l_F$

Proof. Take $d :\Rightarrow F$ $\square$

Formally our derivable objects are Horn implications. It will be seen that this view is fruitful.

3.4.2.2 Strategies of Inverse Method First of all, the language can be restricted. Recall the definition of the sign of a subformula occurrence in a formula: *positive subformulas* occur within the scope of an even number (for example zero) of occurrences of the premises of implication. Non-positive occurrences are *negative*. The following signed subformula property is obvious.

Lemma 1 *If* $d :\Rightarrow F$ *is a derivation in GJ or GJ', and sequent* $A_1, \ldots, A_n \Rightarrow B$ *occurs in* d, *then* $A_1, \ldots, A_n$ *are negative subformulas of* F, *and* B *is a positive subformula of* F.

From now on the language of the system I_F is restricted to sequents of the form

$$l_{A_1}, \ldots, l_{A_n} \Rightarrow l_B \tag{3.1}$$

where $A_1, \ldots, A_n$ are negative subformulas of F, and B is a positive subformula of F .

The previous Lemma shows that this restriction is still *complete*.

Example 3. Complete proof search for the formula $F = a \rightarrow (b \rightarrow a)$ in I_F. In view of the restriction (0.1) only the axiom

$$a \Rightarrow a$$

is possible. No antecedent inference rule is applicable, since there are no composite (non-atomic) negative subformulas of F. Only one succedent rule $(\Rightarrow\rightarrow)$ is applicable to the axiom resulting in

$$a \Rightarrow l_{(b\rightarrow a)}$$

There are two ways of applying the rule $(\Rightarrow\rightarrow)$ to that sequent resulting in

$$\Rightarrow l_F \text{ and } a \Rightarrow l_F$$

and this concludes the search: F is derived.

Example 4. Underivability of the Excluded Middle. Let $F = a \vee \neg a$ where $\neg a = a \rightarrow \bot$. Again the only axiom is $a \Rightarrow a$. Even axiom $\bot \Rightarrow l$ cannot occur in a derivation of l_F since $\bot$ has no negative occurrences in F. The only possible rule produces

$$a \Rightarrow l_F$$

and this concludes the search: no more inferences are possible.

Inversion Strategy and Subsumption Recall that the rules

$$\Rightarrow\rightarrow, \Rightarrow \&, \vee \Rightarrow, \& \Rightarrow \tag{3.2}$$

of the system GJ1 (Section 2.2) are *invertible* : the conclusion is derivable iff all premises are derivable.

Definition 2 *Let* $\circ$ *be a connective (one of* $\vee, \rightarrow, \&$*). We say that the formula* $A \circ B$ *is of the type* $\circ \Rightarrow$ *in the sequent* $A \circ B, \Gamma \Rightarrow D$ *and is of the type* $\Rightarrow \circ$ *in the sequent* $\Gamma \Rightarrow A \circ B$ *. Similar notation is used for labels. (In fact this refers to occurrences of formulas and labels). The label is invertible if it is of one of the types (2).*

Inversion startegy *for* I_F *is the following restriction: if a sequent is not an axiom and contains invertible label, then it is obtained by an invertible rule.*

Note an equivalent reformulation of the inversion strategy for direct chaining: a non-invertible rule cannot be applied if the result contains an invertible label. For example, sequent $l_{A \rightarrow B}, l_{C \& D} \Rightarrow l_{E \rightarrow G}$ can be obtained (according to inversion strategy) by the rules $\& \Rightarrow, \Rightarrow \rightarrow$, but not by the rule $\rightarrow \Rightarrow$. Hence this sequent cannot be generated if the search space contains only two sequents $l_{A \rightarrow B}, l_{C \& D} \Rightarrow l_A$ and $l_B, l_{C \& D} \Rightarrow l_{E \rightarrow G}$.

Lemma 2 *Inversion strategy is complete.*

Proof of the completeness of the inversion strategy for GJ1 can be obtained using standard techniques of proof theory (Curry 1963). Completeness is preserved by our transformation from GJ1 to I_F. $\square$

Refinement. The most important non-invertible propositional inference is $\rightarrow \Rightarrow$. Note that the inference

$$\rightarrow \Rightarrow \quad \frac{A \Rightarrow A \quad A, B, \Gamma \Rightarrow D}{A, (A \rightarrow B), \Gamma \Rightarrow D}$$

is obviously invertible. Corresponding extension of the inversion strategy is also complete: if the antecedent of the conclusion contains $A, A \rightarrow B$ then the rule should be invertible in extended sense, that is, it should introduce the antecedent formula $A \rightarrow B$ or some invertible formula. Similar considerations apply to other inversion criteria known from the literature. The most important of them, rediscovered by many authors, is best known from logic programming. The author learned it from V. Orevkov 1976 for the case $n = 1$, and from the authors of the PRIZ system (Volozh et al. 1983) in general case:

an antecedent formula $a_1 \rightarrow (\ldots (\rightarrow a_n \rightarrow B) \ldots)$ with atomic $a_1, \ldots, a_n$ can be a main formula (i.e. can be analyzed in the bottom-up proof search) only if all $a_1, \ldots, a_n$ are already present in the antecedent:

$$\frac{a_1 \Rightarrow a_1 \ldots \quad a_n \Rightarrow a_n \quad a_1, \ldots, a_n, B, \Gamma \Rightarrow D}{a_1, \ldots, a_n, a_1 \rightarrow (\ldots \rightarrow (a_n \rightarrow B) \ldots), \Gamma \Rightarrow D}$$

Subsumption

Definition 3 *Sequent* $\Gamma \Rightarrow D$ subsumes *the sequent* $\Gamma' \Rightarrow D$ *if* $\Gamma \subseteq \Gamma'$.

Note. It is possible to extend this definition and stipulate that $\Gamma \Rightarrow \perp$ subsumes $\Gamma' \Rightarrow D$ when $\Gamma \subseteq \Gamma'$.

Subsumption strategy allows one to delete from the search space any clause which is subsumed by the remaining clauses. It is complete for the same reason as the analogous strategies for resolution, but its compatibility with other strategies should be verified in each particular case.

3.4.3 Resolution. Propositional case

We reproduce some material from the author's papers (Mints 1985, Mints 1990) and connect it with Section 3.

3.4.4 Intuitionistic clauses

Recall from Section 3.1 that the label l_A stands for a subformula A of the goal formula F. This can be expressed by postulating equivalence

$$l_A \leftrightarrow A$$

or two implications

$$l_A \rightarrow A \qquad A \rightarrow l_A \qquad (3.3)$$

Most often only one of the implications (0.3) will be preserved: $l_A \rightarrow A$ for positive subformulas A, and $A \rightarrow l_A$ for negative A. Some of the implications (0.3) can be simplified, for example $a \lor b \rightarrow c$ can be replaced by two implications $a \rightarrow c$, $b \rightarrow c$. This leads to the following definition, where $p_1 \ldots p_n \rightarrow q$ is understood as a multiple implication:

$$p_1 \rightarrow (\ldots \rightarrow (p_n \rightarrow q) \ldots)$$

Definition 4 *An intutitionistic clause is any implication of the form*

$$(p \rightarrow q) \rightarrow r, \qquad p \rightarrow q \lor r, \qquad p_1 \ldots p_n \rightarrow q \qquad (3.4)$$

where $p, q, r, p_1 \ldots p_n$ are atoms. Initial clauses have $n \leq 2$. $n = 0$ is allowed: $\rightarrow q$ *is identified with q.*

Comment. All non-initial derivable clauses will have the form $p_1 \ldots p_n \rightarrow q$, i.e. they are Horn formulas. Implications $(p \rightarrow q) \rightarrow r$ can be compared to a pair of classical clauses $p \lor r$, $\neg q \lor r$. One cannot have simple reduction to classical clauses (unless PSPACE $=$ NP) since implications $D_1, \ldots D_n \rightarrow a$ where $D_1, \ldots D_n$ are disjunctions of literals and a is an atom, form a Glivenko class in the sense of Orevkov 1971: classical derivability implies intuitionistic derivability.

Throughout this section, clauses will mean intuitionistic clauses. Reduction of arbitrary formula to a clause form is given by the following

Theorem 3 *For any propositional formula F a set Γ_F of initial clauses can be constructed linearly in F by introduction of labels for subformulas such that F is derivable in GJ iff*

$$\Gamma_F \Rightarrow l_F \qquad (3.5)$$

is derivable in GJ.

Proof. The main idea has already been indicated. We introduce labels l_A for subformulas A of F and clauses (0.3) according to the sign of A in F. Then take as Γ_F the sets of introduced clauses. As before, $l_a = a$ for atomic a.

More precisely, define A^* to be A for atomic A, and to be the result of replacing the immediate subformulas B of A by l_B. Let

$$E_A = (l_A \leftrightarrow A^*) \tag{3.6}$$

We express E_A as set of clauses $C_A = C_A^+ \cup C_A^-$, where C_A^+ corresponds to the implication $A^* \to l_A$, and C_A^- corresponds to inverse implication $l_A \to A^*$. Then:
If $A \equiv (B \& D)$ then

$$C_A^+ \equiv \{l_B, l_D \to l_A\} \qquad C_A^- \equiv \{l_A \to l_B, l_A \to l_D\}$$

If $A \equiv (B \vee D)$ then

$$C_A^+ \equiv \{l_B \to l_A, l_D \to l_A\} \qquad C_A^- \equiv \{l_A \to l_B \vee l_D\}$$

If $A \equiv (B \to D)$ then

$$C_A^+ \equiv \{(l_B \to l_D) \to l_A\} \qquad C_A^- \equiv \{l_A, l_B \to l_D\}$$

Now let:

$$\Gamma_F = \cup \{C_A : A \text{ is } non-atomic \text{ } subformula \text{ } of \text{ } F\} \tag{3.7}$$

1. Derivability of (0.5) implies derivability of F. Indeed, replacement of all labels l_A by corresponding subformulas A in (0.5) gives

$$\Gamma_F' \Rightarrow F \tag{3.8}$$

where all formulas in Γ_F' are easily derivable, since they result (by decomposition into clauses) from the formulas of the form $B \to B$. So (0.8) implies F.

2. Derivability of F implies derivability of (0.5). We derive

$$F \to (\Gamma_F \to l_F) \tag{3.9}$$

from

$$\Gamma_F \to (l_F \leftrightarrow F) \tag{3.10}$$

which is obtained by repeated use of the replacement of equivalents

$$(A \leftrightarrow B) \to (G[A] \leftrightarrow G[B]) \tag{3.11}$$

where G is any formula. This concludes the proof of the theorem. $\square$

Example 1. Let $F = \neg\neg(a \vee \neg a)$. Set

$$a' = l_{\neg a}, \ d = l_{a \vee a'}, \ d' = l_{\neg d}$$

Then we have

$$\Gamma_F = \{\neg a \to a', \ a', a \to \bot, \ a \to d, \ a' \to d, \ d \to a \vee a',$$

$$\neg d \to d', \ d', d \to \bot, \ \neg d' \to l_F, \ d', l_F \to \bot\}$$

3.4.4.1 Resolution Calculus *RJ* (Derivable objects): clauses.

Axioms: $a \to a$, $\perp \to a$ for every atom a;

Inference rules:

$$\to^{-} \quad \frac{(p \to q) \to r \quad \Delta, p \to q}{\Delta \to r} \qquad\qquad \to^{-} \quad \frac{(p \to q) \to r \quad \Delta \to q}{\Delta \to r}$$

$$\vee^{-} \quad \frac{p \to q \vee r \quad \Delta \to p \quad \Sigma, q \to s \quad \Pi, r \to s}{(\Delta, \Sigma, \Pi) \to s}$$

$$Res \quad \frac{\Delta \to p \quad p, \Sigma \to q}{(\Delta, \Sigma) \to q}$$

where (Δ, Σ) means as before the result of concatenating Δ and Σ, and contracting repetitions.

Comment. Recall the classical resolution rule (Chang and Lee 1993) :

$$\frac{D \vee L \quad E \vee \neg L}{D \vee E}$$

where the literal L is resolved, and a derived inference (clash rule) where the whole clause is resolved:

$$\frac{L_1 \vee \ldots \vee L_n \quad D_1 \vee \neg L_1 \quad \ldots \quad D_n \vee \neg L_n}{D_1 \vee \ldots \vee D_n}$$

All rules of the system RJ except the first $\to^{-}$ are transformed into a series of standard resolution inferences if sequents $p_1 \ldots p_n \to q$ are translated into classical clauses $\neg p_1 \vee \ldots \vee \neg p_n \vee q$. The rule $\to^{-}$ (which is of course valid classically) reflects specifically intuitionistic features.

Calculus RJ will be used to derive clauses from a fixed set Γ of *input clauses*. The notation is

$$\Gamma \vdash_R C$$

Example 2. Here is a derivation of $a \to b$, $x \to a \vee b$ $\vdash_R x \to b$ by one application of the rule $\vee^{-}$:

$$\frac{x \to a \vee b \quad x \to x \quad a \to b \quad b \to b}{x \to b}$$

Example 3. Consider F, Γ_F from Example 1, and establish $\Gamma_F \vdash_R l_F$.

$$\cfrac{\neg d' \to l_F \quad \cfrac{d, d' \to \perp \quad \cfrac{a' \to d \quad \cfrac{\neg a \to a' \quad \cfrac{d, d' \to \perp \quad a \to d}{d', a \to \perp}}{d' \to a'}}{d' \to d}}{d' \to \perp}}{l_F}$$

Theorem 4 $\Gamma \vdash_R p$ iff the sequent $\Gamma \Rightarrow p$ is derivable in GJ

Proof. All rules of the system RJ are derivable in GJ, which proves one half of the theorem. Proof of the second half will be sketched after the proof of Theorem 5 below. $\square$

The following statement is an extension of the polynomial decidability result for propositional Krom clauses (cf. (Mints 1992)).

Corollary 2 Problem of derivability in GJ of propositional sequents $\Gamma \Rightarrow p$ where Γ consists of clauses (0.4) with $n \leq 1$ is polynomially decidable.

Proof. Note that the condition $n \leq 1$ is stable under resolution: if all premises have it, then the conclusion has it too. But from n atoms one can construct at most $n^2 + 2n$ clauses of this form, hence generation of resolvents stops after this number of steps. $\square$

3.4.4.2 Completeness of resolution: Maslov Transformation To conclude the completeness proof, we describe the transformation GR mentioned in the introduction. It will be applied to a derivation $d :\Rightarrow F$ in the Gentzen-type system GJ' and produce derivation $GR(d) : \Gamma_F \vdash_R l_F$.

Definition 5 Let $d : \Rightarrow F$ in GJ. Consider derivation l_d (Definition 1, Section 3.1). The resulting derivation $GR(d)$ is obtained from l_d by adding "defining clauses" for non-atomic formulas. More precisely, $GR(d)$ is defined by induction on d.

Induction base. d is an axiom $A \Rightarrow A$ or $\bot \Rightarrow A$. Then $GR(d)$ is an axiom $l_A \rightarrow l_A$ or $\bot \rightarrow l_A$.
Induction step. Let d end in the rule L. Consider possible cases.
Case $\Rightarrow$ &. L is

$$\frac{\Gamma \Rightarrow A \quad \Sigma \Rightarrow B}{(\Gamma, \Sigma) \Rightarrow A \& B}$$

By the induction hypothesis we have R-derivations of implications

$$d' : \gamma \rightarrow l_A \quad d'' : \sigma \rightarrow l_B$$

Then $GR(d)$ is the following figure:

$$\frac{l_A, l_B \rightarrow l_{A \& B} \quad d' : \gamma \rightarrow l_A \quad d'' : \sigma \rightarrow l_B}{(\gamma, \sigma) \Rightarrow l_{A \& B}}$$

In the following we show only the rule L and the last inference of the derivation $GR(d)$. Case $\& \Rightarrow$. Consider the third form of the rule.

$$L \quad \frac{A, B, \Gamma \Rightarrow D}{(A \& B, \Gamma) \Rightarrow D} \qquad l_{A \& B} \rightarrow l_B \quad \frac{l_{A \& B} \rightarrow l_A \quad l_A, l_B, \gamma \rightarrow l_D}{\frac{(l_{A \& B}, l_B, \gamma) \rightarrow l_D}{(l_{A \& B}, \gamma) \rightarrow l_D}}$$

Case & $\Rightarrow$. Consider the third form of the rule.

$$L \quad \frac{A, B, \Gamma \Rightarrow D}{(A\&B, \Gamma) \Rightarrow D} \qquad \frac{l_{A\&B} \to l_B \quad \dfrac{l_{A\&B} \to l_A \quad l_A, l_B, \gamma \to l_D}{(l_{A\&B}, l_B, \gamma) \to l_D}}{(l_{A\&B}, \gamma) \to l_D}$$

Case $\to\Rightarrow$

$$L \quad \frac{\Gamma \Rightarrow A \quad B, \Sigma \Rightarrow D}{(A \to B, \Gamma, \Sigma) \Rightarrow D} \qquad \frac{\gamma \to l_a \quad \dfrac{l_{A \to B}, l_A \to l_B \quad l_B, \sigma \to l_D}{(l_{A\to B}, l_A, \sigma) \to l_D}}{(l_{A\to B}, \gamma, \sigma) \to l_D}$$

Case $\Rightarrow\to$

$$L \quad \frac{A, \Gamma \Rightarrow B}{\Gamma \Rightarrow (A \to B)} \qquad \frac{(l_A \to l_B) \to l_{A\to B} \quad l_A, \gamma \to l_B}{\gamma \to (l_A \to l_B)}$$

Case $\Rightarrow \vee$

$$L \quad \frac{\Gamma \to A}{\Gamma \Rightarrow (A \vee B)} \qquad \frac{\gamma \Rightarrow l_A \quad l_A \to l_{A\vee B}}{\gamma \Rightarrow l_{A\vee B}}$$

Case $\vee \Rightarrow$

$$L \quad \frac{A, \Gamma \Rightarrow D \quad B, \Sigma \Rightarrow D}{(A \vee B, \Gamma, \Sigma) \Rightarrow D}$$

$$\frac{l_{A\vee B} \to l_A \vee l_B \quad l_{A\vee B} \to l_{A\vee B} \quad l_A, \gamma \to l_D \quad l_B, \sigma \to l_D}{(l_{A\vee B}, \gamma, \sigma) \Rightarrow l_D}$$

This concludes the definition.

Theorem 5 *(Completeness of resolution).*
(a) If $d : \Rightarrow F$ in *GJ* then $GR(d) : \Gamma_F \vdash_R l_F$.
(b) $\Gamma_F \vdash_R l_F$ iff F is derivable in *GJ*

Proof. (a) was just established. (b) follows from (a), soundness of the rules of RJ and Theorem 4. $\square$

Let us indicate the proof of the second half of Theorem 4 (cf. (Mints 1990)). Let Γ be a finite set of initial clauses and a be an atom. Take arbitrary derivation $d : \Gamma \Rightarrow a$ in *GJ'*. Using permutation of the rules (including inversion) (Kleene 1952, Curry 1963) transform d into a derivation satisfying the following conditions:

1. If the main formula of the rule $\to\Rightarrow$ is of the form $(p \to q) \to r$ then its left-hand side premise is obtained by the rule $\Rightarrow\to$:

$$\frac{\dfrac{\Sigma, p^{\circ} \Rightarrow q}{\Sigma \Rightarrow p \to q} \quad r, \Delta \to D}{((p \to q) \to r, \Sigma, \Delta) \to D}$$

where $\circ$ indicates possible absence of p.

2. If the main formula of the rule $\rightarrow\Rightarrow$ is of the form $p \rightarrow q \vee r$ then its left-hand side premise is obtained by the rule $\vee \Rightarrow$:

$$\frac{\Sigma \Rightarrow p \qquad \dfrac{q, \Delta \Rightarrow D \qquad r, \Pi \Rightarrow D}{(q \vee r, \Delta, \Pi) \Rightarrow D}}{(p \rightarrow q \vee r, \Sigma, \Delta, \Pi) \Rightarrow D}$$

3. If the main formula of the rule $\rightarrow\Rightarrow$ is of the form $p \rightarrow (r \rightarrow q)$, then it is immediately preceded in the right-hand side branch by the rule $\rightarrow\Rightarrow$ introducing $r \rightarrow q$:

$$\frac{\Sigma \Rightarrow p \qquad \dfrac{\Delta \Rightarrow r \qquad q, \Pi \Rightarrow a}{(r \rightarrow q, \Delta, \Pi) \Rightarrow a}}{(p \rightarrow (r \rightarrow q), \Sigma, \Delta, \Pi) \Rightarrow a}$$

Now apply to the resulting derivation in GJ' the transformation similar to GR: delete all members of the list Γ of initial clauses, and then reintroduce them as additional premises of the resolution rules. For example the third form of the rule $\rightarrow\Rightarrow$ considered above will be transformed in the following sequence of three resolution rules:

$$\frac{p, r \rightarrow q \qquad \Sigma \rightarrow p \qquad \Delta \rightarrow r \qquad q, \Pi \Rightarrow a}{(\Delta, \Sigma, \Pi) \rightarrow a}$$

□

3.4.4.3 Strategies of Resolution. Transfer from Genzen-type Systems

We see that the structure of $GR(d)$ is the same as the structure of d. This allows us to carry over strategies. Note that some strategies known in the classical case are obviously incomplete. One example is hyperresolution. A rich source of complete strategies is the transfer from Gentzen-type systems via the transformation GR and its analogs. It allows us in particular to prove the completeness of a powerful analog of hyperresolution due to V. Orevkov 1976.

Example 4. A generalized input strategy is complete. After changing the rules to take account of the pruning originating from the axioms $\bot \rightarrow a$, one can replace this axiom by the rule

$$\bot \quad \frac{\Gamma \Rightarrow \bot}{\Gamma \Rightarrow p}$$

replace the rule Res by two simpler rules

$$\frac{p, q \rightarrow r \qquad \Delta \rightarrow p \qquad \Sigma \rightarrow q}{(\Delta, \Sigma) \rightarrow r} \quad res \quad \frac{p \rightarrow r \qquad \Delta \rightarrow p}{\Delta \rightarrow r}$$

and require that the leftmost premise in every resolution inference except ($\bot$) be an input clause. This system RIp was treated in (Mints 1990).

Consider now strategies for deriving clause forms of the propositional formulas. First, one can simplify this clause form taking into account the signs of subformulas.

Definition 6 *For arbitrary propositional formula F let*

$$\Gamma'_F = \{C^+_A : A \text{ is a positive non} - \text{atomic subformula of } F\}$$

$$\cup\{C^-_A : A \text{ is a negative non} - \text{atomic subformula of } F\}$$

Corollary 3 $\Gamma'_F \vdash_R l_F$ *iff F is derivable in GJ*

Proof. Note that the transformation GR uses only clauses from Γ'_F. $\square$ Example 4. If F is a formula, then the following combination of the inversion strategy and PRIZ strategy is complete for $\Gamma_F \vdash_R l_F$:

conclusion of the rule introducing non-invertible label cannot contain invertible labels except the case, when it introduces antecedent label $l_{a_1,\ldots,a_n \to B}$ with atomic $a_1,\ldots,a_n$ and all $a_1,\ldots,a_n$ are already present in the antecedent.

3.4.5 Intuitionistic Predicate Logic

Let us indicate changes compared to the previous section. Formulas are now constructed by $\&, \vee, \to, \forall, \exists$ from atoms $\bot, P(t_1,\ldots,t_n)$, where P is a predicate symbol and $t_1,\ldots,t_n$ are terms (constructed from individual variables and function symbols).

3.4.6 Clauses

Now label l_A for a non-atomic subformula A of the goal formula F is a new predicate symbol having as arguments free variables of A bound in F. Instead of implications (3) one has

$$\forall \mathbf{y}(l_A(\mathbf{y}) \to A) \qquad \forall \mathbf{y}(A \to l_A(\mathbf{y})) \qquad (3.12)$$

The definition of the intuitionistic clause is extended by two new cases.

Definition 7 *An intutitionistic clause is any implication of the form*

$$(p \to q) \to r, \quad p \to q \vee r, \quad p_1 \ldots p_n \to q, \quad (\forall z p) \to q \quad q \to \exists z p \qquad (3.13)$$

where $p, q, r, p_1 \ldots p_n$ are atoms.

As usual, all free variables are understood to be universally quantified. Reduction of arbitrary formula to a clause form is done exactly as in the proof of Theorem 3 (Section 4.1 with later improvements of Section 4.4). Here we reproduce only additional clauses for the subformulas beginning with quantifiers. If $A \equiv \forall z B(\mathbf{y}, z)$ then (for non-atomic B)

$$C^+_A \equiv \{\forall z l_B(\mathbf{y}, z) \to l_A(\mathbf{y})\} \qquad C^-_A \equiv \{l_A(\mathbf{y}) \to l_B(\mathbf{y}, z)\}$$

If $A \equiv \exists z B(\mathbf{y}, z)$ then (for non-atomic B)

$$C_A^+ \equiv \{l_B(\mathbf{y}, z) \to l_A(\mathbf{y})\} \qquad C_A^- \equiv \{l_A(\mathbf{y}) \to \exists z l_B(\mathbf{y}, z)\}$$

Modification for atomic B is obvious: put B instead of $l_B(\mathbf{y}, z)$.
  Now let:

$$\Gamma_F = \cup\{C_A : A \text{ is non} - \text{atomic subformula of } F\} \qquad (3.14)$$

Instead of (5) (Section 4) we consider now

$$\forall \Gamma_F \Rightarrow l_F(\mathbf{u}) \qquad (3.15)$$

where initial $\forall$ stands for the sequence of universal quantifiers over all free variables in Γ_F which are not free in F, and $\mathbf{u}$ is the list of all free variables of F. It is understood that bound variables are renamed to avoid conflicts. The following statement about derivability in GJ is proved exactly like Theorem 3 (Section 4.1).

Theorem 6 *Formula F is derivable iff the sequent (15) is derivable.*

3.4.6.1 Resolution Calculus RJp for the Intuitionistic Predicate Logic
Derivable objects are clauses. We first introduce a system which does not include unification.

3.4.6.2 Auxiliary calculus RJ'p. Transformation GR'
Axioms and inference rules are the same as in Section 4.2 (with the new notion of atom) plus the following three rules:

$$subst \quad \frac{C}{C[x/t]}$$

$$\forall^+ \;\; \frac{(\forall z p) \to q \quad \Sigma \to p[z/b]}{\Sigma \to q} \qquad \exists^- \;\; \frac{q \to \exists z p \quad p[z/b], \Delta \to r}{(\,q, \Delta\,) \to r}$$

with the standard restriction for substitution $[z/t]$ of a term t for z and standard proviso: variable b is not free in $\Sigma, r, \forall z p$.
  Note. The rules $\forall^+, \exists^-$ are versions of corresponding natural deduction rules, and hence sound.
  Transformation GR (Section 4.3) is extended in an obvious way to the transformation GR' from GJ-derivations into RJ'p-derivations. Following statements are proved like Theorems 4,5 in Section 4. $\vdash'_R$ means derivability in RJ'p.

Theorem 7 . *For arbitrary list Γ of initial clauses and arbitrary atom q*
  $\Gamma \vdash'_R q$ iff the sequent $\forall \Gamma \Rightarrow q$ is derivable in GJ

Let $\mathbf{u}$ be the list of all free variables of the formula F.

Theorem 8 *(a) If $d : \Rightarrow F$ in GJ then $GR(d) : \Gamma_F \vdash'_R l_F(\mathbf{u})$.*
  (b) $\Gamma_F \vdash'_R l_F(\mathbf{u})$ iff F is derivable in GJ

Example 1. Consider $F = \forall y P(y) \to P(x)$, and denote $q = l_{\forall y P(y)}$. We have

$$C_F = \{q \to P(y); \quad \forall y P(y) \to q; \quad (q \to P(x)) \to l_F(x); \quad l_F(x), q \to P(x)\}$$

The derivation of l_F in RJ'p :

$$\cfrac{(q \to P(x)) \to l_F(x) \qquad subst\cfrac{q \to P(y)}{q \to P(x)}}{\to l_F(x)}$$

Example 2. $F = \forall x \exists y (P(x) \& (P(y) \to r)) \to r$. Introduce abbreviations:

$$R = l_{P(y) \to r}, \qquad K = l_{P(x) \& (P(y) \to r)}$$

$$E = l_{\exists y (P(x) \& (P(y) \to r))} \qquad A = l_{\forall x \exists y (P(x) \& (P(y) \to r))}$$

Converting F into clause form taking signs of subformulas into account, we obtain initial clauses

$$R(y), P(y) \to r \qquad K(x, y) \to P(x) \qquad K(x, y) \to R(y)$$

$$E(x) \to \exists y K(x, y) \qquad A \to E(x)$$

The goal $A \to r$ is derived as follows. First we have:

$$\cfrac{A \to E(x)}{A \to E(b)} \quad \cfrac{\cfrac{E(x) \to \exists y K(x, y)}{E(b) \to \exists y K(b, y)} \quad \cfrac{K(x, y) \to P(x)}{K(b, c) \to P(b)}}{\cfrac{E(b) \to P(b)}{A \to P(b)}}$$

Then we obtain:

$$\cfrac{\cfrac{K(x, y) \to R(y)}{K(a, b) \to R(b)} \quad \cfrac{\cfrac{R(y), P(y) \to r}{R(b), P(b) \to r} \quad A \to P(b)}{A, R(b) \to r}}{A, K(a, b) \to r}$$

Finally we obtain:

$$\cfrac{\cfrac{A \to E(x)}{A \to E(a)} \quad \cfrac{\cfrac{E(x) \to \exists y K(x, y)}{E(a) \to \exists y K(a, y)} \quad A, K(a, b) \to r}{A, E(a) \to P(b)}}{A \to r}$$

Unification. Calculus RJp. Now it is easy to introduce unification and give the standard completeness proof by lifting. One of the problems is to adapt unification to unskolemized situation where some of the rules have proviso for eigenvariables.

Let us review notation. *Substitution* is an expression of the form $[x_1 := t_1, \ldots, x_n := t_n]$ where t_i are terms, x_i are distinct variables which do not occur in t_j. If this substitution is denoted by σ, then the result $E\sigma$ of its execution is obtained by replacing all free occurrences of x_i in E by t_i, $i = 1, \ldots, n$.

The *unifier* of the expressions E, F is a substitution σ unifying E and F, i.e., such that $E\sigma = F\sigma$. The *most general unifier* $MGU(E, F)$ is the simplest unifier, that is $E\sigma' = F\sigma'$ implies $\sigma' = MGU(E, F)\sigma''$ for some substitution σ''. The substitution in the right-hand side of the last equation is the result of the successive execution of $MGU(E, F)$ and σ''. $MGU(E_1, \ldots, E_n)$ is the most general unifier of all expressions $E_1, \ldots, E_n$.

$MGU(L_1; \ldots; L_n)$ where $L_1, \ldots, L_n$ are lists of formulas or terms means the most general substitution which unifies L_1 (into one expression), L_2 (into another expression), $\ldots, L_n$.

Consider unification respecting the proviso for eigenvariables, which is suitable for treating non-skolemized existential quantifier in the rules $\forall^+, \exists^-$ below.

For an atomic formula p, list Σ of atomic formulas and expressions E, F we denote by $MGU_{\exists zp, \Sigma}(E, F)$ the most general substitution unifying E, F which does not contain element $z := t$, and such that the $\Sigma\sigma$ does not contain z. It is understood as always that σ does not introduce collision of variables (here with the quantifier over z), i.e., z does not occur in elements $x := t$ with x free in p.

Now we can state the axioms and inference rules of the calculus RJp.

Axioms: $a \to a$, $\qquad \perp \to a$ for every atom a;

Inference rules

$$\to^- \quad \frac{(p \to q) \to r \quad \Delta, p_1 \to q_1}{(\Delta \to r)\sigma} \qquad \sigma = MGU(p, p_1; q, q_1)$$

$$\to^- \quad \frac{(p \to q) \to r \quad \Delta \to q_1}{(\Delta \to r)\sigma} \qquad \sigma = MGU(q, q_1)$$

$$\vee^- \quad \frac{p \to q \vee r \quad \Delta \to p_1 \quad \Sigma, q_1 \to s \quad \Pi, r_1 \to s_1}{((\Delta, \Sigma, \Pi) \to s)\sigma} \qquad \begin{array}{l} \sigma = \\ MGU(p, p_1; q, q_1; r, r_1; s, s_1) \end{array}$$

$$Res \quad \frac{\Delta \to p \quad p_1, \Sigma \to q}{((\Delta, \Sigma) \to r)\sigma} \qquad \sigma = MGU(p, p_1)$$

$$\forall^+ \quad \frac{(\forall zp) \to q \quad \Sigma \to p_1}{(\Sigma \to q)\sigma} \qquad \sigma = MGU_{\exists zp, \Sigma}(p, p_1)$$

$$\exists^- \quad \frac{q \to \exists zp \quad p_1, \Delta \to r}{((q, \Delta) \to r)\sigma} \qquad \sigma = MGU_{\exists zp, \Sigma, r}(p, p_1)$$

$$Fact \quad \frac{p_1, \ldots, p_n, \Sigma \to q}{(p_1, \Sigma \to q)\sigma} \qquad \sigma = MGU(p_1, \ldots, p_n), \quad n \geq 2$$

As usual, for resolution formulation, it is assumed that free variables of premises are renamed before the application of the inference rules to make the result most general.

Factorization rule can be postulated separately or included in other rules.

Lemma 3 *The rules* $\forall_+, \exists_-$ *are sound: universal closures of the premises imply the conclusion.*

Proof. Consider the rule $\forall^+$. Proviso for $\mathrm{MGU}_{\exists zp, \Sigma}(p, p_1)$ implies that

$$p\sigma = p_1\sigma, \qquad (\forall zp)\sigma = \forall z(p\sigma)$$

and z is not free in $\Sigma\sigma$. Hence the following figure is a derivation in GJ'p:

$$\frac{\dfrac{(\forall zp) \to q}{\forall z(p\sigma) \to q\sigma} \quad \dfrac{\Sigma \to p_1}{\Sigma\sigma \to p_1\sigma}}{(\Sigma \to q)\sigma}$$

Consider the rule $\exists^-$. Proviso for $\mathrm{MGU}_{\exists zp, \Sigma, r}(p, p_1)$ implies that

$$p\sigma = p_1\sigma, \qquad (\exists zp)\sigma = \exists z(p\sigma)$$

and z is not free in $(\Sigma, r)\sigma$. Hence the following figure is a derivation in GJ'p:

$$\frac{\dfrac{q \to \exists zp}{q\sigma \to \exists z(p\sigma)} \quad \dfrac{\Delta \to q_1}{\Delta\sigma \to q_1\sigma} \quad \dfrac{p_1, \Sigma \to r}{p_1\sigma, \Sigma\sigma \to r\sigma}}{((\Delta, \Sigma) \to r)\sigma}$$

Remaining rules are treated similarly. $\square$

Definition 8 *Predicate clause $\Gamma' \to p'$ subsumes $\Gamma \to p$ if there is a substitution σ such that $p'\sigma = p$ and $\Gamma'\sigma \subseteq \Gamma$.*

Notation $\Gamma \Rightarrow q$ means that q is derivable from Γ in the system RJp.

The following statements are derived from the Theorems 7,8 (Section 5.2.1) by applying lifting, i.e. by introducing most general unifiers instead of the substitution rule *subst*. Transformation GR is obtained from GR' in the same way.

Theorem 9 . *For arbitrary list Γ of initial clauses and arbitrary atom q sequent $\forall\Gamma \Rightarrow q$ is derivable in GJ iff $\Gamma' \vdash_R q'$ for some $\Gamma' \to q'$ subsuming $\Gamma \to q$.*

Theorem 10 *(a) If $d : \Rightarrow F$ in GJ then $GR(d) : (\Gamma_F)' \vdash_R (l_F(\mathbf{u}))'$ with $(\Gamma_F)' \to (l_F(\mathbf{u}))'$ subsuming $\Gamma_F \to l_F(\mathbf{u})$.*
(b) F is derivable in GJ iff $(\Gamma_F)' \vdash_R (l_F(\mathbf{u}))'$ with $(\Gamma_F)' \to (l_F(\mathbf{u}))'$ subsuming $\Gamma_F \to l_F(\mathbf{u})$.

Examples 3,4. Let us recast derivations of examples 1,2 of Section 5.2.1 into the system RJp. For $F = \forall y P(y) \to P(x)$ one has:

$$\frac{(q \to P(x)) \to l_F(x) \quad q \to P(y)}{\to l_F(x)}$$

For $F = \forall x \exists y (P(x) \& (P(y) \to r)) \to r$ one has first

$$\frac{A \to E(x) \quad \dfrac{E(x) \to \exists y K(x,y) \quad K(x,y) \to P(x)}{E(x) \to P(x)}}{A \to P(x)}$$

Then we obtain:

$$\frac{K(x,y) \to R(x) \quad \dfrac{R(y), P(y) \to r \quad A \to P(x)}{A, R(x) \to r}}{A, K(x,y) \to r}$$

Finally we obtain:

$$\frac{A \to E(x) \qquad \dfrac{E(x) \to \exists y K(x,y) \qquad A, K(x,y) \to r}{A, E(x) \to P(x)}}{A \to r}$$

Example 5. Consider the skolemized version of the previous example. Note that skolemization of the existential quantifier in the prefix of an antecedent formula is sound and faithful in the intuitionistic predicate calculus without equality. $F = \forall x(P(x) \& (P(f(x)) \to r)) \to r$. F can be converted into the following clause form:

$$P(x), \; P(f(x)) \to r \vdash_R r$$

and the derivation is obvious:

$$\frac{P(x) \qquad P(f(x)) \to r}{r}$$

Comparing derivation d in GJ with $GR(d)$, we see that the structure of $GR(d)$ is the same as the structure of d up to lifting. This allows to carry on strategies exactly as in the propositional case.

Conclusion

. Exposition of the inverse method and resolution method in this paper was adapted to the situation when a Gentzen-type cut free system with subformula property is available. Extension of this approach to systems with induction-type axioms, like dynamic logic or temporal logic of linear time requires additional work.

References

Andreoli, J., Paresci, R., Linear Objects: Logical processes with built-in inheritance. New Generation Computing, Special issue, Selected Papers of ICLP'90, (1992)

Chang, C., Lee, R., Symbolic Logic and Mechanical Theorem Proving. Academic Press, New York, (1973)

Curry, H., Foundations of Mathematical Logic. McGraw-Hill, New York (1963)

Dragalin, A., Mathematical Intuitionism - Introduction to Proof Theory, American Math. Society, Providence, R.I.,1981

Dyckoff, R., Contraction-free sequent calculi for intuitionistic logic. Journal of Symbolic Logic, 1992, 57, N3, 795-807

Girard, J.-Y., Linear Logic, Theoretical Computer Science, 1987, 50, 1-102

Gentzen, G., Untersuchungen über das logische Schliessen. Mathematische Zeitschrift, 39, 1934, 176-210, 405-431

Gentzen, G., Die Widerspruchsfreiheit der reinen Zahlentheorie, Mathematische Annalen, 112, 1936, 493-565

Girard, J.-Y., Linear Logic. Theoretical Computer Science, 50:1, 1987, 1-101

Harland, J., Pym D. The Uniform Proof-Theoretic Foundation of Linear Logic Programming. Proceedings of the 1991 International Symposium on Logic Programming. MIT Press, 1991, 304-320

Hodas, J. , Miller, D. Logic Programming in a Fragment of Intuitionistic Linear Logic. Proceedings of sixth Annual IEEE Symp. on Logic in Computer Science, IEEE Computer Society Press, 1991

Hudelmaier, J., Bounds for Cut Elimination in Intuitionistic Propositional Logic, Archive for Mathematical Logic, 31, 331-354, 1992

Kleene, S.C., Introduction to Metamathematics. North-Holland, 1974

Kleene, S.C., Two Papers on the Predicate Calculus, Memoirs of the American Mathematical Society, 10, 1952

Maslov, S. Inverse method of establishing deducibility for logical calculi. Proc. Steklov Inst. of Math. 98, 1968

Maslov, S., Deduction-search tactics based on the unification of order of terms in a favourable set. Seminars in Mathematics, vol. 16, Plenum Press, New York 1971

Maslov, S., The connection between tactics of inverse method and the resolution method. A.O. Slisenko (editor). Zapiski Nauchnykh Seminarov LOMI. v. 16, 1969. English translation in: J. Siekmann, G. Wrightson, eds. Automated Reasoning, Springer-Verlag, Berlin, 1983, v2., 264-27

Maslov, S., Mints, G., Proof Search Theory and the Inverse Method (Russian). Supplement to the Russian translation (Chang, Lee, 1973). Moscow. Nauka, 1983, 310-340

Miller, D., Nadatur, G., Pfennig F., Scedrov A. Proofs as a Foundation for the Logic Programming. Annals of Pure and Applied Logic, 1991, 51, 125-127

Mints, G., Varying of proof search tactics in sequenzen-calculi. Seminars in Mathematics, v.4, Plenum Publishers, 1969, 53-99

Resolution Calculi for Non-classical Logics (Russian), 9th Soviet Symposium in Cybernetics, 1981, v.2, 34-36

Mints, G., Resolution Calculi for Non-classical Logics (Russian). Semiotika i Informatika, 25, 1985, 120-135

Mints, G., Gentzen-type Systems and Resolution Rule. Part I. Propositional Logic. Lecture Notes in Computer Sci. 417, 1990, 198-231

Mints, G., Gentzen-type Systems and Resolution Rule. Part II. Logic Colloquium'90, to be published

Mints, G., Complexity of subclasses of the intuitionistic propositional calculus. BIT, 32, 64-69, 1992

Mints, G., Resolution Calculus for the First Order Linear Logic, Journal of Logic, Language and Information, 2, 59-83, 1993

Mints, G., Selected Papers in Proof Theory, North-Holland-Bibliopolis, 1992

Orevkov, V., On Glivenko sequent classes. - Proc. Steklov Inst. Math., v.98 (1971), p. 143-173 (Translated by AMS, 1971)

Orevkov, V., A specialization of the form of derivations in Gentzen calculi, and some of its applications. J. Soviet Mathematics 6, 1976,N4.

Pliuskevicius, R., On a variant of the constructive predicate calculus without structural deduction rules, Soviet Math. Doklady, v.6, 1965, 416-419

Prawitz, D., Natural deduction, Almquist and Wiksell, 1965

Tammet, T., Proof Search in Linear Logic. Report 70, Programming Methodology Group, Chalmers University, 1993, 36p. Submitted.

Troelstra, A., van Dalen, D., Constructivism in Mathematics, An Introduction, v.2, 1988, North-Holland

Volozh, B., Matskin, M., Mints, B. G., Tyugu, E., PRIZ System and the Propositional Calculus. Kibernetika and Software, 1983

Vorob'ev, N., A new algorithm for derivability in a constructive propositional calculus, American Math. Society Translations, ser.2 v. 94, 1970, 37-71

Voronkov, A., Theorem Proving in Non-standard Logics Based on the Inverse Method. Automated Deduction-11. Lecture Notes in Computer Science, 607, 1992, 648-662, Berlin, Springer-Verlag.

Zamov, N., The Resolution Method without Skolemization, Soviet Math. Dokl., 35, 1987, N2, 399-401

4. Constraint Programming Systems

4.1 Kaleidoscope: A Constraint Imperative Programming Language

Gus Lopez[1], Bjorn Freeman-Benson[2] and Alan Borning[2]

[1]Dept of Computer Science & Engineering, FR-35, University of Washington, Seattle, Washington 98195, USA
{lopez,borning}@cs.washington.edu

[2]School of Computer Science, Carleton University, Herzberg Building, Ottawa, Ontario K1S 5B6, Canada,
bnfb@scs.carleton.ca

Abstract

The Constraint Imperative Programming (CIP) family of languages integrates constraints and imperative, object-oriented programming. In addition to combining the useful features of both paradigms, there are synergistic effects of this integration, such as the ability to define constraints over user-defined domains. We discuss characteristics of the CIP family and provide a rationale for its creation. The synergy of constraints and objects imposes additional challenges for the provision of constructs, such as object identity and class membership, that are well-understood in conventional language paradigms. We discuss the benefits and challenges of combining the constraint and imperative paradigms, and present our current ideas in the context of the design and implementation of the Kaleidoscope'93 language.

4.1.1 Introduction

Imperative programming languages are relatively well understood, used by a large number of programmers, and supported by numerous software tools. However, these languages are often more low-level than one would like. Focusing on interactive graphical applications, we examined a number of user interfaces and

Table 4.1. Imperative versus CIP Code

Imperative	Constraint Imperative

while mouse.button = down do
    old ← mercury.top;
    mercury.top ← mouse.location.y;
    degrees ← mercury.height/scale;
    if old < mercury.top then
        delta_grey(old,mercury.top);
        display_number(degrees);
    elseif old mercury.top then
        delta_white(mercury.top,old);
        display_number(degrees);
    end if;
end while;
	always: degrees = mercury.height/scale;
	always: white_rectangle(thermometer);
	always: grey_rectangle(mercury);
	always: display_number(degrees);
	while mouse.button = down do
	    mercury.top = mouse.location.y;
	end while;

observed that some portions are most clearly and conveniently described using constraints—relations that should be maintained—while other portions are most clearly described using standard imperative constructs. However, none of the imperative languages used to program these interfaces directly supported constraints. Thus, the constraints were encoded implicitly, by hand, and each constraint was enforced by a widely distributed set of small code fragments—a recipe for maintenance headaches.

To address this problem, we proposed constraint imperative programming (CIP), an integration of two disparate paradigms: a standard object-oriented imperative one, and a declarative constraint one (Freeman-Benson 1991; Freeman-Benson and Borning 1992a; Freeman-Benson and Borning 1992b). Compare the two code fragments in Figure 4.1, which allow the user to drag the mercury of a thermometer up and down. The version on the left uses only standard imperative constructs. It requires the programmer to check whether values have changed and if so, to fill or erase the appropriate rectangle increment and then redisplay the temperature value. The constraint version on the right uses of combination of imperative constructs and constraints. Some of the constraints specify relations that must always hold (e.g. temperature = mercury.height / scale), while others specify relations that should hold only while a given condition is true (e.g. the constraint mercury.top = mouse.location.y, which holds only when the mouse button is down). Imperative constructs, such as the **while** statement, are used to control program execution, in particular, when certain constraints should hold.

Consider an object, VerticalLine, represented as two points. If this object were implemented in an imperative language, all operations on VerticalLines would have to ensure that the x fields of both points were equal. Since there is an implicit integrity constraint that these x fields remain equal, it is the programmer's responsibility to maintain this constraint. A CIP implementation of VerticalLine would simply assert this constraint when the object was created (e.g. always: p1.x = p2.x) and maintain it automatically for the programmer.

There are advantages to CIP over approaches based in logic programming: in particular, CIP languages support mutable objects and object identity in a way that is familiar to current users of object-oriented programming. Due to the popularity of imperative programming (and object-oriented programming in particular), CIP offers an evolutionary mechanism (or maybe a Trojan Horse?) for introducing constraint programming.

We have found it useful to extend the constraint paradigm to allow both required and nonrequired (or preferential) constraints. The required constraints must hold for all solutions, while the preferential constraints should be satisfied if possible, but no error condition arises if they are not. A constraint hierarchy can contain an arbitrary number of levels of preference (strengths). The original motivation for this extension was to give a declarative semantics for what to change when perturbing the values in a constraint system. (For example, suppose we have a constraint $A + B = C$, and edit the value of B. Should we change just A, change just C, change both A and C, undo the change to B, or what?) However, constraint hierarchies have additional uses for expressing preferences in planning, layout and other domains. (See (Borning, Freeman-Benson, and Wilson 1992) for more information.)

In addition to constraints of varying strength, Kaleidoscope has constraints of varying duration. Constraint durations specify the period of validity for constraints. The most flexible model would allow constraints to be asserted and retracted at arbitrary points in time. However this would lead to difficulties in predicting behavior, since any piece of code could side-effect which constraints are active. Instead, in our design, the default constraint duration is always, which causes a constraint to remain active forever. A once duration instructs the system to assert the constraint, causing it to be enforced at that moment (and thus potentially affecting values), and then immediately retract it. Finally, the assert/during construct specifies that a constraint should remain in force during the execution of a block or loop. We might make an analogy with the GOTO statement/structured programming controversy of the 60's: GOTO statements are analogous to constructs that allow constraints to be asserted and retracted at arbitrary times, while structured control statements are analogous to the control structures in Kaleidoscope.

Kaleidoscope'93 is a class-based object-oriented language with multi-methods. In a conventional object-oriented language, the method that is executed in response to a message is determined purely by the receiver of the message. For example, if we send the message display to a circle object with a bitmap as an argument, the method to be executed is determined solely by the circle. In contrast, in a language with multi-methods, all arguments potentially may participate in selecting the method; thus in the preceding example, both the circle and the bitmap might participate in the choice of method, allowing a different method to be invoked when displaying on a vector display. The best-known language that supports multi-methods is the Common Lisp Object System (Steele Jr. 1990); another example is Cecil (Chambers 1992).

For traditional object-oriented languages, multi-methods represent a useful but optional extension to the basic mechanism. In contrast, in a CIP language, they are essential, since given a constraint foo(x,y,z), we might be determining a value for an unknown x using the values for y and z—in this case dispatching on the type of x would be a futile endeavor.

Constraint constructors are special procedures that define the meaning of user-defined constraints. In the simplest case, they are equivalent to rewrite rules: for example, when the constructor p1=p2 for two Cartesian points p1 and p2 is executed, it generates two equality constraints, one for the x slots and one for the y slots. In general, though, in keeping with Kaleidoscope's imperative nature, constraint constructors may contain not just calls to other constraint constructors, but arbitrary sequences of imperative code. However, all side effects are restricted to the local variables of the constructor. Viewed from the outside, all the constructor is allowed to do is to place other constraints on its arguments. If satisfied, these further constraints will result in the enforcement of the constraint represented by the constructor.

In the remainder of this paper, Section 4.1.2 outlines the evolution of CIP languages. Section 4.1.3 describes how objects and constraints are combined into a unified language model. Constraint constructors are discussed in Section 4.1.4. Section 4.1.5 presents some of the problems in combining constraints and objects and describes a framework that addresses these problems. The Kaleidoscope'93 implementation, the constraint solvers used by Kaleidoscope'93, and future work are discussed in Sections 4.1.6, 4.1.7, and 4.1.8 respectively.

4.1.2 Background

A number of experimental programming languages include support for constraints. Much of the activity in this area has been based in logic programming, and includes the CLP and cc (concurrent constraint) languages (Cohen 1990; Colmerauer 1990; Jaffar and Lassez 1987; Saraswat 1989; Van Hentenryck 1989; Van Hentenryck, Simonis, and Dincbas 1992; Wilson and Borning 1993). Other constraint languages include Steele's language (Steele Jr. 1980), Bertrand (Leler 1987), and Siri (Horn 1992a; Horn 1992b). (Of these, Siri, another constraint imperative language, is the closest to Kaleidoscope.) For discussions of related work beyond this brief mention, see (Borning, Freeman-Benson, and Wilson 1992; Freeman-Benson and Borning 1992b; Freeman-Benson 1991).

The first version of Kaleidoscope, Kaleidoscope'90, had a Smalltalk-like syntax and served as a proof of concept for CIP. Its successor, Kaleidoscope'91, had several features lacking from Kaleidoscope'90: a conventional Algol-like syntax, multi-methods, and eager constraint solving semantics. These two versions used a refinement model for constraints (as also used in logic programming). In this model, additional constraints further restrict the possible values for variables; however, variables never change values. Refinement semantics and mutable ob-

Table 4.2. Versions of Kaleidoscope

	Kaleidoscope'90	*Kaleidoscope'91*	*Kaleidoscope'93*
Constraint Evaluation	Lazy	Eager	Eager
Variables	Hold streams	Hold streams	Imperative
Concurrent Constraints	Strict	Strict	Non-strict
Syntax	Smalltalk-like	Algol-like	Algol-like
Constraint Model	Refinement	Refinement	Perturbation
Method Dispatching	Single	Multiple	Multiple
Assignment	As a constraint	As a constraint	Destructive

jects were combined by treating variables as streams of values. Each variable had a stream of states of the variable at different points in time. For example, an assignment statement x := x+5 was treated as a constraint between successive states of x: $x_{t+1} = x_t + 5$. Each time a new constraint was added, a constraint was deleted, or some object changed, all constraints were re-executed finding new values for all slots.

In Kaleidoscope'93 we shifted to a perturbation model. In this model, destructive assignment can change the state of objects (perhaps making previously satisfied constraints unsatisfied), and the system perturbs or adjusts values to reach a new state that best satisfies the constraints. Instead of streams of values, variables in Kaleidoscope'93 refer to a single object, as in conventional imperative languages. Assignment in Kaleidoscope'93 is a destructive state change, accompanied by a **once** stay constraint on the assigned variable (to prevent the assignment from immediately being undone by some other constraint).

When implemented in its full generality, the refinement model is a more powerful one, since in particular, it doesn't restrict variables to have a single value. However, the perturbation model seems more natural for imperative programmers, and seems to offer more opportunities for improving the efficiency of our implementation. (The refinement and perturbation models are compared at greater length in (Borning, Freeman-Benson, and Wilson 1992).)

Kaleidoscope'91 had a restriction that concurrent constraints execute in nested time scopes since the effects of constructor execution could not be visible until the completion of the constructor (Freeman-Benson 1991). Concurrent constraints allow such things as variable swapping without a temporary (e.g. y := x || x := y) but we have relaxed these restrictions in Kaleidoscope'93, making nested time scopes unnecessary, although at some cost in expressiveness.

Table 4.2 summarizes these comparisons between the successive versions of the language.

4.1.3 Combining Constraint and Object-Oriented Programming

Kaleidoscope'93 combines constraint and object-oriented programming while preserving a familiar object model from imperative programming. Objects have state and methods, as in most object-oriented languages. Constraints may be placed between objects and object slots, and once a constraint is established, the system attempts to enforce the constraint by filling slots with values. As objects change by assignment, these long-lived constraints re-execute and find new values for their slots.

Adding constraints to an imperative object model adds some complications (Section 4.1.5). Object identity, an important construct in object-oriented languages, has complicated interactions with constraints. The CIP language designer faces a trade-off between expressiveness of the language and problems such as accidental aliasing. Furthermore, circularities can arise if constraints are used to determine classes, values, structure, and identity. (For example, one could imagine a situation in which a given constructor might determine the value of one of its arguments, which determines the class of another argument, which could the choice of constraint constructor, which could affect the value of the argument ...) These circularities also need to be addressed in the language semantics. The VICS constraint framework (Section 4.1.5) handles these and other issues resulting from interactions of different constraint types.

There are also positive synergistic effects of combining constraints and objects. For example, constraints that apply to all members of a class can be enforced automatically when a new instance of the class is created. Consider the following:

```
class HorizontalLine subclass of Object;
  var p1, p2;

  initially

new(Point,p1);

new(Point,p2);

always: p1.y = p2.y;
  end initially;
end HorizontalLine;
```

There is a class invariant constraint between the two points representing a HorizontalLine. This constraint is enforced automatically at object initialization without the need for an explicit constraint call after initialization and without running the risk that a newly initialized member of HorizontalLine does not enforce this invariant.

In the spirit of data abstraction, constraint constructors allow the programmer to define user-defined constraints in terms of other user-defined constraints

or built-in primitive constraints. A user-defined constraint can be used anywhere that a primitive constraint can, and in particular can have a strength in
a constraint hierarchy, and a specified duration. This an important property of
CIP languages, since it does not restrict the programmer to constraints built
into the language.

In the spirit of object-oriented programming, constraint constructors use
multi-method lookup rules to select the appropriate procedure or constructor
based on the classes of the arguments. For example, a constraint j+k=m would
use the + constructor for points if j, k, and m were points, but would use the
constructor for arrays if they were arrays.

4.1.4 Constraint Constructors

As described previously, a constraint constructor provides a means of abstraction for constraints. Constraints can be defined in terms of more primitive constraints, similar to a method defining a message in terms of more primitive
messages. User-defined constraints may invoke other user-defined constraints,
and eventually these constraints are defined in terms of primitive constraints.
For example, the following constructor exploits imperative constructs to set up
constraints between array cells:

```
constructor +(a, b: Array) = (c: Array);
 local i: Integer;
 for i := 1 to a.size do

always: c[i] = a[i] + b[i];
 end for;
end constructor +;
```

As noted previously, both procedures and constraint constructors use multi-
method lookup rules to select the appropriate procedure or constructor based on
the classes of the arguments. However, unlike a procedure call, a constraint does
not necessarily result in just one execution of the corresponding constructor. The
first time a constraint is placed on a set of variables, the multi-method lookup
rules are used to find a constructor that implements that constraint, and the
selected constructor is executed. If any of the variables change by assignment,
then the appropriate constructor is selected using the multiple dispatch rules
(perhaps selecting the same constructor as before, or perhaps a different one).
The constructor is then executed to enforce the constraint. Dynamically binding
constraints to constructors is an important component of the integration of
constraints and objects.

4.1.5 VICS Constraint Framework

While designing Kaleidoscope, we found that a considerable number of our language issues dealt with conflicts between identity, constraints, and classes. The

VICS constraint framework provides a framework for handling these different constraint types. (VICS is an acronym for value-identity-class-structure, the four different types of constraint.)

Following Lisp, Kaleidoscope has several different notions of equality: identity, structural equality, and user defined equality. The identity relation between two variables holds if both variables refer to the same object in the computer's memory. Structural equality maintains that two objects are equal if their slots are equal, and two primitive objects are equal by built-in equality primitives. User defined equality allows the programmer to define the conditions for equality between two objects of the same or different classes (e.g. equality between polar and Cartesian points).

An issue in CIP languages concerns when the classes of objects are determined and when objects are initialized, since constructors can execute at arbitrary points in time (unlike procedures whose execution is determined by a procedure call). Should constructors be allowed to initialize objects? Can constructors create objects automatically for uninitialized argument objects? And if so, what is the class of an argument object? Can a constructor output an object that is a member of a subclass of the annotated argument class? Are class annotations constraints themselves? These issues are discussed in the remainder of this section.

Allowing both the class and the slot values of an object to be constrainable led to a whole host of problems resulting from circularities. If a class constraint can depend on a value constraint and the result of the value constraint depends on the result of a class constraint, there can be class/value circularities. More generally, this happens when different types of constraints are allowed to interdepend on each other.

Are structure constraints yet another form of constraint type? For example, the size of an array, or a mirror constraint between two trees, can be considered constraints on structure rather than values. Do we allow these types of constraints with the full generality of value constraints? If so, how does the language overcome circularities?

VICS addresses these issues pertaining to value, identity, class, and structure constraints, factors these different types of constraints, and provides a semantics for avoiding some of the pitfalls relating to conflicts between these constraint types. VICS attempts to strike a balance between expressiveness and flexibility on the one hand, and understandability and ease of solution on the other. The VICS Vapo-Ware Solver[1] is used in the Kaleidoscope'93 implementation to solve VICS constraints (Section 4.1.7). Each of the following subsections describes how the VICS framework handles different constraint types.

---

[1]Since some readers of this chapter will be from countries other than the United States, we provide a brief explanation of the name. Vicks VapoRub is a common household remedy in the U.S. for children's colds. Vaporware is a pejorative term for software that isn't quite real yet. At one point this term unfortunately also applied to our Kaleidoscope solver, but we hope this time has passed.

4.1.5.1 Value Constraints In VICS, value constraints are constraints that restrict the contents of an object's slot to a particular value in its domain. Value constraints are the most common type of constraint discussed in the research literature. (See Sections 4.1.4 and 4.1.7.) Kaleidoscope'93 provides a collection of primitive value constraints in its libraries, which are solved by local propagation.

Kaleidoscope has a powerful approach to value constraints, in which value constraints continue to be enforced as objects change state. Constraints on mutable objects continue to be enforced by re-executing the constructors implementing these constraints, causing more constructors to re-execute, until primitive constraints are handled by the local propagation solver. This contrasts with constraints in the CLP family of languages, where there is no facility for dynamically re-satisfying constraints to deal with state change.

4.1.5.2 Identity Constraints Object identity is a fundamental feature in standard object-oriented languages. An important situation in which object identity is visible to the user occurs when two variables x and y refer to the same object (i.e. x and y are aliased). In such a situation, a state-changing message sent via x will also be visible when accessing the object referred to by y. In contrast, if x and y refer to equal but not identical objects, changes to the object referred to by x will not affect y.

In a constraint imperative language, many of the effects of intentional aliasing can be achieved more cleanly by using persistent equality constraints (e.g. an **always** x=y constraint). However, persistent equality constraints do not handle constructs that in a conventional imperative language would be handled by updating a pointer to refer to a new object. Examples include a pointer that moves down a linked list, splicing a new element into a list, deleting an element from a list, and in-place insertion of a new node in a tree.

As another kind of example, consider the problem of specifying a circular list with constraints. The desired structure is easy to specify in an imperative language that includes pointers. For example, in Common Lisp we could write

```
(setf a (cons 3 nil))
(setf (rest a) a)
```

In Kaleidoscope we might try writing

```
a.head = 3;
a.tail = a;
```

However, if the constraints only imply equality rather than identity, the preceding pair of constraints can be satisfied by an infinite number of different graph structures (with 1, 2, 3, ... cells forming a circular list, or with a non-circular, infinite list). We might try adding a minimality condition to the Kaleidoscope solver, so that we found the solution with one cons cell—but what if we wanted a list of two cells instead?

It would still be possible to avoid object identity by using a different programming style—but one of the design goals for Kaleidoscope was to provide a familiar model for traditional object-oriented programmers, augmented with constraints. This is perhaps the strongest argument for its inclusion.

Based on such considerations, we decided to support a notion of object identity in Kaleidoscope. A simple way of introducing object identity would be to have a **cell** object that could refer to other objects, and that could be re-directed with a **set** message. However, in keeping with the philosophy of the language, we decided instead to introduce identity constraints, in analogy with equality constraints. In addition to the virtue of consistency, using constraints to specify identity may open up some interesting additional programming idioms, for example, describing constraints that keep the back pointers up-to-date in a bidirectional list, or that automatically maintain the threads a threaded tree. Finally, we decided to allow identity constraints to be bi-directional rather than one-way, again in analogy with equality constraints.

In Kaleidoscope'93, an identity constraint is denoted by ==. Thus, the one-cell list is easily specified by:

```
a.head = 3;
a.tail == a;
```

However, just as pointers can lead to problems in more conventional languages, identity constraints can lead to problems in CIP languages. The primary problem is accidental aliasing. Identity constraints labeled with an **always** duration (which remain in force throughout the program's execution) don't give rise to these difficulties. However, **always** constraints don't allow such common idioms as having a pointer that marches though a list structure, or a list that can have an element deleted. For such uses, we need **once** identity constraints, just as we have other sorts of constraints with a **once** duration.

The aliasing problem arises when the **once** identity constraint is no longer active. Compare

```
new(Point,a);
once: a.x = 0;
once: a.y = 0;
once: a == b;  /* note that this is an identity constraint */
once: a.x = 5;
```

with

```
new(Point,a);
once: a.x = 0;
once: a.y = 0;
once: a = b;  /* note that this is an equality constraint */
once: a.x = 5;
```

In the first example, the **once** identity constraint still has an effect after its duration, since a and b remain identical, so that b.x is also set to 5. In the second example, the once equality constraint has no effect after it is removed, and b.x remains 0.

In Kaleidoscope'93, we have chosen to live with accidental aliasing, despite these problems, since the alternatives we considered led to a less expressive or less intuitive language.

Another issue with object identity concerns circularities. The VICS framework prohibits the constructor for a value constraint from asserting an identity constraint that would invalidate the original choice of constructor for that value constraint. In other words, since the execution of a value constraint cannot depend on an identity constraint executed by that constraint, identity/value circularities are disallowed.

A final issue with object identity is how the identity of uninitialized objects is determined. One approach is to require the programmer to initialize all objects explicitly, and not to allow constructors to create new objects. This is cumbersome, since sometimes we would like constructors to return objects that are created within that constructor. At the other extreme, we considered a very general mechanism (which we called an identitor) that would define the identity rules of arguments for all cases of uninitialized arguments. The drawback of this approach is that constructors became verbose, since they need to include code to handle all the different cases for uninitialized arguments, and so the identitor mechanism was dropped.

The VICS framework uses neither scheme for handling uninitialized variables. It is important to allow constructors to initialize objects, but identitors seemed too powerful, especially considering that most cases for uninitialized arguments will be common cases. The VICS approach is to provide default behavior for uninitialized arguments for these common cases.

Class Object is the root class and LiteObject is a subclass of Object. All uninitialized arguments to a constructor that are annotated as subclasses of LiteObject are automatically initialized upon execution of the constructor. Any arguments which are not annotated as subclass of LiteObject are considered heavyweight objects (e.g. Window). In contrast, these heavyweight objects are not created automatically by the solver; a runtime error is generated if the program tries to invoke an operator on such an uninitialized variable.

As an example, consider the evaluation of p+q=r, where q and r are bound to cartesian points and p is unbound. The constructor for point + will be invoked:

```
constructor +(a, b: Point) = (c: Point);
   a.x + b.x = c.x;
   a.y + b.y = c.y;
end constructor +;
```

with p constrained to be identical to the formal argument a, q to b, and r to c. Since Point is a subclass of LiteObject, a new instance of Point will be created automatically and bound to p.

In contrast, consider is_selected_window(window1,mouse_position). If we evaluate this expression with window1 unbound, since Window is presumably a subclass of Object but not LiteObject, a new window would (correctly) not be created automatically by the constructor, and a runtime error would be signaled if the program attempted to perform an operation on it.

4.1.5.3 Class Constraints A class constraint is a constraint on the class of a variable. Kaleidoscope'90 treated class constraints in a general way, with class constraints being solved as ordinary constraints. Although this scheme was very powerful, it caused the implementation to be inefficient, was semantically confusing, and gave rise to circularities.

VICS simplifies the semantics and implementation by reducing the power of class constraints. The first design decision was how classes for classless variables are determined, and the second was how constructors are chosen given the classes of variables. (A classless variable is one that is not yet constrained to refer to an instance of a particular class.) Classless variables are considered to be of a special class **Bottom**, until the class is set explicitly by assignment, by declaration, or indirectly through identity constraints. **Bottom** is a subclass of all classes. Thus, a variable of class **Bottom** can be used in multiple dispatch constructor lookup. If there is an ambiguous choice of constructors, then a runtime error is signaled. If there is a single constructor choice, despite one or more classless arguments, then constructor execution can proceed.

For efficiency, VICS currently does not allow backtracking. The order of execution of constraints in an expression is arbitrary. If a later constructor executes and has class information that contradicts an earlier constructor executed in the same expression, a runtime error is generated. Programmers can try to avoid this type of runtime error by making variable classes explicit. Circularities with value and identity constraints are avoided with VICS class semantics. The class of a variable is determined prior to establishing the identity of a variable; value constraints are not allowed to select a class for a variable that would force an alternate choice for the value constraint.

4.1.5.4 Structure Constraints Examples of structure constraints include size constraints on arrays, matrix addition (which constrains both the value and structure of matrices), and tree mirror. In some systems these are either treated differently from constraints on values, or not allowed at all. In Kaleidoscope'93, however, constraints on structure are handled in a manner similar to value constraints: either by user-defined constructors, or by primitives (e.g. Array size). Structure and value constraints may be intermingled, as long as the solver can solve the structure constraints by local propagation. (This disallows a cycle through a structure constraint, for example, a constraint on the bounds of an array that depends on the contents of an element of that same array.)

4.1.6 Implementation

The K-machine is a virtual machine for constraint imperative languages, providing low-level functionality that is unavailable from strictly object-oriented

Table 4.3. K-machine Instructions (K-codes)

Operation	Arguments	Description
Branch	BoolVar, NewPC	Conditionally branch to NewPC
CallProc	ProcName, Args	Call a procedure
LoadTemplate	Var, Template	Define a var to refer to a template
AddTemplate	Var	Executes the constraint template
RemoveTemplate	Var	Removes all constraints for the template
Return	none	Returns from a proc. or constructor call
MinStrength	Strgth1, Strgth2	Computes the minimum of two strengths

or strictly constraint-based virtual machines. The interface to the K-machine is similar to that for imperative virtual machines. However, in addition to the standard machine instructions for imperative languages, there are a several instructions pertaining to constraint execution.

An alternative to designing a virtual machine particular to CIP languages would be to use one of the many existing virtual machines for imperative or constraint-based languages. The requirements for CIP support are: object-oriented-support, preferably class-based with inheritance; multi-methods; constraint solving; and dynamically bound constraints. It would be possible, yet extremely awkward, to implement Kaleidoscope with a virtual machine from a conventional object-oriented language with a value-based data store, for example the Smalltalk-80 virtual machine (Goldberg and Robson 1983). However, to do so, the compiler would have to implement the entire semantics of the K-machine in the code generator to ensure that the effect of a constraint-based data store was achieved. This would needlessly complicate the code generator, and would actually reduce the speed of the resulting program. Virtual machines for conventional imperative programming languages are even less suited to CIP languages because they support neither objects nor constraints.

Similarly, it would be possible, yet awkward, to implement Kaleidoscope using the virtual machine for a pure constraint language. For example, CLP($\mathcal{R}$) is a constraint logic programming language whose implementation has a constraint solving engine for constraints over the real numbers (Jaffar, Michaylov, Stuckey, and Yap 1992). The CLAM is the abstract machine used in the CLP($\mathcal{R}$) interpreter, which is based on the WAM, often used in Prolog implementations (Warren 1983). However, to use the CLAM, one would have to translate the Kaleidoscope semantics into one of the object-oriented logic programming schemes. Other constraint-based languages include Bertrand (Leler 1987) and Siri (Horn 1992a). Both Bertrand and Siri are based on an Augmented Term Rewriting virtual machine, which is not powerful enough to support all of the imperative features of Kaleidoscope.

Table 4.3 lists the complete set of K-codes (K-machine instructions). A constraint template sets up a constraint between a set of variables. The execution of a template causes constructors to execute and primitives to be solved. There are three stacks for constraint templates for each of the three durations: once, always, and assert/during. Minstrength is used to compute the minimum of the strength of the currently executing constructor and a second strength (to handle constraints in a constructor that are themselves labeled with a strength).

The key to the semantics of constraint imperative programming is the constraint-based data store and thus, in Kaleidoscope, the object model as well. It is in this constraint-based data store that Kaleidoscope differs from virtual machines for imperative languages. All objects are stored as constraint graph objects. Using the "everything is an object" design principle, stack frames are constraint graph objects as well. Constraints are placed between these constraint graph objects.

The Kaleidoscope'93 implementation is significantly different from the implementation of Kaleidoscope'91. The Kaleidoscope'91 K-machine re-executed all constraints each time a new constraint was added, closely modeling the refinement semantics of the language. The objects as streams of values semantics was mirrored in the implementation by representing variables as streams of objects.

Furthermore, the semantics of Kaleidoscope'91 forced constructors to execute in nested time scopes (Freeman-Benson 1991). Kaleidoscope'91 had an explicit notion of time. In order to prevent the arbitrary advancement of time, the effects within a constructor were local to that constructor via this nested time scope. Handling these nested time scopes led to inefficiencies in the implementation.

In the Kaleidoscope'93 implementation, we have redesigned the K-machine so that constraint constructors execute incrementally. This has improved the performance tremendously, since constructors only need to re-execute when affected by other constraints. Furthermore, objects are no longer represented as streams of values, but persist as mutable objects with a single state, as in conventional imperative virtual machines.

We also eliminated nested time from Kaleidoscope in Kaleidoscope'93, since there is no longer an explicit notion of time. Hence, there are no implementation inefficiencies due to nested time.

4.1.7 Solvers

The VICS Vapo-Ware Solver is a special-purpose solver used by Kaleidoscope'93 to implement the VICS constraint framework. The VICS framework simplifies class constraints, reducing their expressiveness, but allowing more efficient multi-method lookup rules for solving the classes of classless variables.

Value constraints are handled by constructor execution when a constraint is added. For constraints of long duration, the constraint re-executes each time of any of its variables (or the subparts of those variables) changes identity. The execution of a constructor might trigger additional constructors to execute. This process continues until the remaining constraints are primitive constraints, which are solved by SkyBlue (Sannella 1993), the incremental local propagation solver used for Kaleidoscope'93 primitives. (SkyBlue is a new algorithm that extends our earlier DeltaBlue algorithm (Freeman-Benson, Maloney, and Borning 1990; Sannella, Maloney, Freeman-Benson, and Borning 1993) to allow constraints with multiple outputs, and that provides better handling of cycles.)

Structure constraints, as described in Section 4.1.5, are grouped semantically with value constraints, and thus share the same implementation. Hence, there are primitives for structure constraints as well as value constraints.

Identity constraints are solved by special-purpose constructors that establish an identity relation between two variables. For identity constraints of long duration, this constructor is re-executed each time one of these variables changes identity. An unbound variable that is annotated with a subclass of LiteObject is bound at constructor execution time, as specified by the VICS semantics. Finally, there is a predicate that tests whether two variables are identical, also implemented as a constructor.

All primitive constraints are represented as constraint edges in the primitive constraint graph. SkyBlue solves these constraints by executing the primitive constraints and finding values for all variables. As new primitive constraints are added to this graph as a result of constructor execution, SkyBlue re-executes primitives to satisfy all primitive constraints. Since SkyBlue is incremental, constraints that are not affected by changes to the primitive graph do not re-execute.

4.1.8 Future Work

As of this writing, our Kaleidoscope'93 implementation has just become usable. We plan to continue work on the implementation, and as it stabilizes, begin to write larger programs in the language, and feed back the results to the language design and implementation. Another major effort will involve increasing the efficiency of the code produced by the Kaleidoscope compiler, in particular to eliminate runtime constraint satisfaction when possible. Finally, we are about to replace our primitive constraint solver, SkyBlue, with a more powerful solver, CobaltBlue. In addition to local propagation constraints, CobaltBlue will handle simultaneous equations and non-unique constraints.

Acknowledgements

Many people have given help and advice on this work; we would like to thank in particular Craig Chambers, Denise Draper, Jens Palsberg, Michael Sannella, and Michael Schwartzbach. This work was supported in part by the National Science Foundation under Grant No. IRI-9102938, by the Canadian National Science and Engineering Research Council under Grant OGP0121431, by a Fellowship from Apple Computer for Gus Lopez, and by equipment grants from Sun Microsystems.

References

Borning, A., B. Freeman-Benson, and M. Wilson (1992, September). Constraint hierarchies. *Lisp and Symbolic Computation* 5(3), 223–270.

Chambers, C. (1992, June). Object-Oriented Multi-Methods in Cecil. In *Proceedings of the 1992 European Conference on Object-Oriented Programming*, pp. 33–56.

Cohen, J. (1990, July). Constraint logic programming languages. *Communications of the ACM* 33(7), 52–68.

Colmerauer, A. (1990, July). An introduction to Prolog III. *Communications of the ACM*, 69–90.

Freeman-Benson, B. (1991, July). *Constraint Imperative Programming.* Ph. D. thesis, University of Washington, Department of Computer Science and Engineering. Published as Department of Computer Science and Engineering Technical Report 91-07-02.

Freeman-Benson, B. and A. Borning (1992a, April). The design and implementation of Kaleidoscope'90, a constraint imperative programming language. In *Proceedings of the IEEE Computer Society International Conference on Computer Languages*, pp. 174–180.

Freeman-Benson, B. and A. Borning (1992b, June). Integrating constraints with an object-oriented language. In *Proceedings of the 1992 European Conference on Object-Oriented Programming*, pp. 268–286.

Freeman-Benson, B., J. Maloney, and A. Borning (1990, January). An incremental constraint solver. *Communications of the ACM* 33(1), 54–63.

Goldberg, A. and D. Robson (1983). *Smalltalk-80: The Language and its Implementation.* Addison-Wesley.

Horn, B. (1992a, October). Constraint patterns as a basis for object-oriented constraint programming. In *Proceedings of the 1992 ACM Conference on Object-Oriented Programming Systems, Languages, and Applications*, Vancouver, British Columbia, pp. 218–233.

Horn, B. (1992b). Properties of user interface systems and the Siri programming language. In B. Myers (Ed.), *Languages for Developing User Interfaces*, pp. 211–236. Boston: Jones and Bartlett.

Jaffar, J. and J.-L. Lassez (1987, January). Constraint logic programming. In *Proceedings of the Fourteenth ACM Principles of Programming Languages Conference*, Munich.

Jaffar, J., S. Michaylov, P. Stuckey, and R. Yap (1992, July). The CLP($\mathcal{R}$) language and system. *ACM Transactions on Programming Languages and Systems* 14(3), 339–395.

Leler, W. (1987). *Constraint Programming Languages.* Addison-Wesley.

Sannella, M. (1993, February). The SkyBlue Constraint Solver. Technical Report 92-07-02, Department of Computer Science and Engineering, University of Washington.

Sannella, M., J. Maloney, B. Freeman-Benson, and A. Borning (1993, May). Multi-way versus One-way Constraints in User Interfaces: Experience with the DeltaBlue Algorithm. *Software—Practice and Experience* 23(5), 529–566.

Saraswat, V. A. (1989, January). *Concurrent Constraint Programming Languages.* Ph. D. thesis, Carnegie-Mellon University, Computer Science Department.

Steele Jr., G. L. (1980, August). *The Definition and Implementation of a Computer Programming Language Based on Constraints.* Ph. D. thesis, MIT. Published as MIT-AI TR 595, August 1980.

Steele Jr., G. L. (1990). *Common Lisp: The Language* (second ed.). Bedford, Massachusetts: Digital Press.

Van Hentenryck, P. (1989). *Constraint Satisfaction in Logic Programming.* Cambridge, MA: MIT Press.

Van Hentenryck, P., H. Simonis, and M. Dincbas (1992, December). Constraint satisfaction using constraint logic programming. *Artificial Intelligence 58*(1–3), 113–159.

Warren, D. H. D. (1983, October). An abstract prolog instruction set. Technical Report 309, SRI Internatonal, Menlo Park, California.

Wilson, M. and A. Borning (1993, July, August). Hierarchical constraint logic programming. *Journal of Logic Programming 16*(3 & 4), 277–318.

4.2 Constraints in NUT

Jaan Penjam[1] and Enn Tyugu[2]

[1]Institute of Cybernetics, Akadeemia tee 21,
EE0026 Tallinn, Estonia

[2]Inst för Teleinformatik, Kungl Tekniska Högskolan,
Electrum 204, S-16440 KISTA, Sweden

Abstract

NUT is a programming system for knowledge-based programming with facilities for automatic program synthesis. The system allows to specify computational problems in OO style. Concepts and objects can be treated in NUT as functional constraint networks. Constraint satisfaction problems are solved using algorithms for automatic program synthesis described earlier for the PRIZ system.

4.2.1 Introduction

The NUT system is the most advanced representative of the family of programming systems called PRIZ. This family includes systems PRIZ ES, Solver, MicroPRIZ, ExpertPRIZ, NUT etc., which have been developed in the last 20 years in the Institute of Cybernetics of the Estonian Academy of Sciences. All these systems support a knowledge-based programming style and they have been successfully used to solve engineering problems as well as in scientific investigations of AI.

The NUT language was outlined as an extension of an object-oriented programming language with features of automatic program synthesis, and its full description appeared in (Tyugu et al. 1986). The first implementation of a version of the NUT language was done as a part of a Soviet new generation computer project START on the Priz workstations which were developed in the framework of the same project (Kotov et al. 1989) and (Tyugu 1991). In 1990, the NUT system was implemented in various UNIX and X Windows Systems environments (Matskin 1991). The work on implementation of NUT was completed at the Royal Institute of Technology in Stockholm where it is now being used for educational purposes (Matskin and Tyugu 1992).

An attempt is made in the NUT to amalgamate different programming paradigms each of which claims to be a good platform for the future computing: logic programming, object-oriented programming, constraint programming, knowledge-based programming. When one combines different methods

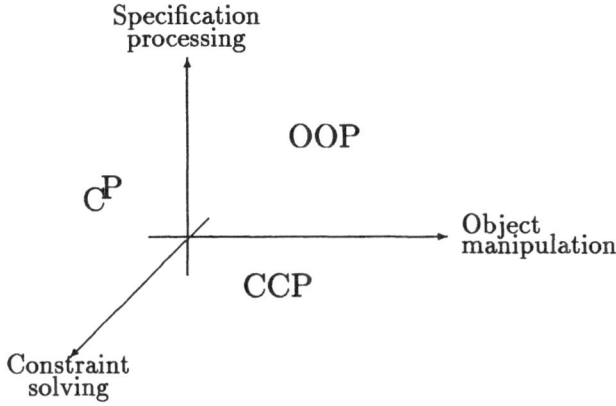

Fig. 4.1. Three dimensions of computing in NUT

and techniques, always a rather natural question arises: how to merge underlying paradigms into a new one which will preserve the merits of all of its constituents. Quite a success has been achieved in combining logic and constraint programming. Two very promising approaches have evolved: constraint logic programming (Jaffar and Lassez 1987) and concurrent constraint programming (Saraswat 1990). A recent work (Smolka et al. 1993) is an example of merging constraint programming with object-oriented programming.

Having a closer look at the NUT system, one can see the following three different modes of computations in it:

- specification processing (inheritance, delegation etc.);

- object manipulation (sending and processing messages);

- constraint solving (synthesizing and running programs on sets of relations).

These are three orthogonal dimensions of computations which can be combined in various ways, Fig. 4.2.1.

The combination of specification processing and object manipulation is what we call object-oriented programming. A coordinate plane determined by the axes of Specification processing and Constraint solving form constraint programming. Combination of object manipulation and Constraint solving is almost covered by concurrent constraint programming and logic constraint programming. This coordinate plane corresponds also to the most interesting and novel part of the NUT system. This is a kind of constraint object programming which is still different from the approach taken in (Smolka et al. 1993), first of all, because it applies a specific technique of constraint solving by program synthesis.

The aim of this article is to present constraint semantics of NUT classes. We describe the way how specifications written in NUT are translated into functional constraint networks suitable for application of different satisfaction techniques. Some of these techniques are described in (Tyugu and Uustalu 1993).

4.2.2 Functional constraints

Let $X = \{x_1, x_2, \ldots x_n\}$ be a set of problem variables. We shall consider constraints as relations over the set X specifying which combinations of values of problem variables are acceptable. Formally, constraints can be written as interpreted formulae in first-order predicate calculus. Let us denote constraints as follows:

$$A_{x_1}(x_1), A_{x_2}(x_2), \cdots, A_{x_n}(x_n),$$
$$A_{x_1,x_2}(x_1, x_2), A_{x_1,x_3}(x_1, x_3), \cdots, A_{x_1,x_n}(x_1, x_n),$$
$$A_{x_2,x_3}(x_2, x_3), A_{x_2,x_4}(x_2, x_4), \cdots, A_{x_2,x_n}(x_2, x_n),$$
$$\vdots$$
$$A_{x_{n-1},x_n}(x_{n-1}, x_n),$$
$$A_{x_1,x_2,x_3}(x_1, x_2, x_3), \cdots, A_{x_{n-2},x_{n-1},x_n}(x_{n-2}, x_{n-1}, x_n),$$
$$\vdots$$
$$A_{x_1,x_2,\ldots,x_n}(x_1, x_2 \ldots, x_n).$$

In special cases, constraints may be simply atomic formulae, i.e. predicates which determine domains of variables (in the case of unary predicates) or "local" relationships between tuples of variables.

A Constraint Satisfaction Problem (CSP) is represented by a conjunction of all constraints involved:

$$\begin{aligned} Q(x_1, x_2, \ldots, x_n) &\equiv A_{x_1}(x_1) \& \cdots \& A_{x_n}(x_n) \\ &\& A_{x_1,x_2}(x_1, x_2) \& \cdots \& A_{x_1,x_2,\ldots,x_n}(x_1, x_2 \ldots, x_n). \end{aligned}$$

The CSP is solvable if the formula

$$\exists x_1, x_2, \ldots, x_n Q(x_1, x_2, \ldots, x_n) \tag{4.1}$$

is constructively derivable. The proof of the solvability of the CSP is called constructive if during derivation individual constants $\bar{x}_1, \bar{x}_2, \ldots \bar{x}_n$ are indicated which satisfy the formula (4.1) for the underlying interpretation.

In general, a CSP may have no complete solution when the amount of usable resources is limited. For efficiency considerations, the partial constraint satisfaction problem is regarded (Freuder and Wallace 1992) or/and additional restrictions are set to the formulae representing expressions and to the interpretation of functional and predicate symbols. Two popular restrictions are that constraints may contain no functional symbols, and domains of potential values of problem variables are finite (Mackworth 1992).

In this paper we shall restrict ourselves to the two following types of constraint formulae:

- ground atoms $A_x(x) \equiv P(x)$ where P is a predicate specifying a domain of x. We call the predicate P the *characteristic predicate* of the class of objects P if the predicate symbol P is interpreted as 'argument x belongs to the class P';

- functional constraints $A_{x_1,\ldots,x_m,y}(x_1,\ldots,x_m,y)$ which has an interpretation where y has at most one value satisfying the relation $A_{x_1,\ldots,x_m,y}(x_1,\ldots,x_m,y)$ for any tuple of values of $x_1,\ldots,x_m$

In the last case, a constraint defines a function $y = f(x_1,\ldots,x_m)$ and can be put down as a formula

$$\mathcal{X}_1,\ldots,\mathcal{X}_m \longrightarrow_f \mathcal{Y} \tag{4.2}$$

where $\mathcal{X}_1,\ldots,\mathcal{X}_m$ are propositions representing computability of $x_1,\ldots,x_m$ respectively. The formula (4.2) itself expresses the property that if the objects $x_1,\ldots,x_m$ have suitable values then one can compute a value for y using function f.

Functions determined by functional constraints may be of the second order as well. This means that a constraint may bind some objects $g_1,\ldots,g_l$ of functional type which stand for arguments of the mapping F of the functional constraint. Formally, a constraint $A_{g_1,\ldots,g_l,x_1,\ldots,x_m,y}(g_1,\ldots,g_l,x_1,\ldots,x_m,y)$ contains the second order functional dependency if the following holds

$$y = F(g_1,\ldots,g_l,x_1,\ldots,x_m).$$

Objects $g_1,\ldots,g_l$ can obtain their values dynamically during solution of the current CSP (Tyugu and Uustalu 1993). In this case, we still may wish to specify type of an object g_i, saying that g_i must be a function computing v_i from $u_{i1},\ldots,u_{ik_i}$. This is expressed by the formula

$$\mathcal{U}_{i1},\ldots,\mathcal{U}_{ik_i} \longrightarrow_{g_i} \mathcal{V}_i.$$

The constraint $A_{g_1,\ldots,g_l,x_1,\ldots,x_m,y}(g_1,\ldots,g_l,x_1,\ldots,x_m,y)$ will then be represented by the following formula:

$$(\mathcal{U}_{11},\ldots,\mathcal{U}_{1k_1} \longrightarrow_{g_1} \mathcal{V}_1),\ldots,(\mathcal{U}_{l1},\ldots,\mathcal{U}_{lk_l} \longrightarrow_{g_l} \mathcal{V}_l),\mathcal{X}_1,\ldots,\mathcal{X}_m \longrightarrow_F \mathcal{Y}. \tag{4.3}$$

Let us notice, that the relation $A_{g_1,\ldots,g_l,x_1,\ldots,x_m,y}(g_1,\ldots,g_l,x_1,\ldots,x_m,y)$ binds the objects $g_1,\ldots,x_1,\ldots,y$, but not the objects $u_{11},u_{12},\ldots,v_1,\ldots$.

Higher order functional constraints provide generality to the language of constraints, and allow some interesting applications, see Sec.4.2.5.2.

4.2.3 The NUT Language

NUT is an object-oriented programming language and environment for specifying problems by means of constraints with built-in methods for solving constraint satisfaction problem. As any object-oriented language, NUT has *class*
and *object* as its basic notions.

Class is a carrier of common features of objects of the same type, i.e. of
objects with similar structure and with the property to react similarly to certain
changes of their environment (receiving the same messages from other related
objects).

Let us introduce a predicate $C(x)$ for every class C which is **true** for any
object x of the class C and **false** otherwise. There are some predefined classes
such as **num**, **text**, **bool** etc. in the NUT system. Hence, there are a number
of unary predicates defined:

- $num(x)$ – x is a rational number, i.e. x is an object of the class **num**;

- $text(x)$ – x is a string of characters;

- $bool(x)$ – x is a boolean value;
  etc.

Similarly, the predicate *triangle(ABC)* means that the object ABC belongs to
the class of triangles. The difference here is that a concept of triangle has to be
specified and stored into the knowledge base by a user as the class `triangle`.

Formally, every object x might be treated as a tuple of its attributes $x =
(x_1, x_2, \ldots, x_n)$ which represents aspects of an object essential for underlying
consideration. A number of attributes considered in any particular situation
is assumed to be finite. A class C determines relationships between attributes
of objects belonging to the class. Each class C has its characteristic predicate
which can be specified as

$$C(x) \quad \equiv \quad \exists x_1, x_2, \ldots, x_n Q(x, x_1, x_2, \ldots, x_n) \qquad (4.4)$$

where $x_1, \ldots, x_n$ are its attributes. This is a constraint specified by the class C.
The matrix Q in the formula (4.4) is the conjunction of "smaller" constraints
representing relations between the attributes. So, using the class mechanism, a
user can build up the hierarchy of constraints.

There are the following means in the NUT system to specify various constraints:

- constraints for structure of objects;

- equational constraints over numeric objects;

- constraints as different kinds of identity relations;

- constraints as messages which may be accepted by an object together with
  its (pre)programmed reaction to the message.

All these constraints can be represented by finite sets of functional constraints.

4.2.3.1 Structural Constraints An object in NUT can have a fixed number of components which are objects again. The names and types of these components are aspects to be specified by the class of the object. Considering objects with complex structure we suppose that there are two different operations one can apply to objects and their components. One can separate a component from the compound object to treat it further independently, and vice versa, one can incorporate objects of proper types into a new object as its components.

For example, the situation where a class Z defines its objects to consist of two components x and y of classes X and Y respectively, can be specified in the NUT language as

```
Class Z:(var x:X; y:Y);
```

This is a structural constraint that binds any object z of class Z with its components which we denote by $z.x$ and $z.y$. Semantically, this means that for every object z of the class Z there exist functions $select_x$, $select_y$ and $compose$ to separate components $z.x$ and $z.y$ from the object z and to unite the two objects into the object of class Z respectively. In other words, belonging to the class Z means for an object z that there are objects $z.x$ and $z.y$, such that the following constraints are satisfied:

$$A_{z.x}(z.x) \equiv X(z.x) \tag{4.5}$$
$$A_{z.y}(z.y) \equiv Y(z.y) \tag{4.6}$$
$$A_{z,z.x}(z, z.x) \equiv select_x(z) = z.x \tag{4.7}$$
$$A_{z,z.y}(z, z.y) \equiv select_y(z) = z.y \tag{4.8}$$
$$A_{z.x,z.y}(z.x, z.y) \equiv \text{true} \tag{4.9}$$
$$A_{z,z.x,z.y}(z, z.x, z.y) \equiv compose(z.x, z.y) = z \tag{4.10}$$

The class Z defines therefore a predicate $Z(z)$ as a conjunction of the formulae (4.5)-(4.10).

The constraints (4.5) and (4.6) determine the domains (given by classes) of components $z.x$ and $z.y$. Other relations are functional constraints and might be reformulated as follows:

$$\mathcal{Z} \longrightarrow_{select_x} \mathcal{Z}.\mathcal{X} \tag{4.11}$$
$$\mathcal{Z} \longrightarrow_{select_y} \mathcal{Z}.\mathcal{Y} \tag{4.12}$$
$$\mathcal{Z}.\mathcal{X}, \mathcal{Z}.\mathcal{Y} \longrightarrow_{compose} \mathcal{Z} \tag{4.13}$$

Constraints (4.7) and (4.8) can be treated as equations defining abbreviation for selection operation $select_x$ and $select_y$ respectively. Afterwards we shall use elsewhere "dotted notation of selection", i.e. $z.x$ instead of $select_x(z)$. To represent computability of such a selected element the proposition Z.X will be used. For example, assuming that abbreviation, one can reduce the definition of the characteristic predicate of class Z as follows:

$$Z(z) = X(z.x) \ \& \ Y(z.y) \ \& \ \mathcal{Z}.\mathcal{X}, \mathcal{Z}.\mathcal{Y} \longrightarrow_{compose} \mathcal{Z}.$$

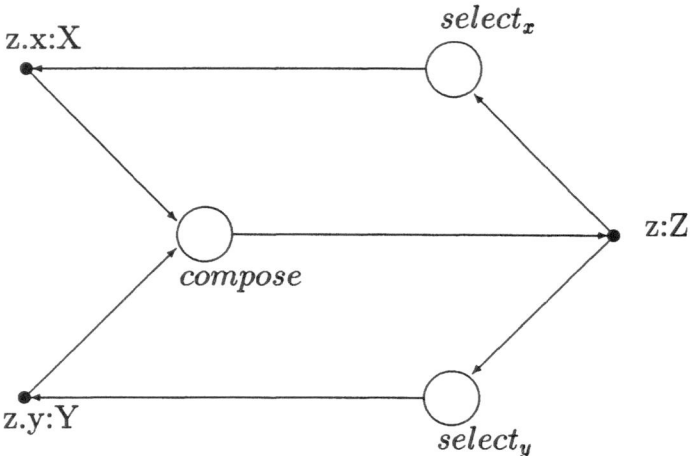

Fig. 4.2. Constraint network of the class Z

On the other hand, a set of implications in the form of formulae (4.11)–(4.13) permits a simple graphical representation of the constraint network. A *constraint network* is a graph where nodes are used for representation of objects involved and functional constraints (implications). The nodes of objects are denoted by names and types (classes) of the corresponding objects and the nodes of constraints are labelled by their names (see next sections) or/and by the functions realizing them. We shall omit some labels, for example classes of objects or function symbols, if there will be no confusion. In Fig. 4.2, the constraints (4.11)–(4.13) are presented as a network.

A hierarchy of classes (and corresponding constraints) can be defined in the manner described above. Besides structural constraints, a class may contain other kinds of conditions to be satisfied. In the following sections we show how these constraints are interpreted as implications in a propositional calculus. Every additional restriction for components of a class will complement its characteristic predicate by one or more atomic constraint.

4.2.3.2 Equations An equation

$$f(x_1, \ldots, x_n) = 0 \tag{4.14}$$

over numeric objects is a constraint which allows us to find some x_i if all other $x_1, \ldots, x_{i-1}, x_{i+1}, \ldots, x_n$ are given. This is valid only when we know the method how to compute x_i from other variables of the equation. Let us denote by f_i^{-1} the function which solves the equation (4.14) in respect of a variable x_i:

$$x_i = f_i^{-1}(x_1, \ldots, x_{i-1}, x_{i+1}, \ldots, x_n)$$

so that

$$f(x_1, \ldots, x_{x-1}, f_i^{-1}(x_1, \ldots, x_{i-1}, x_{i+1}, \ldots, x_n), x_{i+1}, \ldots, x_n) = 0.$$

An equation may be a partially solvable constraint in the sense that it cannot always be solved with respect to all unknowns. For instance, the equation

$$x_1^2 + 2x_1 + 3 = 0$$

cannot be solved in real numbers at all, and the corresponding function f_i^{-1} does not exist. Besides that, we have to accept that sometimes we do not know how to get the function f_i^{-1} even when it exists, as there is no general effective method to solve equations.

The NUT language permits to include equational constraints over numeric components into class declarations. For instance,

```
Class W:(var x,y:num;
         rel
           R: 2*x - y = 0);
```

means that an object of class W has two numeric components x and y constrained by the equation $2x - y = 0$.

The semantics of an equation (4.14) is defined by a conjunction of constraints

$$A_{x_1,\ldots,x_n}^i \equiv \mathcal{X}_1 \& \cdots \& \mathcal{X}_{i-1} \& \mathcal{X}_{i+1} \& \cdots \& \mathcal{X}_n \longrightarrow_{f_i^{-1}} \mathcal{X}_i$$

for every variable x_i for which we know a function f_i^{-1}. In the case of the class W above, the equation R generates two assignments:

$$x := g_1(y) = y/2$$

and

$$y := g_2(x) = 2 * x.$$

Hence, the constraint defined by the class W can be presented as the predicate

$$
\begin{aligned}
W(w) \equiv\ & Num(w.x)\ \&\ Num(w.y) \\
& \&\ W.\mathcal{X}\ \&\ W.\mathcal{Y} \longrightarrow_{compose} W \\
& \&\ W.\mathcal{X} \longrightarrow_{g_1} W.\mathcal{Y} \\
& \&\ W.\mathcal{Y} \longrightarrow_{g_2} W.\mathcal{X}.
\end{aligned}
$$

The constraint network corresponding to the given specification of the class W is shown in Fig. 4.3.

Combining structural and equational constraints permits us to define rather complex concepts as classes of objects of hierarchical structure. For example, the following two classes altogether specify a concept of line segment in two-dimensional space.

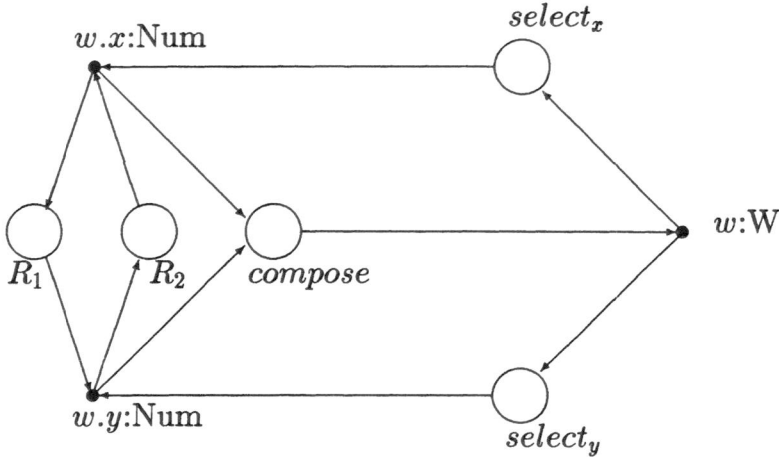

Fig. 4.3. Constraint network of the class W

```
Class  Point:(var x,y:num);

Class  Bar:(var P,Q:Point;
               length, angle:num;
           rel
               (P.x - Q.x)^2 + (P.y-Q.y)^2 = length^2;
               P.y - Q.y = (P.x - P.y) * tan(angle));
```

Here we can point out the expressive power of the NUT language – rather short class descriptions consisting of some equations taken from school textbooks generate a large number of constraints specified. Similarly to the class Z in the previous Section, the characteristic predicate *Point* consists of 5 atomic constraints. Therefore, the declarations of end points P and Q in the specification of the class *Bar* introduce $2 \times 5 = 10$ constraints. Two new constraints will be added by specification of domain *Num* for *length* and *angle*, and 10 more constraints are generated by the two equations as they are solvable with respect to all unknowns. To conclude, the class *Bar* specifies 32 constraints for every object of this class.

This example demonstrates a problem specific for equational constraint systems: equations may not have unique solutions. For instance, there are infinitely many values of variable *angle* which satisfy the last equation in the class *Bar* for fixed valuation of other variables. The NUT system uses some heuristics to choose the solution, however it is recommended to avoid usage of equations with multiple solutions. In many cases specifications with equations of this kind can be transformed into the "equivalent" ones with unique solution. This is mainly a knowledge engineering task we do not consider here; it allows one to use the NUT system for solving practical problems such as they arose in CAD systems or implementing semantics of programming languages (see (Kalja and Pahapill 1992), (Penjam 1990)).

4.2.3.3 Programs as constraints NUT permits a flexible mechanism for message passing between objects. This is used for invoking methods available for an object of a class. Besides that, a method corresponds strictly to a set of functional constraints between the components of the object. A set of constraints

$$\mathcal{X}_1, \ldots, \mathcal{X}_m \longrightarrow_{f_1} \mathcal{Y}_1$$
$$\vdots$$
$$\mathcal{X}_1, \ldots, \mathcal{X}_m \longrightarrow_{f_n} \mathcal{Y}_n$$

where $f = (f_1, \ldots, f_n)$ can be specified in NUT as a method with a name R in the following way:

```
R : x1, ... , xm -> y1, ... , yn { f };
```

Hence, there is correspondence between functional constraints and methods specified by a class.

Let us look at the example:

```
Class compl:(var
            re, im : num;
            mod, arg : num;

        rel
            retomod : re, im -> mod, arg {mod:=sqrt(re^2 + im^2);
                                          arg:=arccos(re/mod)};
            modtore : mod, arg -> re, im {re:=mod * cos(arg);
                                          im:=mod * sin(arg)});
```

The two relations `retomod`, `modtore` of the class `compl` are specified by the following two parts. First, they have external views of constraints which specify their input and output parameters and give some type information, i.e. explicit information about their input and output parameters written to the left and to the right of an arrow:

```
re, im -> mod, arg
mod, arg ->  re, im
```

This external information of constraints is used for planning computations when a constraint problem is solved (see (Tyugu and Uustalu 1993) in this book).

Second, specification of these relations contain programs written in an imperative language which is a part of NUT. These programs implement the methods. This is the semantics of the specifications used in object-oriented computations. The second relation describes a method with an input variables *mod* and *arg* and output variables *re* and *im* which can be invoked by a message *modtore*.

Any method specified in the class defines a node of the constraint network of every object of the class. This node is labelled by the name of the method and there are arcs binding the node with inputs and outputs of the method. If there is an object $C1$ of class *compl*, methods *retomod* and *modtore* give the following two nodes:

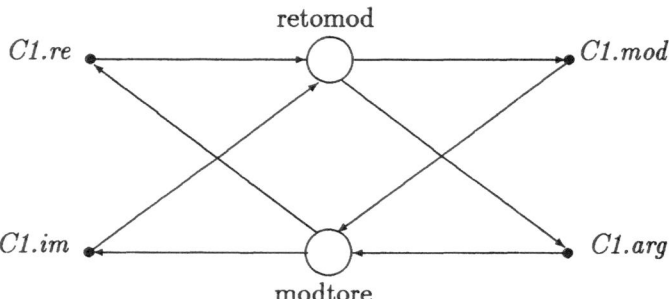

Let us remark that any solvable arithmetic equation can be replaced by a set of specifications of methods representing its functions f_i (cf. previous Sec.). For example the equation $y = 2x$ is equivalent to the following methods:

```
rel
  R1 : x -> y {y:=2*x};
  R2 : y -> x {x:=y/2};
```

4.2.3.4 Identity relations NUT has a large number of specific language constructions that allow to describe specification transformations which are usual for object oriented programming. Some of these features can be effectively specified using different kinds of identity relations.

Identity in the NUT means that two (or more) objects have the same component values. This does not mean automatically that these objects are of the same type, however there must be some correspondence between the types of components of related objects.

In the simplest case when two numeric objects x and y are defined to be identical, it means that there is an equation

$$x = y$$

together with its standard semantics as it was described in previous Section. Identity relation between objects is syntactically specified in the same form, i.e. it looks like an equation. However, the semantics of such a relation is more complicated and depends on the order of components being specified in classes. Omitting here details one can read in (Tyugu 1988, page 78), we demonstrate this feature in the case of binding construction.

Bindings are amendments to types introduced by the specifications of components, and they introduce additional constraints. Let us consider an example where one has defined a triangle as a connection of three line segments:

```
triangle : ( var
                AB : Bar ;
                BC : Bar P=AB.Q;
                CA : Bar P=BC.Q, Q=AB.P;
                perimeter : num;
             rel
                perimeter=AB.length+BC.length+CA.length);
```

The binding P=AB.Q In the specification

```
                BC : Bar P=AB.Q
```

says that the end point of side AB is identical to the first point of side BC, i.e. sides AB and BC have a common point.

Bindings can be considered as syntactic sugar, i.e. they can be syntactically easily transformed into the remaining part of the language, except for the case where type variables are involved. Bindings enable us to write specifications in a shorter form. Let us compare the last class specification with another equivalent one where identity of points is defined explicitly using equation.

```
triangle : ( var
                AB, BC, CA : Bar ;
                perimater : num;
             rel
                AB.Q=BC.P;
                BC.Q=CA.P;
                CA.Q=AB.P;
                perimeter=AB.length+BC.length+CA.length);
```

Despite of different syntax, in both cases, the identity relation AB.Q=BC.P generates two equations, one for both components of the point: $ABC.AB.Q.x = ABC.BC.P.x$ and $ABC.AB.Q.y = ABC.BC.P.y$. Both equations, in turn, generate 2 constraints as this was described in Sec. 4.2.3.2.

4.2.4 Specification of Computational Problems

NUT performs partial constraint satisfaction by means of algorithms for structural synthesis of programs ((Mints and Tyugu 1983) and (Tyugu and Uustalu 1993)). A request for program construction can appear in the NUT system in different forms. First, we discuss the simplest and generally applicable form. A message of the following form can be sent to any object x in the NUT system:

$$x.\texttt{compute}(y, \ldots, z)$$

where y,..., z are components of the object x. This is a request to compute values of y,...,z and to save these values in the object x. In order to compute the values of y,...,z, the class of x, extended with the already existing values of components of x will be used as a specification of this problem. This message fails, if some of the components in the list are not computable from the given specification. Let us consider the following class declarations.

```
Class circle : ( var
                    a, d, p, S : num;
                rel
                    d= 2 * r;
                    S= pi * r ^ 2;
                    p = 2 * pi * d );

Class square : ( var
                    a, d, p, S : num;
                rel
                    d^2 = 2 * a ^ 2;
                    S = a ^ 2;
                    p = 4 * a );


Class problem1 : ( var
                    q : square;
                    c : circle;
                rel
                    c.d=q.a;
                    q.a=13;
                    x=q.S - c.S );
```

Now, after creating an object *fig* by means of the following statement

```
fig:=new problem1
```

we can compute the solution of the problem shown in Fig. 4.4 simply by sending the message

```
fig.compute(x).
```

The list of components in parentheses may be empty:

```
fig.compute().
```

In this case, all components which are computable will be evaluated and the values will be kept in the state of the object **fig**. The message **compute** with empty list of components never fails.

Another possibility to specify a request for program construction is to ask for automatic synthesis of a method. If a class specification contains sufficient information for computing components $y_1,...,y_n$ from other components $x_1,...,x_m$, then a method, let us call it r, with the axiom $x_1,...,x_m \longrightarrow y_1,...,y_n$ can be synthesized, using the following specification in the relations part of the class:

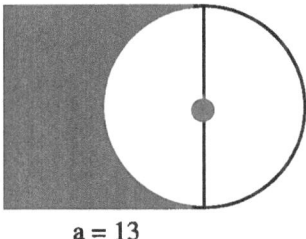

$$a = 13$$

Fig. 4.4. A computational problem

$$r: x1,\ldots, xm \rightarrow y1,\ldots, yn \ \{spec\}$$

The keyword **spec** in the program part is a request for sythesizing a program from the class specification where this keyword is being used. The input and output variables of the program are given in the axiom of the method.

As an example, we can extend the class **problem1** by adding a method for computing the value of the desired result :

```
Class problem2 : ( var
                  q : square a=13;
                  c : circle d=q.a;
                rel
                  result: -> x {spec}
                  x=q.S - c.S );
```

Now the following sequence of statements will compute the result:

```
fig:=new problem2;
fig.result()
```

In order to set a program which solves the problem for an arbitrary value of the side of the square, we have to drop the binding a=13 in the specification of the class, and add the input variable $q.a$ into the axiom of the method result:

```
Class problem3 : ( var
                  q : square;
                  c : circle d=q.a;
                rel
                  x=q.S - c.S;
                  result: q.a -> x {spec} );
```

Then we can write

```
fig:= new problem3;
fig.result(13)
```

for computing the desired result for the side x of the square. One can add more
methods of this kind to the class **problem1**, for example:

```
Class problem4 : ( var
                q : square;
                c : circle d=q.a;
              rel
                x=q.S - c.S;
                result: q.a -> x {spec};
                reverse: x -> q.a {spec};
                fromradius: c.r -> x {spec} );
```

However, in general, every method of the form

$$r: x \to y \ \{spec\}$$

can be modelled by an assignment and the message compute, as shown below
for the method *reverse* in an object w of the class **problem4**:

```
w:= new problem4;
w.x(13);
w.compute(q.a);
```

4.2.5 Some Important Extensions

4.2.5.1 Variables of Type *any* In this section we describe some important
features of NUT language which give it flexibility for specification of constraints.

The type variable **any** provides an interesting form of polymorphism to
the language, which can be used in object-oriented computations as parametric
polymorphism, but has a more general interpretation in specifications – components of an object of type **any** can be referred to before the type of this
object will be concretely specified. The following class represents computationally a concept of maximum of a function. It can be used in a combination with
any class representing a function which has numeric components *arg*, *val* for
representing argument and value of the function.

```
Class max : ( var
              argmax, maxval:num;
              fun:any;
            rel
              r:(fun.arg -> fun.val) -> argmax, maxval {g} );
```

where g is a method for finding maximum of a function. For example, if a
function is represented by the class

```
Class f : ( var
              arg,val:num;
            rel
              val= 1 - arg ^ 2 );
```

then the following class specifies a problem of finding maximum *my* of the function represented by f and the value of the argument *mx* at the maximum of the function:

```
Class problem5 : ( var
                   mx,my ; num;
                   function : f;
                   m : max fun = function,
                           argmax = mx, maxfun = my );
```

4.2.5.2 Higher Order Functional Constraints Let us look at the implementation of the method r in the class *max*:

```
r:(fun.arg -> fun.val) -> argmax, maxval {g};
```

The axiom shows us that the program g, which is an implementation of the method, has one argument and this argument must be a function. The program g can be written directly in the NUT language. It will contain statements which call its functional argument. These statements are called subtask statements of NUT, because a nested implication in an axiom defines a subtask in program construction. In the present example, this is the subtask of finding a function for computing *fun.val* from *fun.arg*, defined by the implication

```
fun.arg -> fun.val
```

In a program, the subtasks are referred to by the number showing their position in the axiom of the program, and their calls have the following form:

```
subtask <integer>(<parameters>)
```

The integer is the subtask number, parameters are passed positionally by value to the variables in the subtask. The subtask statement

```
subtask 1(x, y)
```

in the text of a program g means a call of the function for computing *fun.val* from *fun.arg* synthesized automatically on the class where the method is described. Value of x is passed to *fun.arg* and, after the execution of the function, value of y is received from *fun.val*. There are two kinds of subtasks with subtle but important difference in semantics. A subtask which has the form

```
[<arguments> -> <results>]
```

in an axiom, and has been used above, requests the synthesis of a program on the current state of the object where the method is executed, i.e. it takes into account all values of components available at this time. Another form of the subtask is

```
[<class name> |-- <arguments> -> <results>]
```

This subtask requests synthesis of a program on a new object of the given class and uses purely the properties of the class, ignoring the environment where the request was given.

We demonstrate the usage of a higher order function on an example of a class *map* which models the corresponding functional operator, i.e. it computes an output array b, mapping the function onto elements of an input array a and applying it to them. A virtual component *mapfun* represents the function implicitly. The function must be synthesized according to the subproblem

```
[mapfun.arg -> mapfun.res] .
```

The object *mapfun* has class **any**, but it must contain components *arg* and *res* which represent argument and result values of the mapped function.

```
Class map : ( var
                a,b:array of num;
              vir
                mapfun:any;
              rel
                r:[mapfun.arg -> mapfun.res] a -> b
                       {for i to length(a) do
                               x:=a[i];
                               subtask 1(x,y);
                               b[i]:=y
                       od} );
```

By describing other functional programming operators: *filter*, *reduce* etc., one can easily develop a set of concepts for functional programming in NUT. However, syntax of this functional language will be different from the conventional syntax of functional programming languages.

4.2.5.3 Production Rules

Using purely functional constraints does not allow us to specify abstract features of objects. To overcome this shortage NUT has been extended by Horn clause logic. This is intended for meta-level reasoning about problems and specifications and provides generality and logical power to the NUT system.

Using productions in specifications one can represent facts and rules. Productions can be used for generating new facts and also for computations almost like in Prolog. The following are examples of facts:

```
-> father ( John, Jack ) ;
-> father ( Jack, Jim ) ;
```

and this is a rule:

```
father (@x,@y) & father(@y,@z) -> grandfather (@u,@x,@z);
```

The rules contain metavariables which are identifiers beginning with the character @ and denote objects of the NUT language. The rule given above enables us to produce a new fact:

```
-> grandfather(,John, Jim)
```

from two given facts. The words **father** and **grandfather** denote predicates which can be:

- abstract predicates without any particular realization,

- names of programs,

- names of classes.

In the latter case they are characteristic predicates of classes and this type of predicates is especially useful for describing general laws for classes and objects.

For instance, the following rule

```
point(@u) & point(@v) -> bar(@t, @u, @v)
```

says that if we have two objects of the class *point*, then we can form a new object of the class *bar*. This rather general rule can be applied for extending specifications in solving a number of geometric problems.

Another example of this kind is a rule about distance on a straight line: if the distance from point A to point B is equal to $L1$ and the distance from point B to point C is equal to $L2$, then the distance from A to C is $L1 + L2$. With a class distance:

```
Class distance : ( var
                   A, B : Point;
                   Length : num );
```

we can write a specification of the following from:

```
R: distance A = P, B = Q:
```

or, more briefly:

```
R: distance P, Q:
```

if we use positional binding of components of a class. (P is bound with the first and Q with the second component.)

We can use the class *distance* in a completely different way and write an atomic formula:

```
distance (@x, @y, @z) .
```

This formula contains three variables @x, @y, @z which can be unified with the objects R, P, Q of the specification:

```
R: distance P, Q;
```

and the NUT system can transform it automatically into the following atomic formula:

```
distance (R,P,Q).
```

This can be used as a fact in a production; for example, the law for distance can be written as follows:

```
collinear(@x, @y, @z) &
  distance(@u, @x, @y, @L1) &
    distance(@v, @y, @z, @L2)
      -> distance(@w, @x, @z, @L1 + @L2);
```

This production means that whenever there are three collinear points $@x, @y, @z$ and there is a distance $@u$ of the length $@L1$ between the points $@x$ and $@y$, and another distance $@v$ of the length $@L2$ between the points $@y$ and $@z$, then a new specification for distance can be introduced automatically for the points $@x$ and $@z$.

4.2.6 Summary

Development of NUT is an attempt to incorporate constraint programming into an object-oriented programming framework. This has been done by 1) using classes as a source of information for constraint satisfaction; 2) introducing a special type of messages – the compute messages, which are requests for automatic program construction and execution. This is a dynamic way to apply program synthesis, when existing values of components of objects are taken into account. Methods can be synthesized also purely from class specifications, not taking into account the previous results of computations. This is done, when the keyword **spec** is being used as a body of a message. This is a static approach to program synthesis. Synthesized programs can appear as values of parameters of methods, adding a flavour of higher-orderness to the language, which gives us the most dynamic way to synthesize programs.

Acknowledgements We are much indebted to Mari Kõpp, Mihail Matskin and Benjamin Volozh for polishing the present version of the NUT system. We wish also to express our gratitude to our other colleagues at the Estonian Academy of Sciences by whom the first version of NUT was designed and implemented. The authors would also like to thank Tarmo Uustalu for our fruitful discussions on the NUT system and many helpful comments on this paper.

References

Freuder, E.C., Wallace, R.J. (1992) *Partial Constraint Satisfaction.* – Artificial Intelligence, **58**, pp. 21–70.

Jaffar, J., Lassez J.-L. (1987) *Constraint Logic Programming.* – Proc. of the 14th ACM Symposium on Principles of Programming Languages. Munich, pp. 111–119.

Kalja, A., Pahapill, J. (1992) *Small Knowledge CAD Systems.* – Information Modelling and Knowledge Bases III: Foundations, Theory and Applications, IOC Press, Amsterdam, pp. 347–356 the 14th ACM Symposium on Principles of Programming Languages. Munich, 1987, pp. 111–119.

Kotov, V., Nariniani, A., Tyugu, E. (1989) *The USSR Academy of Sciences START Project.* – Information Processing 89 (IFIP'89). North Holland, pp. 623–626.

Mackworth, A.K. (1992) *The Logic of Constraint Satisfaction.* – Artificial Intelligence, **58**, pp. 3–20.

Matskin, M. (1991) *NUT System papers.* – Computer Science Department. Aarhus University, DAIMI MD–59.

Matskin, M., Tyugu, E. (1992) *The NUT language.* – TRITA-TCS-SE-92-TR. Royal Institute of Technology, Stockholm.

Mints, G., Tyugu, E. (1983) *Justification of the Structural Synthesis of Programs.* – Science of Computer Programming, **2**, no. 3, pp. 215–240.

Mints, G., Tyugu, E. (1988) *The Programming System PRIZ.* – Journal of Symbolic Computations, **5**, pp. 359–375.

Mints, G., Tyugu, E. (1990) *Propositional Logic Programming and the PRIZ system.* – Journal of Logic Programming, **9** no. 2-3, pp. 179–194.

Penjam, J. (1990) *Computational and Attribute Models of Formal Languages.* – Theoretical Comp. Sci., **71**, pp. 241–264.

Saraswat, V. (1990) *Concurrent Constraint Programming.* – Proc. of the 17th ACM Symposium on Principles of Programming Languages. San Francisco, pp. 232–245.

Smolka, G., Henz, M., Wurtz, J. (1993) *Object-Oriented Concurrent Constraint Programming in Oz.* – DFKI RR-933-16. Saarbrucken.

Tyugu, E., Matskin M., Penjam J., Eomois P. (1986) *NUT – An Object-Oriented Language.* – Computers and Artificial Intelligence, **5**, no. 6, pp. 521–542.

Tyugu, E. (1988) *Knowledge-Based Programming.* – Addison-Wesley, N.Y., 1988.

Tyugu, E. (1991) *Three New-Generation Software Environments.* – Communications of the ACM, **34**, pp. 46–59.

Tyugu, E., Uustalu, T. (1993) *Higher-Order Functional Constraint Networks.* – In B. Mayoh, E. Tyugu, J. Penjam (eds.) Constraint Programming. NATO ASI Series F, Vol. 131. Springer-Verlag, Berlin, 1994 (this volume).

4.3 Interval Constraint Programming in C++

Eero Hyvönen, Stefano De Pascale and Aarno Lehtola

VTT, Technical Research Centre of Finland
Information Systems, P.O.Box 1201, 02044 VTT, Finland
{eero.hyvonen | stefano.depascale | aarno.lehtola }@vtt.fi

Abstract

This paper discusses, how to extend C++ language with classes for interval function evaluation and constraint satisfaction. Three portable general purpose libraries for the tasks are being implemented: INT++, IAF++ and INC++. The main innovation of these systems is combination of algebraic and numerical·IA techniques with constraint satisfaction techniques for evaluating interval functions globally and for obtaining better than local solutions for interval constraint satisfaction problems. Our practical goal is to provide the main stream programmer with easy to use, portable C++ libraries that can be used in applications without deep understanding of interval analysis.

Keywords

Constraint programming, interval arithmetic, computer algebra.

4.3.1 Interval programming

Interval arithmetic (IA) (Moore, 1966) generalizes ordinary arithmetic by using intervals in addition to precise numbers. This makes it possible to compute with incomplete, uncertain or partly erroneous data. Since interval arithmetic is largely domain independent, it makes sense to support it by extensions to programming languages or by subroutine libraries. Several systems have been implemented for the task, such as Triplex (Cole, Morrison, 1982), Pascal-SC (Bohlender et al., 1987), Fortran-SC (Kulisch, 1987), IP++ (Alander, 1987), PBasic (Aberth, 1988), VPI (Ely, 1990).

The traditional application focus of IA implementations has been management of rounding errors due to finite machine arithmetic. Artificial Intelligence (AI) research has provided new application fields for interval evaluaton techniques, especially when dealing with various interval labeling (Davis, 1987) or interval constraint satisfaction problems (ICSP) (Hyvönen, 1992). Such problems are encountered if only inexact or incomplete numerical information is available—a typical situation in application fields like scheduling and planning

(Stefik, 1981; Fox, 1983), worst case analysis (Skelboe, 1979), qualitative reasoning (Kuipers, Berleant, 1988), designing (Elias, 1986; Steinberg, 1987; Murtagh, Shimura, 1990), constraint programming (Cohen, 1990) , graphical interfaces (Sutherland, 1963; Borning, 1979; 1986), spreadsheets (Konopasek, Jayaraman, 1984; Hyvönen 1991), mathematical problem solving (Gosling, 1983; Babitchev, 1993). As a result, interval extensions have recently been suggested and implemented into AI programming languages, too, like Lisp (Hyvönen, 1991a), Prolog (Cleary, 1987; Older, Vellino, 1990, 1993) and constraint programming languages CHIP (Lee, van Emden, 1991a) and CLP(R) (Lee, van Emden, 1991b). In contrast to traditional IA implementations, interval extensions in AI languages treat arithmetical expressions declaratively as relational constraints, not as ordinary directed interval functions to be evaluated. In the constraint approach, all variables involved in a function or other expression are evaluated in terms of the others, not only the function value.

This paper discusses implementation of interval function evaluation and constraint satisfaction in C++. Three closely related extensions or tools are discussed:

1. INT++ library implements the notion of interval, and traditional local evaluation of basic interval functions.

2. IAF++ (Hyvönen, De Pascale, 1993) is a library for evaluating interval functions globally in one direction.

3. INC++ (Hyvönen et al., 1993) library makes it possible to evaluate interval expressions and sets of them symmetrically, i.e., to solve interval CSPs.

In comparison with other interval arithmetic systems, the libraries are argued to have several theoretical and practical attractions: First, IAF++ solves the problem of interval function evaluation globally like global optimizers (Ratscheck, Rokne, 1988). This is in contrast with IA extensions such as (Cole, Morrison, 1982; Bohlender et al., 1987; Kulisch, 1987; Alander, 1987; Aberth, 1988; Ely, 1990) that evaluate interval expressions locally (local/global controversy will be discussed in more detail later). IAF++ also has special extensions needed in interval constraint satisfaction tasks, like the possibility of evaluating recursive interval expressions.

Second, a major limitation of current interval constraint satisfaction systems is that only local solutions are found in the general case, not global ones. INC++ is able to determine better than local solutions by applying a combination of numerical interval analysis (Ratscheck, Rokne, 1988), algebraic manipulation (Davenport, 1993) and tolerance propagation techniques (Hyvönen, 1992). For example, a single constraint equation can be solved globally even if it contains multiple variable instances.

Third, from the practical viewpoint, a major problem of current logic programming and Lisp-based systems is that—at least for the time being—they do not integrate well with main stream computing. INT++, IAF++ and INC++ are implemented as portable C++ libraries to overcome problems of integration, portability, and efficiency.

In the following, we first review some IA techniques and present INT++ and IAF++ libraries. After this, problems of solving ICSPs are discussed and solution approaches taken in INC++ are in focus. Finally, current state of research and directions for further work are outlined.

4.3.2 Interval arithmetic techniques

IA usually deals with closed real *intervals* X that are represented as real number pairs: $X = [a, b] = \{x \mid a \le x \le b\}$. Primitive algebraic functions can easily be generalized into the interval case. For example, if $\circ$ is one of the operators $+, -, *, \text{or} /$, then the corresponding interval generalization is defined as:

$$X \circ Y = [x_1, x_2] \circ [y_1, y_2] = x \circ y \mid x_1 \le x \le x_2, y1 \le y \le y_2 \tag{1}$$

For computational purposes, definitions of the functions relating the bounds of argument intervals to the bounds of the resultant interval can be derived:

$$[x, y] + [u, v] = [x + u, y + v] \tag{2}$$

$$[x, y] - [u, v] = [x - v, y - u]$$

$$[x, y] * [u, v] = [\min(xu, xv, yu, yv), \max(xu, xv, yu, yv)]$$

$$[x, y]/[u, v] = [x, y] * [1/v, 1/u], 0 \notin [u, v]$$

The rules follow directly from (1). The same function symbols can be used for both interval and exact value operations. Which operation is in question can be determined by the arguments. These definitions can be generalized also for open intervals, see e.g. (Cleary, 1987). Another possibility is to represent open ends by slightly smaller/larger numbers and use then closed intervals. This simple approach is currently employed in our libraries: Function expressions to be evalutated may contain intervals, like [2,3), but these are converted internally into closed intervals, like [2,2.999···].

4.3.2.1 Interval function evaluation The main problem in evaluating IA functions follows from the fact that IA differs from exact value arithmetic with respect to some algebraic laws. For example, distributive law does not hold in interval arithmetic. Assuming $X = [1, 2]$ we get

$$X * (X - X) = [1, 2] * ([1, 2] - [1, 2]) = [1, 2] * [-1, 1] = [-2, 2]$$

but:

$$X * X - X * X = [1, 2] * [1,] - [1, 2] * [1, 2] = [1, 4] - [1, 4] = [-3, 3]$$

However, for any intervals X, Y, and Z the following *subdistributive* law holds:

$$X * (Y + Z)X * Y + X * Z \qquad (3)$$

This means that equality does not necessary hold between algebraic expression that are equivalent in ordinary algebra. The situation is not as bad as it may seem because of the following results that holds for interval expressions $F(X_1, \cdots, X_n)$ made out of ordinary algebraic functions (rational, exponentials, trigonometric etc. functions) (see e.g. Moore, 1979):

1. If $F(X_1, \cdots, X_n)$ is evaluated by using straightforward definitions of interval operators, then the value Y obtained always contains the actual range of F-values, i.e., $F(X_1, \cdots, X_n) \subseteq Y$. Interval evaluation is safe and never "loses" possible values.

2. It can be shown that if $F(X_1, \cdots, X_n)$ does not have multiple instances of a variable, like in the left hand side of (3), then $F(X_1, \cdots, X_n)$ evaluates the actual range of F-values with any argument intervals.

Hence, functional expressions with unique variable instances like $X * (Y + Z)$ can be evaluated easily by simply applying interval functions like (1) locally, i.e., independently of each other according to the expression. The only problem is functions with multiple variable instances like $X * Y + X * Z$. Evaluating such functions essentially means solving the global unconstrained optimization problem (Ratschek, Rokne, 1988; Horst, Tuy, 1990).

Research in interval arithmetic has produced both numerical and algebraic techniques for evaluating the minimum and maximum of arithmetical functions. A major attraction of these techniques is guaranteed safety. Unlike traditional iterative techniques based on exact values, IA techniques are guaranteed to find bounds for the functions up to arbitrary precision without the fear of losing any feasible solutions. In the following, we review some numerical and algebraic IA techniques that are essential to research in interval constraint satisfaction.

4.3.2.2 Numerical algorithms Numerical interval function evaluation algorithms are needed for evaluating expressions with multiple variable instances. The algorithms used are based on the Skelboe algorithm (Skelboe, 1974) and its various derivatives (Asaithambi et al., 1982; Ratschek, Rokne, 1984, 1988; Moore, 1992). These algorithms employ branch-and-bound search techniques: Argument intervals are inspected in parts and efficiency is gained by identifying and pruning irrelevant subintervals from consideration as early as possible. As pruning criteria, various properties of the function, like the values of its first and second derivatives, and results from earlier evaluations are used.

4.3.2.3 Algebraic techniques Numerical IA algorithms can produce arbitrally close outward approximations for interval function values. However, their computational complexity often dramatically depends on the algebraic representation of the function, i.e., on its *extension*. The most straightforward extensional representation F of a function f is the *natural extension* where the operators of f are simply replaced by corresponding interval operators in F. For example, given $x = [0, 4]$, the natural extension of polynomial

$$y = pow(x, 4) - 10 * pow(x, 3) + 35 * pow(x, 2) - 50 * x + 24 \qquad (4)$$

evaluates $y = [-816, 840]$ although the actual range of values is $[-1, 24]$.

However, there are rules and ways for representing interval extensions that usually evaluate stricter results than the natural extension. The natural extension can be modified by using IA laws. For example, based on the subdistributivity law $I(J + K) \subseteq IJ + IK$ of IA, it is always useful to apply the form $I * (J + K)$ instead of $I * J + I * K$. Another possibility is to use *centred forms* (Moore, 1966) where idea is to shift origin so that argument intervals fall around 0. This minimizes absolute values of interval limits and interval functions are likely to evaluate intervals of less width. In (Ratschek, Rokne, 1984) general canonical representations for rational functions are derived. Still another possibility is to use the *mean value form* (Moore, 1966) Fm. For a single variable function $F(X)$ this form is $F_m(X) = f(c) + F'(X)(X - c)$ where c is the centre of X (or more generally $c \in X$). Mean value form $F_m(X)$ is a simple version of the more general Taylor form (Ratschek, Rokne, 1984) based on the function's Taylor expansion.

There is no general solution to the problem of determining the best extensional form. The excess width of the resultant interval depends both on the properties of the function and on the argument interval values. The most efficient way for determining the actual value of an interval function is heuristic combination of numerical and algebraic techniques discussed above, i.e., to derive efficient extensional forms and to apply numerical interval function evaluation techniques to them, if needed. This is the approach taken in our research.

4.3.3 Local function evaluator INT++

The simplest extension to C++ in our library set is INT++ that implements local interval function evaluation. The library contains class Interval with overloaded operators and definitions for evaluating basic interval arithmetic functions (+, -, *, /, log, exp, etc.) and combined expressions.

Using INT++ library functions is easy. The user simply evaluates arithmetic expressions like in ordinary C++ programming. This is possible because of the overloading facility of C++. For instance, the local value $y = [-816, 840]$ of the polynomial example (4) can be computed and printed as follows:

```
Interval x(0, 4); // Construct an Interval
Interval y = x^4 - 10 * x^3 + 35 * x^2 - 50 * x + 24;
print f("y = [%g, %g] \n", y. Min (), y. Max ());
```

The library also contains a machine independent error management facility. Consider following example:

```
Interval x(-4, -1); // Construct an Interval
Interval y = pow(x, 0.5);
for (int i = 0; i < y. GetErrorCount(); i++)
print f("%s\n", y. GetError(i));
```

Member function GetErrorCount() evaluates here a non-negative value indicating the number of errors encountered during evaluation. Member GetError(i) can then be used to read corresponding error messages. In this case the previous code would print:

```
# Error: Root of negative interval.
```

Interval functions have been implemented in a way that takes into account the finite precision of machine arithmetic. Intervals can be rounded outward to the nearest representable machine number by an explicit call to a rounding function Round() that manipulates the bit representation of the doubles internally. This guarantees that the resultant interval definitely includes all possible values even in cases where rounding errors degenerate results (Forsythe, 1970).

The interval constructor constructs a closed interval by default. If needed, its limits can be opened by members OpenMin(), OpenMax() or Open() that makes both limits open.

4.3.4 Global function evaluator IAF++

IAF++ library (Hyvönen, DePascale, 1993) implements global interval function evaluations in C++. The library provides the user with class IFunction, whose member functions perform necessary tasks for defining and evaluating interval functions.

Communication with IFunction is based on standard C++ data types, string pointers (char *) and doubles. The system is capable of evaluating the actual range of an interval function up to machine precision.

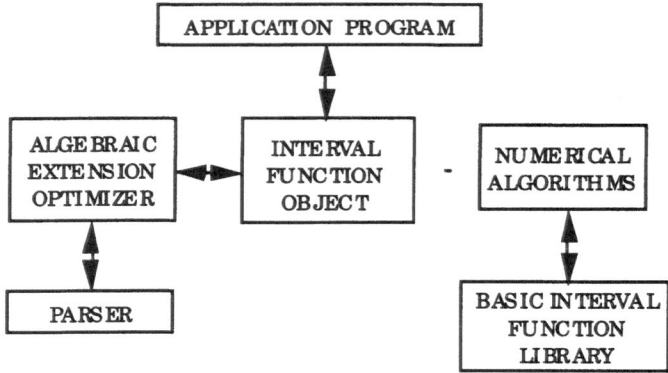

Fig.1 Architecture of IAF++ library.

4.3.4.1 Structure Figure 1 depicts the overall structure of IAF++. Class IFunction makes use of four major modules discussed briefly below.

1. *Parser.* A parser is implemented for transforming interval function expressions into an internal representation. This makes it possible to use ordinary mathematical notation when defining functions. The parser has been produced by using metacompilers Yacc++ and Lex++ of Unix, and can be extended and maintained easily.

2. *Algebraic extension optimizer.* The algebraic extension optimizer transforms the parsed representation into a form optimal for interval arithmetic evaluations. Our system makes use of a set of algebraic transformation rules, canonical representation of polynomials (Davenport et al., 1993) , a symbolic algorithm for rational division, a rule base for optimization, an equation solver, and an algebraic series generator. The optimizer applies heuristic rules to decide what algebraic form to use for different functions. This module is not seen by the end user: IAF++ is designed to be used without deeper knowledge of interval arithmetic.

3. *Basic interval function library.* IAF++ makes use of INT++ library discussed above.

4. *Numerical algorithms.* With functions having multiple variable instances, IAF++ uses numerical interval analysis techniques that depend on the differentiability and other properties of the function. Selecting the method is an automatic internal decision based on heuristics. The computation can be controlled by the user, e.g., by defining sufficient precision level

and a time limit for computations (see below). The system is capable of estimating excess width of the resulting interval.

4.3.4.2 Programming with IAF++ Applications of IAF++ are created simply by including a header file IAF.h in the user program file and by linking the library file with the application. Using an IFunction object involves following steps:

1. Construct an IFunction instance, e.g., one named E.

2. Define (or redefine) the interval function $F(X_1, \cdots, X_n)$ for E, unless not already defined during step (1).

3. Set argument values of $F(X_1, \cdots, X_n)$. If a value is not given, a wide default value is used.

4. Modify optional computational parameters of E if needed.

5. Evaluate E and read the result.

For example, following C++ code would evaluate the so called Goldstein & Price function

$$z = 30 + (2*x - 3*y)^2 * (18 - 32*x + 12*x^2 + 48*y - 36*x*y + 27*y^2) \quad (5)$$

that is known to be difficult for global optimizers:

```
double min, max; // Variables for the result
// Construct a function object
IFunction fn("z = 30 + (2 * x − 3 * y)^2*"
"(18 − 32 * x + 12 * x^2 + 48 * y − 36 * x * y + 27 * y^2)");
fn.SetValue ("x", −2, 2); // Set x = [−2, 2]
fn.SetValue ("y", −2, 2); // Set y = [−2, 2]
// Set optional computational parameters, here precision
fn.SetRelativePrecision (0.001);
fn.SetAbsolutePrecision (0.001);
fn.Evaluate (&min, &max); // Evaluate and read
print f (''The value is: [%g, %g]\n", min, max);
```

The code would print value $[2.99 \cdots, 47830]$. If the natural extension function were evaluated by ordinary local interval arithmetic, the result would have been $[-28570, 47830]$——the local solution is much wider than the global one.

The function object constructed can be redefined and evaluated with different argument and parameter values. Before evaluating the function (step 5 above), optional parameters for the computation can be (re)set by the public member functions of class IFunction. Major computational parameters settable by the user are:

1. Outward rounding

IAF++ can optionally use outward rounding (OR) interval arithmetic. OR makes it possible to eliminate many problems of finite machine precision encountered in various mathematical situations (Forsythe, 1971; Ely 1990). For a simple example, if $Z = X - Y, X = 9.99E34, Y = 9.98E34$, then obviously $Z = 1E32$. However, by using our HP machine and C++ double precision floating point numbers the rounding error is 8.81E18 (!) due to finite machine arithmetic precision. By using OR it is possible to obtain an interval containing the correct result.

2. Precision

IAF++ evaluates interval functions by increasing a downward approximation min- for the minimum and by decreasing upward approximation max$^+$ for the maximum of the function. Computation is terminated and interval [min$^-$, max$^+$] is used as the result, when the approximations are close enough to an in internally maintained interval [min, max] that is known be a subinterval of the final result. This subinterval is obtained as a byproduct of the numerical algorithms used. By comparing the two intervals, IAF++ is able to give inward error estimates for the minimum and maximum. This data may be useful, for example, when computations are terminated due to user specified time limits (see below). Accuracy of the estimate itself depends on the machine arithmetic.

IAF++ uses both absolute and relative precision criteria; either criterion alone may terminate computation. Termination criteria for the absolute case are:

$$\text{min- min}^- \leq \text{precision}$$
$$\text{max}^+ - \text{max} \leq \text{precision I}$$

In the relative case, the criteria are:

$$(\text{min-min}^-) \ / \ \text{min} \leq \text{precision}$$
$$(\text{max}^+\text{-max}) \ / \ \text{max} \leq \text{precision}$$

Relative criteria are useful especially when the absolute values of the interval limits are large, absolute criteria when they are around zero.

Desired precision may not be obtained by using outward rounding arithmetic, if rounding errors due to finite machine precision are greater than the desired precision. IAF++ is capable of terminating computation also in this case and will return an estimate of the error.

3. Time limit

In many applications, response times within predefined limits must be guaranteed (e.g., in real time systems). IAF++ supports such applications by providing a settable time limit. If the resultant interval has not been obtained within the limit, computation is forcibly terminated. Here the last approximation for the result can then be read as the result together with an error estimate for it.

4. Local vs. global evaluation

By default, an interval function is evaluated globally by applying a numerical interval algorithm (if needed) to an algebraically optimized extensional form of the function. However, this global evaluation mode can be switched also to local mode. In local evaluation mode, the algebraically optimized function is evaluated only once without concerning problems of multiple variable instances. This mode can be useful in situations where fast response time is needed even at the price of extra excess width in the result.

Computational parameters of IAF++ make it possible to trade solution precision for computation time. This is essential because interval function evaluations are time consuming and computational time needed cannot usually be estimated before evaluation. In the simplest case, one may only demand the local solution that can be obtained easily. If more accurate results are needed, global techniques can be applied possibly with time limits. Notice that in every case the solution obtained correctly bounds the global solution: Interval constraint reasoning is safe and never loses exact solutions of the problem.

It is also possible for the user to interrupt IAF++ computation dynamically by hitting a control key. After interruption, IAF++ tells the user the current estimate for the result and asks whether he wants to continue or terminate computation.

4.3.4.3 Additional features for constraints Unlike other interval arithmetic evaluators, IAF++ has additional special features useful when applying it to solving interval CSPs.

1. *Setting the function value.* In ordinary systems the user is allowed to give only the values of the arguments X_i of a function $Y = F(X_1, \cdots, X_n)$. In IAF++, (s)he can also set the value variable Y. IAF++ can make use of this information and will usually find the solution more easily.

2. *Recursive functions.* In IAF++ it is the possible to evaluate recursive interval functions of form $X_i = F(X_1, \cdots, X_i, \cdots, X_n)$. For example, if x is solved recursively from the polynomial (4) and the result, say $x = (x^4 - 10 * x^3 + 35 * x^2 + 24)/50$ is evaluated with initial values $X = [-\infty, \infty]$ and $Y = 0$, then IAF++ finds the value $X = [0.999\cdots, 4.00\cdots]$. This is the range of the zeros $x = 1, x = 2, x = 3$,

and $x = 4$ of the original polynomial. Evaluating recursive functions is useful, for instance, in solving interval constraint satisfaction problems globally (Hyvönen, 1992).

3. Splitted intervals. Splitted interval arithmetic used in an earlier Lisp-implementation of ours (Hyvönen, 1991a) is being transported to IAF++, too. IAF++ will be capable of evaluating not only ordinary continuous intervals but more generally discontinuous intervals (Hyvönen, 1992).

4.3.5 Interval CSP evaluator INC++

IAF++ deals with evaluation of interval functions in one predefined direction. INC++ generalizes IAF++ by dealing with *interval constraints*, i.e., with equations and inequations relating a set of mutually dependent variable intervals. A function can be seen as an equation with a variable as either the left or right side; an inequation, say $F(..) >= G(..)$, can be represented as an equation as well, here $[-\infty, 0] = G(..) - F(..)$.

4.3.5.1 Interval CSPs In the general case, an ICSP (Hyvönen, 1992) may involve several constraints:

$$E_1, \cdots, E_n \qquad (6)$$

$$P_1 \in X_1, \cdots, P_m \in X_m$$

Here E_i are equations or inequations, P_j are variables used in them, and X_j are real intervals. The equations can easily be represented as a *constraint net* that consists of a set of variables and function constraints connecting them.

The *tolerance situation* $\{P_1 \in X_1, \cdots, P_m \in X_m\}$ in an ICSP (6) refers to a set of exact value situations $\{P_1 = x_1, \cdots, P_m = x_m \mid x_i \in X_i, i = 1 \cdots m\}$. An ICSP is *admissible* or *feasible* iff its tolerance situation has an exact subsituation satisfying all constraints (i.e., the equations have a solution within the intervals):

$$\exists\{P_1 = x_1 \in X_1, \cdots, P_m = x_m \in X_m\} : E_1, \cdots, E_n \text{satisfied}$$

A variable $P_i \in X_i$ is *consistent* iff *each* interpretation $P_i = x, x \in X_i$, can be satisfied with respect to all constraints by some exact subsituation:

$$\forall x \in X_i \exists\{P_1 = x_1 \in X_1, \cdots, P_i = x, \cdots, P_m = x_m \in X_m\} : E_1, \cdots, E_n \text{satisfied}$$

Intuitively, a tolerance should not contain "extra" values that cannot be satisfied within the given intervals. A tolerance situation is *(globally) consistent*, i.e., it is a (global) *tolerance solution*, iff its every variable is consistent. A variable is *locally* consistent iff it is consistent with respect to all directly connected constraints. Local consistency of a tolerance situation (solution) means that all variables are locally consistent.

In the general case, the solution of an ICSP may not be represented by a single interval solution, but as a set S of them. For reasons of convenience, these solutions can be generalized by the situation $G = \{P_1 \in X_1, \cdots, P_n \in X_n\}$ such that for $i = 1 \cdots n$, min (X_i) is the minimum and max(X_i) is the maximum of all values X_i in the solutions S. Hence, the solution G is the most constrained situation that can be obtained by refining the tolerances from both ends without losing exact value solutions. If splitted intervals are employed, the generalized solution can be represented more accurately by a single slitted interval situation.

4.3.5.2 Single constraint evaluation An important special case of the ICSP is evaluation of a single interval constraint $E(X_1, \cdots, X_n)$. If each variable X_i is solved algebraically from E and represented by a solution function $Y_i = F(X_1, \cdots, X_n)$, constraint E is consistent iff (Hyvönen, 1992):

$$Y_1 \subseteq F_1(X_1, \cdots, X_n), \cdots, Y_n \subseteq F_n(X_1, \subseteq, X_n)$$

INC++ uses an interval algebraic equation solver for extracting and optimizing efficient evaluable IA expressions for the solution functions. By this way INC++ can in principle solve globally any single interval constraint like (4) or (5) up to machine precision. To our knowledge, not other current system is capable of doing this, but constraints are solved more or less locally. For example, if (4) is evaluated with initial values $y = 0$ and $x = [-\infty, \infty]$, a local constraint reasoner cannot constrain x at all, while INC++ returns the global value $x = [0.999\cdots, 4.00\cdots]$.

4.3.5.3 Algebraic globalization In order to solve the ICSP in the general case (with several constraints) globally, dependencies between multiple variable instance in different constraints should be identified and their effects eliminated by either algebraic transformations or numerical techniques. One avenue towards this goal is global tolerance propagation techniques (Hyvönen, 1992).

Currently, only a limited but particularly important algebraic globalization scheme has been experimented with in INC++. This feature can be used to generalize the numerical computations of ordinary spreadsheets (Lotus 1-2-3, EXCEL, Quattro Pro etc.) into the interval case. From the mathematical viewpoint, current spreadsheets can be seen as very simple ICSPs where E_i are functions $Y_i = F_i(\cdots)$. The constraint net is topologically a forest, because it is assumed that F_i are not circularly (i.e., recursively) defined. Initially, each output cell, i.e., a root or an intermediate node in the forest, has value $Y_i = [-\infty, \infty]$ and input cells, i.e., the leafs, have exact values $X_i = [x_i, x_i] = x_i$. During computation, values are propagated from the leafs to the roots via functional constraints in a proper order.

When generalizing this simple computational paradigm into the interval case (Hyvönen, 1991b), a globalization problem is encountered: If functions are evaluated based on local cell definitions, only very wide local values can be obtained; global evaluations are not possible without deeper interval analysis. For example, consider cell functions $A2 = A1 * B1, C2 = B1 * C1$, and $B3 = A2 - C2$ illustrated in figure 2.

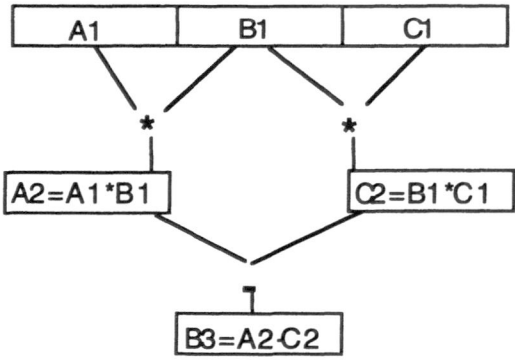

Fig.2 Spreadsheet functions.

If $A1 = C1 = 1$ and $B1 = [1, 2]$, then $B3 = (A1 * B1) - (B1 * C1) = [-1, 1]$ in standard (local) interval arithmetic although the actual range of $B3$ is, of course, $B3 = 1 * B1 - 1 * B1 = 0$.

In INC++, such global dependencies are detected and the system automatically constructs sufficiently, but not unnecessarily large global expressions for evaluating the actual range of values for each cell value in the direction defined by the cell functions. Furthermore, functions in INC++ may be circularly defined (which leads to recursive interval functions). In figure 2, for example, INC++ infers global function B3=B1*(A1-C1) for B3, other cell definitions remain as they are.

Notice that this kind of partial globalization in one direction does not mean that the whole net is completely globalized because the globalized constraints are still treated independently from each other. For a example, in

$$A = X * Y, B = Y/X$$

$$A = 1, B = 1, X \in [1/10, 10], Y \in [1/10, 10]$$

both constraints are globally consistent in separation. The net is locally consistent but not globally, because the global solution is $X = Y = 1$.

4.3.5.4 Programming with INC++ INC++ is based on IAF++. INC++ also makes use of an interval algebraic equation solver and two internal C++ classes. Class IConstraint implements the notion of a single interval constraint and class ICNet provides INC++ with procedures needed for constructing and maintaining larger constraint networks, and for algebraic globalization.

From the programmers point of view, INC++ can be used by calling a single class type Inc. Communication with Inc objects is based on a simple string and number based interface in the same fashion as with IFunction objects in IAF++. An Inc object is used in C++ code as follows:

1. Construct an Inc instance, e.g., one named E.

2. Define ICSP by inserting and/or removing constraints.

3. Set variable values in E.

4. Modify optional computational parameters of E if needed.

5. Evaluate E and read changed variable values, unfeasible constraints detected, or errors.

INC++ functionality becomes available by including a header file Inc.h in the application file and by loading the compiled application with INC++ library. To give an impression of how INC++ is used in an application program, the net of figure 2 is constructed and evaluated below:

```
Inc E;                                  // Construct sheet object
E.InsertConstraint ("1","A2 = A1*B1"); // Define functions
E.InsertConstraint ("2","C2 = B1*C1");
E.InsertConstraint ("3","B3=A2-C2");
E.SetValue ("B1", 1, 2);                // Set values
E.SetValue ("A1", 1);
E.SetValue ("C1",1);
int n = E.Evaluate(); // n indicates changed value count
char *var; // Name for changed variable
double min, max; // Variables for results
for (int i = 0; i<n; i++) {
E.GetChangedValue(i, &var, &min, &max);
printf("%s = [%g, %g]\n",var,min,max);
```

Function Evaluate() returns as its value the number of changed values. Changed variable names and values can then be read by member GetChanged-Value(). If the situation is detected unfeasible, Evaluate() would return a negative number -n indicating that n constraints were unfeasible. Names of these constraints can then be read in the same way as modified variable names in the for-loop above.

User-settable computational parameters used in INC++ are essentially the same as in IAF++ discussed before. One addition is the possibility of evaluating constraints either in one direction, called the *main direction*, or symmetrically. Algebraic globalization can be performed only with respect to the variable in the main direction, i.e, the *main variable*. For a function constraint $Y = F(\cdots)$, the main variable is function value Y. Another added feature is a tolerance relaxation (Hyvőnen, 1991b) scheme for enlargening intervals in infeasible situations in order to make them feasible again. Such a facility is needed, for example, when INC++ is used for interactive problem solving.

In order to test and demonstrate INC++, the library has been integrated with MicroSoft EXCEL spreadsheet program by a set of Dynamic Link Libraries (DLL). The system is a demonstration of a next generation interval spreadsheet

program that can be used not only for computing exact value functions in one direction (as usual) but more generally for evaluating interval functions and for solving interval CSPs.

4.3.6 Conclusions

During our research several experiments with implementing interval constraint satisfaction have been made. The first experiments were implemented in Lisp that allowed rapid prototyping. After getting insight into the problems involved, C++ has been used due to the practical reasons of integration, efficiency and portability. Currently, parts of the system are still under development and more features are being added (like splitted interval arithmetic). In addition, more tuning and empirical testing is needed. However, thus far results form the work seem promising.

A major problem one has to live with when dealing with IA is that the complexity of numerical interval computations is to a large extent unpredictable: It heavily depends on the functions evaluated and initial values used. Our solution to difficult situations is—in addition to trying to make the implementation as efficient as possible—the use of time limits, dynamic interrupts, and the possibility of getting excess width estimates for the returned value.

The main theoretical innovation of IAF++ and INC++ is to apply a combination of interval analysis, algebraic transformations and tolerance propagation techniques for determining local and global interval solutions in an efficient way. The system is planned to be made available to main stream programmers as a set of C++ libraries in MicroSoft Windows and Unix environments.

Acknowledgements

This work has been supported financially by Technology Development Centre of Finland (TEKES). We thank prof. Eero Peltola for discussions and support to our research and Trema Inc. and ViSolutions Inc. for co-operation.

References

Aberth, O. (1988) *Precise Numerical Analysis* (Wm. C. Brown, Dubuque).

Alander, J. (1985) On interval arithmetic range approximation methods of polynomials and rational functions, *Computers & Graphics* **9** (4) 365-372.

Alander, J. (1987) Programmer's manual of interval package IP++, Report TKO B62 (Helsinki University of Technology, Faculty of Information Technology, Espoo, Finland).

Asaithambi, N., Zuhe, S., Moore, R. (1982) On computing the range of values, *Computing* **28** 225-237.

Babichev, A., Kadyrowa, O., Kashevarove, T., Semenov, A. (1993) Unicalc — An intelligent solver for problems with imprecise and subdefinite data. International Conference on Numerical Analysis with Automatic Result Verification, Lafayette, USA, March 1993.

Bohlender, G., Ulrich, C., von Gudenberg, J., Rall, J. (1987) *Pascal-SC, a Computer Language for Scientific Computation* (Academic Press, New York, NY).

Borning, A. (1979) ThingLab - A constraint oriented simulation laboratory, Report CS-79-746 (Stanford University, Department of Computer Science).

Borning, A. (1986) Constraint-based tools for building user interfaces, *ACM Transactions on Graphics* **5** (4) 345-374.

Cleary, J.C. (1987) Logical arithmetic, *Future Computing Systems* **2** (2) 125-149.

Cohen, J. (1990) Constraint logic programming languages, *Comm. ACM* **33** (7).

Cole, A., Morrison, R. (1982) Triplex: A system for interval arithmetic, *Software Practice and Experience* **12** 341-350.

Davenport, J.H., Siret, Y., Tournier, E. (1993) *Computer Algebra - Systems and Algorithms for Algebraic Computation* (Academic Press, New York, NY).

Davis, E. (1987) Constraint propagation with interval labels, *Artificial Intell.* **32** 99-118.

Elias, A.L. (1986) Knowledge engineering of the aircraft design process, in: J.S. Kowalik, ed., *Knowledge Based Problem Solving* (Prentice-Hall, Englewood Cliffs, NJ) 213-256.

Ely, J. (1990) *Prospects for Using Variable Precision Interval Software in C++ for Solving some Contemporary Scientific Problems, dissertation* (The Ohio State University, Ohio).

Forsythe, G. (1970) Pitfalls in computation, or why math book is not enough, *Am. Math. Monthly* **77** 931-956.

Fox, M. (1983) *Constraint-Directed Search: A Case-Study of Job-Shop Scheduling, dissertation* (Carnegie-Mellon University, Department of Computer Science, Pittsburgh, Pennsylvania).

Gosling, J. (1983) *Algebraic Constraints*, dissertation (Carnegie-Mellon University, Department of Computer Science, Pittsburgh, Pennsylvania).

Hansen, E. (1988) An overview of global optimization using interval analysis, in: R. Moore, ed., *Reliability in Computing* (Academic Press, New York, NY) 289-307.

Horst, R., Tuy, H. (1990) *Global Optimization* (Springer-Verlag, Berlin).

Hyvönen, E. (1991a) *Constraint Reasoning with Incomplete Knowledge — The Tolerance Propagation Approach*, dissertation (Publications 72, VTT, Technical Research Centre of Finland, Espoo, Finland).

Hyvönen, E. (1991b) Interval constraint spreadsheets for financial planning, *Proceedings of the first International Conference on Artificial Intelligence Applications on Wall Street* (IEEE Press, New York).

Hyvönen, E. (1992) Constraint reasoning based on interval arithmetic — The tolerance propagation approach, *Artificial Intelligence* **58** 71-112.

Hyvönen, E., De Pascale, S. (1993) IAF++: An interval arithmetic function evaluator in C++, working paper (VTT, Technical Research Centre of Finland, Laboratory for Information Processing, Helsinki, Finland).

Hyvönen, E., De Pascale, S., Lehtola,, A. (1993) Interval constraint satisfaction tool INC++, *Proceedings of 5th International Conference on Tools with Artificial Intelligence*, Boston (IEEE Press, New York,).

Konopasek, M., Jayaraman, S. (1984) *The TK!Solver Book* (McGraw-Hill, Berkeley, California).

Kuipers, B., Berleant, D. (1988) Using incomplete quantitative knowledge in qualitative reasoning, *Proceedings of AAAI-88* (Morgan Kaufmann Publishers, Los Altos, California) 324-329.

Kulisch, U. (1987) FORTRAN-SC, a study of a FORTRAN extension for engineering/scientific computation with access to ACRITH (IBM).

Lee, J., vanEmden, M. (1991a) Numerical computation can be deduction in CHIP, paper (Department of Computer Science, University of Victoria, Canada).

Lee, J., vanEmden, M. (1991b) Adapting CLP(R) to floating point arithmetic, paper (Department of Computer Science, University of Victoria, Canada).

Leler, W. (1988) *Constraint Programming Languages. Their Specification and Generation* (Addison-Wesley, Reading, MA). Moore, R. (1966) Interval Arithmetic (Prentice-Hall, Englewood Cliffs, NJ).

Moore, R. (1979) Methods and Applications of Interval Analysis, SIAM Studies in Applied Mathematics (SIAM, Philadelphia).

Moore, R., Hansen, E., Leclerc, A. (1992) Rigorous methods for global optimization, In: *Recent Advances in Global Optimization* (Princeton University Press, Princeton) 321-342.

Murtagh, N., Shimura, M. (1990) Parametric engineering using constraint-based reasoning, *Proceedings of AAAI-90* (Morgan Kaufmann Publishers, Los Altos, California) 505-510.

Older, W., Vellino, A. (1990) Extending Prolog with constraint arithmetic on real intervals, in: *Proceedings of the Canadian Conference on Electrical and Computer Engineering.*

Older, W., Vellino, A. (1993) Constraint arithmetic on real intervals, in: F. Benhamou and A. Colmerauer, eds., *Constraint Logic Programming, Collected Research* (MIT Press, Cambridge, MA).

Ratscheck, H., Rokne, J. (1984) *Computer Methods for the Range of Functions* (Ellis Horwood, Chichister, England).

Ratscheck, H., Rokne, J. (1988) *New Computer Methods for Global Optimization* (Ellis Horwood, Chichister, England).

Skelboe, S. (1974) *Computation of rational interval functions*, BIT 14 (1) 87-95.

Steele, G.L. (1980) *The Definition and Implementation of a Computer Programming Language Based on Constraints*, dissertation (Massachusetts Institute of Technology, Department of Electrical Engineering and Computer Science, Cambridge, MA).

Stefik, M. (1981) Planning with constraints (MOLGEN: Part 1), *Artificial Intelligence* **16** 111-140.

Steinberg, L. (1987) Design as refinement plus constraint propagation. The VEXED experience. *Proceedings of AAAI-87* (Morgan Kaufmann Publishers, Los Altos, California) 830-835.

Sutherland, I. (1963) Sketchpad: A man-machine graphical communication system, *IFIPS Proceedings of the Spring Joint Computer Conference* 329-346.

4.4 Programming in Timed Concurrent Constraint Languages

Vijay Saraswat, Radha Jagadeesan and Vinheet Gupta

Loyola College, Stanford University, U.S.A.
saraswat@parc.xerox.com

4.4.1 Introduction

The areas of Qualitative Reasoning about physical systems (Weld and de Kleer 1989), reasoning about action and state change (Ginsberg 1987), reactive, real-time computing (Real-time systems 1991) and concurrent programming languages (Milner 1980; Hoare 1985) are areas of inquiry that are fundamentally about the same subject matter — the representation, design and analysis of continuous and discrete dynamical systems.

Surprisingly, no robust, common analyses of this subject matter have hitherto emerged, though these areas have independently been the beneficiaries of vigorous investigation in the past decade(s). The area of reactive, real-time computing has put forth the elegant idea of synchronous programming — languages for specifying and implementing reactive systems that interact "instantaneously" with their environment. The well-developed languages in this family, such as ESTEREL, LUSTRE and SIGNAL, enjoy remarkable mathematical, computational and expressiveness properties. The analysis of concurrency — and, in general, the programme of research into the foundations of computing at the heart of theoretical computer science — has put forth several models for indeterminate, concurrent, communicating systems. And it has developed a methodology for research based on developing an "algebra" of processes, on identifying primitive processes and combinators that are definable in these models and that together (through "full abstraction" results) characterize these models.

The area of non-monotonic reasoning has identified the importance of *defeasible* reasoning — the possibly erroneous "jumping to conclusions" that is the inevitable consequence of the lack of omniscience about a dynamic environment characteristic of all finitary computational systems. (And it has highlighted the paucity of resources at our disposal in attacking these fundamental problems of of *efficient* reasoning in the face of (state) change. The more powerful theories of non-monotonic inference remain hamstrung by artificial model theories or impossibly hard computational problems.) The area of Qualitative Physics has highlighted the importance and centrality of explicit, compositional, declarative, models for simulation, monitoring, diagnosis, control and design of such dynamical systems.

The natural meeting ground for these hitherto non-confluent areas of inquiry is logic — the logic of time and change. Our thrust to this heartland is through the synthesis of (concurrent) constraint programming (CCP) — itself at the heart of the dual logicism and proceduralism of computational logic — with synchronous programming. From the viewpoint of programming language design, we do not claim that there is something profound about the choice of CCP as our starting point. Indeed we believe that the theory of timed computation we develop is robust enough to be applicable to other asynchronous models of computation. However, we have found the notion of an underlying constraint system to be a robust crutch to support our intuitions about the design of powerful computational systems.

CCP is based on the simple idea of a collection of (possibly distributed) agents communicating by imposing and checking pieces of partial information — constraints — on shared variables. Agents are not synchronized, the constraints posted accumulate monotonically — perhaps after arbitrary unbounded delay — in a (possibly mythical) shared store. The computational view is thus asynchronous, monotonic and untimed; the logical view is in terms of deduction in intuitionistic logic.

The fundamental move in the Timed Concurrent Constraint Programming (tcc) framework is to augment the ability of constraint programming to detect "positive information" ("some event is happening", some constraint is derivable) with the ability to detect *negative information* — "some event did not happen", some constraint was *not* derivable on quiescence. Such detection is at the heart of the notion of time-outs that are crucial to reactive, real-time computation and of the notion of "closed world" assumptions that are crucial to reasoning with incomplete information and in the face of change. It also causes the underlying logical view of computation to be in terms of deduction in (fixed-point extensions of) intuitionistic (linear-time) *temporal* logic.

In addition, tcc incorporates a simple idea with its roots in the work in Qualitative Reasoning on model-based simulation of physical systems: the current and future can have no causal impact on the past. Thus, once negative information is detected, it is too late to change the state of affairs that led to the event not happening; all that can be done is to set up for action now and in the future. This idea is instrumental in circumventing the "temporal paradoxes" (Berry and Gonthier 1992) that arise from the confusion between causality and temporality that has hitherto seemed to be an integral part of the synchronous approach to computing. And it is at the heart of our identification of a powerful form of "safe" default reasoning that avoids the complicated mathematical and computational properties of more general forms of non-monotonic reasoning.

This paper explores the expressive power of the tcc paradigm. The origin of the work in the integration of synchronous and constraint programming is described. The basic conceptual and mathematical framework — developed in the spirit of the model-based approach characteristic of theoretical computer science — is reviewed. We show that a range of constructs for expressing timeouts, preemption and other complicated patterns of temporal activity are expressible in the basic model and language-framework. Indeed, we present a single construct on processes, definable in the language, that can simulate the effect of other preemption constructs.

We present Timed Gentzen, a concrete tcc language instantiated over the "generic" constraint system Gentzen that underlies "unification-free" computation in (classical, intuitionistic, linear) logic. Recall that the constraint system Herbrand (Saraswat 1993) originates in the use of "delayed instantiation" of existentially quantified variables on the "right hand side" of a sequent system: in the query $\vdash \exists X.(p(X) \wedge q(X))$ one may think of p and q as processes that dynamically impose constraints on X. The task of the Herbrand constraint system is to express and resolve equalities over uninterpreted terms, through variations of the Herbrand-Martelli-Montanari (first-order) unification algorithm. In contrast, the constraint system we name Gentzen is concerned with solving the core (incremental) inference problem that arises in computing with formulas on the *left* hand side of sequents (e.g., $p(X), \forall Y.p(Y) \to q(Y) \vdash a$). In brief, the "tokens" of the constraint system here are arbitrary (positive) atomic formulas (possibly with "eigen-variables"), and the inference relation is that forced by the non-logical structural rules (identity, cut, permutation, etc.). Thus the computational problem is essentially a database lookup problem, in the face of (1) arbitrary tree-structured data, (2) a monotonically increasing database, (3) universally quantified queries. Somewhat surprisingly, this constraint system has already been used heavily in implemented work in Qualitative Reasoning — it underlies the "active database" viewpoint for organizing problem-solving systems developed by Sussman and his colleagues in the 70's; see (Forbus and deKleer 1993) for a recent expository development.

Subsequently, we present solutions to several representative reactive and synchronous programming problems in Timed Gentzen; also we discuss how some common default inferencing techniques can be represented. In a paper of this form, it is possible only to select and treat a few representative examples.

No paper on programming techniques can be complete without providing the reader with the ability to test and develop new programs. We discuss and include a full working interpreter for Timed Gentzen, written in Prolog, that can be used for running these programs. It is short, under a hundred lines long, but fully functional.

Acknowledgements We gratefully acknowledge extended discussions on various aspects of this work with Danny Bobrow, Jerry Burch, Adam Farquhar, Markus Fromherz, Lalita Jategaonkar, John Lamping, Tim Lindholm, Olivier Raiman, Mark Shirley, Brian Smith and Brian Williams.

4.4.2 Synchronous programming

Reactive systems (Harel and Pnueli 1985; Berry 1989; Halbwachs 1993) are those that react continuously with their environment at a rate controlled by the environment. Execution in a reactive system proceeds in bursts of activity. In each phase, the environment stimulates the system with an input, obtains a response in bounded time, and may then be inactive (with respect to the system) for an arbitrary period of time before initiating the next burst. Examples of reactive systems are controllers and signal-processing systems. The primary issues that arise in programming reactive systems are time-criticality, reliability and maintainability in the face of change.

4.4.2.1 Automata Arguably, the most natural way of programming such systems is in terms of automata with simple loop-free transitions, to ensure bounded response. The transitions of the automaton correspond to simple actions executed by the program at every time step.

Consider for example a simple protocol that implements the controller of a paper-tray of a photo-copier. The function of the controller is to switch the paper tray motor on and off, always trying to keep the position of the top of the stack of paper next to the feeder. There are two sensors, P and E, which are set to 1 when the height of the paper is OK. Whenever the paper level falls, i.e. one of the sensors becomes zero, the motor is activated to push up the paper stack. This protocol can be construed as a finite state machine with two states as in Figure 4.4.2.1.

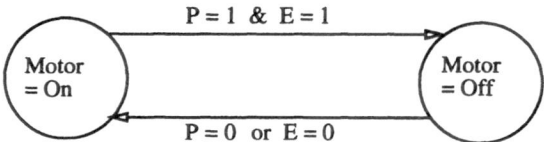

Fig. 4.1. Automaton for a perfect paper-tray

However, automata do not have hierarchical or parallel structure; in particular, small and succinct changes in the specification can lead to global changes in the automaton (Murakami and Sethi 1990). For example, let us say that we want the controller to also be aware of the fact that the sensors may be broken, in which case, it should stop the motor after a certain delay, to prevent it from damaging the copier. An automaton for this protocol is as in Figure 4.4.2.1.

Note that there is no *structural* relationship between the two automata. This makes the maintenance of such code through changes in specification a very onerous task.

4.4.2.2 Process calculi Process calculi (Hoare 1985; Milner 1989; Milner, Parrow and Walker 1989) support parallel composition and communication/synchronization via rendezvous. However, these calculi do not specify the "occurrence time" of the rendezvous. Consequently, program execution is inherently indeterminate. Furthermore, this results in inadequate support for preemption, which is not integrated into the calculi.

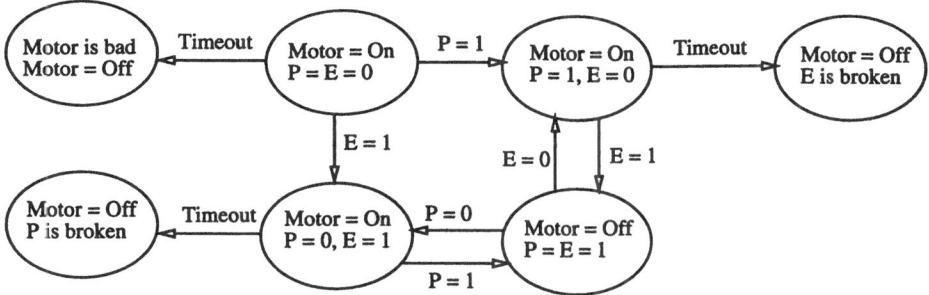

Fig. 4.2. Automaton for a paper-tray with failure modes

4.4.2.3 Temporal logic programming Temporal logic programming languages (Brzoska 1991; Barringer, Fisher, Gabbay $^{+}$1990; Baudinet 89; Moszkowski 1986; Merz 1993) achieve bounded response by imposing syntactic restrictions. This paradigm is inherently nondeterministic. Furthermore, the languages are forced to identify *a priori*, global and fixed notions of "system-variables" and "environment-variables" to ensure true reactivity. This distinction has nebulous logical status, and goes against the algebraic view of parallel composition, where one process is part of the environment of the other process.

4.4.2.4 Synchronous languages The problems with automata leads to the style of synchronous programming; the motivation behind these languages is to achieve the strong real time guarantees of automata in the context of a higher level of system description. The class of synchronous languages (Berry and Gonthier 1992; Halbwachs, Caspi and Pilaud 1991; Guernic, Borgne, Gauthier and Le Maire 1991; Harel 1987) have the following features:

Perfect Synchrony: Program combinators are determinate primitives that respond instantaneously to input. Output at time t is a function of the input at time up to t; at any instant the presence *and* the absence of signals can be detected.

Bounded State: Programs that operate only on "signals" can be compiled into finite state automata with simple transitions.

Multiform Time: Physical time has the same status as any other external event.

Determinacy and synchrony ensure that programs are determinate in the input-output sense as well as the interactive temporal sense. The bounded state property bounds the single step execution time of the program and makes the synchrony assumption realizable in practice. The multiform nature of time allows the combination of programs with different notions of time. There are two classes of languages in this genré: Imperative real time synchronous languages like ESTEREL allow flexible programming constructs, and come with verification tools. The declarative synchronous real time languages, LUSTRE and SIGNAL, inherit elegant equational reasoning from the underlying dataflow model.

The incongruity between internal temporality (there is computation "in between" the stimulus from the environment and the response) and Perfect Synchrony (at each instant a signal is either present or not present, there is no "in between") affects programming language design and implementation. For example,

Temporal paradoxes: One can express programs that require a signal to be present at an instant only if it is not present at that instant. Indeed, the behavioral semantics of (Berry and Gonthier 1992) requires (effectively) complex default reasoning to determine what must happen at each step — in a sense, "stable models" of a default theory must be computed by finding the fixed-points of a system of equations involving non-monotone operators. Approximate static analysis, a calculus of potentials in the case of ESTEREL, is used to eliminate programs with paradoxes (exact analysis is not possible for standard computability reasons). This results, in some cases, in rejecting intuitively correct programs (Halbwachs 1993). Furthermore, this poses problems in constructing process networks with cycles.

Compilation is not compositional: The compilation of a program fragment has to take into account the static structure of the entire program (Halbwachs 1993, Page 93). This is in direct contrast to the standard compilation procedures for traditional programming languages (aho, Sethi and Ullman 1985).

4.4.2.5 Our contributions A re-analysis of the elegant ideas underlying synchronous programming, starting from the viewpoint of asynchronous computation leads us to the framework of *timed concurrent constraint programming*, henceforth called tcc, with the following salient features.

Declarative view: tcc has a fully-abstract semantics based on solutions of equations. tcc programs can be viewed as formulas in an intuitionist linear time temporal logic, and computation can be viewed as generating a "least model" of the program.

Modularity: In the spirit of process algebra, we identify a set of basic combinators, from which programs and reasoning principles are built compositionally.

Expressiveness : tcc supports the *derivation* of a "**clock**" construct that allows a process to be clocked by another (recursive) process; it generalizes the *undersampling* constructs of SIGNAL and LUSTRE, and the preemption/abortion constructs supported by ESTEREL. Thus, tcc encapsulates the rudiments of a theory of preemption constructs. In addition, by selecting an appropriate underlying constraint system (e.g., **Herbrand** underlying (concurrent) logic programming languages), tcc languages can be used to specify cyclic, dynamically-changing networks of processes (c.f. "mobility" (Milner, Parrow and Walker 1989)).

Executability : Under simple syntactic conditions, tcc programs may be compiled into finite state "constraint" automata that have bounded response time.

"Paradox-free" : tcc resolves the tension between synchrony and causality.

4.4.2.6 Basic Intuitions Our starting point is the paradigm of concurrent constraint programming, henceforth called CCP (Saraswat 1993; Saraswat, Rinard and Panagaden 1991). CCP is highly expressive; for example, it generalizes dataflow languages,

CCP is an asynchronous and determinate paradigm of computation. The basic move in this paradigm is to replace the notion of store-as-valuation central to von Neumann computing with the notion that the store is a constraint, that is, a collection of pieces of partial information about the values that variables can take. Computation progresses via the monotonic accumulation of information. Concurrency arises because any number of agents may simultaneously interact with the store. The usual notions of "read" and "write" are replaced by *ask* and *tell* actions. A tell operation takes a constraint and conjoins it with the constraints already in the store; tells are executed asynchronously: thus, it is guaranteed that the store eventually satisfies the constraint, but no assumptions are made on the amount of time taken to achieve this result. Synchronization is achieved via the ask operation: ask takes a constraint (say, c) and uses it to probe the structure of the store: it succeeds if the store contains enough information to entail c; the agent blocks if the store is not strong enough to entail the constraint it wishes to check.

The information accumulated by computation in the CCP paradigm is *positive* information: constraints on variables, or a piece of history recording that "some event happened". The fundamental move we now make is to consider the addition of *negative* information to the computation model: information of the form "an event did not happen". This is the essence of the "time out" notion in real-time programming: some sub-program may be aborted because of the absence of an event.

How can a coherent conceptual framework be fashioned around the detection of negative information? The first task is to identify states of the system in which no more positive information is being generated; the *quiescent* points of the computation. Only at such moments does it make sense to say that a certain piece of information has not been generated. Now *time* can be introduced by identifying quiescent points as the markers that distinguish one time step from the next. This allows the introduction of primitives that can trigger an action in the *next* time interval if some event did not happen through the extent of the *previous* time interval. Since actions of the system can only affect its behavior at current or future time step, the negative information detected is *stable*. Hence there is some hope that a semantic treatment as pleasant as that for the untimed case will be possible. Our basic ontological commitment then is to the following refinement of the Perfect Synchrony Hypothesis — the *Timed Asynchrony Hypothesis*:

Bounded Asynchrony Computation progresses asynchronously in bounded intervals of activity separated by arbitrary periods of quiescence. Program combinators are determinate primitives that respond in a bounded amount of time to the input.

Strict Causality Output at time t is a function of the positive information input upto and including time t and the negative information input at time upto t. The *absence* of a signal in a period can be detected only at the end of a period, and hence can trigger activity only in the next interval.

The Timed Asynchrony hypothesis addresses one practical and mathematical shortcoming of the Perfect Synchrony hypothesis. It is more pleasant and practical to regard the computation at each external clock tick as having a notion of *internal temporality*: it happens *not instantaneously* but over a *very short* — bounded — period of time. This is the reality in any case — sophisticated embedded real-time controllers may require that certain conditions be checked, and then values created for local variables, and then subsequently some other conditions be checked, etc. Indeed, even ESTEREL has such an internal notion of temporality — but it is achieved through a completely separate mechanism, the introduction of assignable variables and internal sequencing (";"). In contrast, tcc does away with the assignable variables of ESTEREL in favor of the same logical (denotational) variables that are used for representing signals. Computation progresses through the asynchronous accumulation and detection of positive information within an interval, and negative information at the end of an interval[1].

To summarize, computation in tcc proceeds in intervals. During the interval, positive information is accumulated and detected asynchronously, as in CCP. At the end of the interval, the absence of information can be detected, and the constraints accumulated in the interval are discarded. We do not provide for the implicit transfer of positive information across time boundaries to maintain the bounded size of the constraint store; this must be done explicitly by the programmer by using the basic combinators.

---

[1]Prima facie, this "monotonic approximation" of ESTEREL may seem to be less powerful than ESTEREL, which can react to negative information at the same clock tick. The variety of programming examples in the rest of the paper support our argument for the expressiveness of tcc.

4.4.3 The tcc model

This section is devoted to reviewing the formalization and technical development of the intuitions discussed in the previous section. Some readers may prefer to look at the more concrete examples in subsequent sections, and consult this section as needed for technical definitions. For this purpose, the syntax, denotational and operational semantics of tcc are summarized in Tables 4.1,4.2,4.3 respectively.

4.4.3.1 Constraint systems Formally, constraint systems C are essentially arbitrary systems of partial information (Saraswat 1992; Saraswat 1993). They are taken to consist of a set D of tokens with minimal first-order structure (variables, substitutions, existential quantification and conjunction), together with an entailment relation $\vdash_C$ that specifies when a token x must follow given the tokens $y_1, \ldots, y_n$ are known to hold. Intuitionistic disjunction can be built in purely formally on top of the underlying constraint system. In particular, the constraint system needs to provide us only with an algorithm that will answer queries of the form "is c entailed by the store S". To answer the query " is $c \vee d$ entailed by the store S", send two different queries for c and d and return yes if either returns yes. Conversely, when a constraint $c \vee d$ is sent to the store, the store appears as if split into two, one receiving c the other d. All subsequent queries are answered successfully only if *both* splits answer successfully.

Examples of constraint systems: (1) **Herbrand** underlying logic programming (variables range over finite trees, tokens specify equality of terms), (2) FD (Hentenryck, Saraswat and Deville 1992) for finite domains (variables range over finite domains, with tokens for equality and for specifying that a variable lies in a given range), etc.

A third example, **Gentzen**, will be the concrete constraint system used in the programming examples in this paper. For this constraint system, we assume that we are given a vocabulary of terms that includes variables, and a vocabulary of predicates with arities. The tokens of the constraint system are then atomic formulas, built out of the predicates and terms. The entailment relation is built out of only structural rules, i.e. is induced by the identity relation on atomic formulas.

In this section, we will take as fixed a constraint system C, with underlying set of tokens D. Let the entailment closed subsets of D be denoted by $|D|$. $(|D|, \subseteq)$ is a complete algebraic lattice; we will use the notation $\sqcup$ and $\sqcap$ for the joins and meets of this lattice. We shall call (finite) sets of tokens *primitive constraints* and designate them by the letters c, d, e. A (finite) *constraint* is an element of $|D|$ generated from a (finite) set of tokens; they will be designated by the letters a, b. For any primitive constraint c, we let $[\![c]\!]$ stand for the constraint generated by c.

4.4.3.2 Denotational intuitions Earlier work (Saraswat, Rinard and Panagaden 1991) identified a cc program with the observations that can be made about the program. The observations of a program are the set of quiescent points – the set of elements of $|D|$ on which the program quiesces without adding any new information. It was further shown that the set S of quiescent points of a program is *determinate* that is, satisfies the property that for any point x, the greatest lower bound (glb) of any non-empty subset of S above x is also in S.[2] Such a model is rich enough to define an "abort" process that, in fact, quiesces on no input (and has hence the empty set of quiescent points).

What should the timed model be? Recall that the execution within a time step is captured by execution in cc and that discrete time is modeled by natural numbers. Combining these two ideas, we conclude that the timed model should be a sequence of models of cc programs. Formally, this is captured by the intuition that "Processes are relations extended over time" (Abramsky 1993).

The formal development follows. First, we extend the set of observations over time:

Definition 4.1 Obs, *the set of observations, is the set of finite sequences of constraints.*

Intuitively, we shall observe the *quiescent sequences* of constraints for the system.

We let s, u, v range over sequences of constraints. We use "ϵ" to denote the empty sequence. The concatenation of sequences is denoted by "$\cdot$"; for this purpose a constraint a is regarded as the one-element sequence $\langle a \rangle$. Given $S \subseteq$ **Obs** and $s \in$ **Obs**, we will write S **after** s for the set $\{a \in |D| \mid s \cdot a \in S\}$ of quiescent points of S in the instant after it has exhibited the observation s.

Definition 4.2 $P \subseteq$ **Obs** *is a* process *iff it satisfies the following conditions:*

1. *(Non-emptiness)* $\epsilon \in P$,

2. *(Prefix-closure)* $s \in P$ *whenever* $s \cdot t \in P$, *and*

3. *(Determinacy)* P **after** s *is determinate whenever* $s \in P$.

We will let **Proc** designate the set of all processes, and let P, Q range over **Proc**.[3]

---

[2]Such a set is said to be determinate because it can be used to define a partial function: associate with every point x in the underlying partial set T, the least element of S above x, if any. These functions are partial *closure operators*, i.e., they are monotone, idempotent and extensive.

[3]An alternate way of thinking of processes is that they correspond exactly to the resting points of partial closure operators on **Obs** (in the lexicographic ordering on sequences) that are *stratified* ($f(s)$, if defined, has the same cardinality as s), and *causal* ($f(s)$ is a prefix of $f(s \cdot a)$, assuming both are defined). Space does not permit discussing this alternate viewpoint in detail.

Syntax.

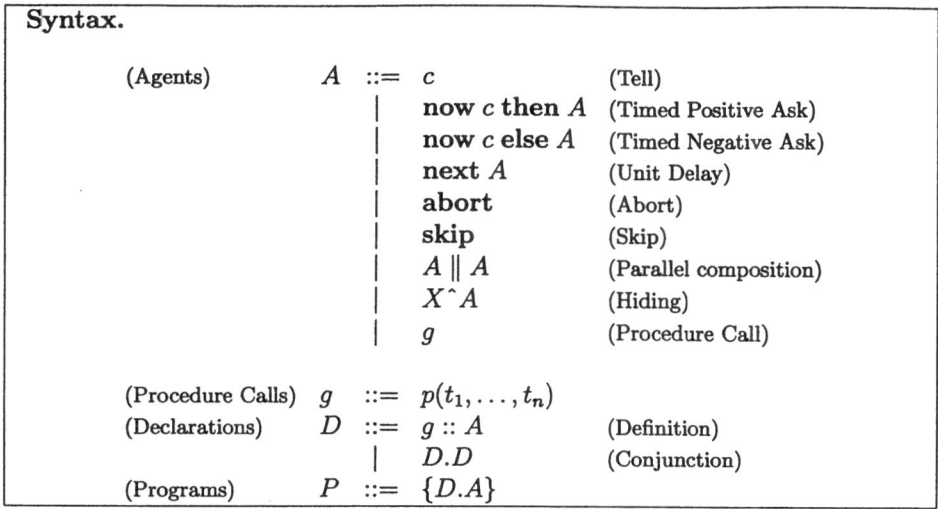

(Agents)	A	$::=$	c	(Tell)
		$\|$	**now** c **then** A	(Timed Positive Ask)
		$\|$	**now** c **else** A	(Timed Negative Ask)
		$\|$	**next** A	(Unit Delay)
		$\|$	**abort**	(Abort)
		$\|$	**skip**	(Skip)
		$\|$	$A \parallel A$	(Parallel composition)
		$\|$	$X \hat{\ } A$	(Hiding)
		$\|$	g	(Procedure Call)
(Procedure Calls)	g	$::=$	$p(t_1, \ldots, t_n)$	
(Declarations)	D	$::=$	$g :: A$	(Definition)
		$\|$	$D.D$	(Conjunction)
(Programs)	P	$::=$	$\{D.A\}$	

Table 4.1. Syntax for tcc languages

4.4.3.3 Process algebra We now identify basic processes and process combinators in the model. The combinators fall into two categories:

CCP constructs: Tell, Parallel composition and Timed Positive Ask are inherited from CCP. These do not, by themselves, cause "extension over time". Parallel composition is the explicit representation of concurrency in the language. Timed Positive Ask and Tell combine to allow synchronization capabilities.

Timing constructs: Timed Negative Ask, Unit Delay, and Abortion that cause extension over time. Unit delay starts a process to be started in the next time instant. Timed Negative Ask is a conditional version of Unit Delay, based on detection of negative information. It causes a process to be started in the the next time instant if on quiescence of the current time instant, the store was not strong enough to entail some information.

The formal description of these combinators follows. We present the denotational and operational semantics simultaneously.

The operational semantics is defined via two binary transition relations $\longrightarrow$, $\rightsquigarrow$ over configurations. $\longrightarrow$ represents transitions *within* a time instant. This relation is intimately related to the transition relation in CCP since it represents computation within a time step. $\rightsquigarrow$ represents a transition from one time instant to the next. A configuration will be simply a (possibly empty) multiset of *agents*, the syntactic representatives of processes. We implicitly represent the store in a configuration: for Γ a multiset of agents, we will let $\sigma(\Gamma)$ be the sub-multiset of tokens in Γ.

Semantic Domain. We take as fixed a constraint system $\mathcal{C}$, with underlying set of tokens D and let the finitary inference relation $\vdash$ record which token follows from which ollection of tokens. Let the $\vdash$-closed subsets of D be denoted by $|D|$. $(|D|, \subseteq)$ is a complete algebraic lattice; we will use the notation $\sqcup$ and $\sqcap$ for the joins and meets of this lattice. A (finite) *constraint* is an element of $|D|$ generated from a (finite) set of tokens. We usually denote (finite) sets of tokens by the letters c, d, e, and constraints by the letters a, b. For any set of tokens c, we let $[\![c]\!]$ stand for the constraint generated by c.

Definition 4.3 Obs, *the set of observations, is the set of finite sequences of constraints.*

Concatenation of sequences is denoted by "$\cdot$"; for this purpose a constraint a is regarded as the one-element sequence $\langle a \rangle$. For any $S \subseteq$ **Obs**, and sequence $s \in$ **Obs**, let S **after** s be the set $\{a \in |D| \mid s \cdot a \in S\}$. A subset S of a partially ordered set T is said to be *determinate* if for every $x \in T$, the subset of S above x is empty or contains a minimum.

Definition 4.4 *A process $P \in$ **Proc** is a non-empty, prefix-closed subset of* Obs *such that P **after** s is determinate for all $s \in P$.*

Semantic Equations. For a sequence of constraints s, by $\exists X.s$ we shall mean the element-wise existential quantification over X.

$$
\begin{aligned}
[\![c]\!] &= \{\epsilon\} \cup \{d \cdot s \in \mathbf{Obs} \mid d \supseteq [\![c]\!]\} \\
[\![\mathbf{now}\ c\ \mathbf{then}\ A]\!] &= \{\epsilon\} \cup \{d \cdot s \in \mathbf{Obs} \mid d \supseteq [\![c]\!] \Rightarrow d \cdot s \in [\![A]\!]\} \\
[\![\mathbf{now}\ c\ \mathbf{else}\ A]\!] &= \{\epsilon\} \cup \{d \cdot s \in \mathbf{Obs} \mid d \not\supseteq [\![c]\!] \Rightarrow s \in [\![A]\!])\} \\
[\![\mathbf{next}\ A]\!] &= \{\epsilon\} \cup \{d \cdot s \in \mathbf{Obs} \mid s \in [\![A]\!])\} \\
[\![\mathbf{abort}]\!] &= \{\epsilon\} \\
[\![\mathbf{skip}]\!] &= \mathbf{Obs} \\
[\![A \parallel B]\!] &= \{s \in \mathbf{Obs} \mid s \in [\![A]\!] \wedge s \in [\![B]\!]\} \\
[\![X\hat{\ }A]\!] &= \{s \in \mathbf{Obs} \mid \exists X.s = \exists X.t, \text{ for some } t \in [\![A]\!]\}
\end{aligned}
$$

The semantics of recursion is handled in the usual way by taking least fixed points of the associated functional.

Table 4.2. Denotational Semantics for tcc languages

Configuration. A configuration is merely a multiset Γ of agents. Multiset union is viewed as parallel composition. We implicitly represent the store in a configuration: for Γ a configuration, $\sigma(\Gamma)$ denotes the sub-multiset of tokens in Γ.

Transition rules. Two binary transition relations $\longrightarrow, \rightsquigarrow$ are defined over configurations. $\longrightarrow$ represents transitions *within* a time instant. $\rightsquigarrow$ represents a transition from one time instant to the next.

Axioms for $\longrightarrow$. The binary relation $\longrightarrow$ on configurations is the least relation satisfying the rules:

$$(\Gamma, \mathbf{skip}) \longrightarrow \Gamma$$
$$(\Gamma, \mathbf{abort}) \longrightarrow \mathbf{abort}$$
$$(\Gamma, A \parallel B) \longrightarrow (\Gamma, A, B)$$
$$(\Gamma, X\hat{\;}A) \longrightarrow (\Gamma, A[Y/X]) \quad (Y \text{ not free in } \Gamma)$$
$$(\Gamma, p(t_1, \ldots, t_n)) \longrightarrow (\Gamma, A[X_1 \mapsto t_1, \ldots, X_n \mapsto t_n])$$

and

$$\frac{\sigma(\Gamma) \vdash c}{(\Gamma, \mathbf{now}\ c\ \mathbf{then}\ A) \longrightarrow (\Gamma, A)}$$
$$\frac{\sigma(\Gamma) \vdash c}{(\Gamma, \mathbf{now}\ c\ \mathbf{else}\ B) \longrightarrow \Gamma}$$

In the case of procedure calls we assume that the underlying program contains a clause $p(X_1, \ldots, X_n) :: A$.

Axioms for $\rightsquigarrow$. The binary relation $\rightsquigarrow$ is the least relation satisfying the single rule:

$$\frac{\Delta, \{\mathbf{now}\ c_i\ \mathbf{else}\ A_i \mid i < n\} \not\longrightarrow}{\Delta, \{\mathbf{now}\ c_i\ \mathbf{else}\ A_i \mid i < n\}, \{\mathbf{next}\ B_j \mid j < m\} \rightsquigarrow \{A_i \mid i < n\}, \{B_j \mid j < m\}}$$

Above, Δ ranges over multisets of agents that do not contain Timed Negative Asks or Unit Delays.

Note that the empty configuration can always make a $\rightsquigarrow$ transition, and that a configuration containing **abort** can never quiesce (that is, if Γ contains **abort**, then there is always a Δ, namely, **abort**, such that $\Gamma \longrightarrow \Delta$). Therefore there are configurations Γ which are such that for no Δ_1, Δ_2 do we have:

$$\Gamma \longrightarrow^* \Delta_1 \rightsquigarrow \Delta_2$$

In that sense $\rightsquigarrow$ is "partial".

Table 4.3. Operational Semantics for tcc languages

4.4.3.4 Timing constructs

Skip. **skip** is the process that does nothing at all at every time instant. Hence every sequence of constraints is quiescent for it. Thus:

$$[\![\text{skip}]\!] \stackrel{d}{=} \mathbf{Obs}$$

Operationally, **skip** has no effect:

$$\Gamma, \text{skip} \longrightarrow \Gamma$$

Abortion. **abort** is the process that instantly causes all interactions with the environment to cease. Hence the only observation that can be made of it is ϵ.

$$[\![\text{abort}]\!] \stackrel{d}{=} \{\epsilon\}$$

Operationally, **abort** annihilates the environment:

$$\Gamma, \text{abort} \longrightarrow \text{abort}$$

Note that this implies that a configuration Γ containing **abort** cannot "$\longrightarrow$-quiesce", that is, reach, through $\longrightarrow$ transitions, a state which has no $\longrightarrow$ transition emanating from it.

Unit Delay. Unit Delay is a variant of the unit delay primitives in synchronous languages (Milner 1983; Berry 1993); intuitively, $A = \textbf{next } B$ is the process that behaves like B in the next time instant. It performs no computation in the present instant. When is $o = a \cdot s$, an arbitrary element of **Obs**, an observation of A? There are no restrictions on a. Since A behaves like B from the next time instant, s must be an observation of B.

$$[\![\textbf{next } B]\!] \stackrel{d}{=} \{\epsilon\} \cup \{a \cdot s \in \mathbf{Obs} \mid s \in [\![B]\!]\}$$

Timed Negative Asks. Timed Negative Ask is the only way to detect "negative information" in tcc. Intuitively, $A = \textbf{now } c \textbf{ else } B$ is the process that behaves like B in the next time instant if on quiescence of the current time instant the store was not strong enough to entail c.[4]

When is $o = a \cdot s$, an arbitrary element of **Obs**, an observation of A? There are two possibilities. Either $a \supseteq [\![c]\!]$ or not. If $a \supseteq [\![c]\!]$, A behaves like **skip**, so s can be any observation whatsoever. If not, A behaves like B from the next time instant; so s must be an observation of A. Thus:

$$[\![\textbf{now } c \textbf{ else } A]\!] \stackrel{d}{=} \{\epsilon\} \cup \{a \cdot s \in \mathbf{Obs} \mid a \not\supseteq [\![c]\!] \Rightarrow s \in [\![A]\!]\}$$

---

[4]In reality, we allow the more general combinator $A = \textbf{now } \{c_1; \ldots; c_n\} \textbf{ else } B$ — it behaves like B provided that the store on quiescence is not above each of the constraints c_i. The details are straightforward.

Operationally, if the current store entails c, then we can eliminate A:

$$\frac{\sigma(\Gamma) \vdash c}{(\Gamma, \mathbf{now}\ c\ \mathbf{else}\ B) \longrightarrow \Gamma}$$

In the following for an agent **now** c **else** A we say that c is the "antecedent" and A the "body".

Operational semantics: the $\rightsquigarrow$ relation. Consider now the situation in which computation in the current time instant has quiesced. This means that all reductions that could have been caused because of the entailment of Positive Asks have been done, all Negative Asks whose antecedents are entailed have been eliminated, and computation has not aborted. Computation can now progress to the next time instant.

The active agents at the next time instant are the bodies of the remaining Negative Ask agents or the bodies of agents within a Unit Delay. All other agents, including the current store, will be discarded. Formally, if Δ ranges over multisets of agents (including constraints) other than Negative Ask or Unit Delay, we can write the transition rule as:

$$\frac{\Delta, \{\mathbf{now}\ c_i\ \mathbf{else}\ A_i \mid i < n\} \not\longmapsto}{\Delta, \{\mathbf{now}\ c_i\ \mathbf{else}\ A_i \mid i < n\}, \{\mathbf{next}\ B_j \mid j < m\} \rightsquigarrow \{A_i \mid i < n\}, \{B_j \mid j < m\}}$$

Note that a configuration Γ can make a $\rightsquigarrow$-transition even if Γ is the empty set of agents; however, it cannot make any $\rightsquigarrow$-transition if it contains **abort**.

Guarded Recursion. A *program* is a pair of declarations D and an agent A; a declaration is of the form $g :: A$, where g is of the form $p(X_1, \ldots, X_n)$, for p a procedure name and X_i variables. (In the following, we let F, G range over programs.) We require that the recursion is guarded, *i.e.* the recursion variable occurs within the scope of an **else** or a **next**. The important consequence of this restriction is that the recursion equations have *unique* solutions, and that computation in each time-step is lexically bounded (i.e., bounded by the size of the program).

To ensure bounded "extension in time" we also need to ensure that recursions are *bounded*, that is, at run-time there are only boundedly many different procedure calls. There are several ways of achieving this. For instance, we could require that procedures take no parameters. This is a familiar restriction in the realm of synchronous programming; for example, the sole recursion construct in ESTEREL is "loop". We shall make the slightly more liberal assumption that any recursive procedure call take exactly the same parameters as the procedure declaration. That is, for any set of mutually recursive declarations:

p(X$_1$, ..., X$_n$) :: A.
q(Y$_1$, ..., Y$_m$) :: B.
...

any call to a procedure p, q, ... in A, B, ... is exactly of the form $p(X_1, \ldots, X_n)$, $q(Y_1, \ldots, Y_n)$, ... (This restriction is equivalent to the parameterless procedures restriction provided that procedure definitions are allowed to be nested within agents, so that bodies of procedure definitions can refer to variables in the lexical scope.)

From a logic programming perspective, this restriction is not as severe as it may seem because constraints are not carried over from one time instant to the next: hence the same variable name may be "reused" at subsequent time-instants. Note that procedures with parameters that take values in finite domains can be compiled away using the parameterless procedure and hiding constructs available in tcc.

The operational and denotational semantics of recursion is standard. In the following, we shall sometimes use the syntax $\mu p.A$ to denote an agent p under the assumption that the program contains a (unique) procedure declaration of the form $p :: A$.

4.4.3.5 Combinators from CCP These combinators follows traditional treatment (Saraswat, Rinard and Panagaden 1991).

Tell. This process adds c in the current store. It is quiescent in any observation that contains at least as much information as c at the first instant.

$$[c] \;=\; \{\epsilon\} \cup \{d \cdot s \in \mathbf{Obs} \mid d \supseteq c\}$$

Since the store is represented in the configuration, there is no explicit operational transition.

Parallel composition. What are the quiescent points of the parallel composition of two agents agents A and B? Exactly those which are quiescent points of A and of B:

$$[A \parallel B] \;=\; [A] \cap [B]$$

Operationally, the idea of parallel composition is already implicit in the "," of multiset union (Berry and Boudol 1990):

$$(\Gamma, A \parallel B) \longrightarrow (\Gamma, A, B)$$

Timed Positive Ask. $B = \mathbf{now}\ c\ \mathbf{then}\ A$ is the process that checks if the current store is strong enough to entail c; and if so, behaves like A. When is $o = d \cdot s$ an arbitrary element of $\mathbf{Obs}$ in $[B]$? There are two possibilities. Either $d \supseteq [c]$ or not. In the first case, B behaves like A; so o must be an observation of A. Otherwise o can be any observation whatsoever — since B will remain quiescent. Thus:

$$[\mathbf{now}\ c\ \mathbf{then}\ A] \;=\; \{\epsilon\} \cup \{d \cdot s \in \mathbf{Obs} \mid d \supseteq [c] \Rightarrow d \cdot s \in [A]\}$$

Operationally, we have:

$$\frac{\sigma(\Gamma) \vdash c}{(\Gamma, \textbf{now } c \textbf{ then } A) \longrightarrow (\Gamma, A)}$$

Hiding. $X \hat{\ } A$ is a process where the variable X is hidden from the environment. At any time step, the agent $\exists X.f$ transforms its input c into the value $c \sqcup \exists X.f(\exists X.c)$. No constraints cross time boundaries. This yields, in terms of fixed points:

$$[\![X\hat{\ }A]\!] \;=\; \{s \in \textbf{Obs} \mid \exists X.s = \exists X.t, \text{for some } t \in [\![A]\!]\}$$

where $\exists X.(c_1.c_2\ldots.c_n) \stackrel{d}{=} (\exists X c_1).(\exists X c_2)\ldots(\exists X.c_n)$.

For the operational semantics, we find a variable Y that does not occur free in the configuration, and substitute it for the bound variable:

$$(\Gamma, X\hat{\ }A) \;\longrightarrow\; (\Gamma, A[Y/X]) \quad (Y \text{not free in } \Gamma)$$

Review. This concludes our discussion of the basic mathematical and operational semantics of tcc constructs. The connections between operational and denotational semantics are straightforward. Indeed, it is not hard to determine that the denotational semantics captures precisely the quiescent sequences of the operational semantics. Full abstraction follows from standard considerations (Saraswat, Jagadeesan and Gupta 1993).

We emphasize that the definitions given above work for *any* constraint system, and are hence very general. While we do not have space to discuss this further (Saraswat, Jagadeesan and Gupta 1993) also provides a sound and essentially complete proof system for establishing inequivalence of programs. Because tcc programs have a logical reading, they may also be used to specify (safety) properties of other tcc programs. Hence this proof system can be used for establishing that programs meet their safety specifications.

(Saraswat, Jagadeesan and Gupta 1993) also discusses a compositional compilation algorithm for tcc programs that takes as input programs with bounded recursion (as discussed above) and outputs a constraint-based FSA. The FSA accepts as input a constraint from the environment, computes (through a bounded number of calls to the underlying constraint system) the constraint that must be output at the current time step, and checks it against a bounded number of other constraints to determine the transition to the next state. The mere fact of such a compilability into FSA's makes possible the use of tcc to program reactive controllers, and the use of powerful analysis techniques for finite state systems.

4.4.4 General programming techniques

We now show how to define some natural patterns of temporal activity in tcc languages. We show that several interesting combinators are definable in the underlying model, and are hence definable for any tcc language.[5] We then present explicit definitions through simplification laws that show how to eliminate the combinators in favor of the basic combinators described in the previous section. (In the following when we write $A = B$, for two agents A and B, we mean that the denotations of these agents are identical processes.)

4.4.4.1 Some simple combinators

Unconditional persistence. Let **always** A be the agent that behaves like A at every time instant:

$$[\![\textbf{always } A]\!] = \{s \in \textbf{Obs} \mid s^i \in [\![A]\!], 0 \leq i \leq |s|\}$$

where $s^0 = s$ and $(d \cdot s)^{n+1} = s^n$. We have the law:

$$\textbf{always } A = A \parallel \textbf{next always } A$$

Thus the agent **always** c ensures that the constraint c will be posted at every time instant.

Conditionals. Let **now** c **then** A **else** B be the agent that behaves like A if c holds in the current time instant; otherwise it behaves like B from the *next* time instant onwards. Its observations are:

$$[\![\textbf{now } c \textbf{ then } A \textbf{ else } B]\!] = \{\epsilon\} \cup \{d \cdot s \in \textbf{Obs} \mid \begin{array}{l} d \supseteq [\![c]\!] \Rightarrow d \cdot s \in [\![A]\!], \\ d \not\supseteq [\![c]\!] \Rightarrow s \in [\![B]\!]\} \end{array}$$

From this we can deduce:

$$\textbf{now } c \textbf{ then } A \textbf{ else } B \;\; = \;\; (\textbf{now } c \textbf{ then } A \parallel \textbf{now } c \textbf{ else } B)$$

Note that the conditional construct will take one branch or the other; there are no conditions under which it can "suspend". In contrast, assuming that the constraint $\neg c$ is definable in the underlying constraint system, the agent (**now** c **then** $A \parallel$ **now** $\neg c$ **then** **next** B) can suspend without executing either A in the current step or B in the next step — exactly in those stores which are not strong enough to entail either c or $\neg c$.[6] This is a reflection of the intuitionistic nature of the implication underlying the **now** c **then** A construct.

---

[5]When we say that a combinator is definable in this model we mean that when it takes processes as arguments it returns a process. Furthermore, unless otherwise discussed all combinators will be monotone and continuous in their process arguments. This means that they can be used freely in recursive definitions.

[6]For example, if c is the constraint X=1, then every store which has no constraints on X will be unable to prove one of X=1 or X ≠ 1.

Multiple Prioritized Waits. Let A be the agent:

$$
\begin{array}{ll}
\textbf{now} & \\
& \textbf{case}\ \ c_1\ \textbf{do}\ A_1 \\
& \textbf{case}\ \ c_2\ \textbf{do}\ A_2 \\
& \quad\cdots \\
& \textbf{case}\ \ c_n\ \textbf{do}\ A_n \\
& \textbf{default}\ \ B \\
\textbf{end} &
\end{array}
\tag{4.1}
$$

defined to behave like A_1 if c_1 is now true, else behaves in the next time instant like A_2 if c_1 is not true, but c_2 was true, and so on, behaving like B if none of the c_i are true. Following the same denotational style reasoning as earlier, A is equivalent to the agent:

$$
\begin{array}{l}
\{\epsilon\} \\
\cup\ \ \{d\cdot s\in\textbf{Obs}\mid d\supseteq[\![c_1]\!], d\cdot s\in[\![A_1]\!]\} \\
\cup\ \ \cup_{2\leq i\leq n}\{d\cdot s\in\textbf{Obs}\mid \forall j<i.\ d\not\supseteq[\![c_j]\!], d\supseteq[\![c_i]\!], s\in[\![A_i]\!]\} \\
\cup\ \ \{d\cdot s\in\textbf{Obs}\mid\ \mid\forall j\leq n.\ d\not\supseteq[\![c_j]\!], s\in[\![B]\!]\}
\end{array}
$$

From the structure of the denotation, it is easy to write down the following equivalent agent in the basic language:

$$
\begin{array}{ll}
& \textbf{now}\ c_1\ \textbf{then}\ A_1 \\
\| & \textbf{now}\ c_2\ \textbf{then}\ \textbf{now}\ c_1\ \textbf{else}\ A_2 \\
\| & \textbf{now}\ c_3\ \textbf{then}\ \textbf{now}\ (c_1;c_2)\ \textbf{else}\ A_3 \\
& \quad\cdots \\
\| & \textbf{now}\ c_n\ \textbf{then}\ \textbf{now}\ (c_1;\ldots;c_{n-1})\ \textbf{else}\ A_n \\
\| & \textbf{now}\ (c_1;\ldots;c_n)\ \textbf{else}\ B
\end{array}
$$

4.4.4.2 Temporal control constructs

Extended Wait. Let **whenever** c **do** A be the agent that suspends until the first time-instant at which c is true; it then behaves like A. Its denotation is:

$$
\begin{array}{ll}
[\![\textbf{whenever}\ c\ \textbf{do}\ A]\!]\ =\ & \{\epsilon\} \\
& \cup\ \{s\cdot d\cdot t\in\textbf{Obs}\mid d\supseteq[\![c]\!], d\cdot t\in[\![A]\!]\} \\
& \cup\ \{s\cdot d\in\textbf{Obs}\mid d\not\supseteq[\![c]\!]\}
\end{array}
$$

with the law:

$$\textbf{whenever}\ c\ \textbf{do}\ A = \textbf{now}\ c\ \textbf{then}\ A\ \textbf{else}\ (\textbf{whenever}\ c\ \textbf{do}\ A)$$

Watchdogs: **do** P **watching** c. The ESTEREL interrupt construct **do** A **watching** S (Berry 1993) cannot be translated precisely into tcc. In ESTEREL the computation of A is aborted at the instant that S is emitted. This leads to semantic complexities — for example, the agent **do** S **watching immediately** S is required to produce S but if it were to produce S it must terminate before producing S! In tcc it is not possible to specify that a computation be aborted in the current instant on receipt of positive information from the environment. Instead, we describe a construct that aborts the computation at the next *stable* instant, that is, at the next moment of quiescence. This is achieved through polling as shown below.

do P **watching** c behaves like P till a time instant when c is entailed; when c is entailed P is killed from the next time instant onwards. (We can similarly define the related *exception handler* primitive, **do** P **watching** c **timeout** B, that also activates a handler B when P is killed.)

In the following, for $s \in \textbf{Obs}$, we use the notation $s \not\geq a$ to mean $b \not\supseteq a$ for every element $b \in s$. Formally,

$$\llbracket \textbf{do } P \textbf{ watching } c \rrbracket \overset{d}{=} \quad \begin{aligned} &\{s \in \textbf{Obs} \mid s \in \llbracket P \rrbracket, s \not\geq \llbracket c \rrbracket \} \\ \cup \ &\{s \cdot a \cdot t \in \textbf{Obs} \mid s \cdot a \in \llbracket P \rrbracket, a \supseteq \llbracket c \rrbracket\} \end{aligned}$$

It satisfies the following laws:

$$
\begin{aligned}
\textbf{do } d \textbf{ watching } c &= d \\
\textbf{do } (A_1 \parallel A_2) \textbf{ watching } c &= \textbf{do } A_1 \textbf{ watching } c \parallel \textbf{do } A_2 \textbf{ watching } c \\
\textbf{do } (\textbf{now } d \textbf{ then } A) \textbf{ watching } c &= \textbf{now } d \textbf{ then } (\textbf{do } A \textbf{ watching } c) \\
\textbf{do } (\textbf{now } d \textbf{ else } A) \textbf{ watching } c &= \textbf{now } (c; d) \textbf{ else } (\textbf{do } A \textbf{ watching } c) \\
\textbf{do } (X\hat{\ }A) \textbf{ watching } c &= X\hat{\ }(\textbf{do } A \textbf{ watching } c)
\end{aligned}
$$

In the last rule, we assume that X is not free in c (this can always be achieved by renaming the bound variable).

We believe that the "monotonic" approximation of asynchronous interrupts afforded by tcc is appropriate for all practical purposes. Consider the example of an Automated Teller Machine (presented in more detail in Section 4.4.6.3). In the case in which the customer presses a **start** button, the action desired (say, A) might be different from that (say B) in which the customer simultaneously presses a **start** and **cancel** button. In tcc the negative information that **cancel** was not pressed must be converted into positive information — and this can only be done at the next time instant. So the action associated with only the **start** button being pressed would be taken for one time step before being aborted.

If the exact functionality of ESTEREL is desired, this can be obtained by sampling the button state at a higher frequency than the frequency driving the main program. (For example, this can be achieved by downsampling from the basic clock — indeed there needs to be a clock more basic than the one associated with button-presses in order to time out an extremely slow customer.) The button sampler would use an adaptation of the mouse protocol (see below) to determine exactly how many buttons were pressed in a given interval and communicate that positive information at the end of the interval to the main program. The main program can then do A on receipt of the information (**start**, ¬**cancel**) and B on receipt of (**start**, **cancel**).

Suspension-Activation primitive: $\mathbf{S}_c\mathbf{A}_e(P)$. This is a preemption primitive that is a variant of *weak suspension* in ESTEREL (Berry 1993). $\mathbf{S}_c\mathbf{A}_e(P)$ behaves like P till a time instant when c is entailed; when c is entailed P is suspended from the next time instant onwards (hence the $\mathbf{S}_c$). P is reactivated in the time instant when e is entailed (hence the $\mathbf{A}_e$). This, for instance, is the behavior of the $(\mathtt{control} - \mathbf{Z}, \mathbf{fg})$ mechanism in Unix.

$$
\begin{aligned}
[\![\mathbf{S}_c\mathbf{A}_e(P)]\!] \quad \overset{d}{=} \quad & \{s \in \mathbf{Obs} \mid s \in [\![P]\!], s \not\sqsupseteq [\![c]\!]\} \\
\cup \quad & \{s \cdot a \cdot t \in \mathbf{Obs} \mid s \cdot a \in [\![P]\!], s \not\sqsupseteq [\![c]\!], a \sqsupseteq [\![c]\!], t \not\sqsupseteq [\![e]\!]\} \\
\cup \quad & \{s \cdot a \cdot t \cdot a' \cdot u \in \mathbf{Obs} \mid \; s \cdot a \cdot a' \cdot u \in [\![P]\!], s \not\sqsupseteq [\![c]\!], \\
& \qquad\qquad\qquad d \sqsupseteq [\![c]\!], t \not\sqsupseteq [\![e]\!], d' \sqsupseteq [\![e]\!]\}
\end{aligned}
$$

Multiform time: **time A on c.** One of the most attractive aspects of the synchronous programming languages is that no particular notion of time is built in. There is no basic signal, say a milli-second clock, with control constructs that are defined explicitly for that signal. (This is done, for instance by Timed CSP (Reed and Roscoe 1986).) Rather, the basic temporal sequencing constructs can be used uniformly with respect to *any* signal that extends over time.

On first glance, it might seem that the introduction of Unit Delay and Negative Ask constructs refer explicitly to an underlying clock and hence do not support a multi-form notion of time. This is however not the case. We shall see shortly that in fact it is possible to uniformly clock arbitrary processes using a general class of processes. For the moment, we concentrate on showing how an arbitrary process A may be exposed to some "sub-sampling" of the basic clock.

Intuitively, **time A on c** should denote a process whose notion of time is the occurrence of the primitive constraint c — A evolves only at the time instants at which the store entails c. Those instants at which c is not entailed by the store should be regarded as completely invisible to A. In particular this implies that the notion of the "next time instant" in A will in fact be the "next time instant at which c holds".

Formally, using the notation $s \downarrow a$ to denote the subsequence of s with all elements $\sqsupseteq a$, we have:

$$
[\![\mathbf{time}\ A\ \mathbf{on}\ c]\!] \quad \overset{d}{=} \quad \{s \in \mathbf{Obs} \mid s \downarrow [\![c]\!] \in [\![A]\!]\}
$$

The laws for **time A on c** are easy to write down. We defer giving an explicit presentation because we now show how to define this construct in terms of the more general **clock** construct.

4.4.4.3 A general clocking construct: the clock combinator

The combinators discussed above have a common basic idea — they allow for the introduction of time steps that are ignored by the underlying agent A. This suggests the introduction of a combinator that directly captures this intuition: **clock B**

do A is a process that executes A only on those instants which are quiescent points of B.

Let P be a process. We identify the maximal subsequence t_P of the sequence t that is an element of the process P. t_P is defined inductively by:

$$\epsilon_P = \epsilon$$

$$(s \cdot a)_P = \begin{cases} (s_P) \cdot a, & \text{if } a \in (P \text{ after } (s_P)) \\ (s_P), & \text{otherwise} \end{cases}$$

Now, recognizing that A is executed only at the quiescent points of B we can state:

$$\textbf{clock } B \textbf{ do } A \;\; \overset{d}{=} \;\; \{t \in \textbf{Obs} \mid t_{[B]} \in [A]\}$$

It is easy to see that **clock** B **do** A is non-empty and prefix-closed if $[B]$ and $[A]$ are. However, **clock** B **do** A may not be determinate for arbitrary $[B]$. A necessary and sufficient condition is that $[B]$ **after** s is upwards-closed, for all $s \in [B]$. (Such processes can be thought of as arising by "extending over time" the basic processes of the form **tell** c.) Accordingly, we identify the syntax for "basic processes" by:

$$
\begin{array}{lll}
\text{(Basic Agents)} & B & ::= \quad c \\
& & \mid \quad \textbf{now } c \textbf{ then next } B \\
& & \mid \quad \textbf{now } c \textbf{ else } B \\
& & \mid \quad \textbf{next } B \\
& & \mid \quad \textbf{skip} \\
& & \mid \quad \textbf{abort} \\
& & \mid \quad B \parallel B \\
& & \mid \quad X\hat{\ }B \\
& & \mid \quad g
\end{array}
$$

$$
\begin{array}{lll}
\text{(Basic Procedures)} & D & ::= \quad g :: B
\end{array}
$$

Note that $[\textbf{always } A]$ and $[\textbf{whenever } c \textbf{ do next } A]$ are basic processes if $[A]$ is.

The **clock** combinator is not monotone or anti-monotone in its first argument. Nevertheless, it is possible to establish

$$\textbf{clock } (\mu g.B) \textbf{ do } A \;\; = \;\; \mu g.\textbf{clock } B \textbf{ do } A$$

using the fact that recursion is guarded and fixed-points are unique.

Table 4.6 in Section 4.4.8 shows how to compositionally reduce programs containing this construct into programs that do not. (The table is given in the syntax of Timed Gentzen, explained in Section 4.4.5.)

We illustrate how some standard temporal constructs can be expressed using **clocks**. Clearly, this construct is in the flavor of the **when** construct (undersampling) in LUSTRE and SIGNAL, generalizd to general processes B instead of boolean streams. The combinators introduced above can be expressed thus:

$$\text{now } c \text{ else } A \ = \ \text{clock (now } c \text{ then next abort) do next } A$$
$$\text{whenever } c \text{ do } A \ = \ \text{clock } c \text{ do } A$$
$$\text{time } A \text{ on } c \ = \ \text{clock (always } c) \text{ do } A$$
$$\text{do } A \text{ watching } c \ = \ \text{clock (whenever } c \text{ do next abort) do } A$$
$$S_c A_e(A) \ = \ \text{clock (whenever } c \text{ do next } e) \text{ do } A$$

Repeated pause/resumptions of a process can be expressed by:

$$\text{clock } (\mu g.\text{whenever } c \text{ do next } (e \parallel \text{next } g)) \text{ do } A$$

4.4.5 The language Timed Gentzen

We now turn to a discussion of Timed Gentzen, a concrete tcc programming language. Subsequently, we shall examine several programming idioms in Timed Gentzen, and discuss a simple implementation.

Syntax. The syntax of the language is summarized in Table 4.4. In general, Prolog lexical and syntactic conventions are followed. For technical reasons, Timed Gentzen source programs are prevented from using the functor '_'/2; this is reserved for internal use.

The syntax {C} is used to say that the constraints (atomic formulas) in C are to be added to the store. The syntax C → A is used for **now** C **then** A, C ↝ A for **now** C **else** A.

Parametric asks are used to communicate "data" with signals: they allow an agent to output in the store an atom with argument structure (e.g. b(2,s)), and another agent to explicitly recover the values: e.g., the agent X\$Y\$(b(X,Y) → A) will cause the generation of the agent A[X ↦ 2, Y ↦ s]. For simplicity of implementation, we require that all the existentially and universally quantified Timed Gentzen variables occurring in a clause are distinct Prolog variables, and distinct from variables occurring in the head of a clause.[7]

The syntax [A1, ..., An] is used to signify the parallel composition of the agents A1, ..., An, for n ≥ 0. In particular, [] stands for **skip**.

Using ";", an agent may check whether the current store entails one of a set of constraints (Positive Ask), or does not entail each of a set of constraints (Negative Ask).

Semantics. Timed Gentzen allows a somewhat more liberal syntax for procedure declarations than we have discussed in Section 4.4.3 for the general tcc framework. The syntax is motivated by programming considerations — in particular, the conventions we adopt below allow for a simple and succinct meta-interpreter for the language.

---

[7]Thus, for example, the body X^A, X^B is considered syntactically ill-formed, as is the clause p(a,X) :: f(X), X^A.

Timed Gentzen allows multiple clauses for a procedure, and allows a clause head to contain (non-variable) terms. In the operational semantics, the first clause whose head can be instantiated to match the call is chosen for procedure reduction.

It is easy to transform any such program into a program that satisfies the procedure declaration syntax for general tcc languages. Assume the program has k clauses p(ti1, ..., tin)::Ai, for $i \in 1 \ldots k$. Assume further that all the variables appearing in clause head i are distinct from those appearing in clause head j, and from the variables X1, ..., Xn. The new program contains a single clause for p/n:

p(X1, X2, ..., Xn) ::
    [V1\$(C1 → A1),
     V2\$(C2 → A2),
     . . .
     Vk\$(Ck → Ak)].

where

- $C1 = D1$,

- $C2 = (D2, \neg \exists V1.D1)$,

- $C3 = (D3, \neg \exists V2.D2, \neg \exists V1.D1)$

- . . .

- $Ck = (Dk, \neg \exists V1.D1, \ldots, \neg \exists V(k-1).D(k-1))$,

and $Di = (X1 \doteq ti1, X2 \doteq ti2, \ldots Xn \doteq tin)$. Here, the usual axioms for equality (Clark's equality theory) are understood to be in force for $\doteq$. However the store is not allowed contain any $\doteq$ assertions. Hence for a particular call p(s1, ..., sn), each equality $sj \doteq tij$ can be evaluated "instantaneously". There are no other agents running simultaneously who can cause more equality assertions to be generated, hence there is no need to "suspend". Either the conditions for a particular clause are applicable or not.

Thus, given the program:

p(a(Y)) :: q(Y).
p(a(Y)) :: s(Y).
p(X) :: r(X).

the goal p(b) will reduce to r(b), the goal p(a(1)) to q(1) (not s(1), and not [s(1),q(1)]).

Other aspects. Three other aspects of Timed Gentzen relevant to (meta-) programming should be pointed out.

First, some rudimentary arithmetic and communication abilities are provided through Ask and Tell operations. Conceptually, one imagines that the store contains the infinite collection of assertions about the extension of the relevant arithmetic relations (e.g, 3 > 2, 2 = 2, etc.). Thus, the program fragment X\$(a(X), X > 3 → proc(X)) will invoke proc only if the store contains an atom a(N) where N is a number great than 3. An ersatz ask-predicate read(X) is provided to input (synchronously) a term from an input channel. Conceptually, one imagines that an external agent places the atom read(t) in the store, if t is the term returned by the read operation. Conversely, some output operations are provided as Tell operations — conceptually, these are thought as being added to the store, and being read by and executed on by some external agent.

Second, each of the combinators:

({}/1, ->/2, ~>/2,next/1,\$/2,^/2,[]/0,'.'/2,::/2)

are also data-constructors. Hence a Timed Gentzen agent is also directly representable as a Timed Gentzen data-structure.

Third, it is assumed that the user program is available in the store, as a collection of assertions of the form (∀)Head :: Body. Asks are allowed to query this database, with the restriction that in all queries of the form t::s in the body of a clause K, all variables occurring in t must occur in the head of K. This ensures that by the time t::s has to be executed in the body of the clause, t will contain no uninstantiated universally quantified variables. Such queries can be implemented by merely doing a lookup of the program stored in a Prolog database, and returning the first answer.[8]

Thus, the following is a legal tcc clause:

tcc(Proc) :: Body\$(Proc :: Body → tcc(Body)).

(and indeed is a crucial clause in the definition of a meta-interpreter for Timed Gentzen, Section 4.4.7.1). Given a procedure call, say tcc(f(3)), the effect of this clause would be to determine the unique body, say B for the procedure call f(3), and invoke tcc(B).

The approach we have chosen to make the program available at run-time is very conservative. Clearly, it is possible to think of the program changing arbitrarily from one time-step to the next, just as the store does. Indeed, conceptually the program and the content of the store are identical — a program happens to have more logical structure in its formulas than the store does. We leave the investigation of this line of approach for future work.

---

[8]Without this restriction, the implementation could be forced to return all possible instantiations of the query. This can become complicated, given the semantics for mutually exclusive clauses above.

(Agents)	A	::=	$\{C\}$	— Constraint Tells
		|	$E \rightarrow A$	— Positive Ask
		|	$(X_1, \ldots, X_n)\$E \rightarrow A$	— Parametric (positive) Ask
		|	$E \rightsquigarrow A$	— Negative Ask
		|	$\texttt{next } A$	— Next
		|	$(X_1, \ldots, X_n)\hat{\ }A$	— Hiding
		|	$\texttt{abort}$	— Process abortion
		|	$[A_1, \ldots, A_n]$	— Parallel composition
		|	$p(t_1, \ldots, t_n)$	— Procedure call
(Tell-Constraints)	C	::=	c	— Primitive constraint
		|	C, C	— Conjunction
(Ask-Constraints)	E	::=	c	— Primitive constraint
		|	E, E	— Conjunction
		|	$E; E$	— Disjunction
(Declarations)	D	::=	$p(t_1, \ldots, t_n) :: A$	— Clause
		|	$D.D$	

$$(4.2)$$

Multiple declarations are allowed per procedure. The first to match is selected. The following defined agents are also accepted:

$$
\begin{array}{lll}
\text{(Agents)} \quad A \quad ::= & \texttt{clock}(A, B) & \\
& \mid \quad \texttt{always}(A) & \\
& \mid \quad \texttt{whenever}(C, A) & \\
& \mid \quad \texttt{watching}(C, A) &
\end{array}
$$

$$(4.3)$$

Table 4.4. Syntax for Timed Gentzen.

4.4.6 Specific programming paradigms

We turn to the examination of various concrete programming problems. Because the origins of tcc were in synchronous programming, we first examine how some typical reactive and synchronous computations may be expressed in Timed Gentzen. Next we consider the representation of some common patterns of default inference.

4.4.6.1 Reactive programming A typical reactive programming task is the programming of controllers. For such tasks, it is crucial that the controller program be compilable into a system with bounded run-time state, e.g. an FSA. The programs presented below for two reactive computation tasks satisfy the conditions for bounded compilability discused in Section 4.4.3. (In particular they do not use embedded parametric asks which also contain the seeds of arbitrary recursion.)

4.4.6.2 A simple mouse controller The task is to program a clock-controller for a mouse (Boussinot and deSimone 1991). The program may assume that it is controlled by the environment using **start** and **stop** signals. The task of the program is to count the number of mouse-clicks that occur during each such interval, and output **none**, **single** or **many** depending on whether there are zero, one or more clicks.

Our solution is similar to the one in (Boussinot and deSimone 1991). A process (**mouse_zero(X)**) is set up whose task is to accumulate in X the number of clicks that occur. (The process ceases looking at the **click** signal once the count reaches two; instead it maintains forever the count two.) The process is aborted by the **stop** signal, which also triggers off a process which generates the appropriate output signal based on the accumulated count.

The program illustrates two common idioms in Timed Gentzen programming. First, note the tandem of **watching(stop,...)** and **whenever(stop, ...)** agents. They are used to get the effect of a do ...**watching** ...**trigger** ... construct in which an agent is activated when a do ...**watching** ... agent is aborted. Second note that the **controller** uses a newly created private channel (X) for communication with its **mouse_n** agents. This allows multiple controllers (perhaps on different mice) to be simultaneously active, without interference.

```
controller(Click, Start, Stop) ::
    X^[watching(Stop, whenever(Start, mouse_zero(X, Click))),
       whenever(Stop,
                [X : 0 → {zero},
                 X : 1 → {one},
                 X : 2 → {many}])].

mouse_zero(X, Click) ::
```

```
watching(Click, always {X : 0}),
whenever(Click, next mouse_one(X, Click)).

mouse_one(X, Click) ::
    watching(Click, always {X : 1}),
    whenever(Click, next mouse_many(X, Click)).

mouse_many(X, _Click) :: always ({X : 2}).
```

A single mouse(Count, X, Click) predicate could have been defined, but the recursion in its definition would not satisfy the syntactic conditions for boundedness.

4.4.6.3 An automated teller machine We present a program for the bank teller machine (ATM) of (Berry, Ramseh and Shyamsunder 1993). This machine accepts an ATM card and verifies the identification number. On receiving an incorrect number thrice, the machine swallows the card; else it asks for an amount, requests the bank's authorization, and releases the money if authorization is received; keeping the card otherwise (!). The customer may cancel the operation at any time.

Our solution is presented below. The structure of the program should be fairly clear. The basic technique of *persistent tells* is used to communicate information between losely coupled subsystems. Consider for example the interaction between the ATM controller and the bank. The ATM has access to the communication channels card and code. It must communicate these channels to the bank, thus allowing the bank to read other messages on the channel. (For example, the display would be expected to add (also using persistent tells) tokens of the form card:N, code:P to the store, for N the bank account number read from the card, and P the password read from the display.) Since there can be no guarantee that the bank will process the information sent to it in the current time instant — for example, the bank may be busy in this time instant servicing some other request — the sender must maintain the item in the store indefinitely. This is achieved by the idiom:

```
watching(received, always {message}).
```

Here, message is the signal being sent to some other agent, and received is the signal that it uses to acknowledge receipt.

The program also illustrates a simple convention. Typically an agent adds to the store a pure "signal" (that is, a 0-ary constant, e.g. auth), together with some messages on the signal (e.g. auth:false). Another agent may detect the signal by suspending on the constant; subsequently the messages associated with the signal may be examined in detail. This technique is particularly useful in situations (such as with the card signal) in which an agent in the environment may be passing a complex (unbounded) data-structure (e.g., card number) *through* the finite state controller to another agent in the environment (e.g., bank). The code for the controller never has to handle the complex data-structure, it merely senses information on a (pure) signal and passes that on. In this way, the mobility of the underlying communication mechanism can be used to maintain boundedness of the controller code.

```
ready ::
   [whenever(card,
     [watching((keep_card ; cancel),
        [verify_code(0),
         whenever(code_ok,
           [{display : enter_amount},
            whenever(amount, verify_funds)])])]),
      whenever((keep_card ; cancel), keep_card ↝ {emit_card})]),
    whenever((keep_card ; emit_card), next ready)].

verify_code(Num) ::
   [Num < 3
     → [{display : enter_code},
         whenever(code,
           [watching(verif,
                     always {bank : verify, bank : verify(card, code)}),
            whenever(verif,
              [verif : true → {code_ok},
               verif : false
               → N1$(N1 is Num + 1 → next verify_code(N1))])
           ])],
    Num = := 3 → {keep_card}].

verify_funds ::
   [watching(auth,
             always {bank : request_auth, bank : request_auth(card, amount)}),
    whenever(auth,
             [auth : true → {delivermoney, emit_card},
              auth : false → {keep_card}])].
```

4.4.6.4 Synchronous programming An obvious application of synchronous programming ideas is in the specification of synchronous circuits, such as those used to describe the operation of systolic algorithms (Kung 1979). Computation is performed by a network of cells connected together by "wires", possibly with finite buffering. Data moves rhythmically through the system, pulsed by an external clock.

It should be clear that an arbitrarily-connected network of cells can be described using an (untimed) **Gentzen** program. The synchronous execution of such a system is then described by merely "extending over time" their operation at a particular time instant. At every instant, the environment may supply input and accept output from interface cells. More powerfully, using Timed Negative Asks, a cell may sense if data was *not* present on a wire in the past cycle, and take subsequent action.

A simple concrete example is provided by the obvious program for computing the Fibonacci sequence. This consists of a single cell containing an adder and a two-place buffer, with the output wired into the input:

```
fib(Val) ::
    [{Val : 0}, next {Val : 1},
     always X$(Val : X
                → (next (Y, Z)$
                    ((Val : Y, Z is X + Y) → (next {Val : Z})))))].
```

A harness for running the program is provided by:

```
main(N) ::
    Index^[watching(Index : N,
                        Val^[fib(Val), counter(Index),
                                output(Val, Index, fib)]),
            whenever(Index : N, abort)].

counter(Init, I) ::
    [{I : Init}, always (X, X1)$((I : X, X1 is X + 1) → next {I : X1})].

output(In1, In2, Op) ::
    always (X, I)$((In1 : X, In2 : I) → {format(' ~ p( ~ p) = ~ p. ~ n', [Op, I, X])}).
```

Clearly, other synchronous algorithms can be implemented in a similar way.

4.4.6.5 Programming with defaults We now turn to some techniques that make explicit use of Timed Negative Asks for defeasible default reasoning.

4.4.6.6 Sieve of Eratosthenes Perhaps the simplest example is provided by the old algorithm for computing the sequence of primes.

Assume that the timed sequence of natural numbers, starting with 2 is produced on Val. The program asserts that each such number N is prime by default — unless there is reason to believe that it is not. If the default is not defeated, an agent sieve is set up that declares every subsequent number X not_prime if it is a multiple of N.

```
primes(Val, Output) ::
    always N$(Val : N → not_prime ⤳ [{Output : N}, always sieve(N, Val)].

sieve(N, Val) ::
    X$(Val : X → X mod N = :=0 → {not_prime}).
```

The overall program is obtained by coupling with the counter from the previous section:

```
primes(Primes) ::
    Val^[primes(Val, Primes), counter(2, Val)].
```

The program may be run in a harness (using watching) in the same way as fib.

4.4.6.7 Persistent assignments The next few examples use a variation of the basic tcc technique of persistent tells to maintain defaults in the face of change.

The basic idea can be explained schematically by a simple example. Suppose we would like to implement the requirement that X should be constrained to be 2 unless stated otherwise. Under the assumption that agents wanting to alter the value of X can declare their intention to do so at least one step in advance, the following technique will work.

The agent that wishes to change the value of X must declare its intention by, say, asserting the token changing(X). The persistence of the default value is then maintained by the agent default(X,M) defined by:

```
default(X, M) :: watching(changing(X), always {X = M}).
```

Once changing(X) is asserted, the asserting agent is guaranteed that the default will not be in effect at the next time instant. It may now establish its own constraints on X, including, perhaps, establishing a default for it:

change(X, N) :: [{changing(X)}, next default(X, N)].

This basic technique may be extended in all sorts of application-dependent ways using the power of tcc combinators. For example, using clock, defaults may be specified to hold exactly during the clock ticks supplied by some arbitrary basic process.

4.4.6.8 Safe defaults The next example is from the domain of Qualitative Reasoning about physical systems. It arises from the goal of constructing compositionally symbolic models of complex, real-time dependent, computational electro-mechanical systems, for the purpose of simulation, control and diagnosis.

The task is to model a portion of the control system for the paper-path of a reprographics machine, such as a photo-copier. In general, the paper-path consists of a sequence of baffles, drives, rollers, gates, and electronic sensors. An electronic module takes input from the sensors and controls the flow of power to various motors. Rollers are driven (through gear-trains) by motors; in normal operation they acquire incoming sheets and move them down-stream. However, rollers may malfunction under a variety of conditions — they may be worn and may slip, or the paper may be greasy and difficult to acquire. Therefore, sensors are installed at various locations to detect whether a sheet dallies unduly at that location. When a sensor signals a jam, the power module immediately cuts power supply to drives, thus halting the paper-path.

We are concerned with building libraries of components models that may be used to assemble a system model given knowledge of system components and structure. In particular, we focus on modeling rollers, sensors and (the control logic for) the power-supply. We would like to use these models to construct a model of a simple system consisting of a pair of rollers in series, with a sensor in the middle:

```
system(R0, S0, R1, M0, M1, M2) ::
    [roller(R0, 10, 11, M0),
     sensor(S0, 11, M1),
     roller(R1, 11, 12, M2),
     power_module].
```

A typical call to system/5 would be: system(r35,s41,r36,ok,ok,ok).

What should such component models look like? The models for roller and sensor are straightforward (uniform extensions over time of point-wise, time-independent, monotone models):

```
roller(_R, Before, After, ok) ::
    always (power → at(Before) : paper → next {at(After) : paper}).

roller(_R, Before, _After, slipping) ::
    always (power → at(Before) : paper → next {at(Before) : paper}).

sensor(_S, Loc, ok) ::
    always (power → at(Loc) : paper → next (at(Loc) : paper → jam)).
```

The **power_module** model is however faced with the problem of lack of omniscience about its environment. A **jam** may be signaled in any of various complicated ways, by any of a collection of subsystems whose identity is not known at model-construction time. The simplest way to model the subsystem, then, is as a mechanism that initiates and maintains the supply of power, subject to *interrupts* by its environment:

```
power_module :: watching(jam, always {power}).
```

The example illustrates the basic idea behind what may be termed *safe defaults*: through its very organization, the program guarantees that any conclusions that are contingent on a default inference cannot in themselves bring about (causally determine) a state of affairs that undermines the applicability of the inference rule. No global reasoning needs to be done, no "default extensions" need to be created. On detection of quiescence, all applicable default rules are fired immediately and irrevocably.

It should be clear, however, that the use of tcc languages for system modeling, simulation and diagnosis is a topic in its own right. Of several remarks possible here, we have space for only three:

- The above model may be used not just for simulation but also diagnosis. Here the problem is: we are given observations of the system (e.g. **jam**) and have to determine the mode of operation of devices consistent with these observations. This is a natural motivation for examining the complexity of the *abduction* problem for tcc programs.

- The above model is stated in the fragment of tcc that can be compiled into FSAs. This suggests that the compositional tcc compilation algorithm can already be used to obtain an "envisionment" of the physical system (that is, a finite, succinct description of all its future behaviors). Standard techniques for model-checking finite state systems may then be used to analyze both component as well as system models constructed in this way.

- It should be clear how some standard problems about reasoning with action and change, such as the Yale shooting problem (Hanks and McDermott 1986) have simple solutions in tcc. In essence, tcc makes it possible to say that the effects of certain actions should persist indefinitely *unless* interrupted by the environment. By computing the least solution above the input supplied by the environment, tcc ensures that there is no *deus ex machina* (no phantom actions such as mysterious "unloadings" of guns) — any deviation from defaults arises solely because of input from the environment.

4.4.7 Explicit Minimization

A common mode for organizing computation is this. In one phase, all agents post whatever constraints they want on the variables of interest. On quiescence it is desired to determine *minimal* values for the particular variable — perhaps *the* minimal one (if it is unique), perhaps *some* arbitrary one (if there are many minimal ones; this is sometimes called a "credulous" choice), perhaps the logical disjunction of all the minimal ones (this is sometimes called "skeptical" choice), while keeping the other variables in the store constant or varying. Various kinds of minimization procedures proposed for logic programming and for default reasoning (e.g., varieties of circumscription) fall into this general paradigm.

The tcc model makes possible the specification of "safe" versions of such primitive processes: it makes sense to perform the minimization only on quiescence of the current phase (the minimization operation is not monotone in its argument, hence cannot be run while its argument is being accumulated); hence the new constraint may be added to the store only at the *next* instant; hence structurally in a way that cannot interact with the actual process of minimization itself.

This leads to the addition of a class of minimization agents to the language. Because of the variability mentioned above, many such agents are definable and interesting. Assume $min(X, c)$ is such a minimization operation — it returns a constraint minimal in X given the information c per some chosen definition of minimization. Then we may define the basic process by:

$$[\![\text{minimize}(\mathtt{X})]\!] \;=\; \{\epsilon\} \cup \{c \in \mathbf{Obs}\} \cup \{c \cdot d \cdot s \in \mathbf{Obs} \mid d \geq min(X, c)\}$$

Of course once the basic agent is introduced into the language, it may be combined with all the other combinators in the language in completely general ways.

Two concrete examples should illustrate the matter further. Consider the *histogram* problem studied by researchers in working on determinate data-flow languages. The problem is to efficiently determine the histogram associated with a given input function f. That is, determine, for each point x in the range of f, the number of points in the domain mapped to x.

The following simple algorithm is expressible in Timed Gentzen augmented with a suitable minimization operation: examine the tuples (Index, Value) in f in parallel, asserting that Index belongs to a set associated with Value. On quiescence, minimize the extension of these sets, and take their cardinality. Concretely:

```
histogram(In, Hist) :: (Temp)^
    [(Index, Value)$((Index, Value) in In → {Index in Temp.Value}),
    minimize(Temp),
    next sizeof(Temp, Hist)].
```

minimize(X) is an example of an "indexical" constraint (Hentenryck, Saraswat and Deville 1992) — a functions from constraints to constraints that is not necessarily monotone. Obviously, several other constraint-system specific indexicals are possible in this vein.

The second concrete example is taken from work on model composition in Qualitative Reasoning and is representative of the kind of default inferencing employed therein. While building component models one may only be able to specify very incomplete information about the relationship between some "global" variable X and some variable V corresponding to the component. For example, one may merely know that X varies monotonically with V (assuming that both vary over some ordered set such as the reals). This can, of course, be achieved by asserting the constraint that the partial derivative of X with respect to V is positive. However, once system structure is completely determined, and the constraints between X and the ensemble of component variables $V_1, \ldots, V_n$ established, another piece of information can be deduced, namely, that X is a function of *just* the inputs $V_1, \ldots, V_n$. Structurally, this is a safe default inference because no inference licensed by this deduction should affect the applicability of the default: once the structure of the system has been determined, it has been determined. That is, the default depends only on predications that are going to remain stable for the rest of the deduction, that are causally independent of the consequences of the conclusion of the default.

Such a safe default rule can clearly be directly expressed in Timed Gentzen, augmented with minimization predicates. Indeed the basic notion of *staged computation* underlying tcc is in completely harmony with the ideas of staged model composition underlying model composition work in Qualitative Reasoning.

4.4.7.1 Meta-programming: A Timed Gentzen meta-interpreter The design of Timed Gentzen makes the description of a meta-interpreter easy:

```
tcc({C}) :: {C}.
tcc(C → A) :: C → tcc(A).
tcc(C ⇝ A) :: C ⇝ tcc(A).
tcc(next A) :: next tcc(A).
tcc(Vars$A) :: Vars$tcc(A).
```

tcc(Vars^A) :: Vars^tcc(A).
tcc([]) :: [].
tcc([A | B]) :: [tcc(A) | tcc(B)].
tcc(Proc) :: Body$((Proc :: Body) → tcc(Body).

Only the last clause is interesting. Note that because of the way sequences of clauses are interpreted in Timed Gentzen, the last clause will be activated only on a agent that does not match any of the other clauses. This can happen only for calls to user-defined procedures. In such a case, the body of the procedure is looked up, using a "clause" meta-call, and passed on to a recursive invocation of the meta-interpreter.

4.4.8 Implementation

We now discuss a simple Prolog interpreter for Timed Gentzen. The implementation is intended to enable users to quickly develop, run, test and debug Timed Gentzen programs, thus getting a feel for the tcc computation model. The emphasis in this implementation is on simplicity rather than efficiency — several well-known techniques that have been developed in the literature on implementations of logic programming languages and problem-solving systems can be used to substantially improve performance.[9]

Separately, we are implementing the FSA compilation algorithm outlined in (Saraswat, Jagadeesan and Gupta 1993) for bounded tcc programs. Clearly that compiler, once it exists, will be the implementation of choice to use in fielding embedded, reactive Timed Gentzen programs.

4.4.8.1 The basic interpreter First we begin with basic operation declarations for symbols that will stand for tcc combinators.

← op(1100, xfy, ' :: ').
← op(975, fy, [next, always]).
← op(950, xfy, [→ , ⤳]).
← op(150, xfy, ['^', '$']).
← use_module(library(ordsets)).
← use_module(library(lists)).

The interpreter keeps track of the following pieces of information:

1. The current agents not yet examined (Pool).

---

[9]For instance, one standard technique is to use partial evaluation to generate from this interpreter a compiler that inputs a source tcc program and outputs Prolog code. This technique was used to generate very similar compiler-based implementations of Concurrent Prolog, GHC and Herbrand.

2. The Positive Asks that have already been discharged (Susp).

3. The Tells that have already been executed (Store).

4. The Nexts that have already been identified (Nexts).

5. The Elses that have already been identified (Elses).

6. The current cycle number (Count).

7. The counter for existential quantifiers (V).

At each step, the next agent from the pool is examined. Obvious things are done in simple cases: a [] agent is discarded, an **abort** agent is Prolog-failed (causing Prolog-failed termination of the entire computation), a parallel composition is repackaged, a **next** agent is pushed onto the Next list, an $\rightsquigarrow$ agent is pushed onto the Else list, a recursive procedure call is unfolded by examining the program database.

The interesting cases are Hiding, (parametric) Asks and Tells. Hiding is implemented by using the counters (and the functor ' _'/2) to generate a unique identifier; this is then bound to the Prolog variable representing the quantified Timed Gentzen variable. In the case of a Tell, the argument of the tell is added to the store. At the same time, all possible instances of the Positive Asks (that have already been discharged) that match this tell are added to the pool. Symmetrically, when a new Positive Ask is being executed, all possible instantiations that reduce against tokens in the store are added to Pool. (This is discussed in more detail below.)

Computation in the cycle terminates when Pool is empty. All the accumulated Elses are now examined to see if they should be rejected or retained for the next cycle. The current Suspended agents and store are thrown away. The next cycle commences.

```
tcc([]) ←!.
tcc([A | Pool]) ←!, tcc(A, Pool, [[], a([], []), [], [], 0, 0]).
tcc(A) ← tcc(A, [], [[], a([], []), [], [], 0, 0]).

tcc([], [Store, _SuspA, Elses, Next, C, _V]) ←!,
    next(Elses, Store, Next, New),
    (New = = []
     → format('˜n Termination at T = ˜p.', [C])
    ; (C1 is C + 1,
    tcc(New, [[], a([], []), [], [], C1, 0]))).

tcc([A | Pool], Rest) ← tcc(A, Pool, Rest).

tcc({(A, B)}, Pool, State) ←!, tcc({A}, [{B} | Pool], State).
```

tcc({C}, Pool, [Store, SuspA | Rest]) ←!,
    install_tell(C, Pool, Store, SuspA, NewPool, NewStore),
    tcc(NewPool, [NewStore, SuspA | Rest]).

tcc((E1, E2) → A, Pool, State) ←!, tcc(E1 → E2 → A, Pool, State).
tcc((E1 ; E2) → A, Pool, State) ←!, tcc(E1 → A, [E2 → A | Pool], State).
tcc(C → A, Pool, [Store, SuspA | Rest]) ←!,
    install_ask(C → A, Pool, Store, SuspA, NewPool, NewSuspA),
    tcc(NewPool, [Store, NewSuspA | Rest]).

tcc(E ↝ A, Pool, [Store, SuspA, Elses | Rest]) ←!,
    tcc(Pool, [Store, SuspA, [E ↝ A | Elses] | Rest]).

tcc(next A, Pool, [Store, SuspA, Elses, Nexts | Rest]) ←!,
    tcc(Pool, [Store, SuspA, Elses, [A | Nexts] | Rest]).

tcc(_X$A, Pool, State) ←!, tcc(A, Pool, State).

tcc(Vars^A, Pool, [Store, SuspA, Elses, Nexts, C, V]) ←!,
    inst_ex_vars(Vars, C, V, NV),
    tcc(A, Pool, [Store, SuspA, Elses, Nexts, C, NV]).

tcc(abort, _Pool, _State) ←!, fail.
tcc([], Pool, State) ←!, tcc(Pool, State).
tcc([A | B], Pool, State) ←!, tcc(A, [B | Pool], State).

tcc(Goal, Pool, State) ←!, (Goal :: Body), !, tcc(Body, Pool, State).

4.4.8.2 The Gentzen constraint system. Consider now the implementation of Ask and Tell operations.

Ask operations A check is made for whether the Ask operation is basic (e.g., an arithmetic routine). If it is, the operation is treated as a Prolog call and fails or succeeds as appropriate.

There are two remaining cases. If the Ask is not parametric, then the store is checked for the match; if there is a match, the Ask is reduced. As an optimization, note that there is no need to record the Ask in Susp since multiple firings will result only in the very same body being fired multiple times. If the Ask is parametric, it is recorded in Susp (multiple firings may potentially be different because of the values bound to variables). A check is made for instantiations in the current store.

The heart of the constraint system operation is this check. The Prolog bagof/3 predicate is used to generate all possible matches of the Ask, and, for each match, to generate the corresponding instantiated body of the Ask. Of importance here is the ability to specify that the query in **bagof** must be existentially instantiated for all the variables that occur in the Ask. (It is for this purpose that Susp actually contains the list T of suspended Asks, together with the list of free variables in T. The call to **vars/6** is used to update this list.) This allows the correct treatment of Timed Gentzen universal variables in Ask-queries (and any Timed Gentzen existential variables in the body of the query). Indeed, the Prolog variables representing Timed Gentzen universal variables will never be instantiated in the course of the computation; **bagof** will use those variables to create copies exactly as needed. (Note that atoms added to the store will always be Prolog-ground, since existential variables are represented as Prolog-ground terms.)

The resulting set of agents is then added to Pool.

```
install_ask(C → A, Pool, Store, a(Var, SuspA), NewPool, NewSusp) ←
    ask_basic(C)
    → (NewSusp = a(Var, SuspA),
        (call(C)
            → NewPool = [A | Pool]
            ; NewPool = Pool))
    ; (vars(A, C, Var, VC, Vs, NewVar),
        (VC = = []
            → (member(C, Store)
                → (NewPool = [A | Pool], NewSusp = a(Var, SuspA))
                ; (NewPool = Pool, NewSusp = a(NewVar, [C → A | SuspA])))
            ; (NewSusp = a(NewVar, [C → A | SuspA]),
              (bagof(A, Vs^member(C, Store), Agents)
                → NewPool = [Agents | Pool]
                ; NewPool = Pool)))).
```

```
ask_basic((_X :: _Y)).
ask_basic(_X is _Y).
ask_basic(_X = : = _Y).
ask_basic(_X<_Y).
ask_basic(_X = <_Y).
ask_basic(_X = _Y).
ask_basic(_X> = _Y).
ask_basic(_X>_Y).
ask_basic(read(_X)).
```

```
vars(A, C, Var, VC, Vs, NewVar) ←
    vars(A, VA),
    vars(C, VC), ord_union(VA, VC, Vars1),
    ord_subtract(VC, VA, Vs),
    ord_union(Vars1, Var, NewVar).
```

```
vars(Term, Vars) ← vars(Term, [], Vars).
vars(X, V, Vars) ← var(X), !, ord_add_element(V, X, Vars).
vars(Term, V, Vars) ←
    functor(Term, _F, A),
    vars_each(0, A, Term, V, Vars).
vars_each(M, N, Term, V, Vars) ←
    M = N
    → V = Vars
    ; (M1 is M + 1,
    arg(M1, Term, Term_M1),
    vars(Term_M1, Var1),
    ord_union(Var1, V, Var2),
    vars_each(M1, N, Term, Var2, Vars)).
```

Tells. Tells are implemented dually to Asks. A basic Tell is simply executed;
note that basic Tells allowed are such that they cannot fail. For non-basic Tells,
a check is made to see if the atom being told is already in the store, in which
case it can be discarded. Otherwise bagof/3 is used to generate the list of
instantiated Ask agents (from Susp) that can now fire; this list is added to
Pool.

```
install_tell(C, Pool, Store, a(Vars, SuspA), NewPool, NewStore) ←
    tell_basic(C)
    → (call(C), NewStore = Store, NewPool = Pool)
    ; (member(C, Store)
        → (NewStore = Store, NewPool = Pool)
        ; (NewStore = [C | Store],
            (bagof(A, Vars^member(C → A, SuspA), Agents)
            → NewPool = [Agents | Pool]
            ; NewPool = Pool))).
```

```
tell_basic(format(_X, _Y)).
tell_basic(ttyflush).
```

Negative Asks. When moving from one time instant to the next, the list of
Negative Ask agents is examined. Those agents whose condition is *not* entailed
are carried over; others are discarded.

```
next([], _Store, Next, Next).
```

---

always(A) :: [A, (next always(A))].

if(Cond, Then, Else) :: [Cond → Then, Cond ⤳ Else].

whenever(C, A) :: [C → A, C ⤳ whenever(C, A)].

watching(_C, D) :: D.
watching(C, D → A) :: D → watching(C, A).
watching(C, D ⤳ A) :: (C ; D) ⤳ watching(C, A).
watching(C, (next A)) :: C ⤳ watching(C, A).
watching(C, Vars^A) :: Vars^watching(C, A).
watching(C, _Vars$A) :: watching(C, A).
watching(_C, abort) :: abort.
watching(_C, []) :: [].
watching(C, [A | R]) :: [watching(C, A) | watching(C, R)].
watching(C, Proc) :: Body$((Proc :: Body) → watching(C, Body)).
time_on(C, A) :: clock(always(C), A).
do_watching(C, A) :: clock(whenever(C, (next abort)), A).
susp_act(C, E, A) :: clock(whenever(C, (next E)), A).

Table 4.5. Timed Gentzen definition of assorted combinators.

next([C ⤳ A | E], Store, Next, Out) ←!,
    (succeeds(C, Store)
        → next(E, Store, Next, Out)
        ; (Out = [A | Out1], next(E, Store, Next, Out1))).

succeeds((C1, C2), Store) ←!, succeeds(C1, Store), succeeds(C2, Store).
succeeds((C1 ; C2), Store) ←!, (succeeds(C1, Store) ; succeeds(C2, Store)).
succeeds(C, Store) ← ask_basic(C) → call(C) ; member(C, Store).

That's it! This completes the description of the interpreter. The general combinators defined in previous sections (e.g. whenever, watching) can be defined as user programs (Tables 4.5, 4.6).

4.4.9 Future work

The ideas above open up a new line of attack on the problem of systematic, model-based design of embedded, reactive, real-time systems, e.g., those used

clock(C, A) :: whenever(C, A).
clock(abort, _A) :: [].
clock(_A, abort) :: abort.
clock([], A) :: A.
clock(_A, []) :: skip.
clock([B | R], A) :: clock(B, clock(R, A)).
clock(B, [A | R]) :: [clock(B, A) | clock(B, R)].
clock(next _B, D) :: D.
clock(next B, D → A) :: D → clock(next B, A).
clock(next B, D ↝ A) :: D ↝ clock(B, A).
clock(next B, next A) :: next clock(B, A).
clock(next B, Vars^A) :: Vars^clock(next B, A).
clock(next B, _Vars$A) :: clock(next B, A).
clock(next B, Proc) :: Body$(Proc :: Body → clock(next B, Body)).
clock((_C → (next _B)), D) :: D.
clock((C → (next B)), (D → A)) :: D → clock((C → (next B)), A).
clock((C → (next B)), (D ↝ A)) :: [(C → clock((next B), (D ↝ A))), ((C, D) ↝ A)].
clock((C → (next B)), next A) :: [(C → (next clock(B, A))), (C ↝ A)].
clock((C → (next B)), Vars^A) :: Vars^clock((C → (next B)), A).
clock((C → (next B)), _Vars$A) :: clock((C → (next B)), A).
clock((C → (next B)), Proc) :: Body$(Proc :: Body → clock((C → (next B)), Body)).
clock((_C ↝ _B), D) :: D.
clock((C ↝ B), (D → A)) :: D → clock((C ↝ B), A).
clock((C ↝ B), (D ↝ A)) :: [(C → (D ↝ A)), ((C, D) ↝ clock(B, A))].
clock((C ↝ B), next A) :: [(C → (next A)), (C ↝ clock(B, A))].
clock((C ↝ B), Vars^A) :: Vars^clock((C ↝ B), A).
clock((C ↝ B), _Vars$A) :: clock((C ↝ B), A).
clock((C ↝ B), Proc) :: Body$(Proc :: Body → clock((C ↝ B), Body)).
clock(Proc, A) :: Body$(Proc :: Body → clock(Body, A)).

Table 4.6. Timed Gentzen definition of clock/2.

to control complex electro-mechanical systems such as airplanes, photo-copiers etc. Considerable work lies ahead on several fronts.

4.4.9.1 Developing methods for generating real-time schedulers from tcc models
An important use of the tcc is in specifying the behavior of simple, computationally-controlled physical mechanisms, such as the paper-path and video-path in a digital photo-copier. This leads to the problem of synthesizing optimal controllers for these physical mechanisms. For example, we can (and, in a slightly different way, have) specify the components of the paper-path in a photocopier and the Xerographic subsystem in tcc. The problem of synthesizing a scheduler is now the problem of synthesizing the time-sequenced control signals that must be input into the system such that the desired output (the properly constituted output job, e.g. 4 double-sided copies, stapled) is produced as early as possible. This can be solved by extracting from the tcc program a constraint problem and solving it using optimization techniques. For example, in the case of some of the scheduling problems we have looked at, the optimization problems generated are a subcase of the integer linear programming problem, and can be solved by dynamic programming. In other cases, we expect considerably harder optimization problems to arise.

Another interesting set of problems arise in re-planning. The schedule, once generated, are pressed into action. Various exceptions can arise at run-time. Sheets may get delayed because a roll is slipping, a video-image may be so complicated as to cause the decompression software to be late in delivering video bits to the output laser, etc. Thus execution has to be monitored, and then, in case of exceptions, subsidiary scheduling problems have to be generated. These are modified versions of the initial problem (with some of the initial commitments in place, and some others contradicted). This naturally motivates examining algorithms for incrementally (re-)solving these optimization problems.

4.4.9.2 Program Verification
The advantages of reasoning with executable specifications is well known; *c.f.* Berry's WYPIWYE principle or executable intermediate representations for compilers. tcc can be viewed as an executable temporal logic, thus permitting programs and properties to be expressed in the same language.

For example, let p be the property "any occurrence of event a must cause b to be true until the next occurrence of event c". The property can be directly expressed as the program:

p :: **whenever** a **do** (**do always** b **watching** c).

An agent A satisfies p iff:
$$A \vdash p$$

Hence, one may use the logic for reasoning about inequivalence of tcc programs for establishing that programs posseses such properties.

We plan to investigate the use of automated tools(theorem provers and model checkers) to solve this verification problem. In particular, since parallel composition is modeled by the logical operation of conjunction, there is hope of performing compositional model checking, thus mitigating the state explosion problem.

For an alternate approach, recall that deterministic safety properties correspond precisely to safety automata (Manna and Pnueli 1990) that have a single designated failure state. Combined with the fact that tcc allows programs and properties to be expressed in the same language, this leads to the promise of reducing general safety properties of tcc programs to checking the reachability of a designated failure state.

From the programming point of view, this suggests a further integration of the logic and programs. At present, tcc allows access only to the *current* value of signal variables. We will investigate the addition of *global* constraints on signal variables, say in the spirit of LUSTRE and SIGNAL. For example, let X, Y, Z be channels that receive one input at each time instant. Then, $\uparrow Z = \uparrow X + \uparrow Y$ would indicate that at all time instants, the value of Z is the sum of the values of X and Y. The utility of this construct for programming and verification needs to be investigated.

4.4.9.3 Towards a theory of preemption In the traditional theory of sequential programming, preemption and abortion constructs have not been investigated separately. The primary reason for this apparent oversight is that control constructs of this form are "compilable" back to traditional combinators, via the continuation passing transform. For example, exceptions in ML are handled this way.

Unfortunately, this oversight has continued in much of the traditional work on process theory, where there is no obvious compilation of preemption constructs back into basic combinators. Indeed, synchronous languages arose in part as an attempt to remedy this flaw. However, the problem is now the plethora of preemption constructs. For example, what is the relationship, if any, between the constructs supported by ESTEREL and those supported by SIGNAL? The unification of the pre-emption combinators in LUSTRE, SIGNAL and ESTEREL achieved by tcc suggests that tcc encapsulates the rudiments of a theory of pre-emption constructs. A fully developed theory would identify the properties of an ambient category of processes that would allow the "orthogonal" addition of pre-emption constructs. A first step would be to explore the connections of tcc with Interaction categories (Abramsky 1993), a general description of synchronous processes.

4.4.9.4 Integration of asynchronous and synchronous computation This paper has focused on synchronous systems; the reason for focusing initially on synchronous systems is that they can be construed as the building blocks for asynchronous systems. Following the route similar to (Berry, Ramseh and Shyamsunder 1993), an asynchronous model of computation can be constructed by message passing between synchronous nodes; message delivery is guaranteed but there are no bounds on message delivery time. In our setting, this translates to a bunch of synchronous nodes running tcc programs, communicating with each other via constraints, where the time taken for stores to incorporate constraints can be unbounded. Thus, indeterminacy arises naturally as the result of abstracting away from timing considerations. From a logical point of view, this idea is captured by the idea of *eventual* tells, modeled by the "Eventual" modality in (linear-time) temporal logic. As in tcc, this program will involve development of foundational and pragmatic aspects.

- From a foundational point of view, this language to satisfy the same strong properties as tcc; namely, the logical and model theoretic readings will enable declarative programming styles and direct specification of complex process descriptions, and their algebraic manipulation.

- From a programming point of view, the language should recover the expressiveness associated with traditional process calculi, for example Hoare's CSP, Occam and Milner's CCS. In fact, since the tcc paradigm already incorporates the ability to "pass channel names" more powerful calculi, say Milner's Pi-calculus, should be mimicked. The significant difference from programming in traditional process calculi will be twofold: firstly, the ability to program declaratively that is made possible by the logical foundations of the language; and secondly, the integration of real time into programming and reasoning.

References

S. Abramsky. Interaction categories. Available by anonymous ftp from papers/Abramsky:theory.doc.ic.ac.uk, 1993.

A. V. Aho, R. Sethi, and J. D. Ullman. *Compilers – Principles, techniques and tools.* Addison-Wesley, 1985.

H. Barringer, M. Fisher, D. Gabbay, G. Gough, and R. Owens. Metatem: A framework for programming in temporal logic. In J. W. de Bakker, W. P. de Roevere, and G. Rozenberg, editors, *Stepwise Refinement of Distributed Systems– Models, Formalisms, Correctness.* LNCS 430. Springer-Verlag, 1990.

M. Baudinet. Temporal logic programming is complete and expressive. In *Proc. of ACM conference on Principles of Programming languages*, 1989.

G. Berry and G. Boudol. The chemical abstract machine. In *Proceedings of the 17th Annual ACM Symposium on Principles of Programming Languages*, 1990.

F. Boussinot and R. de Simone. The ESTEREL language. *Proceedings of the IEEE*, 79(9):1293–1304, 1991.

G. Berry. Real-time programming: General purpose or special-purpose languages. In G. Ritter, *Information Processing 89*, pages 11–17. Elsevier. (North-Holland), 1989.

G. Berry. Preemption in concurrent systems. In *Proc. of FSTTCS*. LNCS 781. Springer-Verlag, 1993.

G. Berry and G. Gonthier. The ESTEREL programming language: Design, semantics and implementation. *Science of Computer Programming*, 19(2):87–152, November 1992.

G. Berry, S. Ramesh, and R.K. Shyamsunder. Communicating reactive processes. In *Proceedings of Twentieth ACM Symposium on Principles of Programming Languages*, pages 85–98, 1993.

C. Brzoska. Temporal logic programming and its relation to constraint logic programming. In V. A. Saraswat and K. Ueda, editors, *Logic Programming: Proceedings of the 1991 International Symposium*, pages 661–677, 1991.

K. Forbus and J. deKleer. *Building Problem Solvers*. MIT Press, 1993.

P. Le Guernic, M. Le Borgne, T. Gauthier, and C. Le Maire. Programming real time applications with SIGNAL. In *Special issue on Another Look at Real-time Systems*, Proceedings of the IEEE, September 1991.

Matthew Ginsberg, editor. *Readings in Nonmonotonic Reasoning*. Morgan Kaufmann, 1987.

N. Halbwachs. *Synchronous programming of reactive systems*. The Kluwer international series in Engineering and Computer Science. Kluwer Academic Publishers, 1993.

N. Halbwachs, P. Caspi, and D. Pilaud. The synchronous programming language LUSTRE. In *Special issue on Another Look at Real-time Systems*, Proceedings of the IEEE, Special issue on Another Look at Real-time Systems, September 1991.

S. Hanks and D. McDermott. Default reasoning, nonmonotonic logics, and the frame problem. In *Proceedings of Fifth National Conference on Artificial Intelligence*, pages 328–333, 1986.

D. Harel. Statecharts: A visual approach to complex systems. *Science of Computer Programming*, 8:231 – 274, 1987.

D. Harel and A. Pnueli. On the development of reactive systems,In: K. R. Apt (ed.) *Logics and Models of Concurrent Systems*, pages 471–498. NATO ASI Series F, Vol. 13. Springer-Verlag, 1985.

C. A. R. Hoare. *Communicating Sequential Processes*. Series in Computer Science. Prentice-Hall International, London, 1985.

C.A.R. Hoare. *Communicating Sequential Processes*. Prentice-Hall International Series in Computer Science. Prentice-Hall, 1985.

P. Van Hentenryck, V. A. Saraswat, and Y. Deville. Constraint processing in cc(fd). Technical report, Computer Science Department, Brown University, 1992.

H.T. Kung. Let's design algorithms for VISI systems. Technical Report 151, CMU-CS, Jan 1979.

Z. Manna and A. Pnueli. A hierarchy of temporal properties. In *Proceedings of the ACM SIGPLAN conference on Principles of Programming Languages*, 1990.

R. Merz. Efficiently executing temporal logic programs. In M. Fisher and R. Owens, editors, *Proc. of IJCAI*, 1993.

R. Milner. *A calculus of communicating systems*. LNCS 92, Springer-Verlag, 1980.

R. Milner. *Communication and Concurrency*. Prentice-Hall, 1989.

R. Milner. Calculi for synchrony and asynchrony. *Theoretical Computer Science*, 25:267–310, 1983.

B. Moszkowski. *Executing Temporal Logic Programs*. Cambridge Univ. Press, 1986.

R. Milner, J. G. Parrow, and D. J. Walker. A calculus for mobile processes, part I and II. LFCS Report ECS-LFCS-89-85, University of Edinburgh, 1989.

G. Murakami and R. Sethi. Terminal call processing in esterel. Technical Report 150, AT& T Bell Labs, 1990.

Special issue on real-time systems, 1991.

G.M. Reed and A.W. Roscoe. A timed model for communicating sequential processes. In *Proceedings of ICALP '86*,LNCS 226 Springer-Verlag, 1986.

Vijay A. Saraswat. The Category of Constraint Systems is Cartesian-closed. In *Proc. 7th IEEE Symp. on Logic in Computer Science, Santa Cruz*, 1992.

Vijay A. Saraswat. *Concurrent Constraint Programming*. Logic Programming and Doctoral Dissertation Award Series. MIT Press, March 1993.

Vijay Saraswat, Radha Jagadeesan, and Vineet Gupta. Foundations of timed concurrent constraint programming. Technical report, Xerox Palo Alto Research Center, December 1993. Submitted for publication.

Vijay A. Saraswat, Martin Rinard, and Prakash Panangaden. Semantic foundations of concurrent constraint programming. In *Proceedings of Eighteenth ACM Symposium on Principles of Programming Languages, Orlando*, January 1991.

D.S. Weld and J. de Kleer. *Readings in Qualitative Reasoning about Physical Systems*. Morgan Kaufmann, 1989.

4.5 An Introduction to AKL A Multi-Paradigm Programming Language

Sverker Janson and Seif Haridi

Swedish Institute of Computer Science
Box 1263, S-164 28 KISTA, Sweden
E-mail sverker@sics.se, seif@sics.se

4.5.1 Introduction

AKL is a multi-paradigm programming language based on a concurrent constraint framework (Janson and Haridi 1991), directly or indirectly supporting the following paradigms.

- processes and process communication,

- object-oriented programming,

- functional and relational programming,

- constraint programming.

These aspects of AKL are cleanly integrated, and provided using a minimum of basic concepts, common to them all. AKL agents will serve as processes, objects, functions, relations, or constraints, depending on the context.

AKL is a programming language kernel. Some aspects of a complete programming language, a user language, have been omitted, such as type declarations and modules, a standard library, and direct syntactic support for some of the programming paradigms; but the programming paradigms and the basic implementation technology developed for AKL will carry over to any user language based on AKL.

In the following sections, we will introduce AKL, then describe process programming in AKL, object-oriented programming in AKL, functional and relational programming in AKL, and constraint programming in AKL. Finally, it will be shown how these aspects may be integrated in an application.

4.5.2 Concurrent Constraint Programming

AKL is based on the concept of concurrent constraint programming, a paradigm distinguished by its elegant notions of communication and synchronisation based on constraints (Saraswat 1993).

In a concurrent constraint programming language, a computation state consists of a group of *agents* and a *store* that they share. Agents may add pieces of information to the store, an operation called *telling*, and may also wait for the presence in the store of pieces of information, an operation called *asking*. The information in the store is expressed in terms of *constraints*, which are statements in some constraint language, usually based on first-order logic, e.g.,

$$X < 1, Y = Z + X, W = [a, b, c], \ldots$$

If telling makes a store inconsistent, the computation fails (more on this later). Asking a constraint means waiting until the asked constraint either is *entailed* by (follows logically from) the information accumulated in the store or is *disentailed* by (the negation follows logically from) the same information. In other words, no action is taken until it has been established that the asked constraint is true or false. For example,

$X < 1$ is obviously entailed by
$X = 0$ and disentailed by
$X = 1$.

Constraints restrict the range of possible values of variables that are shared between agents. A variable may be thought of as a container. Whereas variables in conventional languages hold single values, variables in concurrent constraint programming languages may be thought of as holding the (possibly infinite) set of values consistent with the constraints currently in the store. This extensional view may be complemented by an intensional view, in which each variable is thought of as holding the constraints which restrict it. This latter view is often more useful as a mental model.

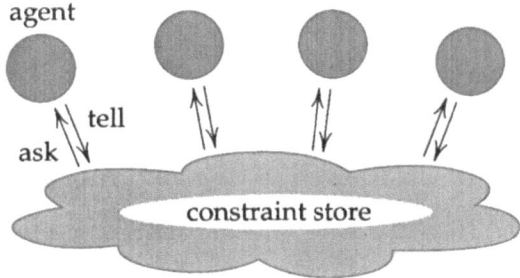

Fig. 4.1. Agents interacting with a constraint store

The range of constraints that may be used in a program is defined by the current *constraint system*, which in AKL, in principle, may be any first-order theory. In practice, it is necessary to ensure that the telling and asking operations used are computable and have a reasonable computational complexity. Constraint systems as such are not discussed here. For the purpose of this introduction, we will use a simple constraint system with a few obvious constraints, which is essentially that of Prolog and GHC to which arithmetic has been added.

Thus, constraints in AKL will be formulas of the form

$$\langle expression \rangle = \langle expression \rangle$$
$$\langle expression \rangle \neq \langle expression \rangle$$
$$\langle expression \rangle < \langle expression \rangle$$

and the like. Equality constraints, e.g.,

X = 1, are often called *bindings*, suggesting that the variable
X is *bound* to 1 by the constraint.

Correspondingly, the act of telling a binding on a variable is called *binding* the variable. Expressions are either *variables* (alpha-numeric symbols with an upper case initial letter), e.g.,

$$X, Y, Z, X1, Y1, Z1, \ldots$$

or *numbers*, e.g.,

1, 3.1415, -42, ...

or *arithmetic expressions*, e.g.,

1 + X, -Y, X * Y, ...

or *constants*, e.g.,

a, b, c, ...

or *constructor expressions* of the form

$$\langle name \rangle (\langle expression \rangle, \ldots, \langle expression \rangle)$$

where $\langle name \rangle$ is an alpha-numeric symbol with a lower case initial letter, e.g.,

s(s(0)), tree(X, L, R), ...

There is also the constant [] , which denotes the empty list, and the list constructor [$\langle expression \rangle | \langle expression \rangle$].

A syntactic convention used in the following is that, e.g., the expression [a | [b | [c | d]]] may be written as [a, b, c | d], and the expression [a | [b | [c | []]]] may be written as [a, b, c]. In addition we assume that constraints *true* and *false* are available, which are independent of the constraint system and may be identified with their corresponding logical constants.

4.5.3 Basic Concepts

The agents of concurrent constraint programming correspond to statements being executed concurrently. Constraints, as described in the previous section, are atomic statements known as *constraint atoms* (or just constraints). When they are asked and when they are told is discussed in the following.

A *program atom* statement of the form

$$\langle name \rangle (X1, \ldots, Xn)$$

is a defined agent. In a program atom, $\langle name \rangle$ is an alpha-numeric symbol and n is the arity of the atom. The variables

X1, ..., Xn are the *actual parameters* of the atom. Occurrences of program atoms in programs are sometimes referred to as *calls*. Atoms of the above form may be referred to as $\langle name \rangle / n$ atoms, e.g.,

$$\text{plus(X, Y, Z)}$$

is a plus/3 atom. Occasionally, when no ambiguity can arise, "$/n$" is dropped. The behaviour of atoms is given by *(agent) definitions* of the form

$$\langle name \rangle (X1, \ldots, Xn) := \langle statement \rangle.$$

The variables X_1, ..., X_n must be different and are called *formal parameters*. During execution, any atom matching the left hand side will be replaced by the statement on the right hand side, with actual parameters replacing occurrences of the formal parameters. A definition of the above form is said to define the $\langle name \rangle / n$ atom, e.g.,

$$\text{plus(X, Y, Z)} := Z = X + Y.$$

is a definition of plus/3.

A *composition* statement of the form

$$\langle statement \rangle, \ldots, \langle statement \rangle$$

builds a composite agent from a sequence of agents. Its behaviour is to replace itself with the concurrently executing agents corresponding to its components.

A *conditional choice* statement of the form

$$(\langle statement \rangle \rightarrow \langle statement \rangle \; ; \; \langle statement \rangle)$$

is used to express conditional execution. Let us call its components condition, then-branch, and else-branch, respectively. (Later a more general version of this statement will be introduced.)

Let us, for simplicity, assume that the condition is a constraint. A conditional choice statement will ask the constraint in the condition from the store. If it is entailed, the then-branch replaces the statement. If it is disentailed, the else-branch replaces the statement. If neither, the statement will wait until either becomes known. If the condition is an arbitrary statement, the above described actions will take place when the condition has been reduced to a constraint or when it fails. The concept of failure is discussed later.

A *hiding* statement of the form

$$X1, \ldots, Xn : \langle statement \rangle$$

introduces variables with local scope. The behaviour of a hiding statement is to replace itself with its component statement, in which the variables
X1, ..., Xn have been replaced by new variables.

Let us at this point establish some syntactic conventions.

- Composition binds tighter than hiding, e.g.,

$$X : p, q, r$$

  means

$$X : (p, q, r)$$

  Parentheses may be used to override this default, e.g.,

$$(X : p), q, r$$

- Any variable occurring free in a definition (i.e., not as one of the formal parameters, nor introduced by a hiding statement) is implicitly introduced by a hiding statement enclosing the right hand side of the definition, e.g.,

$$p(X, Y) := q(X, Z), r(Z, Y).$$

  where Z occurs free, means

$$p(X, Y) := Z : q(X, Z), r(Z, Y).$$

  in which hiding has been made explicit.

- Expressions may be used as arguments to program atoms, and will then correspond to bindings on the actual parameters, e.g.,

$$p(X+1, [a, b, c])$$

  means

$$(\; Y, Z : Y = X+1, Z = [a, b, c], p(Y, Z) \;)$$

where the new arguments have also been made local by hiding.

It is now time for a first small example: an append/3 agent which is used to concatenate two lists.

append(X, Y, Z) :=
   (X = [] → Z = Y
   ; X = [E|$X1$], append($X1, Y, Z1$), Z = [E|$Z1$]).

It will initially suffice to think about constraints in two different ways, depending on the context in which they occur. When occurring as conditions, constraints are asked. Elsewhere, they are told.

In append/3, the condition X = [] is asked, which means that it may be read "as usual". If it is entailed, the then-branch is chosen, in which Z = Y is told. If the condition is disentailed, the else-branch is chosen. There, X = [E—X_1] is told. Since X is not [], it is assumed that it is a list constructor, in which E is equal to the head of X and X_1 equal to the tail of X. The recursive append call makes Z_1 the concatenation of X_1 and Y. The final constraint Z = [E—Z_1] builds the output Z from E and the partial result Z_1.

Note how variables allow us to work with incomplete data. In a call

   append([1, 2, 3], Y, Z)

the parameters Z and Y can be left unconstrained. The third parameter Z may still be computed as [1, 2, 3 | Y], where the tail Y is unconstrained. If Y is later constrained by, e.g., Y = [], then it is also the case that Z = [1, 2, 3].

Variables are also indirectly the means of communication and synchronisation. If a constraint on a variable is asked, the corresponding agent, e.g., conditional choice statement, is suspended and may be restarted whenever an appropriate constraint is told on the variable by another agent.

At this point it seems appropriate to illustrate the nature of concurrent computation in AKL. The following definitions will create a list of numbers, and add together a list of numbers, respectively.

list(N, L) :=
   (N = 0 → L = []
   ; L = [N |$L1$], list(N − 1,$L1$)).

sum(L, N) :=
   (L = [] → N = 0
   ; L = [M|$L1$], sum($L1,N1$), N = $N1$ + M).

The following computation is possible. In the examples, computations will be shown by performing rewriting steps on the state (or configuration) at hand, unfolding definitions and substituting values for variables, etc., where appropriate, which should be intuitive. In this example we avoid details by showing only the relevant atoms and the collection of constraints on the output variable N. Intermediate computation steps are skipped. Thus, list(3, L), sum(L, N)

is rewritten to

list(2, $L1$), sum([3|$L1$], N)

by unfolding the list atom, executing the choice statement, and substituting values for variables according to equality constraints. This result may in its turn be rewritten to

list(1,$L2$), sum([2|$L2$],$N1$), N $= 3 + N1$

by similar manipulations of the list and sum atoms. Further possible states are

list(0, $L3$), sum([1|$L3$], $N2$), N $= 5 + N2$
sum([], $N3$), N $= 6 + N3$
N $= 6$

with final state N $= 6$.

The list/2 call produces a list, and the sum/2 call is there to consume its parts as soon as they are created. The logical variable allows the sum/2 call to know when data has arrived. If the tail of the list being consumed by the sum/2 call is unconstrained, the sum/2 call will wait for it to be produced (in this case by the list/2 call).

In this example, a particular execution order was chosen, but observe that the final result is quite independent of the execution order.

The simple set of constructs introduced so far is a fairly complete programming language in itself, quite comparable in expressive power to, e.g., functional programming languages. If we were merely looking for Turing completeness, the language could be restricted, and the constraint systems could be weakened considerably. But then important aspects such as concurrency, modularity, and, of course, expressiveness would all be sacrificed on the altar of simplicity.

In the following sections, we will introduce constructs that address the specific needs of important programming paradigms, such as processes and process communication, object-oriented programming, relational programming, and constraint satisfaction. In particular, we will need the ability to choose between alternative computations in a manner more flexible than that provided by conditional choice.

4.5.4 Don't Care Nondeterminism

In concurrent programming, processes should be able to react to incoming communication from different sources. In constraint programming, constraint propagating agents should be able to react to different conditions. Both of these cases can be expressed as a number of possibly non-exclusive conditions with corresponding branches. If one condition is satisfied, its branch is chosen.

For this, AKL provides the *committed choice* statement

$$(\ \langle statement \rangle \mid \langle statement \rangle$$
$$; \ldots$$
$$; \langle statement \rangle \mid \langle statement \rangle \ )$$

The symbol "|" is called *commit*. The statement preceding commit is called a *guard* and the statement following it is called a *body*. A pair

$$\langle statement \rangle \mid \langle statement \rangle$$

is called a *(guarded) clause*, and may be enclosed in hiding as follows.

$$X1, \ldots, Xn : \langle statement \rangle \mid \langle statement \rangle$$

The variables $X_1, \ldots, X_n$ are called *local variables* of the clause.

Let us first, for simplicity, assume that the guards are all constraints. The committed-choice statement will ask all guards from the store. If any of the guards is entailed, the composition of its constraint and its corresponding body replaces the committed-choice statement. If a guard is disentailed, its corresponding clause is deleted. If all clauses are deleted, the committed choice statement fails. Otherwise, it will wait. Thus, it may select an arbitrary entailed guard, and commit the computation to its corresponding body.

If a variable Y is hidden, an asked constraint is preceded by the expression "for some Y" (or logically, "∃Y"). For example, in

$$X = f(a), (\ Y : X = f(Y) \mid q(Y) \ )$$

the asked constraint is $\exists Y(X = f(Y))$ ("for some Y, $X = f(Y)$"), which is entailed, since there exists a Y (namely "a") such that $X = f(Y)$ is entailed.

List merging may now be expressed as follows, as an example of an agent receiving input from two different sources.

```
merge(X, Y, Z) :=
        ( X = [] | Z = Y
        ; Y = [] | Z = X
        ; E, X1 : X = [E|X1] | Z = [E|Z1], merge(X1, Y, Z1)
        ; E, Y1 : Y = [E|Y1] | Z = [E|Z1], merge(X,Y1, Z1) ).
```

A merge agent can react as soon as either X or Y is given a value. In the last two clauses, hiding introduces variables that are used for "matching" in the guard, as discussed above. These variables are constrained to be equal to the corresponding list components.

4.5.5 Don't Know Nondeterminism

Many problems, especially frequent in the field of Artifical Intelligence, and also found elsewhere, e.g., in operations research, are currently solvable only by resorting to some form of search. Many of these admit very concise solutions if the programming language abstracts away the details of search by providing don't know nondeterminism.

For this, AKL provides the *nondeterminate choice* (or *don't know choice*) statement.

$$(\ \langle statement \rangle \ ? \ \langle statement \rangle$$
$$; \dots$$
$$; \ \langle statement \rangle \ ? \ \langle statement \rangle \ )$$

The symbol "?" is called *wait*. The statement is otherwise like the committed choice statement in that its components are called *(guarded) clauses*, the components of a clause *guard* and *body*, and a clause may be enclosed in hiding.

Again we assume that the guards are all constraints. The nondeterminate choice statement will also ask all guards from the store. If a guard is disentailed, its corresponding clause is deleted. If all clauses are deleted, the choice statement fails. If only one clause remains, the choice statement is said to be determinate. Then the composition of the constraint in the remaining guard and its corresponding body replaces the choice statement. Otherwise, if there is more than one clause left, the choice statement will wait. Subsequent telling of other agents may make it determinate. If eventually a state is reached in which no other computation step is possible, each of the remaining clauses may be tried in different copies of the state. The alternative computation paths are explored concurrently.

Let us first consider a very simple example, an agent that accepts either of the constants a or b, and then does nothing.

p(X) :=
        (X = a ? true
        ; X = b ? true).

The interesting thing happens when the agent p is called with an unconstrained variable as an argument. That is, we expect it to produce output. Let us call p together with an agent q examining the output of p.

q(X, Y) :=
        (X = a → Y = 1
        ; Y = 0).

Then the following is one possible computation starting from

        p(X), q(X, Y)

First p and q are both unfolded.

$$(\; X = a \; ? \; true \; ; \; X = b \; ? \; true \;), \; (\; X = a \rightarrow Y = 1 \; ; \; Y = 0 \;)$$

At this point in the computation, the nondeterminate choice statement is non-determinate, and the conditional choice statement cannot establish the truth or falsity of its condition. The computation can now only proceed by trying the clauses of the nondeterminate choice in different copies of the computation state. Thus,

$$X = a, \; (\; X = a \rightarrow Y = 1 \; ; \; Y = 0 \;)$$
$$Y = 1$$

and

$$X = b, \; (\; X = a \rightarrow Y = 1 \; ; \; Y = 0 \;)$$
$$Y = 0$$

are the two possible computations. Observe that the nondeterminate alternatives are ordered in the order of the clauses in the nondeterminate choice statement. This ordering will be used later.

Now, what could possibly be the use of having an agent generate alternative results? This we will try to answer in the following. It will help to think of the alternative results as a sequence of results. Composition of two agents will compute the intersection of the two sequences of results. This will be illustrated using the member agent, which examines membership in a list.

member(X, Y) :=
$$(\; Y1 : Y = [X|Y1] \; ? \; true$$
$$; \; X1, Y1 : Y = [X1|Y1] \; ? \; member(X, Y1) \;).$$

The agent

$$member(X, [a, b, c])$$

will establish whether the value of X is in the list $[a, b, c]$. When the agent is called with an unconstrained X, the different members of the list are returned as different possible results (in the order a, b, c, due to the way the program is written). The composition

$$member(X, [a, b, c]), \; member(X, [b, c, d])$$

will compute the X that are members in both lists. When two nondeterminate choice statements are available, the leftmost is chosen. In this case it will enumerate members of the first list, creating three alternative states

$$X = a, \text{member}(X, [b, c, d])$$
$$X = b, \text{member}(X, [b, c, d])$$
$$X = c, \text{member}(X, [b, c, d])$$

The members in the first list that are not members in the second are eliminated by the failure of the corresponding alternative computations. A computation that fails leaves no trace in the sequence of results, and the two final alternative states will be

$$X = b$$
$$X = c$$

In fact, the sequence of results may become empty, as in the case of the following composition

$$\text{member}(X, [a, b, c]), \text{member}(X, [d, e, f])$$

Such complete failure is also useful, as discussed in the following.

4.5.6 General Statements in Guards

Although we have ignored it up to this point, any statement may be used as a guard in a choice statement. The behaviour presented above has been that of the special case when conditions and guards are constraints. This will now be generalised.

Before we proceed, we introduce the general conditional choice statement.

$$(\ \langle statement \rangle \rightarrow \langle statement \rangle$$
$$; \ldots$$
$$; \langle statement \rangle \rightarrow \langle statement \rangle \ )$$

The symbol "$\rightarrow$" is called *then*. Again, the statement is otherwise like the other choice statements in that its components are called *(guarded) clauses*, the components of a clause *guard* and *body*, and a clause may be enclosed in hiding.

The previously introduced version of conditional choice is, of course, merely syntactic sugar for the special case

$$(\ \langle statement \rangle \rightarrow \langle statement \rangle$$
$$; \text{true} \rightarrow \langle statement \rangle \ )$$

The case where the guard of the last clause is "true" is common enough to warrant general syntactic sugar, thus

$$(\ \langle statement \rangle \rightarrow \langle statement \rangle$$
$$; \ldots$$
$$; \text{true} \rightarrow \langle statement \rangle \ )$$

may always be abbreviated to

$$(\ \langle statement \rangle \ \rightarrow \ \langle statement \rangle$$
$$; \dots$$
$$; \langle statement \rangle \ )$$

For the last time we make the simplifying assumption that the guards are all constraints. The conditional choice statement asks the constraint of the first guard. If it is entailed, the composition of it and its body replaces the choice statement. If it is disentailed, the clause is deleted, and the next clause is tried. If neither, the statement will wait. These steps are repeated as necessary. If no clauses remain, the conditional choice statement fails.

When a more general statement is used as a guard, it will first be executed locally in the guard, reducing itself to a constraint, after which the previously described actions take place. To illustrate this before we descend into the details, let us use append in a guard (a fairly unusual guard though).

$$(\ append(X, Y, Z) \rightarrow p(Z)$$
$$; true \rightarrow q(X, Y) \ )$$

If we supply constraints for X and Y, e.g., $X = [1]$, $Y = [2, 3]$, a value will be computed locally for Z, and the resulting choice statement is

$$(\ Z = [1, 2, 3] \rightarrow p(Z)$$
$$; true \rightarrow q(X, Y) \ )$$

with its above described behaviour.

Formally, the computation in the guard is a separate computation, with local agents and its own local constraint store. Constraints told by local agents are placed in the local store, but constraints asked by local agents are asked from the union of the local store and external stores. Locally told constraints can thus be observed by local agents, but not by agents external to the guard.

When the local computation terminates successfully, the constraint asked for the guard is the conjunction of constraints in its local constraint store. This coincides with the behaviour in the special case that the guard was a constraint. In fact, the behaviour of a constraint atom statement is always to tell its constraint to the current constraint store.

If the local store becomes inconsistent with the union of external stores, the local computation fails. The behaviour is then as if the computation had terminated successfully, its constraint had been asked, and it had been found disentailed by the external stores.

The scope of don't know nondeterminism in a guard is limited to its corresponding clause. New alternative computations for a guard will be introduced as new alternative clauses. This will be illustrated using the following simple nondeterminate agent.

one_or_one(X, Y) :=
        (X = 1 ? true
        ; Y = 1 ? true).

Let us start with the statement

        (one_or_one(X, Y) | q)

The one_or_one atom is unfolded, giving

        ((X = 1 ? true ; Y = 1 ? true) | q)

Since no other step is possible, we may try the alternatives of the nondeterminate choice in different copies of the closest enclosing clause, which is duplicated
as follows.

        (X = 1 | q
        ; Y = 1 | q)

Other choice statements are handled analogously.

    Before leaving the subject of don't know nondeterminism in guards, it
should be clarified exactly when alternatives may be tried. A (possibly local)
state with agents and their store is *(locally) stable* if no computation step other
than copying in nondeterminate choice is possible, and no such computation
step can be made possible by adding constraints to external constraint stores
(if any). Alternatives may be tried for the leftmost possible nondeterminate
choice in a stable state.

    By only executing a nondeterminate choice in a stable state, don't know
nondeterministic computations will be synchronised in a concurrent setting in
a manner not unlike the synchronisation achieved by conditional or committed
choice. For example, the agent

        member(X, Y)

will unfold to

        (Y1 : Y = [X|Y1] ? true
        ; X1, Y1 : Y = [X1|Y1] ? member(X, Y1))

By adding constraints to the environment of this agent, it is possible to continue
execution without copying, e.g., by adding X = 1 and Y = [2|W].

    Thus, while there are active agents in its environment that may potentially
tell constraints on Y, the above agent is unstable.

4.5.7 Bagof

Finally, we introduce a statement which builds lists of sequences of alternative results. It provides powerful means of interaction between determinate and non-determinate code. It is similar to the corresponding construct in Prolog, and a generalisation of the list comprehension primitive found in functional languages (e.g., Haskell).

A *bagof* statement of the form

$$\text{bagof}(\langle variable \rangle, \langle statement \rangle, \langle variable \rangle)$$

builds a list of the sequence of alternative results from its component statement. The different alternative bindings for the variable in the first argument will be collected as a list in the variable in the last argument. The statement will be executed within the bagof statement in a manner not unlike the execution of a guard. Don't know nondeterminism is not propagated outside it.

For example, the composition

$$\text{member}(X, [a, b, c]), \text{member}(X, [b, c, d])$$

has two alternative results $X = b$ and $X = c$. By wrapping this composition in a bagof statement, collecting different alternatives for X in Y

$$\text{bagof}(X, (\text{member}(X, [a, b, c]), \text{member}(X, [b, c, d])), Y)$$

the result becomes

$$Y = [b, c]$$

as could be expected. Bagof exists in two varieties: ordered (the default) and unordered. The don't know nondeterministic alternatives are, as usual, ordered in the order of clauses in the nondeterminate choice. Thus,

$$((X = a ; X = b) ; (X = c ; X = d))$$

generates alternatives for X in the order a, b, c, d. So,

$$\text{bagof}(X, ((X = a ; X = b) ; (X = c ; X = d)), Y)$$

yields $Y = [a, b, c, d]$. However,

$$\text{unordered\_bagof}(X, ((X = a ; X = b) ; (X = c ; X = d)), Y)$$

ignores this order, and collects an alternative in the list as soon as it is available. Depending on the implementation, this could lead to a different order, e.g., $Y = [d, c, b, a]$.

4.5.8 More Syntactic Sugar

Analogously to what is usually done for functional languages, we now introduce syntactic sugar that is convenient when the guards in choice statements consist mainly of pattern matching against the arguments, as is often the case.

A definition of the form

$$p(X1, \ldots, Xn) :=$$
$$(\; g1 \; \% \; b1$$
$$; \ldots$$
$$; \; gk \; \% \; bk \;).$$

where % is either $\rightarrow, |$, or ?, may be broken up into several clauses

$$p(X1, \ldots, Xn) :- g1 \; \% \; b1.$$
$$\ldots$$
$$p(X1, \ldots, Xn) :- gk \; \% \; bk.$$

which together stand for the above definition.

The main point of this transformation into clausal definitions is that the following additional syntactic sugar may be introduced, which will be exemplified below: (1) Free variables are implicitly hidden, but here the hiding statement encloses the right hand side of the clause (i.e., to the right of ":–"), and not the entire definition. (2) Equality constraints on the arguments in the guard part of a clause may be folded back into the heads $p(X1, \ldots, Xn)$ of these clauses. (3) If the remainder of the guard is the null statement "true", it may be omitted. (4) If the guard is omitted and the guard operator is wait "?", it may also be omitted. (5) If the guard operator is omitted, and the body is the null statement "true", a clause may be abbreviated to a head.

As an example, the definition

$$\text{member}(X, Y) :=$$
$$(\; Y1 : Y = [X|Y1] \; ? \; true$$
$$; \; X1, Y1 : Y = [X1|Y1] \; ? \; member(X, Y1) \;).$$

may be transformed to clauses

$$\text{member}(X, Y) :-$$
$$Y = [X|Y1]$$
$$? \quad true.$$
$$\text{member}(X, Y) :-$$
$$Y = [X1|Y1]$$
$$? \quad member(X, Y1).$$

where hiding is implicit according to (1). The equality constraints may then be folded back into the head according to (2), and the remaining null guards may be omitted according to (3), giving

member(X, [X|Y1]) :–
   ?   true.

member(X, [X1|Y1]) :–
   ?   member(X, Y1).

which may be further abbreviated to

member(X, [X|Y1]).
member(X, [X1|Y1]) :–
      member(X, Y1).

according to (4) and (5). We exemplify also with the append and merge definitions.

append([], Y, Z) :–
  →   Y = Z.
append(X, Y, X) :–
  →   X = [E|X1],
      Z = [E|Z1],
      append(X1, Y, Z1).

merge([], Y, Z) :–
  | Y = Z.
merge(X, [], Z) :–
  | X = Z.
merge([E|X], Y, Z) :–
  | Z = [E|Z1],
      merge(X, Y, Z1).
merge(X, [E|Y], Z) :–
  | Z = [E|Z1],
      merge(X, Y, Z1).

The examples should make it clear that some additional clarity is gained with
the clausal syntax, which prevails in the logic programming community. We end
this section with a few additional remarks about the syntax.

As syntactic sugar, the underscore symbol "_" may be used in place of a
variable that has a single occurrence in a clause. All occurrences of "_" in a
definition denote different variables.

In an implementation of AKL, the character set restricts our syntax. The
then symbol "→" is there written as "-¿", and subscripted indices are not
possible. For example, append would be written as

append([], Y, Z) :–
  ->   Y = Z.
append(X, Y, Z) :–
   ->   X = [E|X1],
      append(X1, Y, Z1),
      Z = [E|Z1].

which is a program that can be compiled and run in the AKL Programming System (Janson and Montelius 1992). However, to make programs as readable as possible, we will continue to use "→" and indices.

4.5.9 Processes and Process Communication

Agents may be thought of as processes, and telling constraints on shared variables may be thought of as communicating on a shared channel. The basic principles supporting the idea of communicating processes were discussed in the previous sections. Here we will expand the discussion by explaining many of the concurrent programming idioms. These are inherited from concurrent logic programming (see, e.g., (Shapiro 1987)).

4.5.9.1 Communication and Streams The underlying idea is that a logical variable may be used as a *communication channel*. On this channel, a message can be sent by a producer process by binding the variable to some value.

$$X = a$$

A conditional or a committed-choice statement may be used by a consumer process to achieve the effect of waiting for a message. By imposing suitable constraints on the communication variable in their guards, these statements will require the value of the variable to be defined before execution may proceed. Until the value has been produced, the statement will be suspended.

$$(\ X = a \mid this$$
$$; X = b \mid that \ )$$

However, as soon as the variable is constrained, the guard parts of these statements may be executed, and the appropriate action can be taken. Message arguments can be transferred by binding the variable to a constructor expression.

$$X = f(Y)$$

Likewise, the argument can be received by matching against a constructor expression.

$$(\ Y : X = f(Y) \mid this(Y)$$
$$; Y : X = g(Y) \mid that(Y) \ )$$

Again, note the scope of the hiding statement. It is limited to each guarded statement. If Y were given a wider scope, the first guard would instead be that the value of X should be equal to $X = f(Y)$, for some given value of Y. The above use has the reading "if there exists a Y such that $X = f(Y) \ldots$", and it allows Y to be constrained by the guard.

Contrary to what is the case in the above examples, communication is not restricted to a single message between a producer and a consumer. A message can be given an argument that is the variable on which the next message will be sent. Usually, the list constructor is used for this purpose. The first argument of the list constructor is the message, and the second argument is the new variable. A sequence of messages can be sent as follows.

$$X0 = [M1|X1], X1 = [M2|X2], X2 = [M3|X3], \ldots$$

The receiver waits for a list constructor, and expects the message to arrive in the first argument, and the variable on which further messages will be sent in the second argument. Observe that the above example is simply the construction of a list of messages. When used to transfer a sequence of messages between processes, a list is referred to as a *stream*. Just like a list, a stream may end with [], which indicates that the stream has been closed, and that no further messages will be sent.

Understood in these terms, the list-sum example above is a typical *producer-consumer* example. The list agent produces a stream of messages, each of which is a number, and the sum agent consumes the stream, adding the numbers together.

4.5.9.2 Basic Stream Techniques In the previous section, we discussed the notions of producers and consumers. The list-agent is an example of a producer, and the sum-agent is an example of a consumer. Further basic stream techniques are stream transducers, distributors, and mergers.

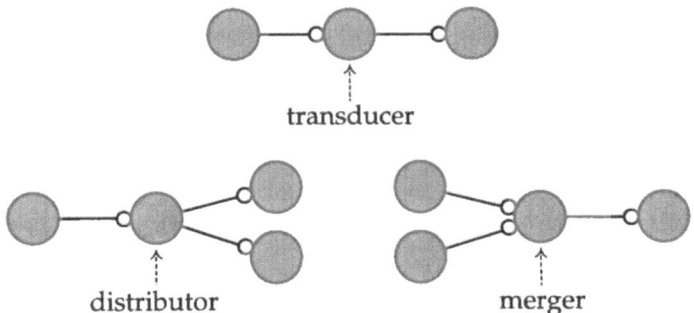

Fig. 4.2. Transducer, distributor, and merger

A stream *transducer* is an agent that takes one stream as input and produces another stream as output. This may involve computing new messages from old, rearranging, deleting, or adding messages. The following is a simple stream transducer computing the square of each incoming message.

```
squares([], Out) :-
    →    Out = [].
```

```
squares([N|Ns], Out) :-
    →    Out = [N*N|Out1],
         squares(Ns, Out1).
```

A stream *distributor* is an agent with one input stream and several output streams that directs incoming messages to the appropriate output stream. The following is a simple stream distributor that sends apples to one stream and oranges to the other.

```
fruits([], As, Os) :-
    →    As = [],
         Os = [].
fruits([F|Fs], As, Os) :-
         apple(F)
    →    As = [F|As1],
         fruits(Fs, As1, Os).
fruits([F|Fs], As, Os) :-
         orange(F)
    →    Os = [F|Os1],
         fruits(Fs, As, Os1).
```

A stream *merger* is an agent with several input streams and one output stream that interleaves messages from the input streams into the single output stream. The following is the standard binary stream merger, which was also shown in the language introduction.

```
merge([], Ys, Zs) :-
    |    Zs = Ys.
merge(Xs, [], Zs) :-
    |    Zs = Xs.
merge([X|Xs], Ys, Zs) :-
    |    Zs = [X|Zs1],
         merge(Xs, Ys, Zs1).
merge(Xs, [Y|Ys], Zs) :-
    |    Zs = [Y|Zs1],
         merge(Xs, Ys, Zs1).
```

Note that all the above definitions can also be seen as simple list-processing agents. However, they are more interesting when one considers their behaviour as components in concurrent programs.

4.5.9.3 Process Structures Process networks can be used for storing data. This is an example of an objectoriented reading of processes. The technique is best introduced by an example. We will show how a dictionary can be represented as a binary tree of processes.

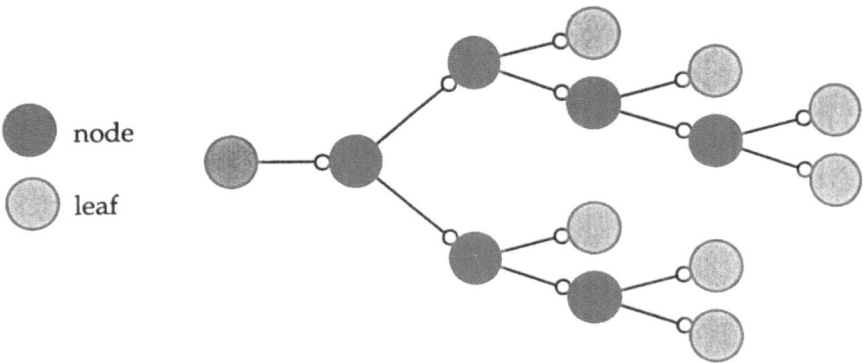

Fig. 4.3. Tree of node and leaf processes

The tree is built from leaf processes and node processes. A leaf process has one input stream from its parent. A node process has one input stream from its parent and two output streams to its children. In addition, it has two arguments for holding the key and the value of the data item stored in the node.

Thus, the processes correspond to equivalent data-structures. In their default state, these processes are waiting for messages on their input streams. The messages may be of the kind insert(Key, Value), with given key and value that should be inserted, lookup(Key, Result), with a given key and a sought for result (an unconstrained variable), and the closing of the stream which means that the tree should terminate (deallocate itself).

This technique, to include a variable in the message for the return value, is common enough to warrant a name of its own: *incomplete messages*.

The computed result is wrapped in the constructor found(Value), if a value corresponding to a key is found, and is otherwise the constant "not_found". When a node process receives a request, it compares the key to the key held in its argument, and either takes care of the request itself, or passes the request along to its left or right sub-tree, depending on the result of the comparison. A leaf process always processes a request itself.

```
dict(S) := leaf(S).

leaf([]) :-
    →    true.
leaf([insert(K,V)|S]) :-
    →    node(S, K, V, L, R),
         leaf(L),
         leaf(R).
leaf([lookup(K,V)|S]) :-
    →    V = not_found,
         leaf(S).

node([], _, _, L, R) :-
```

```
    →    L = [],
         R = [].
node([insert(K1, V1)|S], K, V, L, R) :-
    →    (           K1 = K
         →    node(S, K, V1, L, R)
         ;           K1 < K
         →    L = [insert(K1, V1)|L1],
                     node(S, K, V, L1, R)
         ;           K1 > K
         →    R = [insert(K1, V1)|R1],
                     node(S, K, V, L, R1) ).
node([lookup(K1, V1)|S], K, V, L, R) :-
    →    (           K1 = K
         →    V1 = found(V),
                     node(S, K, V, L, R)
         ;           K1 < K
         →    L = [lookup(K1, V1)|L1],
                     node(S, K, V, L1, R)
         ;           K1 > K
         →    R = [lookup(K1, V1)|R1],
                     node(S, K, V, L, R1) ).
```

In the following section on object-oriented programming, we will relate this programming technique to conventional object-oriented programming and its standard terminology.

4.5.10 Object-Oriented Programming

In this section, the basic techniques that allow us to do object-oriented programming in AKL are reviewed. Like the programming techniques in the previous section, they belong to logic programming folklore.

There is more than one way to map the abstract concept of an object onto corresponding concepts in a concurrent constraint language. The first and most widespread of these will be described here in detail (Shapiro and Takeuchi). It is based on the process reading of logic programs. Several embedded languages have been proposed that support this style of programming (e.g., (Kenneth M. Kahn and Bobrow 1987; Yoshida and Chikayama 1988; Davison 1989)). They are typically much less verbose, and they also provide more explicit support for objectoriented concepts.

As will be seen, in this framework there is no real need for an implementation of objects, unlike the case when one is adding object oriented support to a language such as C. Following an object-oriented style of programming is a very natural thing.

4.5.10.1 Objects An *object* is an abstract entity that provides services to its clients. Clients explicitly request services from objects. The request identifies the requested service, as well as the objects that are to perform the service.

Objects are realised as processes that take as input a stream (a list) of requests. The stream identifies the object. The data associated with the objects are held in the arguments of the process. An object definition typically has one clause per type of request, which performs the corresponding service, and one clause for terminating (or deallocating) the object. Thus, clauses correspond to methods.

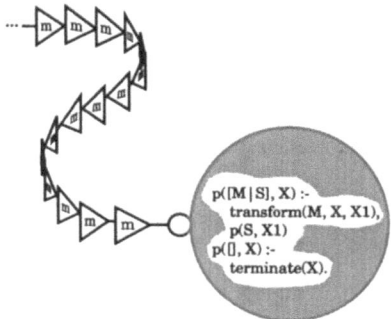

Fig. 4.4. An object consuming a list of messages

The requests are typically expressions of the form name(A, B, C), where the constructor "name" identifies the request, and A, B, and C are the arguments of the request.

The process description, the agent definition, is the class, the implementation of the object. The individual calls to this agent are the instances. A standard example of an object is the bank account, providing withdrawal, deposits, etc.

make_bank_account(S) :=
          bank_account(S, 0).

bank_account([], _) :–
     →   true.
bank_account([withdraw(A)|R], N) :–
     →   bank_account(R, N – A).
bank_account([deposit(A)|R], N) :–
     →   bank_account(R, N + A).
bank_account([balance(M)|R], N) :–
     →   M = N,
          bank_account(R, N).

A computation starting with

make_bank_account(S),
S = [balance(B1), deposit(7), withdraw(3), balance(B2)]

yields

B1 = 0, B2 = 4

A bank-account object is created by starting a process bank_account(S, 0) given as initial input an unspecified stream S (a variable) and a zero balance. The stream S is used to identify the object. A service deposit(5) is requested by binding S to [deposit(5)|S_1]. The next request is added to S_1, and so on. In the above example, only one clause will match any given request. When it is applied, some computation is performed in its body and a new bank_account process replaces the original one. The requests in the above example are processed as follows. Let us start in the middle.

bank_account(S, 0), S = [deposit(7), withdraw(3), balance(B2)].

The bank_account process is reduced by the clause matching the first deposit request, leaving some computation to be performed.

N = 0+7, bank_account(S1, N), S1 = [withdraw(3), balance(B2)].

This leaves us with.

bank_account(S, 7), S1 = [withdraw(3), balance(B2)].

The rest of the requests are processed similarly.

Finally, there are a few things to note about these objects. First, they are automatically encapsulated. Clients are prevented from directly accessing the data associated with an object. In imperative languages, this is not as self-evident, as the object is often confused with the storage used to store its internal data, and the object identifier is a pointer to this storage, which may often be used for any purpose.

Second, requests are entirely generic. The expression that identifies a request may be interpreted differently, and may therefore involve the execution of different code, depending on the object. This does not involve mandatory declarations in some shared (abstract or virtual) ancestor class, as in many other languages.

Third, becoming another type of object is extremely simple. Instead of replacing itself with an object of the same type, an object may pass its stream, and appropriate parameters, on to a new object. An example of this was given in the section on process structures, where a leaf process became a node process when a message was inserted into a binary tree.

4.5.10.2 Inheritance In the object-oriented paradigm, objects can be classified in terms of the services they provide. One object may provide a subset of the services of another object. This way an interface hierarchy is formed.

It is of course important, from a software engineering point of view, that the descriptions of objects higher up in the hierarchy can be reused as parts of the descendant objects. This is either done by inheritance or by delegation. Delegation is easily achieved in the framework we describe. However, since requests are completely generic, it is also possible to design an interface hierarchy without inheritance or delegation, if so desired.

Delegation is achieved by creating instances of the ancestor objects. The object identifier of (the stream to) this ancestor object is held as an argument of the derived object. The object corresponding to the ancestor could appropriately be called a subobject of the derived object. The derived object filters incoming requests and delegates unknown requests to its subobject.

Delegation is not restricted to unknown requests. We may also define what is elsewhere known as after- and before-methods by filtering as well. The derived object may perform any action before passing a request on to a subobject.

Let us derive from the bank_account class a kind of account that does some form of logging of incoming requests. Let us say that it also adds a get_log service that returns the log. This is easy.

```
make_logging_account(S) :=
            make_bank_account(O),
            make_empty_log(Log),
            logging_account(S, O, Log).
logging_account([get_log(L)|R], O, Log) :-
     →      L = Log,
            logging_account(R, O, Log).
logging_account([Req|R], O, Log) :-
     →      O = [Req|O1],
            add_to_log(Req, Log, Log1),
            logging_account(R, O1, Log1).
logging_account([], O, _) :-
     →      O = [].
```

With delegation, it is cumbersome to handle the notion of self correctly. Modern forms of multiple inheritance, based on the principle of specialisation, are also difficult to achieve. Instead, it is quite possible to view inheritance as providing the ability to share common portions of object definitions by placing them in super-classes, which are then implicitly copied into sub-class definitions. To exploit this view, syntactic support has to be added to the language, e.g., along the lines of Goldberg and Shapiro (Goldberg and Shapiro). This view corresponds closely to that of conventional object-oriented languages.

4.5.10.3 Ports for Objects *Ports* are a special form of constraints, which, when added to AKL, or to any concurrent logic programming language, will solve a number of problems with the approach to object-oriented programming presented above, problems that we have avoided mentioning so far. This section provides a preliminary introduction to ports. They, and the problems they solve, are described in great detail elsewhere (Sverker Janson and Montelius 1993).

A port is a binary constraint on a bag (a multi-set) of messages and a corresponding stream of these messages. It simply states that they contain the same messages, in any order. A bag connected to a stream by a port is usually identified with the port, and is referred to as a port. The open_port(P, S) operation relates a bag P to a stream S, and connects them through a port. The stream S will usually be connected to an object. Instead of using the stream to access the object, we will send messages by adding them to the port. The send(M, P) operation sends a message M to a port P. To satisfy the port constraint, a message sent to a port will immediately be added to its associated stream, first come first served.

When a port is no longer referenced from other parts of the computation state, when it becomes garbage, it is assumed that it contains no more messages, and its associated stream is automatically closed. When the stream is closed, any object consuming it is thereby notified that there are no more clients requesting its services.

Thus, to summarise: A port is created with an associated stream (to an object). Messages are sent to the port, and appear on the stream in any order. When the port is no longer in use, the stream is closed, and the object may choose to terminate.

A simple example follows.

$$\text{open\_port}(P, S), \text{send}(a, P), \text{send}(b, P)$$

yields

$$P = \langle a \ port \rangle, \ S = [a, b]$$

Here we create a port and a related stream, and send two messages. The messages appear in

S in the order of the send operations in the composition, but it could just as well have been reversed. The stream is closed when the messages have been sent, since there are no more references to the port.

Ports solve a number of problems that are implicit in the use of streams. The following are the most obvious.

- If several clients are to access the same object, their streams of messages have to be merged into a single input stream. With ports, no merger has to be created. Any client can send a message on the same port.

- If objects are to be embedded in other data structures, creating, e.g., an array of objects, streams have to be put in these structures. Such structures cannot be shared, since several messages cannot be sent on the same stream by different clients. However, several messages can be sent on the same port, which means that ports can be embedded.

- With naive binary merging of streams, message sending delay is variable. With ports, message sending delay is constant.

- Objects based on streams require that the streams are closed when the clients stop using them. This is similar to decrementing a reference counter, and has similar problems, besides being unnecessarily explicit and low-level. A port is automatically closed when there are no more potential senders, thus notifying the object consuming messages.

4.5.11 Functions and Relations

Functions and relations are simple but powerful mathematical concepts. Many programming languages have been designed so that one of the available interpretations of a procedure definition should be a function or a relation. AKL has well-defined subsets that enjoy such interpretations, and provide the corresponding programming paradigms.

4.5.11.1 Functions The functional style of programming is characterised by the determinate flow of control and by the non-cyclic flow of data. There is no don't care or don't know nondeterminism: a single result is computed; and agents do not communicate bi-directionally; an agent takes input from one agent and produces output to another agent. The latter point is weakened somewhat if the language has a non-strict semantics, in which case "tail-biting" techniques are possible.

Many of the AKL definitions are indeed written in the functional style. For example, the "append", "squares" and "fruits" definitions in the preceding sections are essentially functional, although the latter two were introduced as components in a process-oriented setting.

The basic relation between functional programs and AKL definitions is illustrated by an example, written in the non-strict, purely functional language Haskell. (The appropriate type declarations are supplied with the functional program for clarity.)

```
data (BinTree a) => (Leaf a) | (Node (BinTree a) (BinTree a))

flatten :: (BinTree a) -> [a]

flatten (Leaf x) l = x:l
flatten (Node x y) l = flatten x (flatten y l)
```

In AKL, a corresponding program is phrased as follows.

```
flatten(leaf(X), L, R) :-
    →    R = [X|L].
flatten(node(X, Y), L, R) :-
    →    flatten(Y, L, L1),
         flatten(X, L1, R).
```

The main differences are that an explicit argument has to be supplied for the output of the "function", and that nested function applications are un-nested, making the output of one the input of another.

AKL is not a higher-order language, and does not provide "definition variables", but does provide the same functionality (modulo currying) in a simple manner. The technique has been known in logic programming for a long time [Warren 1981]. A term representation is chosen for each definition in a program, and an agent apply is defined, which given such a term applies it to arguments and executes the corresponding definition.

One possible scheme for AKL is as follows. Let a term $p(n, t_1, \ldots, t_m)$ represent a definition $p/(n-m)$, which when applied to $n-m$ arguments t_{m+1}, $\ldots, t_n$ calls p/n with $p(t_1, \ldots, t_n)$.

To give an example relating to the above programs, the term flatten(3) corresponds to the function flatten, and the term flatten(3, Tree) to the function (flatten tree) (where Tree and tree are equivalent trees). A corresponding agent

```
apply(flatten(3), [X,Y,Z]) :-
    →    flatten(X, Y, Z).
apply(flatten(3,X), [Y,Z]) :-
    →    flatten(X, Y, Z).
apply(flatten(3,X,Y), [Z]) :-
    →    flatten(X, Y, Z).
apply(flatten(3,X,Y,Z), []) :-
    →    flatten(X, Y, Z).
```

is also defined. In practice, it is convenient to regard apply as being defined implicitly for all definitions in a program, which is also easily achieved in an implementation. This functionality may now be used as in functional programs as follows. We define an agent

map/3, which maps a list to another list.

```
map(P, [], Ys) :-
    →    Ys = [].
map(P, [X|Xs], Ys0) :-
    →    Ys0 = [Y|Ys],
         apply(P, [X, Y]),
         map(P, Xs, Ys).
```

and may then call it with, e.g., map(append(3,[a]), [[b],[c]], Ys) and get the result Ys = [[a,b],[a,c]].

Although by no means necessary, expressions corresponding to lambda expressions can also be introduced. Let an expression

$$(X1, \ldots, Xk)\backslash A$$

where
   A is an AKL agent with free variables
   Y1, ...,
   Ym, stand for a term

$$p((m + k), Y1, \ldots, Ym)$$

where
   p/$(m + k)$ is a new agent defined as

$$p(Y1, \ldots, Ym, X1, \ldots, Xk) := A.$$

We may now write, e.g.,
   map((X,Y)\append(X, Z, Y), [[b],[c]], Ys) and get the result
   Ys = [[b|Z],[c|Z]]. Finally, the syntactic gap to the functional notation can
be closed even further by introducing the syntax

$$P(X1, \ldots, Xk)$$

standing for

$$apply(P, [X1, \ldots, Xk])$$

Obviously, the terms corresponding to functional closures may be given more
efficient representations in an implementation.

4.5.11.2 Relations The relational paradigm is known from logic programming as well as from from database query languages. Most prominent of logic
programming languages is Prolog, which is entirely based on the relational
paradigm. A large number of powerful programming techniques have been developed. Prolog and its derivatives are used for data and knowledge base applications, constraint satisfaction, and general symbolic processing. AKL supports
Prolog-style programming.
   Characteristic of the relational paradigm is the idea that programs interpreted as defining relations should be capable of answering queries involving
these relations. Thus, if a parent relation is defined, the program should be
able to produce all parents for given children and all children for given parents,
enumerate all parents and corresponding children, and verify given parents and
children. The following definition clearly satisfies this condition.

parent(sverker, adam).
parent(kia, adam).
parent(sverker, axel).
parent(kia, axel).
parent(jan_christer, sverker).
parent(hillevi, sverker).

Maybe less intuitive, but just as appealing, is the following: a simple parser of a fragment of the English language. The creation of a parse-tree is omitted.

s(S0, S) := np(S0, S1), vp(S1, S).

np(S0, S) := article(S0, S1), noun(S1, S).

article([a|S], S).
article([the|S], S).

noun([dog|S], S).
noun([cat|S], S).

vp(S0, S) := intransitive_verb(S0, S).

intransitive_verb([sleeps|S], S).
intransitive_verb([eats|S], S).

The two arguments of each atom represent a string of tokens to be parsed as the difference between the first and the second argument. The following is a sample execution.

> s([a, dog, sleeps], S)
> np([a, dog, sleeps], S2), vp(S2, S)
> article([a, dog, sleeps], S1), noun(S1, S2), vp(S2, S)
> noun([dog, sleeps], S2), vp(S2, S)
> vp([sleeps], S)
> intransitive_verb([sleeps], S)
> S = []

The relation defined by s is

> s([a, dog, sleeps|S], S)
> s([a, dog, eats|S], S)
> s([a, cat, sleeps|S], S)
> s([a, cat, eats|S], S)
> s([the, dog, sleeps|S], S)
> s([the, dog, eats|S], S)
> s([the, cat, sleeps|S], S)
> s([the, cat, eats|S], S)

for all S, and will be generated as alternative results from

> s(S0, S)

The idea of a pair of arguments representing the difference between lists is important enough to warrant syntactic support in Prolog, the DCG syntax, which allows the above definitions to be rendered as follows.

s -> np, vp.

np -> article, noun.

article -> [a].
article -> [the].

and so on. The example is naive, since real examples would be unwieldy, but the state of the art is well advanced, and the literature on unification grammars based on the above simple idea is rich and flourishing.

4.5.12 Constraint Programming

Many interesting problems in computer science and neighbouring areas can be formulated as constraint satisfaction problems (CSPs). To these belong, for example, Boolean satisfiability, graph colouring, and a number of logical puzzles (a couple of which will be used as examples). Other, more application oriented, problems can usually be mapped to a standard problem, e.g., register allocation to graph colouring. Often, these problems are NP-complete; any known general algorithm will require exponential time in the worst case. Our task is to write programs that perform well in as many cases as possible.

A CSP can be defined in the following way. A *(finite) constraint satisfaction problem* is given by a sequence of variables $X_1, \ldots, X_n$; corresponding sequence of (finite) domains of values $D_1, \ldots, D_n$; and a set of constraints $c(X_{i_1}, \ldots, X_{i_k})$. A *solution* is an assignment of values to the variables, from their corresponding domains, which satisfies all the constraints.

For our purposes, a constraint can be regarded as a logical formula, where satisfaction corresponds to the usual logical notion, but formalism will not be pressed here. Instead, AKL programs are used to describe CSPs, and their intuitive logical reading provides us with the corresponding constraints. Each agent is regarded as a (user-defined) constraint, and will be referred to as such. The agents are typically don't know nondeterministic, and the assignments for which the composition of these agents does not fail are the solutions of the CSP.

The example to be used in this section is the n-queens problem: how to place n queens on an n by n chess board in such a way that no queen threatens another. The problem is very well known, and no new algorithm will be presented. The novelty, compared to solutions in conventional languages, lies in the way the algorithm is expressed. The technique used is due to Saraswat (Saraswat 1993).

Each square of the board is a variable
V, which takes the value
0 (meaning that there is no queen on the square) or
1 (meaning that there is a queen on the square).
The basic constraint is that there may be at most one queen in each row, column, and diagonal. Given that n queens are to be placed on an n by n board, a derived constraint, which we will use, is that there must be exactly

one queen in each row and column. Note that the exactly-one constraint can be decomposed into an at-least-one and an at-most-one constraint. We now proceed to define these constraints in terms of smaller components. The problem is not only to express the constraints, which is easy, but to express them in such a way that an appropriate level of propagation will occur, which will reduce the search space dramatically.

The at-most-one constraint can be expressed in terms of the following agent.

xcell(1, N, N).
xcell(0, _, _).

Note that this agent is determinate if the first argument is known, or if the last two arguments are known and different. For a sequence of squares V_1 to V_k, we can now express that at most one of these squares is 1 using the xcell agent as follows.

> xcell(V1, N, 1),
> xcell(V2, N, 2),
> ...,
> xcell(Vk, N, k)

If more than one V_i is 1, the variable N will be bound to two different numbers, and the constraint will fail. Let us call this constraint at_most_one($V_1, \ldots, V_k$), thus avoiding the overhead of having to write a program to create it.

An at_most_one constraint will clearly only have solutions where at most one square is given the value 1, but note also the following propagation effects. If one of the V_i is given the value 1, its associated xcell agent becomes determinate, and can therefore be reduced. When it is reduced, N is given the value i, and the other xcell agents become determinate, and can be reduced, giving their variables the value 0.

The at-least-one constraint can be expressed in terms of the following agent.

ycell(1, _, _).
ycell(0, S, S).

Note that this agent too is determinate if the first argument is known, or if the other two arguments are known and different. For a sequence of squares V_1 to V_k, we can express that at least one of these squares is 1 using the ycell agent as follows.

> S0 = begin,
> ycell(V1, S0, S1),
> ycell(V2, S1, S2),
> ...,
> ycell(Vk, Sk − 1, Sk),
> Sk = end

If all the squares are 0, a chain of equality constraints, $S_0 = S_1$, $S_1 = S_2$, ...,
will connect "begin" with "end" by equality constraints, and the constraint will
fail. This constraint we call at_least_one(V_1, ..., V_k).

Again note the propagation effects. If a variable is given the value 0, then its
associated ycell agent becomes determinate. When it is reduced, its second and
third arguments are unified. If all variables but one are 0, the second argument of
the remaining ycell agent will be "begin" and its third argument will be "end",
and it will therefore be determinate. When it is reduced, its first argument will
be given the value 1.

Thus, not only will these constraints avoid the undesirable cases, but they
will also detect cases where information can be propagated. When no agent
is determinate, and therefore no information can be propagated, alternative
assignments for variables will be explored by trying alternatives for the xcell
and ycell agents.

A program solving the n-queens problem can now be expressed as follows.

- For each column, row, and diagonal, consisting of a sequence of variables
  V_1, ..., V_k, the constraint at_most_one(V_1, ..., V_k) has to be satisfied.

- For each column and row, consisting of a sequence of variables V_1, ...,
  V_n, the constraint at_least_one(V_1, ..., V_n) has to be satisfied.

- The composition of these constraints is the program.

Note that when information is propagated, this will affect other agents, making
them determinate. This will often lead to new propagation. One such case is
illustrated below.

1	0	0	0
0	0	V_{23}	V_{24}
0	V_{32}	0	V_{34}
0	V_{42}	V_{43}	0

The above grid represents the board, and in each square is written the variable
representing it, or its value if it has one. We will now trace the steps leading to
the above state. Initially, all variables are unconstrained, and all the constraints
have been created. Let us now assume that the topmost leftmost variable (V_{11})
is given the value 1. It appears in the row V_{11} to V_{14}, in the column V_{11} to V_{41},
and in the diagonal V_{11} to V_{44}. Each of these is governed by an at_most_one
constraint. By giving one variable the value 1, the others will be assigned the
value 0 by propagation.

A second case of propagation is the following, where V_{12} and V_{24} are assumed to contain queens, and propagation of the above kind has taken place.

0	1	0	0
0	0	0	1
V_{31}	0	0	0
V_{41}	0	V_{43}	0

Here we examine the propagation that this state will lead to. Notice that in row 3, all variables but V31 have been given the value 0. This triggers the at_least_one constraint governing this row, giving the last variable the value 1, which in turn gives the variables in the same row, column, or diagonal (only V_{41}) the value 0. Finally, V_{43} is given the value 1 by reasoning as above.

The above program is reasonably good. The programs usually written for constraint logic programming languages with finite domain constraints do not exploit the fact that both rows and columns should contain exactly one queen (e.g., (Van Hentenryck 1989)). A very good solution can be obtained if the xcell and ycell agents are ordered so that those governing variables closer to the centre of the board come before those governing variables further out. If at some step alternatives have to be tried for an agent, values will be guessed for variables at the centre first. This happens to be a good heuristic for the n-queens problem, even better than the so called first-fail principle, which is usually employed.

4.5.13 Integration

So far, the different paradigms have been presented one at a time, and it is quite possibly by no means apparent in what relation they stand to each other. In particular the relational and the constraint satisfaction paradigms have no apparent connection to the process paradigm. Here, this apparent dichotomy will be bridged, by showing how a process-oriented application based on the solver for the n-queens problem could be structured.

The basic techniques for interaction with the environment (e.g., files and the user) are shown first, and then a program structure is introduced which is somewhat inspired by the Smalltalk Model-View-Controller paradigm.

4.5.13.1 Interoperability The idea underlying interoperability is that an AKL agent sees itself as living in a world of AKL agents. The user, files, other programs, all are viewed as AKL agents. If they have a state, e.g., file contents, they are closer to objects, such as those discussed above. It is up to the AKL implementation to provide this view, which is inherited from the concurrent logic programming languages.

A program takes as parameter a port to the "operating system" (OS) agent, which provides further access to the functionality and resources it controls. An interface to foreign procedures adds glue code that provides the necessary synchronisation, and views of mutable data structures as ports to agents. The examples use imaginary, although realistic, primitives, as in the following.

```
main(P) :=
        send(create_window(W, [xwidth=100, xheight=100]), P),
        send(draw_text(10, 10, 'Hello, world!'), W).
```

Here it is assumed that the agent main is supplied with the "operating system" port P when called. The OS provides window creation, an operation that returns a port to the window agent, which provides text drawing, and so on.

For some kinds of interoperability, a consistent view of don't know nondeterminism can be implemented. For example, a sub-program without internal state, such as a numerical library written in C, does not mind if its agents are copied during the course of a computation. For particular purposes, it is even possible to copy windows and similar "internal" objects. But the real world does not support don't know nondeterminism. It would hardly be possible to copy an agent that models the actual physical file-system; nor would it be possible to copy an agent that models communication with another computer.

The only solution is to regard this kind of incompleteness as acceptable, and either let attempts to copy such unwieldy agents induce a run-time error, or give statements a "type" which is checked at compile-time, and which shows whether a statement can possibly employ don't know nondeterminism.

4.5.13.2 Encapsulation To avoid unwanted interaction between don't know nondeterministic and process-oriented parts of a program, the nondeterministic part can be encapsulated in a statement that hides nondeterminism. Nondeterminism is encapsulated in the guard of a conditional or committed choice and in bagof. When encapsulated in a guard, a nondeterministic computation will eventually be pruned. In a conditional choice, the first solution is chosen. In a committed choice, any solution may be chosen. When encapsulated in bagof, all solutions will be collected in a list.

More flexible forms of encapsulation can be based on the notion of engines. An engine is conceptually an AKL interpreter. It is situated in a server process. A client may ask the engine to execute programs, and, depending on the form of engine, it may interact with the engine in almost any way conceivable, inspecting and controlling the resulting computation. A full treatment of engines for AKL is future work.

4.5.13.3 Model-View-Controller The Model-View-Controller (MVC) paradigm for assigning different responsibilities to the components of an object-oriented program is easily realised in AKL, as in any object- or process-oriented language. In AKL it also localises and encapsulates don't know nondeterminism in the relevant part of the program, which is usually the model.

In the next section, MVC will be applied to the structuring of an n-queens application, using imaginary OS primitives.

4.5.14 An N-Queens Application

Assume the existence of a don't know nondeterministic n-queens agent

n_queens(N, Q) := ....

which returns different assignments Q to the squares of an N by N chess board. It is easily defined by adding code for creation of constraints for different length sequences, and code for creating sequences of variables corresponding to rows, columns, and diagonals on the chess board. No space will be wasted on this trivial task here. We proceed to the MVC structure with which to support the application.

```
main(P) :=
          initialise(P, W, E),
          view(V, W),
          controller(E, M, S, V),
          model(M, S).
```

The initialise agent creates a window accepting requests on stream W and delivering events on stream E. The view agent presents whatever it is told to by the controller on the window using stream W. The model delivers solutions on the stream S to the n-queens problems submitted on stream M. The controller is driven by the events coming in on E. It submits problems to the model on stream M and receives solutions on stream S. It then sends solutions to the view agent on V for displaying.

Let us here ignore the implementation of the initialise, view, and controller agents. The interesting part is how the don't know nondeterminism is encapsulated in the model agent. We assume that we are satisfied with being able to get either one or all solutions from the particular instance of the n-queens problem, or getting the reply that there are no solutions (for $N = 2$ or $N = 3$).

```
model([], S) :-
     →    S = [].
model([all(N)|M], S) :-
     →    bagof(Q, n_queens(N, Q), Sols),
          S = [all(Sols)|S1],
          model(M, S1).
model([one(N)|M], S) :-
     →    ( Q :       n_queens(N, Q)
            →    S = [one(Q)|S1]
          ;          S = [none|S1] ),
          model(M, S1).
```

As described above, don't know nondeterminism within bagof and choice statements is not propagated further. The MVC part of the program can be kept entirely free of nondeterminism.

4.5.15 Current and Future Work

Current and planned topics at SICS include efficient sequential and parallel implementations parametrised with user-definable constraint systems (in C), implementations of various constraint systems, extensions of the basic framework, such as engines for meta-level programming, program analysis and program transformation, inter-operability with conventional languages and operating systems, and investigation of formal properties.

An experimental AKL programming system is available from SICS for research and educational purposes.

Acknowledgements

The authors wish to thank the other members of the Concurrent Constraint Programming group at SICS for their contributions to this work. Discussions with Vijay Saraswat and David H. D. Warren during the design phase were very valuable.

References

Davison, A. (1989). POLKA: A Parlog Object-Oriented Language. Ph. D. thesis, Department of Computing, Imperial College, London, May.

Goldberg, Y. and E. Shapiro. Logic programs with inheritance.

Janson, S. and S. Haridi (1991). Programming paradigms of the Andorra Kernel Language. In Logic Programming: Proceedings of the 1991 International Symposium. MIT Press.

Janson, S. and J. Montelius (1992). The design of the AKL/PS 0.0 prototype implementation of the Andorra Kernel Language. *ESPRIT deliverable, EP 2471 (PEPMA)*.

Kenneth M. Kahn, Eric Dean Tribble, M. S. M. and D. G. Bobrow (1987). *Vulcan: Logical concurrent objects*. MIT Press.

Saraswat, V. A. (Ed.) (1993). Concurrent Constraint Programming Languages. MIT Press.

Shapiro, E. (Ed.) (1987). Concurrent Prolog: Collected Papers. MIT Press.

Shapiro, E. and A. Takeuchi. Object-oriented programming in Concurrent Prolog. Journal of New Generation Computing 1.

Sverker Janson, S. H. and J. Montelius (Eds.) (1993). Research Directions in Concurrent Object-Oriented Programming In Ports for Objects in Concurrent Logic Programs. MIT Press.

Van Hentenryck, P. (1989). Constraint Satisfaction in Logic Programming. MIT Press.

Yoshida, K. and T. Chikayama (1988). A'UM—a stream-based concurrent object-oriented language. In *In Proc. Fifth Generation Computer Systems 1988, ICOT*, Tokyo.

Appendix

Contents of technical report CS57/93 of the Institute of Cybernetics, Estonian Academy of Sciences, 21 Akadeemia tee, EE-0026 Tallinn, Estonia (see Preface):

NATO ASI Series F

Including Special Programmes on Sensory Systems for Robotic Control (ROB) and on Advanced Educational Technology (AET)

NATO ASI Series F

NATO ASI Series F

Including Special Programmes on Sensory Systems for Robotic Control (ROB) and on Advanced Educational Technology (AET)

NATO ASI Series F